DIBRE ABOTH HA-OLAM.

SAYINGS

OF

THE JEWISH FATHERS.

THE LIBRARY

OF

JEWISH CLASSICS

Edited by

Gerson D. Cohen

SAYINGS

OF

THE JEWISH FATHERS

COMPRISING

PIRQE ABOTH

IN HEBREW AND ENGLISH

WITH NOTES AND EXCURSUSES.

EDITED FOR THE SYNDICS OF THE CAMBRIDGE UNIVERSITY PRESS

BY

CHARLES TAYLOR D.D.

MASTER OF ST JOHN'S COLLEGE CAMBRIDGE.

Second Edition with Additional Notes and a Cairo fragment of
Aquila's version of the Old Testament.

PROLEGOMENON BY
JUDAH GOLDIN

KTAV PUBLISHING HOUSE, INC.

NEW YORK

1969

REPRINT BY PERMISSION OF CAMBRIDGE UNIVERSITY PRESS

FIRST PUBLISHED 1897

LIBRARY OF CONGRESS CATALOG CARD NUMBER: 75-79492
MANUFACTURED IN THE UNITED STATES OF AMERICA

PROLEGOMENON

*On Charles Taylor's Sayings of the Jewish Fathers**

> . . . I . . . accustomed myself to read a chapter of the
> tractate Aboth every day. Do ye the same at table, before
> Grace after meals, read a chapter daily till you know the
> whole tractate by heart. This practice will habituate and at-
> tract you to saintliness.

From the Testament of Judah Asheri (1270-1349)

Like his extraordinary commentary and notes on Pirqe Aboth,
Charles Taylor (1840-1908) seems to have been extraordinary
as a person too. For twenty-seven years, from 1881 on, he
served as Master of St. John's, one of the very distinguished
colleges of Cambridge; nevertheless, for almost two decades before then, and later during all the years of his Mastership, he continued actively as a serious scholar, studying closely and inter-
preting ancient texts, and communicating his enthusiasm for
original research to others. We read that as Master of his College,

---

* I would like to express my thanks to the Rev. Professor J. S. Boys Smith,
Master of St. John's College, Cambridge, for providing me with suggestions
and material on Taylor's life. For the convenience of readers of this volume,
all references to Pirqe Aboth and transliterations are in accordance with
Taylor's usage.

v

"Taylor left details of administration to others." Clearly, however, from the little known of him—"The Taylors were not given to talking about themselves"—it could never be said that he shirked official duties or responsibilities. His participation in university affairs was no slight matter: he took part in the discussions on the revision of the statutes of the college; he was a member of the council of the university; from 1873 on he held the appointment of College Lecturer in Theology; for two full years he served as the Vice-Chancellor of the University, for six years was one of the two university aldermen in the borough council; in more ways than one might expect, he revealed his concern for the first of the Cambridge College Missions in south London, for "secondary school" education, and so on.

This combination of the studious and the official and practical suggests something or someone formidable, discouraging intimacy and light conversation. A time was to come when he would be close to Solomon Schechter; yet to the end, in his letters to Schechter, Taylor, we are told, addressed him only as "Dear Sir." With everyone, apparently, Taylor was reserved and even stiff in manner: ". . . he was at his best in his own rooms with a single friend or two, or on a country tramp." "His courtesy, in small matters as in great, might be called old-fashioned." These are typical remarks about the man by some of his contemporaries. They go on to say, however, that there was nothing of the recluse or the exaggeratedly otherworldly in his conduct or tastes. He was a warm host—breakfasts seem to have been one of his favorite times for entertaining! As a student he rowed in his college boat-races. He was always fond of sculling, long exploratory walks, mountain climbing. And his generosity was striking, "constant and lavish," to quote one of the members of the College. "His gifts to the College," said another, "were almost princely. . . . It was characteristic of him that if after one of these donations a College meeting attempted to thank him, he would proceed with promptitude to the next business." As is well known, it is thanks to his munificence, "to the enlightened generosity of this great student and patron of Hebrew literature . . .," in the words of Schechter, that the contents of the Cairo Genizah were transferred to Cambridge. This is the historic Taylor-Schechter Collection for which Jewish scholars especially continue to be profoundly grateful. Whole chapters of Jewish history and of Mediterranean society have been rewritten and written as a result of this great treasury of manuscripts and documents.*

Let us return, however, to his intellectual preoccupations and industry. In part, they need not surprise us. For example, it is easy to presume that if a scholar is attracted by the epigrammatic sayings of Aboth, he would very likely find classical Hebrew Wisdom literature attractive. Thus in 1874 there is Taylor putting out *The Dirge of Coheleth in Ecclesiastes XII*, rejecting the anatomical rendering of verses 2-7 of that chapter, and defending their literal sense and poetic force. Years later, in 1899, he published portions of the Hebrew Ben Sira in collaboration with Schechter.

Moreover, since Taylor was a learned Christian divine (he was ordained deacon in 1866 and priest in 1867), we might well expect from him a work like *The Gospel in the Law* (1869); he even made use of it subsequently as a basis for a course of sermons in the church he served as curate. Several other titles are also telling: *The Teaching of the Twelve Apostles* (1886); *An Essay on the Theology of the Didache* (1889); *The Witness of Hermas to the Four Gospels* (1892); *The Oxyrhynchus Logia and the Apocryphal Gospels* (1899); *The Oxyrhynchus Sayings of Jesus* (1905). These learned studies would recommend themselves naturally to a scholarly clergyman who, as a student, had

---

* Taylor's shyness and (what must have been) ingrained reluctance to have attention called to his generosity, inhibit even one writing about him, even more than half a century after Taylor's death. I would therefore like to report in a footnote three other benefactions of his; taken together, perhaps they make partially visible an interior *douceur* of mind, a hospitality toward all human exercise in wholesomeness, in refinement of body and spirit. Taylor provided the Lady Margaret Club with the site for its boat-house and sent the eight to Henley. He owned several sets of the Babylonian Talmud; and one of these he gave as outright gift to a *Hevrah Shas* in a poor London synagogue when he learned that the men in that Talmud-study group could not afford to buy the volumes, because he considered himself duty-bound to come to their assistance. To his University Library he presented a fine copy of the *Kandjur,* and thus helped make of Cambridge a leading repository of Buddhist texts.

obtained a second class in the classical tripos and, three years after that, a first class in the theological examination. Incidentally, apparently Taylor also planned a new edition of the *Chronicle of Bar Hebraeus,* but nothing seems to have come of that.

What does occasion surprise (and this may even account for Taylor's failure to obtain a first class in the classical tripos—but Taylor was never the man to "read with an eye to the class list . . . to make getting marks [his] end and aim") is that to begin with he devoted himself mainly to mathematics, and his deep interest in this field he never gave up, even while he engaged in painstaking studies of Hebrew and Greek and Syriac and theological literature. He was ninth wrangler in 1862. In 1863 he published *Geometrical Conics, Including Anharmonic Ratio and Projection.* His textbook, *The Elementary Geometry of Conics,* published in 1872, went through several editions. In 1881 appeared an even larger treatise, *An Introduction to the Ancient and Modern Geometry of Conics,* which included a sketch of the early history of geometry. The article on "Geometrical Continuity" in the 1902 edition of the Encyclopaedia Britannica was his, and it was reprinted in 1910. It is estimated that he wrote about thirty or forty mathematical papers, principally on geometry, in addition to his more ambitious contributions to the field. No less an authority than A. E. H. Love said of Taylor's mathematical writings that they are "marked by elegance, conciseness, a rare knowledge of the history of the subject, and a veneration for the great geometers of the past."

This, then, is something of the man who in 1877 published the first edition of *Sayings of the Jewish Fathers,* and in 1897 put out a second edition of this work with some sixty pages of additional notes; and in 1900 brought out the Appendix Volume with its fastidious descriptions of 170 manuscripts of Aboth text, and of Aboth text and commentary—in this last volume he included his critical Notes on the Text which replaced the Critical Notes that had preceded the Translation in the first edition. The work is a storehouse of learning, and no student of Pirqe Aboth, once he has used Taylor, is likely to forget it or to pass it by or neglect to consult it. It is even possible that long after Taylor's other writings are forgotten, his *Sayings of the*

Jewish Fathers will continue to keep his memory alive, beyond the English-speaking world, too. To the work's special merit we shall turn in a moment; first, however, we must clear away what may otherwise prove to be a huge stumbling-block, and that is (of all things!) Taylor's *translation*. It is almost unbelievable.

For example: *We-hewe mit'abeq ba-'afar raglehem* is rendered by "And powder thyself in the dust of their feet." Never mind the sixties of the twentieth century, which in any event are hardly the court of final appeal, even for the sixties. However, even in Victorian England, did anyone ever speak like that? "Five disciples were there to Rabban Jochanan ben Zakai, and these were they. . . . Hatred of the creatures put[s] a man out of the world. . . . Whoso receives upon him the yoke of Torah, they remove from him the yoke of royalty and the yoke of worldly care. . . . Lo! he is not guilty, till he has sat down and suffered [the words of Thorah] to depart from his mind. . . . Whosesoever wisdom is in excess of his works, to what is he like. . . . Ten things were created between the suns. . . ." Such translation ought never to be visited on any text, but above all on the Aboth sayings! One big reason for the enduring popularity of Pirqe Aboth, both among *hoi polloi* and philosophers, is certainly the idiomatic polish, the graceful compactness of its sayings. There are difficult clauses and whole sentences in Aboth, and to decide what they mean is far from easy, despite the many and superb Jewish (Hebrew and Arabic) commentaries on this treatise. But nothing in Pirqe Aboth is wooden, or tortured, or ponderous. Compared to the original, Taylor's *translation* is a lexical servitude.

Apparently this was nineteenth-century academic fidelity to the original. Even in the twentieth century there have been scholars, sensitive and gifted, who have translated ancient texts, Hebrew ones and of other languages, which read like nothing except A. E. Housman's caricature of translations of Greek tragedy:

> O, suitably-attired-in leather-boots
> Head of a traveller, wherefore, seeking whom
> Whence by what way how purposed art thou come
> To this well-nightingaled vicinity?

Taylor's translation is not to be defended (this is true, by the way, not only of Taylor's but of a number of others' too; that's a story, however, for another day). At the same time, it would be grossly unfair to imply that he is unreadable, that from beginning to end his translation is useless. No, even this is far too grudging—the translation is very, very often forthright even if not sparkling. The very passion for precision which brought him in the end into clumsy and pedestrian expression has at least this virtue: it reflects the severe honesty with which Taylor treated the basic units, the very words and syntax, of his text. To repeat, however: Although something can be gained by studying the English words Taylor adopts for the Hebrew ones, his translation fails to convey the *ḥen*, the felicity and the literary grace of Pirqe Aboth.

On the other hand, the commentary immediately accompanying the translation and the discussions in the Additional Notes, the five Excursuses and *their* additional notes, and the critical Notes on the Text and the detailed comments on the manuscripts—these are first rate and in them Taylor is at his best. Like a talmudical commentator, with remarkable erudition he explores Talmud and Midrash, early and late post-talmudic exegesis, all the resources of the long Jewish intellectual tradition, to make intelligible the teachings of Aboth. He moves surefootedly in the world of the Rabbis and draws on their discourse, mastering their interpretations, selecting the relevant passage or passages, introducing those explanations which naturally, legitimately relate to the Aboth saying and make it understandable. In his statement on Elisha' ben Abiyyah, he even finds it interesting to report that there is a Hebrew rendering of Goethe's *Faust*. We come face to face with Taylor as erudite commentator at once, in his very first comment (on the concept of "fence," *seyag*): he calls our attention to passages in Jebamoth, Rosh ha-Shanah, Aboth de-Rabbi Nathan, Rashi; and in his Additional Note (pp. 134-135) continues explaining in the light of still other sources, the Midrash Tehillim, Pesiqta Rabbathi, Tosefta, Mekhilta. And it's not only talmudic sources he refers to, but also Septuagint, Apocrypha, New Testament, apostolic and post-apostolic literature, and modern discussions too. For his purposes he enlists whatever is germane, whatever is genuinely expository, whatever will help establish the *peshat,* the primary, the literal and reasonably implicit intention of the saying.

Or, here, for example, is part of his comment on "Love work" (I.11); "Whosoever does not teach his son a business, or 'work,' teaches him robbery (Qiddushin 29a)." Then comes a quotation from Ephesians in the original Greek.* Resuming Taylor: "R. 'Aqiba said: 'Make thy sabbath weekday, and be not dependent upon the creatures' (Shabbath 118a; Pesachim 112a, 113a. Cf. Ecclus. xl.28, 9). A man should hire himself out to 'ABODAH ZARAH, rather than become dependent upon his fellows. Not literal idolatry, it is added, but service which is strange to him. Flay a carcase in the street and receive pay; and say not, I am Cahana (*or* priest), and a great and learned man (Pesachim 113a; Baba Bathra 110a). Cf. Aboth R. N. XI. The Shekinah was not to dwell with Israel till they had made a sanctuary (Ex. xxv.8). 'Six days *must* (not *mayest*) thou labour, and do all thy work': labour if poor, but find 'work' to do even if rich. A wife is relieved from household work in proportion to the number of maidservants she brings her husband. If she brings him four 'she sits in a chair.' R. Eli'ezer says, If she brings him a hundred she must still work in wool, since idleness occasions lewdness. R. Sh. ben Gamaliel says, that he who has exempted her by a vow from all work may as well divorce her (Kethuboth v.5). Great teachers, as Hillel, acted up to the precept, 'Hate not laborious work' (Ecclus. vii.15). St Paul engaged in manual labour (Acts xviii.3; I Cor. iv.12). Contrast: 'The wisdom of a learned man cometh by opportunity of leisure; and he that hath little business shall become wise. How can he get wisdom that holdeth the plough? . . . they shall not sit on the judges' seat, nor understand the sentence of judgment; and they shall not be found where parables are spoken. But they will maintain the state of the world, and (all) their desire is in the work of their craft' (Ecclus. xxxviii.24-34. Cf. xxvi.29)."

* I am not reproducing the Greek because it would add to the cost of printing, and the reader will find it easily in the text below, pp. 18f. For the same reason I have chosen a passage in which Taylor does not quote the Hebrew original.

(The student will find it interesting, I believe, to compare Taylor's comment with that in Maḥzor Vitry, 471.)

There is no need to quote additional examples, for the reader now once again has in his hands the Taylor volumes—have they been out of print these many years because readers were disheartened by the translation?—and can examine the comments personally (and thus also observe the way Taylor quotes the original sources). But it is worth spelling out what is extraordinary in such commentary. In his own time, as well as today or any day, even though Taylor's scholarship in Christian sources would be noteworthy, in that regard he would not be singular. What makes Taylor stand out is his Jewish scholarship, his being at home in that vast domain of post-biblical *Hebrew* literature, from Midrash and Talmud through the works of the great exegetes—Vitry, Maimonides, Duran, Abarbanel, and so on and on. And it is touching to find his own Hebrew style affected by the manners of speaking of the classical rabbinic scholars he has diligently studied: like a Tosafist he will introduce a question by *we-'im tomar* and the answer by *we-yesh lomar,* abbreviations and all (see, for example, his note 7 on the foot of page 3 of the Hebrew text). And how he loves to make Hebrew words his own! He will speak of peraqim, of seder, and won't even italicize; very often he does not bother even to transliterate or translate: the Hebrew word will be presented in its own alphabet. (However, in this way he loves also the Greek and Latin words.) I have been unable to find out who taught Taylor rabbinic Hebrew; was it Schiller-Szinessy? According to the Jewish Encyclopaedia, he came to Cambridge in or about 1863, but Taylor was already in residence at St. John's in the autumn of 1858! At all events, Taylor reads his Hebrew as though he had acquired it "by attendance upon the wise, by discussion with associates, by the argumentation of disciples."

The same excellence distinguishes the discussions in his five excursuses (pp. 105-130, 173-192). He is constantly summoning the evidence of fundamental texts, critically evaluating their testimony, carefully taking note of their specific vocabulary. To this day those discussions remain instructive.

Needless to say, in the almost-a-century since Taylor's *Say-*

ings first appeared, Judaica scholarship has advanced considerably; it is no wonder therefore that there will be disagreement with some of his renditions or interpretations. While he understands the word *peras* in the saying of Antigonus as "recompense," we know today (thanks to E. J. Bickerman) that something like "rations" or "allowance" is the more accurate explanation. The way he reads Ele'azar ben 'Arak's saying in II.18 (although he appreciated that the word "Thorah" was "of doubtful genuineness," and that is why he italicized it—see his introductory remark at the head of Chapter I) is most likely not to be accepted, and the correct original version is more likely to have been, "Be diligent to learn wherewith thou mayest answer," etc. Hillel's saying, "He who serves himself with the tiara perishes," he fails to comment on at all, and his brief reference to it in the Notes on the Text is hardly satisfying. In neither version of Aboth de-Rabbi Nathan is it interpreted as in Aboth IV.9, although, truth to say, Version B of Aboth de-Rabbi Nathan is somewhat ambiguous in this connection. In other words, high praise of Taylor does not mean that one will always agree with him—Taylor would have been the first to dismiss meaningless tribute with disdain. But even when one disagrees with him, one learns a lot from him, all the time. It has happened more than once or twice that twentieth-century scholars have in the course of their own researches come upon a striking textual variant, or decided upon a possible "new" interpretation, only later to discover that the reading had already been noted by Taylor, or that that interpretation had already occurred to, or been encountered in the earlier literature by Taylor. There are many rewards for the scholar who will patiently examine the Notes on the Text; and the descriptions of the manuscripts are an education not only in Hebrew bibliography but in textual criticism as well.

For about Pirqe Aboth there is still a great deal to be learned, even in connection with details that have been observed before and for which explanations have been proposed. For example: What is Aboth doing in the fourth seder, the fourth order of the Mishnah, Neziqin? Is it indeed as Maimonides suggested, that, first, after several treatises of the Mishnah have outlined what judges and institutions of justice require, Aboth now comes along to demonstrate that the teachings of the Sages on this score are not inventions of their own, but an uninterrupted tradition reaching back to the Revelation at Sinai; and, second, that the ethical exhortations in the Sayings of Aboth, while important for all human beings, are eminently so for those who act as judges, and therefore they above all should learn well these lessons? Or consider the following: At the beginning of Chapter II, Rabbi (Judah the Prince) advises us to "consider three things" in order to escape falling into the hands of transgression; at the beginning of Chapter III an earlier Sage, 'Aqabiah ben Mahalaleel, also counsels "consider three things" in order to escape transgression. But the three things recommended by the one are not the same as the three recommended by the other. Is it only individual temperament which distinguishes the one man from the other? Or one final example: The fifth chapter begins with a statement that "By ten Sayings the world was created." But what were those ten sayings, those utterances? And if the answer to the question is far from self-evident, as talmudic uncertainty itself reveals, why did not the Mishnah go on to state plainly what they were, as for instance, it does in a later statement regarding the ten miracles wrought in the Sanctuary, or regarding the ten things that were created "at the time of transition from the 'six days of creation' to the sabbath?" Every serious reader of Aboth will find ample opportunity for questions and further reflection, even after he's consulted the commentators. Frequently the test of a great commentator is not so much his answer to questions which perplex him, as his ability to make us aware of problems which, left to our own devices only, we might never have noted. Were it not for Taylor's Notes, we might remain unaware of many fine points. See, for example, his critical note on the name Matthai (the Arbelite) on page 136 of the Appendix Volume.

In the brief biographical sketch of Taylor which Sir J. E. Sandys, the author of the *History of Classical Scholarship*, drew up after Taylor's death, we read: "His college sermons, delivered in a quiet, level tone, with no rhetorical display, were marked by a solid grasp of fact and a patient elaboration of detail." Essentially the same was said in an obituary by another of Taylor's

colleagues: "In all his work . . . there is evidence not only of a
wide and massive learning, but also of an alert ingenuity, which
is only equaled by his inexhaustible patience in the examination of details." One more witness: "The true meaning of a text
was a vital question to him, and he shrank from no sacrifice in-
volved in honest research, and what he searched for was accurate
information and exact knowledge." This thoroughness, this re-
jection of ostentatious or gaudy expression, this determined devotion to detail and exactitude—all are beautifully exemplified
in Taylor's *Sayings of the Jewish Fathers, Dibre 'Aboth ha-'Olam.*
These sayings which so impressed him, he did not come to
praise or to criticize, to recommend or to refute. Their merit
was vivid the moment they were understood: they "will flame
out, like shining from shook foil." Taylor undertook to make
them understandable, just that, understandable. His *Sayings*
therefore is not only "the most important contribution to [tal-
mudic and rabbinic] studies made by any Christian Scholar
since the time of Buxtorf"; it belongs to that body of literature
from Aboth de-Rabbi Nathan down through the centuries, which
teaches us the meaning of Pirqe Aboth, and is read and studied
and consulted and quoted whenever Aboth is read. When is
Aboth read, however? One answer to this question is available
on the first page of Charles Taylor's Introduction (and Sar
Shalom is ninth century). Still others are to be found in the
Zunz reference Taylor lists in the first footnote of that page. But,
as we saw at the outset, there are also additional answers.

February 1969   Judah Goldin
                                                     Davenport College
                                                     Yale University

Postscript:

For a bibliography of modern critical literature on **Pirqe
Aboth**, see the forthcoming article on 'Abot in the Encyclopaedia
Judaica, the first volume of which is scheduled to appear in the
near future. For the time being, cf. Sh. Shunami, *Bibliography of
Jewish Bibliographies,* Jerusalem, 1965, the entries under Abot,
Pirke, in the Index on p. 835.

PREFACE.

The Second Edition of *Dibré Aboth ha-Olam* or *Sayings of the Jewish Fathers* may be shortly described as a reprint of the work as published in 1877, with a section of ADDITIONAL NOTES. Interspersed with the reprint are insertions in square brackets, a few things are omitted, and short new notes fill up pages 26, 41, 77, 98. With the two titles of the book compare *Shebach* ABOTH OLAM in the Hebrew of Ecclesiasticus and its Greek rendering Πατέρων ὕμνος.

An Appendix not yet published contains the CATALOGUE of Manuscripts referred to in the *Introduction*, which was announced as undertaken "with especial reference to disputed readings," followed by critical *Notes on the Text of Aboth**. It is complete as first planned, but awaits a supplement describing Manuscripts examined or to be examined by Mr Schechter, Reader in Talmudic and Rabbinic in the University of Cambridge, to whose learning and acumen I am indebted for the suggestion of additions and improvements throughout the work.

The collection of Manuscripts lately brought from Egypt by Mr Schechter, with the generous consent of the Grand Rabbi

---

* No. 170 in the Catalogue analyses a commentary on Aboth which has been ascribed on slight grounds to R. Meshullam ben Qalonymos. See *Semitic Studies in mem.* Dr A. KOHUT, art. *On Codex de-Rossi* 184 (Berlin 1897). An old Cairo fragment of Aboth omits the *baba* or verse באשתו אמרו כו' (I. 6). Readings of this fragment are ענוים with *pathach* under the *nun* (I. 5, cf. Aboth R. N.), רחק for הרחק & תתיואש with *vau* (I. 8), דרך הארץ *bis* with art. (III. 26), שנפיו *bis* for שענפיו & באת ופוכרתו והופכתו (III. 27), החכם & הגיבור with art. (IV. 1, 2). Another fragment in the same hand reads סוד (?) with *vau* (II. 10), שלושה שלושה *bis* (II. 12, 13), שבכלל דבריו מדבריכם *bis* (II. 11), מבריע הוא מה שתשיב את without לך (II. 16), ירושה without דברים (II. 14), (II. 18). The scribe used irregular scraps of parchment, and had to make some lines shorter than they should have been.

of Cairo*, includes some fragments of the Old Testament in Greek with the Tetragrammaton written repeatedly in Hebrew characters οὐ τοῖς νῦν ἀλλὰ τοῖς ἀρχαιοτάτοις, in accordance with the remark of Origen on Psalm ii. (*Opp.* II. 539) that it so stood ἐν τοῖς ἀκριβεστέροις τῶν ἀντιγράφων, and the confirmatory testimony of St Jerome (*Praef. in Sam. et Malachim*) "Et nomen Domini tetragrammaton in quibusdam Graecis voluminibus usque hodie antiquis expressum litteris invenimus." The Name is so written in the annexed specimen of Aquila's version of the Old Testament (p. viii.).

In the same collection is being found more and more of the long lost original Hebrew of Ecclesiasticus (p. 169), a book which furnishes not a few apt illustrations of Aboth†, although the precise degree of its affinity in thought and diction to the New Hebrew is still under discussion.

Of the innumerable works on Aboth it must suffice to make mention here of Professor Dr H. L. Strack's concise and thoroughly practical edition *Die Sprüche der Väter.*

---

* See the *Times* for Aug. 3, 1897, art. *A Hoard of Hebrew Manuscripts* by Mr Schechter, followed by Mr F. C. Burkitt's notice of a fragment of Aquila's version of 2 Kings. On the supposed inaccuracy of Origen and Jerome's statements above-mentioned see Gesenius *Gesch. d. hebr. Sprache und Schrift* p. 176 (Leipz. 1815), Migne *P. L.* on Jerome *l.c.*

† With Aboth vi. 9 (p. 103) compare Ecclus. xli. 12 כי הוא ילוך כו׳ *for that will accompany thee more than thousands of precious treasures.* Professor Margoliouth in the *Athenaeum* for July 31, 1897 finds κάρδαμον translettered in Ecclus. xl. 16 כרדמות and Aboth iv. 9 קרדום לאכול. In connexion with the chariot (p. 169) and with ὁ πονηρός (p. 192) see *Semitic Studies in mem.* Kohut art. *The Testament of Job* by Dr K. Kohler, *Texts and Studies* vol. v. no. 1.

C. TAYLOR.

13th August 1897.

CONTENTS.

* With plates of *recto* and *verso* to follow and face the transcript.

Fragment of Aquila's version of the Old Testament transcribed from a Cairo Palimpsest*.

Psalm xc. 6. απο δηγμου δεμ[ονιζοντος μεσημβριας].   *recto*

7. παισειται απο πλαγιου σ[ου χιλιας]
κ αι μυριας απο δεξι[ων σου]
προς σε ου προσεγγ[ισει].

8. εκτος εν οφθαλμοις [σου επιβλε]ψεις
και αποτισιν † ασεβων οψη.

9. οτι σοι יהוה ελπις μου
υψιστον εθηκας οικητηριον σου.

10. ου μεταχθησεται προς σε κακια
και αφη ουκ εγγισει εν σκεπη σου.

11. οτι αγγελοις αυτου εντελιται σε
του φυλαξαι σε εν πασαις οδοις σου.

12. επι ταρσων αρουσιν σε
μηποτε προσκοψη εν λιθω [πους σου].

13. επι λεενα και ασπιδα πατησεις.

Psalm xci. 4. [εν κι]θαρα.   *verso*

5. [οτι ηυφρανας με יה]וה εν κατεργω σου
[εν ποιημασι] χειρων σου αινεσω.

6. [ως εμεγαλυνθη] ποιηματα σου יהוה
σφοδρα [εβαθυνθ]ησαν λογισμοι σου.

7. [ανηρ] ασυνετος ου γνωσεται
και ανοητος ου συνησει συν ταυτην.

8. εν τω βλαστησαι ασεβεις ομοιως χλοη
και ηνθησαν παντες κατεργαζομενοι
ανωφελες
εκτριβηναι αυτους εως ετι.

9. και σοι υψιστος εις αιωνα יהוה.

10. ιδου οι εχθροι σου יהוה ‡
ιδου οι εχθροι σου απολουνται
[σκορπι]σθησονται παντες κατεργαζο
[μενοι ανωφελες].

* Above the Greek is part of T. J. Moed Qat. ii. 4—iii. 1.
† Ἀπότισις is extant here only in the Old Testament.
‡ The Name is written in archaic Hebrew characters.

RECTO (PS. XC. 6-13)

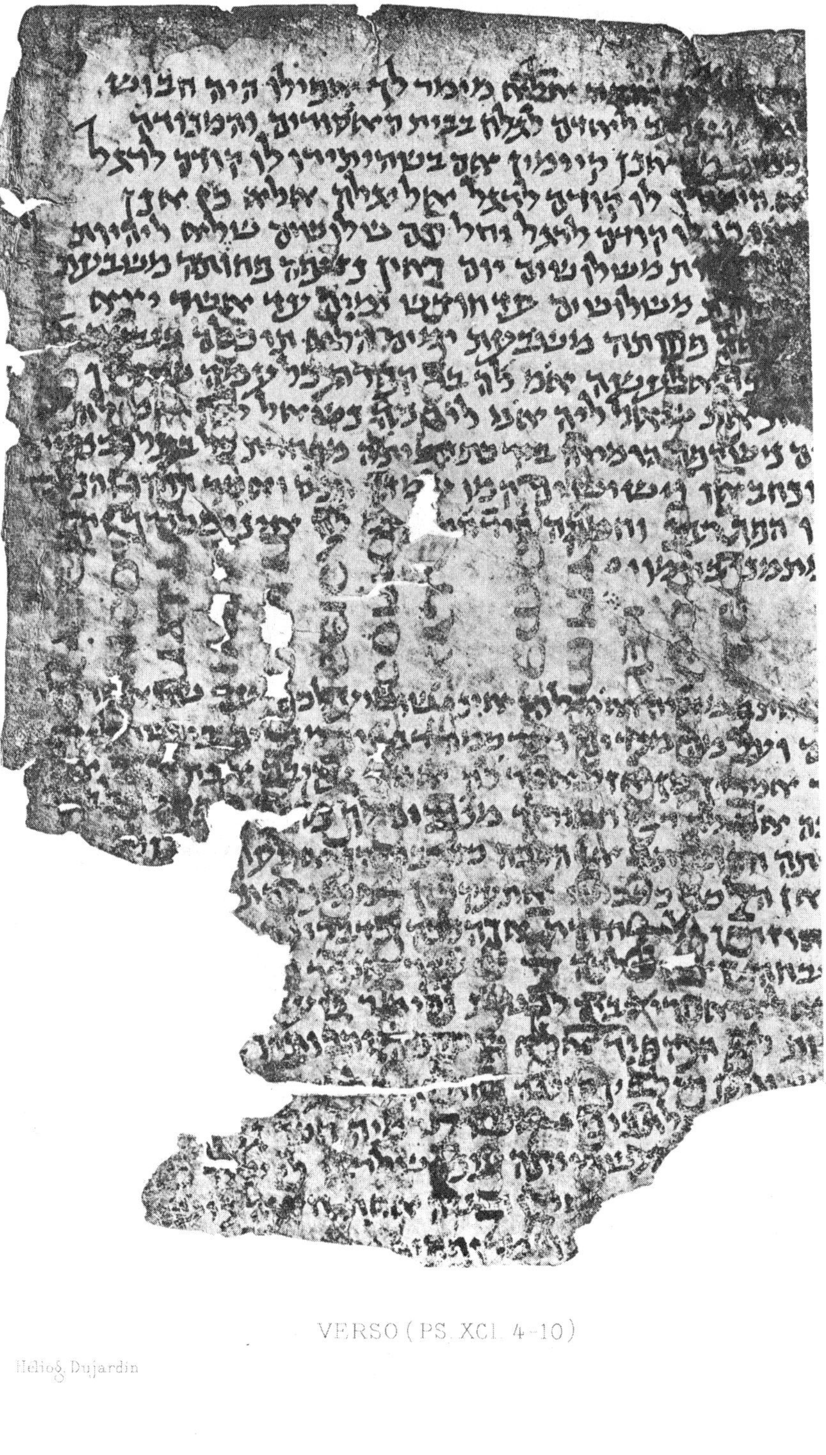

VERSO (PS. XCI. 4-10)

Héliog. Dujardin

INTRODUCTION.

INTRODUCTION.

MASSEKETH ABOTH, best known [with the addition of Pereq
Rabbi Meir] as Pirqe Aboth, or Chapters of the Fathers, is a
Mishnah Tract in Seder Neziqin, where it stands between
'Abodah Zarah and Horaioth. It takes its name from the fact
that it consists to a great extent of maxims of the Jewish
FATHERS whose names are mentioned in its pages, and is
chiefly valued as a compendium of practical ethics, although it
is not without a mystical element in portions of its Fifth and
concluding Chapter. Its simplicity and intrinsic excellence
have secured for ABOTH a widespread and lasting popularity,
and have led to its being excerpted from the Talmud and used
liturgically in the Synagogue, at certain seasons, from an early
period. "It was the custom," writes Sar Shalom Gaon[1], "in
the house of our Rabbi in Babel, to recite ABOTH and (the
supplementary sixth chapter) QINYAN THORAH, after evening
prayer upon the Sabbath;" and the "Six Chapters" are found
at the present day in Prayer Books of the Ashkenazic[2] rite.

The Talmudic saying that *Whosoever would be pious
must fulfil the dicta of the* FATHERS is quoted by Rabbinic
commentators in their introductions to Pirqe Aboth, and the
Tract has been described, with reference to this saying, as
"Mishnath ha-Chasidim," a course of instruction for the pious.

[1] Quoted by RASHI in ספר הפרדס סימן ד׳. On the various uses, see ZUNZ
Die Ritus des synagogalen Gottesdienstes p. 85.

[2] German, Polish, &c.

The First Chapter opens with the statement that Moses, having received the Law from Sinai, handed it down to Joshua, and he in turn to the Elders, and the Elders to the men of the Great Synagogue. The Mosaic succession having been thus far established, the men of the Great Synagogue speak their three WORDS, which express the aim and function of the new school of Soferim: "Be deliberate in judgment; and raise up many disciples; and make a hedge to the Law." Next comes Simon Justus, with his saying, that the three pillars of the world are Revelation, Worship, and Humanity; and after him the first teacher of Greek name, Antigonus, whose inculcation of disinterested service is described in a Jewish tradition as the ultimate source of the negative tenets of the Sadducees, or "Sons of Zadok." From this point onward to the end of the Fourth Chapter we have a series of moral sayings, which are put into the mouths of Rabbis who lived within the period from two centuries before to two centuries after CHRIST.

The Fifth Chapter is characterised by something of a more speculative tendency. It touches upon the cosmogony; upon miracles, and their relation to the order of nature; upon the connexion between the moral and the physical; upon the varieties of men, and minds, and motives; upon the antitheses of the good and the evil dispositions. In form it is a series of groups of ten, seven, four, and three things; its sayings, unlike those in preceding chapters, take the form of historical narrative, or of systematic classification; and it makes no mention of the name of any Mishnah Teacher, until we come, at or near the end, to a saying which is ascribed to Jehudah ben Thema: "Be bold as a leopard, and swift as an eagle, and fleet as a hart, and strong as a lion, to do the will of thy FATHER WHICH IS IN HEAVEN."

Of commentaries upon ABOTH, the best known is that of Maimonides, which is found—sometimes in the original Arabic, but more commonly in Hebrew—in separate Manuscripts, or

in his work on the whole Mishnah, or in Jewish Prayer Books
of the Italian rite. Another great commentary, which has been
ascribed to R. Jacob ben Shimshon, to R. Shemuel ben Meir,
a grandson of Rashi, and even to Rashi himself, is found likewise in separate Manuscripts, and in a great number of Prayer
Books, especially of the Franco-German rite. In its most complete form[1] it belongs apparently to the beginning of the thirteenth century, but it is based upon traditions of a much earlier
date. A third work which is indispensable for the criticism
of ABOTH is the Arabic commentary of 'R. Israel' of Toledo,
which has hitherto been supposed to have perished, except in
so far as it was embodied in the Hebrew commentary of his
descendant, Isaac ben R. Shelomoh; but a manuscript of R.
Israel's work has been lately purchased for the Bodleian Library
[1875], and will be found described and identified in [No. 90 of]
the forthcoming Catalogue of MANUSCRIPTS OF THE TEXT OF
ABOTH AND OF COMMENTARIES UPON IT.

The printed text of the Five Peraqim[2] is from an important
manuscript of the MISHNAH, [which was purchased for the
Cambridge University Library in 1869, and has been edited
by Mr W. H. Lowe, of Christ's College]. The sixth Pereq is
taken from a modern Ashkenazic Prayer Book.

The *Comparative Index of the Mishnah* gives the title of
each Tract[3] according to the MS., with its positions in the MS.
itself and in the well-known edition of Surenhusius respectively. The *Index* is followed by extracts from the Mishnah

---

[1] That is to say, in the form in which it appears in the so-called MACHAZOR
VITRY, which has been cited under that name in the notes. But, as will be
shewn in the *Catalogue of MSS. of Aboth*, this title, although given by S. D.
Luzzatto, is inaccurate.

[2] Each chapter in the MS. forms a continuous paragraph. But the printed
text [of the five chapters in *Sayings of the Jewish Fathers*] has been subdivided
according to the punctuation of the MS. [except that chap. v. 13—14, from
חרב בא to השמט הארץ, should have formed one verse only, as in No. 98 of
the *Catalogue*], and numbers have been added for convenience of reference *within
the edition itself*.

[3] Notice especially מסכת נזיקין.

including two complete specimen pages[1], which, with the exception of the headings, have been transcribed literally and line by line from the MANUSCRIPT. [The *Index* and the extracts above-mentioned are now transferred to the APPENDIX.]

St John's College,
April 9th, 1877.

---

[1] Notice in the first extract the reading ואכילת פסחים, which a comparison of the two Gemaras shews to be characteristic of the "Jerushalmi." The reading in the extract from Sanhedrin, omitting כל ישראל יש להם חלק כו׳ and beginning אלו—*not* ואלו, is confirmed by the Gemara. ABOTH itself is one of the Tracts not found in other copies of the "Jerushalmi."

Extracts from page 1 of the First Edition of
Sayings of the Jewish Fathers.

The following Manuscripts are referred to :

British Museum MSS.

A. Addit. 27201
B. Orient. 1003
C. Addit. 27070
D. ,,   27072
E. ,,   17057
F. ,,   27115

Cambridge MSS.

𝔄. University, Addit. 470
𝔅. St John's College, K. 7
ℭ. University, Addit. 667
𝔇. ,,   ,,   1200
ℭ. ,,   ,,   561
𝔉. A Machazor.

A* denotes the Oxford MS., *Bodl.* 145. It contains the same commentary as A (Machazor Vitry). A† is a third copy of the same commentary. A† and 𝔉 are in the possession of the Editor.

Bar S. denotes Isaac Bar Shelomoh, the author of the commentary in B, 𝔅.

The text of Aboth is taken from 𝔄; Pereq VI from an edition of the Ashkenazic Prayer Book.

In citations from the Talmud the letters T. J. are prefixed to those which are from the Jerushalmi. The rest are from the Babli.

The Hebrew letters, תת,   ת,   ט,   צ,   ע,   ק,   כ,   ח,
are transliterated,   *tth,* *th,* *t,* *ç,* '*,*   *q,*   *k,*   *ch,*
except in some cases in which familiar forms are retained.

The following Translation and Commentary with the Excursuses occupied pages 25—145 in the First Edition. To
find the corresponding pages in the Second Edition, subtract
fourteen, or in the case of the last page only *fifteen*. For the
Critical Notes on the Text which preceded the Translation
and Commentary in the First Edition see under *Notes on the
Text* in the APPENDIX.

PIRQE ABOTH.

האי מאן דבעי למהוי חסידא

לקיים

מילי דאבות

PIRQE ABOTH.

CHAPTER I.

Some passages of doubtful genuineness are printed in italics. Omissions of the manuscript of Chapters I—V are supplied in smaller type. On words in thick type see the Excursuses at the end of Chapter VI.

1. Moses received the **Thorah** from Sinai, and he delivered it to Jehoshua‘, and Jehoshua‘ to the elders (Josh. xxiv. 31 ; Jud. ii. 7), and the elders to the prophets, and the prophets delivered it to the men of the **Great Synagogue.** They said three things: Be deliberate in judgment; and raise up many disciples; and make a fence[1] to the Thorah.

[1] Impose additional restrictions so as to keep at a safe distance from forbidden ground : "ושמרתם את משמרתי (Lev. xviii. 30), make a *mishmereth* to my *mishmereth*" (Jebamoth 21 a). "To what is the matter like ? To a man watching a garden. If he watches it from without, it is all watched ; if he watches it from within, the part in front of him is watched; and the part behind him is not watched." The סייג (III. 20 ; VI. 6) lies at the root of the Rabbinic system. Its application to holy days gives rise to the principle מוסיפין מחול על קדש (R. ha-Shan. 9 a), in connexion with which compare Rashi on Gen. ii. 2, where it is said that whereas man must sanctify the Sabbath in advance, not knowing the instant of its commencement, the Creator "enters upon it to a hair's breadth," and even seems to finish "*on* the seventh day" itself. For other examples see Aboth de R. Nathan I., II., where it is said *inter alia* that Adam misapplied the principle of the סייג, and gave occasion to the Tempter, by superadding the prohibition, *Neither shall ye touch it*, and representing this to Eve as part of God's command, which was only, *Thou shalt not eat of it* (Gen. ii. 17; iii. 3). [Gen. ii. 2 Sept. ἕκτῃ *sixth*, to exclude work on the *seventh*.]

2.   Shime'on ha-Çaddiq[2] was of the remnants of the Great Synagogue. He used to say, On three things the world is stayed[3]; on the Thorah[4], and on the Worship[5] (Rom. ix. 4), and on the bestowal of Kindnesses[6].

[2] Various traditions have gathered round the name of Simon Justus. "Seine Persönlichkeit tritt im Andenken der spätern Rabbinen ins Dunkel der Fabel zurück" (Jost, *Geschichte des Judenthums und seiner Secten*, A. 110). He is said in Joma 9 a, 39 a, 69 a, to have served as high-priest for forty years, and to have gone out in procession to meet "Alexander of Macedon," as Jaddua' is related (Jos. *Ant.* XI. 8. 5) to have done. Various miracles were wrought during his priesthood. In Menachoth 109 b he predicts his own death; and there follows an account of the building of a temple in "Alexandria of Egypt" (Is. xix. 19) by his son Onias, or נחוניו (A in Menach. XIII. 10). But see Jos. *Ant.* XIII. 3. 3. Simon has been made contemporary with נסקלנס (? Gaïus Caligula. Cf. Jost, A. 359), who attempted to set up his statue in the temple at Jerusalem. See Megillath Tha'anith XI. ; T. J. Sotah IX. 13 ; Babli 33 a ; Jos. *Ant.* XVIII. 8 ; and Jos. ben Gorion II. 6, where this tale likewise is told of Alexander. See also 3 Macc. i. ii. The eulogy in Ecclus. l. has been applied by some to Simon I., son of Onias, called Simon Justus in Jos. *Ant.* XII. 2. 5 ; and by others to Simon II., also son of Onias. The latter Simon is identified in Bar Hebr. Chronicon Eccles. (col. 22, ed. Abbeloos et Lamy) with the Συμεών of Luke ii. 25, who is characterised as δίκαιος. Herzfeld concludes that the allusion in the text is to Simon II., and that the date of his high-priesthood was 226—198 B.C. Zunz (*Die Got-*

tesdienstlichen Vorträge d. Juden, p. 36) gives the date 221—202 B.C.

[3] These three things are regarded as bases or *pillars* of the world. Cf. Ps. lxxv. 4 ; Prov. ix. 1 ; and (?) 1 Tim. iii. 15. [Chagigah 12 b.]

[4] See Nedar. 32 a. The world, it is said, was only created for the sake of the Thorah and its learners. The notion of design in creation is brought out in a striking way at the beginning of Bereshith Rabbah. Thorah, or Wisdom (Prov. viii. 1), was God's agent or instrument (cf. Aboth III. 23), and plan. As a human king does not build a palace of himself without an artificer ; nor he of himself without drawings and plans ; so God looked into the Thorah and created the world, כן הקב״ה היה מביט בתורה ובורא את העולם. Seven things were created before the world, or existed as concepts in the mind of the Creator ; *Thorah*, Gehenna, the Garden of Eden, the Throne of Glory, the Sanctuary, Repentance, and the Name of Messiah. Thorah counselled God to create the world. "Hence the wise have said, A kingdom without counsellors is no kingdom at all" (Pirqe R. Eli'ezer III.). See also Nedarim 39 b.

[5] This in the mouth of a high-priest means the service and sacrifices of the temple which was then standing. Cf. Megillah 31 b, Tha'anith 27 b. In Pirq. R. Eliez. XVI. it is proved from Prov. xv. 8, by identifying *prayer* with *'abodah*; since what other service (Dan. vi. 16) could there be in Babel ? But the primary meaning is more appropriate here ; and the fact

3. **Antigonus** of[7] Soko received from Shime'on ha-Çaddiq. He used to say, Be not as slaves that minister to the lord with a view to receive recompense; but be as slaves that minister to the lord without a view to receive[8] recompense; and let the fear of Heaven be upon you.

that *prayer*, which *is not enjoined in the Pentateuch*, תפילה אינ׳ דבר תורה (T. J. Berakoth I. 5), is not mentioned and brought into prominence in the sayings of this Pereq may perhaps be taken as one sign of their superior antiquity. [Aboth R. N. *A* iv., *B* v.]

[6] This is connected in Aboth R. N. iv. with עולם חסד יבנה (Ps. lxxxix. 3). It was declared in the beginning more acceptable (Hos. vi. 6) than the sacrifices which Israel were destined to offer (Pirq. R. Eliez. xvi.). It is not to be restricted to the *requital* of benefits, but is as far reaching, and at the same time as undefinable (Peah I. 1), as a man's "duty to his neighbour." While its fruits are enjoyed in this world, the principal remains for the world to come (cf. 1 Tim. iv. 8). With *çedaqah* — a treasure laid up not on earth but in heaven, over which the hand (of the spoiler) has no power—it counterpoises all the precepts of the Thorah. But it is greater than çedaqah, as having to do alike with person and property, rich and poor, dead and living. It includes the duties of sympathy (χαίρειν μετὰ χαιρόντων, κλαιειν μετὰ κλαιόντων, Rom. xii. 15)—of attending the wedding and the funeral. It is more beloved even than the study of Thorah. (T. J. Peah I. 1; Sukkah 49 b.) The Thorah itself begins and ends with it (Sotah 14 a); for God *clothed* Adam and Eve (Gen. iii. 21), and "he *buried* him (Moses) in a valley" (Deut. xxxiv. 6). He who occupies himself in Thorah and *gemiluth chasadim*, and buries his children, is forgiven all his

iniquities (Berakoth 5 b).

[7] The title איש סוכו is said (A; bar S.) to imply that Antigonus was *vir magnus* in his city. Cf. איש ישראל (Jud. vii. 14). For other examples of this usage in the Mishnah, see Aboth I. 4, 5; III. 9, 10; IV. 7, 28; Challah IV. 10; 'Orlah II. 5, 12; Gittin VI. 7; 'Edioth VI. 2; Middoth I. 2.

[8] Serve God from pure motives, with a view which is not that of receiving recompense. Serve, however, from a sense of duty, and be not like voluntary workers who sometimes will, and sometimes will not, labour. So bar S. on the last clause, with the suggestion that it did not belong to the original saying, but was added later to prevent future generations from drawing extreme negative inferences like "Çadoq and Baithus." 𝕰 omits the clause, *but be, &c.*, probably through homœoteleuton; but it is possible that the original saying consisted of one clause only: *Be not, &c.* Antigonus inculcates disinterested service without expressly enunciating any doctrine positive or negative concerning a future state of retribution. He does not add: "in order that your reward may be double in the world to come" (Aboth R.N. v.); with which compare the principle: למד מאהבה וסוף הכבוד לבא "Learn out of love, and honour will come eventually" (Nedarim 62 a). The question is raised in Sotah v. 5: "Did Job serve out of love?" and it is worthy of remark that the discussion in the Gemara turns upon the double reading לא (קרי לו) איחל (Job xiii. 15), which

4. Jose ben Joʻezer of Çeredah and Jose ben Jochanan of Jerusalem[9] received from them. Jose ben Joʻezer of Çeredah[10] said, Let thy house be a meeting-house for the wise; and powder thyself in the dust of their feet[11]; and drink their words with thirstiness.

is illustrated by צר (קרי לו) לא (Is. lxiii. 9).

[9] The תנאים from § 4 to § 13 are named two and two as σύνζυγοι. In Peah II. 6 the chain of tradition is given compendiously: the "pairs" received from the prophets, and they from Moses. In Chagigah II. 2 each pair is represented as divided on one and the same question. It is added that the first mentioned in each pair held the office of *nasi*, or president of the Sanhedrin, and the second that of *ab beth din*, or vice-president. Their chronology cannot be precisely determined. Herzfeld (*Gesch.* II. 140) gives their dates B. C. as follows: (α) The two Josephs, 170; (β) Jehoshuaʻ and Matthai, 140—110; (γ) Jehudah, 100; Shimeʻon, 90; (δ) Shemaʻiah and Abtalion, 65—35; (ε) Hillel, 30. The last date (=100 years before the destruction of the temple) is given in Shabbath 15 a. Zunz (*Gottesd. Vorträge*, 37, note *c*), assuming a hiatus after Antigonus (190 B.C.), dates the pairs as follows: (α) 140—130; (β)**; (γ) 90—80; (δ) 60 —50; (ε) z. *Zeit des Herodes*.

[10] Joseph ben Joʻezer was a priest of pre-eminent piety (Chagigah II. 7). "From the time when the two Josephs died the *clusters* (Mic. vii. 1) ceased" (Sotah 47 a). The word *eshkol* is explained in Themurah 15 b, by איש שהכל בו. By some it is identified with σχολή. It is said (Them. 15 a) that at the death of J. ben Joʻezer the *eshkoloth* ceased to learn Thorah like Moses. Up to that time, but no longer,

they were free from reproach. The sayings of ben Joʻezer indicate that he used his best endeavours to revive the respect for traditional teaching, and to establish "schools" of the wise. The sayings attributed to particular teachers are not, according to the pseudo-RASHI, to be regarded as necessarily originating with them. It is only meant that they were commonplaces in their mouths (Berakoth 17 a). Cf. Aboth IV. 26.

[11] Cf. Luke x. 39; Acts xxii. 3. Although entertaining scholars in thy house assume not a position of superiority, but sit at their feet as a learner. Cf. also the metaphorical expression, אבק לשׁון הרע (Baba Bathra 165 a). That the hearer, especially in the case of a large audience, should be placed at a lower level than the teacher was a matter of obvious convenience; but J. ben Joʻezer recommends it as a sign of humility. The posture of a teacher and his scholars is discussed from a different point of view in Megillah 21 a: "Whence is it that a Rab must not sit on a couch and teach his disciples on the floor?—but both he and they must sit on the couch, or both stand (Rashi). It is because it is said (Deut. v. 31), Stand thou here WITH ME. From the days of Moses to Rabban Gamliel, they always learned Thorah standing. After his death sickness came down to the world, and they learned Thorah sitting. It is said that Moses *sat* (Deut. ix. 9), and also that he *stood* (Deut. x. 10): in the one case, said

5. Jose ben Jochanan of Jerusalem said, Let thy house be opened wide ; and let the needy be thy household; and prolong not converse with woman[12] ($\tau\hat{\eta}$ γυναικί).

6. (*His own wife, they meant, much less his neighbour's*

Rab, to receive the law, and in the other to announce it. According to R. Chaninah, he neither sat nor stood, but crouched. R. Jochanan says, וישב in the former passage only meant that he stayed...*Easy things are learned standing, and hard things sitting*." That it was customary in the time of Gamaliel II. for the scholars in the *beth ha-midrash* to sit not on the ground but on *subsellia*, appears from the statement (Berakoth 28 a) that after his deposition 400 or 700 additional ספסלי were required. The תנא also sat, whilst an אמורא, or "dragoman" (תרגמן), who stood before him, repeated his words, with or without comment, for the benefit of those who sat at a distance. In certain cases it might be convenient for teacher or taught to stand (Acts xiii. 16 ; Matt. xiii. 2) ; but the evidence of the New Testament and of the Talmud shews that it was more usual to sit. The word ישיבה, *sessio*, is even used of students (II. 8). The public reader of the book Esther might either stand or sit (Megillah IV. 1). On the mutual respect of RAB and THALMID see Aboth IV. 17.

[12] This saying might be applied to a man's wife in particular (as in § 6), or to woman in general, καὶ ἐθαύμαζον ὅτι μετὰ γυναικὸς ἐλάλει (Joh. iv. 27). Cf. Eccl. vii. 28. Man takes precedence of woman in various ways, though "The man is not without the woman, nor the woman without the man, nor both of them without the Shekinah" (Bereshith Rabbah VIII. Cf. 1 Cor. xi. 11). The Thorah in its

entirety is for the man ; whereas the woman is exempt from those positive precepts which are to be fulfilled at stated times (Qiddushin I. 7). She is not to learn Thorah—much less to teach (1 Tim. ii. 12)—not being included in such passages as Deut. xi. 19 : "And ye shall teach them your SONS." How then shall woman make out her title to salvation ? Σωθήσεται ...διὰ τῆς τεκνογονίας (1 Tim. ii. 15; v. 14). Her work is to send her children to be taught in the synagogue : to attend to domestic concerns, and leave her husband free to study in the schools : to keep house for him till he returns. Cf. Berakoth 17 a, נשים במאי זכיין באקרויי בנייהו לבי כנישתא ובאתנויי גברייהו בי רבנן ונטרן לגברייהו עד דאתו מבי רבנן : Women, slaves and children are mentioned together in Berakoth III. 3 ; Sheqalim I. 5. Another remarkable grouping is found in the Jews' Morning Prayer, where the men in three consecutive Benedictions bless God " who hath not made me a GENTILE...a SLAVE...a WOMAN." This affords an illustration (the more striking on account of its indirectness) of a characteristic saying of St Paul : οὐκ ἔνι Ἰουδαῖος οὐδὲ Ἕλλην, οὐκ ἔνι δοῦλος οὐδὲ ἐλεύθερος, οὐκ ἔνι ἄρσεν καὶ θῆλυ, πάντες γὰρ ὑμεῖς εἷς ἐστε ἐν Χριστῷ Ἰησοῦ (Gal. iii. 28). Women could not in general be witnesses (עדים) ; but they had their rights of property. In the case of inheritance, if the property is small "filiæ aluntur, et filii mendicabunt" (Kethuboth XIII. 3 ; Baba Bathra IX. 1). [Chagigah T. B. 3 a & T. J. 75 d.]

wife.) Hence the wise have said, Each time that the man prolongs converse with the woman he causes evil to himself, and desists from words of Thorah, and in the end he inherits Gehinnom[13].

7. Jehoshua' ben Perachia and Matthai[14] the Arbelite received from them. Jehoshua' ben Perachiah said[15], Make unto thyself a master; and possess thyself of an associate; and judge every man in the scale of merit[16].

8. Matthai the Arbelite said, Withdraw from an evil neighbour; and associate not with the wicked[17];. and grow not thoughtless[18] of retribution.

---

[13] Cf. υἱὸν γεέννης (Matt. xxiii. 15).

[14] On the reading, see *Crit. Note*. Little of importance is known of this "pair," except that (Jost, *Gesch.* A. 233) "aus ihren Lehrsätzen, die man von Mund zu Mund weiter überlieferte, ist zu erkennen dass sie dahin strebten dem *mündlichen* Gesetz gegen die hervorgetretene *sadducäische Ansicht* mehr Eingang zu verschaffen."

[15] Jehoshua' counsels a man to place himself under the direction of a traditional teacher, and to associate himself with a worthy companion. There was a proverbial saying, "Companionship or death" (Tha'anith 23 a), companionship even with such friends as those of Job (Baba Bathra 16 b). "Two are better than one" (Eccl. iv. 9), in Thorah as in other matters, since when two study together their words are "written in the book of remembrances" (Berakoth 6 a). Cf. Prov. xxvii. 17. Nay, more, חרב אל הבדים ונאלו (Jer. l. 36), which is turned: "a sword is against the *solitary*, and they are stultified" (see p. 44). The word *chaber*, a companion, came to be used especially of men of learning. It is sometimes equivalent to "colleague," in an official sense; or to "fellow," or "associate,"

of a learned society; and it is contrasted with עם הארץ, which denotes the vulgar herd (Taharoth vii. 4). An interpretation of pseudo-Rashi is: "Make to thyself a Rab, to learn orally; and buy thyself חבר ספרים," buy *books* and make them a *chaber*.

[16] Give a suspected person, whoever he may be, the benefit of the doubt. Let the scale in which he is weighed have a bias towards the side of merit or acquittal. He who thus judges others will thus himself be judged, הדן חברו לכף זכות דנין אותו לכף זכו'. See Shabb. 127 b, where the saying follows upon an enumeration of the things which profit in both worlds. The saying in Shabbath might give rise to the doubt, "who is my *chaber*?" but the words of the text apply to all men. It may serve as a μνημόσυνον to remark that the zodiacal Libra (Bemidbar R. xvi.) corresponds to the month of Judgment, Thishri; as טלה (Pirq. R. Eliez. vii.) to ניסן.

[17] Woe to the wicked! woe to his neighbour! (Nega'im xii. 6). The dry wood sets fire to the green (Sanhedrin 93 a). [See Wetstein's note on St Luke xxiii. 31.]

[18] Cf. Prov. xxviii. 14. The word usually means to despair, give up

9. Jehudah ben Tabai and Shime'on ben Shatach[19] received from them. Jehudah ben Tabai said, Make not thyself as them that predispose the judges[20]; and while the litigants stand before thee, let them be in thine eyes as guilty; and when dismissed from before thee let them be in thine eyes as righteous, because that they have received the doom upon them.

hope of a thing; but the caution is not to presume upon immunity. Even here, however, some commentators endeavour to retain the usual meaning, "despair not of good," if evil come upon thee. 𝔄 wrongly repeats the clause at the end of § 11. Bar S. aptly quotes Eccl. viii. 11 ; adding the remark that *pithgam* does not mean *dabar*, but '*onesh*, "for Qoheleth did not speak ארמית."

[19] In a narrative which there is reason to suspect of inaccuracy, it is said that in the time of Sh. ben Shatach one תודום איש רומי introduced the practice of eating נדיין מקולסין, or quasi-passovers, at Rome; and that Shime'on wrote to him: "Wert thou not Theodos I would pass judgment of נדוי upon thee," &c. (Berakoth 19 a). Bar S. relates that this pair escaped to Alexandria from Jannai the king; and that then arose (?) the sect of the Qaraites, who learned the written Law, the oral Law having been forgotten. At length Jehudah was recalled, and made *nasi*. See T. J. Sanhedrin vi. 9. The Machazor Vitry gives also the alternative view that his colleague was *nasi*, referring to Sanhedrin vi. 4, where, in the course of a discussion whether women who have been stoned should be hanged, Shime'on ben Shatach is said to have hanged eighty women at once in Ashqalon, although even two persons should not be condemned in one day; whereupon the Gemara (46 b) remarks that, when occasion requires, punishments beyond those in the Thorah may be inflicted, as a "fence" to the Thorah. Jehudah did not always practise the judicial impartiality which he recommends. Having once (Makkoth 5 b), out of opposition to the Sadducees, put a false witness to death before the condemned had been executed, he appealed to his colleague, who charged him with having shed innocent blood, and added that neither of two false witnesses was to be punished unless they had both been convicted. Thereupon Jehudah vowed never again to pronounce a decision except in the presence of Shime'on.

[20] The attitude of a judge should be one of impartiality. Be not therefore as partisans who plead the cause of one of the litigants, and thus prejudice the case *before it comes into court*. While the suit is being tried the judge should not look upon either party with favour, but should examine both sides thoroughly and suspiciously. When it is over he should regard both as innocent; whether as having been proved to be in the right, or as having paid the penalty of wrong-doing. The difficult phrase עורכי הדיינים, "disposers or arrangers of the judges," occurs in Kethuboth 52 b, 86 a (cf. pseudo-Rashi on Aboth), and is explained in the commentary as above; it occurs also in Shabbath 139 a, where it is explained of those who teach the

3

10. Shime'on ben Shatach said, Make full examination of the witnesses; but be guarded in thy words, perchance from them they may learn to lie.

11. Shema'iah and Abtalion[21] received from them. Shema'iah said, Love work[22]; and hate lordship[23]; and make not thyself known to the government[24].

litigants to deceive. A slight change of reading would give the meaning, "disposers of *suits* (הדינין)," or special pleaders; but the explanation adopted above gives a more natural sequence. There is another reading (with א for ע), which gives the sense "as *arch*-judge, or *arch*-judges." Jost (*Gesch.* A. 241) renders: "Als Richter sei nicht Sachwalter der Parteien, den andern Richtern gegenüber."

[21] Shema'iah and Abtalion, who were said to be descendants of Sancherib or of Haman (Gittin 57 b; Sanhedrin 96 b), have been identified with the Sameas and Pollio of Josephus, who writes (*Ant.* xv. 1. 1): "But Pollio the Pharisee and Sameas a disciple of his were honoured by (Herod) above all the rest; for when Jerusalem was besieged they advised the citizens to receive Herod; for which advice they were well requited. But this Pollio (or SAMEAS, xiv. 9. 4) at the time when Herod was once upon his trial of life and death foretold in a way of reproach to Hyrcanus and the other judges, how this Herod whom they suffered now to escape would afterwards inflict punishment on them all." In the account of the trial in Sanhedrin 19 a, Jost (*Gesch.* A. 252) would read: "SHEMA'IAH (for *Shime'on ben Shatach*) said to him, Herod (for *King Jannai*), stand on thy feet, &c."; and he adds the following important remarks on the court of the Sanhedrin, and on the status of the pairs (note 9) in relation to it: "Die Schilderung

dieses Gerichtes ist in mehrfacher Hinsicht merkwürdig. Erstens berufen sich die Ankläger auf das Recht der Juden, dass selbst anerkannte Verbrecher nicht eher gestraft werden dürfen als ein *Synedrion* den Spruch erlassen habe. Ein Beweis dass die Synedrial-Einrichtung allerdings schon wurzelte. Zweitens wird von *dem Synedrion* (also dem bestimmten, offenbar dem einzigen) in Jerusalem gesprochen, vor dessen Schranken Hyrkan den Herodes lud. Drittens führte Hyrkan, nicht aber die beiden Schulhäupter, wie man erwarten sollte, den Vorsitz; wie denn *Sameas* auch nur als *einer der Richter* bezeichnet wird, welcher den Muth hatte den Fürsten und die erschrockenen Mitglieder an ihre Pflicht zu erinnern."

[22] Whosoever does not teach his son a business, or "work," teaches him robbery (Qiddushin 29 a). Ὁ κλέπτων μηκέτι κλεπτέτω μᾶλλον δὲ κοπιάτω κ.τ.λ. (Eph. iv. 28). R. 'Aqiba said: "Make thy sabbath weekday, and be not dependent upon the creatures" (Shabbath 118 a; Pesachim 112 a, 113 a. Cf. Ecclus. xl. 28, 9). A man should hire himself out to 'ABODAH ZARAH, rather than become dependent upon his fellows. Not literal idolatry, it is added, but service which is strange to him. Flay a carcase in the street and receive pay; and say not, I am Cahana (*or* priest), and a great and learned man (Pesachim 113 a; Baba Bathra 110 a). Cf. Aboth R. N. xi. The Shekinah was not to dwell with Israel till they

12. Abtalion said, Ye wise, be guarded in your words; perchance ye may incur the debt of exile, and be exiled to the place of evil waters; and the disciples that come after you may drink and die[25], and the Name of Heaven be profaned.

had made a sanctuary (Ex. xxv. 8). " Six days *must* (not *mayest*) thou labour, and do all thy work" : labour if poor, but find " work " to do even if rich. A wife is relieved from household work in proportion to the number of maidservants she brings her husband. If she brings him four " she sits in a chair." R. Eli'ezer says, If she brings him a hundred she must still work in wool, since idleness occasions lewdness. R. Sh. ben Gamaliel says, that he who has exempted her by a vow from all work may as well divorce her (Kethuboth v. 5). Great teachers, as Hillel, acted up to the precept, " Hate not laborious work" (Ecclus. vii. 15). St Paul engaged in manual labour (Acts xviii. 3 ; 1 Cor. iv. 12). Contrast : " The wisdom of a learned man cometh by opportunity of leisure : and he that hath little business shall become wise. How can he get wisdom that holdeth the plough?... they shall not sit on the judges' seat, nor understand the sentence of judgment : they cannot declare justice and judgment ; and they shall not be found where parables are spoken. But they will maintain the state of the world, and (all) their desire is in the work of their craft" (Ecclus. xxxviii. 24—34. Cf. xxvi. 29).

[23] By Rabbanuth some understand " das Rabbi-Wesen " (Matt. xxiii. 8). But it should perhaps be understood of social or political dignity. The Machazor Vitry explains it by *malkuth*. Be like Saul who " hid himself among the stuff" (1 Sam. x. 22) to avoid

being made king. Lordship brings to an early grave, so that Joseph dies before all his brethren, and one prophet outlasts several kings (Ex. i. 6 ; Isaiah i. 1 ; Pesachim 87 b). R. Jonah connects this clause with the preceding by means of Prov. xii. 9. Dr Michael Cahn aptly recites from Plato, *Repub.* 347 D : ἐπεὶ κινδυνεύει, πόλις ἀνδρῶν ἀγαθῶν εἰ γένοιτο, περιμάχητον ἂν εἶναι τὸ μὴ ἄρχειν ὥσπερ νυνὶ τὸ ἄρχειν. A man should not crown himself. "Let another man praise thee, and not thine own mouth" (Prov. xxvii. 2). When the first man rose to his feet, והיה מתואר בדמות אלהים, the creatures were for worshipping him as their Creator ; but Adam said, " Let us go, I and you, and make Him, who created us, king ; for the people appoint the king, and no king appoints himself independently of the people" (Pirqe R. El. xi.).

[24] Avoid growing great, and coming under the notice of the " rashuth " (= ἐξουσία, concretely), in such a way as to excite jealousy or suspicion. Or : " ne nimium familiaris fias principibus "—such associations being thought *corrupting* as well as dangerous. Cf. ii. 3 ; iii. 8; James ii. 6.

[25] The name Abtalion is sometimes explained Aramaically by " pater adolescentium," in allusion to the " disciples" mentioned below. His sayings are transcendental, with historical reference. Scholars must take heed to their doctrine, lest they pass over into the realm of heresy, and inoculate their disciples with deadly error. The

13. Hillel[26] and Shammai received from them. Hillel said, Be of the disciples of Aharon[27]; loving peace, and pur-

penalty of untruth is untruth, to imbibe which is death. Historically regarded, the Israelite's captivity amongst worshippers of strange gods was the judgment upon him for irreligiousness. Abarbanel here credits Abtalion with a prescience that the second Temple was to be destroyed. Since it is contemplated that the wise themselves may be enthralled, the caution is not to be thought of as directed merely against loose or insufficiently explained expressions, nor against the opposite extreme (cf. Chagigah II. 1) of the too free unveiling—reading ותגלו as pi'el, and comparing גלות with גלוי (cf. Abarbanel)—of סתרי תורה, which Moses delivered by word of mouth without comment. As regards the figures employed, (1) WATERS may stand for doctrine (§ 4), or for peoples (Is. xl. 15). Streams while they flow upon הארץ (an expression used especially of the Holy *Land*), are good, and blessed, and sweet, and of profit to the world; but when mingled with the sea they become accursed and bitter...So Israel, when they swerve to heathen customs, become accursed and evil; and as the rivers are food for the sea, so are they for the fire of hell (Pirqe R. El. IX.): (2) DEATH is thought of as in Rom. vii. 9—11, where there is a reference to Gen. ii. 17; iii. 3. Contrast Prov. iii. 18, and cf. Aboth I. 14; II. 15; III. 7; IV. 9; Baruch iii. 4—14: "hear now the prayers of the DEAD Israelites"; Jalqut 762 (on Numb. xix. 14): "Words of Thorah are established only when a man kills himself on their behalf." [Shabbath 83 b.]

[26] Hillel was called, *ha-Gadol*, or *ha-Zaqen*, or *ha-Babli* (Berakoth 4 b; Sukkah 28 a; Pesachim 66 a). The

name is in Jud. xii. 13. He studied Thorah while yet in Babylon, and at length, for its more exclusive study, separated from his trading brother Shebna; whereupon there came forth *Bath Qol* and said, "If a man would give all the substance of his house for love, &c." (Cant. viii. 7). If a man excuses himself from Thorah-study on the ground of poverty, it will be said to him, "Wast thou poorer than Hillel?" Of his small daily earnings a moiety went to the gatekeeper at the schools. Once he had earned nothing, and was shut out. He climbed up and sat at the window to hear the words of the living God from Shema'iah and Abtalion. It was sabbath eve in Tebeth, and the snow covered him three cubits deep. Said Shema'iah to Abtalion in the morning, Why is the house so dark to-day? it must be cloudy. They spied Hillel: they brought him in: and attended to his wants, saying, He is worthy that the sabbath should be profaned for him (Joma 35 b). The tale of his appointment as "nasi" is told in T. J. Pesachim VI. 1, and more briefly in Babli 66 a. The principle that Passover sets aside Sabbath when they clash had escaped the elders, or *sons*, of Betheira (? Sadducees). Hillel, being interrogated, said that it followed *a fortiori* from the fact that more than 200 minor "Passovers" (= sacrifices) in the year set aside the Sabbath; and he argued his point from every side, but in vain, since Thorah without traditional authority is no Thorah, כל תורה שאין לה בית אב אינה תורה. At length he said, It occurs to me that thus I heard from Shema'iah and Abtalion; and they arose and appointed him

suing peace; loving mankind[28], and bringing them nigh (Deut. xxx. 14; Eph. ii. 17)[29] to the Thorah.

"nasi." He was in fact the head and founder of a school, called after him, "Beth Hillel," the opponents in controversy of "Beth Shammai," to whom however they frequently made concessions. With the appointment of Hillel, " ein ganz neues, bis dahin als untergeordnet betrachtetes Princip der Lehrweise zur Geltung kam, nämlich die beständige Unterstützung der Ueberlieferung durch logisches Verfahren, so oft man sich nicht auf unmittelbare Behauptungen angesehener Lehrer berufen konnte " (Jost, *Gesch.* A. 257). Hillel had 80 disciples, of whom 30 were worthy, as Moses, that the Shekinah should rest upon them : 30, that the sun should stand still for them, as for Joshua : and 20 were of medium capacity. The least was Jochanan ben Zakkai : the greatest, Jonathan ben 'Uzziel, whose fire in the study of Thorah burnt up the birds that flew over him (Sukkah 28 a). Hillel, Shime'on, Gamliel and Shime'on held office in the period 30 B.C.—70 A.D.; and the pair Jose, Jose (§ 4) much earlier (Shabbath 15 a). At the end of Bereshith Rabbah, the age of Moses is divided into three periods of 40 years (Acts vii. 23 ; Ex. vii. 7); and amongst " six pairs " whose lives were equal are included (besides Moses) HILLEL HA-ZAQEN, R. Jochanan ben Zakkai, and R. 'Aqiba. [Sifré, ed. Fr. 150 a.]

[27] Seek peace at home, and pursue it abroad (Bemidbar Rabbah XIX.). The words of Mal. ii. 5, 6 : "*My covenant was with him* (Levi) *of life and peace...* and (he) did turn many away from iniquity," came to be applied especially to Aaron [Aboth R. N. XII.]. He was one of seven fathers who made covenants. Of " Phinehas, the son of Elea-

zar, the son of Aaron," it is said : " Behold I give unto him my covenant of peace " (Numb. xxv. 12) ; and to him also Mal. ii. 5, 6 is applied. Aaron was so beloved that he was bewailed by כל בית ישראל (Numb. xx. 29), men and women ; but Moses, by the *sons* of Israel alone (Deut. xxxiv. 8). Peace-making like *gemiluth chasadim* profits in both worlds (Peah I. 1). The Day of Atonement clears from transgressions against God, but not from those against one's neighbour, till he has been reconciled (Joma, *end*). For more on peace see Bem. Rabbah, *loc. cit.*, where it is said, אין כלי מחזיק ברכה אלא שלום, " no vessel but peace can hold blessing," a saying found also at the end of the Mishnah in some editions (Surh. VI. 503) ; but 𝔄 omits the whole paragraph, *Dixit R. J. &c.*

[28] Lit. τὰς κτίσεις. Cf. Mark xvi. 15, and (?) Rom. viii. 19.

[29] See the anecdotes of Hillel in note 33. For an illustration (Bereshith Rabbah XXVIII. ; Chazitha, on Cant. i. 4) which may be found to throw a new light on Matt. xxiii. 15 (περιάγετε τὴν θάλασσαν καὶ τὴν ξηρὰν ποιῆσαι ἕνα προσήλυτον), I am indebted to Dr Schiller-Szinessy, who informs me that he called attention to it in a lecture "nearly 30 years ago." I find it also in Jellinek's *Bet-ha-Midrasch*, Wien 1873, V. p. XLVI.: א׳ר חנין נעשה בכרכי הים מה שלא נעשה בדור המבול. הוי יושבי חבל הים גוי כרתים. גוי שהוא ראוי כרת. ובאי זה זכות הן עומדין. בזכות גוי אחד (נ״א גר אחד). בזכות ירא שמים אחד. שהן מעמידין בכל שנה. ר׳ לוי פתר לו לשבח. גוי שכרת ברית. המד׳א וכרות עמו הברית: " Said R. Chanin(a), There was done

14. He used to say, A name made great[30] is a name destroyed; he who increases not decreases[31]; and he who will

(? said) with respect to the districts of the sea what was not done with respect to the generation of the Flood: Ho! dwellers on the sea-coast, nation of Kerethim (Zeph. ii. 5), nation deserving of excision. And by what merit do they stand? By the merit of ONE PROSELYTE: by the merit of one fearer of Heaven, whom they raise up in every year. R. Levi explained it in a good sense, of a heathen who has made (cf. Neh. ix. 8) a covenant." The parallel passage in Midrash Chazitha varies in detail from the above, and runs as follows: א״ר חנינא נאמר . . . שלא נאמר . . . גוי שחייב כרת. ובזכות מי ניצל. בזכות ירא שמים אחד שמעמידין בכל שנה ושנה. ר' לוי פתר ליה כו': Hence it would appear that there was a custom of making one representative proselyte annually, to typify the salvability of the Gentiles. The final cause of Israel's captivities was that that they might make proselytes (Pesach. 87 b. Cf. Rom. xi. 11); but it does not clearly appear that the scribes were actuated by a missionary spirit, or that they were overhasty in receiving such proselytes as presented themselves (Jebamoth 47 b; Jost, Gesch. A. 448). The Jew was bound to attract men to the Thorah by his good example, but not in the ordinary sense of the word to proselytise (Joma 96 a). The universality of the Thorah is expressed by the saying that it was originally given in all the languages of the world. "Every word that went forth from the mouth of the Holy One was divided into seventy tongues," כל דיבור ודיבור שיצא מפי (Shabbath 88 b. Cf. Berakoth 13 a, Thosaph. הקב״ה נחלק לשבעים לשונות·

on בכל לשון)—which seventy tongues had their representatives in the ship that carried Jonah (Pirqe R. El. x.). "The whole Thorah was spoken in every tongue" (Sotah 33 a). In like manner the expressions מסיני. משעיר. מהר פארן. מרבבת קדש· (Deut. xxxiii. 2) are interpreted in Sifre of a fourfold revelation in Hebrew, Greek, Arabic, and Aramaic. It is added that God revealed himself from the four winds; and "not upon Israel only was He revealed, but upon all the nations. First he went to the sons of Esau and said, Will ye receive the Thorah?" On their refusal it was offered to others, and at last to Israel.

[30] Some commentators have assumed from the dialect of this Mishnah (cf. II. 7; v. 33) that it dates from the time when Hillel was in Babel. The word נגד in Aramaic means to draw, or extend. It stands for נטה or משך in Targ. Gen. xxxix. 21; Ps. xxxvi. 11; but cf. the Biblical נגיד. The saying is illustrated by Is. ii. 17; Prov. xxix. 23; Matt. xxiii. 5—12. The Holy One exalts him who humbles himself, and humbles him who exalts himself. Greatness flees from him who follows after it, and follows after him who flees from it. A man should not "force the hour," but bide his time ('Erubin 13 b, cf. 54 a; Nedarim 55 a). The saying is otherwise explained, as ps-Rashi remarks, of one who continually draws the NAME of the Holy One into all his occupations; or of one who משך שמה של תורה עליו שלא עסק בה לשמה (C).

[31] He who learns from his teacher and adds not to his words, not having intelligence to go beyond what he has

not learn (*or* teach) deserves slaughter; and he who serves himself with the tiara perishes.

15. He used to say, If I am not for myself[32] who is for me? and being for my own self what am I? If not now when?

16. Shammai said[33], Make thy Thorah an ordinance[34]; say

been expressly taught, will *come to an end*, "his mother will bury him"; or will *bring to an end* and lose what he has learned by rote. Cf. Matt. xxv. 29. He who refuses to impart his knowledge (or "who will not learn at all"), commits a deadly sin. So too does he who utilises the crown of the Thorah, or of the Holy NAME, by teaching (or studying) for his own profit and glorification. Cf. IV. 9, 19.

[32] A man must be self-reliant; but must not live for himself (Rom. xiv. 7). According to another interpretation: "I must work out my own salvation, yet how weak are my unaided efforts" (Phil. ii. 12, 13). ἰδοὺ νῦν καιρὸς εὐπρόσδεκτος (2 Cor. vi. 2).

[33] Shammai, or Shamai, the successor of Hillel's colleague Menachem (Chagigah II. 2), generally has the first word in controversy (v. 25); but tradition does not credit him with the same readiness as Hillel to give every man a patient hearing. "A man should be gentle like Hillel, and not irritable like Shamai" (Shabbath 30 b). The Talmud goes on to relate how a man undertook for a wager to exhaust Hillel's patience, but failed. One day a foreigner came to Shamai to be proselytised, on condition of accepting the Written and dispensing with the Oral Thorah. Shamai dismissed him with a rebuke. He appealed to Hillel, who on the first day taught him the letters of the alphabet (in the usual order), and on the morrow gave them in reverse order. But, said the would-be-proselyte, did

you not tell me so and so yesterday? If you relied on me for that, retorted Hillel, rely upon me likewise for the Oral Law. Another came to Shamai to be converted provided that he could be taught the whole Thorah whilst he stood on one foot. Shamai beat him away, and he went to Hillel, who said: "What is hateful to thyself do not *to thy fellow;* this is the whole Thorah, and the rest is commentary; go, study." Cf. ὃ μισεῖς μηδενὶ ποιήσῃς (Tobit iv. 15), and the converse, Matt. vii. 12. A third overhearing the description of the high-priest's vestments which was being read in a synagogue, came to Shamai to be made a proselyte in order that he might become high-priest. Shamai beat him away. He went to Hillel, who said, Do they appoint as king one who knows not the ordinances of the kingdom? Go, learn them. He read as far as Numb. i. 51: "And the stranger that cometh nigh shall be put to death." He said to him, This scripture, of whom is it spoken? He said to him, Even of David, King of Israel. A fortiori of me, argued the stranger; for if of Israel, God's son and first-born (Ex. iv. 22), such a thing is written, much more of a worthless proselyte who has come with his staff and with his wallet... After a time the three met together. They said, The irritability of Shamai sought to drive us from the world: the gentleness of Hillel BROUGHT US NIGH under the wings of the Shekinah.

[34] Contrast II. 17. Make thy study

little and do much[35]; and receive every man with a pleasant expression of countenance (III. 18).

17. Rabban Gamliel[35] said, Make to thyself a master, and be quit of doubt; and tithe not much by estimation[36].

18. Shime'on[37] his son said, All my days I have grown up

of Thorah a *fixture*: a thing to be engaged in daily at stated times, and to which secular engagements must give way. 'Obadiah ben Jacob of Sforno takes the words of Shamai as addressed to his predecessor: "Though thou hast gone forth, O Menachem, to the service of the king, it is fitting that thou shouldest fix times for Thorah." Ps-Rashi is not content with stated times, but demands the whole day for Thorah.

[35] Be like Abraham, who only promised a MORSEL OF BREAD, but "fetcht a CALF TENDER AND GOOD" (Gen. xviii. 5, 7).

The next link in the chain of tradition is given in II. 9. In the interval there is a digression to the descendants of Hillel, who himself reappears in II. 5. The first Gamliel (or, in the Greek form, Γαμαλιήλ), son of Shime'on, and grandson of Hillel, is called Rabban; but the title may have been permanently connected with his name only by a later generation, for (1) like Hillel, who was not called Rabban, he is distinguished as HA-ZAQEN; and (2) he is called simply GAMALIEL both in Acts v. 34, xxii. 3 (under circumstances which make it improbable that a customary title of respect should have been omitted), and likewise in Shabbath 15 a: "Hillel, and Shime'on, GAMALIEL, and Shime'on held the office of nasi, while the temple was standing, for 100 years." For his opinion in what cases the Sabbath strictness might be relaxed, see 'Eru-

bin 45 a. Cf. Beçah II. 6. The high esteem in which he was held is shewn by the saying, that "from when R. G. ha-Zaqen died the glory of the Thorah ceased, and purity and פרישות (III. 20) died" (Sotah IX. 15). His death is placed eighteen years before the destruction of the temple. From Acts v. 39 a tradition arose that he died a Christian. He was not the author of the "heretic-benediction."

[36] In the case of a thing whereof the value and dimensions are not precisely laid down it becomes necessary to form a special estimate or *measurement*. Hence the root *amad* gives the sense "conjecture." In Sanhedrin IV. 5, אומד (ﬡ עומד) is used of "circumstantial" evidence in a capital charge, in parallelism with *hearsay*. Let duties be defined as far as may be by rule: let doubts be resolved by authority: leave as little scope as possible for personal bias and the temptations of self-interest.

[37] For a defence of Simon ben Gamaliel I. against the aspersions of Josephus (*Life* § 38), see Jost, *Gesch.* A. 443. Rabbinic commentators suggest that he is not here called Rabban because his sayings date from the time of his pupilage, when Jochanan ben Zakai (II. 9) was ראש ישיבה. But see note 35, and II. 1. Simon was one of the peace-party in the closing years of the Jewish state, and he suffered "den Märtyrertod...kurz vor oder bei der Einnahme Jerusalems." For his saying on proselytism in Va-jiqra Rabbah II. see Jost, A. 447.

amongst the wise, and have not found aught good for a man but silence[38]; not learning but doing is the groundwork; and whoso multiplies words occasions sin.

19. Rabban Shime‘on[39] ben Gamliel said, On three things the world stands; on Judgment, and on Truth, and on Peace[40].

[38] Qoheleth Rabbah, v. 5, cites as a saying of R. Jehoshua‘: "Speech for a sheqel—silence for two; (it is) like a precious stone"; and adds (referring to this Mishnah) a saying of Rabbi, סמא דמילתא משתוקא, Silence is the cure of a thing. But both Talmuds have סמא דכולא, a panacea (T. J. Berakoth ix. 1; T. B. Megillah 18 a). The caution against undue loquacity is applied to sacred things. RR. Jochanan and Jonathan found a provincial chazan extemporising in his synagogue, and they silenced him, on the ground that *he had no right to add to the Benedictions which were already fixed by authority*. The Babli here refers the תפלה to the Great Synagogue. He who talks overmuch even in praise of the Holy One is "swallowed up," or rooted out of the world, for it is said (Job xxxvii. 20), היספר לו ...כי יבלע. Cf. Matt. vi. 7; Eccl. v. 2; Ecclus. vii. 14; Berakoth 61 a. SILENCE is His praise (Ps. lxv. 2).

[39] The R. Sh. b. G. here spoken of was the son of Gamaliel II., who was the grandson of Gamaliel I. The second Gamaliel (80—115 A.D.) was a man of liberal views, but self-willed and overbearing. It is related that he justified his conduct in frequenting a bath in ‘Akko which contained a statue of Aphrodite on the ground that the statue was made as an ornament for the bath, and not the bath as an ornament for the statue (‘Abodah Zarah iii. 4). His treatment of the venerable R. Jehoshua‘, who ventured to differ from him on more than one occasion (R. ha-Shanah ii. 9; Berakoth 27 b), at length aroused the popular indignation to such an extent that he was deposed from his presidency, and succeeded by the youthful Ele‘azar ben‘Azariah,on the memorable day frequently alluded to in the Talmud in the phrase בו ביום (cf. "*that same year,*" in Joh. xi. 49; xviii. 13); but after a time a compromise was effected, and the two presided alternately. His son Shime‘on at length succeeded him, and became the teacher of many illustrious men. To this age (remarks Jost) belong the sayings of Meir, Jehudah, Jose, and Simon b. Gamliel in the Mishnah. "Sein Todesjahr ist nicht näher bestimmt, doch fällt es in die Zeit der parthischen Kriege in den ersten Jahren des Marcus Aurelius (um 164). Seine Bestrebungen gediehen zum Abschluss durch seinen berühmten Sohn JEHUDAH."

[40] Justice, truth, and peace (§ 13) are collectively the σύνδεσμος of society, a threefold cord which is not quickly broken (Eccl. iv. 12). They are a system of internal forces by which the world is held together, though the pillars of the former αἰών (§ 2) have been shaken, and the Temple itself has fallen. So the heavenly bodies are said to be kept in their orbits by the attractions of חמדה and אמונה, which draw them to אהיה. Peace plays an important part in the New Testament. In connexion with αὐτὸς γάρ ἐστιν ἡ εἰρήνη ἡμῶν (Eph. ii. 14; Mic. v. 4), and ὁ Θεὸς τῆς

εἰρήνης (Rom. xvi. 20), observe that PEACE is a Talmudic Name of God. The etymological affinity in Hebrew, of peace and perfectness, הכל יושלם בשלום, "everything is PERFECTED BY PEACE," gives a clue to the genesis of some Pauline expressions. Compare ἐν ἀγαπῇ...ἐν τῷ συνδέσμῳ τῆς εἰρήνης (Eph. iv. 3), with τὴν ἀγάπην ὅ ἐστιν σύνδεσμος τῆς τελειότητος (Col. iii. 14), which may be explained by supposing ἀγάπη to have replaced εἰρήνη, peaceableness, in Εἰρήνη...σύνδεσμος τῆς τελειότητος. In Col. iii. 15 occurs the paradox, ἡ εἰρήνη τοῦ Χριστοῦ βραβευέτω, which may have been suggested by the expression ומשפט שלום of Zech. viii. 16, a verse which is cited at the end of this Pereq in many copies. The Qabbalists state the general theorem that all the attributes of God are in unison; and they work out the idea in their own peculiar way by so manipulating the Divine Names as to identify them all by alphabetical permutations. Thus PEACE, LOVE, MIGHT or JUDGMENT, and FEAR are made severally equivalent to the TETRAGRAMMATON, and therefore to one another (Berith Menuchah, ed. Amsterdam, 1648, fol. 3 a). [Jud. vi. 24; Shabbath 10 b; Pereq ha-Shalom.]

---

p. 11. *Moses*] At the beginning of the Mekhilta, with the emendation כלי לדברות for כלול לדברות proposed by Dr Israel Lewy in *Ein Wort über die Mechilta des R. Simon* (Breslau 1889) and again by Mr Schechter, we read that "As Moses was a *vessel* for λόγια so Aaron was a *vessel* for λόγια," cf. iv. Ezra iv. 11 *quomodo poterit uas tuum capere altissimi uiam?*, Acts ix. 15 σκεῦος...τοῦ βαστάσαι τὸ ὄνομά μου, 2 Cor. iv. 7 "We have this treasure in earthen vessels," Nedarim 50 b "Fair Torah in foul vessel."

p. 11. *Thorah*] Without מעמדות (Ta'an. 27 b) or תורה (Nedar. 32 a) heaven and earth would not stand.

p. 11. *delivered*] Mekhilta כי תשא (Fr. 103 b, 104 a), "The sabbath was delivered to you and ye were not delivered to the sabbath," illustrates St Mark ii. 27.

p. 11, n. 1] Gen. ii. 2 is one of the "ten" passages altered by the LXX for king Ptolemy. See Megillah T. B.

9 a & T. J. i. 9 (71 *d*), Mekhilta בא (15 b), Tanchuma שמות (Buber ii. 6 a), Mas. Soferim i. (Müller pp. ii. & 14).

p. 15, n. 12] With reference to this note Prof. Mayor, in a paper read to the Cambridge Philological Society (Nov. 8, 1883), writes as follows: "It seems highly probable that St Paul had distinctly in his mind a saying current in the Greek schools, variously ascribed to Thales or Socrates (D. L. i. 33) or Plato (Plut. Marius 46. § 1). Lactantius gives it thus (iii. 19. § 17), *non dissimile Platonis illud est, quod aiebat se gratias agere naturae, primum quod homo natus esset potius quam mutum animal; deinde quod mas potius quam femina; quod Graecus quam barbarus; postremo quod Atheniensis et quod temporibus Socratis.*"

p. 22, n. 29] See M. Joel *Blicke in die Religionsgeschichte* ii. 50, n. 1 (Breslau 1883); Bernays *Gesammelte Abhandlungen* ii. 71 sq. (Berl. 1885) on "Die Gottesfürchtigen bei Juvenal."

CHAPTER II.

1. Rabbi[1] said, Which is the right course that a man should choose for himself? Whatsoever is a pride to him that pursues it[2], (and) brings him honour (Phil. iv. 8) from men. And

[1] Rabbi, which is equivalent to "my lord," or διδάσκαλε (Joh. i. 39), is properly a vocative, but came to be used as a title also, the possessive affix being disregarded. As a title it is superior to Rab (which is applied especially to Babylonian doctors, whereas Rabbi is applied to those of Palestine), but inferior to Rabban (a title given to seven or eight descendants of Hillel and to Jochanan ben Zakai). It is said [Kohut A. C. i. 7a] that Rabbi is greater than Rab, and Rabban than Rabbi, yet GREATER THAN RABBAN IS HIS NAME, גדול מרבן שמו, i.e. the greatest glory is to need no title at all, but to be sufficiently distinguished by one's name alone, like Hillel, Ezra, and the prophets. Another form, רבון, occurs in Targum and Gemara as a Divine title, and is also used with the affix "my" in much the same way as Rabbi. Cf. Mark x. 51; Joh. xx. 16, ῥαββουνί, ὃ λέγεται διδάσκαλε. This form רבוני occurs once in the Mishnah (Tha'anith iii. 8) according to the manuscript ℳ, instead of רבונו של עולם, "Lord of the world," which is found in other copies.

The title of RABBI κατ᾿ ἐξοχήν was given to Jehudah ben Simon III., who was also called Jehudah ha-Nasi (§ 2), and Rabbenu ha-Qadosh, or the holy. To him is attributed the compilation of the MISHNAH; but the MISHNAH as we have it is a later recension, as may be inferred from the way in which "Rabbi" himself is introduced (cf. Menachoth vi. 3; viii. 6, &c.). He is thought to have been born about 140 A.D., shortly after the execution of R. 'Aqiba, and to have died at Sepphoris, after 17 years of ill health, at the age of 80, in 219 or 220 A.D. (Jost, Gesch. B. 118); but by some he is placed earlier. It is remarked that "from the days of Moses to Rabbi we have not found Thorah and greatness in one place" (Gittin 59 a); for there was not his like in Israel for greatness in Thorah and wealth. "From when Rabbi died, meekness and the fear of sin ceased" (Sotah ix. 15). Little is known of the details of his literary and administrative work.

[2] The interpretation of this somewhat doubtful clause varies according to the reading, and also according to the meaning assigned to עושה. The rendering given above involves a departure from the text of ℳ, and is adapted to the usual reading ותפארת.

be attentive to a light precept as to a grave, for thou knowest not the assigned reward of precepts[3]; and reckon the loss for a duty against its gain, and the gain by a transgression against its loss. And consider three things, and thou wilt not fall into the hands of transgression (III. 1): know what[4] is above thee—a seeing eye, and a hearing ear (1 Pet. iii. 12), and all thy deeds written in a book (Dan. vii. 10).

2. Rabban Gamliel, son of R. Jehudah ha-Nasi[5], said,

Jost renders "welcher ihm in seinen eigenen Augen und in denen der Menschen zum Ruhme gereicht." Taking the former תפארת as subjective compare מעשה ידי להתפאר (Is. lx. 21). The second תפארת is illustrated by Jud. iv. 9: "notwithstanding the JOURNEY that thou takest shall not be for THINE HONOUR." R. 'Obadiah of Sforno—cf. Baba Bathra 16 b—remarks that a man should choose a business to which he can devote himself *con amore*, for, "happy is he whose business is perfumery, and woe to him whose business is tanning." Bar S. objects to the usual interpretation that תפארת cannot be taken subjectively, and that עשה does not apply well to דרך (but cf. Jud. xvii. 8); and he proposes the interpretation: "Whatsoever is done for the honour of a man's Maker (לעושהו) will bring the man honour from his fellows." Cf. Matt. vi. 33; Aboth iv. 10. A third interpretation, which presupposes the usual reading, is: "Whatsoever is to the glory of God, AND also has the approval of men." Cf. Prov. iii. 4 (cited by R. Elijah of Wilna): "So shalt thou find favour and good understanding in the sight of God and man." [Nedarim 22 b; Tamid 28 a.]

[3] Cf. NEDARIM 39 b. It is remarked that a reward (length of days) is specified in the case of two extreme precepts, the gravest of the grave: "Honour thy father and thy mother,"

and the lightest of the light: "Thou shalt not take the dam with the young. But thou shalt in any wise LET THE DAM (האם) GO, and take the young to thee; that it may be well with thee, and that thou mayest prolong thy days." It is inferred in Sifre (Deut. xxii. 7), that if this light precept is singled out for such a reward, *a fortiori* will the fulfilment of other precepts be rewarded. ℬ remarks that *negative* precepts do not come under consideration here, since there is no שכר for them.

[4] Or, omitting מה: "Know (that) above thee is a seeing eye, &c." This concise reading is found in ℭ.

[5] R. Jehudah is said (Kethuboth 103 b) to have nominated his (elder) son Gamaliel to succeed him as Nasi. The first part of this Gamaliel's saying relates to individuals as such, and counsels them to combine secular occupation with Thorah study. The expression *derek ereç*, or *via terræ*, may denote the conduct of worldly business, or an acquaintance with, and conformity to, the usages of society, "good-manners," &c. The phrase occurs not only in Rabbinic, but (with a variation) in the Bible, in senses readily determined by the context. Cf. Gen. xix. 31; Josh. xxiii. 14; 1 Kings ii. 2. The second part of the saying recommends individuals, regarded as members of the congregation of Israel, to act εἰς δόξαν τοῦ Θεοῦ (Rom. xv. 7), re-

Excellent is Thorah study together with worldly business, for the practice of them both puts iniquity out of remembrance; and all Thorah without work must fail at length, and occasion iniquity[6]. And let all who are employed with the congregation act with them in the name of Heaven, for the merit of their fathers sustains them, and their righteousness stands for ever. And ye yourselves shall have reward reckoned unto you[7] as if ye had wrought.

3. Be cautious with (those in) authority, for they let not a man approach them but for their own purposes; and they appear like friends when it is to their advantage, and stand not by a man in the hour of his need.

4. He used to say, Do His will as if it were thy will[8], that He may do thy will as if it were His will. Annul thy will before His will, that He may annul the will of others before thy will[9].

5. Hillel said, Separate not thyself from the congregation, and trust not in thyself until the day of thy death[10]; and judge

lying upon the merit of the patriarchs. Cf. ἀγαπητοὶ διὰ τοὺς πατέρας (Rom. xi. 28). With the conclusion of the saying compare Rom. iv. 4, τῷ δὲ ἐργαζο-μένῳ ὁ μισθὸς οὐ λογίζεται κατὰ χάριν, ἀλλὰ κατὰ ὀφείλημα.

[6] The usual reading, וגוררת, is simplest.

[7] Literally, according to the text of 𝔄 (but see *Crit. Note*), "THEY reckon unto you." The indefinite THEY, which occurs so frequently in Rabbinic, is interpreted of the של (or ב"ד) פמליא מעלה, the "upper" or celestial "familia" (or tribunal). Cf. Eph. iii. 15. The Holy One, blessed is He, does nothing without consulting the *familia superna*, for it is said (Dan. iv. 17), "This matter is by the decree of the watchers, and the demand by the word of the holy ones" (Sanhedrin 38 b). Cf. Dan. iv. 25, 32; "And THEY shall drive thee from men." The same construction is found in the New Testament. Cf. δώσουσιν εἰς τὸν κόλπον

ὑμῶν (Luke vi. 38).

[8] Ἐάν τις θέλῃ τὸ θέλημα αὐτοῦ ποιεῖν κ.τ.λ. (Joh. vii. 17). Cf. Ps. xl. 9. "It is revealed and known before Thee that our will is to do Thy will. And who hindereth? The leaven in the dough, and servitude to the kingdoms," &c. (Berakoth 17 a).

[9] "At the time when Israel do the will of God their work is done by the hand of others, for it is said, And strangers shall stand and feed your flocks, and the sons of the alien shall be your plowmen and your vinedressers (Is. lxi. 5); and at the time when Israel do not the will of God their work is done by their own hand, for it is said (but cf. the context), And thou shalt gather in thy corn, &c. (Deut. xi. 14). Nay more, the work of others is done by their hand, for it is said (Deut. xxviii. 48), And thou shalt serve thine enemies" (Berakoth 35 b).

[10] BERAKOTH 29 a illustrates this saying by the case of one Jochanan

not thy friend until thou comest into his place; and say not of a word which may be heard[11] that in the end it shall be heard; and say not, When I have leisure I will study; perchance thou mayest not have leisure.

6. He used to say, No boor[12] is a sinfearer; nor is the vulgar[13] pious; nor is the shamefast apt to learn, nor the pas-

---

who after ministering as high-priest for 80 years became a Çaduqi. Rabbinic writers do not countenance the opinion that the priestly party were to a great extent, or normally, Sadducaic. Cf. Excursus III. The Machazor Vitry (see *Crit. Note*) remarks that the title "R." should not be read, as in 𝔄, before the name of HILLEL. He is identified with Hillel ha-Zaqen by comparing Sukkah 53 a, where the saying about the "skull" (§ 7)—omitting the word סוף (ed. Lemberg)—is attributed to him: "They said of Hillel ha-Zaqen that when he was sharing in the festivity of the שואבה—sc. at the feast of Tabernacles [Kohut *A.C.* II. 85; Delitzsch *Iris*, p. 198, Edinb. 1889]—he said, If I am here, all are here; and if I am not here, who is here? He used to say thus, Whatsoever place I take pleasure in, thither My feet lead me. If thou wilt come to My house, I will come to thy house: if thou wilt not come to My house, I will not come to thy house (Exod. xx. 24). Moreover he saw a skull that floated on the surface of the water, and he said to it, Because thou drownedst they drowned thee, AND they that drowned thee shall be drowned."

[11] This is well explained by the Machazor Vitry in accordance with the context. If a word of Thorah MAY BE HEARD—if a man has leisure to attend to the call of duty at once, let him do so, and not make the excuse that it may be attended to at some future time, that ITS END IS TO BE HEARD; and even if he is pressed with business, let him find time for it, and not say that when he has leisure he will attend to his Thorah, for that more convenient season may never come.

According to the more usual *negative* reading and interpretation the saying is a caution against propounding far-fetched, paradoxical, not-to-be-heard-of doctrines, even though they may in the end perhaps be susceptible of a rational interpretation. Speak not words which *prima facie* CANNOT be heard, though ultimately they may be heard: words which require elaborate explanation before they can be accepted; "Alles was du vorträgst musz mit Klarheit...geschehen" (Paulus Ewald). Cf. Maimonides, who is followed by very many of the moderns. The *negative* reading and interpretation, in some form, is usually adopted; but that of the Machazor Vitry has strong claims to acceptance. For the various reading אפשר (אי) in the Mishnah see also Parah vi. 1; vii. 5; Makshirin III. 5—7; Sotah v. 3; 'Erakin viii. 7; Themurah v. 4.

[12] The word בור, of which BOOR may be employed as a transliteration, is used of "incultus, sylvestris ager." In Prov. xii. 1: "but he that hateth reproof is BRUTISH," the Targum has בורא, for Heb. בער.

[13] The expression *'am ha-areç* is used in Rabbinic to denote the vulgar herd, ὁ ὄχλος οὗτος ὁ μὴ γινώσκων τὸν νόμον (Joh. vii. 49). Cf. Ezek. vii. 27...

sionate to teach[14]; nor is every one that has much traffic wise. And in a place where there are no men endeavour to be a man[15].

7.　Moreover he saw a skull (Matt. xxvii. 33) which floated on the face of the water, and he said to it, Because thou drownedst[16] they drowned thee, and *in the end* they that drowned thee shall be drowned.

8.　He used to say, More flesh, more worms : more treasures, more care : more maidservants, more lewdness : more menservants, more theft : more women[17], more witchcrafts (Nah. iii.

καὶ αἱ χεῖρες τοῦ λαοῦ τῆς γῆς παραλυθήσονται. In this Mishnah, and *passim*, it is used as a singular to denote ONE of the ὄχλος. So גוי, the singular of גוים, ἔθνη, is used to denote an individual heathen.

[14] An ἐπίσκοπος should be διδακτικός, and not ὀργίλος (1 Tim. iii. 2; 2 Tim. ii. 24; Tit. i. 7).

[15] A man should bear himself manfully when left to his own resources (cf. I. 15). It is added in Berakoth 63 a: "In a place where there is a man, there be not a man": refrain from undue self-assertion.

[16] He who has suffered violence must have been a wrong-doer; and they that have done the man violence will themselves come to an untimely end. Cf. πάντες γὰρ οἱ λαβόντες μάχαιραν ἐν μαχαίρῃ ἀπολοῦνται (Matth. xxvi. 52). The above saying of Hillel —which, like some others attributed to him (cf. I. 14), is in Aramaic—is one of the many ways of expressing the great principle of retribution: "as thou hast done, it shall be done unto thee" (Obadiah 15). It is a common saying in the Talmud that "with what measure a man measures, THEY (cf. note 7) measure to him": Samson, who followed after the desire of his eyes, was blinded by the Philistines: Absalom, who prided himself upon his hair, was hanged up by his hair

(Sotah I. 7, 8). The bribed judge will live to grow blind (Peah, *end*), "for a gift doth blind the eyes of the wise" (Deut. xvi. 19). On the other hand, when the member that sinned has suffered, the curse is removed. Thus, sentence of slavery is pronounced, because "Ham the father of Canaan ...SAW...and TOLD" (Gen. ix. 22)— thereby sinning with eyes and teeth: and contrariwise the slave is set at liberty (Ex. xxi. 26, 7) when he has suffered the loss of eye or tooth (Bereshith Rabbah xxxvi.).

[17] Cf. Ex. xxii. 18. Woman is regarded as a medium of temptation. Man is to woman as שכל to חמר—as νοῦς to ὕλη, or αἴσθησις: as upper to lower: as right to left: as the Divine to the human. Philo writes (de Mundi Opificio, Vol. I. pp. 39, 40, ed. Mangey): τὰς δὲ γοητείας καὶ ἀπάτας αὐτῆς ἡ ἡδονὴ τῷ μὲν ἀνδρὶ οὐ τολμᾷ προσφέρειν, τῇ δὲ γυναικί, καὶ διὰ ταύτης ἐκείνῳ· πάνυ προσφυῶς καὶ εὐθυβόλως. Ἐν ἡμῖν γὰρ ἀνδρὸς μὲν ἔχει λόγον ὁ νοῦς, γυναικὸς δ' αἴσθησις, κ.τ.λ. It is disputed whether σαρκός, in Joh. i. 13, where it is contrasted with ἀνδρός, refers especially to the female. The contrast "right" and "left" (Zohar on Gen. i. 2, col. 14) is explained by the doctrine that the (left) hand of God created earth, and the right hand heaven, according to an

4): more Thorah, more life (Prov. iii. 1, 2): *more wisdom, more scholars*[18]: *more righteousness, more peace.* He who has gotten a good name has gotten it for himself[19]. He who has gotten to himself words of Thorah, has gotten to himself the life of the world to come.

9. Rabban Jochanan ben Zakai[20] received from Hillel and

interpretation (given also in Pirqe R. El. xviii.) of Is. xlviii. 13, אף ידי יסדה ארץ וימיני טפחה שמים. The man is εἰκὼν καὶ δόξα θεοῦ· ἡ δὲ γυνὴ δόξα ἀνδρός ἐστιν (1 Cor. xi. 7). The congregation of Israel is personified as a γυνή, in relation to God.

[18] The teacher who increases his wisdom will increase his *consessus* of scholars (R. Jonah). Bar S. cites Maimonides as favouring this reading. The usual reading: *Viel Schule, viel Weisheit* (P. Ewald), may mean either (1) that wisdom increases with *study*, or (2) that it increases with the *consessus* of scholars, who sharpen not only one another (Prov. xxvii. 17), but also their Rab, by their discussions. So ℭ, bar S. &c., citing the well-known saying: "I have learned much from my teachers: more from my associates: but from my disciples most of all." Cf. iv. 1.

[19] Φρόντισον περὶ ὀνόματος, αὐτὸ γάρ σοι διαμένει ἢ χίλιοι μεγάλοι θησαυροὶ χρυσίου (Ecclus. xli. 12).

[20] Jochanan ben Zakai, or Zakkai (Ζακχαῖος), was the "least" of the disciples of Hillel (cf. Pereq i. note 26). His learning is described in Baba Bathra 134 a: at his death "splendor sapientiæ" ceased (Sotah ix. 15). "Durch ihn ward *Jamnia* zum Sitz der gesetzgebenden Versammlungen, zu einem neuen *Jerusalem:* während er seine Lehrschule an einem kleinen Orte in der Nähe hielt" (Jost, *Gesch.* B. 17). He was distinguished as a scrupulous adherent to the old paths, rather than as a

theoretical reformer. The strictness of his moral code is intimated by the remark attributed to him in Chagig. 5 a (on Mal. iii. 5), that *levia* are reckoned as *gravia*. (It is added, on ומטי גר, that he who perverts the cause of the stranger, is as if he perverted that of Heaven, כל המטה דינו של גר כאלו מטה דינו של מעלה.) In Chagigah *l. c.* Jochanan remarks further, on the last verse of Ecclesiastes, that sins of inadvertence and of wilfulness are put on a par. In Chagigah 13 a, he urges the futility of speculating, with our finite capacities, upon the secrets of the universe: "What answer gave *bath qol* to that wicked one who said (Is. xiv. 14), I will ascend above the heights of the clouds, I will be like the most High?... The years of man are only seventy, whereas from earth to the firmament is a journey of 500 years, and the thickness of the firmament is a journey of 500 years, and the interval between each firmament and the next is a journey of 500 years." His view of the religious status of the heathen is brought out in Baba Bathra 10 b, where he infers from Prov. xiv. 34, that moral goodness may atone for them, as the sin-offering (חטאת) for Israel. They said of R. Jochanan ben Zakai that he was always beforehand in saluting even a heathen in the street (Berakoth 17 a. Cf. Aboth iv. 22). When he was at the point of death some of his disciples came to visit him. He wept. They said, Why dost thou, the light of Israel...weep? He said

from Shammai. He used to say, If thou hast practised Thorah[21] much, claim not merit to thyself, for thereunto wast thou created (Luke xvii. 10; 1 Cor. ix. 16).

10.   Five disciples[22] were there to Rabban Jochanan ben Zakai, and these were they: R. Li'ezer[23] ben Hyrqanos, and R. Jehoshua' ben Chananiah, and R. Jose the Priest, and

(Berakoth 28 b), Were they bringing me before an earthly king, whose wrath is transient: who, should he put me to death, the death would not be eternal: whom, moreover, I might hope to persuade or bribe... even then I should weep; How then can I but weep, when they are bringing me before...Him whose wrath is 'eternal': who, if He puts me to death, the death is 'eternal': and whom I cannot hope to move with words or bribes? They say to him, Bless us; and accordingly he prays paradoxically that *the fear of Heaven may be upon them as the fear of flesh and blood:* the transgressor has a real fear of detection by his fellows: would that he could equally realise the truth that he is seen by God. There was a belief that dying saints were sometimes visited in their last moments by the spirits of the departed. In accordance with this belief, R. Jochanan is represented as directing his assembled disciples to prepare a seat for Hezekiah who was coming. "Es ist sehr zu beklagen, dass weder die Dauer seiner Wirksamkeit *nach* der Zerstörung des Tempels, noch sein Todesjahr, welches vermuthlich in Domitians Regierungszeit fällt, angemerkt worden."

[21] The reading of modern editions is: "If thou hast *learned* (note א) much Thorah." The better attested עשה may include both acquisition and practice. The MSS. favour the reading: "If thou hast wrought much at ᴛʜʏ Tʜᴏʀᴀʜ." Bar S. illustrates the

saying as follows: "Why was the book Ezra not called by the name of Nehemiah? Because he insisted upon his merits, as it is said, Remember me, O my God, concerning this, and wipe not out my good deeds" (Neh. xiii. 14). But see Sanhedrin 93 b.

[22] The same five disciples attempt to comfort R. Jochanan on the death of his son (Aboth R.N. xɪᴠ.), and Ele'azar again bears off the palm. After the death of his master he withdrew to Emmaus, but failed to draw disciples after him. According to Shabbath 147 b, he yielded to the enervating influences of the place, and his learning deserted him: then they prayed for him and it returned. His case is adduced in illustration of the principle that a man should betake himself to a place of Thorah (ɪᴠ. 20), and not presume upon his own power to raise up a school for himself in a place where Thorah is not already studied.

[23] La'zar (Λάζαρος), and Li'ezer (cf. *Crit. Note*) are colloquial abbreviations. R. Eli'ezer—who was a preceptor of R. 'Aqiba—is described as a faithful preserver of traditions received: Ele'azar, as a teacher of original power and inexhaustible fertility of invention, "who adds to what he has heard (cf. ɪ. 14), and draws inferences; whereas El. b. Hyrqanos, as we find in Sukkah, never spoke a word that he had not heard from his Rab" (A*). For the metaphor of the spring, cf. John iv. 14, πηγὴ ὕδατος ἀλλομένου εἰς ζωὴν αἰώνιον. [Psalm xxxvi. 10.]

5

R. Shimeʿon ben Nathanael, and R. Eleʿazar ben ʿArak. He used to recount their praise: Eliʿezer ben Hyrqanos is a plastered cistern, which loseth not a drop; Jehoshuaʿ ben Chananiah —happy is she that bare him; Jose the Priest is pious[24]; Shimʿeon ben Nathanael is a sinfearer; Eleʿazar ben ʿArak is a welling spring.

11.   He used to say, If all the wise of Israel were in a scale of the balance, and Eliʿezer ben Hyrqanos[25] in the other scale, he would outweigh them all.   Abba Shaul said in his name, If all the wise of Israel were in a scale of the balance, and Eliʿezer ben Hyrqanos with them, and Eleʿazar ben ʿArak in the other scale, he would outweigh them all.

[24] The *chasid* is of greater excellence than the *çaddiq* (δίκαιος). Cf. the gradation: "Three things are said of nail-parings, He who burns them is חסיד; He who buries them is צדיק; He who throws them away is רשע" (Niddah 17 a).   The term *chasid* is used in the text in connexion with the designation "the Priest." So Jose ben Joʿezer (I. 4) is called חסיד שבכהונה (Chagigah II. 7). There is a certain halo of antiquity about the word in the phrase חסידים הראשונים (Berakoth v. 1). One of the conjectures about the name Essene, or ʾΕσσαῖος, identifies it with חסיד (regardless of the ד). But the Essenes were opposed to sacrifice, and the *chasid* might be a priest.

[25] The typical traditionalist Eliʿezer is balanced against the man of genius. In favour of tradition ℂ quotes, סיני ועוקר הרים סיני עדיף, when the choice lies between "Sinai" and an "uprooter of mountains," the preference is given to Sinai. See the discussions in Berakoth 64 a and Horaioth 14 a, where R. Joseph is described as סיני, and Rabah as עוקר הרים. Cf. also R. ʿObadiah of Sforno, in the Bologna Machazor, who adds that the "uprooter of mountains" has the advantage in criticism, as "a pungent grain of pepper is better than a basketful of gourds." [Megillah 7 a; Chagigah 10 a.   Cf. Matt. xvii. 20.]

R. Eliʿezer incurred excommunication through his opposition to the opinion of the majority. Cf. IV. 12. Shortly afterwards he retired from Lydda to Cæsarea.   On his death-bed he apostrophised his arms: "Alas! my two arms, which are like two books of Thorah rolled up." He added, that he had learned and taught much Thorah, but had not by learning lessened his teachers' store by so much as a dog laps from the sea; nor had his own disciples taken away from him, אלא כמכחול בשפופרת. He had laid down the law (said he) times innumerable, when his decisions had been received without a question (Sanhedrin 68 a); and indeed notwithstanding the ban under which he lay, the Mishnah has preserved more than 330 of his sayings—"mehr als von irgend einem seiner Gefährten" (Jost, *Gesch.* B. 35). His respect for authority is further shewn by his counsel (§ 14) to warm oneself by, and yet keep at a respectful distance from, the fire of the wise. After him is named the work, *Pirqe Rabbi Eliʿezer ben Hyrqanos.*

12.   He said to them, Go and see which is the good way
that a man should cleave to.   Rabbi Li'ezer said, A good eye[26]:
R. Jehoshua' said, A good friend[27]: and R. Jose said, A good
neighbour: and R. Shime'on said, He that foresees what is to
be[28]: R. La'zar said, A good heart.   He said to them, I approve
the words of Ele'azar ben 'Arak rather than your words, for his
words include your words.

13.   He said to them, Go and see which is the evil way that
a man should shun.   R. Li'ezer said, An evil eye[29]: and
R. Jehoshua' said, An evil companion: and R. Jose said, An
evil neighbour: and R. Shime'on said, He that borroweth and
repayeth not[30]—he that borrows from man is the same as if he
borrowed from God (blessed is He)—for it is said, The wicked
borroweth, and payeth not again, but the righteous is merciful
and giveth (Ps. xxxvii. 21): R. La'zar said, An evil heart.
He said to them, I approve the words of Ele'azar ben 'Arak

---

[26] "He that hath a bountiful eye
(טוב עין) shall be blessed; for he giveth of his bread to the poor" (Prov.
xxii. 9).   On טוב לב (Prov. xv. 15)
see Sanhedrin 100 b. [Aboth R. N.
xiv. לב טוב לשמים ולב טוב לבריות.]

[27] CHABER is a familiar friend, colleague, or associate: SHAKEN, simply a
neighbour. Cf. i. 7, 8; Luke xv. 6,
καλεῖ τοὺς φίλους καὶ τοὺς γείτονας.

[28] Cf. לעם נולד (Ps. xxii. 32).   The
saying is explained in A* as denoting
a man of insight, who considers the
consequences of things beforehand,
and thereby regulates his actions, ba-
lancing the sacrifice for a duty against
its reward (§ 1).

[29] "Eat thou not the bread of him
that hath an evil eye (רע עין)...Eat
and drink, saith he to thee; but his
heart is not with thee" (Prov. xxiii. 6,
7). "He that hasteth to be rich is
איש רע עין" (Prov. xxviii. 22). The
evil eye denotes especially niggardli-
ness, envy, or jealousy. Cf. Aboth v.

19; Matt. xx. 15.   Compare also § 15,
where the "evil eye" perhaps corresponds to הקנאה (Aboth iv. 30).
R. Jonah brings out the connexion
between this saying of R. Shime'on
and the former by remarking that the
borrower should consider whether he
is able to repay, for the day of reckoning will surely come.

[30] "He that hath pity upon the poor
lendeth unto the Lord" (Prov. xix. 17).
ἐφ' ὅσον ἐποιήσατε ἑνὶ τούτων τῶν ἐλα-
χίστων, ἐμοὶ ἐποιήσατε (Matt. xxv. 40).
The character here condemned is that
of a man wanting in insight, who incurs responsibilities which he is not
able to meet and who views things
from an external standpoint, not seeing the significance of commonplace
actions, whereas ὁ ἐν ἐλαχίστῳ ἄδικος
καὶ ἐν πολλῷ ἄδικός ἐστιν (Luke xvi. 10).
Another explanation (bar S.) is that
all wealth belongs to God (Haggai ii.
8), and men are His stewards.   Hence
the borrower borrows from God.

rather than your words, for your words are included in his words[31].

14. And they said (each) three things. R. Li'ezer[32] said, Let the honour of thy friend be dear unto thee as thine own; and be not easily provoked; and repent[33] one day before thy death. And warm thyself before the fire of the wise, but beware of their embers, perchance thou mayest be singed, for their bite is the bite of a fox[34], and their sting the sting of a scorpion, and their hiss the hiss of a fiery-serpent, and all their words are as coals of fire (Jer. v. 14).

[31] Ἔσωθεν γὰρ ἐκ τῆς καρδίας...ὀφθαλμὸς πονηρός κ.τ.λ. (Mark vii. 21, 22). The "heart" has not now quite the same significance as formerly. Cf. "Ephraim also is like a silly dove without HEART" (Hosea vii. 11); and notice the remarkable expression, τοὺς ὀφθαλμοὺς τῆς καρδίας (Eph. i. 18; Clem. ad Cor. I. 36, 59).

[32] The three sayings of R. Li'ezer are variously reckoned. Rambam regards: "And warm thyself, &c." as an extraneous addition, and takes the caution against anger as the second; whereas "Rashbam" and others make it part of the first, since irritability tends to discourtesy. According to the latter reckoning the sayings are, (1) "Let the honour, &c."; (2) "Repent, &c."; (3) "Warm thyself, &c." The connexion between anger and the dishonouring of a man's neighbour might be illustrated by Matt. v. 22, πᾶς ὁ ὀργιζόμενος τῷ ἀδελφῷ αὐτοῦ ἔνοχος ἔσται τῇ κρίσει...ὃς δ' ἂν εἴπῃ, Μωρέ, ἔνοχος ἔσται εἰς τὴν γέενναν τοῦ πυρός. "Whosoever is angry, punishments of Gehinnom come upon him, for it is said (Eccl. xi. 10), Remove כעם from thy heart, and put away evil from thy flesh. And 'evil' is Gehinnom, for it is said (Prov. xvi. 4),...the wicked for the day of evil" (bar S.) By

three things a man is tested, בכוסו ובכיסו ובכעסו, by his cup, and his purse, and his temper. [This saying is in 'Erubin 65 b.]

[33] R. 'Obadiah establishes a connexion between this clause and the preceding by remarking that if anger has got the better of a man he should repent at once. The saying is quoted in Shabbath 153 a, and explained as meaning that a man should repent to-day because he may die to-morrow: "Let thy garments be always white" (Eccl. ix. 8). A parable of Jochanan ben Zakkai is added: A king invited his servants to a banquet without specifying the time: the wise (פיקחין) dressed themselves and sat at the gate: the foolish went to their work: suddenly the guests were summoned: the king was pleased with the wise, and angry with the foolish: he said, They that dressed themselves for the banquet shall sit and eat, and they that did not shall stand and look on. The son-in-law of R. Meir said that all shall sit, but the wise shall eat and drink, and the foolish shall be hungry and thirsty (Is. lxv. 13).

[34] Bar S. mentions a reading נחש, which perhaps crept in from a commentary in which it was used below to explain שרף.

15. R. Jehoshua' said, An evil eye[35], and the evil nature[36],

[35] The expression עַיִן הרע might be rendered, *oculus mali*, since עַיִן is usually feminine; but see *Crit. Note*. It occurs in many other places. Observe that the saying on ὀφθαλμὸς πονηρός in § 13 is attributed to Eli'ezer, not Jehoshua'.

Jehoshua' frequently appears in controversy with 'Aqiba, Gamliel (p. 25), Eli'ezer, &c. "Wir haben von ihm in der Mischnah gegen 130 Aussprüche...Er war zur Zeit des Tempels schon erwachsen, und Schüler des Jochanan b. Zachai. Als Levit gehörte er zu den Sängern des Tempels, kurz vor dessen Zerstörung er seinem Lehrer ins Lager der Römer folgte" (Jost, *Gesch.* B. 71). When, in sorrow for the destruction of the Temple, many Pharisees refused to eat flesh and drink wine, which were no longer offered on the altar, he shewed them that logically they must abstain likewise from bread, and fruit, and water, and admonished them to desist from excessive demonstrations of grief on the ground that no burden should be put upon the congregation which the majority could not bear (Baba B. 60b), שאין גוזרין גזירה על הצבור אלא א׳כ רוב צבור יכולין לעמוד בה. He had the reputation of being a faithful observer of the Law, but an opponent of extravagant developments. "Die Juden liebten ihn sehr, und sein Wort bewirkte Beruhigung der Gemüther in der Zeit furchtbarer Aufregung unter *Trajan's* Regierung."

[36] The omission of the article before יצר may be abundantly illustrated from Rabbinic. Cf. חסידים הראשונים (Berakoth v. 1), &c. The omission is also Biblical (Gen. i. 31).

The word יצר denotes (1) formation, or a thing formed (Ps. ciii. 14; Is.

xxix. 16), and (2) διανοία, especially in connexion with לב. Cf. Gen. vi. 5; viii. 21, יצר לב האדם רע מנעריו. The יצר רע is the evil nature or disposition in or of a man: the יצר טוב his good nature or disposition. These —cf. the παλαιὸς and καινὸς ἄνθρωπος (Eph. iv. 22, 23)—are frequently personified. The dualism of man's nature is evolved from Gen. ii. 7, where it is said, וַיִּיצֶר כו׳ (with *two yods*), He formed man with two יצרים, the one, טוב י׳, and the other, רע י׳ (Berakoth 61 a). A curious "parable" is given in connexion with the murder of Abel: A thief effected a robbery in the night, escaping the vigilance of the gatekeeper, who however caught him on the morrow and began to reproach him for his dishonesty. The retort was, I am a thief, and thou art the watchman: I have not neglected my business, but thou hast neglected thine. So Cain said to God, Thou didst create in me יצר הרע, and in consequence I slew Abel: why didst Thou, that art the keeper of all, let me slay him? It is Thou that hast slain him, Thou that art called אנכי (see Excursus on Shema'), for hadst Thou accepted my offering like his, I should not have been jealous of him (Tanchuma on Gen. iv. 9). The Targum and Midr. Rab. on Eccl. ix. 14, 15 make the *little city* the heart of man: the *great king* that comes against it, the יצר רע: and the *poor wise man* that delivers the city, the יצר טוב. This reminds us of the ἰσχυρός, spoiled by the ἰσχυρότερος, and at the same time of the indwelling ἀκάθαρτον πνεῦμα (Luke xi. 21—26).

The evil יצר (Eccl. x. 1, Targ.) lies at the door of the heart like a דבובא, "instar muscæ" (Berakoth 61 a); in

and hatred of the creatures put a man out of the world[37] (αἰών).

16.   R. Jose said, Let the property (Luke xvi. 11, 12) of thy friend be precious unto thee as thine own; set thyself to learn Thorah, for it is not an heirloom unto thee[38]; and let all thy actions be to the name of Heaven[39].

17.   R. Shime‘on said, Be careful in reading the **Shema**‘[40], *and in Prayer;* and when thou prayest[41], make not thy prayer

connexion with which compare Geiger's *Urschrift und Uebersetzungen der Bibel, &c.* p. 53, where BEELZEBUB is explained as meaning ENEMY, not "fly-god": " Die ägyptisch-griechischen Uebersetzer setzen daher für diesen Eigennamen der Philistäer ganz allgemein ' Fremdstammige ' (ἀλλόφυλοι). Ihre Nationalgottheit Baal-Sebub (2 Kön. 1, 2. 3. 16) wird daher später mit aramäischer Aussprache als Beelzebub (o.—bul), als feindliche Gottheit überhaupt, als Gegengott, Satanas, Haupt der Dämonen schlechtweg gebraucht (Matth. 10, 25. 12, 24 u. 27, vgl. 9, 34. Marc. 3, 22. Lucas 11, 15 u. 19). Ja dieser Sprachgebrauch ist so geläufig geworden, dass dieses Wort in etwas abweichender aramäischer Form, nämlich als Beel-Debab (בעל דבבא), wie die syr. hexapl. Uebersetzung bereits für Baal-Sebub setzt, in sämmtlichen aramäischen Dialekten ganz einfach einen 'Feind' bedeutet, und daraus mit Wegwerfung des Beel ein neuer Stamm דבב sich bildet für: hassen, anfeinden."

[37] Cf. πᾶς ὁ μισῶν τὸν ἀδελφὸν αὐτοῦ …οὐκ ἔχει ζωὴν αἰώνιον ἐν αὐτῷ μένουσαν (1 Joh. iii. 15). The term "creatures" (I. 13) was in common use in the sense MANKIND.

[38] Contrast Deut. xxxiii. 4. The knowledge of Thorah is not inherited, but must be purchased at the cost of a man's own labour. A* remarks that the clause is dotted above, to shew

that it should be omitted.

[39] Cf. 1 Cor. x. 31. A* &c. refer to the blessing of Jael, in illustration of the principle that even evil done from a good motive is better than good done from an evil motive.

[40] The portion of Thorah thus called, from its initial word שמע (Deut. vi. 4), is appointed to be read or recited morning and evening by every Jew.

The first tract of the Mishnah commences with a question about the time for reading the שמע, or "audi," in the evening (Berak. I. 1). It was regarded as including the Decalogue. See Excursus IV.; and cf. Mark xii. 29, where the ἐντολὴ πρώτη is said to be, Ἄκουε, Ἰσραήλ. Κύριος ὁ Θεὸς ἡμῶν Κύριος εἷς ἐστί. καὶ ἀγαπήσεις Κύριον τὸν Θεόν σου, κ.τ.λ. For him who reads the AUDI with scrupulous precision as regards its several letters "They cool Gehinnom," for it is said (Ps. lxviii. 15), "When the Almighty *scattered* kings in it, it was white as *snow* on Zalmon;" where take פרש in the sense, *separate,* or make distinct, and read צלמות, *shadow of death,* for צלמון (Berakoth 15 b).

[41] Prayer is not to be said merely at set times and as a duty, but is to be the expression of a heartfelt desire: " He who makes his prayer קבע, his prayer is not תחנונים, δέησις" (Berakoth IV. 4). "There is no set time (קבע) for the evening prayer"

an ordinance, but an entreaty before God[42], blessed is He, *for it is said, For God is compassionate and easily-entreated,*

(Berakoth 26 a). If it is doubtful whether a man has read the AUDI he is required to read it, but not so with prayer. R. Jochanan said, Oh! that a man would pray all the day long (Berakoth 21 a; Pesachim 54 b). A man when he prays should not stand in a high place but in a low place, for it is said (Ps. cxxx. 1), Out of the *depths*, &c. (Berakoth, 10 b). Although prayer is not directly commanded in the Pentateuch (Pereq I, note 5), the duty of praying three times in the day (Ps. lv. 18; Dan. vi. 11) is made to rest upon the authority of Abraham, Isaac, and Jacob. Abraham established the morning prayer (Gen. xix. 27), since *standing* is to be identified with *thefillah* (Ps. cvi. 30). Two other times of prayer, under the names שיחה, and פגיעה, are referred to Isaac and Jacob (Gen. xxiv. 63; xxviii. 11). See Bereshith Rabbah LXVIII. On the "ten" names of prayer, and on תחנונים, cf. Deut. Rab. II. On תפילין, meaning φυλακτήρια, see Buxtorf, s.v. פלל.

[42] The word MAQOM, from QUM, to stand, denotes that in which things exist, i.e. place or space. It is constantly used in Rabbinic writings as a name of God, who is regarded as the ἐν ᾧ or *locus* of existence (Acts xvii. 28), and as *filling* all space: "All the earth is full of His glory" (Is. vi. 3). Both of these meanings of the name are mentioned in Jalqut 117 (on ויפגע במקום, Gen. xxviii. 11), where it is said that God is so called, מפני שהוא מקומו של עולם ואין העולם מקומו, because He is the PLACE of the world, and not the world His place—so ℔, commenting upon § 12—according to the Scriptures, Ex. xxxiii.

21, הנה מקום אתי; Deut. xxxiii. 27; Ps. xc. 1, "Lord, thou hast been our dwellingplace" (מעון, καταφυγή). The words מקום and יהוה are also equated by a species of Gematria (III. 28), the letters of the former amounting to 186, and the sum of the *squares* of those of the latter $(10^2 + 5^2 + 6^2 + 5^2)$ being likewise 186. See Buxtorf, *Lex. Chald.* col. 2001. Bar S. cites this from R. Israel. In accordance with the above uses, God the Father is spoken of in the New Testament both as containing and as filling all. The like is also said of the Son—cf. the Pauline ἐν Χριστῷ on the one hand, and ἵνα πληρώσῃ τὰ πάντα (Eph. iv. 10) on the other. Since space and its complement are correlatives, the use of MAQOM, τόπος, naturally suggests a doctrine of a πλήρωμα. Moreover, since MAQOM is an ordinary Hebrew Name of God, it is not necessary to assume that its correlative πλήρωμα was originally a product of GNOSTICISM. As testimony (1) to the antiquity of this remarkable use of τόπος, (2) to the natural affinity of the expression to πλήρωμα, and (3) to the applicability of the conception to the Λόγος, compare the following from Philo, *De Somniis Lib. I.* (Vol. I. p. 630, ed. Mangey): Τριχῶς δὲ ἐπινοεῖται τόπος· ἅπαξ μὲν χώρα ὑπὸ σώματος ἐκπεπληρωμένη· κατὰ δεύτερον δὲ τρόπον ὁ θεῖος λόγος, ὃν ἐκπεπλήρωκεν ὅλον δι' ὅλων ἀσωμάτοις δυνάμεσιν αὐτὸς ὁ θεός...κατὰ δὲ τρίτον σημαινόμενον αὐτὸς ὁ θεὸς καλεῖται τόπος, τῷ περιέχειν μὲν τὰ ὅλα, περιέχεσθαι δὲ πρὸς μηδενὸς ἁπλῶς, καὶ τῷ καταφυγὴν τῶν συμπάντων αὐτὸν εἶναι· καὶ ἐπειδήπερ αὐτός ἐστι χώρα ἑαυτοῦ, κεχωρηκὼς ἑαυτὸν καὶ ἐμφερόμενος μόνῳ ἑαυτῷ. Ἐγὼ μὲν οὐκ εἰμὶ τόπος, ἀλλ' ἐν τόπῳ, καὶ ἕκαστον

longsuffering, and plenteous in grace[43]; and be not wicked unto thyself[44].

18. R. La'zar said, Be diligent to learn *Thorah*, wherewith thou mayest make answer (1 Pet. iii. 15) to Epicurus[45]; and know before whom thou toilest[46]; and who is the Master of thy work.

19. R. Tarphon[47] said, The day is short, and the task is

τῶν ὄντων ὁμοίως· τὸ γὰρ περιεχόμενον διαφέρει τοῦ περιέχοντος, τὸ δὲ θεῖον, ὑπ' οὐδενὸς περιεχόμενον, ἀναγκαίως ἐστὶν αὐτὸ τόπος ἑαυτοῦ.

[43] The Scripture proof was probably a later addition. 𝔄 apparently mixes up Joel ii. 13 and Ps. lxxxvi. 15.

[44] [Cf. Ecclus. vii. 16 μὴ προσλογίζου σεαυτὸν ἐν πλήθει ἁμαρτωλῶν, Qiddushin 4 b & Tosefta, Joma 2 b בפני עצמו, *by itself.*]

[45] The Greek name Epicurus is used to denote a heretic or unbeliever, whether Jewish or foreign. On this word, and on מין, *heretic*, see Buxtorf, *Lex. Chald.* The latter is supposed by some to be from מאני, Manes, and to denote primarily a Manichee; early Jewish writers used it especially for *Christian*, but in later times, owing to the tendency to expunge antichristianisms, it was frequently crossed out, or replaced by some other word, as Çaduqi or Kuthi ; and to such an extent has this been done that wherever there has been a suspicion of an allusion to Christianity the text can seldom be entirely depended upon.

The reading of the text implies that the Thorah itself, if diligently studied, will supply the required answer to the "Epicurean," who must therefore be regarded as a Jew-heretic. The reading of bar S. is susceptible of the same interpretation : "Study Thorah, *that thou mayest know* what answer to make to an Epicurus;" or it may mean, if ודע be taken disjunctively:

"Study Thorah, *and also know* how to answer Epicurus." The latter is the interpretation of R. Israel, who says that the student should first be well-grounded in Thorah and Talmud, and then learn *scientias exterorum*, that he may be able to refute those who go astray from the truth ; and he remarks upon the saying (Berakoth 28 b), "Be careful of the honour of your associates, *and restrain your sons from meditation* (ההגיון), and set them between the knees of a scholar ; and when ye pray, know before whom ye stand ; and so shall ye be counted worthy of the life of the world to come"—that a man is not required to restrain himself from speculation, but only his sons who have not come to maturity. In the same way he understands the injunction not to teach one's *son* "Greek science" (Sotah 49 b); and he holds that there is no Divine command not to teach one's son Thorah in Greek.

[46] R. 'Obadiah writes on this clause that a man should work strenuously *for the glory of God.* The final clause, especially with the longer readings (note ר), introduces the idea of *reward.* Thus the required number of three sayings (§ 14) is made up. This may also be done by dividing the first saying, and joining ומי כו to what precedes.

[47] R. Tarphon, Trypho, or "Teraphon," a contemporary of the above-mentioned five, was one of those pre-

great, and the workmen are sluggish[48], and the reward is much, and the Master of the house is urgent. He said, It is not for thee to finish the work[49], nor art thou free to desist therefrom; if thou hast learned much Thorah, they give thee much reward; and faithful is the Master of thy work, who will pay thee the reward of thy work, and know that the recompence of the reward of the righteous is for the time to come[50].

sent at the death of R. J. ben Zakkai.

[48] This Mishnah has points of contact with the Parable of the Vineyard in Matt. xx., where the οἰκοδεσπότης says to the labourers whom he finds unemployed, Τί ὧδε ἑστήκατε ὅλην τὴν ἡμέραν ἀργοί; Bar S. remarks that since man is a microcosm containing all the affairs of the world in miniature, the affairs of the αἰών are here likened to those of the individual.

[49] Although "ars longa vita brevis,"

a man must neither despair nor yield to idleness, for he is not called upon to finish the work singlehanded, and yet is bound to contribute to the best of his ability; and in proportion to his work he will be rewarded, if not at once, in the time to come.

[50] This expression, like ὁ αἰὼν ὁ μέλλων, has its ambiguity. It may refer, as here, to the future life; or, as in 'Erubin IX. 3, to the future in this life. [Heb. x. 35 μισθαποδοσία.]

---

p. 29, § 4] In 'Abodah Zarah 19 a, in connexion with the saying of Antigonus in Aboth I. 3, there is a discussion of Psalm i. 2, "But his delight is in the law of the Lord; and in his law doth he meditate day and night." At first the law (תורה) is called God's; but afterwards נקראת על שמו, it is called by his (the man's own) name. He has made the law of God his law.

p. 31, n. 17] Cf. Clem. *Hom.* II. 16 ἐν ἀρχῇ ὁ Θεὸς εἷς ὤν, ὥσπερ δεξιὰ καὶ ἀριστερά, πρῶτον ἐποίησε τὸν οὐρανὸν εἶτα τὴν γῆν καὶ οὕτως ἐξῆς πάσας τὰς συζυγίας.

p. 33, n. 23] Codex Bezae reads "*Lazar* amicus noster mortuus est" in St John xi. 14. The Old Latin Cod. *a* likewise has the form *Lazar*, as Mr Rendel Harris points out in *A Study of Codex Bezae* p. 183 (Camb. *Texts and*

Studies II. no. 1). The form Λάζαρ occurs in chap. 2 of *Acta Pilati* literally retranslated into Greek from an Armenian manuscript by Mr Conybeare (Oxf. *Studia Biblica et Ecclesiastica* IV. 61, 85).

p. 35, § 13] To be בדרך רחוקה (T. J. Joma, end) is to be in an evil way, "far from God." The phrase in its literal sense is found in Num. ix. 9 (cf. Sifré I. § 69).

p. 36, n. 31] *The heart has eyes*, as it is said in *Midrash Alpha Betha de-R. 'Aqiba*, לאדם יש לו עינים אף ללב יש לו עינים (Jellinek *Bet-ha-M.* III. p. 34). *The heart sees*, for it is said ולבי ראה הרבה (Eccl. Rab. i. 16). Maimonides writes in *Hilkoth Yesodé ha-Torah* IV. 7, "Forms without matter are not visible to the eye, but they are known by the eye of the heart."

CHAPTER III.

1. 'Aqabiah ben Mahalaleel[1] said, Consider three things[2], and thou wilt not come into the hands of transgression (II. 1). Know whence thou camest; and whither thou art going; and before whom thou art about to give account and reckoning[3].

[1] We read in the Mishnah that 'Aqabiah ben Mahalaleel testified concerning four things: they said, Retract, and we will make thee *Ab Beth Din* to Israel: he said, It were better for me to be called fool all my days than to be made wicked before HA-MAQOM for one hour, so that they may not say that for the sake of office he retracted. He persisted in his views, and was excommunicated. When at the point of death he counselled his son to retract the four things, saying that he himself had received them by tradition from the many, but his son, who received them from him alone, must yield to the majority of his contemporaries ('Edioth v. 6, 7), for the halakah is according to the many as against the one (Berakoth 9 a, 37 a). This principle is "propped," not very securely, upon the words, אחרי רבים להטות (Ex. xxiii. 2), which are rendered by Onqelos, בתר סניאי שלם דינא, *give judgment according to the majority*. The verse from which they are taken is usually rendered: "Thou shalt not follow a multitude to do evil; neither shalt thou speak in a cause *to decline after many to wrest* judgment."

[2] The three things to be considered are matters of observation or revelation. Contrast the warning against speculation: "Whosoever considers four things, What is *above, below, before, behind*, it were better for him that he had not come into the world" (Chagigah II. 1).

[3] This Mishnah is cited in T. J. Sotah II. 2; Va-jiqra Rabbah xviii.; Qoheleth Rabbah, on Eccl. xii. 1. R. 'Aqiba expounded the clause, וזכר נא את בוראיך, so as to include the three things mentioned above, thus: "Remember בראך · בורך · בארך, thy *source*, thy *grave*, thy *Creator*." It may be remarked here that Rabbinic citations of Scripture are not intended always as absolute proofs of the doctrines and ideas in connexion with which they are adduced. A citation is often a mere μνημόσυνον, and as such may even be the more effective in proportion to the non-naturalness of its application. That citations cannot have been always intended as proofs may be gathered from an examination of a number of instances. But over and above this we have an express statement in the Mishnah in relation to a certain question: "Quamvis rei

Know whence thou camest: from a fetid drop; and whither
thou art going: to worm and maggot[4] (Job xxv. 6); and before
whom thou art about to give account and reckoning: before the
King of the kings of kings, blessed is He.

2.   R. Chananiah, prefect of the priests[5], said, Pray for the
peace of the kingdom[6] (1 Tim. ii. 1, 2), since but for fear thereof *we* had swallowed up each his neighbour alive.

3.   R. Chananiah ben Thradyon said, Two that sit together
without words of Thorah are a session of scorners, for it is said,
Nor sitteth in the seat of the scornful[7] (Ps. i. 1); but two that
sit together and are occupied in words of Thorah have the
Shekinah[8] among them, for it is said, Then they that feared the
Lord[9] spake often one to another, &c. (Mal. iii. 16).

4. *One that sits and studies, the Scripture imputes to him as if he fulfilled the whole Thorah, for it is said, He sitteth alone and keepeth silence, because he hath borne[10] it upon him* (Lam. iii. 28).

שכנתיה, *the glory of His Shekinah* (Gen. iii. 24, Targ. Jerus.)—which "glory" manifests itself in flaming fire on Sinai (Ex. xix. 18)—or ש' יקרא (Ps. lxviii. 19). We find ש' קודשא in Targ. Jonathan on Numb. v. 3, &c. The Shekinah is especially connected with the tabernacle (*mishkan*), and the sanctuary, but it is not to be restricted to a visible and local symbol of the Divine Presence. This is only one of the applications of the word, which is used with much greater latitude. It is said by R. Ishmael and others (Baba Bathra 25 a) that שכינה is in every place, although in the course of the discussion other opinions are advanced. The Thosaphoth, in connexion with the view that the Shekinah was especially in the west, remark that its face was eastward, or in the direction in which Israel worshipped, and that hence the points of the compass N. S. E. W. are called *left, right, before, behind*. It may be noticed here (cf. p. 31) that the *left* side is connected with evil. So the *north*, for (Jer. i. 14) מצפון תפתח הרעה. The text (cf. § 9) speaks of an invisible Shekinah which may be present anywhere, and it affords an illustration of Matt. xviii. 20, οὗ γάρ εἰσι δύο ἤ τρεῖς συνηγμένοι εἰς τὸ ἐμὸν ὄνομα, ἐκεῖ εἰμὶ ἐν μέσῳ αὐτῶν. The Shekinah may even rest upon an individual (pp. 21, 48). The righteous in the world to come sit with crowns on their heads, ונהנים מזיו השכינה (Berakoth 17 a). SHEKINAH is sometimes practically equivalent to MEMRA, λόγος (v. 1), but we may distinguish between them by regarding the one as the medium of a

passive, the other of an *active*, manifestation: the one as creative, the other as "overshadowing" or indwelling. The two are brought together by St John, in whose theology the conceptions assume a new definiteness, and the medium becomes a Mediator: ὁ Λόγος σὰρξ ἐγένετο, καὶ ἐσκήνωσεν ἐν ἡμῖν (Joh. i. 14). The word σκηνή and its derivatives are chosen on account of their assonance with the Hebrew to express the *Shekinah* and its dwelling with men—compare especially Rev. xxi. 3: Ἰδοὺ ἡ σκηνὴ τοῦ Θεοῦ μετὰ τῶν ἀνθρώπων, καὶ σκηνώσει μετ' αὐτῶν—and indeed so closely does Shekinah resemble σκηνή, that the former has even been thought of as a transliteration of the latter. The word is rare in the Mishnah, but occurs frequently in Midrash and Gemara.

[9] The MS. **א** expresses יהוה by יי followed by a vertical stroke or flourish wholly above the line. In some MSS. a ו is inserted in order to make up the numerical value of יהוה, viz. 26. The shorter Name יה is identified by Gematria (§ 28) with the longer Name by writing out the names of its letters, הא, יוד, which are thus made to amount to 10 + 6 + 4, and 5 + 1. The saying, "two that sit, &c." is repeated in § 9.

[10] The word *natal* is used of "bearing off" a reward. The whole saying is probably an interpolation. There is a saying of an opposite tendency which may be noticed here: "The Thorah is acquired only בחבורה, by association" (Berakoth 63 b). "A sword is against the solitary, &c." (p. 16). A man's wits are sharpened by his friend

5. R. Shime'on said, Three that have eaten at one table, and have not said over it words of Thorah, are as if they had eaten of sacrifices of (the) dead[11], for it is said, For all tables are full of vomit and filthiness without MAQOM[12] (Is. xxviii. 8).

6. But three that have eaten at one table, and have said over it words of Thorah, are as if they had eaten of the table of MAQOM, blessed is He, for it is said, And he said unto me, This is the table that is before the Lord (Ezek. xli. 22).

7. Chananyiah ben Chakinai said, He who awakes by night, and he who is walking alone by the way, and[13] turns aside his heart to idleness, is "guilty of death."

8. R. Nechonyiah ben ha-Qanah said, Whoso receives upon

(Prov. xxvii. 17). The Thorah is like fire: fire does not burn alone, with nothing to feed it: so words of Thorah, אין מתקיימין ביחידי. A great scholar profits from association with the meanest, as "the small wood is used to set on fire the large": a disciple may even be his master's best teacher (Tha'anith 7 a; Makkoth 10 a). See p. 63.

[11] Idols are "dead" (Is. viii. 19), and powerless, in contrast with God THE LIVING ONE; and as "corpses" they also defile by contact. Cf. Ps. cvi. 28.

[12] The expression naturally means, "without place," with no spot clear from defilement; but the use of ὁ τόπος as a name of God (p. 39) suggests a secondary meaning: "without mention of the Name of God." The idea of §§ 5, 6 is illustrated by 1 Tim. iv. 4: ὅτι πᾶν κτίσμα Θεοῦ καλόν, καὶ οὐδὲν ἀπόβλητον, μετὰ εὐχαριστίας λαμβανόμενον· ἁγιάζεται γὰρ διὰ λόγου Θεοῦ καὶ ἐντεύξεως. Compare Εἴτε οὖν ἐσθίετε, εἴτε πίνετε, εἴτε τι ποιεῖτε, πάντα εἰς δόξαν Θεοῦ ποιεῖτε (1 Cor. x. 31).

[13] He who is sleepless at night should think on words of Thorah (Ps. lxiii. 7): if even at such a time he turns his mind to idleness and idle thoughts, he incurs guilt. So with

the solitary traveller. Compare...ἵνα εἴτε γρηγορῶμεν, εἴτε καθεύδωμεν, ἅμα σὺν αὐτῷ ζήσωμεν (1 Thess. v. 10). The Mishnah thus interpreted forms an apposite sequel to §§ 5, 6. According to another reading (והמפנה) and interpretation the meaning is, that (1) he who is wakeful at night, (2) he who frequents solitary places, and (3) he who indulges in idle thoughts, deserve condemnation; in explanation of which "Rashbam" is quoted as remarking that at night time, and in desert places, and in unguarded moments, a man is especially liable to assaults of the מזיקין, or evil spirits. This notion might indeed be illustrated from the Talmud, but the first interpretation better suits the context. Thorah study is incumbent upon a man at all available times..."when thou sittest in thine house, and when thou walkest by the way, and when thou liest down, and when thou risest up" (Deut. vi. 7: xi. 19). "At midnight I will rise to give thanks unto Thee..." (Ps. cxix. 62). A man should "increase" his time of study by making inroads upon the night (Crit. Note I. 14). When he walks by the way he must let nothing interrupt his "mishnah" (§ 11).

him the yoke[14] of Thorah, they remove from him the yoke of
royalty and the yoke of worldly care; and whoso breaks from
him the yoke of Thorah, they lay upon him the yoke oɪ royalty
and the yoke of worldly care.

9. R. Chalaftha of Kaphar-Chananiah said, When ten sit
and are occupied in words of Thorah the Shekinah is among
them, for it is said, God standeth in the CONGREGATION[15] of the

[14] Ἄρατε τὸν ζυγόν μου ἐφ' ὑμᾶς, καὶ
μάθετε ἀπ' ἐμοῦ...ὁ γὰρ ζυγός μου χρη-
στός, καὶ τὸ φορτίον μου ἐλαφρόν ἐστιν
(Matt. xi. 29, 30). The yoke of malkuth stands for the burdens, as of tax-
ation, put upon a man by the government under which he lives, or the
oppression which he may suffer at the
hands of the great. The yoke of derek
ereç is the anxiety which a man suf-
fers in the struggle for existence: the
cares of labour, poverty, or discontent
with his condition. Every man (writes
bar S.) is by nature continually rest-
less and changeable, saying in winter,
would that it were summer, and in
summer, would that it were winter: he
longs for children if he has none, and
if his family increases he is impatient
of the care of rearing them, &c. From
over anxiety on all such matters an
absorbing devotion to Thorah frees a
man. The Tables of the Law are a
charter of freedom (vi. 2). For a paraphrase of this Mishnah see Aboth R.
N. xx.

The word עוֹל may be used absolutely,
as in T. J. Peah i. 1. It likewise enters into several Rabbinic expressions
analogous to those in the text. Thus
we read of a yoke of malkuth shamayim,
and of miçvah (Berakoth 13 a): a yoke
of flesh and blood (Aboth R. N. xx.): a
yoke of הקב"ה.

[15] Ten is the number which consti-
tutes a congregation (עֵדָה), since it is
said (Numb. xiv. 27), How long shall I
bear with this evil congregation? From

the twelve spies take away Joshua and
Caleb, and there remain ten, which is
therefore the number of an 'edah. A
"great" city is one that contains ten
batlanim, or men of leisure, to make a
congregation (Megillah i. 3). A place
containing less than ten is a kaphar.
Omitting from the text the words in
italics as probably interpolated, we
pass on to the number THREE, which
is connected with אֲגוּדָה, fasciculus.
Compare Baba Meçi'a i. 8, where an
אֲגוּדָה of documents is explained to
mean three or more tied together, while
the corresponding word תכריך, invo-
lucrum, means three or more rolled
together. In like manner A* connects
אֲגוּדָה with the number three, referring inter alia to Ex. xii. 22, where
Rashi interprets אֲגוּדַת אֵזוֹב as a
bundle of three stalks. The number
five is not mentioned in the similar
passages of Berakoth 6 a; Mekiltha,
Jethro xi.; Jalqut i. 305, where the
series of sayings springs naturally out
of a context. From the verse Ex. xx.
24, בְּכָל הַמָּקוֹם אֲשֶׁר אַזְכִּיר אֶת שְׁמִי
וכו', the question arises under what
circumstances is the Shekinah present with men? "In every place...
where I am revealed to thee, בֵּית
הַבְּחִירָה, in the chosen house (or
Temple). Hence they have said, The
incommunicable NAME [iii. n. 35] must
not be uttered in the provinces. Hillel
(cf. p. 30) said, If thou wilt come to
My house, I will come to thy house,
and if thou wilt not come to My house,

mighty (Ps. lxxxii. 1). *And whence (is it proved of) even five*[16]?
Because it is said, He judgeth among gods. And whence
even three ? Because it is said,...and hath founded his TROOP
in the earth (Amos ix. 6). And whence even two ? Because it

I will not come to thy house, To the
place that my heart loves thither my
feet lead me. Hence they have said,
Every ten men that are assembled in
the synagogue, the Shekinah is with
them, for it is said, God standeth in
the 'edah, &c. And whence even three
that JUDGE, because it is said, He
judges among gods, &c." Here an entirely new case, suggested by the second
hemistich of the same verse, is brought
under consideration. It is granted
that the Shekinah is with an ἐκκλησία,
a congregation assembled for the discharge of religious duties: but is the
Shekinah present likewise at secular
functions? Yes! where three are gathered to administer justice, the Shekinah is in the midst. From the public meeting of a *beth din* (=three), we
pass next to the private meeting of
two friends to study and discuss Thorah,—this transition is most clearly
marked in Berakoth—and thence to
the case of the individual. Berakoth
then takes the numbers in reverse
order. If the Shekinah is with one,
why make separate mention of two?
Because the words of two are written
in the book of remembrances: discussion is required to make a lasting impression. But why should three be
mentioned? To show that JUDGMENT
is THORAH, a sacred and not merely a
secular function. Lastly, why mention
ten? If דין is תורה, what advantage
has the 'edah over the *beth din?* It is
that the Shekinah comes to the three
only when they are seated, but comes
beforehand to the place of the 'edah:
the "congregation" intend *ab initio* to
perform a sacred function, but דיּן is

only *ex post facto* תורה. It may be
remarked that Jonathan targumises
Ex. xx. 24: "In whatsoever place I
cause my Shekinah to rest, and thou
worshippest before ME, there I will
send upon thee my blessing and will
bless thee." As some have found a
difficulty in אזכיר את שמי, and wish
to read תזכיר, observe that R. Josiah
in Jalqut calls the verse מסורס, and
reads in inverse order, In what place
soever I come unto thee, there will I
cause my NAME to be mentioned.

[16] The great mass of MSS. retain
the number five, but some connect it
with *judgment*—making up the number by adding two litigants to three
judges; while others connect it with
the *fasciculus,* which is assumed to be
that which can be grasped with the
five fingers of a hand. The simplest
hypothesis (suggested by Ⓔ) is that the
parallels from Berakoth, Mekiltha, and
Jalqut (see note 15) give the original
reading, and that the number five
should be expunged. The clause
בקרב כו׳ is the second hemistich of
the verse already quoted for the 'edah,
and would therefore probably be quoted, if at all, in the second place. The
mention of *judgment* could then scarcely fail to suggest the number three (see
Crit. Note). The "mishnah" in question is an adaptation of a series of
sayings on Thorah and other matters
to the case of *Thorah alone.* Accordingly the scripture proof for the number three is struck out, since it brings
in the inappropriate notion of judgment, and a new proof for the same
number, viz. from the *aguddah*, is inserted.

is said, Then they that feared the Lord spake often one to another (§ 3). And whence even one? Because it is said, In all places where I record my name I will come unto THEE, and I will bless thee (Ex. xx. 24).

10. R. La'zar ben Jehudah of Barthotha said, Give Him of what is His, for thou and thine are His[17]; and thus he saith in David[18], For all things come of Thee, and of thine own have we given thee (1 Chron. xxix. 14).

11. R. Jacob said, He who is walking by the way and studying, and breaks off his study[19] (Mishnah) and says, How fine is this tree! how fine is that tree! and how fine is this fallow! they account it to him as if he were "guilty of death."

12. R. Dosithai[20], son of R. Jannai, said in the name of R. Meir, When a scholar of the wise sits and studies, and has forgotten a word of his Mishnah, they account it unto him as if he were "guilty of death," for it is said, Only take heed to thyself, and keep thy soul diligently, lest thou forget the words which thine eyes have seen (Deut. iv. 9). Perhaps his Mishnah

---

[17] Cf. Joh. xvii. 9, 10: ἀλλὰ περὶ ὧν δέδωκάς μοι, ὅτι σοί εἰσι. καὶ τὰ ἐμὰ πάντα σά ἐστι, κ.τ.λ.

[18] Compare the formula of citation "in David" in Heb. iv. 7.

[19] The word שׁנה means to change, or to repeat, and hence generally to study or learn. The Aramaic form of the word is תנא, on which see the lexicons. The word משׁנתו is pointed with a horizontal stroke under the נ. This sign, which is now appropriated to Pathach, served in an older system of punctuation, out of which that now in use was developed, for Qameç also. The latter then came to be distinguished by a dot placed under the "Pathach" (⁻); and finally the dot was brought into contact with the "Pathach," and the modern "Qameç" (ᴛ) arose. The citation from the Cambridge University MS. Oo I. 19, fol. 12 b, in the Rabbinic footnote, may

serve as a μνημόσυνον of this fact.

[20] "R. Israel writes that this wise man is mentioned in the Mishnah only here and in 'Erubin" [v. 4] (bar S.).

Forgetfulness is regarded as sinful in so far as it arises from carelessness and neglect of δευτέρωσις. A man is not to be blamed for a forgetfulness arising from sickness or any cause beyond his control. In Berakoth 8 b, an old man who has forgotten his "Thalmud" מחמת אונסו is compared to the shattered tables of the Law, and it is said, לוחות ושׁברי לוחות מונחות בארון, the tables and the fragments of the tables were laid up in the Ark. So the broken-down scholar is to be treated with respect. Of prayer it is said in Berakoth v. 5 that to make a mistake in it is סימן רע לו, an evil sign to a man. The expression דברים (Deut. iv. 9) does not mean merely written "words."

has but grown hard[21] to him? What need then to say, "And lest they depart from thy heart all the days of thy life"? Lo! he is not guilty, till he has sat down and suffered them to depart from his mind.

13. R. Chananiah ben Dosa said, Whosoever fear of sin precedes his wisdom[22], his wisdom stands; *and whosoever wisdom precedes his fear of sin, his wisdom stands not.*

14. He used to say, Whosoever works are in excess of

---

[21] Some commentators understand תקף as of wine which has turned sour or lost its flavour; but it is unnecessary to bring in this meaning here. The case under consideration is that of a man who has not absolutely forgotten, but does not remember readily; his Mishnah is not *fluent in his mouth.* Compare Berakoth 34 b: "They said of R. Chanina ben Dosa that he used to pray over the sick, and say, This one lives, and that one dies. They said to him, Whence knowest thou? He said to them, If my prayer is fluent in my mouth, אם שגורה תפלתי בפי, I know that it is accepted, and if not, I know that it is rejected." Bar S., quoting Sifre, writes that a man should be as careful to preserve his Thorah as his money, for it is hardly gotten, as *gold,* and perishes easily, like *glass,* זכוכית (Job xxviii. 17). He who learns Thorah and does not "repeat" is as one who sows and does not reap. He who learns and forgets is like a mother that bears and buries. Sanh. 99 a.

[22] Different meanings are assigned to the precedence of the fear of sin to "wisdom." The saying is taken to denote either that a man's fear of sin should be instinctive, rather than a result of calculation; or that the fear of sin should be a motive urging him to the acquisition of knowledge as a safeguard against transgressions into which his ignorance might betray him.

The former interpretation is to be preferred: a man should build upon the foundation of religious feeling, rather than of philosophy.

It may be conjectured that the second clauses of §§ 13—15 are later additions. They are not found in Aboth R. N. xxii., and their omission is partly favoured by the reading of the Machazor Vitry in § 14. Compare also note א on § 15. Aboth R. N., after the first clause of § 13, refers to Ps. cxi. 10: "The fear of the Lord is the *beginning* (?) of wisdom." Then follows the first clause of § 14, with a scripture proof from Ex. xxiv. 7: We will DO, and we will HEAR. "They said before Rabban Jochanan ben Zakkai, A wise man and a sinfearer, what is he? He said to them, Lo! he is a workman, with his tools in his hand. A wise man but not a sinfearer, what is he? He said to them, He is a workman who has not his tools in his hand. A sinfearer but not wise, what is he? He said to them, He is no workman, but has his tools in his hand." A* quotes this *baraitha,* with some remarks upon his reading of it. Another comparison is given, from Joma: A man with wisdom but without the fear of Heaven is like a man with the key of an inner court, but unable to enter because he has not the key of the outer court.

his wisdom[23], his wisdom stands; *and whosesoever wisdom is in excess of his works, his wisdom stands not.*

15. He used to say, With whomsoever the spirit of men is pleased[24], the Spirit of God is pleased ; *and with whomsoever the spirit of men is not pleased, the Spirit of God is not pleased.*

16. R. Dosa ben Horkinas said, Morning sleep, and mid-day wine[25], and the babbling of youths[26], and frequenting

---

[23] " Thalmud " and practice—cf. the controversy on Faith and Works—are frequently set against one another in discussions. Aboth I. 18 decides for the latter. On the other side see the remarks of Sifre upon Deut. xi. 13: "If ye shall hearken diligently unto my commandments," where it is said: And ye shall learn them, and ye shall observe to do them (Deut. v. 1). The scripture shews that doing depends on learning, and not learning on doing, שהמעשה תלוי בתלמוד ואין תלמוד תלוי במעשה.

[24] For the expression compare Baba Bathra VIII. 5, where it is said that when a man has left his property to strangers and passed over his sons, what he has done is done, but his act is not approved, "*sapientium spiritus non requiescit in eo.*" The sayings in the text may be compared with 1 Joh. iv. 20: ὁ γὰρ μὴ ἀγαπῶν τὸν ἀδελφὸν αὐτοῦ ὃν ἑώρακε, τὸν Θεὸν ὃν οὐχ ἑώρακε πῶς δύναται ἀγαπᾶν; This Mishnah is taken by bar S. as exemplifying the doctrine that there is a correspondence in all respects between the upper world and the lower: " Whatever exists above, exists also below." Thus there is an archetypal and celestial Adam analogous to the lower Adam, and made literally in the *image of God.* There is also a *familia* above corresponding to the human *familia* below, with respect to which it is said: " May it be thy pleasure, O Lord our God, to make peace in the family above, and in the

family below" (Berakoth 16 b, 17 a). The condition or action of either of these communities must have its analogue in the other. " He who occupies himself in Thorah for its own sake makes peace in the family above and in the family below, for it is said יעשה שלום לי שלום יעשה לי... (Is. xxvii. 5). Rab said, It is as if he built a palace above and below...Moreover he protects the whole world, &c., and brings the redemption nigh" (Sanhedrin 99 b).

[25] A man must not sleep beyond the time of reading the morning *Shema*': nor drink wine early, and so indispose himself alike for Thorah and business. In connexion with the drunkenness of Noah, we read in Midrash Tanchuma that there are four stages from sobriety to intoxication. A man before drinking is innocent as a lamb, and like a sheep which is dumb before its shearers: after drinking enough he is strong as a lion, and says that there is no one like him in the world: in the next stage he becomes a hog: when thoroughly drunken he is like an ape, and dances and jests and talks nonsense and knows not what he is doing. If all this happened to righteous Noah, how must it be with ordinary men? Noah cursed his own descendants, saying, Cursed be Canaan, &c. The children of Ham, because he *saw* the nakedness of his father, and *told* his brethren, had their eyes reddened, and their lips deformed, according to the

the meeting houses[27] of the vulgar, put a man out of the world.

17. R. Li'ezer ha-Moda'i said, He that profanes things sacred[28], and contemns the festivals, and annuls the covenant of Abraham our father, and acts barefacedly against the Thorah[29], even though he be a doer of good works, has no portion in the world to come.

18. R. Ishma'el said, Be pliant of disposition (*or* to a chief)

divine decree, מדה כנגד מדה, measure for measure.

[26] Constant association with young men tends to frivolity, and withholds a man from serious study. Rehoboam took the counsel of young men (1 Kings xii. 8), and caused the disruption of the kingdom. There is a proverb, בנין נערים סתירה וסתירת זקנים בנין, young men's construction is destruction, and old men's destruction is construction.

[27] Bar S. confirms the omission of בתי by reference to his "ancient Mishnaioth." The synagogue served for meetings not merely "precum et sacrorum causa," but for general educational purposes. It served *inter alia* as a schoolhouse for the young (p. 15), in contrast with *beth ha-midrash*, the college for those of riper years. Here, however, the primary reference is to Thorah. Everything which leads the mind astray from it is to be avoided as destroying a man's soul, and putting him out of the world (αἰών). On the other hand, "he that increases Thorah increases life" (II. 8). Ἐρευνᾶτε τὰς γραφάς, ὅτι ὑμεῖς δοκεῖτε ἐν αὐταῖς ζωὴν αἰώνιον ἔχειν (Joh. v. 39).

[28] The fifth Seder of the Mishnah, called *Qodashim*, treats of holy things, and the second, *Mo'ed*, of festivals.

He who despises sacred things, and repudiates the covenant of circumci-

sion, and acts in defiance of the Thorah, cannot be saved by moral excellence. The sense is impaired by reading: "*Thorah and* good works." The text gives a more effective contrast. "He who acts impudently against the Thorah," &c., cannot be saved by good works. The expression מגלה פנים is explained in T. J. Peah I. 1 as meaning, "one who says that the Thorah was not given from Heaven." Buxtorf s. v. גלא writes: "*Revelat faciem contra legem*, id est, proterve, impudenter agit vel insurgit contra eam.*" The unveiled face may also denote confidence in a good sense (2 Cor. iii. 18).

[29] In Sifre on Numb. xv. 31, where this Mishnah is quoted, the clause והמגלה כו' is omitted, but it occurs and is explained in the context. He who hath "*despised the word of the Lord*" is there said to be a Çaduqi; and he who hath "broken (הפר) His commandment," an Epicurus. Another explanation is then given, in which the former expression is rendered, in the words of our text, המגלה פנים בתורה, and the second by המפר ברית בשר. Then follows this Mishnah, with the ending, אע"פ שיש בידו מצוות הרבה כדי הוא לדחותו מן העולם, however many precepts he may perform, he merits expulsion from the world.

and yielding to impressment[30] (Matt. v. 41), and receive every man with cheerfulness.

[30] The text of 𝔄 has the peculiar reading, *Be light of head &c.* The usual reading, which is given in the footnote א, is generally taken to mean: Be pliant towards a great man, and easy in thy bearing with the young—*Esto levis sive velox erga caput, et facilis erga juventutem sive juvenem* (Buxtorf, *Lex. Chald.* s. r. שחר, col. 2372); but some of the older commentators assign very different meanings to the expressions used, and especially to the rare word rendered *juventutem*.

תשחורת] The meaning YOUTH is supported by the analogy of Eccl. xi. 10, כי הילדות והשחרות הבל, and is derived either from *dawn*, or *blackness* (of hair), both of which meanings are found under the root שחר. It has also been deduced from שחר, *petere*. Cf. בחור, *electus*. Pseudo-Rashi assigns to it the opposite meaning SENECTUS, quoting in favour of this view the same verse Eccl. xi. 10. A third meaning, which is well supported, is FORCED SERVICE or ἀγγαρία ('Aruk; "Rashbam"; &c.). For a corresponding use of the verb cf. Onqelos on Num. xvi. 15: שחרית מנהון דחד חמרא לא, *Nullius asinum unquam petii.* There is a saying, quoted in the Machazor Vitry and elsewhere, "Attach thyself to an ἀγγαρεύς, and they will do thee homage," הדבק לשחוור וישתחוו לך. The meaning MELANCHOLY has also been assigned to the word. Midrash Rabbah on Lam. ii. 11 is ambiguous. We read there of three kinds of tears, "but the tear of merriment (שחוק) is the best of all." It is added that there are three kinds of evil tears, "but that of תשחורת is hardest of all." Then follow tales of a man and of a woman each of whom had בן תשחורת,

and he died &c. The commentaries on the Midrash are at variance; some give the meaning *juventus*, but the מתנות כהונה quotes the interpretation of the 'Aruk with approval.

נוח ל] This expression is used in relation (i) to *actions*, (ii) to *persons*. The latter construction is chiefly found in such sayings as, נוח לו שלא נברא, It were *better for him* that he had not been born. For examples of the former construction see II. 14; v. 17; and compare Bereshith Rabbah xvii., where it is said that man is *open to persuasion*, נוח להתפתות, and woman is not *open to persuasion*, because man was formed of earth, which a little water easily dissolves, but woman was made of bone, which will not melt. In the passage under discussion, the construction will be unexceptionable if תשחורת—preceded by ל (see *Crit. Note*)—be interpreted ἀγγαρία, but not so if it be taken concretely of a person, *juvenis.*

קל ראש] [Most] MSS. with the exception of 𝔄 read לראש, but the passage is quoted as in the text in a MS. of the 'Aruk, Cambridge University *Additional* 471.2, where s. v. קל, we find immediately after קלות ראש the words בפ׳ עקביה הוי קל ראש . בר׳ דמאי כו׳; but another MS. of the 'Aruk, *Additional* 376, reads ... קל לראש ראש דמאי... and a third MS., *Additional* 473. 2, has the brief reading הוי קל ראש דמאי... In this case a confusion has arisen from the immediately following reference to the "beginning of Demai." The reading of 𝔄 gives the most natural construction, since קל ל is used of an *action* (v. 30), but not usually of a *person:* on the other hand,

19.　R. ʿAqibah[31] said, Merriment, and lightness of disposition[32], accustom a man to lewdness.

it is open to the objection that it recommends levity, which is condemned in § 19 and elsewhere. This however is partly in favour of the reading, which from its paradoxical nature would be in danger of corruption by the copyists. It may have been intended to contrast the "lightness" which is condemned in general terms in § 19 with a "lightness" which is lawful or expedient under certain circumstances. In like manner bashfulness is condemned from a certain point of view in II. 6, but is singled out for the highest praise in v. 31; and שׂחוק has both a good sense and a bad sense. Compare, also, the praise of "impudence" and shameless pertinacity: "Impudens et importunus vincit hominem malum, quanto magis Deum, qui bonitas mundi ipsa est" (Jalq. II. 550, on Jonah iii. 8); which illustrates Luke xviii. 4—8, and Matt. xi. 12. Cf. Buxtorf, Lex. s. v. חצף, a word which is used for עז in the Targum on Prov. vii. 13. If, as is probable, קלות ראש denotes primarily an ἐλαφρία (2 Cor. i. 17) which results from want of deliberation (note 32), the reading of the text may be explained as meaning that a man should be *hasty*, and yielding to ἀγγαρία. When such a service is put upon him, he should not pause to deliberate, but should take it upon him at once, and yield himself unreservedly to the exaction, in accordance with the saying: καὶ ὅστις σε ἀγγαρεύσει μίλιον ἕν, ὕπαγε μετ᾽ αὐτοῦ δύο (Matt. v. 41). The Machazor Vitry (quoted in *Crit. Note*) paraphrases the saying as follows: "*Lighten thy head* and be pliant as a reed which sways hither and thither, and prompt as a man that is quick to oblige the *head*

of the city and its judges"; thus combining two interpretations.

Other interpretations are as follows: "Be deferential in the presence of a great man, but *sedate* and not too affable towards the young" (Rambam). "When thou art young be קל towards the Creator, and likewise in the time of thine *age* be נוח לו" (Rashi, as quoted by bar S.). "Be קל to the *chief*, or first in rank, and נוח to his ἀγγαρεύς" (R. Jonah). On the whole there is a fair amount of authority for the meaning ἀγγαρία. This being adopted, the expressions קל ראש ונוח may either be taken both together as describing a man's attitude towards ἀγγαρία, or we may read, הוי קל לראש, *Esto velox erga caput*, and take נוח לתשחורת, "yielding to ἀγγαρία," as a separate clause. Levy (*Chald. Wörterbuch* s. v. שׁחר) renders: "sei dienstfertig gegen einen Vornehmen und schmiegsam gegen die Regierung (den Regierer)."

[31] R. ʿAqiba(h) ben Joseph, though descended from non-Jewish parents, and until middle age averse from study, became one of the greatest lights of Judaism both before and after the death of Gamaliel II., with whom, as with R. Jehoshuaʿ (see p. 37), he is brought into connexion in Sukkah III. 9 and elsewhere. In his early years he kept the flocks of the wealthy Kalba Shebuaʿ of Jerusalem, whose daughter he at length married. He espoused the cause of bar Kokba, or Koziba (Sanhedrin 97 b), and acknowledged his claim to the Messiahship: was led captive(?) at the destruction of Bethar (135 A.D. See Jost, *Gesch.* B. 81 note) by Severus: and was

20.   He used to say, Tradition[33] **is a fence to Thorah ;** tithes

put to death, after a long imprison-
ment, by tortures which he bore with
heroic constancy. When the " Greek "
[read *wicked*] kingdom had decreed
that Israel should not occupy themselves in Thorah, Pappus ben Jehudah came and found 'Aqiba holding
large public assemblies for Thorah-
study. He said to him, 'Aqiba, art
thou not afraid of the kingdom?
'Aqiba answers by a parable of a fox
which was walking by the river side.
He sees the fishes clustering from
place to place, and asks them from
what they are fleeing. They say,
From the nets which men are bringing
upon us. He asks, Is it your pleasure
to come up on to the land, that I and
you may dwell together, as my fathers
dwelt with your fathers? They said
to him, Most foolish of beasts, if we
are afraid in the place of our life, how
much more in the place of our death !
So Israel may be distressed even in
their native element of the Thorah,
which is " thy life and the length of
thy days," but to leave it is certain
death... When 'Aqiba was being led
out to execution, it was the time of
reading the *Shema'*, and they were
combing his flesh with combs of iron,
and he was receiving upon him the
yoke of the kingdom of Heaven (i.e.
reciting the *Shema'*). To his disciples
who remonstrate : "Thus far, thou
hast endured enough "; " all my days
(said he) I have been troubled about
this verse: Thou shalt love the Lord
...*with all thy soul*, even if He should
take away thy spirit. When, said I,
will it be in my power to fulfil this?
Now that I have the opportunity shall
I not fulfil it?" As he was protracting
the word אחֿד, ONE, till he expired,
the heavenly voice, BATH QOL, went
forth and said: " Happy art thou R.

'Aqiba that thy spirit went forth at
אחֿד " (Berakoth 61 b). The ministering angels said before the Holy One,
" such is Thorah and such (*a death*)
is its reward " (cf. Menachoth 29 b),
according to Ps. xvii. 14, ממתים ידֿך
'יֿ ממתים כו. BATH QOL went forth
and said, Happy art thou R. 'Aqiba,
that thou art invited to the life of the
world to come. [Midr. Prov. ix.]

'Aqiba learned tradition from Eli'e-
zer ben Hyrqanos, and acquired the
minutiæ of scholarship from Nachum
of Gimzo, with whom he studied for
22 years, investigating the uses of par-
ticles, as גם, אֿת, רק, אֿך, wherever they
occurred in Scripture (Chagigah 12 a ;
Pesachim 22 b ; Bereshith Rabbah i.).
Once when the chazan summoned him
to read Thorah to the congregation,
he excused himself on the ground that
he had not read over the portion twice
(or four times), privately, in accordance with the example of the Holy
One (Midrash Tanchuma on Ex. xx.
1 ; Bereshith Rabbah xxiv.), who first
thinks His words over and meditates
upon them, and then communicates
them to men, for it is said (Job xxviii.
27, 28), אֿז ראֿה כו, and afterwards,
ויֿאמר לֿאֿדם. In like manner it is
written in Ex. xx. 1: And God spake
all these words saying, &c. i.e. He
SPAKE to Himself, and then SAID to
men. It is said in T. J. Sotah ix. 10,
17 that there arose no *eshkol* (see p.
14) before R. 'Aqiba, and that the
springs of wisdom ceased with him.
He was one of the four who " entered
Paradise " (IV. 1). As a compiler
and systematiser of traditions he was
the forerunner of Jehudah ha-Nasi
(who was born shortly after his death),
but his work has not been preserved in writing in its original

are a fence to wealth[34]; vows a fence to sanctity[35]; a fence to wisdom is silence.

form. Amongst the thousands of his hearers were "*Meir* (eigentlich *Measa*) *Judah* b. Ilai, *Jose* b. Hilpetha, *Simon* b. Jochai, *Eliezer* b. Jakob." Together with his contemporary and rival R. Jehoshua', he was enrolled by posterity amongst the Patres Mundi.

[32] Qalluth rosh, or lightness of head, denotes unbecoming *levity*. It is indeed explained in the 'Aruk as meaning *lifting up of the* head, the opposite of humility; but it is more likely that its proper meaning is quickness and thoughtlessness, and that its opposite, "gravity of head," means slowness and deliberation, or *mens composita*, as it is well rendered in Berakoth v. 1, ed. Surenhusius: "Non assurgunt ad precandum nisi *mente composita*, מתוך כובד ראש. Sancti prisci precabantur horam prius *morati*, ut animum in Deum intenderent." It is said in Berakoth ix. 5: לא יקל את ראשו כנגד שער המזרח, a man should not "lighten his head" before the eastern gate. Since הקל also means *hold in light esteem*, or *dishonour*, and since קלות ראש is especially to be avoided in *prayer*, we may perhaps compare the expression καταισχύνει τὴν κεφαλήν, which is used in relation to *prayer* in the doubtful passage, 1 Cor. xi. 4, 5. A man must not rise to pray, nor must he part from his friend, "from the midst of שחוק, and קלות ראש, and vain words" (Berakoth 31 a). But שחוק is not universally condemned. Cf. Ps. cxxvi. 2: "Then was our mouth filled with *laughter*, and our tongue with joy." A non-natural interpretation is given to the above verse in Berakoth 31 a: "It is forbidden to a man to fill his mouth with שחוק, for it is said, *Then shall* our mouth be &c., אז ימלא שחוק פינו. When? In the time when the nations shall say, The Lord hath done great things &c." Some commentators remark upon § 19, that such שחוק only as is combined with "lightness of head" is condemned; but others take the expressions separately.

[33] Masorah, or Massoreth, is used of tradition in general, and is correlative to Qabbalah (i. 1). The expression, "from their fathers" in Job xv. 18, is expanded by the Targumist into: "from the tradition, מסורתא, of their fathers." This form of expression is also found in the Mishnah. Cf. Sheqalim vi. 1, where it is said that there was a מסורת in the possession of the houses of R. Gamliel and Chananiah, sagan of the priests, with regard to the place in which the Ark was hidden. The allusion in the text is to the oral Tradition by which the written Thorah is supplemented or interpreted. Masorah in the modern sense is especially a system of rules for the reading of the text of the Hebrew Scriptures. The view that these rules are referred to here has the support of A†, ℭ, and R. Jonah; but although the beginnings of the textual "Masorah" were of ancient date, there is nothing in the Mishnah to limit the generality of the word מסורת.

[34] The clause omitted by 𝕬 is illustrated by the proverbial saying, עשר בשביל שתתעשר (Shabbath 119 a).

[35] The meaning of פרישות is "separation" from defilement, and hence *sanctity* of life. It is used in the Mishnah in parallelism with טהרה, *purity*, at the end of Sotah, where it is said that,—"From when Rabban

21. He used to say, Beloved is man that he was created
"in imagine"; greater love (was it that it) was made known to him that
he was created "in imagine Dei," as it is said, For in the image of
God[36] made He man (Gen. ix. 6).

Gamliel ha-Zaqen died, the glory of
the Thorah ceased, and purity and
פרישות died." For a satirical classification of the various kinds of Pharisees, see T. J. Berakoth ix. 7, and
Buxtorf, Lex. s. r. פרש. Under the
same root is found the expression שם
המפורש for the NAME יהוה. [Compare
Wisdom xiv. 21 τὸ ἀκοινώνητον ὄνομα,
the incommunicable name.]

[36] Man is beloved by God in whose
image (Gen. i. 27; ix. 6), or likeness
(Gen. v. 1), he was created; and he
should be beloved by his fellow-men
as a consequence of this love towards
God Himself. This principle is brought
out by the verse partly cited in the
text: "Whoso sheddeth man's blood,
by man shall his blood be shed: for
in the image of God made He man,"
on which R. 'Aqiba remarks (Bereshith
Rab. xxxiv.); "Whosoever sheddeth
blood, they reckon it to him as if he
diminished THE LIKENESS." See also
Excursus on Shema' (ii. 17). "On
these two commandments (Love God,
Love thy neighbour) hang all the law
and the prophets" (Matt. xxii. 40).
The second of these is included in the
first, according to Bereshith Rabbah,
xxiv. (end), where, "Thou shalt love
thy neighbour as thyself," is brought
into connexion with the saying of Gen.
v. 1: "In the likeness of God made He
him." Hence the contrast in James
iii. 9: ἐν αὐτῇ εὐλογοῦμεν τὸν Κύριον
καὶ πατέρα, καὶ ἐν αὐτῇ καταρώμεθα τοὺς
ἀνθρώπους τοὺς καθ' ὁμοίωσιν Θεοῦ
γεγονότας. Compare 1 Joh. iv. 21: καὶ
ταύτην τὴν ἐντολὴν ἔχομεν ἀπ' αὐτοῦ,
ἵνα ὁ ἀγαπῶν τὸν Θεὸν ἀγαπᾷ καὶ τὸν
ἀδελφὸν αὐτοῦ.

The Midrash is full of speculations
on the creation of the world and of
man, some of which serve to illustrate
the language of the New Testament
Scriptures, as may be seen from the
following examples.

'Ο πρῶτος ἄνθρωπος ἐκ τῆς γῆς, χοϊκός·
ὁ δεύτερος ἄνθρωπος ἐξ οὐρανοῦ (1 Cor.
xv. 47). A conception which pervades
the Midrash literature is that there is
an "upper" and a "lower" Adam: a
celestial man, made strictly in the
image of God, and a terrestrial man
corresponding in detail to his archetype, of which he is the material
adumbration. This twofold conception
makes it difficult at times to estimate
the precise value of the brief enig-
matical sayings of the Rabbis on the
Creation and the Fall. The matter is
further complicated by their tendency
to ignore the distinction between the
potential and the actual: between the
embryo and its development: between the "idea" and its temporal
manifestation. There are two aspects
of the statement that man was made
in the çelem, or image, of God, according as we regard the resemblance to
God as predicated of the actual man
or of his archetype; and as a consequence of this there are also two ways
of regarding the Fall, viz. (1) as a loss
of the Divine image in which man was
actually created, and (2) as a falling
away of the terrestrial Adam from
his archetype. In the "Book of the
generations of Adam" the Divine likeness is described as not wholly lost
but perpetuated (cf. James iii. 9):
"God created man in the LIKENESS of
God...Adam begat a son in his own

22. Beloved are Israel that they are called children of

LIKENESS, after his image" (Gen. v. 1, 3); on which Ramban remarks: "It is known that all that are born of living beings are in the likeness and image of their parents; but because Adam was exalted in his likeness and his image, for it is said of him that, In the likeness of God made He him, it says expressly here that his off-spring likewise were in that exalted likeness, but it does not say this of Cain and Abel, not wishing to dilate upon them, &c." This agrees with the Targum of Jonathan which intro-duces the remark that "before this Eve bare Cain who was not like him (Adam), &c." The Midrash dwells with much emphasis on the word *tholedoth*, "generations" or offspring, and regards the human race as com-prised in Adam as embryo or *golem*. To this is applied Ps. cxxxix. 16: "Thine eyes did see my *golem*, and in thy book they all were written, יָמִים יֻצָּרוּ וְלֹא אֶחָד בָּהֶם." "He created him *golem*, an unshapen mass: and he was extended from one end of the world to the other." (Bereshith Rab-bah xxiv.) "Everything that was created in the six days of *Bereshith* needs 'making' (i.e. preparation or concoction). The mustard for ex-ample needs sweetening: lupines (θέρ-μοι) need sweetening: wheat needs to be ground: even man needs תִּקּוּן, amendment" (B. Rabbah xi.). Ac-cording to this view the "image" and "likeness" is that to which man ap-proximates, and which is found in greater perfection in the תּוֹלְדוֹת אָדָם than in Adam himself.

The saying that the first man was coextensive with the world is found in various places of the Talmud and the Midrash. The old philosophic concep-tion that the world is a μέγας ἄνθρω-πος, and man a microcosm, is adopted by Philo and the Rabbis. The con-stituents of man were gathered from all parts of the earth (Pirqe R. El. xi.). The faculties of the earth correspond to his (Qoheleth Rabbah on Eccl. i. 4): "Whatsoever the Holy One, blessed is He, created in man, He created its analogue in the earth. Man has a *head*: the earth has a head (Prov. viii. 26). Man has *eyes* and *ears*, &c., &c.: the earth has eyes and ears, &c., &c. (Ex. x. 15; Is. i. 2)." "Why was man created alone? To teach thee that whosoever destroys one soul of Israel, it is reckoned to him as if he destroyed a whole world; and whoso-ever preserves one soul of Israel, it is reckoned to him as if he preserved a whole world" (Jalq. i. 15). [Sanh. iv. 5.] Man, who at first stretched from end to end of the world, was diminished by the hand of God, for it is said, "Thou didst form me אָחוֹר וָקֶדֶם, and didst *lay thine hand upon me*" (Ps. cxxxix. 5). See Chagigah 12 a, where it is also said, that *the first man extended from the earth to the firmament*, for it is said that he was created עַל הָאָרֶץ, *upon* or *above* the earth. "Twice didst thou form me (writes the commentator), at first high, then low." The primal man fell short of the Creator's מַחֲשָׁבָה, or *idea*, of which the realization will be in the future, when the Son of Man bridges the chasm between heaven and earth (Joh. i. 52). In like manner the φῶς ἀληθινόν which was created in the be-ginning was withdrawn from the gene-rations that were unworthy of it (Job xxxviii. 15), and remains hidden away for the righteous in the time to come, when "the light of the moon shall be

God[37]; greater love (was it that it) was made known to them that they are called children of God, as it is said, Ye are the children of the LORD your God (Deut. xiv. 1).

23. Beloved are Israel that there was given to them the instrument with which the world was created[37]; greater love

as the light of the sun, and the light of the sun shall be sevenfold, כאור שבעת הימים, as the light of THE SEVEN DAYS" (Is. xxx. 26) of the CREATION WEEK (Bereshith Rabbah III., XI., XII., XLII.; Chagigah 12 a). With this light the first Adam saw from end to end of the world. The world itself was created by it (B. Rabbah XII., אותה האורה שבה נברא העולם). Compare Joh. i. 5—10; καὶ τὸ φῶς ἐν τῇ σκοτίᾳ φαίνει, καὶ ἡ σκοτία αὐτὸ οὐ κατέλαβεν…ἦν τὸ φῶς τὸ ἀληθινὸν ὃ φωτίζει πάντα ἄνθρωπον ἐρχόμενον εἰς τὸν κόσμον· ἐν τῷ κόσμῳ ἦν, καὶ ὁ κόσμος δι᾽ αὐτοῦ ἐγένετο, καὶ ὁ κόσμος αὐτὸν οὐκ ἔγνω.

A doctrine of progressive creations culminating in the present order is propounded in Beresh. Rabbah III., IX.: "And God saw all that He had made, and behold IT WAS VERY GOOD... R. Tanchuma said, The world was created in its season: the world was not fit to be created before that. Said R. Abuhu, This signifies that the Holy One, blessed is He, was creating worlds and destroying them, and creating worlds and destroying them, till he created these. He said, These are satisfactory to me; those are not satisfactory to me."

[37] Compare 1 Joh. iii. 1, 2: Ἴδετε ποταπὴν ἀγάπην δέδωκεν ἡμῖν ὁ πατήρ, ἵνα τέκνα Θεοῦ κληθῶμεν....ἀγαπητοί, νῦν τέκνα Θεοῦ ἐσμεν, καὶ οὔπω ἐφανερώθη τί ἐσόμεθα· οἴδαμεν δὲ ὅτι ἐὰν φανερωθῇ ὅμοιοι αὐτῷ ἐσόμεθα, ὅτι ὀψόμεθα αὐτὸν καθώς ἐστι. The sonship of Israel implies their possession of the Divine likeness in a higher degree

than Adam, or man in general. There is a progression from § 21 to § 23. The primal man, the embryo of the race, is created an adumbration of Elohim: Israel is singled out for the distinction of sonship to יהוה: and not only do they resemble the Creator passively, but their work is likened to His, for they have in their hands the creative instrument, the Thorah, by which the world was made, and by which the Divine image is perpetuated. R. ʻObadiah of Sforno dilates upon man's faculty of acquiring a perfection with which he was not specifically created. He remarks that the expression, "according to (as it were) our likeness" (Gen. i. 26) is approximative, and signifies, כמו דמותנו לא כדמותנו האמתי; and that "In imagine &c." implies the twofold possibility (1) of rising to perfection by means of wisdom through which the love and fear of God are acquired, and (2) of lapsing into chaos and perishing, according to the words of the Psalmist, אדם ביקר ולא יבין כו' (Ps. xlix. 21), if he will not understand, he will be like the beasts that perish; for if man had been wholly spiritual he might have been called actually Elohim, a word which is applied not only to God but to intellectual and incorporeal beings, as angels, and also to judges, in respect of the νοῦς, or חלק שכלי, which properly belongs to them; but since he is in part material he is described not as Elohim, but, in lower terms, as "in the image of Elohim." In favour of this view is Gen. iii. 5,

(was it that it) was made known to them that there was given to them the instrument with which the world was created, as it is said, For I give you good doctrine, forsake ye not MY LAW (Prov. iv. 2).

24.   Everything is foreseen[38]; and freewill is given.   And the world is judged by grace; and everything is according to work.

25.   He used to say, Everything is given on pledge ($\dot{\alpha}\rho\rho a\beta\dot{\omega}\nu$); and the net (Eccl. ix. 12) is cast over all the living.   The office is open; and the broker gives credit[39]; and the ledger

---

where, notwithstanding the original creation "*In imagine,*" temptation is presented in the form, "Ye shall be *as Elohim,* &c."

[38] This Mishnah touches upon two great controversies, and affirms that the opposites, PREDESTINATION and FREEWILL, MERCY and JUSTICE, are reconcileable. The word צפוי might indeed mean only that the affairs of the world are *known* to God, καὶ οὐκ ἔστι κτίσις ἀφανὴς ἐνώπιον αὐτοῦ (Heb. iv. 13), but it seems best to take it here as including *fore*knowledge, in accordance with the remarks of R. Jonah, who quotes Ps. cxxxix. 1, 2: "O Lord, thou hast searched me, and *known* me. Thou knowest my downsitting and mine uprising, thou understandest my thought *afar off.*" We have thus a sharply defined contrast between the foreknowledge of God, and the freedom of will which is nevertheless given to man. The reading of the text, which gives a parallel contrast between the χρηστότης of God (Rom. xi. 22) and His just judgment of men according to their works, is to be preferred to the negative reading: "*not* according to work." The insertion of רוב, which is strongly supported, gives the meaning, that everything is according to the *preponderance*

of work; that is to say, a man's good deeds are set off against his evil deeds, and he is condemned or acquitted according as the latter or the former are found to be the more weighty or numerous.

[39] The words חנוני and שולחני are found in Ma'aser Sheni iv. 2. The latter denotes a *numularius;* the former has the more general meaning *tabernarius,* and is also used for *numularius,* which perhaps best suits the reading of the text—but see note א. The world is likened to the office of a merchant, or of a money-broker: the *tabernarius,* or *numularius,* the Lord of the world, gives credit, but records the obligations incurred; in due time the collectors, who are daily going their rounds, exact payment from each debtor: in the case of a defaulter they have the arm of the law to rest upon, and its sentence will be according to truth.

On the meaning of מקיף see Levy's *Chaldäisches Wörterbuch,* s.r. נקף. The word is used in Qiddushin 40 a: "They *give no credit* in the case of profanation of the NAME"; they grant the offender no respite, but punish him at once. It is used also in the passage cited in note 35 from the Jerushalmi, in explanation of פרוש ניקפי (one of the seven kinds of Pharisees), who

($\pi\iota\nu\alpha\xi$) is open; and the hand writes; and whosoever will borrow comes and borrows; and the bailiffs go round continually every day, and exact from a man whether he wills or not; and they have whereon to lean; and the judgment is a judgment of truth.   And everything is prepared for the BANQUET[40].

26. R. La'zar ben 'Azariah[41] said, No Thorah, no culture;

says, אקיף לי ואנא עביד מצוה, "warte (eig. leihe mir Zeit), ich muss zuvor ein gottgefälliges Werk verrichten."

[40] The enjoyment of the world to come is figuratively spoken of in Rabbinic writings as THE BANQUET. In the New Testament compare: Μακάριοι οἱ εἰς τὸ δεῖπνον τοῦ γάμου τοῦ ἀρνίου κεκλημένοι (Rev. xix. 9). The Talmud cites Ex. xxiv. 11: "And upon the nobles of the children of Israel he laid not his hand: also they saw God, and did eat and drink"—in the sense that the vision of God, or of the Shekinah, was meat and drink to them: "It was a commonplace in the mouth of Rab, that in the world to come there is neither eating, nor drinking, nor procreation, nor barter, nor envy, nor hatred, nor strife; but the righteous sit with their crowns on their heads, and enjoy the splendour of the SHE-KINAH, for it is said, And they saw God, and did EAT and DRINK" (Berakoth 17 a). The word akal, to eat, is frequently used in a secondary sense, as in the saying of R. Hillel: "There is no Messiah for Israel, since they have already eaten him in the days of Hezekiah" (Sanhedrin 98 b, 99 a). The ministering angels, who are flaming fire, are fed on the splendour of the Shekinah, מזיו שכינה הם נזונין (Be-midbar Rabbah xxi.), for it is said (Prov. xvi. 15), "In the light of the king's countenance is life." Lower down in the same chapter the Holy One is represented as saying to Israel:

"In this world ye offer before me the shewbread and oblations. In the world to come I will spread for you a great table, and the nations of the world shall behold and be confounded, for it is said, Thou wilt prepare a table before me in the presence of mine enemies (Ps. xxiii. 5)...Behold, my servants shall eat, but ye shall be hungry: behold, my servants shall drink, but ye shall be thirsty" (Is. lxv. 13). The female Leviathan is preserved for the banquet of the righteous in the world to come (Baba Bathra 74 b). "At the fourth hour the Holy One, blessed is He, sits and plays with leviathan, for it is said (Ps. civ. 26), That leviathan whom thou hast made to play with him, לשחק בו" ('Abodah Zarah 3 b). Compare Targ. on Ps. civ. 26, where it is said to have been created, למנחך ביה לצדיקיא בסעורדת בית מדוריה. Cf. also, πεποιημένον ἐγκαταπαίζεσθαι ὑπὸ τῶν ἀγγέλων αὐτοῦ (Job xl. 14; xli. 24), in the LXX. description of behemoth. [Lagarde omits ביה.]

[41] The rich and influential Ele'azar, or (?) Eli'ezer, ben 'Azariah, was chosen, notwithstanding his youth, to succeed the second Gamaliel on his deposition from the presidency; whereupon R. 'Aqiba remarked: "It is not that he excels me as a son of Thorah, but as a son of great men" (T. J. Berakoth iv. 1). Ben 'Azariah, who is said to have been but 17 years of age, describes himself as prematurely aged: "Lo, I am as a son of 70 years, but am not a son of

no culture, no Thorah. No wisdom, no fear (of God); no fear (of God), no wisdom. No knowledge, no discernment[42]; no discernment, no knowledge. No meal, no Thorah; no Thorah, no meal[43].

27. He used to say, Whosoever wisdom is in excess of his works, to what is he like?[44] To a tree whose branches are abundant, and its roots scanty; and the wind comes, and uproots it, and overturns it. And whosoever works are in excess of his wisdom, to what is he like? To a tree whose branches are scanty, and its roots abundant; though all the winds come upon it, they stir it not from its place.

28. R. La'zar Chasmah said, "Qinnim" and "Pith_eché

---

70 years" (T. B. Berakoth 28 a). THAT DAY they removed the doorkeeper and gave free admission to all, whereas Gamaliel had excluded every disciple who was not the same inwardly as outwardly. It is added that when anything is recorded as having happened בו ביום, the occasion of ben 'Azariah's accession is referred to; and the day is described as one in which all the pending controversies were decided. It should rather be described as the day on which the *principle of decision* in accordance with the opinion of the majority (IV. 12), to which even Gamaliel gave in his adhesion, came at length to be distinctly recognised. On the restoration of Gamaliel they did not depose ben 'Azariah (T. J. *loc. cit.*) [Berak. 7 *d*], but made him *Ab beth din*. According to the Babli, three sabbaths (or weeks) in the month were assigned to Gamaliel as president, and the fourth to ben 'Azariah. Hence it is said: "Whose Sabbath is it? The Sabbath of R. El. ben 'Azariah."

[42] Prov. ix. 10: "The FEAR of the Lord is the beginning of WISDOM: and the KNOWLEDGE of the holy is UNDER-

STANDING." [The Torah itself teaches דרך ארץ (Joma 4 b).]

[43] The want of "corn," or, generally, of the means of sustenance, prevents a man from obtaining instruction, and studying Thorah. The converse, taken literally, would imply that Thorah fits a man for the discharge of secular duties, and brings worldly prosperity in its train: "Seek ye first the kingdom of God, and his righteousness; and all these things shall be added unto you" (Matt. vi. 33). But "Wisdom," which is sometimes identified with Thorah, provides sustenance also in a spiritual sense: "Come, eat of my bread, and drink of the wine which I have mingled...For by me thy days shall be multiplied, and the years of thy life shall be increased" (Prov. ix. 5, 11). [Ecclus. xv. 1—3 ἄρτον συνέσεως καὶ ὕδωρ σοφίας.]

[44] The Rabbinic parables, like those of the New Testament, are commonly introduced by some such formula as *Mashal* למה"ר, *to what is the matter like?* [Cant. Rab. i. 1 § 8 teaches that parables are wanted to draw out the sense of Torah.]

Niddah" are essentials of *Thorah*[45]; canons *of* astronomy and Gematria[46] are aftercourses of wisdom[47].

[45] The fifth Seder of the Mishnah contains a tract called קנים, or *nests;* and the sixth contains a tract called נדה. QINNIM relates to the young *birds* which men and women were required to offer in certain cases (Luke ii. 24; Shebi'ith VIII. 8). NIDDAH relates to the uncleannesses of women.

[46] גמטריא, a Hebraised form of γεω-μετρία, denotes an *arithmetical* method of exegesis, in which the numerical values of the Hebrew letters—which, like the Greek, are used to denote numbers—are taken into account. Thus one word may be substituted for another to which it is numerically equivalent, as in Bereshith Rabbah LXVIII., where Jacob's *ladder* is identified with mount *Sinai*, since סלם (60 + 30 + 40) is equal to סיני (60 + 10 + 50 + 10). For other examples of this species of gematria see Buxtorf's *Lex. Chald.* s.v. The Egyptian Bondage was to last 210 years, because it is said in Gen. xlii. 2: "*go down* thither," the letters of רדו, *go down*, amounting to 200 + 4 + 6. The first Temple was to stand 410 years, for it was said (Lev. xvi. 3): "*Thus* (בזאת) shall Aaron come into the holy place"; or, by gematria, "(2+7+1+400) years shall he come into it." This example and the preceding are quoted by the so-called Rashbam in illustration of the received interpretation of gematria. The antiquity of the method of GEMATRIA may be gathered from Rev. xiii. 17, 18. [Mr Burkitt (*Camb. Philolog. Soc.* March 5, 1896) suggests that Tyconius (fl. 380 A.D.) in his lost commentary on the Apocalypse had in mind the figure ⚡ as being the *mark*

and representing the *number* (*v. l.* 616) of the beast. It "is a combination of X' = 600, I' = 10, and ⌐ (the older form of the *Episemon* ϛ') = 6." It would suit Antichrist as being like the Monogram for ΧΡΙϹΤΟϹ reversed, "*anti* enim *contra* dicitur" (Beatus). This "may have been that explanation of 616 which S. Irenaeus (*Haer.* v 30) does not think fit to explain to his readers. In that case it would afford the earliest trace of the use of the Monogram as a symbol of Christ."]

[47] The things first mentioned are "corpora legis," essentials of Thorah, as opposed to the refinements of "Gematria," and astronomical calculations. On תקופה, *revolution, orbit*, see Levy's *Chald. Wörterbuch.* According to the usual interpretation, פרפראות denotes "Deliciæ, Cupediæ, Edulium vel obsonium ex rebus minutis et delicatis, quod vel ante cibum sumitur excitandi appetitus causa, vel post cibum, voluptatis causa"; and accordingly *Gematria* and the like are described either (1) as intellectual delicacies which stimulate the appetite for wisdom, or (2) with greater probability, as small and unimportant matters in comparison with the *pièces de résistance* mentioned above. According to another view (given in note ח), *Gematria* &c. belong merely to the outer circle of wisdom—they are the περιφέρεια, not the centre, of the Thorah. Or they are the *dress* or *adornment* (fr. πορφύρα) of wisdom, according to an improbable interpretation which "Rashbam" mentions with approval, referring to "Rab Nathan who compiled the 'Aruk."

CHAPTER IV.

1. Ben Zoma[1] said, Who is wise? He that learns from every man; for it is said, From[1] all my teachers I gat understanding (Ps. cxix. 99).

2. Who is mighty? He that subdues his nature[2]; for it

---

[1] Shime'on ben Zoma, a younger contemporary of 'Aqiba, belonged to the school of the mystics, and, from being profoundly versed in theosophic speculation, was said to have entered Paradise (Chagigah 14 b; Cant. Rab. i. 4). [Ezek. xxviii. 13.] Three others entered with him: 'Aqiba, ben 'Azai, and Elisha' ben Abuyah (III. 19; IV. 27). "Things which were not revealed to Moses were revealed to R. 'Aqiba and his companions" (Bemidbar Rabbah XIX.). Ben Zoma, according to Chagigah, "looked, and became demented," from indulging too freely in the "honey" (Prov. xxv. 16) of metaphysics. "He who sees ben Zoma in a dream may expect wisdom" (Berakoth 57 b). With him the *darshanim* ceased, according to Sotah 49 b.

The verse cited in proof of ben Zoma's first saying is rendered in its original context: "I have MORE understanding THAN all my teachers." R. Israel has some remarks on the love of wisdom for its own sake. It is written, "If thou seekest her as silver, and searchest for her as for hid treasures; Then shalt thou understand the fear of the Lord, and find the knowledge of God" (Prov. ii. 4, 5). As a man seeks silver wherever it is to be found, and values it all the same whether he obtains it by the help of high, low, rich, or poor, so let him seek wisdom for its own sake, and from any teacher who is able to teach him.

Why is Thorah like water? because as a great man is not ashamed to say to an inferior, Give me a drink of water, so a great man is not ashamed to say to an inferior, Teach me one pericope, one word, one verse, or even one letter (Chazitha, on Cant. i. 2). And why is it like ξύλον (Prov. iii. 18)? because, as small wood kindles the great, so little scholars sharpen great ones (Tha'anith 7 a). Then follows the oft quoted saying (cf. Makkoth 10 a): *I have learned much from my masters; and from my associates more than from my masters; and from my disciples more than from them all.* Bar S. observes, that the man who struggles against the evil nature within him has a harder warfare than he who fights against an external foe, since his enemy never leaves him.

[2] "The wicked watcheth the righteous, and seeketh to slay him" (Ps. xxxvii.

is said, He that is slow to anger is better than the mighty; and he that ruleth his spirit than he that taketh a city (Prov. xvi. 32).

3. Who is rich? He that is contented with his lot; for it is said, When thou eatest the labour of thy hands, happy art thou, and it shall be well with thee (Ps. cxxviii. 2). "Happy art thou" in this world; "and it shall be well with thee" in the world to come[3].

32). The "wicked" is man's evil nature (Sukkah 52 b), which he must subdue, yet not wholly destroy and eradicate, for this would be to ruin the body by the destruction of the psychic force. The evil yeçer rules over the animal soul, which a man is commanded to preserve: "Take heed to thyself, and keep thy *soul* diligently" (Deut. iv. 9); and in order to do this, he must to a certain extent follow the promptings of the yeçer. Even the evil yeçer is good, for it is said: "And God saw everything that he had made, *and*, behold, it was very good" (Gen. i. 31). The good יצר was VERY GOOD, *and* so was the evil יצר, but for which a man would never build a house, nor marry, nor beget, nor trade (Bereshith Rabbah ix.). The evil nature, and a child, and a woman are things which the left hand should repel, and the right bring near. [Sanhedrin 107 b.]

The evil nature is called "yeçer" absolutely from its existing originally, and for a long time alone, for "the *imagination* of man's heart is *evil* from his youth" (Gen. viii. 21), whereas yeçer ha-tob, which is presided over by νοῦς, is added later, and then only coexists with the evil, which is thirteen years older (Midrash Qoheleth ix. 14; Aboth, *Addenda*). The strong and great man is he in whom the evil nature is strong; "and therefore our wise men, of blessed memory, have said, In the place, where penitents stand, the faultlessly righteous stand not," for it is said (Is. lvii. 19), Peace, peace to him that is far off, and to him that is near: to the far off first, and afterwards to the near (Berakoth 34 b).

[3] It is a characteristic of Talmudic exegesis, that, as far as possible, every expression of Holy Scripture is regarded as having a separate significance. In such texts as the above the *darshan* allows no mere cumulation of phrases for the sake of symmetry or emphasis, but he sees distinct allusions in אשריך and טוב לך to the present and future worlds. Such twofold allusions are continually being pointed out in the Talmud and Midrash. In the text we may perhaps suppose a play upon the words, *ashreka*, thy happiness, and '*oshreka*, thy wealth. With this saying compare 1 Tim. vi. 6: ἔστι δὲ πορισμὸς μέγας ἡ εὐσέβεια μετὰ αὐταρκείας. The three sayings may be taken as a commentary on Jer. ix. 23: "Let not the WISE man glory in his wisdom, neither let the MIGHTY man glory in his might, let not the RICH man glory in his riches."

It is said in Berakoth ix. 5, that all the benedictions in the Temple used to end simply with A SECULO; but from the time when the Epicureans (א reads *ha-minim*) cavilled and said, There is but one world, it was ordered to conclude with A SECULO IN SECULUM.

4. Who is honoured? He that honours mankind; for it is said, For them that honour me[4] I will honour, and they that despise me shall be lightly esteemed (1 Sam. ii. 30).

5. Ben 'Azzai[5] said, Hasten to a slight precept, and flee from transgression; for precept induces precept, and trans-

[4] In the original context the speaker is God; but the verse is here applied to establish the principle of reciprocity more generally. One interpretation is, that he who honours men is reckoned as honouring God himself, in whose image they were created (III. 21), in accordance with a well-known Rabbinic principle, which may also be illustrated from the New Testament. Observe that the evil is not attributed to God: it is not said, "I will despise them," but, *they shall be despised.* "If one comes for defilement, they suffer him; if he comes for purification, they help him" (Joma 38 b): the naphtha seller lets his customer measure for himself: the perfumer says, Let me help you with the balsam, that we may both enjoy its fragrance. "The memory of the just is blessed" (Prov. x. 7) by his neighbour: "but the name of the wicked shall rot" of itself.

"Great is כבוד הבריות, which supersedes a negative precept of the Thorah" (Berakoth 19 b).

[5] Shime'on ben 'Az(z)ai, prospective son-in-law of R. 'Aqiba, appears to have separated from his wife for more complete devotion to study, although recognising the religious duty, as the Jews regard it, of marriage and פריה ורביה, in accordance with the command, "Be fruitful and multiply," to abstain from which is as murder: "Whosoever (says ben 'Azai, in Bereshith Rabbah xxxiv.) abstains from procreation, the Scripture reckons it unto him as if he shed blood, and

diminished the likeness," for it is forbidden to shed the blood of a man *because* he was created in the image of God (Gen. ix. 6), and in the very next verse it is said, And you, be ye fruitful, and multiply.

Ben 'Azai was one of the four who entered Paradise (note 1). "He looked, and perished": i.e. he died prematurely, worn out by his preternatural activity. With him the *shaqdanim* came to an end (Sotah 49 b). "He who saw ben 'Azai in a dream might hope for *chasiduth*" (Berakoth 57 b).

"Ben 'Azai was sitting and commenting, and the fire was flaming about him. They went and said to R. 'Aqiba, Rabbi, ben 'Azai sits and comments, and the fire flames about him. He went to him, and said to him, I have heard that thou wast commenting, and the fire was flaming about thee. He said to him, Yea, yea! He said to him, Perchance in the recesses of the CHARIOT thou wast employed. He said to him, Nay, I was but sitting and concatenating in Thorah, and from Thorah onward to the Prophets, and from the Prophets to the Scriptures; and the words were as pleasing as at their proclamation from Sinai, and sweet as when they were originally given" (Chazitha, on Cant. i. 10) out of the midst of the fire.

[6] Habits are formed by the repetition of single acts. When a man discharges or disregards a duty he thereby predisposes himself for a like course of action on a future occasion.

9

gression induces transgression[6]; for the reward of precept is precept, and the reward of transgression is transgression[7].

6. He used to say, Despise not any man, and carp not at any thing; for thou wilt find that there is not a man that has not his hour, and not a thing that has not its place.

7. R. Levitas of Jabneh said, Be exceeding lowly of spirit, for the hope of man is the worm. R. Jochanan ben Baroqah said, Whoso profanes the name of Heaven in secret, they punish him openly. The erring is as the presumptuous, in profanation of the NAME[8].

The passing act of transgression leads up to a settled course of evil. He who first "WALKS in the counsel of the ungodly" (Ps. i. 1), next "STANDS in the way of sinners," and at length "SITS in the seat of the scornful." The passage cited from Sifre in Excursus I. 2 (ix.), cf. Sukkah 52 a, and Sanhedrin 99 b— interprets Is. v. 18: "Woe unto them that draw iniquity with CORDS OF VANITY, and sin as it were with a cartrope," as meaning that the band of sin is at first slender, like a spider's thread, but afterwards becomes thick and strong as a cartrope. It is added: R. said, He who performs one precept for its own sake, let him not rejoice over that precept (alone), for in due course it will draw after it many others; and he who commits one transgression, let him not deplore that (only), for it will be the cause of many others, For "precept leads on to precept, and transgression to transgression."

[7] Welldoing is the fruit of welldoing, and evildoing the fruit of evildoing. This is interpreted by R. Jonah as meaning, not that "virtue is its own reward," and the consciousness of wickedness its sole punishment, but that a man is responsible for his actions, inasmuch as one action is consequent upon another, and he has thus

the power of educating and predisposing himself for good or evil. The performance of duty is rewarded by an increased facility of subsequent performance.

[8] In the case of profanation of the Name of God, no allowance is made for inadvertence, but the man is punished forthwith. Sins of ignorance and those committed deliberately are reckoned as one and the same. "On account of what was Gechazi punished? Because he called his master by his name, for it is said, And Gechazi said, My lord, O king, this is the woman, and this is her son, whom Elisha restored to life" (2 Kings viii. 5; Sanhedrin 100 a). A feeling of reverence leads the Jews to avoid, as far as possible, all mention of the Names of God. This feeling is manifested, not only in the case of שם המפורש (p. 56), for which *Adonai* or *Elohim* is substituted in the reading of Scripture, but, in their post-canonical literature, even with regard to less sacred, and not incommunicable Divine names. In the Talmud and Midrash, and (with the exception of Prayer Books) in the Rabbinic writings generally, it is the custom to abstain from using the Biblical names of God, *except in citations from the Bible;* and even when *Elohim* is necessarily brought in, it is often

8. R. Ishma'el his son said, He that learns in order to

intentionally misspelt, *Elodim*, or *Elo-qim*. For יהוה again, especially in Qabbalistic works, we find the spellings, יהוד and ירוד. In the treatise Pirqe Aboth, as the reader may easily verify for himself, all direct mention of "God" is avoided, except in Biblical quotations, and in an interpolated liturgical formula (v. 31).

שמים] HEAVEN is one of the usual substitutes for the Name of God. Cf. I. 3, 12; II. 2, 16; IV. 7, 16 (note), 17; v. 24, 25. It is a well-known characteristic of St Matthew's Gospel that, amongst other Hebraisms, it makes frequent use of the phrase ἡ βασιλεία τῶν οὐρανῶν, instead of ἡ βασιλεία τοῦ Θεοῦ. Compare also Matt. xxiii. 22: καὶ ὁ ὀμόσας ἐν τῷ οὐρανῷ ὀμνύει ἐν τῷ θρόνῳ τοῦ Θεοῦ, καὶ ἐν τῷ καθημένῳ ἐπάνω αὐτοῦ. St Paul again writes, πάντα εἰς δόξαν Θεοῦ ποιεῖτε (1 Cor. x. 31), the equivalent of which in the Mishnah language is, "Let all thy deeds be to the name of Heaven" (Aboth II. 16).

המקום] PLACE, or Space, is another Name of God which was in common use. Cf. II. 13, 17; III. 5, 6, 15, 22; v. 7. There is external evidence for its antiquity in Philo's use of ὁ τόπος, on which see note 42, p. 39. This use of ὁ τόπος throws light upon the periphrasis of the LXX. in Ex. xxiv. 10: καὶ εἶδον τὸν τόπον οὗ εἰστήκει ὁ Θεός.

השם] THE NAME (IV. 7; v. 14) was used as a substitute for יהוה, or "God." Traces of this usage are found in ὑπὲρ τοῦ ὀνόματος ἀτιμασθῆναι (Acts v. 41), and ὑπὲρ γὰρ τοῦ ὀνόματος ἐξῆλθον, μηδὲν λαμβάνοντες ἀπὸ τῶν ἐθνικῶν (3 John 7). Since τὸ ὄνομα was used as a synonym for "God," the actions of God himself appeared to be attributed to the Name of God. Hence the Qabbalistic mode of expres-

sion, according to which a power and efficacy was attributed to the most holy NAME, which was regarded as an instrument in the hand of the initiated.

הקב"ה] THE HOLY ONE, *blessed is He*, is used as a Name of God, either as a supplement to other expressions (III. 1; IV. 32), or alone (v. 6). The use of a benediction, as ברוך הוא, or יתברך, at the mention of God is thought to be required by Prov. x. 7: "The memory of the just is blessed," the mention of the Holy One should be accompanied with benediction. (The hemistich is also quoted by its initials when reference is made to a "just" man who is no longer living. The use of these initials, ז"צל—or briefly ז"ל, *beata memoria ejus*—indicates that the person whose name they follow is dead.) But הק' is found alone, without ב"ה, in the Machazor Vitry. Compare Job vi. 10: "for I have not concealed קדוש, the words of the Holy One." In like manner ὁ ἅγιος is used in the book of Ecclesiasticus, καὶ ὀνομασίᾳ τοῦ ἁγίου μὴ συνεθισθῇς (xxiii. 9). On the other hand, ὁ εὐλογητός stands alone as a Name of God in Mark xiv. 61.

The pronunciation of יהוה was thought to be prohibited by Lev. xxiv. 16: "And he that *blasphemeth* the name of the Lord, he shall surely be put to death, and all the congregation shall certainly stone him: as well the stranger, as he that is born in the land, when he *blasphemeth* THE NAME, shall be put to death." The Jews here render נקב not *blaspheme*, but *pronounce distinctly*. So the LXX., Ὀνομάζων δὲ τὸ ὄνομα Κυρίου θανάτῳ θανατούσθω. The non-pronunciation of יהוה, which was already an established practice when the LXX. version was

teach[9], they grant him the faculty to learn and to teach: he that learns in order to practise, they grant him the faculty to learn, and to teach, and to practise.

9. R. Çadoq said, Make them[10] not a crown, to glory in them; nor an ax, to live by them. And thus was Hillel wont to say, And he who serves himself with the tiara perishes (I. 14). Lo, whosoever makes profit from words of Thorah removes his life from the world.

10. R. Jose said, Whosoever honours the Thorah[11] is himself held in honour with men; and whosoever dishonours the Thorah is himself dishonoured with men.

11. R. Ishma‘el said, He that refrains himself from judgment, frees himself from enmity, and rapine, and false swearing[12]; and he that is arrogant in decision[13] is foolish, wicked, and puffed up in spirit.

---

made, may be regarded as the germ of the Qabbalistic theosophy, in which God was removed to an infinite distance from the material world, and the interval was populated with a succession of intermediate creations, or emanations from the Deity.

[9] It is said in Sanhedrin 99 a, that he who learns Thorah and does not teach it, he it is that "hath despised the word of the Lord" (Numb. xv. 31).

The initial letters of the words על מנת ללמד form the word עמל. Conversely, by one of the Rabbinic artifices of exegesis, Job v. 7 (as noticed by P. Ewald) is made to mean, not that "man is born to trouble," but that he is born to learn in order to teach. Another example of the method of ראשי תבות or initials, is afforded by the word אמן, Amen, which is Qabbalistically explained as an abbreviation of אל מלך נאמן, God is a Faithful King.

[10] Another reading is: "Make IT (the Thorah) not a crown, &c." The reading of the text is explained in two ways, either (1) make not words of Thorah a crown, or (2) make not thy disciples a crown, &c. The latter explanation may be supported by St Paul's use of στέφανος in Phil. iv. 1, and 1 Thess. ii. 19. "On account of what was Abraham our father punished, and his sons subjugated to Egypt for 210 years? Because he impressed scholars into his service" (Gen. xiv. 14; Nedarim 32 a) in his expedition for the rescue of Lot.

[11] Pseudo-Rashi gives the following explanations of, Whosoever honours the Thorah; "He who does not leave the book of the Thorah on the floor, or on a bench; and some say, He who inclines his ear to the book of the Thorah, and does not talk while the Chazan is reading it; and some say, He who does not leave it open, and go out."

[12] He who arbitrates between contending parties incurs the enmity of those who are disappointed by his decisions. He also runs the risk of

12. He used to say, Judge not alone, for none may judge alone save One; and say not, Accept ye my opinion, for they are free-to-choose[14], and not thou.

13. R. Jochanan said, Whosoever fulfils the Thorah in poverty[15], will at length fulfil it in wealth; and whosoever neglects the Thorah in wealth, will at length neglect it in poverty (Luke vi. 21, 25).

14. R. Meir said, Have little business, and be busied in Thorah; and be lowly in spirit unto every man; and if thou idlest from the Thorah, thou wilt have idlers many against thee[16]; and if thou labourest in the Thorah, He[17] hath much reward to give unto thee.

15. R. Li'ezer ben Jacob said, He who performs one precept has gotten to himself one advocate[18]; and he who

doing injustice by erroneous judgments, and of giving occasion to falsehood and perjury on the part of the litigants. Compare i. 10, where the judge is admonished to be on his guard whilst examining the witnesses in a suit: "be guarded in thy words, perchance from them they may learn to lie."

[13] "He who puffs up his heart, thinking within himself that he knows how to decide in a cause without fail, behold, he is foolish. He is called foolish because he is wise in his own eyes, than which there is no greater folly, for (Prov. xxvi. 12; xxix. 20) there is more hope of a fool than of him" (R. Jonah). To exemplify the use of the word הוראה, cf. Horaioth 3 b: "Whatsoever *decision* has gone forth publicly in the congregation, an individual who practises it is released, because *decision* was only given to distinguish between the erring and the presumptuous."

[14] It rests with thy colleagues to choose whether they will adopt thy opinion: it is not for thee to force it upon them.

[15] "Whosoever 'blackens his visage' for the sake of words of Thorah in this world, the Holy One, blessed is He, will make his splendour to shine in the world to come, for it is said (Cant. v. 15), His countenance is as Lebanon, excellent as the cedars...... Whosoever starves himself for the sake of words of Thorah in this world, the Holy One, blessed is He, will satiate him in the world to come, for it is said (Ps. xxxvi. 8), They shall be abundantly satisfied with the fatness of thy house; and thou shalt make them drink of the river of thy pleasures" (Sanhedrin 100 a).

[16] He who is watchful [Jer. i. 12] in the study of Thorah has given to him שקדנין כנגדו, and he who idly desists from Thorah study has given to him בטלנין כנגדו—as lions, bears, thieves, and robbers. See Aboth R. N. xxix. [p. 87].

[17] Here again the good only, and not the evil, is attributed directly to God. See note 4.

[18] We have here in a Hebrew form the word παράκλητος, or ADVOCATE (1 Joh. ii. 1), one who is called to a

commits one transgression has gotten to himself one accuser. Repentance and good works[19] are as a shield against punishment.

person's aid, which is rendered, perhaps wrongly, COMFORTER in Joh. xiv. 16, 26; xv. 26; xvi. 7. With this Mishnah compare Shemoth Rabbah XXXII.: "If a man performs one precept, the Holy One, blessed is He, gives him one angel to guard him, for it is said (Ps. xxxiv. 7): The angel of the Lord encampeth round about them that fear Him. If he performs two precepts He gives him two angels to guard him, for it is said (Ps. xci. 11): For He shall give His angels charge over thee, to keep thee in all thy ways. If he performs many precepts He gives him the half of His host, for it is said (Ps. xci. 7): A thousand shall alight at thy side, and ten thousand at thy right hand: that is the half of his host, for it is said (Ps. lxviii. 17): The chariots of God are twenty thousand, even thousands of angels."

[19] "It was a commonplace in the mouth of Raba that, The perfection of wisdom is repentance" (Berakoth 17a). "When a man has been wholly wicked all his days, and has repented at last, the Holy One, blessed is He, receives him." This follows from Ezek. xxxiii. 19: But if the wicked turn from his wickedness, and do that which is lawful and right, he shall live thereby. Said R. Jochanan, Nay, more. All the transgressions which he has committed are imputed to him as merits, as is proved by Ps. xlv. 9: Myrrh and aloes and cassia are all thy בגידות: all the *transgressions* which thou hast committed against me are as myrrh and aloes and cassia (T. J. Peah I. 1). A similar play on בגדיו, in Gen. xxvii. 27, which may be pointed so as to mean *transgressions* or *transgressors*,

is implied in Bereshith Rabbah LXV. Penitents are set above "just persons which need no repentance" in a saying quoted in note 2.

Repentance was created before the world (Nedarim 39 b. Cf. p. 12): without it the world could not stand: the repentance of one man brings forgiveness to the whole world. On the efficacy of repentance, and of sacrificial Atonement, see the end of Mishnah Joma, and the Gemara upon it. For certain sins, repentance gives a respite, and the day of atonement atones; but he who sins against his neighbour must first be reconciled to him. The unpardonable sin, in the case of which repentance gives not respite, nor does the day of atonement atone, nor have sufferings a purgatorial efficacy, but these together only give respite, till DEATH purges (Is. xxii. 14), is PROFANATION OF THE NAME (Joma 86 a).

The wise man, יצר טוב, delivers the citadel of the body from יצה"ר by means of repentance and good works (Nedarim 32 b). Said R. Ele'azar b. R. Jose, All the righteousness and piety that Israel perform in this world make great peace and great PARACLETES between Israel and their Father which is in Heaven...Great is righteousness, which brings the redemption nigh... Ten hard things were created in the world. *Rock* is hard, but *iron* cuts it: *fire* fuses iron: *water* quenches fire: *clouds* bear water: *wind* scatters clouds: the *body* bears the wind: *fear* shatters the body: *sleep* dissipates wine; and death is harder than all of them, but RIGHTEOUSNESS delivers from death (Prov. x. 2; Baba Bathra 10 a).

16.   R. Jochanan Sandalarius said, Whatsoever assemblage is in the name of duty[20] will in the end be established; and that which is not in the name of duty will not in the end be established.

17.   R. La'zar said, Let the honour of thy disciple be dear unto thee as the honour of thine associate[21]; and the honour of

[20] Or "of Heaven," according to the usual reading. Aboth R. N. xl. reads מצוה, and illustrates the saying from the Great *Synagogue*, on the one hand, and the Generation of the *Dispersion* (Gen. xi. 8) on the other.

[21] The climax is broken by the reading: "Dear unto thee *as thine own*," which may have arisen from assimilation to other passages, as ii. 17.

R. Jonah remarks that a man is not enjoined to honour his disciple precisely as he honours his associate, but rather to be equally scrupulous in according to each the honour due to him, "each one according to his honour." Fear includes honour, but honour does not include fear. The two words are brought together in Mal. i. 6: "A son honoureth his father, and a servant his master: if then I be a father, where is mine HONOUR? and if I be a master, where is my FEAR?" With the concluding words of this Mishnah compare St Paul's τῷ Κυρίῳ (Eph. vi. 7).

The claims of a man's Father and his Teacher to precedence in certain cases are laid down in Baba Meçi'a ii. 11: "Si res sua perdita sit et patris sui, tum sua præcedit; si sua et magistri ipsius res perdita sit, tum sua præcedit. Si patris et magistri ipsius …res magistri præcedit, nam pater eum quidem produxit in hunc mundum, sed magister ejus, qui ipsum sapientiam docuit, traduxit ipsum in mundum futurum. Sin autem pater ipsius fuerit sapiens, res patris præcedit. Si pater et magister ipsius ferant onus, onus magistri prius deponet, et deinde onus patris. Si pater et magister fuerint in captivitate (et non habuerit quo utrumque redimat) prius redimet magistrum ipsius, et deinde patrem. Si pater ipsius fuerit sapiens, redimet prius patrem, et deinde magistrum suum." "A scholar must not rise up before his master except twice in the day, morning and evening, in order that the honour of his master may not exceed that of Heaven" (Qiddushin 33 b), where allusion is made to the practice of saying the *Shema'* morning and evening. [See כסף משנה on Maim. *Hilkoth Talmud Torah* vi. 8.]

The scholar who controverts his Rab is as if he controverted the Shekinah (Sanhedrin 110 a): he who engages in strife with his Rab is as if he engaged in strife with the Shekinah: he who speaks, or thinks, evil against his Rab is as if he did it against the Shekinah.

God himself is the great Chief Rabbi, and diligently studies and teaches Thorah. "Then began the Synagogue of Israel to utter praise to the Lord of the world, and thus she spake, That God it is my delight to serve, who is clad by day in a robe white as snow, the Divine glory of whose face flames like fire from greatness of wisdom and thought, who originates new lessons every day, and will announce them to his people in the great day" (Targ. Cant. v. 10). "Said Moses the pro-

thine associate as the fear of thy master; and the fear of thy master as the fear of Heaven.

18.   R. Jehudah said, Be careful in Thalmud, for error in Thalmud amounts to sin[22].

19.   R. Shime'on said, There are three crowns: the crown of Thorah, and the crown of Priesthood, and the crown of Royalty (Ex. xxv. 10, 11 ; xxx. 1, 3 ; xxv. 23, 24); but the crown of a good name[23] *mounts* above them (Eccl. vii. 1).

20.   R. Nehorai said, Betake thyself to a place of Thorah, and say not that it shall come after thee; for[24] thine associates

phet, When I went up to the height, I saw there the Lord of all the worlds, יהוה, quartering the day into four parts.   Three hours He was employed in Thorah: three in judgment: three in provisioning the world: and three in uniting man and wife (Targ. Jerus. Deut. xxxii.).   The fourfold division is given, with a variation, in 'Abodah Zarah 3 b : during the fourth quarter of the day, according to one statement, " He sits and teaches school children [Rashi שמתו] Thorah" (Is. xxviii. 9; Jalqut 302), a work which is of such importance that it must not be stopped even for the building of the sanctuary (Shabbath 119 b).

[22] Forgetfulness, or mistake in study, is here said to be equivalent to a deliberate sin, in order to impress upon the student the duty of constant repetition with a view to ensure accuracy.   Compare the expression used above in § 7, where it is said that no distinction is made between unintentional and deliberate profanation of THE NAME.   So in Chagigah 5 a, it is said, with reference to the last verse of Ecclesiastes, "He weighs out to him errors as deliberate sins."   He who forgets his Thalmud commits a deadly sin (III. 12).   "Action depends on Thalmud, and not Thalmud on action" (Sifre, עקב).

[23] A "good name" in general is here called a crown.   In like manner the Name of God is compared to a crown, as in Pirqe R. Eli'ezer XLVII., where it is said that at the giving of the Law six hundred thousand angels descended, and crowned each one of the sons of Israel with the crown of *Shem ha-mephorash*.   As long as they wore these crowns they were holier than the angels of God, and the angel of death had no power over them.   It is said [ib. IV.] that the Holy One sits in heaven with the crown of the ineffable Name upon His head.   [Cf. Shab. 88 a, Targ. Jon. Ex. xxxii. 25.]

[24] A man should frequent a place where there are facilities for instruction, and should not trust to himself for the acquisition of the knowledge of Thorah.   He must go to the Thorah, and not expect the Thorah to come to him.   If he associates himself with scholars he will be well grounded in it by their aid, for the knowledge of it is acquired by association.   See pp. 16, 33.

According to another view of the latter part of this Mishnah, a man must *not* trust to his companions for instruction: "Say not that thine associates will establish it in thine hands: depend not upon thine associates, who have themselves gone to learn, to

will confirm it unto thee; and lean not unto thine own understanding (Prov. iii. 5).

21. R. Jannai said, Neither the security of the wicked, nor the afflictions of the righteous, are in our hand[25].

22. R. Matthiah ben Charash said, Be beforehand in saluting[26] every man; and be a tail to lions, and not a head to foxes[27].

23. R. Jacob said, This world is like a vestibule[28] before

come and teach thee; for thou thyself must go with them and pursue after Thorah, if thou wouldest know it. But lean not unto thine own understanding: although thou learnest, and betakest thyself to a place of Thorah, and growest wise, lean not unto thine own understanding. Depend not upon thine opinion, but do all that thou doest by the advice of the wise." So R. Jonah, agreeing with A†.

[25] We are unable to answer the questions: Why do the wicked flourish? Why do the righteous suffer?

[26] Literally, Anticipate the Peace of every man; "Peace" being the usual form of greeting. "Whosoever knows that his friend is accustomed to salute him, let him anticipate his salutation, for it is said, Seek peace, and pursue it (Ps. xxxiv. 15). And if he salutes him, and he does not return it, he is called a spoiler, for it is said (Is. iii. 14), For ye have eaten up the vineyard; the spoil of the poor is in your houses" (Berakoth 6 b). "They said of R. Jochanan ben Zakkai that no man ever anticipated him in salutation, not even a Gentile in the street" (Berakoth 17 a).

[27] "Be a tail to lions, and not a head to foxes." "Thy glory is to make thyself a tail, and to abase thyself, and follow after a scholar of the wise, rather than to be a head unto foxes, to worthless men, who are accounted only as foxes. And I have found a Scripture

proof for it, for it is said (Prov. xiii. 20), He that walketh with wise men shall be wise" (A†). Compare Eccl. vii. 5: "It is better to hear the rebuke of the wise, than for a man to hear the song of fools."

[28] The word rendered vestibule is generally identified with πρόθυρον, which however it does not resemble quite so closely as might have been expected. Bar S. (see *Crit. Note*) adopts the view that it should be written with final *Daleth*, for *Resh*. [This reading is to be preferred.]

Sinners who have been companions in this world will be separated in the world to come; he who repents before death will be numbered with the righteous, and he who does not repent, with the wicked. The latter will say, Were we not together in the world? did we not steal and do all manner of evil works together? why then are we separated? is there then respect of persons with God? They will answer, that it is repentance which has made the separation between him and his companion. "Suffer me then," he will say, "to go and repent"; but it will be answered that the time for repentance has gone by, for "this world is like a sabbath, and the world from which thou camest is like the sabbath eve: if a man provides not on the sabbath eve, what shall he eat on the sabbath? The world from which thou camest is like

the world to come; prepare thyself at the vestibule, that thou mayest be admitted into the hall[29].

24. He used to say, Better is one hour of repentance and good works in this world than all the life of the world to come[30]; better is one hour of refreshment of spirit in the world to come than all the life of this world.

25. R. Shime'on ben Ele'azar said, Conciliate not thy friend in the hour of his passion; and console him not in the hour when his dead is laid out before him; and "interrogate" him not in the hour of his vow; and strive not to see him in the hour of his disgrace.

26. Shemuel ha-Qatan said[31], Rejoice not when thine

dry land, and this world like sea: if a man provides not for himself on the land, what shall he eat on the sea? This world is like a wilderness, and the world from which thou camest is like inhabited land: if a man provides not for himself from the inhabited land, what shall he eat in the wilderness?" See Midrash Qoheleth, i. 15; Midrash Ruth, cap. III.

[29] This word is sometimes rendered "palace"; but it is really a transliteration of τρικλίνιον.

[30] Repentance and amendment in this life are accounted an equivalent for the life to come; they are the price paid for it, and a means by which it is secured to a man. On the other hand the joys of the world to come are such that "one hour" of them outweighs all the enjoyment of the present world, in the same way that, as the Psalmist says of the sanctuary: "A day in thy courts is better than a thousand."

[31] The saying ascribed to Shemuel consists, according to the best-attested reading, of an extract from the book of Proverbs, without note or comment, which "he was accustomed to repeat." It is found also at the end of Pereq v. in some copies.

SHEMUEL is placed in the same category with Hillel in T. J. Sotah IX. 13: "The elders entered into Beth Gadia in Jericho, and Bath Qol went forth and said to them, There is among you a man worthy of the Holy Spirit, only that the generation is unfit; and they cast their eyes upon Hillel ha-Zaqen. And when he died they used to say of him, Alas! meek pious one, disciple of 'Ezra! And again, the elders entered into an upper chamber in Jabneh, and Bath Qol went forth and said to them, There is among you one worthy of the Holy Spirit, only that the generation is unfit; and they cast their eyes on Shemuel ha-Qatan. And why was his name called Qatan? Because he made himself little. But some say, because he was scarcely less than Shemuel ha-Ramathi. And when he died, they used to say of him, Alas, meek pious one, disciple of Hillel ha-Zaqen!" He is said to have drawn up the "Heretic Benediction" (Berakoth 28 b) still found in the Jewish ritual. Gamaliel ha-Zaqen himself is sometimes alluded to as perhaps the author of the "Benediction"; but what appears from the passage of Berakoth above alluded to is that Gamaliel II., desiring to have a *birkath*

enemy falleth, and let not thine heart be glad when he stumbleth (Prov. xxiv. 17).

27. Elisha' ben Abiyyah[32] said, He who learns as a lad, to what is he like? to ink written on fresh paper; and he who learns when old, to what is he like? to ink written on used paper[33].

28. R. Jose ben Jehudah of Kaphar ha-Babli said, He who learns from the young, to what is he like? to one that eats unripe grapes, and drinks wine from his vat; and he who learns from the old, to what is he like? to one that eats ripened grapes, and drinks old wine.

29. R. said, Regard not the flask, but what is therein; there is a new flask that is full of old (wine), and an old one in which there is not even new[34].

ha-minim added to the Eighteen Benedictions, asked if there was anyone able to draw up such a formula; and, in answer to his appeal, Shemuel supplied the required form of words, as a modification (it is thought) of an older "Sadducee-Benediction," to the satisfaction of Gamaliel.

[32] The usual form is Elisha' ben Abuyah, but Abiyyah is a Biblical name. [1 Kings xiv. 1 Abijah.]

The tendency of this Elisha's speculations was destructive: when he entered Paradise (note 1), he began to "destroy the plants therein." He ultimately apostatised, and became a derider of Judaism; and accordingly, in the Talmudic account of the entry of the four into Paradise, his name is suppressed, and he is only indirectly alluded to as אחר, a certain "other."

Dr Ad. Neubauer, in a report on "Talmudical and Rabbinical Literature" (Philological Society, 1876), notices a Hebrew rendering of Goethe's Faust, in which "The dramatis personæ are taken from Jewish history; for instance, the learned and dissatis-

fied Faust is represented by the Talmudical Elishah, son of Abuyah, who, searching too deeply for the solution of theosophical problems, was finally driven to apostasy...The translator, the late Dr Letteris, has in our judgment in many respects surpassed the original." The title of the rendering, which was published in Vienna in the year 1865, is Ben Abuyah, Goethe's Faust, eine Tragoedie in einer hebräischen Umdichtung.

[33] R. Sh. ben Gamliel further compares one who learns Thorah in his youth to a young man who marries a maiden well suited to him (Aboth R. N. xxiii.). Learning in youth is also likened to graving upon stone; and learning in old age, to tracing characters upon the sand.

[34] The saying of Rabbi is a corrective of that of Jose ben Jehudah, which immediately precedes. R. Jose describes the learning of the young as crude and immature, like new wine: Rabbi shews by another comparison that this is not always the case. On the contrary, as a new flask may contain old wine, so the mind of the

30. R. Li'ezer ha-Qappar said, Jealousy, and lust, and ambition, put a man out of the world[35].

31. He used to say, The born are to die; and the dead to revive; and the living to be judged; for to know, and to notify, and that it may be known[36], that He is the framer, and He the

young may even be more mature than that of his elders; the mind of the aged is not necessarily stored with reflection, but may be like an empty vessel. R. Jonah connects the two Mishnioth in question by means of Job xxxii. 6—9: "And Elihu the son of Barachel the Buzite answered and said, I am young, and ye are very old; wherefore I was afraid, and durst not shew you mine opinion. I said, Days should speak, and multitude of years should teach wisdom. But there is a spirit in man: and the inspiration of the Almighty giveth them understanding. Great men are not always wise: neither do the aged understand judgment." With Rabbi's parable of the קנקן [Othello II. 3 canakin] compare Matt. ix. 17: οὐδὲ βάλλουσιν οἶνον νέον εἰς ἀσκοὺς παλαιούς, κ.τ.λ. [A.V. bottles, R.V. wine-skins. Read once leather bottles, comparing Hen. VI(3). II. 5 "His cold thin drink out of his leather bottle," and then bottles.]

The comparison of Thorah to water, WINE, oil, honey and milk, is dwelt upon in Sifre (עקב), on Deut. xi. 22, and in Midrash Chazitha, on the words, "For thy love is better than WINE" (Cant. i. 2). Thorah is like water, which is grateful to the thirsty, is ubiquitous, gives life to the world, comes down from heaven, purifies, works its way by constant dripping, seeks its level, is kept in earthen vessels...and drowns those who cannot swim. But water grows bad if kept long in a vessel. Is this likewise the case with Thorah? Nay, it is like WINE, which improves

as it grows old in the bottle, כל זמן שהוא מתישן בקנקן. Or is it like water, which does not rejoice the heart of man? Nay, like WINE, which does rejoice the heart of man. Is it then like wine, which is sometimes bad for the head and for the body? Nay rather, like oil, which is good for both, &c. "Thy love is better than WINE," interpreted by Gematria (III. 28), signifies that Israel is more beloved than the ι + ι + ν (= 70) nations of the world. [In vino veritas, for יין is by Gematria סוד, secret ('Erub. 65 a).]

[35] The same is said in II. 15 of the evil eye [Ecclus. xiv. 10 ὀφθαλμὸς πονηρός], the evil yeçer [xv. 14 διαβουλίου], and misanthropy. Compare also the three heads under which worldliness is summed up in 1 Joh. ii. 16: ἡ ἐπιθυμία τῆς σαρκός, καὶ ἡ ἐπιθυμία τῶν ὀφθαλμῶν, καὶ ἡ ἀλαζονεία τοῦ βίου.

קנאה] This word, like ζῆλος, is also used in a good sense, as in Baba Bathra 21 a: "The emulation of Soferim increases wisdom."

[36] Truths which in this world men are taught and then teach others "will in the world to come be known of themselves without a teacher," according to the prophetic description of the coming age: "And they shall teach no more every man his neighbour, and every man his brother, saying, Know the Lord: for they shall all know me, from the least of them, unto the greatest of them, saith the Lord" (Jer. xxxi. 34). Τότε δὲ ἐπιγνώσομαι, καθὼς καὶ ἐπεγνώσθην (1 Cor. xiii. 12). [Ecclus. xv. 19 ἐπιγνώσεται.]

creator, and He the discerner[37], and He the judge, and He the witness, and He the "adversary," and He is about to judge with whom there is no iniquity, nor forgetfulness, nor respect of persons, nor taking of a bribe, for all is His, and know that all is according to plan.

32. Let not thine imagination assure thee that the grave is an asylum; for perforce thou wast framed (Jer. xviii. 6), and perforce thou wast born, and perforce thou livest, and perforce thou diest, and perforce thou art about to give account and reckoning before the King of the kings of kings, the Holy One, blessed is He.

[37] "He *fashioneth* their hearts alike; he *considereth* all their works" (Ps. xxxiii. 15). The world is to be judged by One who, as Judge, and Witness, and 'Αντίδικος, possesses power and knowledge, and will exact strict justice (Matt. v. 25). Cf. Rom. viii. 33, 34. [Midr. Ps. xvii. (p. 127 ed. Buber) What is the bribe that He takes from the wicked in this world? תשובה ותפלה וצדקה.]

---

p. 63, § 2 הכובש את יצרו] Ecclus. xxi. 11 ὁ φυλάσσων νόμον κατακρατεῖ τοῦ ἐννοήματος αὐτοῦ, Midr. Ps. cxix. 11.

p. 64, § 3] To be truly rich one must be αὐτάρκης. Compare 2 Cor. vi. 10, Philippians iv. 11 (ed. Lightfoot), Clem. *Paed.* ii. 3 πλοῦτος δὲ ἄριστος ἡ τῶν ἐπιθυμιῶν πενία.

p. 66, n. 7 שכר מצוה מצוה] Cf. καὶ χάριν ἀντὶ χάριτος (Joh. i. 16, ed. Westcott), Rom. i. 17, and Mr C. G. Montefiore's *Florilegium Philonis* in the *Jewish Quarterly Review* (vii. 540).

p. 67, n. 8 שמים] On *shamayim* as a designation of God see Lightfoot *Hor. Hebr.* on Matt. iii. 2. "Everything is in the hands of *shamayim* except the fear of *shamayim*" (Megillah 25 a), Dan. iv. 23 (26) די שליטין שמיא, *that the heavens do rule.*

ib. מקום] Ezek. iii. 12 ברוך כבוד יהוה ממקומו, "Blessed *be* the glory of the LORD from His place." Cf. in *The History of John the son of Zebedee* in Wright's *Apocryphal Acts of the Apostles* (ii. 39, 1871), "And straightway these two angels came and hovered over the water, and were crying *Holy, holy, holy, Father and Son and Spirit of holiness* after him" [Syr. *from His place*]. Joma 38 a מקום כבוד עכשיו במקומו, *now the glory of Maqom is in its place.*

ib. השם] Cf. T. J. Makkoth iii. 32 *b₆* & Sifra קדשים, he is not guilty עד שיכתוב שם השם *until he writes the name of the Name* (Lev. xix. 28). In Lev. xxiv. 11 A.V. "the name" is expanded into "the name *of the Lord*," cf. St James v. 14 (ed. Mayor p. 161, 1892). The author of the *Bundle of Myrrh* notes that the law of Moses is the law *of God*, משה being an anagram of and equal by Gematria to השם.

CHAPTER V.

1. By ten Sayings[1] the world was created. And what is learned therefrom? for could it not have been created by one

[1] The world is described as created by SAYINGS, because in Genesis the acts of creation are introduced by א' ויאמר, "and God SAID." כי הוא אמר ויהי כו' (Ps. xxxiii. 9). In the Jalqut, which commences with the paragraph Aboth v. 1, NINE occurrences of ויאמר are reckoned, and the tenth is said to be implied in בראשית, "*In the beginning* God created the heavens and the earth," since it is said that " by the word of the Lord (בדבר יי)" the heavens were created (Ps. xxxiii. 6). [Rosh ha-Shanah 32 a.] In Pirqe R. El. III., TEN *va-yomer's* are reckoned (Gen. i. 3, 6, 9, 11, 14, 20, 24, 26, 29; ii. 18), the last being that which leads up to the creation of woman. In Bereshith Rabbah xvii., the first "Saying" is taken as implied in בראשית: the second in ורוח א' (i. 2): then follow eight of those specified above, from Gen. i. 3 to i. 26, ending with the creation of man; but it is added that Menachem bar Jose excludes ורוח כו', and replaces it by iii. 18. In Chagigah 12 a, it is said in the name of Rab, that by ten "things," or דברים, the world was created: some of the ten things specified, as *chochmah, chesed, geburah,* being found also among the ten Sephiroth of the Qabbalists.

The point of view in the text is that the grandeur of Creation is more impressively portrayed as the outcome of repeated acts of power, than as the immediate result of a single fiat of omnipotence. "God laboured so much in creating the world by ten sayings" in order to emphasize the guilt of the sinners who mar His work, and the merit of the righteous who preserve it. But elsewhere creation is described as requiring the least conceivable effort on the part of God: read not בהבראם, "on their being created," but (as two words) בה' בראם [Gen. Rab. xx. 2], He created them by the letter H; "by the breath of His mouth."

Various other ways of representing the creative process are found in the Rabbinic writings. THORAH, which is identified with Wisdom (Prov. viii. 1), and with Ἀρχή (ver. 22), is introduced as the speaker in Gen. i. 1: "*By me, who am* Ἀρχή, *God created, &c.*"— where the first word is read as two, בי ראשית (Jalqut 2). The ideal ISRAEL is also said to be the creative agent: "By the merit of Israel, who are called RESHITH (Jer. ii. 3), God created the heavens and the earth." "R. Berekiah said, By the merit of MOSES the world was created, &c." "From each word, דבור, that proceeded from the mouth of the Holy

Saying? But it was that vengeance might be taken on the wicked, who destroy the world that was created by ten Sayings; and to give a goodly reward to the righteous, who maintain the world that was created by ten Sayings.

2. Ten generations were there from Adam to Noach[2], to shew how great was His longsuffering (1 Pet. iii. 20); for all

One, blessed is He, there was created an angel, for it is said (Ps. xxxiii. 6): By the word of the Lord were the heavens made; and *all the host of them* by the breath of His mouth" (Chagigah 14 a).

The subjects of בראשית, and of מרכבה, *the chariot* (cf. Ezek. i.), were made a nucleus of theosophic speculations, which were only to be communicated with the greatest caution, for it is said: "Honey and milk are under thy tongue (Cant. iv. 11), things which are sweeter than honey should be under thy tongue" (Chagigah 13 a), or should not be revealed. "Non exponunt...opera creationis cum duobus, neque currum cum uno, nisi fuerit sapiens qui sensum intelligit. Quicunque considerat quatuor causas, ei melius fuisset quod nunquam intrasset mundum; nempe id quod supra est, quod infra est, et quod ante est, et quod post est. Et quicunque non attendit ad honorem Creatoris sui, ei melius fuisset quod non intrasset mundum" (Chagigah ii. 1).

In connexion with the subject of esoteric doctrine and mysticism it may be remarked that the name 'Εσσαῖος (cf. ii. 10; v. 16), or Essene, not improbably denotes *secret*, or *mystic;* for (1) the word חשאי, *secret*, or *silent*, would naturally be transliterated 'Εσσαῖος, in the same way that חשן, as Jost remarks (*Gesch.* A. 207, Note), is by Josephus transliterated 'Εσσήν, and (2) "We may illustrate

this derivation by Josephus' description of the Essenes, *B. J.* ii. 8. 5, τοῖς ἔξωθεν ὡς μυστήριόν τι φρικτὸν ἡ τῶν ἔνδον σιωπὴ καταφαίνεται, and perhaps this will also explain the Greek equivalent θεωρητικοί, which Suidas gives for 'Εσσαῖοι. The use of the Hebrew word חשאים in Mishna Shekalim v. 6, though we need not assume that the Essenes are there meant, will serve to show how it might be adopted as the name of the sect." See Professor Lightfoot's recent edition of St Paul's Epistle to the Colossians [1875], where a full account of the conflicting theories about the Essenes is given.

[2] Ten generations are reckoned (Gen. v. 3—29), including both Adam and Noah. It is said of *dor ha-mabbul* the generation of the deluge, that they have no portion in the world to come (Sanhedrin xi. 3). The thought that God, after bearing so long with the wickedness of those evil generations, did at length bring the flood upon the earth, should assure Israel that He will in due time put an end to their captivity, and requite their oppressors according to their works (R. Jonah). "What is the meaning of the *seven days* (of respite): For yet seven days, and I will cause it to rain upon the earth, Gen. vii. 4, 10? They were the days of mourning for Methuselah, to teach thee that the death of the righteous hinders punishments from coming" (Sanhedrin, 108 b).

the generations were provoking Him, till He brought the deluge upon them.

3. Ten generations were there from Noach to Abraham[3], to shew how great was His longsuffering; for all the generations were provoking Him, till Abraham our father came, and received the reward of them all.

4. With ten temptations[4] was Abraham our father tempted,

---

[3] The ten generations are reckoned (Gen. xi. 10—26), excluding Noach. "Our Rabbis have said, that when Noah died Abraham our father was 58 years old; yet if thou number the descendants, thou wilt find ten generations between them, for although Noah prolonged his days ten generations, the generations are reckoned to shew how great was His longsuffering, for all the generations were provoking Him, till Abraham our father came. And they have not said here, Till He took vengeance on them, for Abraham our father made up for all their shortcomings, and wrought good which counterpoised all their evil, and delivered them from punishments" (R. Jonah). But the like is not said of Noah, who was only relatively righteous: he was "perfect in his own generations" (Gen. vi. 9), but not in the generations of others (Sanhedrin 108 a).

[4] The temptations of Abraham are reckoned in more than one way. A †, referring to "Pirqe R. Eli'ezer ben Hyrqanus," gives the following computation. 1. Nimrod sought to slay him, and he hid himself in the earth thirteen years. 2. Nimrod cast him into the *fiery* furnace, because he would not worship his idols, and the fire had no power over him to burn him (Targ. Jonathan, Gen. xi. 28; Bereshith Rabbah xxxviii.). This, says R. Jonah, is not expressly stated in

the Thorah, but it is elicited from the expression, "*Ur* (=fire) of the Chaldees." 3. "Get thee out of thy country, and from thy kindred" (Gen. xii. 1). 4. "And there was a famine in the land" (xii. 10). 5. His wife "was taken into Pharaoh's house" (xii. 15). 6. He waged war with Chedorlaomer (xiv. 14). 7. The bondage of his posterity was predicted (xv. 13). 8. At the age of ninety he was circumcised. 9. He is commanded to cast out the bondwoman and her son (xxi. 10). 10. He is commanded to sacrifice Isaac (xxii. 2). For other ways of making up the number of the trials A † refers to *Midrash Thillim*, and to the "Mishnah of R. Nathan" (Aboth R.N. xxxiii.), which reckons them as follows: *Two* in Gen. xii. 1, "Get thee out, &c.;" *Two* with respect to his two sons; *Two* with respect to his two wives; *One* in his war with "the kings"; *One* in בין הבתרים (Gen. xv.); *One* in Ur of the Chaldees; *One* in his circumcision. "And why was he tried with ten trials, neither more nor less? It was with reference to the ten מאמרות by which the world was created. Abraham, having been tried with ten trials, and being found perfect, was fitted to uphold the world which was created by ten מאמרות," and he was rewarded by corresponding decads of miracles which were wrought for his sons in Egypt, and by the Sea.

and he withstood them all; to shew how great was the love of Abraham our father.

5. Ten miracles were wrought for our fathers in Egypt; and ten by the sea[5].

6. *Ten plagues[6] brought the Holy One, blessed is He, upon the Egyptians in Egypt; and ten by the Sea.*

7. With ten temptations did our fathers tempt God in the wilderness, for it is said, And they have tempted me now these ten times[7], and have not hearkened to my voice (Numb. xiv. 22).

8. Ten miracles were wrought in the Sanctuary[8]. No

---

[5] The ten miracles wrought for Israel in Egypt were the ten plagues which fell upon their oppressors. The ten by the Sea are made out in various artificial ways from the account of the passage of the Israelites through the Sea, and the drowning of the Egyptians. Thus it is said in Mekiltha (מס׳ בשלח ד׳), that 1. The sea was cleft; 2. It was divided into twelve parts; 3. It was made dry land, &c. Amongst the miracles are reckoned, that "He gave them fresh water out of the midst of salt," and that "The sea became like glass vessels, for it is said, The depths were congealed in the heart of the sea" (Ex. xv. 8). Compare Midrash Thanchuma *in loc.*; Jalqut 234; Aboth R. N. xxxiii; Pirqe R. Eli'ezer xlii; and see the notes in Surenhusius, Vol. iv. p. 466.

[6] On the doubtful genuineness of this saying see *Crit. Note.* The plagues brought upon the Egyptians may be identified with the miracles wrought on behalf of the Israelites.

[7] This verse is cited in 'Erakin iii. 5, where the heinousness of slander is dwelt upon, and it is said that "sentence was passed upon our fathers in the wilderness only on account of the evil tongue." If the spies, it is added,

were condemned for slandering trees and stones, how much more is he to be condemned who slanders his neighbour! The ten temptations wherewith the Israelites tempted God are reckoned as follows: "with respect to the sea, *two* (before and after the passage); the waters, *two;* the manna, *two;* the quails, *two;* the calf, *one;* the wilderness of Paran, *one.*" Further details are given by the way (fol. 15). In Aboth R. N. xxxiv. God is represented as tempting the Israelites with ten temptations, "In all of which they were found not perfect."

[8] "These miracles were wrought likewise in the second temple, although the state of Israel was not in every respect perfect, and their heart was not firm with Him. But it shews that, for all this, the Divine grace had not desisted from working miracles with them contrary to nature in His Holy city whilst His sanctuary was still in the midst of it" (R. Obadiah ben Jacob of Sforno).

Of miracles not specified in this place, the miracle of the scarlet thread, לשון של זהורית, which changed colour on the day of Atonement, may be mentioned: "Originally they used to bind a scarlet thread upon the door of

woman miscarried from the scent of the holy meat[9]; and the
holy meat never stank ; and an uncleanness befel not the
highpriest[10] on the day of the Atonement ; and a fly[11] was not
seen in the slaughterhouse ; and a defect was not found in the
sheaf[12]; nor in the two loaves[12]; nor in the shewbread[13]; *and*

the porch, without. If it grew white
they rejoiced : if it grew not white
they were troubled. They arranged
to bind it on the door of the porch
within : and still they watched, and
looked. If it grew white they rejoiced:
if not they were troubled. They arranged to bind half of it to the rock,
and half of it between the horns of
the scapegoat...*Forty years before the
temple was destroyed the scarlet thread
did not grow white, but remained red*"
(Rosh ha-Shanah 31 b).   Compare
Joma 67 a, &c. The whitening of the
thread is connected with Is. i. 18 in
Joma VI. 8: "Lingua coccinea alligata
erat ad portas templi, et cum hircus
ad desertum accessisset, albescebat
quia dicitur ; *Si fuerint peccata vestra
sicut coccinum, sicut nix albescent.*"

[9] "No woman ever miscarried
through a vain longing to partake of
the flesh offered in sacrifice, or reserved for the priests alone."

[10] Ishmael b. Qimqith, having become disqualified, was replaced by
his own brother, so that their mother
saw two of her sons high-priests on
the same day. The wise asked how
she had merited such an honour. She
replied, that *the walls of her house had
never seen the hair of her head* (Aboth
R. N. xxxv.). Her modesty was still
further rewarded according to Joma
47 a, by her having not two only but
seven sons, all of whom ministered in
the high-priesthood.

[11] The ZEBUB was a symbol of im-
purity. "Behold, now, I perceive that
this is an holy man of God" (2 Kings

iv. 8). How did she discover this?
From the fact that no FLY crossed the
table of Elisha'. A Thorah-flame, an
אש דת (Deut. xxxiii. 2), goes forth
from the righteous, and purifies the
air around. Cf. pp. 21, 65.

"Said Rab, The evil *yeçer* is like
a fly, for it is said (Eccl. x. 1), Flies
of death cause the ointment of the
apothecary to send forth a stinking
savour" (Berakoth 61 a). The Targum on the same verse compares the
evil nature to a *debuba*, which lies at
the doors of the heart (p. 37) and
causes death, and corrupts a good
name, which is like ointment.

[12] By *'omer* is meant either a
measure, the tenth part of an ephah
(Ex. xvi. 36), or a sheaf. The 'omer
was offered at the time of the Passover, and consisted of first fruits of
the barley harvest. At Pentecost,
fifty days later, "the two loaves," the
first fruits of the wheat harvest, were
offered : "And ye shall count unto
you from the morrow after the sabbath, from the day that ye brought
the sheaf of the wave offering; seven
sabbaths shall be complete : Even unto the morrow after the seventh sabbath shall ye number fifty days: and
ye shall offer a new meat offering unto
the Lord. Ye shall bring out of your
habitations two wave loaves of two
tenth deals : they shall be of fine
flour; they shall be baken with leaven;
they are the first fruits unto the Lord"
(Lev. xxiii. 15—17).

For further details see the Mishnah,
Menach. x. [al. VI.] The *'omer* was to be

rains quenched not the pile; and the wind prevailed not against the pillar of smoke[14]; they stood serried, and bowed down at ease[15]; and serpent and scorpion harmed not in Jerusalem; and a man said not to his fellow, The place is too strait for me (Is. xlix. 20) to lodge in Jerusalem.

9. Ten things were created between the suns[16]. The

taken from the vicinity of Jerusalem, unless the crops there were not sufficiently ripened at the time appointed for the offering. "A tale is told of its being taken from the gardens of Çerefim, and the two loaves from the valley of עֵין סוכר," which probably denotes the neighbourhood of Συχάρ (Joh. iv. 5). [Surh. v. 98.]

[13] The shewbread consisted of "twelve cakes" of fine flour, which were "set in order before the Lord" every sabbath, and remained till they were replaced by others on the following sabbath (Lev. xxiv. 5—9). "A great miracle used to be wrought on the shewbread: its taking away was as its setting in order, for it is said (1 Sam. xxi. 7), To put hot bread in the day when it was taken away" (Joma 21 a), that is to say, that the bread was still *hot on the day of its being taken away*, חם ביום הלקחו.

[14] At the conclusion of the last day of the feast all watched the smoke of the altar-pile (Joma 21 b; Baba Bathra 147 a). If it inclined toward the NORTH, the poor rejoiced, and the householders were troubled, because it was to be a rainy year, so that the crops would rot if kept: if it inclined to the SOUTH, the poor were troubled, and the householders rejoiced, because it was to be a dry year, &c.: toward the EAST, all rejoiced: toward the WEST, all were troubled.

The straightness of the column of smoke was sometimes regarded as a sign of the acceptance of prayer and

sacrifice: the broken column betrayed hypocrisy (Berith Menuchah 11 b).

[15] On the occasions of the great festivals for which the people at large came up to Jerusalem, although the worshippers were so closely packed in the 'azarah that they had scarcely room to stand upright, nevertheless by a miracle they had ample space to bow down, so that no man incommoded his neighbour; and no one was ever unable at such time to find lodging and maintenance in the city, however great the concourse of people.

The "ten miracles," though wrought in relation to the Temple festivals, did not all take place in the Temple itself, but פתח במקדש וסיים בירושלם, "he begins with the Temple, and ends with JERUSALEM." See Joma 21 a, where it is discussed how the ten (cf. *Crit. Note*) are to be reckoned, and additional marvels are mentioned, such as the miraculous disappearance of the fragments of earthenware, &c.

[16] Ten things were created between the evenings, or at the time of transition from the "six days of creation" to the sabbath. It is felt to be impossible to define their relation to the course of nature, to which, however, everything, not excepting the miraculous, belongs. They are no part of the normal work of the creation period: at the same time they can only be thought of as preordained ἀπὸ καταβολῆς κόσμου. "It saith, that these things were created between the suns, for indeed although God, blessed

mouth of the earth[17]; and *the mouth of* the well[18]; and the

be He, wrought great signs and wonders contrary to the nature of things, such as the plagues of Egypt, and the miracles at the Red Sea, &c., at all events He did not create anything after the six days of Bereshith, as it saith, And God ended on the seventh day, and rested; and as it saith, There is nothing new under the sun; and therefore, concerning these ten things, which are not mentioned in the account of the work of Bereshith, he saith that they were created then without doubt; and the explanation of their not being mentioned with the rest of the work of Bereshith, is because it was impossible to tell us the time of their creation, for in fact it was at a transition period, between two days which could not fitly be reckoned with either of them" ('Obadiah Sforno).

R. Israel finds a difficulty in the numbering of the rainbow amongst the ten things, " in all of which were miracles out of the course of nature, and all of which moreover appeared in time of need, whereas the bow may be seen any day."

As in the case of other groups of " ten things," it is disputed how the number is to be made up. According to one reckoning, (1) the writing in the abstract; (2) the writing in the concrete, or the writing-instrument (*maktheb*); and (3) the tables themselves, are reckoned separately as three of the ten things; but this distinction is not made in the Targum of Jonathan, as cited in note 18. The ram which Abraham sacrificed instead of Isaac is said in Bemidbar Rabbah xvii. to have been created " between the suns." [Rev. xiii. 18.]

[17] " But if the Lord make a new thing, and the earth open *her mouth*,

and swallow them up, &c." (Numb. xvi. 30). "Said the Holy One, blessed is He, to Moses, What seekest thou? He said before Him, Lord of the world אם בריאה כו', If Thou hast created a mouth to the earth, well: if not, let the Lord now create her a mouth" (Bemidbar Rabbah xviii.). Compare Sanhedrin 110 a; Nedarim 39 b, where the seven things created before the world (p. 12) are specified.

[18] Although the expression, "mouth of the באר," in connexion with the "mouth of the earth" which *swallowed up* Korah (Numb. xvi. 32), suggests a reference to Ps. lxix. 15: "Neither let the deep swallow me up, and let not the pit shut her mouth upon me," nevertheless the allusion is, doubtless, as it is generally supposed to be, to some other באר. "THE MOUTH OF THE WELL. According to Rashi's (?) interprétation, it opened its mouth and uttered a song (Numb. xxi. 17). But some understand the rock which Moses smote, i.e. the באר which went about with Israel in the wilderness" (Bar S.). Compare also Bemidbar Rabbah xix. In either case there is some difficulty in accounting for the expression, "*the mouth* of the well."

The difficulty may be solved by reading הבאר alone, without פי, (1) according to the Targum of Jonathan on Numb. xxii. 28: "Ten things were created after the finishing of the world, at the coming in of the sabbath, between the suns: The manna; and THE WELL (ובירא); and the staff of Moses; and the shamir; and the bow; and the clouds of glory; and the MOUTH of the earth; and the writing of the tables of the covenant; and the demons; and the speaking MOUTH of the ass"; and (2) according also to

mouth of the ass; and the bow (Gen. ix. 13); and the manna; and the rod[19]; and the shamir-worm[20]; and the character; and the writing[16]; and the tables.   And some say, the spirits[21]

Pesachim 54 a, where the ten things are: "THE WELL; and the manna; and the bow; and the כתב; and the מכתב; and the tables; the grave of Moses; and the cave in which Moses and Elijah stood; the opening of the mouth of the ass; and the opening of the mouth of the earth to swallow up the wicked. And some say likewise the rod of Aaron, its almonds, and its buds; and some say likewise the spirits; and some say likewise the vesture of the primal Adam." [Gen. R. xx. 12.]

[19] The ROD which was made "between the suns" was given to Adam, and handed down from generation to generation, till, after the death of Joseph, it passed into the hands of Pharaoh. Moses alone could read the letters upon it—it was inscribed *inter alia* with *Shem ha-mephorash* (p. 56) and he was thus designated as the future deliverer of Israel (Pirqe R. Eli'ezer XL.).

[20] The SHAMIR (see Buxtorf, *Lex. Chald.*) was a small worm which split or cut stones upon which it was placed. Moses used it to engrave the stones of the ephod. First he wrote upon them in ink: then he "shewed them" the shamir, or passed it over the lines which he had traced, and the stones were cleft, without loss of substance, as a fig is split by the sun, or as a channel is formed by water. The shamir was created משֶׁשֶׁת ימי בראשית. Nothing, however hard, can stand against it.   Solomon, having got possession of it with the help of Asmodeus, king of the devils, used it to cut the stones for the temple, for it is said (1 Kings vi. 7) that no tool of iron was heard in the house while it was in building (Gittin 68 a; Sotah 48 b).

[21] The demons, or שׂדרים, are commonly called "*mazziqin*," or *nocentes*. "The Holy One, blessed is He, had created their souls, and was about to create their bodies, when the sabbath set in, and He did not create them" (Bereshith Rabbah VII.). Hence it is that they are invisible to the human eye, being simply נפש חיה (Gen. i. 24) "If power were given to the eye to see, no creature could exist because of the spirits...Each of us has a thousand at his left hand, and ten thousand at his right hand (Ps. xci. 7). Said Raba, It is from them that comes the crowding in the assemblage, and weakness of knees, and the wearing out of the clothes of students, and colliding with the feet.   He who wishes to know about them must take sifted ashes, and sprinkle them by his bed, and in the morning he will see marks as of cocks' feet.   He who wishes to see them must take the caul of a black she-cat, daughter of a black one: a firstborn, the daughter of a firstborn: and burn it in the fire, and pulverise it, and fill his eyes with it, and he will see them.   Let him put the rest into an iron tube, and seal it with a signet of iron, that they may not steal it away, and let him seal its mouth that he may not be harmed. Rab Bibi bar Abaye did this. He saw, and was harmed. Our Rabbis prayed for mercy on him, and he was healed" (Berakoth 6 a). The spirits helped Solomon to find the shamir, and to build the temple. They frequent desolate places, and are especially to be feared in the night time.

also; and the sepulchre of Moses (Deut. xxxiv. 6); and the ram of Abraham our father (Gen. xxii. 13). And some say, tongs also, made with tongs[22].

10.   Seven things are in a clod, and seven in a wise man. The wise man speaks not before one who is greater than he in wisdom; and does not interrupt the words of his companion; and is not hasty to reply; he asks according to canon, and answers to the point[23]; and speaks on the first thing first, and on the last last; of what he has not heard he says, I have not heard; and he acknowledges the truth[24]. And their opposites are in the clod.

Jochanan ben Zakkai understood the talk of devils (Baba Bathra 134 a). Members of the SANHEDRIN were to be בעלי כשפים, or skilled in magic (Sanhedrin 17 a; Menachoth 65 a), that they might be in a position to give judgment in cases which came before them.

[22] The chain of secondary causes is endless. The instrument צבת presupposes another, with the help of which it was made, and so on *in infinitum*. Speculation, failing to reach the ultimate, must rest upon the doctrine that God is the Creator: He made the first. Cf. Pesachim 54 a.

The difficulty is presented in another form in Chagigah 12 b: "R. Jose said, Woe to the creatures, that see, and know not what they see: that stand, and know not on what they stand. On what stands the earth? on the pillars (Job ix. 6): and the pillars upon the waters (Ps. cxxxvi. 6): and the waters upon the mountains (Ps. civ. 6): and the mountains upon the wind (Amos iv. 13): and the wind upon the storm (Ps. cxlviii. 8): and the storm depends upon the arm of the Holy One, for it is said (Deut. xxxiii. 27), Underneath are the everlasting arms."

[23] The reading of the text is thus explained by A†: "If he has occasion to ask a question, he asks *according to the halakah* with which they are occupied; and if any one asks of him, he answers his interrogator according to the matter which he asked him, and does not digress to another matter. And if one has asked him two or three things, he replies in order." The usual reading (see note ג) signifies, that his inquiries have relation to the subject in hand, and his replies are in accordance with the received canons of interpretation.

[24] R. 'Obadiah of Sforno illustrates this Mishnah from the book of JOB. 1. The wise man will not speak before his superior in wisdom: so Elihu refrained from speaking when in the presence of his seniors, for "I said, Days should speak, and multitude of years should teach wisdom" (xxxii. 7). 2. He does not interrupt his companion, but is like Elihu, who "waited till Job had spoken" (xxxii. 4); unlike his friends, with whom Job had to expostulate: "Suffer me that I may speak; and after that I have spoken, mock on" (xxi. 3). 3. He is not hasty to answer before he has properly heard his friend's opinion, like Bildad, who said; "Doth God pervert judgment?" (viii. 3), and was rebuked by

11. Seven kinds of punishments come on account of seven main transgressions[25]. When some men tithe, and some do not tithe, dearth from drought comes: some of them are hungry, and some of them are full. When they have not tithed at all, a dearth from tumult[26] *and from drought* comes. And when they have not offered the dough-cake, a deadly dearth comes.

Job for misapprehending his meaning, for "I know it is so of a truth, &c." (ix. 2). 4. He interrogates to the point, unlike Eliphaz (iv. 7); and answers according to *halakah*, unlike Job's three friends, to whom God said: "Ye have not spoken of me the thing that is right" (xlii. 7). 5. He deals with each point in its proper order, like Elihu (xxxiii. 8, &c.). 6. He does not profess to know what he does not know, like Zophar: "But oh that God would speak, and open his lips against thee. And that he would shew thee the secrets of wisdom, &c." (xi. 5, 16). 7. And he admits the truth, unlike the three friends of Job, against whom Elihu's wrath was kindled, "because they had found no answer, and yet had condemned Job" (xxxii. 3).

[25] The phrase גופי עברות, or "bodies of transgressions," denotes (says Bar S.) such as comprise many subdivisions, as the body is divided into many members. On the idiomatic uses of גוף see the lexicons. "And it saith, For seven *bodies* of transgressions, to teach that though they are more than seven, nevertheless they are called seven, as being comprised in seven bodies, i.e. *kinds* or *species* (Leb Aboth)."

The seven punishments are, three degrees of famine; the pestilence; the sword; the noisome beast; and exile. The seven main transgressions are committed, according to Sforno, in relation to tithing; judgment; pro-

fanation of the NAME; strange worship; sensuality; bloodshed; and the sabbatical year; but the sins are differently reckoned by other commentators, who endeavour to make them correspond to the seven punishments, each to each. For a series of discussions bearing upon this subject see the Gemara on Shabbath II. 6; and cf. Lev. xxvi.

[26] The three degrees of famine are apportioned as follows. 1. Partial neglect of tithing is punished by partial famine resulting from *drought* (Jer. xvii. 8). As it is said in Amos iv. 7: "And I caused it to rain upon one city, and caused it not to rain upon another city." 2. The universal neglect of tithing is punished by famine "of מהומה" or of that and drought combined, according to the usual reading. The former reading is favoured by Aboth R. N. xxxviii.; which however has תורמין, instead of מעשרין, in this clause. Famine "of מהומה" is either (i) a famine of war and *tumult*, through which the land is untilled (R. Jonah), or the crops are ruined by marauders; or (ii) a famine causing *destruction*: "...and shall destroy them with a mighty *destruction*, until they be destroyed" (Deut. vii. 23). 3. A famine of entire consumption results from neglect of the ordinance: "Ye shall offer up a *cake* of the first of your dough for an heave offering" (Numb. xv. 20). The rains fail utterly: "thy heaven that is over thy head shall be brass, and the earth that is under

12.   Pestilence comes into the world for the capital crimes mentioned in the Thorah, which are not brought before the tribunal[27]; and for the seventh year fruits.

13.   The sword comes upon the world for suppression of judgment; and for perversion of judgment; and for explaining Thorah not according to canon.

14.   Noisome beasts come into the world for vain swearing; and for profanation of the NAME.

Captivity comes upon the world for strange worship; and for incest; and for shedding of blood; and for (not) giving release to the land[28].

15.   At four seasons[29] the pestilence waxes: in the fourth

---

thee shall be iron" (Deut. xxviii. 23). "I will even appoint over you *terror*" (Lev. xxvi. 16): read not *behalah*, but *bechallah*, on account of the *challah*, or *cake* (Shabbath 32 b). The Divine judgments are "measure for measure" (Is. xxvii. 8).

[27] The terrestrial court is not commissioned with respect to precepts whereof the reward is specified. See Mekiltha (בחדש ח), on the "Fifth Commandment."

PESTILENCE is sent as a judgment for capital crimes which have not come under the jurisdiction, or cognisance, of the *beth din*, but are reserved for judgment by the hand of God. But deaths which the tribunal is authorised to inflict are, even then, superseded only by analogous deaths; thus he who deserves to be stoned, falls from a housetop, or is trampled on by a beast: he who deserves burning is stung by a serpent: he who deserves beheading is killed by robbers: he who deserves hanging is drowned, or dies of συνάγχη. See A†, ₵.

Pestilence, though resulting naturally from bad water, food, air, and other intelligible causes, is none the less sent by Divine Providence. But know that, for all this, we do not sin

in fleeing because of it to some place where there is no pestilence; for he who flees does not deny the omnipresence of God, but bows his uncircumcised heart and bears the yoke of migration as a punishment for his sins. And let him not embolden himself to stand against his King, when he is angry with him, or designs to tempt him (Leb Aboth).

[28] "But in the seventh year shall be a sabbath of rest unto the land, a sabbath for the Lord: thou shalt neither sow thy field, nor prune thy vineyard. That which groweth of its own accord of thy harvest thou shalt not reap, neither gather the grapes of thy vine undressed: for it is a year of rest unto the land. And the sabbath of the land shall be meat for you; for thee, and for thy servant, &c." (Lev. xxv. 4—6). The seventh year was called, the year of *ha-she-mittah*, the release (Deut. xv. 9; xxxi. 10).

[29] At four seasons of the septennial cycle disease is prevalent owing to the appropriation of what should have been devoted to the poor.

The neglect of the poor's tithe in the third and sixth years of the septennium leads to pestilence in the

(year); in the seventh; at the ending of the seventh; and at the ending of the Feast in every year. In the fourth (year), on account of the poor's tithe in the third; in the seventh, on account of the poor's tithe in the sixth; and at the ending of the seventh[30], on account of the seventh year fruits; and at the ending of the Feast[31] in every year, on account of the largesses of the poor.

16. There are four characters[32] in men. He that saith,

years immediately following. The מעשר עני is enjoined in Deut. xiv. 28, 29: "At the end of three years thou shalt bring forth all the tithe of thine increase the same year, and shalt lay it up within thy gates: And the Levite (because he hath no part nor inheritance with thee), and the stranger, and the fatherless, and the widow, which are within thy gates, shall come, and shall eat and be satisfied; that the Lord thy God may bless thee in all the work of thine hand which thou doest." The third year is called "the year of tithing" (Deut. xxvi. 12). In this year, as Rashi remarks, the Levite received his tenth (Numb. xviii. 21), as in other years, but the *Second*, or Festival, *Tithe* (Deut. xiv. 23), was devoted to the poor. On these tithes see the Mishnah-Tracts named after them, in Seder Zera'im.

[30] In the "eighth" year, which is called the "goings out of the seventh" (A†, ℂ), pestilence prevails owing to neglect of the preceding year of release. "And six years thou shalt sow thy land, and shalt gather in the fruits thereof: But the seventh year thou shalt let it rest and lie still; *that the poor of thy people may eat:* and what they leave the beasts of the field shall eat" (Ex. xxiii. 10, 11).

[31] After "the Feast" of Tabernacles, or of Ingathering, in each year judgment comes for having deprived the poor of the donations due to them, which were פאה . שכחה . לקט, that is, *spicilegium, oblivio,* and *angulus.* Cf. Levit. xix. 9: "And when ye reap the harvest of your land, thou shalt not wholly reap the CORNERS of thy field, neither shalt thou gather the GLEANINGS of thy harvest;" and Deut. xxiv. 19: "When thou cuttest down thine harvest in thy field, and hast FORGOT a sheaf in the field, thou shalt not go again to fetch it: it shall be for the stranger, for the fatherless, and for the widow: that the Lord thy God may bless thee in all the work of thine hands."

[32] MIDDAH denotes *measure*, and hence, standard, characteristic, quality, virtue, &c. The title of Aristotle's "Ethics" is rendered ספר המדות. The first of the "middoth" here described is that of the man who neither gives nor takes: is neither self-sacrificing, nor yet grasping, or dependent upon his neighbours. This character is said to be neither good nor bad, but *intermediate.* Others, however, regard it as a spirit of haughty independence, and indifference to the welfare of others: "Behold, this was the iniquity of thy sister Sodom, pride, fulness of bread, and abundance of idleness was in her and in her daughters, neither did she strengthen the hand of the poor and needy" (Ezek. xvi. 49). The second standard is worldly and utilitarian:

12

Mine is mine, and thine is thine, is an indifferent character;
but some say, It is the character of Sodom: (he that saith,)
Mine is thine, and thine is mine, is 'am ha-areç: Mine and
thine are thine, pious: Thine and mine are mine, wicked.

17.　There are four characters in dispositions.　Easily provoked, and easily pacified, his gain is cancelled by his loss[33]:
hard to provoke and hard to pacify, his loss is cancelled by his
gain: hard to provoke, and easily pacified, pious: easily provoked, and hard to pacify, wicked.

18.　There are four characters in scholars.　Quick to hear
and quick to forget, his gain is cancelled by his loss: slow to
hear and slow to forget, his loss is cancelled by his gain: quick
to hear, and slow to forget, is wise: slow to hear, and quick to
forget, this is an evil lot.

19.　There are four characters in almsgivers[34].　He who is

the man acts with a view to recompense: he lends to those from whom he
hopes to receive (Luke vi. 34); οὐχὶ
καὶ οἱ τελῶναι οὕτως ποιοῦσιν (Matt.
v. 46); "He is called 'am ha-areç
(here used as a *singular*, see II. 6),
because he aims at the establishment
of the world, desiring to take and
give, for thereby love increases between them; and although it is a
good *middah* for the establishment of
the world, it does not spring from
wisdom, for 'He that hateth gifts
shall live' (Prov. xv. 27), and the
good *middah* is to give and not to
receive" (R. Jonah). He who gives,
"hoping for nothing again," is *chasid*,
or pious. The selfish, grasping man,
who receives and makes no return, is
"wicked."

בנונית] It may be remarked on the
use of this word, which means *intermediate*, that the "via media," and
the "καθ' ὑπερβολὴν ὁδός" of excellence, are regarded as widely divergent.
Maimonides, who attempts to reduce
the ethics of the Mishnah to the Aris-
totelian standard, regards the *chasid*

as one who inclines a little to one
extreme, and performs works of su-
pererogation which it would be hazard-
ous for ordinary people to attempt.
See his *Shemonah Peraqim*, § 4.

חסיד] The word *chasid* here denotes
the opposite of "wicked," and cannot
be shewn to carry any allusion to
a particular sect, the *Essenes* (p. 34),
as some have endeavoured to make
out. For a less improbable derivation
of 'Εσσαῖος see note 1. "Von חסיד es
fortzuleiten wäre sprachlich nicht zu
rechtfertigen" (Jost, *Gesch.* A. 207,
Note). "For although, in spite of
all the attempts which have been
made to explain it, the meaning of
this name is quite uncertain, it certainly cannot be connected with that
of the חסידים" (Kuenen).

[33] A various reading interchanges
the words *loss* and *gain*, and thus
reverses the estimates of the first and
second tempers.

[34] The first character has an evil
or grudging eye with respect to the
things of others. He is unwilling
that they should share with him the

willing to give, but not that others should give, his eye is evil towards the things of others: that others should give, and he should not give, his eye is evil towards his own: he who would give and let others give, is pious: he who will not give nor let others give, is wicked.

20. There are four characters in college-goers[35]. He that goes and does not practise, the reward of going is in his hand: he that practises and does not go, the reward of practice is in his hand: he that goes and practises is pious: he that goes not and does not practise is wicked.

21. There are four characters in those who sit under the wise; a sponge; a funnel; a strainer; and a bolt-sieve[36]. A

credit of liberality: or he is a misanthrope, who is jealous lest his neighbours' possessions should be blessed by their almsgiving, and lest they should enjoy favour with God and man. The truly liberal, on the contrary, is he who "counsels" liberal things (Is. xxxii. 8): who is not only liberal himself, but moves others to be so (Abarbanel).

[35] The relative values of Thalmud and Practice come once more under consideration in this Mishnah. The first character is ἀκροατὴς λόγου, the second ποιητής (James i. 23), the third is both, the last neither. A different turn is given to the "reward of going," in Berakoth 6 b, where it is said אגרא דפרקא רהטא, "the profit of the lecture is the running:" the unintelligent majority profit more by their zeal in going to hear it, than by the teaching as such.

[36] By נפה is meant a fine sieve "of leather or hair," which was made use of in some way for "dressing" meal, and separating the seconds from the fine flour. Cf. Shebi'ith v. 9; Shabbath viii. 2; Menachoth vi. 7, x. 4; Kelim xxvii. 5. Such sieves were used in preparing soleth for the minchah. Thirteen, of different degrees of fineness, were to be used in preparing the 'omer, according to a "halakah to Moses from Sinai:" twelve, for the two loaves: eleven, for the shewbread; or, according to R. Shime'on, the number of siftings was not prescribed, but the soleth was re-sifted as many times as was found necessary. See Menachoth 76 b. It is said by the commentators upon this Mishnah, that the corn was first partially crushed in a bean mill: the husk and powder were then sifted out: and what remained was ground over again, and became SOLETH. The word קמח may denote meal in general (III. 26); but it is here (?) identified with the "dust" of the Menachoth (viii. 2), which was not altogether refuse, but was unfit for SOLETH. Compare the following from the Jalqut on Canticles: "Song most bepraised and exalted of Songs: Rabbi Ele'azar ben 'Azariah made a comparison of it to a man who brings a measure of wheat to a baker, and says, Produce from it QEMACH; and after that produce me from it SOLETH; and after that produce me from it a cake. Thus out of all the wisdom of Solomon there is no SOLETH to Israel except Song of Songs. All the

sponge, which sucks up all; a funnel, which lets in here and lets out there; a strainer, which lets out the wine and keeps back the dregs; a bolt-sieve, which lets out the pollard and keeps back the flour.

22.   All love which depends on some thing[37], when the thing ceases, the love ceases; and such as does not depend on anything, ceases not for ever.

23.   What love is that which depends on some thing? the love of Amnon and Thamar[38]; And that which does not depend on anything? this is the love of David and Jonathan.

Songs are holy: Song of Songs is Holy of Holies." The scholar who treasures up only what is most precious is certainly, *qua* learner, of the highest class; and in this Mishnah he is generally thought to be so regarded. There are, however, some commentators who give precedence to the "strainer"; regarding him as a teacher, who gives out a still more refined doctrine than he has received; whilst the SIEVE typifies the perverted mind which "turns light to darkness, and darkness to light, and feeds others with refuse." See the commentaries תפארת ישראל and יין לבנון. The latter urges, in favour of this view, the analogy of the five preceding groups of fours, in all of which the pious, and the wise, are mentioned third in order. But in Aboth R. N. xl. the order here is different.

Another view is adopted in לב אבות, where the third scholar is taken to be the man who speculates on theosophic mysteries; and the last is the discriminating traditionalist. The comparison is taken, in the one case from wine which drives a man out of his mind, מוציא האדם מדעתו: in the other from bread which strengthens man's heart; but "*the parable of the* SIEVE *seems to me very difficult; for if it were like that which we use*

now, and which LETS THROUGH *the* סולת, *it would not be right, &c.*" It is not easy to render the clause satisfactorily. The word "sieve" alone is inadequate, since it might be used with as much propriety to symbolize the mind which retains the refuse; and indeed it is *prima facie* most natural to think of the fine flour as falling through the sieve, whilst the coarser sort is retained. The commentators quoted at the beginning of this note make SOLETH mean, not precisely "fine flour," but that which after re-grinding becomes fine flour. The technical words *bolter, bolting-cloth,* BOLT-SIEVE, do not embody this idea, but they satisfy the requirements of the case indirectly to a certain extent. A bolter which I have seen sifts the ground corn at once into three sorts. The corn in the bolter descends an incline, passing first over a fine cloth, and then over a coarser cloth: the former lets through the fine flour, *which is caught in a receptacle attached to the machine:* the process is repeated at the second cloth: the third quality, coarse bran, *passes out at the end of the bolter.*

[37] The love which is to be lasting must be disinterested, and independent of all extrinsic considerations. It may be remarked that *ha-dabar* is

24. Whatsoever gainsaying is for the name of Heaven will in the end be established; and that which is not for the name of Heaven[39] will not in the end be established.

25. What gainsaying is that which is for the name of Heaven? the gainsaying of Shammai and Hillel[40]. And that

sometimes τὸ πρᾶγμα in the idiomatic sense of 1 Thess. iv. 6.

[38] "Then Amnon hated her exceedingly; so that the hatred wherewith he hated her was greater than the love wherewith he had loved her" (2 Sam. xiii. 15).

[39] Compare the distinction in Bereshith Rabbah iv. between controversy which is for the ordering of the world, and that which is for its disordering. "To the Name of Heaven, means, for the establishment of the truth of a matter, or to convince of transgression; and not to shew superiority, or to gain a reputation" (A†). For the expression cf. εἰς ὄνομα προφήτου... δικαίου...μαθητοῦ (Matt. x. 41, 42), and see IV. 16. Direct mention of GOD is avoided by the use of שׁמים, as in IV. 7 and elsewhere.

[40] The controversies of Shammai and Hillel, and of their followers, fill a large space in the Talmud. Shammai is self-asserting, and Hillel yielding (p. 23), but the canon is according to Hillel. "Said R. Abba, Said Shemuel, Three years disputed Beth Shammai and Beth Hillel: these said, The halakah is according to us, and these said, The halakah is according to us. Bath Qol went forth and said, These and those are words of the Living God, and the halakah is according to Beth Hillel. But if these and those were words of the Living God, how did Beth Hillel merit that the halakah should be fixed according to them? Because they were yielding and lowly, and taught their own

words and those of their opponents together. Nay, more, *they placed the words of Beth Shammai before their own words* (see *Crit. Note*)...Two years and a half disputed Beth Shammai and Beth Hillel: these said, Better for a man not to have been created than to have been created; and these said, Better for a man to have been created than not to have been created. They concluded, Better for a man not to have been created than to have been created: now that he has been created, let him look well to his doings" ('Erubin 13 b). "From the time when Bath Qol went forth, the halakah is always according to Beth Hillel, and whosoever transgresses the words of Beth Hillel deserves death...And where did Bath Qol go forth? R. Bibi in the name of R. Jochanan said, At Jabneh went forth Bath Qol" (T. J. Sotah III. 4).

"Beth Shammai said, The heavens were created first, and afterwards the earth was created, for it is said, In the beginning God created the heavens and the earth (Gen. i. 1). And Beth Hillel said, The earth was created first, and afterwards the heavens, for it is said, In the day that the Lord God made the earth and the heavens (Gen. ii. 4)...And 'the wise' have said, This and that were created together, for it is said (Is. xlviii. 13), Mine hand also hath laid the foundation of the earth, and my right hand hath spanned the heavens: when I call unto them, they stand up together" (Chagigah 12 a. See above, pp. 31, 32; and cf.

which is not for the name of Heaven? this is the gainsaying of Qorach (Jude 11).

26. Whosoever makes the many[41] righteous, sin prevails not over him; and whosoever makes the many to sin[42], they grant him not the faculty to repent.

27. Moses was righteous, and made the many righteous, and the righteousness of the many was laid upon him[43], for it is said, He executed the justice of the Lord and His judgments, WITH Israel (Deut. xxxiii. 21).

Jerobe'am[42] sinned, and caused the many to sin, (and) the sin of the many was laid upon him, for it is said, Because of the sins of Jerobe'am who sinned, and made Israel to sin (1 Kings xiv. 16, &c.).

28. In whomsoever are three things, he is a disciple of Abraham; and three (other) things, a disciple of Bile'am.

29. A good eye, and a lowly soul, and a humble spirit (belong to) the disciple of Abraham: an evil eye[44], and a

Bereshith Rabbah, XII.); that is to say the (left) hand created the earth, and the right hand at the same time created the heavens.

The Hillelite theory corresponds to 1 Cor. xv. 46: ἀλλ' οὐ πρῶτον τὸ πνευματικόν, ἀλλὰ τὸ ψυχικόν, ἔπειτα τὸ πνευματικόν. The three views propounded above may be taken as texts for three philosophies, of *idealism, evolutionism,* and *dualism.* Matter was in some systems regarded as essentially evil; and its creation, according to a prevalent symbolism, is fitly attributed to the *left hand,* as YAD is taken to mean.

[41] Sin prevails not over him who leads the many to righteousness, since it would be unseemly that the master should be in Gehinnom whilst his disciples are in Paradise (Joma 87 a). *Ha-rabbim,* οἱ πολλοί (Rom. v. 19), denotes the public, or "the general," and, like *çibbur,* the congregation, is contrasted with *ha-yachid,* ὁ εἷς. "*Reshuth ha-rabbim*" is equivalent to "locus publicus." See Mishnah

Surenhusius, Vol. II. p. 1.

[42] This saying, in the form כל מי שחטא והחטיא כו', is cited in Sotah 47 a (cf. Sanhedrin 107 b); and it is added that a magnet suspended the Sin [Rashi *calves*] of Jerobe'am between heaven and earth. "Three kings have no portion in the world to come...Jerobe'am, Achab, and Manasseh" (Sanhedrin XI. 2). "*After* this thing Jeroboam returned not from his evil way. What is, *After?* Said R. Abba, After the Holy One, blessed is He, had taken him by his raiment, and said, Turn thee! and I, and thou, and the son of Jesse will walk in the Garden of 'Eden. He said to Him, Who at the head? The son of Jesse at the head! If so, I had rather not." (Sanhedrin 102 a; 1 Kings xiii. 33.)

[43] Moses is reckoned as cooperating with Israel in all their acts of righteousness: "consequently the זכות of the many depends upon him."

[44] The evil eye corresponds to הקנאה (IV. 30): the soul, ψυχή, is the seat of תאוה, or "appetite": the

swelling soul, and a haughty spirit, to the disciple of Bile'am. And what difference is between the disciples of Abraham and the disciples of Bile'am? The disciples of Bile'am go down to Gehinnom[45], for it is said, But thou, O God, shalt bring them down into the pit of destruction (Ps. lv. 24); but the disciples of Abraham inherit the Garden of 'Eden, for it is said, That I may cause those that love me to inherit SUBSTANCE[45]; and I will fill their treasures (Prov. viii. 21).

30.   R. Jehudah ben Thema said, Be bold as a leopard, and swift as an eagle, and fleet as a hart, and strong as a lion[46], to do the will of thy **Father which is in Heaven.**

spirit, the seat of ambition, and of the desire for כבוד. Compare the threefold classifications in 1 Joh. ii. 16; Aboth II. 15. The three evil qualities in question are ascribed to Bile'am in "Midrash R. Thanchuma" (cited by A†), and in Bemidbar Rabbah xx. He had an evil eye, for it is said: "And Balaam lifted up his eyes, and he saw Israel, &c." (Numb. xxiv. 2). He had a grasping soul, for it is said: "If Balak would give me his house full of silver and gold, &c." (xxii. 18). He had a haughty spirit, for, instead of confessing to the messengers of Balaq that God had altogether forbidden him to go, and to curse the people, he said to them: "Get you into your land: for the Lord refuseth to give me leave to go *with you*" (xxii. 13). "He said to me, It is not consistent with thy honour to go with these, but with their superiors; for he desired my honour. And Balak sent yet again princes, more, and more honourable than they" (ver. 15).

[45] "Four ἰδιῶται have no portion in the world to come...Bile'am, and Doeg, and Achithophel, and Gechazi" (Sanhedrin XI. 2).

"How many years old was Bile'am? It is not expressly written, but from what is written, Bloody and deceitful men shall not live out *half* their days (Ps. lv. 24), he must have been 33 or 34 (that is less than the half of 70) years old. Well hast thou replied to my question! Bile'am's escutcheon appeared to me, and there was written on it, Son of thirty and three years was Bile'am the lame, when captain Phinechas slew him" (Sanhedrin 106 b). This estimate of the age of Bile'am controverts a previous statement that he was living at the time of Pharaoh's edict: "Every son that is born, &c." (Ex. i. 22). He is regarded as a "bloody man," because he occasioned the death of twenty-four thousand Israelites by his advice to Balaq (Numb. xxv. 9; Rev. ii. 14). SUBSTANCE is by Gematria 310 (ש״י) æons (Sanhedrin 100 a).

[46] This saying is quoted, in connexion with 'Aqiba's עשה שבתך חול, כו׳, in Pesachim 112 a; but "Rashi" refers to the Pereq, מקום שנהגו (iv. instead of x.), and ℬ, citing "Rashi," refers to Zebachim. For another application of the saying, see Bemidbar Rabbah on the sepulchre of Moses, toward the end of *Seder Balaq*. The Machazor Vitry makes Masseketh אבות end, very appropriately, at the words, אביך שבשמים.

31. *He used to say, The bold of face to Gehinnom[47]; and the shamefaced[48] to the garden of 'Eden. May it be well-pleasing in thy sight, Lord, our God, and the God of our fathers, that thy city may be built in our days; and give us our portion in thy Thorah.*

32. *Ben Bag-bag said, Turn it, and again turn it; for the all is therein[49], and thy all is therein: and swerve not therefrom, for thou canst have no greater excellency than this.*

[47] The saying 'כו פנים עז(ות) was probably borrowed in the first instance from Masseketh Kallah, together with other matter from which it was afterwards detached. Although now regarded as part of Aboth, it is not found after 'כו כנמר עז הוי in Aboth R. N. xli.: ℭ has a double reading which confirms the suspicion of its spuriousness; and in Masseketh Kallah there is no evidence that it is quoted from Aboth.

[48] "Bashfulness is a good sign." It it said that a man who has a sense of shame will not readily sin, במהרה לא חוטא הוא: "and he who has not פנים בושת, of a surety his ancestors stood not on mount Sinai." (Nedarim 20 a; Jalqut I. 301; Mekiltha, בחדש 'ט). [Ta'anith 7 b.]

For prayers against פנים עזות see Excursus v.

[49] Everything is contained in the Thorah: it was the plan according to which the world itself was created (p. 12). "In it, without doubt, are history and tale: proverb and enigma: correction and wisdom: knowledge and discretion: poetry and word-play: conviction and council: dirge, entreaty, prayer, praise, and every kind of supplication; and all this in a Divine way superior to all the prolix benedictions in human books; to say nothing of its containing in its depths the Names of the Holy One, blessed is He, and secrets of being without end"

(Leb Aboth). Some commentators remark that works on science and philosophy are not needed by the diligent student of Thorah, which contains, not only "all things necessary to salvation," but "all the wisdom of the world." Study Thorah, "and thou wilt not need the books of the philosophers of the nations, and their investigations" (Sforno). Thorah is cheaply purchased by the sacrifice of worldly advantage, "for the whole world and its fulness was created in six days, but the Thorah was only given after forty days" (Shemoth Rabbah xlvii.; Va-jiqra R. xxx.; Chazitha, Cant. viii. 7).

"There is none poor but in knowledge. They say in the West (in Palestine):

דרא ביה כולא ביה דלא דא ביה מה ביה
דא קני מה חסר דא לא קני מה קני :

In whom this is, there is all: in whom this is not, what is there? Hath one gotten this, what lacks? hath he not gotten this, what hath he gotten?" (Nedarim 41 a.)

The ending בה וכולך of this clause in 𝔄 may be illustrated by such expressions as האדם כל זה, This is the whole of man (Eccl. xii. 13); "She is thy life (Prov. iv. 13), and (Deut. xxx. 20) the length of thy days." Compare also the obscure verse Is. xxxviii. 16. The striking reading of the text (cf. "totus in illis")

33. *Ben He-he*[50] *said, According to the toil is the reward.*

would account for the occurrence in MSS. of וֹבה תהוי, "and be in it." In many good MSS. והפך is pointed as pi'el. It may accordingly be taken as a frequentative.

[50] The names of בן בג בג and בן ה' ה' are identified by Gematria. Their sayings are apparently ascribed to Hillel in Aboth R. N. [*A* xii. p. 55], from whom, however, "Bar H. H." is distinguished in Chagigah 9 b. According to one explanation, ב'ג ב'ג denotes, *Son of proselyte parents* גר וגיורת. According to a note in the so-called Machazor Vitry, בן ה' ה' denotes a proselyte, one who has become a *Son of Abraham and Sarah*, whose names were changed by the introduction of the letter ה'. It is added, that "They allude to Ben Bag-bag in Qiddushin and Baba Qamma, and to Ben He-he in הכל חייבין." [Qiddush. 10 b, Baba Q. 27 b, Chagigah 9 b.]

The saying of Ben He-he, like i. 14; ii. 7, is in Aramaic. Final ה is often found for א. Cf. כולה in § 32. In Aboth R. N. xii. [but see *B* xxvii.] the saying, besides being attributed to Hillel (with the addition of לכולהון), is immediately afterwards retorted upon Hillel, when he is surprised to find that wheat costs two dinars a measure in one place, and three dinars at a place more remote. It forms an admirable conclusion to the Masseketh, but was doubtless a proverbial saying not peculiar to ABOTH. [1 Cor. iii. 8 ἔκαστος—κατὰ τὸν ἴδιον κόπον.

ADDENDA.

THE AGES OF MAN.

He used to say, At five years old, Scripture: at ten years, Mishnah: at thirteen[1], the Commandments: at fifteen[2], Thalmud: at eighteen, the bridal: at twenty[3], pursuits: at thirty, strength: at forty, discernment: at fifty, counsel: at sixty, age: at seventy, hoariness: at eighty[4], power: at ninety, decrepitude: at a hundred, it is as though he were dead, and gone, and had ceased from the world.

A metrical paraphrase of the above is given in the commentary *Leb Aboth.* The Midrash on Qoheleth i. 2 reckons seven "vanities," corresponding to the seven æons of man. The child of a year is like a KING, adored by all: at two or three he is like a SWINE, dabbling in filth: at ten he bounds like a KID: at twenty he is like a HORSE, neighing and spirited, and desires a wife: when he has married a wife, behold he is like an ASS: when children are born to him, he is shameless as a DOG in procuring the means of sustenance: when he has grown old he is like an APE—if, at least, he is *'am ha-areç;* but a son of Thorah, like David, is a king though old (1 Kings i. 1). [Joma 22 b Saul when made king was like a *ben shanah* (1 Sam. xiii. 1).]

13

SOLON, and HIPPOCRATES "the physician," in Philo *De Mundi Op.* (Vol. I. 25, 26 ed. Mangey), divided the life of man into *Ten* and *Seven* hebdomads respectively. [See also *Die Lebensalter in der Jüdischen Literatur* by Leopold Löw, Szegedin 1875.]

[1] After THIRTEEN YEARS the boy becomes a *bar miçvah* υἱὸς ἐντολῆς, and enters upon the responsibilities of the higher life. Why (asks the Midrash, on Eccl. ix. 14) is the evil *yeçer* personified as a "great" king? Because it is thirteen years older than the good *yeçer*. [See p. 37, Aboth R. N. XVI. p. 62, ib. p. 166, Midr. Ps. ix. (Buber p. 82), Maim. *Moreh Nebukhim* III. 22.]

[2] It is commonly said that GEMARA, in the sense "completion," properly denotes the series of discussions upon the "Mishnah," which, with the Mishnah itself, made up the "Thalmud." But it is probable that the root גמר should be taken in the sense "learn" by rote, in contrast with סבר *to speculate*: a man should first learn, and afterwards speculate, מאי קמ"ל דליגמר איניש והדר ליסבר (Shabbath 63 a). A† remarks that when he has, in the course of five years, learned the settled Mishnah, which is the גמרא of the Thannaim, he should then proceed to learn סברא, that is "our Thalmud," which we call גמרא. Gemara (cf. Gamra), in the dialect of the Amoraim who arose in Babel, means the unexplained *text of the Mishnah*.

[3] At the age of TWENTY, according to one view, he *is pursued* by "precepts and punishments." So ℭ, rejecting the interpretation that *he pursues* or labours to obtain the means of sustenance for his family. But since in what follows the man's intrinsic qualities are described, it seems best to interpret the phrase as meaning that this is the time of life at which man is most eager in the pursuit of his ideal: it is the age of activity and enthusiasm, in contradistinction to the later ages of settled strength, wisdom, and influence.

[4] The OCTOGENARIAN *must have possessed* great natural power and vigour, which is now, however, well-nigh exhausted, ואם בגבורת שמונים שנה כו' (Ps. xc. 10). [Or if he lives longer it is בגבורתו של מקום]

---

thirteen] He is "minorennis" until *fourteen*, or "In Ecclesiasticis" until thirteen (Buxt. 1364 on נער). Cf. Shulchan 'Arukh *Orach Chayim* 199. 10. The בן י"ג is called איש *man*, for so was Levi at that age (Gen. xxxiv. 25), and in Is. xliii. 21 "This people have I formed" זו *this* is by Gematria thirteen (Magen Aboth). Cf. Löw *Lebensalter*, Machsor Vitry, Niddah 46 a.

twenty] There is a saying that the celestial *beth din* do not punish a man until twenty, see Magen Aboth, Löw *Lebensalter*, Rashi on Num. xvi. 27, Shabbath 89 b, T. J. Bikkur. II. 1 (64 c), T. J. Sanh. XI. 7 (30 b₃₆) ed. princeps or XI. 5 ed. Zitomir 1865, Gen. Rab. 58. 1, Zohar II. 98 a₁. He then "comes of age" for *pursuit* or prosecution מן השמים. Abarbanel in *Nachalath Aboth* gives the interpretation that the בן כ' is quick and impulsive שהס קלי המרון והסס רותח. Another view is that twenty is the age for military service (Machsor Vitry p. 551, Num. i. 3, Deut. xxiv. 5), cf. in Shakespeare's Seven Ages of Man *Then a soldier*. Heb. Auth. P. B. ed. Singer p. 204 (cf. Löw p. 24, Strack on Aboth) "at twenty for seeking a livelihood.'

CHAPTER VI.

PEREQ R. MEIR.

ON THE ACQUISITION OF THORAH.

All Israel have a portion in the world to come[1], for it is said, Thy people also shall be all righteous: they shall inherit the land for ever, the branch of my planting, the work of my hands, that I may be glorified (Sanhedrin xi. 1; Isaiah lx. 21; Rom. xi. 26).

Wise men have taught in the Mishnah tongue; blessed is He that made choice of them and their Mishnah:

1. RABBI MEIR said, Whosoever is busied in Thorah for its own sake merits many things; and not only so, but he is worth the whole world: he is called friend, beloved: loves God, loves mankind: pleases God, pleases mankind. And it clothes him with meekness and fear, and fits him to become righteous, pious, upright and faithful: and removes him from sin, and brings him toward the side of merit. And they enjoy from him counsel, and sound wisdom, understanding, and strength, for it is said, Counsel is mine, and sound wisdom: I am understanding; I have strength (Prov. viii. 14). And it gives him kingdom, and dominion, and faculty of judgment. And they reveal to him the secrets of Thorah; and he is made, as it were, a spring that ceases not, and as a river that flows on increasing. And he becomes modest, and long-suffering, and forgiving of insult. And it magnifies him and exalts him over all things.

2. Said Rabbi Jehoshua' ben Levi, Every day Bath Qol goes forth from Mount Choreb, and makes proclamation and says, Woe to the creatures for contempt of Thorah, for who-

---

[1] This saying is repeated before each of the six Peraqim.

soever does not occupy himself in Thorah is called " blame-worthy[1]," for it is said, As a jewel of gold in a swine's snout, so is a fair woman which is without discretion (Prov. xi. 22). And it saith, And the tables were the work of God, and the writing was the writing of God, graven upon the tables (Ex. xxxii. 16); read not[2] CHARUTH, graven, but CHERUTH, freedom, for thou wilt find no freeman but him who is occupied in learning of Thorah; and whosoever is occupied in learning of Thorah, behold he exalts himself, for it is said, And from Matthanah to Nachaliel: and from Nachaliel to Bamoth (Numb. xxi. 19).

3. He who learns from his companion one section, or one canon, or one verse[3], or one word, (or) even one letter, is bound to do him honour; for thus we find with David king of Israel, who learned not from Achithophel but two things only, that he called him his master, his guide, and his acquaintance,

---

[1] Nazuf serves as a "not(a)riqon" of נֶזֶם זָהָב בְּאַף. An example of another species of נוטריקון occurs in Jalqut I. 298 (Mekiltha בחדש 'ח), where: " Honour thy father and thy mother, that thy days may be long," is said to carry with it the alternative, וְאִם לָאו לְמַעַן יִקְצְרוּן. This latter species is overlooked by Buxtorf s. v., and by his modern editor.

[2] Compare Joh. viii. 32; James i. 25, ii. 12: and see Aboth III. 8; 'Erubin 54 a; 'Abodah Zarah 5 a; Bemidbar Rabbah XVI.; &c.

The exegetical device אל תקרי, " Read not " so but so, is often used in the Talmud, when it is desired to attach a preconceived idea to a Scriptural expression by way of μνημόσυνον. The אל תקרי is not to be taken as evidence that an actual various reading was current. The words to which it is prefixed are confessedly the true reading, with which the darshan makes free for a special purpose.

[3] Some system of reckoning by VERSES was employed by the Jews at a very early period (Qiddushin 30 a); but the present division of the Old Testament into chapters and VERSES was introduced later by the Christians, and adopted from them by the Jews. See the Cambridge University MS. *Additional* 465, of which the " Leaves 245 a—246 a are occupied by a Table of the Christian division of the several books of the Hebrew Bible, drawn up by R. Solomon b. Ishmael...it cannot well be later than the early part of the XIVth century, or at least a hundred years before the date of R. Isaac Nathan, whose concordance, begun in 1437, is usually considered the first instance of the Jewish adoption of the Christian chapters for any purpose. The introduction shews that it was here used for the purpose of ready reference in the continually recurring controversies with the Christians " (Schiller-Szinessy's CATALOGUE, Vol. I. p. 17, on MS. No. 13).

for it is said, But it was thou, a man mine equal, my guide, and mine acquaintance (Ps. lv. 14). And is there not an argument from the greater to the less, that as David king of Israel, who learned not from Achithophel but two words only, called him his master, his guide, and his acquaintance, he who learns from his companion one section, or one canon, or one verse, or one word, or even one letter, is so many times the more bound to do him honour? And honour is nothing but *Thorah*, for it is said, The wise shall inherit honour (Prov. iii. 35). And the perfect shall inherit good (Prov. xxviii. 10). And good is nothing but Thorah, for it is said, For I give you good doctrine, forsake ye not my Thorah (Prov. iv. 2).

4. This is the path of Thorah: A morsel with salt[1] shalt thou eat; Thou shalt drink also water by measure (Ezek. iv. 11); and shalt sleep upon the ground, and live a life of painfulness, and in Thorah shalt thou labour. If thou doest thus, Happy shalt thou be, and it shall be well with thee (Ps. cxxviii. 2): "happy shalt thou be" in this world; "and it shall be well with thee" in the world to come (IV. 3).

5. Seek not greatness for thyself, and desire not honour. *Practise more than thou learnest.* And lust not for the table of kings, for thy table is greater than their table, and thy crown greater than their crown, and faithful is thy task-master who will pay thee the wage of thy work.

6. Greater is Thorah than the priesthood, and than the kingdom; for the kingdom is acquired by thirty degrees, and the priesthood by four and twenty, and the Thorah is acquired by forty and eight things. And these are they, by learning, by a listening ear, by ordered speech, by discernment of heart, by dread, by fear, by meekness, by cheerfulness, by pureness, by attendance upon the wise, by discussion with associates, by the argumentation of disciples, by sedateness; by Scripture, by Mishnah; by little traffic, by little intercourse, by little luxury, by little sleep, by little converse, by little merriment; by long-suffering, by a good heart, by faith in the wise, by acceptance of chastisements; he that knows his place, and that rejoices in his portion, and that makes a fence to his

[1] This is a Talmudic phrase for a poor man's fare (Berakoth 2 b).

words, and does not claim merit to himself; he is loved, loves
God, loves mankind, loves righteousnesses, loves uprightness,
loves reproofs; and retires from honour, and puffs not up
his heart with his learning, and is not forward in decision;
bears the yoke with his associate, and inclines him to the
scale of merit, and grounds him upon the truth, and grounds
him upon peace (I. 19); and settles his heart to his study;
asks and answers, hears and adds thereto; he that learns in
order to teach, and that learns in order to practise; that makes
his master wiser, and that considers what he has heard, and
that tells a thing in the name of him that said it. Lo, thou
hast learned that whosoever tells a thing in the name of him
that said it, brings redemption to the world, for it is said,
And Esther told it to the king in the name of Mordekai
(Esth. ii. 22).

7.   Great is Thorah, which gives life to those who practise
it in this world and in the world to come, for it is said, For
they are life unto those that find them, and health to all
their flesh (Prov. iv. 22); and it saith, It shall be health to
thy navel, and marrow to thy bones (Prov. iii. 8); and it saith,
She is a tree of life to them that lay hold upon her: and
happy is every one that retaineth her (Prov. iii. 18); and it
saith, For they shall be an ornament of grace unto thy head,
and chains about thy neck (Prov. i. 9); and it saith, She
shall give to thine head an ornament of grace: a crown of
glory shall she deliver to thee (Prov. iv. 9); and it saith,
For by me thy days shall be multiplied, and the years of thy
life shall be increased (Prov. ix. 11); and it saith, Length of
days is in her right hand; and in her left hand riches and
honour (Prov. iii. 16): and it saith, For length of days, and
years of life, and peace, shall they add to thee (Prov. iii. 2).

8.   Rabbi Shime'on ben Jehudah, in the name of Rabbi
Shime'on ben Jochai, said, Comeliness, and strength, and
wealth, and honour, and wisdom, and age, and hoariness,
and sons, are comely to the righteous, and comely to the
world, for it is said, The hoary head is a crown of glory;
it is found in the way of righteousness (Prov. xvi. 31); and
it saith, The glory of young men is their strength: and the

beauty of old men is the grey head (Prov. xx. 29); and it saith, Sons' sons are the crown of old men; and the glory of sons are their fathers (Prov. xvii. 6); and it saith, Then the moon shall be confounded, and the sun ashamed, when the Lord of hosts shall reign in mount Zion, and in Jerusalem, and before his ancients gloriously (Is. xxiv. 23).

Rabbi Shime'on ben Manasia said, These (?) seven qualities which the wise have reckoned to the righteous were all of them confirmed in Rabbi and his sons.

9. Said Rabbi Jose ben Qisma, Once I was walking by the way, and there met me a man, and he gave me "Peace"; and I returned him "Peace." He said to me, Rabbi, from what place art thou? I said to him, From a great city of wise men, and doctors, am I. He said to me[4], Rabbi, should it be thy pleasure to dwell with us in our place, I will give thee a thousand thousand dinars of gold, and goodly stones, and pearls. I said to him, If thou shouldest give me all the silver, and gold, and goodly stones, and pearls that are in the world, I would not dwell but in a place of Thorah; and thus it is written in the book of Psalms, by the hands of David, king of Israel, The law of thy mouth is better unto me than thousands of gold and silver (Ps. cxix. 72). Moreover in the hour of a man's decease not silver, nor gold, nor goodly stones, and pearls accompany the man, but Thorah and good works alone, for it is said, When thou goest, it shall lead thee; when thou sleepest, it shall keep thee; and when thou awakest, it shall talk with thee (Prov. vi. 22). "When thou goest, it shall lead thee," in this world: "when thou sleepest, it shall keep thee," in the grave: "and when thou awakest, it shall talk with thee," in the world to come. And it saith, The silver is mine, and the gold is mine, saith the Lord of hosts (Hagg. ii. 8).

10. *Five*[5] possessions possessed the Holy One, blessed is He,

---

[4] Observe the absence of conjunctions: "I said to him...said he to me," &c. The same peculiarity is found in parts of the New Testament. Cf. Joh. iv. xxi., which are quite in the Talmudic style in this respect.

[5] The text of ℭ reads FOUR possessions, instead of FIVE. Cf. note א. Gen. xiv. 19 is not a good proof that Abram was a קנין.

in his world, and these are they: THORAH, one possession; HEAVEN AND EARTH, one possession; *Abraham, one possession;* ISRAEL, one possession; THE SANCTUARY, one possession. Thorah, whence? because it is written, The Lord possessed me in the beginning of his way, before his works of old (Prov. viii. 22); Heaven and Earth, whence? because it is written, Thus saith the Lord, The heaven is my throne, and the earth is my footstool: where is the house that ye build unto me? and where is the place of my rest (Is. lxvi. 1)? and it saith, O Lord, how manifold are thy works! in wisdom hast thou made them all: the earth is full of thy possessions (Ps. civ. 24); Abraham, whence? because it is written, And he blessed him, and said, Blessed be Abram of the most high God, possessor of heaven and earth (Gen. xiv. 19); Israel, whence? because it is written, Till thy people pass over, O Lord, till the people pass over, which thou hast possessed (Ex. xv. 16); and it saith, To the saints that are in the earth, and to the excellent, in whom is all my delight (Ps. xvi. 3); The Sanctuary, whence? because it is written, The place, O Lord, which thou hast made for thee to dwell in, the sanctuary, O Lord, which thy hands have established (Ex. xv. 17); and it saith, And he brought them to the border of his sanctuary, even to this mountain, which his right-hand had possessed (Ps. lxxviii. 54).

11. Whatsoever the Holy One, blessed is He, created in his world, he created not but for his glory, for it is said, Every one that is called by my name: for I have created him for my glory, I have formed him; yea, I have made him (Is. xliii. 7); and it saith, The Lord shall reign for ever and ever (Ex. xv. 18).

Rabbi Chanania ben 'Aqashia said[1], The Holy One, blessed is He, was pleased to give merit to Israel: therefore he multiplied unto them Thorah and precepts, for it is said, The Lord is well pleased for his righteousness' sake; he will magnify the law, and make it honourable (Is. xlii. 21).

[1] This saying is repeated at the end of each of the six Peraqim.

EXCURSUS I.

Thorah. Qabbalah. The Decalogue. (See I. 1, p. 11.)

1. It is very important to notice some of the uses of the words Thorah and Qabbalah. Those of the latter are especially striking.

" We have two Thoroth (said Shammai in reply to a would-be proselyte), the written Thorah, תורה שבכתב, and the oral Thorah, תורה שבעל פה " (Shabbath 31 a). Some things were communicated by mouth, and some things were communicated by writing, and we should not know which of them are the more precious but for what is said: "...for after the tenor of (עַל פִּי) these words I have made a covenant with thee and with Israel " (Ex. xxxiv. 27). This shews that those which were BY MOUTH (בפה) are the more precious (T. J. Peah II. 6. Cf. T. J. Megillah IV. 1 ; T. B. Gittin 60 b). In T. J. Berakoth I. 7 it is said in the course of a discussion, in the name of R. Jochanan : " Words of Soferim are akin to words of Thorah and more beloved than words of Thorah, for (Cant. i. 2), Thy LOVE is better than WINE (sc. of the Thorah)" :

דודים דברי סופרים לדברי תורה וחביבים יותר מד״ת. כי טובים דודיך מיין.

It is added that whereas the Thorah contains both *light* and *weighty* precepts, the words of the Soferim are all of the latter class, חמורים. He who transgresses their words deserves death, for " whoso breaketh an HEDGE, a serpent shall bite him" (Eccl. x. 8). In 'Abodah Zarah ii. 5 it is discussed whether the reading in Cant. i. 2 is דּוֹדֶיךָ or דּוֹדַיִךְ, and the decision is given in favour of the former[1]. That is to say, the congregation of Israel addresses God (not *vice versa*), and says, as it is further explained in the Gemara (35 a) : "LORD of the world, the words of Thy love are sweeter unto me than the wine of Thorah." The authority of the Thorah was final, and its decisions without appeal, as is expressed for example by the saying, *That which is of the Thorah needs not confirmation*, ודאורייתא לא בעי חיזוק (Rosh ha-Shanah 19 a, cf. Jebamoth 85 b), whereas words of Soferim do need חיזוק, *confirmation*. Upon the latter compare Kethuboth 83 b, 84 a, where it is said that, " The wise have confirmed, or given force (עשו חיזוק) to, their words more than—or as much as—to those of Thorah." In R. ha-Shanah 19 a it is said by ר' אשי, that "words of Qabbalah are like to words of Thorah." Other sayings tending to the exaltation of παράδοσις and scribe-law might be given ; but in drawing inferences from them allowance must be made for their rhetorical and

[1 So Agadath Shir Hashirim line 251 (ed. Schechter from Cod. De Rossi 541, Camb. 1896), giving the pointing דּוֹדֶיךָ.]

14

dialectic character. They are commonly put forward as private opinions in debate, rather than as authoritative decisions.

The word **Thorah** has a special application to the Pentateuch, or Law of Moses (Deut. i. 5; Josh. viii. 31; 1 Kings ii. 3; Luke xxiv. 44; Joh. i. 17); but it is also applied to the remaining Scriptures. Thus in Sanhedrin 91 b the verses Josh. viii. 30; Ps. lxxxiv. 5; Is. lii. 8 are cited as Thorah. But the preeminence of Thorah as compared with the remaining Scriptures is brought out by the saying of R. Jochanan in T. J. Megillah i. 7: "The Prophets and the Hagiographa will cease but the five books of Thorah will not cease." Resh Laqish adds that the book Esther likewise and the הלכות of the oral Thorah will never cease, for הליכות עולם לו (Hab. iii. 6).

2. The word **Qabbalah** means διαδοχή, and denotes *tradition* (παράδοσις), regarded from the point of view of reception. It is applied not only to what is generally understood by TRADITION, but even to the Prophetic Scriptures and the Hagiographa[1], as below:

(i)   MISHNAH Tha'anith II. 1 (Joel ii. 13):

ובקבלה הוא אומר וקרעו לבבכם ואל בגדיכם.

and in QABBALAH he saith, And rend your heart, &c.

(ii)   T. J. Kilaim IX. 1 (Ezek. xliv. 17):

פירש בקבלה ולא יעלה עליהם צמר בשרתם כו'.

(iii)   T. J. Niddah III. 3 (Ps. cxxxix. 16):

ועליו הוא מפורש בקבלה גולמי ראו עיניך כו'.

(iv)   Rosh ha-Shanah 7 a (Zech. i. 7):

אמר רבינא דבר זה מתורת משה רבינו לא למדנו מדברי קבלה למדנו ביום עשרים וארבעה לעשתי עשר חדש הוא חדש שבט.

Said Rabina, This matter we have learned not from the Thorah of Mosheh our lord: from words of QABBALAH we have learned it, "Upon the four and twentieth day of the eleventh month, which is the month Sebat..."

(v)   Niddah 25 a (Job x. 10):

ועליו מפורש בקבלה הלא כחלב תתיכני וכגבינ' תקפיאני כו'.

(vi)   Mekiltha, מס' דפסחא ה' (Cant. iv. 12):

ועליהם מפורש בקבלה גן נעול אחותי כלה גל נעול מעין חתום.

(vii)   Mekiltha, מס' דפסחא י"ד (Jer. ii. 2):

ועליהם מפורש בקבלה הלוך וקראת באזני ירושלם.

(viii)   Sifra, מס' דמלואים (Mal. ii. 5):

ומנין שאהרן רודף שלום בישראל שנאמר ויראו כל העדה כי גוע אהרן ויבכו את אהרן שלשים יום כל בית ישראל...וכן הכתוב מפורש על ידי אהרן בקבלה בריתי היתה אתו החיים והשלום שהיה רודף שלום בישראל כו'.

---

[1] See Excursus III. § 4; Zunz *Gottesdienstl. Vorträge* pp. 44, 353 (1832).

And whence (appears it) that Aaron pursued peace in Israel? Because it is said, "And when all the congregation saw that Aaron was dead, they mourned for Aaron thirty days, even all the house of Israel" (Numb. xx. 29, see p. 21) ... And thus is the SCRIPTURE[1] interpreted of Aaron in QABBALAH : "My covenant was with him of life and peace," because he pursued peace in Israel.

(ix)   Sifre on Numb., פסקא קי"ב (Ps. l. 20; Is. v. 18):

עליו מפורש בקבלה תשב באחיך תדבר בבן אמך תתן דופי אלה עשית והחרשתי
דמית היות אהיה כמוך כסבור אתה שמא כדרכי בשר ודם דרכי המקום
אוכיחך ואערכה לעיניך בא ישעיה ופירש בקבלה הוי מושכי העון בחבלי השוא
וכעבותות העגלה חטאה· תחילתו של חטא הוא דומה לחוט של כוביא
אבל סופו (להיות) כעבותות העגלה חטאה· ר' אומר העושה מצוה אחת לשמה
אל ישמח על אותה מצוה שלסוף גוררת מצות הרבה והעובר עבירה אחת אל
ידאג עליה לסוף שגוררת עבירות הרבה שמצוה גוררת מצוה ועבירה גוררת
עבירות :

It is expressly said thereupon in QABBALAH, "Thou sittest and speakest against thy brother, &c." ... Isaiah came and interpreted in QABBALAH, "Woe unto them that draw iniquity with cords of vanity, and sin as it were with a cartrope." (The remainder of the passage illustrates Aboth IV. 5, q. v.)

(x)   Sifre on Deut., פסקא מ"ח (Eccl. x. 8):

בא שלמה ופירש עליו בקבלה ופורץ גדר ישכנו נחש· הא למדת שכל הפורץ
גדרים של חכמים לסוף פורעניות באים עליו· ר"ש בן יוחי אומר הרי הוא נפש
שבעה תבום נופת כו'·

Solomon came and interpreted it in QABBALAH, "and whoso breaketh an hedge, a serpent shall bite him." Lo! thou hast learned that whoso breaketh hedges (cf. I. 1) of the wise, eventually punishments come upon him. R. Sh. ben Jochai said, Behold he is "A full soul that loatheth an honeycomb" (Prov. xxvii. 7).

In the above examples, to which more might be added, we find quoted as QABBALAH, or tradition, Isaiah, Jeremiah, Ezekiel, Joel, Zechariah, Malachi, Psalms, Job, Song of Songs, Ecclesiastes. The Pentateuch being called THORAH (iv), or SCRIPTURE (viii), the other Books are expressly described as being, on the contrary, QABBALAH. This mode of speaking may be assumed to be a survival from a remote period at which the Pentateuch alone had been accepted as canonical; for it could scarcely have *arisen* in comparatively recent times. It must be taken into account in the discussion whether the Sadducees rejected "tradition" only, for a difficulty may arise in defining accurately what was understood by "tra-

---

[1] Miqra also is used specially of the Pentateuch. See below § 3. iii. *b*.

dition." Granted that they accepted all the canonical books, what weight would they have allowed, when their distinctive tenets were at stake, to an argument from a Prophet which appeared to contradict the Thorah or Pentateuch, to which a marked preeminence was and is assigned by Jews in general? Cf. Excursus III.

3. On the Jewish division of the **Decalogue,** which differs from our division of the so-called "Ten Commandments," see Excursus IV.

The Decalogue is sometimes singled out as the revelation to Moses from Sinai. At other times the conception of revelation is idealised, and it is said that all Scripture, Mishnah, and Gemara were made known to Moses. A connecting link between these extremes is the view that the entire Law is latent in the Decalogue; in accordance with which view special treatises have been written—as by Sa'adiah Gaon (cf. Rashi on Ex. xxiv. 12), and the author of the anonymous treatise in the Cambridge University MS. *Additional* 493—in which each of the 613 commandments is referred to some one of the "Ten Words" of the Decalogue. The number of the commandments is given in Makkoth 23 b : "613 commandments were spoken to Moses—365 *negative*, according to the number of days in the solar-year; and 248 *positive*, corresponding to the members of the human body... תורה by Gematria is equal to the number 611. The other two, אנכי and לא יהיה לך (i.e. the first and second of the Ten Words), *we* heard מפי הגבורה." The next page gathers up the whole 613 successively into 11, 6, 3, 1, as follows. First comes David who rests them all upon eleven, according to clauses of Ps. xv. 2—5, from הולך תמים to ושחד כו'. Then Isaiah (xxxiii. 15) rests them on six. Micah (vi. 8) on three. Amos (v. 4) on the one, "seek ye ME." But this, says Rab Nachman bar Isaac, may mean, דרשוני בכל התורה כולה; and he prefers to rest them upon a saying in Hab. ii. 4, which assumes great prominence in the New Testament likewise (Rom. i. 17; Gal. iii. 11; Heb. x. 38), וצדיק באמונתו יחיה, And the just shall live by his "FAITH."

The following are some of the statements which have to be taken into account in estimating the Rabbis' views of revelation. It is evident that some of their dicta were not intended to be taken literally, but are the paradoxes of idealists, which leave us in some doubt as to how much they supposed to have been revealed explicitly to Moses.

(i) T. J. Megillah iv. 1 :

מקרא משנה ותלמוד ואגדה ואפילו מה שתלמיד וותיק עתיד להורות לפני ..

רבו כבר נאמ' למשה מסיני.

Scripture, Mishnah, and Thalmud, and Agadah, and even that which the diligent scholar was destined to point out before his master, were already spoken to Moses from Sinai.

(ii) T. B. Megillah 19 b :

‎...מאי דכתיב ועליהם ככל הדברים אשר דבר ה׳ עמכם בהר· מלמד שהראהו
‎הקב״ה למשה דקדוקי תורה ודקדוקי סופרים ומה שהסופרים עתידין לחדש·

(iii) Berakoth 5 a :

‎...מאי דכתיב ואתנה לך את לוחות האבן והתורה והמצוה אשר כתבתי
‎להורותם· לוחות אלו עשרת הדברות· תורה זה מקרא· והמצוה זו משנה· אשר
‎כתבתי אלו נביאים וכתובים· להורותם זה הגמרא· מלמד שכולם נתנו למשה
‎מסיני·

What means the Scripture : "And I will give thee (a) the tables of
stone ; (b) the Thorah ; (c) the commandment ; (d) which I have written ;
(e) that thou mayest teach them" (Ex. xxiv. 12) ? The expressions signify,
(a) the Decalogue ; (b) Miqra (= Scripture, or Pentateuch) ; (c) Mishnah ;
(d) Prophets and Hagiographa ; (e) Gemara—all of which are shewn to
have been given to Moses from Sinai.

(iv) Shemoth Rabbah XXVIII. :

"And God spake ALL these words, saying—" Said R. Isaac, What the
prophets were about to prophesy in every generation they received from
Mount Sinai, for thus Moses said to Israel (Deut. xxix. 14), ‎ואת אשר איננו
‎פה עמנו היום, not ‎עמנו עומד היום, but simply ‎עמנו היום. These are
the souls (of those) about to be created, who had no substance, and of
whom "standing" could not be predicated. Although they existed not in
that hour, each one of them received his own. Cf. Mal. i. 1, "...IN THE
HAND OF Malachi" (not IN THE DAYS OF Malachi), because the prophecy was
already IN HIS HAND from Mount Sinai, but till that hour authority had
not been given him to prophesy. And so Isaiah (xlviii. 16) says, ‎מעת היותה
‎אני, from the day that the Thorah was given on Sinai there I was, and
received this prophecy, "and now the Lord God and His Spirit hath sent
me." Till then authority had not been given him to prophesy. And not
all the prophets only, but also the sages that were to arise in successive
generations, each one of them received his own from Sinai, according to
the scripture : "These words the LORD spake unto all your assembly...with
a great voice, AND HE ADDED NO MORE" (Deut. v. 22). R. Jochanan said,
Each voice was divided into seven voices, and they were divided into
seventy tongues.

(v) Jalqut I. 285 (cf. Mekiltha and Thanchuma) :

"All the Ten Words were spoken superhumanly with a single utterance
(‎דבור)...It is said that all the ‎דברות in the Thorah were spoken with
a single ‎דבור."

The oral Halakhoth given to Moses on Sinai are said in T. J. Peah II. 6
to have been all embodied in the Mishnah : but elsewhere we read that
very much of the original tradition is lost.

EXCURSUS II.

The Great Synagogue. (See I. 1, p. 11.)

1. *The period of the* MEN OF THE GREAT SYNAGOGUE.

From statements in Aboth about the Great Synagogue it would seem that it was regarded as comprising a *succession* of teachers, for (1) the "Prophets" previously spoken of belonged to successive generations, and (2) Simon Justus himself is said to have been one of the last of the Great Synagogue, which must therefore have covered the interval between the cessation of "prophecy" and the date, or supposed date, of Simon. That the chain was intended to be continuous appears likewise from Peah II. 6 (𝔄, fol. 4 a) where it is said (see p. 14) that the PAIRS received from the PROPHETS :

אמ' נחום הלבלר מקובל (?) מר' מיאשא שקיבל מאבא שקיבל מן הזוגות
שקיבלו מן הנביאים הלכה למשה מסיני הזורע את שדהו כו'.

In Aboth R. N. I. the line of succession from Moses is given in the form : *Joshua : Elders : Judges : Prophets : Hag., Zech., Malachi : G.S.*

The **Great Synagogue** (as we may conclude in accordance with a prevalent tradition, which attributes its establishment to Ezra) arose some time after the return from the Captivity, and included "*alle die bis zum Simon an der Spitze der Gesetzlehre in Judäa standen*" (Jost, *Gesch.* A. 42). It was natural however that later generations —led partly by the popular tendency to simplify the more obscure parts of history by the summation of scattered events, and partly by the desire to make the Great Synagogue seem still greater, and its decisions more venerable—should have come to regard the various Traditions relating to it as marking a single epoch. It is accordingly said to have been a college consisting of 120 contemporaries, all of whose names are recorded in the Holy Scriptures. Their number is determined from a comparison of Berakoth 33 a with Megillah 17 b ; the expression אבה"ג in the one passage corresponding to מאה ועשרים זקנים, ובהם כמה נביאים, "120 elders, including several prophets," in the other. The number of 120 is made up from the 84 (or 83, LXX. and T. J. Chagigah III. 8) signatories mentioned in Neh. x. 2—28 : the 33 (or 34) "prophets" supposed to be named in Neh. viii. 4, 7 and ix. 4, 5 ; and the 3, Chaggai, Zekariah, and MALACHI (whom Targum Jonathan on Mal. i. 1 identifies with EZRA). To account for the number of 85 (for 84) "elders" in T. J. Megillah I. 7 it has been proposed to insert a name before וישוע in Neh. x. 10, or to include Ezra. In T. J. Berakoth II. 4 the number 120 is said to include upwards of 80 prophets. Herzfeld, to whose *Geschichte* &c. (I. 381, Excurs. 12) the reader may be referred for additional details, rightly regards the number 120 as fictitious, whether it be assumed to be

the number of the Great Synagogue at any one epoch, or the sum total of
its numbers in successive periods. In the pages following he attempts to
identify it with the Synhedrin. Its name is not mentioned by Josephus or
Philo; but some have imagined a reference to it in 1 Macc. vii. 12; xiv. 28.
Little, however, is known about the MEN OF THE GREAT SYNAGOGUE, except
that the Mishnah regards them as having received the Tradition from the
Prophets, and preserved it down to the age of Simon Justus. The passage
of Aboth which gives the lower limit is cited, together with I. 19, in T. J.
Megillah III. 7 :

תמן תנינן שמעון הצדיק היה משירי כנסת הגדולה הוא היה אומר על ג'
דברים העולם עומד על התורה ועל העבודה ועל גמילות חסדים וישלשתן בפסוק
אחד ואשים דברי בפיך כו'.

תמן תנינן רבן שמעון בן גמליאל אומר על ג' דברים העולם עומד על הדין
ועל האמת ועל השלום ושלשתן דבר אחד ... אמר רבי מנא ושלשתן בפסוק
אחד אמת ומשפט שלום כו' :

2.   *The work of the* GREAT SYNAGOGUE.

...וכיון שעמדו אכה"ג החזירו הגדולה ליושנה

And when the men of the Great Synagogue arose, they restored the
GREATNESS to its pristine state.

T. J. Berakoth VII. 4; Megillah III. 8.

In a parallel passage of the Babli (Joma 69 b) we find : "Why was their
name called the men of the Great Synagogue ? Because they restored the
CROWN to its pristine state, שהחזירו עטרה ליושנה," where the crown might
refer to THE NAME, or to the Thorah (Aboth IV. 19); but, as in the "Jerushalmi," the Scripture-proofs adduced favour the reading גדולה rather than
עטרה. Their work, as suggested by their "Three Words" in Aboth I. 1,
was to define, to teach, and to develope, the Law. Their first saying, "Be
deliberate in judgment," is applied in Aboth R. N. I. to the gradual formation of the Canon. "At first it was said that PROVERBS, SONG OF SONGS,
QOHELETH[1] were apocryphal, because they spoke παραβολάς, and that they
were not of the Kethubim, until the men of the Great Synagogue arose and
interpreted them." It is said that they "wrote down (כתבו) EZEKIEL, and
the TWELVE (minor prophetical books), DANIEL, and MEGILLATH ESTHER"
(Baba Bathra 15 a); and that they composed *inter alia* the "18 Benedictions" of the Jews' Prayer-Book. The Masorah also is attributed to them
(Buxt. Tiber. Pt. I., cap. x.). Lastly, besides fixing the Canon it was necessary
to "make a fence to the Thorah": to surround it with a MARGIN of casuistry :
to evolve the principles which underlay its words : to develope and apply
its decrees, accommodating them to the varied requirements of the time.

---

[1] This book was long disputed, "QOHELETH does not defile the hands,
according to Beth Shammai: but Beth Hillel say it defiles the hands"
('Edioth v. 3).

Antigonus. Zadok. Sadducee. (See I. 3, p. 13.)

1. According to a Jewish tradition, it was the saying of Antigonus, in Aboth I. 3, which gave rise to Sadduceeism. The great authority for this view of the case is Aboth de-Rabbi Nathan, Chapter V. :

אנטיגנוס איש סוכו קבל משמעון הצדיק הֹהֹא אל תהיו כעבדים המשמשין
את הרב עֹמֹ לקבל פרס אלא היו כעבדים המשמשין את הרב שלא עֹמֹ לקבל
פרס ויהי מורא שמים עליכם כדי שיהיה שכרכם כפול לעתיד לבא. אנטיגנוס
איש סוכו היו לו שני תלמידים שהיו שונין בדבריו שונין היו לתלמידים
ותלמידים לתלמידיהם עמדו ודקדקו אחריהן ואמרו מה ראו אבותינו לומר
אפשר שיעשה פועל מלאכה כל היום ולא יטול שכרו ערבית אלא אלו יודעין
אבותינו שיש העולם הבא ויש תחיית המתים לֹא הֵיו אומרי׳ כך עמדו ופרשו
מן התורה ונפרצו מהם שתי פרצות צדוקין וביתוסין. צדוקין על שם צדוק
ביתוסין על שם ביתוס שהיה משתמש בכלי כסף וכלי זהב כל ימיו לֹא היתה
דעתו גסה עליו אלא צדוקין אומ׳ מסורה בית פרושין שהן מצערין עצמן בעולם
הזה ובעולם הבא אין להן כלום[1] :

"Antigonus of Soko received from Shime‘on ha-Çaddiq. He used to say, Be not as slaves that serve the Rab on the terms of receiving recompense; but be as slaves that serve the Rab not on the terms of receiving recompense; and let the fear of Heaven be upon you; that your reward may be doubled for the time to come.

Antigonus of Soko had two disciples, who repeated his words: and they repeated them to (their) disciples, and their disciples to their disciples. THEY AROSE, and refined after them, and said, What did our fathers imagine, in saying that a labourer might do work all the day and not receive his reward at evening? Nay, but if our fathers knew that there was the world to come, and that there was a revival of the dead, they would not have spoken thus. THEY AROSE and separated from the Thorah; and two sects were formed from them, Çaduqin and Baithusin; Çaduqin, after the name of Çadoq: Baithusin, after the name of Baithos, who was served in vessels of silver and vessels of gold all his days: his mind was not puffed up (or

---

[1] For a transcript of the above from a Bodleian MS. (No. 408, fol. 72) I am indebted to Dr Neubauer. [From שהיה to the end (al. ׳והיו כו) is a *tosefeth*, cf. Ab. R. N. p. 26 ed. Schechter. On *Das Trihäresion* see Graetz *Gesch. d. Juden* III. n. 10 (1878).]

were served all *their* days : *their* mind &c.) : but the Çaduqin said, The Pharisees have a tradition that they must worry themselves in this world ; and in the world to come there is naught for them."

The above, which is also cited in the 'Aruk, seems to represent Sadduceeism &c. as having arisen from the perversion and misunderstanding of the saying of Antigonus, not immediately, but after the lapse of a considerable period. If, however, Çadoq and Baithus, or Boethus, were not the actual originators of the heresies in question, why were those heresies named after them ? But Maimonides on Aboth i. 3, and 'Obadiah of Bertinoro on Jadaim iv. 6, describe Çadoq and Baithus as the actual heresiarchs. It is an open question whether Aboth R. N. v. embodies an authentic tradition, or a mere theory based upon an assumption that Judaism had been in the same phase of development from time immemorial, and that Sadduceeism could never have been otherwise than reactionary.

2. *The Sadducees* "SONS OF ZADOQ."

Geiger's theory[1] was that the Çadoqites were a sacerdotal conservative party, named after the Çadoq who anointed Solomon (1 Kings i. 39). Ezekiel several times speaks of the SONS OF ÇADOQ, בני צדוק, and he expressly describes them as the priestly family κατ᾽ ἐξοχήν, to the exclusion of other Levites : " And the Levites that are gone away far from me, when Israel went astray, which went astray away from me after their idols ; they shall even bear their iniquity...they shall not come near unto me, to do the office of a priest unto me...But I will make them keepers of the charge of the house, for all the service thereof, and for all that shall be done therein. But THE PRIESTS the Levites, THE SONS OF ZADOK[2], that kept the charge of my sanctuary when the children of Israel went astray from me, they shall come near to me to minister unto me, and they shall stand before me to offer unto me the fat and the blood, saith the Lord God" (Ezek. xliv. 10—15). Passing on to the New Testament, we find the Sadducees mentioned in the Synoptic Gospels as opponents of the Pharisees : in St John's Gospel they are not mentioned at all, but the combination CHIEF PRIESTS and Pharisees (vii. 32, 45 ; xi. 47, 57 ; xviii. 3) occurs instead of Pharisees and SADDUCEES (Matt. iii. 7 ; xvi. 1—12 ; Acts xxiii. 7) ; and the identification of the Sadducees with the sacerdotal party seems to be completed by Acts v. 17, ἀναστὰς δὲ ὁ ἀρχιερεὺς καὶ πάντες οἱ σὺν αὐτῷ, ἡ οὖσα αἵρεσις τῶν Σαδδουκαίων, κ.τ.λ. We see then that Çadoq was a venerable priestly name of the age of Solomon: that the sons of Çadoq were singled out as THE priestly line from the captivity and thenceforward ; and that the Çadoqites were still the priestly party in Apostolic times. Hence it may be granted

---

[1] *Urschrift* pp. 20 &c.

[2] Cf. 2 Chron. xxxi. 9, 10 : " Then Hezekiah questioned with the priests and the Levites concerning the heaps. And Azariah THE CHIEF PRIEST OF THE HOUSE OF ZADOK answered him..."

that Geiger's theory is not devoid of probability, although on the other side it is urged, "that not a single trace of this supposed designation of Sons of Zadok occurs in the Jewish post-exile literature—which would be altogether inexplicable, had that name been in general use."

3. According to the last mentioned theory, Sadduceeism was of ancient growth: according to Aboth R. N. v. it was a comparatively modern phase of opinion. The two theories have been combined by supposing that the "Sadducees" belonged to the ancient Zadoq-party, but that their views were coloured at a later period by an infusion of GREEK thought.

4. *The tenets of the* SADDUCEES.

The Sadducees said, μὴ εἶναι ἀνάστασιν (Matt. xxii. 23), and our Lord answers by an indirect argument from the Pentateuch[1], instead of bringing proofs of a more obvious and direct kind from other parts of Holy Scripture. Hence it has been inferred that they accepted the Pentateuch only, and rejected the Nebiim and Kethubim. On the other side it is asserted that this inference is wholly inaccurate: that they accepted the three divisions of the Old Testament, and rejected only the extra-Scriptural "Tradition," and scribe-law. The truth, perhaps, lies *in medio*. The Jews in general esteemed, and still esteem, the Pentateuch more highly than the Prophets and the Hagiographa:

ולכך אני אומ'[2] שנקראו נביאים וכתובים דברי קבלה שהיו מקובלין [בהן]
ובאין מימות משה ומכל מקום אינן שוין לחמשה ספרים שכולן מצות וחוקים כו':

"And therefore I say that the PROPHETS and HAGIOGRAPHA are called words of QABBALAH, because they were received by διαδοχή, and they came from the days of Moses; *and by no means are they equal to the* FIVE BOOKS, which are all precepts and ordinances, &c."

If the Sadducees were of the number of those who insisted most strongly upon the superior authority of the Pentateuch, it might in certain cases be nearer to the truth to say that they rejected the Prophets and Hagiographa than to say that they accepted them. If a Prophet were quoted in opposition to Moses, they would have questioned the authority of the Prophet. For an example of such contrariety see Makkoth 24 a:

א'ר יוסי בר חנינא ארבעה גזרות גזר משה רבינו על ישראל באו ארבעה
נביאים ובטלום כו':

"Said R. Jose bar Chanina, Four גזרות pronounced Moses our Lord upon Israel: four prophets came and made them void[3]. Moses said (Deut. xxxiii. 28), Israel then shall dwell in safety...Amos (vii. 5), Cease, I beseech Thee, &c. Moses said (Deut. xxviii. 65), And among these nations

---

[1] For illustrations, see Lightfoot's *Hor. Hebr.* on Matt. xxii. 32; Joh. iv. 25.
[2] See col. 2 of the commentary on ABOTH in the MS. A†. A omits בהן. [In Machsor Vitry 462₁₅ ed. Hurwitz read משה for יהושע.]
[3] Νόμον οὖν καταργοῦμεν (=בטל) διὰ τῆς πίστεως; (Rom. iii. 31).

thou shalt find no rest: Jeremiah (xxxi. 2), Israel, when I went to cause him to rest. Moses said (Exod xx. 5), *Visiting the iniquity of the fathers upon the children :* Ezekiel (xviii. 20), *The soul that sinneth, it shall die.* Moses said (Lev. xxvi. 38),.And ye shall perish among the heathen : Isaiah (xxvii. 13), And it shall come to pass in that day, that the great trumpet shall be blown..."

It would follow that a party answering more or less closely to the description of the Sadducees must have existed, under some name or other, before the times of Antigonus, if we might assume that there was a time at which the Pentateuch was the whole BIBLE, and the other books had not as yet been fully recognised as canonical; but their comparative depreciation of the other books would have a tendency to diminish in course of time, when these had once been generally received into the Canon. "The Sadducees," writes Josephus (*Ant.* XIII. 10. 6), "are able to persuade none but the rich, and have not the populace obsequious to them." Their influence was on the wane, and it received a fatal blow in the destruction of Jerusalem. Their power as a sacerdotal oligarchy then vanished, and in after times the name Sadducee was freely used (p. 40) as a synonym for a heretic, regarded as one who *receded* from an acknowledged standard of orthodoxy.

5. *The* BOOKS *of the Sadducees.*

a. We have no authentic remains of Sadducee literature; but it has been suggested, with a certain plausibility, that the book ECCLESIASTICUS approximates to the standpoint of the primitive Çaduqin, as regards its theology, its sacerdotalism, and its want of sympathy with the *modern* Soferim. The name of EZRA is significantly omitted from its catalogue of worthies : "It remains singular," remarks Kuenen, "that the man whom a later generation compared, nay made almost equal, to Moses, is passed over in silence...Is it not really most natural that a Jesus ben Sirach did not feel sympathy enough for the first of the Scribes, to give him a place of honour in the series of Israel's great men ?" The modern SCRIBE was to Ben Sirach an unworthy descendant of the primitive WISE, in accordance with Eli'ezer ha-Gadol's lament over the degeneracy of a later age :

מיום שחרב בית המקדש שרו חכימיא למהוי כספריא כו' :

"Ex quo Templum devastatum est[1], cœpere SAPIENTES similes esse SCRIBIS ; Scribæ ædituis ; Æditui, vulgo hominum ; Vulgus vero hominum in pejus indies ruit, nec quis rogans, aut quærens, superest. Cui ergo innitendum ? Patri nostro cœlesti."

b. In Sanhedrin 100 b, the BOOKS OF SADDUCEES, and the BOOK OF BEN SIRA, are placed side by side on the *Index expurgatorius :*

תנא בספרי צדוקים רב יוסף אמר בספר בן סירא נמי אסיר למיקרי :

---

[1] MISHNAH, Sotah IX. 15 (Surenhusius, Vol. III. p. 308). 𝔄 reads תלמידיא, for חזניא : עמא, for דארעא 'ע : &c. See fol. 100 b.

EXCURSUS IV.

Qeriyath Shema'. The Decalogue. (See II. 17, p. 38.)

1. The **Shema'**, or **Audi**, is a portion of Scripture which commences:
"**Hear**, O Israel, &c."; and is commonly understood to comprise the
following passages :

DEUTERONOMY vi. 4—9 :

Hear, O Israel: The LORD our God *is* one LORD[1]: And thou shalt love
the LORD thy God with all thine heart, and with all thy soul, and with all
thy might. And these words, which I command thee this day, shall be
in thine heart : And thou shalt teach them diligently unto thy children,
and shalt talk of them when thou sittest in thine house, and when thou
walkest by the way, and when thou liest down, and when thou risest up.
And thou shalt bind them for a sign upon thine hand, and they shall be as
frontlets between thine eyes. And thou shalt write them upon the posts
of thy house, and on thy gates.

DEUTERONOMY xi. 13—21 :

And it shall come to pass, if ye shall hearken diligently unto my commandments which I command you this day, to love the LORD your God,
and to serve him with all your heart and with all your soul, That I will
give *you* the rain of your land in his due season, the first rain and the
latter rain, that thou mayest gather in thy corn, and thy wine, and thine
oil. And I will send grass in thy fields for thy cattle, that thou mayest eat
and be full. Take heed to yourselves, that your heart be not deceived,
and ye turn aside, and serve other gods, and worship them ; And *then* the
LORD'S wrath be kindled against you, and he shut up the heaven, that there
be no rain, and that the land yield not her fruit ; and *lest* ye perish quickly
from off the good land which the LORD giveth you. Therefore shall ye lay
up these my words in your heart and in your soul, and bind them for a sign
upon your hand, that they may be as frontlets between your eyes. And ye
shall teach them your children, speaking of them when thou sittest in thine
house, and when thou walkest by the way, when thou liest down, and when
thou risest up. And thou shalt write them upon the door-posts of thine
house, and upon thy gates : That your days may be multiplied, and the
days of your children, in the land which the LORD sware unto your fathers
to give them, as the days of heaven upon the earth.

[1] The Authorized Version gives an impossible construction, as is at once
seen when "LORD" is replaced by the יהוה of the original. Read, YHVH is ONE,
or sole, comparing Zech. xiv. 9.

NUMBERS XV. 37—41 :

And the LORD spake unto Moses, saying, Speak unto the children of Israel, and bid them that they make them fringes in the borders of their garments throughout their generations, and that they put upon the fringe of the borders a ribband of blue : And it shall be unto you for a fringe, that ye may look upon it, and remember all the commandments of the LORD, and do them ; and that ye seek not after your own heart and your own eyes, after which ye use to go a whoring : That ye may remember, and do all my commandments, and be holy unto your God. I *am* the LORD your God, which brought you out of the land of Egypt, to be your God : I *am* the LORD your God.

But the *first* of the above passages is the שמע proper : the *second* is called, from its commencement, וְהָיָה אִם שָׁמֹעַ : and the *third*, פרשת ציצת, or ויאמר. The order of the three is accounted for in Berakoth II. 2, " Said R. Jehoshua' ben Qorchah, Why does שמע come before והיה אם שמע ?— why but that one may RECEIVE UPON HIM THE YOKE OF THE KINGDOM OF HEAVEN[1] first, and after that receive upon him the yoke of the command-ments ? And והיה כו' before ויאמר ? because the former is employed day and night, and the latter only in the daytime."

The opening words of the Audi are written with two *literæ majus-culæ*,

שְׁמַע יִשְׂרָאֵל יְהוָֹה אֱלֹהֵינוּ יְהוָֹה אֶחָד :

which have been accounted for in various ways[2]. But it was obviously intended that the syllables which they conclude should be pronounced with the utmost clearness and emphasis ; and that the copyist should be guarded against all possibility of error, especially as regards the Daleth, since, as it is said at the beginning of Midrash Thanchuma, " If thou make Daleth into Resh thou destroyest the whole world, for it is said (Ex. xxxiv. 14), כי לא תשתחוה לאל אחר, For thou shalt worship no *other* God."

They cool the flames of hell (p. 38) for him who reads the AUDI ומדקדק באותיותיה. And what is this *diqduq othiyoth?* it is the distin-

---

[1] The above is a common expression (cf. p. 54) for reciting the AUDI, which contains an acknowledgement of the sole kingship of YHVH. Let a man, when he has cleansed himself, lay his Tefillin, and recite the Audi, and pray. This is the " *complete kingdom of Heaven,* מלכות שמים שלימה " (Berakoth 15 a).

[2] For other meanings which have been assigned to the two large letters in the Shema', see BA'AL HA-TURIM *in loc.*, and Buxt. TIBERIAS, Pt. 1, Chap. XIV. The two together make the word 'ED, *witness*, and indicate that, if Israel are not God's witnesses (Is. xliii. 10 ; xliv. 8), He will be a quick witness against them (Mic. i. 2 ; Mal. iii. 5, &c.). Taken separately they indicate that יהוה is the One God in the ד quarters of the earth, and over its ע (= 70) nations, all of whom are summoned to hear (Is. xxxiv. 1): that Israel has ע names: the Thorah ע " faces," aspects, or interpretations, &c.

guishing clearly between the lameds in בכל לבבכם, or between *mem* and *mem* in ואבדתם מהרה, &c. (Debarim Rabbah II.).

2. *The* DECALOGUE *embodied in the* SHEMA'.

שעשרת הדברות הן הן גופה של שמע :

In St Mark's Gospel (xii. 29) the opening words of the AUDI are said to constitute the πρώτη ἐντολή, which, according to note 36, p. 56, comprises all the precepts of the Thorah. In the Jerusalem Talmud, *loc. cit.*, the several Λόγοι or Ῥήματα of the Decalogue are discovered in the Shema':

"Why do they read these two (?) sections every day? R. Simon said, Because there is written in them, 'lying down,' and 'rising up.' R. Levi said, Because the Ten Words are contained in them:

(i) *I,* YHVH, *am thy God.*

     Hear, O Israel, YHVH *is our God* (Deut. vi. 4).

(ii) *Thou shalt have no other gods but* ME.

     YHVH *is One* (Deut. vi. 4).

(iii) *Thou shalt not take the Name of* YHVH *thy God in vain.*

     And thou shalt love YHVH *thy God* (Deut. vi. 5): he who loves the King will not swear by his Name, and lie.

(iv) *Remember the Sabbath day to keep it holy.*

     That ye may remember, &c. (Num. xv. 40): R. says, This is the Sabbath precept, which counterpoises all the precepts of the Thorah, for it is written (Neh. ix. 14), And madest known unto them thy holy Sabbath, and commandedst them precepts, and statutes, and Thorah—shewing that it counterpoises all the precepts of the Thorah.

(v) *Honour thy father and thy mother.*

     That your days may be multiplied, and the days of your children (Deut. xi. 21).

(vi) *Thou shalt do no murder.*

     And lest ye perish quickly (Deut. xi. 17): he that slays is slain.

(vii) *Thou shalt not commit adultery.*

     And that ye seek not after your own heart and your own eyes (Num. xv. 39): Said R. Levi, The heart and the eye are two negotiators of sin. It is written (Prov. xxiii. 26), My son, give me thine heart, and let thine eyes observe my ways: the Holy One, blessed is He, saith, If thou hast given me thy heart and thine eye, I know that thou art MINE.

(viii) *Thou shalt not steal.*

That thou mayest gather in thy corn (Deut. xi. 14): thy corn, and not thy neighbour's corn.

(ix) *Thou shalt not bear false witness against thy neighbour.*

I, YHVH, am your God (Num. xv. 41). And it is written, ויהוה אלהים אמת (Jer. x. 10). What means אמת (*Truth*)? R. Abuhu said, That He is a living God, and King of the world. R. Levi said, The Holy One, Blessed is He, saith, If thou hast witnessed false witness against thy neighbour, I impute it unto thee as if thou hadst witnessed against Me, that I created not heaven and earth.

(x) *Thou shalt not covet thy neighbour's house.*

And thou shalt write them upon the door posts of thine house (Deut. xi. 20): thine house, and not thy neighbour's house."

3. *The public daily reading of the* DECALOGUE *discontinued.*

It may interest the Liturgiologist to notice that the daily recital of the Decalogue is said, in both Talmuds, to have been at one time customary, and to have been discontinued later for anti-christian reasons.

T. J. BERAKOTH I. 8 [*al.* 5]:

בדין הוה שיהו קורין עשרת הדברות בכל יום ומפני מה אין קורין אותן מפני טענת המינין שלא יהו אומ' אלו לבד' ניתנו לו למשה בסיני :

"Of right they should read the Ten Words every day. And on account of what do they not read them? on account of the cavilling of the heretics, so that they might not say, These only were given to Moses on Sinai."

T. B. BERAKOTH 12 a:

וקורין עשרת הדברות שמע והיה אם שמוע ויאמר אמת ויציב ועבודה וברכת כהנים· אמר רב יהודה אמר שמואל אף בגבולין בקשו לקרות כן אלא שכבר בטלום מפני תרעומת המינין· תניא נמי הכי רבי נתן אומר בגבולין בקשו לקרות כן אלא שכבר בטלום מפני תרעומת המינין רבה בב"ח סבר למקבעינהו בסורא אמר ליה רב חסדא כבר בטלום מפני תרעומת המינין אמימר סבר למקבעינהו בנהרדעא א"ל רב אשי כבר בטלום מפני תרעומת המינין :

"And they read the Ten Words, and Shemaʻ, &c. Said Rab Jehudah, Said Shemuel, In the provinces also they sought to read them, only that they had already stopped them on account of the murmuring of the heretics..."

4. *The division of the so-called* TEN COMMANDMENTS.

The choice is generally supposed to lie between the present Anglican, and the Roman, mode of dividing the Decalogue; but "An arrangement, probably of very early date, unlike either of these, is found in the common text of the Targum of Palestine, and has been adopted by Maimonides, Aben-Ezra, and other Jewish authorities down to the present day. The First *Word* is identified with, *I am the* LORD *thy God which brought thee out of the land of Egypt* (which cannot of course be properly called a *Commandment*), and the second Word is made...to include what is divided in our Prayer Book into the First and Second Commandments. The subject-matter itself seems to suggest grave and obvious objections to (this arrangement). There is a clear distinction between polytheism and idolatry which entitles each to a distinct commandment." (*Speaker's Commentary*, Ex. xx. 21.)

But (*a*) the latter objection to the Hebrew division—however true the remark may be in itself—is not confirmed by the language of the Pentateuch[1]; and (*b*) the former likewise, which is based upon the use of the word 'Commandment,' is seen to be of little force when it is noticed that the original דבר is not adequately represented by *Commandment* or ἐντολή. The latter is the rendering of מצוה, a term which is not specially[2]

---

[1] The second WORD, taken as above, runs thus: "There shall not be to thee אלהים אחרים beside Me——(thou shalt not make unto thee a graven image, &c.)——thou shalt not BOW DOWN TO THEM, nor serve them; for I, יהוה, thy God, am A JEALOUS God, &c." It is unnatural to cut off the statement, "For I...am a jealous God," from its relation to the "other Elohim," to whom it is forbidden in express terms to "bow down." Compare Ex. xxxiv. 14, which illustrates this view in the most striking way: כי לא תשתחוה לאל אחר כי יהוה קנא שמו אל קנא הוא. In like manner Deut. vi. 14, 15 forbids to "go after OTHER GODS"..."for the Lord thy God is a JEALOUS God." The assumed distinction between the Elohim and the images which are forbidden in the second WORD, is overthrown by their identification in ver. 23 of the very same chapter of Exodus which contains the Decalogue: "Ye shall not make with me GODS OF SILVER, neither shall ye make unto you GODS OF GOLD." Compare: "Up, make us gods...These be thy gods, O Israel, which brought thee up out of the land of Egypt...And MOSES returned unto the Lord and said, Oh, this people have sinned a great sin, and have made them GODS OF GOLD" (Ex. xxxii. 1, 4, 8, 23, 31). "Thou shalt make thee no molten gods" (Ex. xxxiv. 17). The value of Philo's testimony—which is adduced (see Suicer *Thesaurus s. v.* Δεκάλογος) in favour of the distinction between the Elohim and the images—must be allowed to be somewhat reduced by his known predilection for refinements.

[2] But amongst the 613 Commandments, the First, Second, &c. "Words" are reckoned. See Excursus I. § 3. The root צוה is also used in the Bible in *relation to* the Ten Words, but not directly *of* them.

applied to the DECALOGUE. The Jews do not speak of "The Ten Commandments," but of "The ten דברים" (Ex. xxxiv. 28, &c.) or עשרת הדברות; and they regard אנכי not merely as a separate one of THE TEN WORDS, or Divine utterances, but as the greatest of them all.

In favour of the Hebrew division may be cited:

(1) T. J. Berakoth I. 8. See above, § 2.

(2) Targum 'Jonathan,' Ex. xx. 2, 3. [Notice the readings in "Machsor Vitry" ed. Hurwitz p. 337.]

דבירא קדמאה כד הוה נפיק מן פום קודשא יהי שמיה מברך הי כזיקין
והי כברקין והי כשלהוביין דינור למפד דינור מן ימיניה ולמפד דאישא מן שמאליה
פרח וטייס באויר שמיא וחזר ומתחמי על משיריתהון דישראל וחזר ומתחקק על
לוחי קיימא דהוון יהיבין בכף ידוי דמשה ומתהפיך בהון מן סטר לסטר ובכן
צווח ואמר עמי בני ישראל אנא הוא אלהכון די פרקית ואפיקית יתכון פריקין
מן ארעא דמצראי מן בית שעבוד עבדיא :

דבירא תניינא כד הוה נפיק כו' הוה צווח ואמר עמי בית ישראל לא יהוי
לך אלהא אוחרן בר מני :

"**The First Word**, when it had gone forth from the mouth of the Holy One, blessed be his Name, was like sparks, and lightnings, and flames of fire; a torch of fire was on its right hand, and a torch of flame on its left hand: it flew and hovered in the air of the heavens, and returned and was seen over the encampments of Israel; and returned and graved itself upon the tables of the covenant which were given into the hands of Moses; and turned itself upon them from side to side, and cried out thus, and said, My people, sons of Israel, I *am your God*, who freed you, and brought you out freed from the land of the Egyptians, from the bondage-house of slaves."

"**The Second Word**, when it had gone forth...cried and said, My people, house of Israel, there shall not be to thee another God, beside Me."

(3) Jalqut I. 2. [Othioth de R. 'Aqiba, p. 55 b, Warsaw 1885.]

"And whence is it that Aleph is called One? because it is said (Deut. xxxii. 30), איכה ירדף אחד אלף. And whence is it that ha-Qadosh, blessed is He, is called One? because it is said (Deut. vi. 4), Hear, &c. יהוה אחד. And whence is it that the Thorah is called One? because it is said (Num. xv. 29), תורה אחת יהיה לכם. אנכי (is at the) head of all the דברות, and Aleph (is at the) head of all the letters, אנכי ראש כל הדברות ואלף ראש כל האותיות:"

(4) Midrash Chazitha (Cant. v. 11).

"For twenty-six generations was the letter Aleph making complaint before the Holy One, blessed is He: LORD of the world, Thou hast set me

at the head of the letters, and didst not create the world by me, but by
Beth, for it is said, בְּרֵאשִׁית God created the heaven and the earth. The
Holy One, blessed is He, said to it, My world and its fulness were not
created but by the merit of Thorah (Prov. iii. 19). To-morrow I shall
be revealed, and shall give the Thorah to Israel, and I will set thee at the
beginning of all the דברות, and will open with thee first."

(5) Mekiltha, דבחדש ח׳ מס׳; Jalqut I. 299.

" How were the TEN WORDS given ? five on this Table, and five on that.
(i) There was written, *I, YHVH, am thy God ;* and opposite to it, *Thou shalt
do no murder.* The Scripture shews that, whosoever sheds blood, the
Scripture imputes to him as if he diminished THE LIKENESS of the King.
A parable of a king of flesh and blood, who entered into a province, and
they set up effigies, and made images, and sunk dies to him. After a time,
they overturned his effigies, shattered his images, and effaced his dies,
and they 'diminished the likeness' of the king. So, whosoever sheds
blood, the Scripture imputes to him as if he diminished THE LIKENESS of
the King, for it is said (Gen. ix. 6), Whoso sheddeth man's blood, &c.
(ii) It was written, *Thou shalt have no other, &c. ;* and it was written
opposite to it, *Thou shalt not commit adultery.* The Scripture shews that,
whosoever practises strange worship, the Scripture imputes to him as if he
committed adultery from God, for it is said (Ezek. xvi. 32), As a wife that
committeth adultery, which taketh strangers instead of her husband. And
it is written (Hos. iii. 1), Then said the Lord unto me, Go yet, love a
woman beloved of her friend, and an adulteress, &c. (iii) It was written,
Thou shalt not take the Name of the Lord thy God in vain ; and opposite
to it was written, *Thou shalt not steal.* It shews that whosoever steals
will at last come to false swearing, for it is said (Jer. vii. 9), Will ye steal,
murder, and commit adultery, and swear falsely? And it is written
(Hos. iv. 2), By swearing, and lying, and killing, and stealing, and commit-
ting adultery. (iv) It was written, *Remember that thou keep holy the sabbath day ;* and opposite to it was written, *Thou shalt not bear false witness.*
The Scripture shews that whosoever profanes the sabbath witnesses before
Him who spake, and the world was, that He did not create his world in six
days, and did not rest on the seventh ; and whosoever keeps the sabbath
witnesses before Him who spake, and the world was, that He created his
world in six days, and rested on the seventh, for it is said (Is. xliii. 10), Ye
are my witnesses, saith the Lord. (v) It is written, *Honour thy father
and thy mother ;* and opposite to it is written, *Thou shalt not 'covet.'* The
Scripture shews that whosoever 'covets,' at last begets a son that curses his
father and his mother, and honours one who is not his father. Therefore
were the TEN WORDS given, five on this Table, and five on that. So says
R. Chanina ben Gamliel. And the wise say, Ten on this Table, and ten on
that Table, for it is said (Deut. v. 22), These words the Lord spake, &c.
and He wrote them in two Tables of stone."

The above examples will suffice to shew that the present Hebrew division of the Decalogue is not without "adequate authority." According to Josephus (Suicer I. 831) the First Word *teaches* ὅτι θεός ἐστιν εἷς, καὶ τοῦτον σέβεσθαι μόνον, and the Second Word *commands* μηδενὸς εἰκόνα ζῴου ποιήσαντας προσκυνεῖν. This arrangement, as regards the Second Word, is preferred by many Christians on the ground that it more distinctly forbids image-worship. But it is open to the objection that it seems to admit the existence of real "other gods," who are not to be classed with elílím, or idols proper, like "all the gods of the nations" in Psalm xcvi. 5 (p. 120).

[According to the Mekhilta, the Words on the two Tables respectively (Ex. xx. 2—12, 13—17) were or commenced :

כבד.	זכור.	לא תשא.	לא יהיה.	אנכי.
לא תחמד.	לא תענה.	לא תגנב.	לא תנאף.	לא תרצח.

Thus each of the five Words on the first Table and none on the second mentions יהוה אלהיך "the LORD thy God." In the Midrash לקח טוב or "Pesikta Sutarta" of R. Tobiah ben Eliezer (II. p. 139 ed. Buber, Wilna 1880) there is a plan of the two Tables with the Ten Words written briefly as above, five on each.

Philo (*De Decalogo & Quis r. d. Haeres?*), Josephus (*Ant.* III. 6), and Irenaeus (II. 36 ed. Harvey) likewise divide the Ten Words into two Fives, the former of which, according to Philo, is the ἀμείνων πεντάς. This, he says, begins *a Deo patre* and *desinit in parentes qui ad illius imitationem gignunt particulariter* (Suicer 832). In Qiddushin 30 b the honour of parents is likened to that of God, and it is said, as also in Niddah 31 a, that *three are* שותפין באדם *partners in* the making of *a man*, the Holy One (who contributes the breath of life) and the father and the mother.

On the Ten Words see also Friedmann's edition of the "Pesikta Rabbati," 98 b—125 b (Wien 1880), noticing the comparison of them to the Ten Sayings by which the world was created (108 a).]

EXCURSUS V.

The Lord's Prayer. (See v. 30, p. 95.)

The expressions and ideas of the Lord's Prayer (Matt. vi. 9—13, cf. Luke xi. 2—4) may be illustrated from the Rabbinic writings, and for the most part they rest ultimately on the Old Testament itself.

Πάτερ ἡμῶν ὁ ἐν τοῖς οὐρανοῖς[1]] "Is not he thy Father ?" (Deut. xxxii. 6). "Doubtless thou art our Father...thy Name is from everlasting" (Is. lxiii. 16; lxiv. 8). Both אבינו alone and אבינו שבשמים are found in Jewish forms of Prayer. [See *The Authorised Daily Prayer Book of the United Hebrew Congregations of the British Empire* edited by Mr Singer.]

"R. Ele'azar ben 'Azariah expounded, That ye may be clean from all your *sins before the Lord* (Lev. xvi. 30); transgressions between a man and HA-MAQOM the day of expiation expiates: transgressions between a man and his fellow the day of expiation expiates not, until he reconcile his fellow. Said R. 'Aqiba, Happy are ye, Israel; before whom do ye purify yourselves? Who purifies you? YOUR FATHER WHICH IS IN HEAVEN" (Joma VIII. 9).

"On whom have we to lean? on OUR FATHER WHICH IS IN HEAVEN" (Sotah IX. 15).

... to do the will of thy Father which is in Heaven
(Aboth v. 30).

ἁγιασθήτω τὸ ὄνομά σου] The NAME of God is an especially Hebraic expression (p. 67), and it is often used to avoid express mention of God. Cf. משכן שמך (Ps. lxxiv. 7). 'Holiness' is an attribute of God's Name in the Bible *passim*. "Neither shall ye profane my holy Name; but I will be hallowed among the children of Israel: I am the Lord which hallow you" (Lev. xxii. 32). "They shall SANCTIFY MY NAME, and sanctify the Holy One of Jacob, and shall fear the God of Israel" (Is. xxix. 23). "And I will sanctify my great Name, which was profaned among the heathen" (Ezek. xxxvi. 23).

"Any benediction which is without mention of HA-SHEM (i.e. יהוה) is no benediction at all" (Berakoth 40 b).

ἐλθέτω ἡ βασιλεία σου] The coming of the KINGDOM, and the sanctifying of the NAME, are brought together in some passages of the Old Testament, thus: "And the Lord *shall be king* over all the earth: in that day shall there be one[2] Lord, and HIS NAME[3] one" (Zech. xiv. 9).

---

[1] In St Luke *l.c.* Westcott and Hort omit ἡμῶν ὁ ἐν τοῖς οὐρανοῖς, and the petitions γενηθήτω κ.τ.λ., ἀλλὰ ῥῦσαι κ.τ.λ.

[2] Or "YHVH shall be ONE."

[3] The Qabbalists equate שמו to רצון by Gematria.

"Any benediction which is without MALKUTH (kingdom—mention of God as KING) is no benediction at all" (Berakoth 40 b).

γενηθήτω τὸ θέλημά σου, ὡς ἐν οὐρανῷ καὶ ἐπὶ γῆς] "Whatsoever the Lord pleased, that did he in heaven, and in earth" (Ps. cxxxv. 6).

"And what is this 'oratio brevis'? R. El. said, Do thy will in heaven above, and give rest of spirit to them that fear Thee *beneath* [Tosefta Zuck. p. 7₂ בארץ *on earth*]; and do what is good in thine eyes. Blessed art Thou, O Lord, that hearest prayer" (Berakoth 29 b).

On the correspondence between the heavenly and the earthly, see p. 50. Cf. Matt. xvi. 19; xviii. 10, 18; Luke xv. 10. "May it be thy will, O Lord, our God[1], to make peace in the family above, and in the family below" (Berakoth 16 b—17 a).

τὸν ἄρτον ἡμῶν τὸν ἐπιούσιον δὸς ἡμῖν σήμερον[2]] This petition, addressed to Πάτερ ἡμῶν ὁ ἐν τοῖς οὐρανοῖς, corresponds to Ex. xvi. 4: "Behold, I will rain BREAD FROM HEAVEN for you; and the people shall go out and gather דבר יום ביומו, τὸ τῆς ἡμέρας εἰς ἡμέραν, A CERTAIN RATE EVERY DAY." The occurrence of several allusions (Ps. lxxviii. 24; cv. 40; Nehem. ix. 15; Sap. Sol. xvi. 20; &c.) to the corn, or bread, of heaven makes it sufficiently probable *a priori* that the Lord's Prayer also should have some reference to the giving of the manna. Compare Joh. vi. 32: "Verily, verily, I say unto you, Moses gave you not that bread from heaven; but MY FATHER GIVETH YOU the true BREAD FROM HEAVEN"; and notice that in Sap. Sol. xvi. 27—28 the gathering of the manna is associated with prayer and thanksgiving, "For that which was not destroyed of the fire, being warmed with a little sunbeam, soon melted away (Ex. xvi. 21): That it might be known, that we must prevent the sun to give thee thanks, and at the day-spring **pray unto Thee.**"

The expression דבר יום ביומו—which is found again in 2 Kings xxv. 30, Jer. lii. 34, Dan. i. 5—is discussed in Mekiltha ויסע פ״ב מס' (Jalqut I. 258) on Ex. xvi. 4:

"*From heaven:* from the good treasure of heaven, for it is said (Deut. xxviii. 12), The Lord shall open unto thee his good treasure, the heaven. Rabban Shime'on ben Gamliel said, Come and see how beloved were Israel before HA-MAQOM! and because they were beloved before him he changed on their account the order of nature: he made for them the lower upper, and the upper lower. Hitherto the bread had come up from the earth, and the dew down from heaven, for it is said (Deut. xxxiii. 28), A land of corn and wine; also his heavens shall drop down dew. But now the things are changed: the bread comes down from heaven, and the dew ascends from the earth, for it is written, *I will rain bread from heaven for you*, and it is written (ver. 14) ותעל שכבת הטל.

And the people shall go out and gather:—not that they were to go

---

[1] יהי רצון מלפניך ה' אלהינו שתשים שלום בפמליא של מעלה ובפמליא של מטה.

[2] Or...δίδου ἡμῖν τὸ καθ' ἡμέραν (Luke xi. 3).

out to the enclosures and gather, but they were to go out to the ἔρημοι and gather.

A certain rate every day: Rabbi Jehoshua' said, *So that a man should gather on the day for the morrow, as on sabbath eve for sabbath.* R. El. ha-Moda'i said, *So that a man should not gather on the day for the morrow, as on sabbath eve for sabbath,* for it is said, דבר יום ביומו, matter of a day in its day[1], He who created the day created its provision (פרנסתו). Hence R. El. ha-Moda'i said, Whosoever has what to eat to-day, and says, What shall I eat to-morrow? lo! such an one is wanting in faith, for it is said, That I may **prove** him, whether he will walk in my law, or not. Rabbi Jehoshua' said, If a man studies two canons at morning, and two at evening, and attends to his business all the day, they reckon to him as if he fulfilled the whole Thorah altogether. Hence Rabbi Shime'on ben Jochai used to say,

לא נתנה תורה לדרוש אלא לאוכלי המן

Thorah was not given to search into, except to the eaters of the manna.

How? Can a man sit and search, and not know whence he is to eat and to drink, and whence to be clad and covered (Matt. vi. 31)? The Thorah was not given to search into, except to the eaters of the manna; and second to them are (the priests,) the eaters of the Therumah."

On the meaning of ἐπιούσιος.

The stricter etymological view requires that ἐπιούσιος should be derived from ἐπιέναι, rather than from ἐπεῖναι. The much controverted derivation from ἐπιέναι through the medium of ἡ ἐπιοῦσα ἡμέρα may be said to be *prima facie* less simple than one which refers the word more directly to its assumed root. But it is proposed here merely to illustrate the more direct interpretation of ἐπιούσιος from a Hebrew standpoint.

L. DE DIEU, according to *Poli Synopsis*, gives the explanation:

"Panis ἐπιούσιος est panis *succedaneus*, hoc est, qui pani jam absumpto succedit, et ut succedat, natura corporis postulat."

According to this view, ἄρτος ἐπιούσιος is לחמא ܠܚܡܐ ܐܡܝܢܐ, תדירא, or לחם תמיד, bread which is successive or continual. It is natural to pray πάντοτε [תמיד] δός ἡμῖν τὸν ἄρτον τοῦτον (Joh. vi. 34): "Let thy lovingkindness and thy truth תמיד יצרוני, continually[2] preserve me" (Ps. xl. 12); and, at the same time, to pray that in each day so much

---

[1] The manna was gathered in the morning to supply the needs of the on-coming day. It was given "with a bright countenance," in the light, because it was prayed for rightly; whereas the quails were given "with a dark countenance," and in the darkness, because they were not prayed for rightly. See Mekiltha, and Rashi, on Ex. xvi. 8, 21.

[2] Cf. היום ובכל יום in the prayer cited below from Berakoth 60 b (p. 129).

only may be given as is needed for that day. Compare: "And he did eat bread continually [תמיד] before him all the days of his life. And his allowance was a continual allowance given him of the king, a daily rate for every day, all the days of his life" (2 Kings xxv. 29—30, Jer. lii. 34), Ex. xxix. 38, Numb. xxviii. 3, Is. lii. 5. [Aboth III. 25 "continually every day."]

[Notice in the *Birkath ha-Mazon* "And by His great goodness *continually* hath food not failed us, and may it not fail us for ever and ever for His great name's sake...We thank Thee...for the food wherewith Thou dost feed and sustain us *continually every day* ובכל עת ובכל שעה," and compare Auth. P. B. p. 37 "Who...in Thy goodness renewest the creation *every day continually*," ib. 232 "and to such as are hungry and thirsty give bread and water unfailingly," Heb. תן לחמם ומים נאמנים give their bread and water sure (Is. xxxiii. 16). Cureton (*Remains of a very antient recension of the Four Gospels in Syriac*, 1858) renders the Old Syriac ולחמן אמינא of Matt. vi. 11 "*And our bread constant of the day give us*," comparing Num. iv. 7 התמיד Syr. *aminoith*. See also Dict. of Bible art. *Syr. Versions* by S. P. T. (1863).]

καὶ ἄφες ἡμῖν τὰ ὀφειλήματα ἡμῶν, ὡς καὶ ἡμεῖς ἀφήκαμεν τοῖς ὀφειλέταις ἡμῶν] The principle, "As thou hast done, it shall be done unto thee" (Obadiah 15), is fully accepted by the Rabbis, and pervades their literature. See p. 31. Ἄφες ἀδίκημα τῷ πλησίον σου, καὶ τότε δεηθέντος σου αἱ ἁμαρτίαι σου λυθήσονται (Ecclus. xxviii. 1—5).

"May it be Thy will, O Lord, my God, and God of my fathers, that I may not be harsh with my companions, nor my companions be harsh with me. That we may not make defiled the pure, nor make pure the defiled. That we may not BIND THE LOOSED, NOR LOOSE THE BOUND, that I should be shamed for this αἰών, and for the αἰών to come[1] (T. J. Berakoth IV. 2).

"May it be Thy will... that hatred of us may not come into the heart of man, nor hatred of man come into our heart; and that envy of us may not come into the heart of man, nor envy of man come into our heart: and may Thy Thorah be our work all the days of our life, and may our words be תחנונים before Thee" (T. J. *loc. cit.*).

καὶ μὴ εἰσενέγκῃς ἡμᾶς εἰς πειρασμόν] The word πειρασμός is used in the New Testament to denote outward and physical, no less than inward and spiritual, trials. The words למען אנסנו in Ex. xvi. 4 are an additional connecting link between that verse and the Lord's Prayer. The Jews' Morning Prayer (cf. Berakoth 60 b) has the petition ואל תביאנו...לידי נסיון.

"Said Rab, Never should a man bring himself into the hands of temptation; for behold David, King of Israel, brought himself into the hands

---

[1] Καὶ ὃ ἂν δήσῃς ἐπὶ τῆς γῆς, ἔσται δεδεμένον ἐν τοῖς οὐρανοῖς (Matt. xvi. 19). Lightfoot illustrates the common Hebrew expressions *bind*, *loose* by "a double decad" of examples. The example in the text is noteworthy on account of its allusion to the two worlds.

of temptation, and stumbled : he said…(Ps. xxvi. 2) Examine me, O Lord, and PROVE me" (Sanhedrin 107 a).

ἀλλὰ ῥῦσαι ἡμᾶς ἀπὸ τοῦ πονηροῦ] *But deliver us from the evil.* It is disputed whether THE EVIL is ὁ πονηρός (1 Joh. v. 18, &c.), or τὸ πονηρόν. Compare 2 Thess. iii. 3 ; 2 Tim. iv. 18 ῥύσεταί με ὁ Κύριος ἀπὸ παντὸς ἔργου πονηροῦ, καὶ σώσει εἰς τὴν βασιλείαν αὐτοῦ τὴν ἐπουράνιον· ᾧ ἡ δόξα εἰς τοὺς αἰῶνας τῶν αἰώνων. ἀμήν.

The word רע, in the Old Testament, is applied to *things* and to *persons*. Compare : "The angel who redeemed me רע מכל" (Gen. xlviii. 16). "And hath kept his servant מרעה" (1 Sam. xxv. 39). "Depart מרע¹, and do good" (Ps. xxxiv. 15). "I make peace, and create רע" (Is. xlv. 7). "Deliver me, O Lord, רע מאדם" (Ps. cxl. 2). "The adversary and enemy is this המן הרע" (Esth. vii. 6). If THE EVIL be masculine, it does not at once follow that the allusion is to the 'wicked *One*²' alone.

Compare the following Talmudic prayers, especially No. 3.

1.

"May it be thy will, O Lord, our God, and the God of our fathers, to deliver us from the shameless, and from shamelessness : from EVIL man, and from EVIL hap, from EVIL *yeçer*, from EVIL companion, from EVIL neighbour, and from Satan the destroyer : from hard judgment, and from a hard 'adversary,' whether he be a son of the covenant, or not a son of the covenant" (Berakoth 16 b).

2.

"It is revealed and known before Thee, that our will (Aboth II. 4) is to do Thy will. And who hinders ? The leaven that is in the dough, and servitude to the kingdoms. May it be Thy will to deliver us from their hand" (Berakoth 17 a).

3.

"And cause me to cleave to Thy commandments. *And bring me not into the hands of* sin, nor into the hands of iniquity, nor into the hands of *temptation*³, nor into the hands of disgrace. And bow my *yeçer* to be subservient to Thee. And remove me from EVIL man, and from EVIL companion. And cause me to cleave to the good *yeçer*, and to a good companion (Aboth II. 12, 13), in Thy world. And give me, THIS DAY AND EVERY DAY, to grace, and to favour, and to lovingkindness, in Thine eyes and in the eyes of all that behold me" (Berakoth 60 b).

---

¹ Note that τὸ πονηρόν, instead of πονηρόν, may stand for רע without the article, as in Eccl. viii. 11, 12 לעשות רע τοῦ ποιῆσαι τὸ πονηρόν.

² Μὴ ἀντιστῆναι τῷ πονηρῷ (Matt. v. 39).

³ This, which illustrates the Lord's Prayer in several particulars, is found also, in a slightly varied form, in the Jews' Morning Prayer : " …and bring us not into the hands of sin, nor into the hands of *transgression*, and iniquity, nor into the hands of temptation, nor into the hands of contempt. And let not the evil yeçer *have dominion* over us, and remove us from evil man, &c."

4.

"And remove us from all that Thou hatest; and bring us nigh unto all that Thou lovest" (T. J. Berakoth IV. 2).

1.

BERAKOTH 16 b:

רבי בתר צלותיה אמר הכי יהי רצון מלפניך ה׳ אלהינו ואלהי אבותינו
שתצילנו מעזי פנים ומעזות פנים **מאדם רע ומפגע רע מיצר רע מחבר
רע משכן רע** ומשטן המשחית מדין קשה ומבעל דין קשה בין שהוא בן ברית
ובין שאינו בן ברית·

2.

BERAKOTH 17 a:

ר׳ אלכסנדרי בתר צלותיה אמר הכי יר״מ ה׳ אלהינו שתעמידנו בקרן אורה
ואל תעמידנו בקרן חשכה ואל ידוה לבנו ואל יחשכו עינינו איכא דאמרי הא
רב המנונא מצלי לה ורבי אלכסנדרי בתר דמצלי אמר הכי רבון העולמים גלוי
וידוע לפניך שרצוננו לעשות רצונך **ומי מעכב שאור שבעיסה ושעבוד
מלכיות יר״מ שתצילנו מידם** ונשוב לעשות חקי רצונך בלבב שלם :

3.

BERAKOTH 60 b:

**ויר״מ יי׳ אלהי שתרגילני בתורתך ודבקני במצותיך ואל
תביאני לא לידי חטא ולא לידי עון ולא לידי נסיון ולא לידי
בזיון וכוף את יצרי להשתעבד לך ורחקני מאדם רע ומחבר
רע ודבקני ביצ״ט ובחבר טוב בעולמך ותנני היום ובכל יום
לחן ולחסד ולרחמים בעיניך ובעיני כל רואי :**

4.

T. J. BERAKOTH IV. 2:

רבי חייא בר אבא מוסיף ותייחד לבבינו ליראה את שמך **ותרחקנו מכל
מה ששנאת ותקרבינו לכל מה שאהבת** ותעשה עמנו צדקה למען
שמך :

The two factors of man's nature are יצר הרע or יצרא בישא (pp. 37, 64) and יצר הטוב or יצרא טבא. The evil *yeçer* is sometimes called *yeçer* simply. Although this is primarily the man's own evil nature, 'the imagination of his heart,' it is personified as an external energy that attacks his heart (p. 64), and all manner of evil is spoken of as brought about by its machination. "Lest mine enemy say, I have prevailed against him" (Ps. xiii. 5), becomes in the Targum, "Lest יצרא בישׁא say, &c." "They shall bear thee up in their hands, lest thou stumble against (יצרא בישׁא, which is like) a stone" (Ps. xci. 12). "There shall no *strange god* be in thee, neither shalt thou worship any strange god (Ps. lxxxi. 10). What is the אל זר that is in a man's body (*or* self)? He used to say, It is יצר הרע" (Shabbath 105 b). In Sukkah 52 a, the evil *yeçer* is first taken in the sense of διαλογισμὸς πονηρός (cf. Matt. xv. 19), and it is added, that "in the time to come, the Holy One, blessed is He, will bring the evil *yeçer*, and slay him in the presence of the righteous and the wicked...Seven names has יצר הרע. The Holy One, blessed is He, called it EVIL, for it is said (Gen. viii. 21), For the *yeçer* of man's heart is evil from his youth. Moses called it UNCIRCUMCISED (Deut. x. 16). David called it, by implication, UNCLEAN (Ps. li. 12). Solomon called it ENEMY (Prov. xxv. 21). Isaiah called it STUMBLINGBLOCK (Is. lvii. 14). Ezekiel called it STONE (Ezek. xxxvi. 26). Joel called it צפוני (Joel ii. 20), that is יצר רע, which is HIDDEN, and stands, in the heart of man...The greater the man, the greater his יצר... Said R. Jonathan, The evil *yeçer* seduces a man in this world, and will testify against him in the world to come...With four things the Holy One, blessed is He, was vexed that He had created them; and these are they, Captivity, Kasdim, Ishmaelites, and יצר הרע" (Sukkah 52 a—b). The evil יצר is identified *inter alia* with Satan, and with the Angel of death. (Baba Bathra 16 a, Job ii. 7.) [Maim. Moreh Nebukhim III. 22.]

["The evil" deprecated in the petition ῥῦσαι ἡμᾶς ἀπὸ τοῦ πονηροῦ should include the evil *yeçer*, in accordance with St James i. 13—15. The Syriac version ܡܢ ܒܝܫܐ *men bisha* may also have been the original of ἀπὸ τοῦ πονηροῦ, if "The Prayer" was given in Aramaic. If it was originally in Hebrew, we must make choice apparently between רע πονηρός or πονηρόν, and רשׁע πονηρός.]

The following words of ST CLEMENT OF ROME (*Ad Corinth.* I. 60, pp. 106, 107 ed. Bryennius, Constant. 1875) serve as a very ancient paraphrase of the words of the Prayer from ἄφες ἡμῖν to ἀπὸ τοῦ πονηροῦ.

...ἄφες ἡμῖν τὰς ἀνομίας ἡμῶν καὶ τὰς ἀδικίας καὶ τὰ παραπτώματα καὶ πλημμελείας. Μὴ λογίσῃ πᾶσαν ἁμαρτίαν δούλων σου καὶ παιδισκῶν, ἀλλὰ καθαρεῖς ἡμᾶς τὸν καθαρισμὸν τῆς σῆς ἀληθείας, καὶ κατεύθυνον τὰ διαβήματα ἡμῶν ἐν ὁσιότητι καρδίας πορεύεσθαι καὶ ποιεῖν τὰ καλὰ καὶ εὐάρεστα ἐνώπιόν σου καὶ ἐνώπιον τῶν ἀρχόντων ἡμῶν. Ναί, δέσποτα, ἐπίφανον τὸ πρόσωπόν σου ἐφ᾽ ἡμᾶς εἰς ἀγαθὰ ἐν εἰρήνῃ, εἰς τὸ σκεπασθῆναι ἡμᾶς τῇ χειρί σου τῇ κραταιᾷ καὶ ῥυσθῆναι ἀπὸ πάσης ἁμαρτίας τῷ βραχίονί σου τῷ ὑψηλῷ, καὶ ῥῦσαι ἡμᾶς ἀπὸ τῶν μισούντων ἡμᾶς ἀδίκως.

ADDITIONAL NOTES.

ADDITIONAL NOTES.

1.

p. 11, I. 1 תורה [קבל תורה in Rabbinic may stand for התורה (*Crit. Note*). On νόμος and ὁ νόμος see Romans ed. Gifford *App. to Introduction*, Thayer *N. T. Lex.* s.v. νόμος. Notice the saying אין מוקדם ומאוחר בתורה (Pesach. 6 b). Josephus *contra Ap.* 8 (Ryle *Can. of O.T.*) writes of the books of Scripture, "We have but two and twenty...And of these, five are the books of Moses... From the death of Moses to the (death) of Artaxerxes, king of Persia, the successor of Xerxes, the prophets who succeeded Moses wrote the history of the events that occurred in their own time, in thirteen books. The remaining four documents comprise hymns to God and practical precepts to men. From the days of Artaxerxes to our own time every event has indeed been recorded. But these recent records have not been deemed worthy of equal credit on account of the failure of the exact succession of the prophets." It is sometimes said briefly that the זוגות (cf. Luke x. 1 ἀνὰ δύο, Phil. iv. 3 σύνζυγε) "received" from the prophets, and they from Moses (p. 110 & *Crit. Note*); or that a man received from his teacher, ורבו מרבו, up to Moses ('Ed. viii. 7, Yad. iv. 3, Chag. 3 b).

If Moses actually received all that he is said by Rabbis of old time to have received, his Torah included the fence which the men of the Great Synagogue instructed their disciples to make to it.

"Moses received Torah" rather means that he received כללות *generalia* (Sotah 37 b), which in a sense comprised particulars deducible therefrom, as the progenitor, ὡς ἔπος εἰπεῖν, contains the race (Heb. vii. 9—10). Artificial rules of exegesis were a means of making it appear that literally *kulla bah* (v. 32) everything was in the Torah. "In the Bible absolutely everything is to be found in outline" are words of a Christian preacher. Church Fathers, as Justin and Clement of Alexandria (Kaye chap. iv.), found the substance and the source of Greek philosophy in the Hebrew Scriptures.

It is said in the passage cited below that Moses delivered the Law orally and for oral transmission to seventy wise men. After the Assumption of Moses, however, it was written down by someone who did not foresee what would happen to it, and was repeatedly lost or destroyed:

Clem. *Hom.* III. 47 καὶ ὁ Πέτρος ʿΟ τοῦ θεοῦ νόμος διὰ Μωϋσέως ἑβδομή-
κοντα σοφοῖς ἀνδράσιν ἀγράφως ἐδόθη παραδίδοσθαι, ἵνα τῇ διαδοχῇ πολι-
τεύεσθαι δύνηται, μετὰ δὲ τὴν Μωϋσέως ἀνάληψιν ἐγράφη ὑπό τινός, οὐ μὴν ὑπὸ
Μωϋσέως· ἐν αὐτῷ γὰρ τῷ νόμῳ γέγραπται Καὶ ἀπέθανεν Μωϋσῆς καὶ ἔθαψαν
αὐτὸν ἐγγὺς οἴκου Φογόρ, καὶ οὐδεὶς οἶδεν τὴν ταφὴν αὐτοῦ ἕως τῆς σήμερον. οἷόν
τε ἦν ἀποθανόντα Μωϋσῆν γράφειν Ἀπέθανεν Μωϋσῆς; ἐπεὶ ἐν τῷ μετὰ Μωσέα
χρόνῳ (ὥς γε ἔτη που πεντακόσια ἢ καὶ πρός) ἐν τῷ καθαρισθέντι ναῷ κειμένος
εὑρίσκεται, καὶ μεθ᾽ ἕτερά που πεντακόσια ἔτη φέρεται καὶ ἐπὶ τοῦ Ναβουχοδονόσορ
οὕτως ἐνπρησθεὶς ἀπόλλυται. καὶ ὅμως μετὰ Μωϋσῆν γραφεὶς καὶ πολλάκις
ἀπολωλὼς τὴν τοῦ Μωϋσέως πρόγνωσιν καὶ οὗτος ὡμολόγησεν, ὅτι τὸν ἀφανισμὸν
αὐτοῦ προειδὼς οὐκ ἔγραψεν· οἱ δὲ γράψαντες, τῷ τὸν ἀφανισμὸν μὴ προεγνω-
κέναι ἐπ᾽ ἀγνωσίας ἐλεγχθέντες, προφῆται οὐκ ἦσαν.

Much of what was received as the Law was impugned on the authority
of Christ, who (ib. III. 51) τὰ πρὸ οὐρανοῦ καὶ γῆς παρερχόμενα ἐσήμανεν
μὴ ὄντα τοῦ ὄντως νόμου. See Paul de Lagarde *Clementina* 1865.

2.

p. 11, n. 1 סִיג] Syr. ܣܝܳܓܳܐ, φραγμός (Whish *Clavis Syr.* Matt. xxi.
33), cf. Ecclus. xxviii. 24 περίφραξον, xxxvi. 25 φραγμός, Eph. ii. 14, 15 τὸ
μεσότοιχον τοῦ φραγμοῦ...τὸν νόμον τῶν ἐντολῶν ἐν δόγμασιν, Midr. Ps. ii.
(Buber p. 32) *wall..fence &c.* Another word for *s'yag* is *gader* (Excurs.
I. 2. x.). An excessive fence of tradition (III. 20) may make the
commandment "of none effect": a man must therefore not make the
gader יותר מן העיקר, lest it fall and destroy the plants (Aboth R. N. *B* I,
p. 3). Solomon's wisdom was "as the sand" (1 Kings iv. 29),
which is a fence against the sea: so a man's wisdom is a fence or wall to
his *yeçer* (Prov. xxv. 28, Pesiqta Rabbathi פרה f. 59 ed. Friedmann).

Clem. *Strom.* I. 20 (Potter p. 377) makes Greek philosophy a φραγμός
to the truth, and quotes as Scripture the saying υἱέ, μὴ γίνου ψεύστης,
ὁδηγεῖ γὰρ τὸ ψεῦσμα πρὸς τὴν κλοπήν, which belongs, as Bryennius pointed
out, to the section of the Didaché beginning " My child, flee from all evil
and from all that is like to it." Cf. *Strom.* II. 23 ὁδὸς δὲ ἐπ᾽ ἀναισχυντίαν
ἡ αἰσχρολογία καὶ τέλος ἀμφοῖν ἡ αἰσχρουργία (p. 506, n. 4), ib. IV. 21 ἀποχὴ
κακῶν is the way to the Gospel and to welldoing (p. 623), Chullin 44 b
הרחק מעליה דרכך כו', ib. Tosefta (Zuck. p. 503) הרחק מן הכיעור ומן הדומה לו
(Prov. v. 8), Aboth R. N. II. *A* & *B*. Note that הכיעור is τὸ αἰσχρόν,
the ungraceful and disgraceful, comparing Gen. xli. 3, 4, 19, 20. In theory
and practice the law required a fence, as a written Torah needs a margin
to safeguard the edges of the text.

A fence to an ordinance may take the form of a margin of time added
to keep men at a safe distance from transgression, as we have seen in the
case of the Sabbath. For another example see Mekhilta on Ex. xii. 12
בלילה הזה (fol. 6 ed. Friedmann), where it is said with reference to ver. 10
until the morning, "And why have they said *until midnight*? To keep a

man far from transgression and to make a fence to the law"; and see the first *mishnah* or *baba* or verse of the Mishnah and the Gemara upon it (T. B. Berakh. 4 b).

The Gemara l.c. gives as *baraitha* "The wise have made a fence to their words." Aboth R. N. (p. 3 ed. Schechter) says "Make a fence to thy words," as did the Holy One, and likewise Adam, Torah, Moses, Job, Prophets, Kethubim, and (the) wise. Ben Sira may have known the saying and worked it up with others in Ecclus. xxviii., where he writes "Look that thou *hedge* thy possession about with thorns; bind up thy silver and thy gold; And make a balance and a weight for *thy words*; and make a door and a bar for thy mouth" (ver. 24—25). Notice in verses 14 & 15 " A *third* person's *tongue* &c.," cf. Buxt. 1160 לשון שלישי, Midr. Ps. xii. יכרת ה' כל שפתי כו', Edersheim on Ecclus. in the Speaker's Commentary. On the tongue see also St James iii. ἡ γλῶσσα πῦρ κ.τ.λ. (p. 105 ed. Mayor 1892) comparing Is. v. 24 לשון אש lit. *tongue of fire.*

Dr C. H. H. Wright on *Koheleth* quotes the opinion of Bloch "that the sense of making a fence to the Law was to separate the books which were of Divine origin from those which had merely a human source," the Torah or Law being taken to mean the Hebrew Scriptures generally, see under "Fence round the law" Index p. 509 (1883), and cf. Aboth III. 20.

3.

p. 12, n. 3 (cf. p. 26) *pillars of the world*] See Midr. Rab. Ex. 47. 4, Lev. 25. 8, Num. 10. 1, Cant. v. 15. Deut. Rab. 5. 1, reading עומד for קיים in I. 19, speaks of the three *feet* of the world.   Sayings on Wisdom (Prov. viii., ix.) and the Torah combined with speculations on the *tetrad* may have led up to the sayings on the Gospel and the Four Gospels in Iren. III. 11. 11—12 (ed. Harvey), cf. *The Witness of Hermas to the Four Gospels* (1892), *The Four Gospels and the Four Elements* (Journ. of Philol. XXI. 69).   Irenaeus, who describes his four pillars as πνέοντας κ.τ.λ. undique *flantes* incorruptibilitatem, may have had in mind *The Book of Enoch* XVIII. 1—3 (p. 88 ed. Charles 1893), " And I saw the chambers of all the winds, and I saw how He had furnished with them the whole creation and the firm foundations of the earth. And I saw the cornerstone of the earth, I saw the four winds which bear the earth and the firmament of the heaven. And I saw how the winds stretch out the vaults of heaven and have their station between heaven and earth: these are the pillars of the heaven."   Predecessors of Irenaeus acquainted with the cosmogony of "Enoch" may have compared the Four Gospels to "the four winds which bear the earth and the firmament of heaven "; and this may have been done at any time after or even in anticipation of the express recognition by the Church of four and four only.

Prof. Mayor compares Baehrens *XII Panegyrici Latini* (1874), *Pan.* v. 4 (Constantio Caesari), where it is proved after the manner of Irenaeus that there must needs be four rulers: "Et sane praeter usum curamque rei publicae etiam illa Iouis et Herculis cognata maiestas in Iouio Herculioque principibus totius mundi caelestiumque rerum similitudinem requirebat, quippe isto numinis uestri numero summa omnia nituntur et gaudent: *elementa quattuor et totidem anni uices et orbis quadrifariam duplici discretus oceano et emenso quater caelo lustra redeuntia et quadrigae solis et duobus caeli luminibus adiuncti Vesper et Lucifer.*"

The following reasons assigned for the observance of the four Ember weeks are quoted in Hook's *Lives of the Archbishops of Canterbury*, vol. I. ch. 5 (p. 186 ed. 1), "Because the world consists of four quarters, east, west, south, and north; and man is compounded of four elements, fire, air, water, and earth; and the mind is governed by four virtues, prudence, temperance, fortitude, and justice; and the four rivers of Paradise, as types of the four Gospels, water the whole earth; and the year turns on the four seasons, spring, summer, autumn, and winter; and this number, four, is on all hands acknowledged to be the number of perfection; therefore the old fathers instituted the four Ember weeks, according to God's law; as also holy men and apostolical doctors have done under the New Testament."

The commentator Bachja writes on Aboth I. 19 that prayer is the עמידה and עמוד of the world, cf. Buxt. 1622. The term *amidah* (pl. *-oth*) is used for certain forms of prayer to be said standing (Heb. Auth. P. B. pp. 44, 115, &c.), especially the SHEMONAH ESREH or *eighteen* benedictions. See in *The Apocalypse of Baruch* II. 2 (ed. Charles 1896) "Because your works are to this city as a firm pillar and your prayers as a strong wall," with the note that the verse is reproduced in The Rest of the Words of Baruch i. 2 in the form αἱ γὰρ προσευχαὶ ὑμῶν ὡς στῦλος ἑδραῖος ἐν μέσῳ αὐτῆς καὶ ὡς τεῖχος ἀδαμάντινον περικυκλοῦν αὐτήν. Worship (I. 2) includes prayer, which is עבודה בלב (T. J. Berakh. IV. 1 *init.*).

אנשי המעמד *viri stationis*. In Mishnah Ta'an. IV. (T. B. 26 a) 𝔄 64 b omits the words from *Viri stationis quatuor dies in hebdomade jejunabant* bracketed by Surenhuis (II. 379). Herm. *Sim.* v. 1. 1—2 στατίωνα κ.τ.λ., cf. Bingham's *Antiquities*.

On what stands the earth?...upon the wind &c. (p. 86). So MIDRASH HA-GADOL (col. 3 in the forthcoming edition by Mr Schechter) with the addition that some say the world stands upon twelve pillars *according to the number of the children of Israel* (Deut. xxxii. 8), some say on seven (Prov. ix. 1), some on one whose name is צדיק for *the righteous is* יסוד עולם (Prov. x. 25). This means that the world stands not but by the merit of the righteous. Said R. Chiya bar Abba ראה הקב"ה כו' the Holy One saw that the righteous were few and He arose and planted them in every generation, for they are the pillar of the world.

On the *four feet* of the throne of God, which is established *by mercy* (Is. xvi. 5), see the parable in Midr. Ps. lxxxix. כי אמרתי עולם חסד יבנה.

4.

p. 15, l. 5—6 אישה] R. 'Aqiba teaches in Sotah 17 a איש ואישה זכו
שכינה ביניהן לא זכו אש אוכלתן *man and wife if they be deserving have
the Shekhinah between them if not fire devours them*, for איש and אשה
together contain the Name י׳ה, but without *yod* and *hé* they reduce
to אש אש, fire devouring fire (1 Cor. vii. 9 πυροῦσθαι, xi. 11 ἐν κυρίῳ).
Woman takes fire more quickly and burns more fiercely than man, for the
letters of אש *fire* come together in אשה *woman* but are separated by the
yod of the Shekhinah in איש *man*. See Buxt. 76, Kohut i. 307, Pirqé
R. El. xii. with Loria's commentary, Ecclus. ix. 9 Syr. in *Crit. Note*.

The Rabbinic view of Marriage. It is deduced from Gen. i. 28 that
פריה ורביה is a duty, cf. Pesach. 113 b, Qiddush. 29 b, Jebam. 63 a "a *man*
without a wife is not a man"—the reading *Jew* is due to the censors of the
press, see *Lectures on Teaching of 12 Apost.* pp. 84 sq. It does
not follow that marriage was regarded as of "superior sanctity" (Lightfoot
Coloss. p. 139, 1875) to celibacy, notwithstanding the use of a word meaning
sanctificationes for *sponsalia* (Buxt. 1980 on קדּוּשׁ). In respect of פריה
ורביה, which is for this world only (p. 60, n. 40) and is a work of the evil
yeçer (p. 64, n. 2), man is akin to the lower creatures and not to the angels
(Ab. R. N. xxxvii. p. 109). The Holy One (Midr. Ps. viii.) explains to the
angels that the Torah was not given to them because they could not keep
it, "for with you there is no increasing and multiplying, and no uncleanness,
and no death and sickness" (p. 74 ed. Buber). The mystic, like
ben Azzai (Jebam. 63 b), could allegorize the duty of marriage by making
אשה mean תורה, cf. Sifré ii. § 345 on מורשה קהלת יעקב. Eccl. ix. 9
ראה חיים עם אשה is made to mean that a man should combine a business
or אומנות with Torah study (Rashi), in accordance with Aboth ii. 2.
Qiddush. 30 b proves by Eccl. *l.c.* that a man is bound to teach his son a
craft, whether *isshah* means wife or Torah, cf. p. 75, n. 33. With
Aboth i. 6 מדברי תורה כו׳ compare 1 Cor. vii. 32 sq. τὰ τοῦ κυρίου κ.τ.λ.

It may be said in one sense that the evil יצר does and in another that it
does not exist בבהמה in the beast, see Aboth R. N. xvi. (Schechter p. 64),
Berakh. 61 a מתקיף לה ר״׳נ בר יצחק כו׳. The Torah was not given
to the angels for (they are asked) יש ביניכם יצר הרע (Shabb. 89 a), a question
to be answered in the negative.

Gentile...slave...woman. See p. 26 and *Class. Review* x. 191, Heb.
Auth. P. B. pp. 5—6, Maim. *Hilk. Tefillah* vii. 6, Tur *Orach Chayim* 46,
Tosefta Berak. 7 (Zuck. p. 16), Chagigah i. 1 (Streane pp. 1—15), Menachoth
43 b where it is taught that a man should bless God daily that He
made him an Israelite, not a woman, not בור (Ab. ii. 6). After discussion
slave replaces *boor*. Gentiles, slaves and women are classed together as of
lower religious status than the בן תורה, women and slaves being exempt
from positive precepts for which there are set times (Streane p. 12).

St Paul declares them all equal "in Christ Jesus," apparently presupposing the Rabbinic grouping of them as not "one" in respect of Torah.

The like grouping is implied in St Peter's quotation from Joel in Acts ii. 17—18, "I will pour out of my Spirit *upon all flesh*...your *daughters* shall prophesy...Yea and on my *servants*...I will pour out in those days of my Spirit," Heb. וגם על העבדים *the* not *my* slaves (Joel iii. 2). Cf. Ab. R. N. *B* xliii. (p. 120) וגם לרבות בני אדם חיה ועוף, *all flesh* (not man only) is to see the salvation of God (Is. xl., Rom. viii.). On the judgment of "the soul of man on account of the souls of beasts in the world to come" see *The Book of the Secrets of Enoch* ch. 58 (p. 73 ed. Charles, 1896), and on the covenant (Hos. ii. 18) to be made with the animals in the Messianic times see Ex. Rab. 15. 21 (Wünsche p. 119).

Since writing the above I have noticed the passage in Joel *Blicke* I. 119, "Die Stelle die dem Plato nachsagt er habe täglich Gott gedankt dass er ihn zum Hellenen, nicht zum Barbaren, zum Freien, nicht zum Sklaven, zum Manne und nicht zum Weibe geschaffen, kann ich augenblicklich nicht finden. Thatsächlich entspricht das aber drei talmudisch für die Liturgie vorgeschriebenen Segenssprüchen. Die Meinung über die Frau die in diesen Segenssprüchen sich ausspricht, ist daher nicht jüdisch (orientalisch), sondern griechisch, und geht auf Platon's Aeusserungen im Timäus zurück, der das Eingehen *in eines Weibes Natur* für eine Art von Strafe bezeichnet."

Weiss in like manner, in his Hebrew work דור דור ודורשיו on the History of Jewish Tradition (Part II. chap. xv. p. 147), makes R. Meir say in Menachoth 43 b that a man should give thanks daily that he was not made גוי or אשה or בור, having no tradition or Torah for it, but *knowing* כי כן היה מנהגו כו' *that so it was the practice of Socrates the Greek to bless daily.* These benedictions in Menachoth are properly ascribed to R. Jehudah and not to R. Meir. See Bacher's *Die Agada der Tannaiten* II. 202 (1890).

R. Judah's benedictions are given also in T. J. Berakhoth ix. 2 (13 *b*) *Béni soit Dieu de ne pas m'avoir créé païen, ni stupide, ni femme*...de n'être pas une femme parce qu'elles ne remplissent pas tous les préceptes religieux (Schwab p. 158, 1871).   The word בור *stupide* has the sense of בער (p. 30, n. 12), which stands in parallelism with בהמות in Ps. lxxiii. 22 *So* brutish *was I, and ignorant; I was as a* beast *before thee.* Was בור, which has given place to "slave," a substitute for ἄλογον τῇ φύσει θηρίον (*Class. Review l.c.*)?   Women ranked with slaves in respect of certain "préceptes religieux." How numberless are the times that that occurs in the Talmudic pandect...נשים ועבדים *Women, servants and children are not bound to these things* (Lightfoot *Hor. Hebr.* Matt. iii. 7).

Professor Mayor (cf. p. 26) cites the following five passages in the *Classical Review* x. 191 (May 1896):

Plutarch life of Marius 46 § 1: Πλάτων μὲν οὖν ἤδη πρὸς τῷ τελευτᾶν γενόμενος ὕμνει τὸν αὑτοῦ δαίμονα καὶ τὴν τύχην, ὅτι πρῶτον μὲν ἄνθρωπος, εἶτα Ἕλλην, οὐ βάρβαρος οὐδὲ ἄλογον τῇ φύσει θηρίον γένοιτο, πρὸς δὲ τούτοις ὅτι τοῖς Σωκράτους χρόνοις ἀπήντησεν ἡ γένεσις αὐτοῦ.

Lact. iii 19 § 17 : non dissimile Platonis illud est, quod aiebat se gratias agere naturae : primum quod homo natus esset potius quam mutum animal, deinde quod mas potius quam femina, quod Graecus quam barbarus, postremo quod Atheniensis et quod temporibus Socratis.

Diogenes Laertius i § 33 (under Thales): Ἕρμιππος δ᾽ ἐν τοῖς βίοις εἰς τοῦτον ἀναφέρει τὸ λεγόμενον ὑπό τινων περὶ Σωκράτους. ἔφασκε γάρ, φησί, τριῶν τούτων ἕνεκα χάριν ἔχειν τῇ τύχῃ· πρῶτον μὲν ὅτι ἄνθρωπος ἐγενόμην καὶ οὐ θηρίον· εἶτα ὅτι ἀνὴρ καὶ οὐ γυνή· τρίτον ὅτι Ἕλλην καὶ οὐ βάρβαρος.

Ep. Gal. 3 28 : οὐκ ἔνι Ἰουδαῖος οὐδὲ Ἕλλην· οὐκ ἔνι δοῦλος οὐδὲ ἐλεύθερος· οὐκ ἔνι ἄρσεν καὶ θῆλυ· πάντες γὰρ ὑμεῖς εἷς ἐστε ἐν Χριστῷ Ἰησοῦ.

Ep. Col. 3 11 : ὅπου οὐκ ἔνι Ἕλλην καὶ Ἰουδαῖος, περιτομὴ καὶ ἀκροβυστία, βάρβαρος, Σκύθης, δοῦλος, ἐλεύθερος· ἀλλὰ τὰ πάντα καὶ ἐν πᾶσι Χριστός.

Plato according to Plutarch, who was a younger contemporary of St Paul, lauds his own daemon and Fortune for that he was a civilised human being and had been a contemporary of Socrates, and says nothing about women or slaves.

The tradition from Hermippus in Diogenes Laertius makes Thales or Socrates give thanks that he was *a man and not a woman &c.*

Lactantius, who brings together sayings as on the *Two Ways* (Journ. of Philol. XXI. 247) from various sources, had in mind perhaps *inter alia* Gal. iii. 28 *non est* MASCULUS *neque femina.* Bünemann on Lactantius *l.c.* refers to Plutarch, Diogenes Laertius, and the Jews' Morning Prayer.

From "undesigned coincidences" between the New Testament and Rabbinic writings we may sometimes infer the antiquity of sayings in the latter. In quoting Gal. iii. 28 (1877) I meant to suggest that it testified to an existent Jewish grouping of women * with slaves and Gentiles in respect of Torah. At a still earlier date Greek thought may have influenced Rabbinism in this as in other matters.

For the remainder of this note I am indebted to Professor Bywater :

Dio Chrysostom (i.e. the pseudo Dio Chrysostom if the editors are right in their view of this oration, which is certainly ancient and cannot be separated from the genuine writings of Dio by any great number of years) writes in *Or.* LXIV. p. 597 M., Σωκράτης γοῦν ἐπὶ πολλοῖς αὐτὸν ἐμακάριζε, καὶ ὅτι ζῷον λογικὸν καὶ ὅτι Ἀθηναῖος.

The interest in the statement in Dio is not in what he actually says (for he is obviously abridging a fuller statement) but in the fact that he tells the story of Socrates, of whom according to Hermippus it was sometimes told. The saying in some form was certainly current in connexion with Thales, Socrates, and probably Plato in the 3rd century B.C. Hermippus (surnamed Callimacheus) mentions the death of Chrysippus which occurred in B.C. 207, and may be presumed to have written not later than B.C. 200. The fragments of his book are edited by Müller (1849) in the Didot series.

* Philo *Hypothetika* (Mangey II. 629) γυναῖκας ἀνδράσι δουλεύειν κ.τ.λ.

Greek literature is full of attacks on women, cf. Stobaeus *Flor.* 73.
Aristotle describes woman and the slave in *Poetics* 15 as τὸ μὲν χεῖρον
τὸ δὲ ὅλως φαῦλον.

5.

p. 16, ɪ. 8 *the wicked*] Aboth R. N. *B* xvi. ברח *flee* from an evil neighbour and be not companion to *the wicked* (sing.), that is (p. 36) יצה'ר the Evil
Impulse, which sits *at the door* (Gen. iv. 7) of the heart. When a man is
bent upon transgression it sways all his members, for it is king over them
(Eccl. v. 9). It is by Gematria הרשע ὁ πονηρός (Magen Elohim).

Psalm xxxvii. 32 " *Wicked* watcheth *the righteous* and seeketh to slay
him." Here Sukkah 52 b *init.* makes "wicked" (lit. πονηρός without the
article) the Evil Impulse, Deut. Rab. 11. 11 (Wünsche p. 114) makes "the
righteous" mean Moses, and "wicked" the most wicked of all the Satans
סמאל הרשע Samael ὁ πονηρός.   Compare Wisdom ii. 12, 20.

In Job ix. 24, "Earth is given into hand of *wicked*: he covereth
the faces of the judges thereof," Baba Bathra 16 a interprets *wicked* (sing.)
by Satan; and Ex. Rab. 21. 7 (Wünsche p. 170) interprets עויל "ungodly"
in the same way in Job xvi. 11 "God delivereth me to *ungodly* (sing.),
and casteth me into hands of *wicked* (pl.)."

These are of course mere homiletical applications. When in Targum,
Talmud or Midrash a word meaning *wicked* and with or without the article
is said to denote יצרא בישא or Satan or Samael the Wicked One, it no
more follows that this is its primary sense than that צדיק "just" means (as
it is made to mean) God in Prov. x. 7, where it is said that the memory of
the deceased just person is blessed.

Typical human enemies of Israel, as well as the Evil Impulse and Satan,
were called THE WICKED and THAT WICKED ONE in the Rabbinic writings.
Buxtorf writes רשיעא...*Hoc titulo hostes quidam Israëlitarum in Targum
insigniuntur*, and gives examples. Compare Midr. Ps. xxii. (Buber p. 192)
we learn them from *the parashah of* אותו רשע i.e. the Pentateuch Lesson
about Shechem, Aboth R. N. *A* xvi. *that wicked one* (fem.).

On the book of Job and on the good and the evil inclinations see
Maimonides *Moreh Nebukhim* iii. 22—23 (pp. 93—111 ed. Friedländer,
1885).   In 1 Cor. vii. 5 ἵνα μὴ πειράζῃ ὑμᾶς ὁ Σατανᾶς a Rabbinic name
of the Tempter would be יצר הרע. See Schoettgen *Hor. Hebr.*, Nork
Rabbinische Quellen und Parallelen zu N. T. Schriftstellen (Leipzig 1839).

6.

p. 19, ɪ. 12 *drink and die*] Cf. Gen. ii. 17, St John xi. 26 (ed. Westcott),
1 Cor. xv. 31 καθ' ἡμέραν ἀποθνήσκω, 1 Tim. v. 6 ζῶσα τέθνηκεν.

Sifré ɪɪ. § 32 ובכל נפשך (Deut. vi.), even though he take away thy soul.
כי עליך הורגנו כל היום, God accounts the righteous as slain every day.

Tamid 32 a on Aboth ɪv. 3 השמח בחלקו, What should a man do that he may live? He should slay himself (N.T. θανατοῦτε, νεκρώσατε). What should a man do that he may die? He should quicken himself, יחיה את עצמו (N.T. ζωοποιεῖν). What should a man do that he may be acceptable to the creatures? יסני מלכו ישלטן (Ab. I. 11). See Mr Montefiore's Hibbert Lectures p. 568. T. J. Berak. II. 3 (4 *d*) "*For the living know that they shall die,* these are the righteous who even in their death are called living : but the dead know *not anything*, these are the wicked who though living are called dead, for it is said *For I have no pleasure in the death of* המת" (see on Eccl. ix. 5 in Schiffer *Kohel. nach Talm. u. Midr.*), cf. Buber's Tanchuma, end.

But whosoever drinketh of the water that I shall give him shall never thirst (Joh. iv. 14). Compare Aboth I. 4 And drink their words with thirstiness, Chagigah 3 a (Streane p. 8) We are thy disciples and of thy waters we drink, Schoettgen, Nork, Wünsche *Erläuterung der Evv. aus Talm. u. Midr.* on St John *l.c.*, King *Yalkut on Zech.* p. 121 With joy shall ye receive a New Law &c. (Targ. Is. xii.). ib. *but the water that I shall give him shall be in him a well of water springing up into everlasting life.* Compare Midr. Ps. civ. 1 (Buber p. 440) כמעיין הנובע, where the Jalqut adds לעתיד לבוא.

7.

p. 19, n. 22 *manual labour*] On this subject see S. Meyer *Arbeit und Handwerk im Talmud* (Berlin 1878), Delitzsch *Handwerkleben zur Zeit Jesu* (Erlangen 1868), *Jewish Artisan Life &c.* translated from the German of Delitzsch by Mrs Philip Monkhouse, *The Dignity of Labour as taught in the Talmud* by Rabbi H. Gollancz in the *Imperial and Asiatic Quarterly Review* (July 1891).

Creatures which do not work for their living are classed with thieves and robbers, cf. chap. IV. n. 16, *Epist. Barn.* 10. 4 οἵτινες οὐκ οἴδασιν διὰ κόπου καὶ ἱδρῶτος ἑαυτοῖς πορίζειν τὴν τροφήν, ἀλλὰ ἁρπάζουσιν κ.τ.λ.

8.

p. 21, n. 28 τὰς κτίσεις] *Didaché* 16 ἡ κτίσις τῶν ἀνθρώπων, 1 Pet. ii. 13 —18 " Submit yourselves πάσῃ ἀνθρωπίνῃ κτίσει for the Lord's sake : whether it be to the king, as supreme ; Or unto governors...Honour all *men*...Servants, be subject to your masters...iii. Likewise, ye wives &c.", cf. Eph. v. 21 ὑποτασσόμενοι ἀλλήλοις ἐν φόβῳ Χριστοῦ. The natural rendering of πάσῃ ἀνθρωπίνῃ κτίσει is *to every human creature*, sc. in authority, but κτίσις here is usually assumed to mean "ordinance," cf. Huther in Meyer's *N. T. Kommentar.* "When students sit and are subject (נכבשין) one to another, God attends to their words" (Midr. Ps. xxx., Buber p. 236). The honour to be rendered to all men is "the honour of *the creatures*" (p. 65, n. 4). R. 'Aqiba said ואל תצטרך לבריות, be independent of *the creatures* (p. 18, n. 22). Aboth R. N. xxxvII. "There are seven κτίσεις one above

another &c." Buxt. 350, Midr. Ps. cii. לְעַם נברא, "to a people created
בריאה חדשה " (N.T. *new creature*).

For the Lord's sake. Shabbath 50 b A man washes his face, hands and
feet every day בשביל קונו for his Maker's sake (Rashi *to the honour of his
Maker...He created everything* לכבודו).

9.

p. 22, n. 29 *into seventy tongues*] See Midr. Ps. lxviii. (Buber p. 317)
on המבשרות צבא רב "great was the company of the preachers."

10.

p. 23, l. 15 *who is for me?*] The commentary Midrash Shemuel points
out that מי, which is by Gematria *fifty*, the number of the gates of בינה, is
taken by the Zohar for a name of God in Is. xl. 26 מי ברא אלה Who *created
these things*. Such was His name before the creation. After it He was
immanent in and revealed as Elohim by "these things," for the word
אלהים is made up of מי and אלה. Another Qabbalistic name of God is אין,
cf. Irenaeus I. 14. 1 ed. Mass. ἀνούσιος (vol. I. pp. 129, 131 ed. Harvey).

11.

p. 23, n. 33 [דעלך סני כו'] On Jewish and other forms of the so-called
Golden Rule (Gibbon *Decline and Fall* ch. 54, n.) see Selden *De Jure
Naturali et Gentium* VII. 12, Wetstein on Matt. vii. 12, Bernays (*Gesam.
Abhandl.* I. 262—282) on Philo's *Hypothetika*, Lazarus *Zur Charakt. der
Talmud. Ethik* p. 10, n. (Breslau 1877), Neubauer's Chaldee *Tobit* (Oxf.
1878), Güdemann *Nächstenliebe*, Delitzsch *Jesus u. Hillel*, Edersheim *The
Life and Times of Jesus the Messiah,* and the *Didaché* ed. Harnack, Harris,
Funk and others.

Buxtorf under סנא quotes the saying attributed to Hillel דעלך סני כו',
*Quod odiosum est tibi proximo tuo ne feceris. Haec est Lex tota : caetera
nil sunt nisi ejus explicatio,* and Matt. vii. 12.　　　　　The Aramaic
form of the rule in Neubauer's *Tobit* is דסאני לך לחורני לא תעביד (p. 8),
Heb. אשר תשנא לנפשך כו' (p. 24).　　　　　Philo (Euseb. *Praep. Evang.*
viii. 7) gives it in the short oblique form ἅ τις παθεῖν ἐχθαίρει μὴ ποιεῖν αὐτόν.

These forms point to a common original מא את סאני לך כו' (with pael
part. *sané*) ὃ σὺ ἐχθαίρεις σεαυτῷ κ.τ.λ. In ὅσα μὴ θέλετε ἑαυτοῖς γίνεσθαι
(*Did.* 1) a "would not" takes the place of "hate." It remains to derive
the saying, which is "Lex tota," from the Torah*. A. ben Ezra (and simi-
larly Ramban) explains Lev. xix. 18 ואהבת לרעך כמוך, lit. ἀγαπήσεις τῷ
κ.τ.λ., by שיאהב הטוב לחברו כמו לנפשו, a man should *love* τὸ ἀγαθόν *for
his fellow* as for himself. So Targ. pseudo-Jonathan (ed. Netter 1859)

---

* With *on one foot* (p. 23) cf. Horace *Sat.* I. 4. 10 stans pede in uno.

ותרחמיה לחברך דמן אנת סַגִי לך לא תעביד ליה אנא יי' (ver. 18), cf.
ותרחם ליה כוותך דמא את סָגִי לך לא תעביד ליה (ver. 34), a man should
shew love *to* his fellow by not doing *to* him what he dislikes when done *to*
himself. Thus the saying in question is accounted for as an explanation of
ואהבת followed by ל *to*, instead of את as in Deut. vi. 5, xi. 1. Detaching
it from its context and explaining ליה by לחברך, we get מא את סאני
לחברך תעביד לא לך (or דאת סָגִי), ὃ σὺ μισεῖς σεαυτῷ οὐ ποιήσεις τῷ
πλησίον σου, cf. Ecclus. xv. 11 ἃ γὰρ ἐμίσησεν κ.τ.λ. The saying may
have been known to Ben Sira. The principle of it is in Ecclus. viii. 5—7
...Remember that we all...For some of us also &c., xxxi. 15 R.V. Consider
thy neighbour's *liking* by thine own.

Philo (Mangey II. 629) introduces it thus, Μύρια δὲ ἄλλα ἐπὶ τούτοις, ὅσα
καὶ ἐπὶ ἀγράφων ἐθῶν καὶ νομίμων. κἂν τοῖς νομίμοις [Viger νόμοις] αὐτοῖς.
Ἅ τις παθεῖν ἐχθαίρει μὴ ποιεῖν αὐτόν. Ἅ μὴ κατέθηκεν μηδ' ἀναιρεῖσθαι.
This illustrates St Luke xix. 21 αἴρεις ὃ οὐκ ἔθηκας (Bernays p. 274). On
the unwritten law see also *The Apocalypse of Baruch* LVII. 2.

12.

p. 24, l. 16 *countenance*] "And the Lord spake unto Moses face to face."
The word *panim* is plural, and is used twice. Hence there were four
"faces," a stern, a neutral, a pleasant and a laughing *face*, pointing to
Miqra, Mishnah, Talmud, Agadah (Mass. Sof. XVI. 2).

13.

p. 25, l. 18 *silence*] Compare Ignat. *Magnes.* 8 ὅς ἐστιν αὐτοῦ λόγος ἀπὸ
σιγῆς προελθών, Iren. I. 8 (Mass. 14). 1 *Colorbasi* silentii. Dr M. Joel
explains *colorbas* as a faulty reading of the words קלא ברת (Aram. for
Bath Qol, Buxt. 322) in reverse order, with ת pronounced *s*.

14.

p. 27, n. 1 גדול מרבן שמו] For this saying in the 'Arukh see under אבי'
(Kohut I. 7 a_6), where it is taken from a letter of R. Sherira Gaon. See
also Neubauer *Mediaeval Jewish Chronicles*, pref. p. xii (1887).

15.

p. 29, II. 5 אל תפרוש מן הציבור] Heb. x. 25, Ta'anith 11 a, Isocr. *ad
Demonicum* 13 τίμα τὸ δαιμόνιον ἀεὶ μέν, μάλιστα δὲ μετὰ τῆς πόλεως, cf.
Ecclus. iv. 7 Get thyself the love of the congregation, vii. 7 Sin not against
the multitude of the city. ib. *until the day of thy death.* See
Ecclus. xi. 28, Dict. of Bible art. *Ecclesiastes* I. 834 a (ed. Smith & Fuller,
1893), Midr. Ps. xvi. (Buber p. 120) *Sanctus benedictus* does not canonise
His saints until they are בארץ in the earth.

16.

p. 30, n. 10 בית השואבה (ℨ 58 a שאבה without *vau*)] Kohut II. 85
Fackelhaus. It is also explained as *domus hauriendi*, "because therefrom
they draw the Holy Spirit" (Is. xii. 3, T. J. Sukkah v. 55 *a*, Buxt. 2299).
See Lightfoot *Hor. Heb.* on St John vii. 38—39 "as the scripture hath said,
out of his belly shall flow rivers of living water. But this spake he of the
Spirit, which they that believe on him should receive," comparing Ps. xl.
9 ותורתך בתוך מעי ἐν μέσῳ τῆς καρδίας (al. κοιλίας) μου. It is a question
what "scripture" is referred to.

Aboth vi. 1 likens the recipient of Torah to a spring פוסק שאינו and a
river שמתגבר והולך, that goes "from strength to strength," cf. Prov. v.
15—16 שתה מים מבורך כו', 'Abodah Z. 19 a, "Machsor Vitry" ed. Hurwitz
p. 555. At first he drinks from a "cistern," then from an unfailing "well."
Finally his Torah becomes "rivers of waters in the streets," a great נהר
which flows out from him. "The reception of the blessing leads at once to
the distribution of it in fuller measure" (Westcott on St John *l.c.*). So in
Aboth R. N. xiv. R. Jochanan calls El'azar ben 'Arakh שוטף כו נחל, with
reference to the Scripture יפוצו כו' (Prov. *l.c.*), lit. *to establish what is said.*

See also Midr. Ps. i. דבר אחר כי אם בתורת יי' חפצו כו', as waters fall
drop by drop and become נחלים, so words of Torah: a man learns one
halakhah to-day and another to-morrow, till he abounds like a spring.
Ecclus. xxi. 13 "The knowledge of a wise man shall be made to abound as
a flood; and his counsel as a fountain of life," xxiv. 30—31 "And, lo, my
stream became a river." *The Book of Enoch* xlix. 1 For wisdom is poured
out like water, li. 3 and all the secrets of wisdom will stream forth from
the counsels of his mouth (pp. 136, 140 ed. Charles).

Jacob's Well. Gen. xxix. 1—3 Then Jacob lifted up his feet, and
came to the land of the children of the east. And he looked, and behold a
well in the field, and, lo, three flocks of sheep lying there by it; for out of
that well they watered the flocks: and the stone upon the well's mouth was
great. And thither were all the flocks gathered: and they rolled the stone
from the well's mouth, and watered the sheep, and put the stone again
upon the well's mouth in its place. See Gen. Rab. 70. 8, Jalqut i. 123 on
Gen. *l.c.*, ii. 741 on Ps. xlii., Pesiqta Rabbathi psq. 1, St John iv. 6, Wünsche
Erläuterung der Evv. p. 512 (1878).

Lifted up his feet. A sound heart is the life of the בשרים σάρκες (Prov.
xiv. 30). When a man hears glad tidings (בשורה), then טעין ליביה ית רגלוהי
his heart carries his feet, or הכריסא טענא רגלי'א the *belly carries the feet*,
as "the creatures say in their parables" (Matt. Kehunnah). In Menenius
Agrippa's fable of the Belly and the Members the former holds the position
of dignity, and (as in St John vii.) it is the source of supply.

A well in the field. That is "The Well," namely *that which went with
Israel in the wilderness* (Matt. Kehunnah). The mention of this well's
mouth helps to account for פי הבאר in Aboth v. 9.

The Midrash gives several interpretations of the passage cited, and (like T. J. Sukkah *l.c.*) explains שמשם היו שואבים רוח הקודש by בית השואבה because therefrom they drew the Holy Spirit. In one of these the well is the synagogue and the *great stone* the Evil Impulse, which is rolled away as the congregation enter to hear Torah and returns to its place when they go out In another the well is Sinai from which they heard עשרת הדברות the decalogue, and the great stone is the Shekhinah. Psq. Rabbathi *l.c.* and Jalq. Ps. xlii. refer to Is. lxvi. 23 וֹהיה מדי חדש בחדשו כו׳, speak of the pilgrims' appearing and seeing the face of the Shekhinah at the great feasts, and derive שואבה as above from שאב.

Menenius Agrippa's famous comparison of the human body and the body politic is given by Livy and Dionysius of Halicarnassus as below, and briefly in Plutarch's *Vita Coriolani* § 6.

Livy II. 32...nullam profecto nisi in concordia civium spem reliquam ducere : eam per aequa per iniqua reconciliandam civitati esse. sic placuit igitur oratorem ad plebem mitti Menenium Agrippam, facundum virum et, quod inde oriundus erat, plebi carum. is intromissus in castra prisco illo dicendi et horrido modo nihil aliud quam hoc narrasse fertur : *Tempore quo in homine, non ut nunc omnia in unum consentiebant, sed singulis membris suum cuique consilium, suus sermo fuerat, indignatas reliquas partes sua cura suo labore ac ministerio ventri omnia quaeri, ventrem in medio quietum nihil aliud quam datis voluptatibus frui. conspirasse inde, ne manus ad os cibum ferrent, nec os acciperet datum, nec dentes quae conficerent. hac ira dum ventrem fame domare vellent, ipsa una membra totumque corpus ad extremam tabem venisse. inde apparuisse ventris quoque haud segne ministerium esse, nec magis ali quam alere reddentem in omnis corporis partes hunc, quo vivimus vigemusque, divisum pariter in venas maturum confecto cibo sanguinem.* comparando hinc, quam intestina corporis seditio similis esset irae plebis in patres, flexisse mentes hominum.

Dionys. Hal. *Antiq. Roman.* VI. 86 ἔοικέ πως ἀνθρωπείῳ σώματι πόλις. σύνθετον γὰρ ἐκ πολλῶν μερῶν ἐστιν ἑκάτερον, καὶ οὔτε δύναμιν ἔχει ἕκαστον τὴν αὐτὴν τῶν ἐν αὐτοῖς μερῶν, οὔτε χρείας παρέχεται τὰς ἴσας. εἰ δὴ λάβοι τὰ μέρη τοῦ ἀνθρωπείου σώματος ἰδίαν αἴσθησιν καθ᾽ αὐτὰ καὶ φωνήν, ἔπειτα στάσις ἐν αὐτοῖς ἐμπέσοι καθ᾽ ἓν γενομένοις τοῖς ἄλλοις ἅπασι πρὸς τὴν γαστέρα μόνην, καὶ λέγοιεν οἱ μὲν πόδες, ὅτι πᾶν ἐπ᾽ αὐτοῖς ἐπίκειται τὸ σῶμα· αἱ δὲ χεῖρες, ὅτι τὰς τέχνας ἐργάζονται καὶ τἀπιτήδεια ἐκπορίζουσι καὶ μάχονται πολεμίοις, καὶ ἄλλα πολλὰ ὠφελήματα παρέχουσιν εἰς τὸ κοινόν· οἱ δὲ ὦμοι, ὅτι τὰ ἄχθη πάντα ἐπ᾽ αὐτοῖς κομίζεται· [τὸ δὲ στόμα, ὅτι φθέγγεται·] ἡ δὲ κεφαλή, ὅτι ὁρᾷ καὶ ἀκούει καὶ τὰς ἄλλας αἰσθήσεις περιλαβοῦσα πάσας ἔχει, δι᾽ ὧν σώζεται τὸ πᾶν· εἶτα φαῖεν πρὸς τὴν γαστέρα· Σὺ δέ, ὦ χρηστή, τί τούτων ποιεῖς; ἢ τίς ἐστιν ἡ σὴ χάρις ἡμῖν καὶ ὠφέλεια; ἀλλὰ σύ γε τοσοῦτον ἀπέχεις τοῦ πράττειν τι καὶ συγκατορθοῦν ἡμῖν τῶν κοινῇ χρησίμων, ὥστε καὶ ἀντιπράττεις καὶ ἐνοχλεῖς καὶ πρᾶγμα ἀφόρητον ὑπηρετεῖν ἀναγκάζεις καὶ φέρειν ἀπανταχόθεν, εἰς τὴν ἐκπλήρωσιν τῶν σεαυτῆς ἐπιθυμιῶν. φέρε, τί οὐ μεταποιούμεθα τῆς ἐλευθερίας κ.τ.λ.

19

With this compare *Civitas parva homo est &c.* in St Jerome on Eccl. ix. (p. 150), and the Rabbinic, Scriptural and other parallels.

17.

p. 31, n. 16 *As thou hast done*] Clem. *Cor.* 13 "most of all remembering the words of the Lord Jesus...*As ye do so shall it be done to you &c.*," Lev. xxiv. 19 *as he hath done so shall it be done to him,* Gen. ix. 6 'שופך דם כו, ·Rev. xiii. 10.   Compare Wisdom xi. 16—17 δι' ὧν τις ἁμαρτάνει διὰ τούτων κολάζεται, xvi. 1 δι' ὁμοίων, Didaché 16 σωθήσονται ὑπ' αὐτοῦ τοῦ καταθέματος, Psq. Rabbathi אנכי אנכי הוא מנחמכם (with the parallels in ed. Friedm. 156 b) "Saith the Holy One... בו בדבר שאני מכה אני מרפא...for it is said *and I will heal thee* ממכותיך (Jer. xxx. 17) *of* and by *thy wounds,*" Zohar on Ex. יתרו (f. 83 b₂₄ Lublin 1882) Torah study saves מאשא אחרא דגיהנם, Heb. Auth. P. B. p. 49 n., 1 Pet. iii. 21 σώζει βάπτισμα & 2 Pet. iii. 6 ὕδατι ἀπώλετο.   Note that נחש *serpent* is by Gematria משיח *Messiah.*

18.

p. 31, ll. 8 *more women*] Or *Qui multiplicat* UXORES *multiplicat veneficas.* So Orelli in *Opuscula Graecorum veterum sententiosa et moralia* II. 455 (1821), cf. Sanh. 100 b, Schechter in *J. Q. R.* III. 691 & *Studies in Judaism* no. 13, Maim. *Moreh Nebukhim* III. 37. The Christian view of woman is implicitly contained in the Old Testament.

מרבה שלום. Ecclus. i. 18 The fear of the Lord is the crown of wisdom, making peace and perfect health to flourish, Syr. *et multiplicans pacem ac vitam atque sanitatem,* Hebrew perhaps מרבה שלום ומרפא.

19.

p. 33, ll. 9 עשית תורה] Josh. xxii. 5 לעשות את המצוה ואת התורה, Neh. ix. 34 לא עשו תורתך. Sifra קדושים Lev. xx. 16 (92 d ed. Weiss 1862) compares trees שעושין את הפירות and man שעושה את התורה, cf. Lev. Rab. 27. 1 הצדיקים עושים פירות.   Ecclus. xix. 20 ποίησις νόμου, 1 Macc. ii. 67 ποιητὰς τοῦ νόμου.   The verb "do" in Hebrew is ordinarily followed by מצוה, דברי תורה (Rom. ii. 14 τὰ τοῦ νόμου) &c. rather than by תורה.   Midr. Ps. xv. (p. 119 ed. Buber) כאלו עשה כל המצות, but Ps. cxix. (p. 492) אם עשית את התורה כל ימי חייך. Ps. xvii. (p. 132) מצוה is to תורה as a candle to the sun (Prov. vi. 23).

Although מעשי התורה (Heb. N.T.) is an obvious rendering of "works of the law," it does not appear that it was a current phrase in Rabbinic. Torah is not exactly νόμος, and "faith" as well as good "works" (III. 17) was required for the fulfilment of the Torah. Compare Ecclus. xxxii. 24 R.V. He that believeth the law giveth heed to the commandment, St Mark i. 15 believe in the gospel, Sanday and Headlam on Rom. iii. 3 ἠπίστησαν.

For the collective singular מעשה (Rom. ii. 15 τὸ ἔργον τοῦ νόμου) see III.

24 המעשה לפי והכל, Sukkah v. 4 (Surh. II. 277) מעשה ואנשי חסידים, Berak.
7 a אבותיהם מעשה, Sanh. 44 b זמרי מעשה. A Midrash תורה מעשה is
printed in *Kol Bo* § 118 (Venice 1547), and in Jellinek's *Bet ha-Midrasch*.

For מעשה in the sense *historia rei gestae* see Buxt. 1678, Menach. x. 2
(p. 83, n. 12), cf. תורה מעשי in Ben Jacob's *Oçar ha-Sefarim* p. 358, no.
1929 (Wilna 1880).

20.

p. 35, II. 12—13 *good way...evil way*] See *The Two Ways in Hermas
and Xenophon* (Journ. of Philol. XXI. 243—258). The Torah is likened
(p. 257) in T. J. Chagigah II. 1 to two paths, the one of אור *fire* the other
of שלג *snow*, cf. Aboth R. N. XXVIII. (Schechter p. 86) To what is the
matter like? to an army marching between ways of fire and snow &c.,
Ecclus. xv. 16 He hath set fire and water before thee : thou shalt stretch
forth thy hand unto whichsoever thou wilt. See also *The Book of the
Secrets of Enoch* p. xxi. and chap. xxx. 15 ed. Charles (1896).

Hermas harps upon the same theme with variations when he speaks of
the two Angels that accompany a man, and of his personified good Ἐπιθυμία
and evil Ἐπιθυμία. Compare in Maim. *Moreh Nebukhim* III. 22 (Friedländer p. 100) "According to our Sages the evil inclination, the adversary
(*satan*), and the angel [of death] are undoubtedly identical, and the adversary being called "angel" because he is among the sons of God, and the
good inclination being in reality an angel, it is to the good and the evil
inclinations that they refer in their well-known words, *Every person is
accompanied by two angels, one being on his right side, one on his left*,"
and see the passage of Baba Bathra cited near the end of Excursus V.

On the next folio (Baba B. 17 a) it is said that *the angel of death had
no power over* certain persons. "But," remarks Dr Friedländer in a note
on *Moreh Nebukhim* III. 51 (p. 293), "Maimonides holds that *angel of
death* and *evil inclination* are identical, and accordingly in the passage
referred to the Patriarchs and Moses, Aaron and Miriam are said to have
been free from evil inclination." Such a result shews that the
expressions said to be synonymous are not merely different names for the
same thing.

On the other hand compare St James i. 13—14 μηδεὶς πειραζόμενος κ.τ.λ.
with Ecclus. xxi. 27 *When the ungodly curseth Satan he curseth his own
soul*, on which Dr Edersheim writes in the *Speaker's Commentary*, "This
certainly accords with an exceptional Rabbinic view, which identifies Satan
with the *Yetser ha-Ra*, the evil inclination." Cf. Ecclus. xv. 11—12.

As the evil יצר is in the end to be slain by the Holy One (p. 130), so
ἔσχατος ἐχθρὸς καταργεῖται ὁ θάνατος (1 Cor. xv. 26). As Satan is
called σκάνδαλον (Matt. xvi. 23), so the evil יצר (p. 130), which is also connected with אבן אפל (Job xxviii. 3) in Gen. Rab. 89. 1 and Jalq. II. 915.

Hermas, so to say, makes the evil Ἐπιθυμία an Angel of Death which delivers εἰς θάνατον, calls it τοῦ διαβόλου θυγάτηρ, says that if resisted φεύξεται ἀπὸ σοῦ μακράν, and says the like of the Devil. See *Mand.* XII. 1, 2, 5, St James iv. 7.

21.

p. 36, n. 31 (cf. p. 41) *heart*] St Mark xii. 30 quotes Deut. vi. 5 "with all thine heart, and with all thy soul, and with all thy might" with the explanatory addition of διανοίας κ.τ.λ., and St Matt. xxii. 37 keeps "mind" and omits "might." Sifré II. § 32 (Fr. 73 a) explains בכל לבבך by בשני יצריך with thy two natures or impulses, the evil and the good, cf. Midr. Ps. ix. 2. On the heart see also Midr. Eccl. i. 7 "all the rivers run into the sea."

On *Cor malignum* in IV. Ezra iii. 21 see Sanday and Headlam on Romans v. 12—14 (p. 137, 1895).   The *yeçer* being "the imagination of the thoughts of the *heart*," as the heart is called uncircumcised so the evil *yeçer* is called uncircumcised (p. 130).

Heart and heart. See Ps. xii. 3 בלב ולב ידברו, 1 Chron. xii. 33, 38 not of *heart and heart*...but with *a perfect heart*. This idiom suggests an explanation of Prov. xxi. 8 הפכפך דרך איש וזר וזך ישר פעלו, A.V. "The way of man is froward and strange : but as for the pure, his work is right," R.V. "The way of him that is laden with guilt [Arab. *wzr*] is exceeding crooked : but as for the pure, his work is right (marg. *straight*)." On this difficult verse the commentary קב ונקי has the following note נתן גדר הפכפך, לא׳ש הפכפך והוח ס׳ם לו לפעמ׳ס דרך א׳ס ולפעמ׳ס דרך זר the is a person whose way is sometimes one man's and sometimes another's, at times his own at times a stranger's. Compare the Homeric γναθμοῖσι γελοίων ἀλλοτρίοισιν, they laughed "with alien lips." He is, as we may say, א׳ש לב ולב, a man of two hearts or δίψυχος, in contrast with זך the *pure*. St James, possibly referring to the verse, writes "a doubleminded man, unstable in all his ways...and purify your hearts, ye doubleminded" (i. 8, iv. 8). There is apparently no adjective διπλοκάρδιος corresponding to διπλοκαρδία, which is found in chap. 6 of the Didaché.

22.

p. 37, ll. 15 (cf. pp. 63, 70, 77, 82, 98, 130) יצר הרע *in Ecclesiasticus and the New Testament*] *Test.* 12 *Patr.* Aser 1, 5 (pp. 183, 185 ed. Sinker 1869) suggests that Ecclus. xxxiii. 15 πάντα...δύο δύο ἐν κατέναντι τοῦ ἑνός includes the δύο διαβούλια, the evil *yeçer* and the good *yeçer*.

Prof. Margoliouth finds *yeçer* and יצר הרע in other verses of Ecclus. (*Inaug. Lect. & Expositor* 1890). Thus, while in Ecclus. xvii. 6 διαβούλιον (Syr. *creavit*) seems to be a rendering of the verb יצר mistaken for the noun יֵצֶר, this was apparently the original of ἐννόημα (p. 77) in Ecclus. xxi. 11 "He that keepeth the law becometh master of his *yeçer* (Syr. ܢܘܗܩ)." The Torah is said to be an antidote or condiment to the evil *yeçer* in Sukkah 52 b, Qiddush. 30 b, Baba B. 16 a, Gen. Rab. 22. 6, Aboth R. N. xvi. Note that כבש has the sense *condire* (Buxt. 1010).　　We may assume that יצר הרע כו' was the original of Ecclus. xxxvii. 3 ὦ πονηρὸν ἐνθύμημα [*imagination...evil* Gen. vi., viii.] πόθεν ἐνεκυλίσθης; Syr. *Inimicus et sceleratus quorsum creati sunt?*, and that Syr. read צר by error for יצר. Syr. and Vulg. suggest ἐκτίσθης [om. εν after πόθεν] for ἐκυλίσθης. Note that "enemy" is a name of יצר הרע, comparing St Paul's ἔχθρα and ἔσχατος ἐχθρός, and that God repented that He had created it (p. 130, Gen. vi. 5—6).　　While the New Testament psychology rests more or less upon the Torah (Eph. iv. 24 ed. Ellicott), it may contain Rabbinic elements. If יצר הרע was known to Ben Sira, we shall perhaps find some of its many names (p. 130) in the earliest Christian writings.

The two Men in Man. We have seen that the πονηρός is sometimes interpreted יצר הרע. Sukkah 52 b deduces from 2 Sam. xii. 4, "And there came *a traveller* unto the rich man, and he spared to take of his own flock and of his own herd, to dress for *the wayfaring man* that was come unto him; but took the poor man's lamb, and dressed it for *the man* that was come to him," that the evil *yeçer* comes to a man at the first as a *traveller*, then becomes a *guest* (ארח ξένος), and at last the *man*, comm. בעל הבית οἰκοδεσπότης, or we may say that it becomes the man himself, for the "nature" which the strong man overcomes is "self," cf. Gen. Rab. 22. 6 (Wünsche p. 101). The evil and the good יצר together make two ἄνθρωποι in man. Compare St Jerome's application of Levit. xvii. ἄνθρωπος ἄνθρωπος quoted below, and St Paul's ἔσω and ἔξω, and his "old" and "new" ἄνθρωπος. The ἔσω [Plato ἐντὸς] ἄνθρωπος and the κρυπτὸς τῆς καρδίας ἄνθρωπος (1 Pet. iii. 4) correspond to the good *yeçer*, whereas in the Talmud the evil *yeçer* is called κρυπτός (p. 130), in accordance with St Mark vii. 21 ἔσωθεν γὰρ ἐκ τῆς καρδίας κ.τ.λ. (Gen. vi. 5).

Aboth R. N. xvi. (Schechter p. 64) has a parable, "Whereunto is the matter like? The evil *yeçer* is like two men who went into an inn." One was arrested for brigandage and asked who was with him. Unwilling to die alone, he informed against his companion. So too says *yeçer ha-ra'*, "Seeing that I am to perish in the world to come [p. 130], I will destroy the whole body."

Joma 69 b quotes Zech. v., where a woman represents wickedness. They say, Since it is καιρὸς εὐπρόσδεκτος let us pray for pardon for the spirit (יצרא) of transgression. If thou kill him (or that גברא *man*), the world perisheth (*comm.* because there would be no increasing and multiplying). For *Variae Lectiones* and parallels see Rabbinovicz ד"ס iv. 201 (1871). Whether expressly called גברא or not, the Evil Impulse is here depicted anthropomorphically.

The two Minds in Man. St Paul's word φρόνημα, synonyms of which are used to render יצר, may itself have been suggested by it. On φρόνημα σαρκός see Art. IX. *De Peccato Originali*, comparing Buxt. 973 יצר הרע *Concupiscentia mala...qua homo naturaliter ad malum propendet & in*

malum inclinat.   Tertullian writes in *De Anima* 41 that
"naturae corruptio *alia natura* est, habens suum deum et patrem, ipsum
scilicet corruptionis auctorem." According to Shabbath 105 b the evil
yeçer is a "strange god" within a man (Phil. iii. 19), and "idolatry" is
among its works (Gal. v. 20).   Another word for יצר is ἐπιθυμία,
desire. The two Desires are personified in Herm. *Mand.* XII. The good
one is to be put on (ἐνδεδυμένος...ἐνδύσαι), like the "new man" (Eph. iv. 24),
with which it is thus connected. Qiddush. 81 b יצר אלבשה her *yeçer*
clothed her.   See also Note 20, and Rom. ii. 15 τῶν λογισμῶν
κατηγορούντων κ.τ.λ. with Schoettgen's note.

St Jerome on Ecclesiastes (cf. *The Jews in the Works of the Church
Fathers* by Dr S. Krauss in *J. Q. R.* VI.) :

Eccl. iv. *Melior est puer pauper et sapiens quam rex senex et stultus
qui nescit providere in posterum. Quoniam de domo vinctorum &c....*
Hebraeus meus, cujus saepe facio mentionem, cum Ecclesiasten mecum
legeret, haec Baracibam [Rab. Aqiba], quem unum vel maxime admi-
rantur, super praesenti loco tradidisse testatus est. Melior est interior
homo, qui post quartum decimum [p. 98] pubertatis annum in nobis
exoritur, exteriore homine, qui de matris alvo natus est, qui nescit
recedere a vitio, et qui de domo vinctorum, de utero videlicet materno,
ad hoc exivit ut regnaret (*al.* regnet) in vitiis. Qui etiam in potestate
sua pauper effectus est, mala omnia perpetrando. Vidi eos qui in priore
homine vixerunt, et cum secundo homine postea versati sunt, eo videlicet
qui pro priore decessore generatus est : intellexique omnes in homine
priore peccasse antequam, secundo nascente, duo homines fierent. Quia
vero ad meliora conversi, et post Y litteram philosophorum, sinistro
tramite derelicto, ad dextrum apicem contenderunt, et secundum, id est,
novissimum hominem sunt secuti, non laetabuntur in eo, id est, in priore.
Hos duos homines et Apostolus contestatur (2 Thess. ii.) et Leviticus
non tacet: *Homo, homo* [Sept. ἄνθρωπος ἄνθρωπος] *si voluerit* illud vel
illud (Levit. xvii.).

Eccl. ix. *Civitas parva et viri in ea pauci &c....*Aliter Hebraeus ita
hunc locum interpretatus est : Civitas parva homo est, qui etiam apud
philosophos minor mundus vocatur. Et viri in ea pauci, membra de
quibus homo ipse contexitur. Cum autem venerit adversus eam rex
magnus diabolus, et quaesierit locum per quem possit irrumpere, invenitur
in ea humilis et sapiens, et quieta *cogitatio interioris hominis*, et servat
urbem quae obsessa ab hostibus cingebatur.

Midr. Tillim on Ps. ix. explains "with my whole heart" as meaning
with יצר טוב and יצר רע, and finds these in Eccl. iv. 13, where (it says)
the one is called *puer pauper et sapiens* because it is joined to a man
only from and after his thirteenth year, is not obeyed, and sets men in
good ways, and the other is called *rex senex et stultus* because all the
members of the body obey it, it is with a man from birth to old age, and it
sets men in evil ways (cf. Targ. & Midr. Eccl., Nedar. 32 b, Ab. R. N.

xvi.). St Jerome's *cogitatio* (al. *sensus*) of the ἔσω ἄνθρωπος is the good יצר, cf. Gen. viii. 21 Vulg. *Sensus enim et cogitatio humani cordis in malum prona sunt ab adolescentia sua*, that is " de matris alvo" according to T. J. Berak. III. 6 d_{16}, cf. Gen. R. 34. 10 (Wünsche p. 152).

In Rom. vi. 12—14, " Let not sin therefore reign in your mortal body... Neither yield ye your members as instruments of unrighteousness unto sin...For sin shall not have dominion over you," there may be an allusion to the "rex senex" who reigns over the members, as well as to Gen. iv. 7, which is also possibly referred to in other passages of the New Testament, as Luke xxii. 31, 1 Pet. v. 8. From חטאת *fem.* followed by רובץ *masc.* it is inferred that the evil *yeçer* is first weak then strong (Gen. R. 22. 6, Wünsche p. 101). In Nedar. 32 b it is made out by Gematria that the Holy One made Abram king at first over 243 members and afterwards, when he was called Abraham, over all the 248 members of the body.

Abraham was פרוש אהבה, a Pharisee of the highest class. He made the evil *yeçer* good, and made a covenant with him. His heart was נאמן לפניך (Neh. ix. 8), whereas David's was חלל within him (Psalm cix. 22). See T. J. Berakh. IX. 7 (14 b).

The two Treasures. In Matt. xii. 35 (Luke vi. 45) ὁ ἀγαθὸς ἄνθρωπος ἐκ τοῦ ἀγαθοῦ θησαυροῦ [Deut. xxviii. 12] ἐκβάλλει ἀγαθά, καὶ ὁ πονηρὸς ἄνθρωπος ἐκ τοῦ πονηροῦ θησαυροῦ ἐκβάλλει πονηρά, the evil אוצר may have been suggested by the evil יצר, cf. *Test.* Aser 1 ὁ θησαυρὸς τοῦ διαβόλου, al. διαβουλίου (*yeçer*). Cf. Zech. xi. 13 "to the potter," with Mr W. H. Lowe's note on the reading.

The Book of the Secrets of Enoch. On ch. xxx. 16, " I knew his nature, he did not know his nature. Therefore his ignorance is a woe to him that he should sin, and I appointed death on account of his sin," Mr Charles in a note remarks that this ignorance "is not first and directly an ignorance of moral distinctions, but of his nature with its good and evil impulses (יצר הרע and יצר הטוב)." Comparing the text with Deut. xxxi. 21 For I know את יצרו, and Ps. ciii. 14 For He knoweth יצרנו (Aboth R. N. xvi. *sub fin.*), we may suppose that "Enoch" refers as the note suggests to יצה"ר and יצה"ט.

On the Evil Impulse see also Baba B. 78 b " *Wherefore they that* SPEAK IN PROVERBS *say &c.* (Num. xxi. 27). These are they that RULE (המושלים) over their *yeçer*," Midr. Ps. ix. (Buber p. 80) & Aboth IV. 2 n. טוב מאד includes יצה"ר, Ps. xxxiv. (p. 246) & Gen. Rab. 54. 1 If thine enemy the Evil Impulse hunger feed him with bread of Torah &c., Ps. cxix. (p. 492) It has no power over one who has the Torah in his heart ולא נוגע בו, cf. καὶ ὁ πονηρὸς οὐχ ἅπτεται αὐτοῦ (1 Joh. v. 18), and see Aboth R. N. ed. Schechter pp. 30, 70, 158 &c.

The Speaker's Commentary on Ecclesiasticus. Ecclus. xv. 14—15 "He himself made man from the beginning, and left him in the hands of his COUNSEL," διαβουλίου for Heb. יצר (Edersheim). Mr Schechter compares MIDRASH HA-GADOL on Gen. iv. 6—7 (col. 107) :

ואם לא תיטיב לפתח חטאת רבץ. הרי את מסור בידו של יצר
הרע שהוא רובץ על הפתח.

Hence and from the Syriac of Ecclus. *l.c.* ואשלם אנון ביד יצרהון it appears
that Ben Sira probably wrote that the Creator מסר delivered man into the
hand of his יצר with its tendency to evil, cf. Qiddush. 30 b and if ye be not
occupied in Torah ye are נמסרים בידו. With this agrees Rom. i. 24, 26, 28
παρέδωκεν [מסר] αὐτοὺς ὁ θεός, cf. 1 Cor. v. 5.   Notice the saying
Apoc. Baruch LIV. 19 each one of us has been the Adam of his own soul.

Midrash ha-Gadol continues *If thou doest not well*, the consequence will
be שאת *a rising* (Lev. xiv. 56), that is leprosy; and adds that the verse
Gen. iv. 7 is one of five of doubtful punctuation, for שאת may also be taken
with תיטיב.   Supposing it to mean שאת פנים in contrast with
נפלו פניך, a possible construction gives the sense, Sin COUCHETH [Gen.
xlix. 9 *he couched as a lion*] at the door, watching אם תיטיב שאת ואם לא
כו׳ whether thou wilt or wilt not (cf. Eccl. xii. end) recover from thy
passion. Ecclus. xxvii. 10 *As the lion lieth in wait...so sin &c.* serves as
a link between Gen. iv. 7 *sin coucheth* and 1 Pet. v. 8—9 ὡς λέων ὠρυόμενος
...ᾧ ἀντίστητε κ.τ.λ. Compare St James iv. 7.

Ecclus. xvii. 6 *Counsel* &c. "In omitting the word the Syriac is probably faithful to the original" (Edersheim). Say rather with Prof. Margoliouth that it rightly renders יצר as a verb, cf. Ps. xciv. 9 יוצר עין *He that
formed the eye.*

Ecclus. xxi. 11 He that keepeth the law *getteth the mastery* [rule]
over his INCLINATION (Edersheim), Syr. אלין יצרה. Cf. Aboth IV. 2 הכובש
את יצרו. Mastery of inclination by means of Torah is a favourite theme of
the Rabbis. All things were created in syzygies and Torah is an opposite
of יצה״ר. See Eccl. vii. 14, Ecclus. xxxiii. 14—15, Chagigah 15 a, Midrash
Temurah in Jellinek *Bet ha-Midrasch* I. 108 שכל דבר שברא בשתים ובשתוף,
Baba B. 16 a He created the Evil Impulse and Torah as תבלין thereto.

On Ecclus. xxi. 27 *When the ungodly curseth Satan* see Note 20.

Ecclus. xxxvii. 3 O WICKED IMAGINATION. Syr. read צר ורע by mistake for יצר הרע (Margoliouth). The context is about friends who are
false or have turned to foes. Such mischief (Midr. Ps. xxxiv.) is wrought
by the Evil Impulse, himself the most inveterate of enemies, who after
associating with a man all his life will trip him up at forty, fifty, sixty if he
can. היש לך שונא גדול מזה canst thou have a greater enemy than this ?

23.

p. 40, n. 45 [מין] See Levy, Kohut. Benjamin Musafia makes המינים an
abbreviation of המאמינים *the believers* (N.T. πιστεύοντες, πιστοί). This
suggests that מין might be rendered *misbeliever*, cf. *miscreant.*

In Rosh ha-Shan. 17 a the "Minim und Denuncianten" [Buxt. 1234] are condemned for ever מפני שפשטו ידיהם בזבול because they stretched forth their hands against the Temple: their judgment is to outlast Gehinnom (Midr. Ps. xlix. מזבול לו, Buber p. 278). In explanation of this Dr M. Joel (cf. Graetz *Gesch. d. Juden*) quotes Gen. Rab. 64. 10 (Wünsche p. 308), where it is said that, when the wicked kingdom in the days of Jehoshua ben Chananiah (II. 10)—that is Rome under Hadrian— had decreed the rebuilding of the Temple, the Kuthim, in the words of their predecessors (Ezra iv. 13), opposed it.

The Ebionites (Joel *Blicke* I. 26) according to Irenaeus I. 22 (Mass. 26) adored Jerusalem *quasi domus sit Dei*. In *Epist. Barn.* 16 (Lightft.-Harmer p. 284, 1891) we read "Moreover I will tell you likewise concerning the temple, how these wretched men being led astray set their hope on the building...as being a house of God...*Behold they that pulled down this temple themselves shall build it* [Is. xlix. 17]...Now also the very servants of their enemies shall build it up." Cf. Psq. Rabbathi (Friedmann 149 b) ואתה צריך לבנותה כו'. Those who felt with Barnabas would have looked with disfavour upon the rebuilding of the Temple at Jerusalem.

It is said in T. J. Megillah I. 11, 71 c_9 that the Torah cannot be adequately translated אלא יוונית except into Greek. The Gemara continues בורגני אחד בידא להם ארמית מתוך יוונית he made an Aramaic Targum *from the Greek*. It has been thought that Targ. "Onkelos" was so named as being based upon Aquila's Greek rendering of the Torah. See Graetz *History of the Jews* II. 589 (trans. by B. Löwy 1891).

The injunction not to teach one's son Greek (Sotah IX. 14, Surh. III. 304) dates from the war of Quietus (𝔄 105 b_7 ed. Lowe קיטם, Surh. טיטום). For examples of Hebrew words in the Bible read Rabbinically as Greek see Dr M. Sachs *Beiträge* I. 19 (Joel *Blicke* I. 51). The Munich MS. reading ההוא פילוספא for ההוא פלנספא קבא in Shabbath 116 a is conjecturally explained by "a certain אפסקבא *ἐπίσκοπος*" in Mr Lowe's *Fragment of T. B.* p. 68 *b*.

24.

p. 43, III. 1 *whence...whither*] Clem. *Cor.* 38 ἐκ ποίας ὕλης ἐγενήθημεν κ.τ.λ., Mekhilta *Shir.* נורא תהלות (Fr. 42 a), הקב״ה צר צורה במים כו', Heracliti Ephes. *Reliq.* 68 (ed. Bywater 1877) ἐξ ὕδατος δὲ ψυχή. Sotah 5 a makes רימה (שאול or) סרוחה, בושה of נוטריקון a (בשר or) בסר, see Buxt. 329 & פחד יצחק. Midr. Ps. xvi. 10 כו' שלא ימס בשרו, cf. Acts ii. 29—31.

25.

p. 44, n. 8 מצפון] Midr. *Elleh ha-Debarim Zuta* (p. 22 ed. Buber) Messiah is to come from the north, Lev. Rab. 9. 6 מלך משיח שנתון בצפון.

26.

p. 44, n. 8 SHEKINAH] Compare Ecclus. xxiv. 8 " Then the Creator of all
things gave me *Wisdom* a commandment ; and he that created me made
my tabernacle to rest, and said, Let thy tabernacle be in Jacob, and thine
inheritance in Israel."

27.

p. 45, III. 7 *by night*] How did Moses on the mount know when it was
day and when night ? Because he was taught Scripture by day and
Mishnah or Oral Law by night. See Midr. Ps. xix. יום ליום (Buber p. 166),
Tanchuma כי תשא ל/ו (I. 127 b Warsaw 1879), Pirqe R. El. 46, Magen Aboth
on the Ages of Man. Or he learned Torah in the daytime and repeated it
by himself at night, to teach Israel that they should be working at Torah
day and night. During the forty days he was fed מזיו השכינה, or he ate
bread of Torah and drank water of Torah (Prov. ix. 5, Is. lv. 1). See
Buber's Tanchuma כי תשא 60 a, Buxt. 1861 on פשט.

28.

p. 48, n. 19 *punctuation*] RISH, that is R. Jacob Shimshoni or ben
Shimshon, in the so-called Machsor Vitry (Hurwitz p. 462) writes of things
revealed to Moses " And not these only were said to Moses from Sinai by
word of mouth according to what we learn in the *pereq* [of the Mishnah
commencing] אין בין המודר &c." On this "famous passage
in Nedarim 37 b *sq.*" see Mr I. Harris on *The Rise and Development of
the Massorah* in the *Jewish Quarterly Review* (I. 138, 1889)*. On the
authority of Rab the verse Nehemiah viii. 8 is made in Nedar. *l.c.* to allude
to הפסוקים the "versual divisions," and פיסוק טעמים the "pausal divisions"
or punctuation of verses by accents, or as some think the מסורות.
" Obviously the Talmud is not referring to written signs of any kind, for
Nehemiah viii. 8 is describing a public recital of the Law. The divisions
spoken of must therefore be of the nature of elocutionary pauses."
RISH *l.c.* says that points are not Mosaic but were invented by the scribes,
which accounts for the existence of three systems of ניקוד *pointing*
in his time. Compare Dr M. Friedländer's notice of *A Third System of
Symbols for the Hebrew Vowels and Accents* in the *Jewish Quarterly
Review* VII. 564 *sq.* (1895).

Rab's interpretation of Neh. viii. 8 is found also in Megillah 3 a, and
Bachja on the Pentateuch gives it s.v. אדני (Gen. xviii. 3) with ניקוד in
place of פסקי טעמים. "They forgot these מסורות and restored them
again " (Megil. *l.c.*).

---

* See also Prof. W. Bacher's *Contribution to the History of the term
"Massorah"* at the end of *J. Q. R.* vol. III. (1891), and the same writer's article
on *The Origin of the word Haggadah (Agada)* in *J. Q. R.* IV. 406—429.

R. Tobiah ben Eliezer (cent. x.) in his commentary Leqach Tob on Canticles interprets Job xxviii. 27 אז ראה כו' (doubtless on the authority of some Midrash) as referring to *Miqra, Targum, Accentuation, Pointing.* See the Cambridge University MS. Additional 378, fol. 25 a.

On cases of punctuation by accents see also p. 152, *Crit. Note* III. 21, Joma 52 a & 31 b Tos. ד"ה ופשט on Gen. iv. 7 שאת, Ex. xxv. 33 משוקדים, Ex. xvii. 9 מחר, Gen. xlix. 7 ארור, Deut. xxxi. 16 וקם. In T. J. Abodah Z. II. 7, 41 c & d these five references are given in their Biblical order and R. Tanchuma adds Gen. xxxiv. 7. Cf. Sanhedrin 90 b, Mekhilta עמלק par. 1 (Fr. 54 a), Gen. Rab. 80. 6 (Wünsche p. 393), Cant. Rab. i. 2 כי טובים כו'.

29.

p. 50, III. 16] Targ. Eccl. x. 16 *Woe to thee O land of Israel when the wicked Jeroboam shall reign over thee...and thy magnates eat bread before they offer the morning sacrifice.* Midr. Shocher Tob (Buber p. 19) & R. D. Qimchi (p. 7 ed. Schiller-Szinessy) on Ps. i. "his *leaf* shall not wither," even the שיחה of the wise is instructive, cf. *Epist. Barn.* 11. 8 "*Folia*...hoc est quia omnis sermo &c.," and see Schechter on A Jewish Boswell in *Studies in Judaism.*

30.

p. 55, n. 32 1 Cor. xi. 4—5 ἀκατακαλύπτῳ τῇ κεφαλῇ κ.τ.λ. (cf. p. 82)] For parallels and contrasts see J. J. Wetstenii *Nov. Test. Graecum.* Compare Juvenal *Sat.* VI. 390 *Pro cithara velare caput* i.e. sacra facere capite velato. See also Brüll *Jahrbücher für jüd. Gesch. u. Litteratur* VIII. 51 art. *Die Haarbedeckung der jüd. Frauen,* Abrahams *Jewish Life in the Middle Ages* p. 278.

Plutarch *Quaest. Rom.* 14 διὰ τί τοὺς γονεῖς ἐκκομίζουσιν οἱ μὲν υἱοὶ συγκεκαλυμμένοι αἱ δὲ θυγατέρες γυμναῖς ταῖς κεφαλαῖς καὶ ταῖς κομαῖς λελυμέναις; "The custom still obtains in West Cumberland for the male mourners to wear their hats in Church at a Funeral. Within the last 20 years the men observed the same practice in Church on the Sunday but one after the Funeral, but I have not seen them do it lately. All the mourners however remain seated during the whole service on both days" (Signed J. T. POLLOCK *Vicar of Brigham, Cumberland.* 16 Nov. 1896).

1 Cor. xi. 7 ἀνὴρ...δόξα θεοῦ ὑπάρχων (cf. Heb. i. 3). See *J. Q. R.* III. 695 art. by Mr Schechter *The Quotations from Ecclesiasticus in Rabbinic Literature* no. 19 הדר אלהים בני אדם והדר בני אדם כסותו *sons of men are God's glory, a son of man's is his raiment,* cf. Ps. xxix. 2 בהדרת קדש.

1 Cor. xi. 10 ἐξουσίαν. A crown or cap ἐπὶ τῆς κεφαλῆς may signify possession of or subjection to authority. H. A. W. Meyer *Kommentar über das N. T.* "*Hitzig* aber in d. theol. Jahrb. 1854 p. 129 ff. das Wort für ein *judengriechisches* ausgiebt, und zwar aus ἐξ ἴσου entstanden, da der

Schleier zwei vorne und hinten im Gleichgewichte überhangende Hälften gehabt habe."

1 Cor. xi. 10 διὰ τοὺς ἀγγέλους. Granted that it was comely for a woman to have her head veiled in the presence of men, why should she when praying (ver. 5) even in private have it veiled διὰ τοὺς ἀγγέλους ? St Paul, himself conscious of being a spectacle both to angels and men (1 Cor. iv. 9), would have others no less awake to the presence of the unseen witnesses, cf. Heb. xii. 1 νέφος μαρτύρων κ.τ.λ. Everyone, it was said, was accompanied by two angels (Note 20). When a man desired absolute privacy, he begged his angels to leave him for a season (Berak. 60 b *init.*). A woman praying or prophesying was to think of her angels as close at hand, and to veil herself before them as if they were men.

Gen. Rab. 21. 9 (Wünsche p. 98) on Gen. iii. 24 המתהפכת teaches that angels change their shapes and appear at different times as men, women [Zech. v. 9], winds or spirits, angels.

For THEGRI (al. *Hegrin*) as the name of the angel in Herm. *Vis.* IV. 2. 4 Dr J. Rendel Harris has proposed to read, and Dr Harmer accordingly reads, SEGRI from Dan. vi. 22 סגר. Note that one of the three names of רוח פסקונית (comm. *which is Gabriel*) in Sanhed. 44 b (cf. Jalq. II. 353 *init.*) is סיגרון from סגר (Kohut *A. C.* VI. 22). Brüll *Jahrbücher für Jüdische Geschichte* I. 158 (1874) art. *Fremdsprachliche Wörter in Talm. u. Midr.* identifies סיגרון with Σκίρων (or Σκείρων), and refers on רוח פסקונית to *Tanchuma Wesot-habracha* § 6 (125 b, Warsaw 1879).

31.

p. 56, n. 35 *the incommunicable name*] On the Tetragrammaton or Name of Four Letters יהוה see *Dict. of Bible* art. JEHOVAH by Mr Aldis Wright (1863), Kuenen *The Religion of Israel* and *Hibbert Lectures* n. 4, *Studia Biblica* I. art. 1 by Prof. Driver (1885), Leopold Löw *Gesammelte Schriften* I. (Szegedin 1889) art. 7 *Die Aussprache des vierbuchstabigen Gottesnamens* 1867, Maim. *Moreh Nebukhim* I. 62.

The Tetragrammaton יהוה may be older than יהו, יו, יה, and יהו may have been derived from it by apocopation. As the verb-form יִשְׁתַּחֲוֶה with ו conversive reduces to יִשְׁתַּחוּ, so from יהוה (it is said) may have come יהו, and thence יו and יה. " There are no grammatical objections to this."

But in proper names are found some of the archaisms which are classed as exceptions to modern rules. For example, " Similar to the Aramaic is the Hebrew form, which appears in its integrity in the proper name חֹוְי; but ordinarily ai has passed into ĕ, and we get the form חֹוֶה." See the late Prof. W. Wright's *Lectures on the Comparative Grammar of the Semitic Languages* p. 269 (Camb. 1890), and ib. p. 255 " We now proceed to the large and important class of verbs in which the weak letter occupies the third place in the root. In our Hebrew Grammars these are generally called verbs ל"ה, but as the ה is merely a vowel letter, I prefer speaking of

them as verbs ל״ו or ל״ע, according to circumstances. Verbs ל״ה, strictly
so called, are such as גָּבַהּ, which pertain to a quite different class, *verba
tertiae gutturalis*." A ל״ה verb not strictly so called is שׁחה, " Hithpal.
הִשְׁתַּחֲוָה (tertia radicali geminata...) fut. apoc. יִשְׁתַּחוּ, in pausa יִשְׁתָּחוּ "
(Gesen. *Thesaur.*). Accordingly we may say that the root in question is
properly not שׁחה but שׁחו׳, and that in "fut. apoc. יִשׁתחו" it becomes
itself again, after conversion to a pseudo ל״ה form and expansion therefrom
to שׁחוה in יִשׁתחוה. In any case the quadriliteral שׁחוה must have grown
out of some more elementary form of the root. Hence the comparison of
יהוה, יִשׁתחוה and יהו, יִשׁתחו suggests that יהו is perhaps not merely an
apocopated form of יהוה. Something still remains to be said in support of
the view that the longer is not the older form of the Name.

For ways of reading יהוה see also Bp Pearson on the words *Our Lord*
in the Creed, *Heb. Words and Synonyms* by Dr E. G. King (1884), *The
Gnostics and their Remains* by C. W. King (ed. 2 1887), Irenaeus ed.
Harvey II. 58. 1 (vol. I. p. 386) "Eodem modo et Jaωth [Jaωh], extensa
cum aspiratione novissima syllaba, mensuram praefinitam manifestat ; cum
autem per ο Graecam corripitur, ut puta Jaoth [Jaoh], eum qui dat fugam
malorum significat," cf. in Walton's Polyglot "Jaoth, vel potius Jaoh."
The emendation is confirmed by a reading *Jacob*, with *cob* for ωh.

In a note on Iren. I. 1. 7 Harvey suggests that the name IAΩ, which he
hesitates (p. 34, but see p. 230) to identify with יהוה, is "indicated in
the A and Ω of the Apocalypse," see Rev. i. 8 Ἐγώ εἰμι τὸ Ἄλφα καὶ τὸ
Ὦ, λέγει Κύριος, ὁ θεός, ὁ ὢν καὶ ὁ ἦν καὶ ὁ ἐρχόμενος, ὁ παντοκράτωρ.

The verse cited quotes from Ex. iii. 14 Ἐγώ εἰμι ὁ ὢν and adds καὶ
ὁ ἦν καὶ ὁ ἐρχόμενος, cf. Heb. xiii. 8 Jesus Christ is "the same yesterday,
and to day, and for ever." If at the time of the writing of the Apocalypse
the word יהוה was regarded as comprising הָיָה הֹוֶה יְהְיֶה, ἦν ὤν ἔσται, this
would have been expressed as nearly as might be in Greek by the use of A
and Ω, taken from the name IAΩ, as symbols of past and future eternity.
We have only to conjecture that this name, however much it may have
differed therefrom, was understood to be the Greek for יהוה.

Qiddushin 71 a relates in the name of R. Jochanan that the secret of
the שם בן ד׳ אותיות (Rashi קריאתו וכתיבתו ופירושו) used to be communicated to disciples once, or some say twice, in a *septennium*. The word
שבוע, which has been inappropriately rendered *week*, is now understood to
have the same meaning here as in Chullin 91 b. The ministering angels
say a song only once in a day, ואמרי לה פעם א׳ בשבת וא״ל פעם א׳ בחודש
וא״ל פעם א׳ בשנה וא״ל פעם א׳ בשבוע וא״ל פעם א׳ ביובל וא״ל פעם א׳ בעולם
or once in a *week*, month, year, *septennium*, jubilee or aeon.

Mr Schechter writes in the *Jewish Quarterly Review* VI. 427 (referring
to *Tosephta Berachoth* ix. ed. Schwartz, and Graetz *Gesch. d. Juden*), that
"At a certain period in history, when the heresy of the new sects was
threatening to affect larger classes, the Rabbis even enforced the utterance

of the Tetragrammaton in every benediction," that there might be no doubt Who was addressed.

R. Mosheh of Cordovero makes a suggestion which is quoted with approval in Tosafoth Yom Tob on Joma VI. 2 ואולי טעם הדבר כמו שכתב החכם מה״ר משה קרדואר״ו בסוף עבודת יום הכפורים שבכל יוס ה׳ו מזכירין הכהנים אותו בברכת הכהנים בנקוד אל״ף דל״ת דהיינו וכו׳ וביוס זה היה מזכיר בנקוד חול״ס סגו״ל קמ״ץ סגו״ל (Berl. 1861) i.e. that the priests in their daily blessing pronounced the TETRAGRAMMATON with the pointing of ADONAI, "that is &c.," but the high priest on the Day of Atonement pronounced it with the pointing cholem, segol, qameç, segol.

In MISHNAH Sotah VII. 6 (Surh. III. 264) on the sacerdotal blessing Num. vi. 24—26 it is said that "In Sanctuario τετραγράμματον efferebatur secundum literas: sed in Provinciis substituebatur cognomen"; but it is not said that "incurvabant se et adorabant et in facies decumbebant" at the utterance of the Name, except when they heard it "ex ore Sacerdotis magni" on the Day of Atonement (Joma l.c. Note 41). It is in order to account for this that R. Mosheh of Cordovero makes his suggestion that יהוה was not fully pronounced except by the high priest on the Day of Atonement. The pronunciation which R. Mosheh gives for it is YŏHĕWĀHĕ, an abbreviation of the complete spelling of the Name. Compare the equation of יה, that is יו״ד ה״א, by Gematria to יהוה (26).

The question of the pronunciation of the TETRAGRAMMATON is twofold. What is the correct, grammatical vocalisation of יהוה? and how was it pronounced by the high priest on the Day of Atonement? Doubtless he pronounced it not in a plain colloquial way, but with a musical intonation as in a chant or song, Heb. נעימה (Kohut A. C. v. 358 a). If it was rendered with a number of notes in excess of its proper grammatical complement of vowels, this would account for the traditional view which makes it a comprehensive שם הויה nomen essentiae, signifying that יהוה is הֹוֶה וּמְהַוֶּה, ever existent and the cause of existence. See Ex. iii. 14 with Targ. & comm., Pirqe R. El. 40 end, Tur Orach Chayim § 5, Judah ben Barzilai on יצירה ס׳ pp. 112, 116 (1885), Heb. Auth. P. B. p. 3.

The words of Irenaeus l.c. "extensa cum aspiratione novissima syllaba" evidently convey, as far as they go, a true tradition. The end of the word for ONE in the "Hear O Israel" was to be emphasised and dwelt upon (pp. 54, 117), and in the words of lamentation in Jeremiah xxii. 18 הוי אדון והוי הדה it may have been intended that the aspirated last syllable should be prolonged in like manner.

32.

p. 56, III. 21 in imagine] There is a benediction in Kethuboth 8 a and in the Hebrew Marriage Service (Auth. P. B. p. 299) " Blessed art thou, O Lord our God, King of the universe, who hast made man in thine image, after thy likeness, and hast prepared unto him, out of his very self, a

perpetual fabric, אשר יצר את האדם בצלמו בצלם דמות תבניתו והתקין
לו ממנו בנין עדי עד," in which the expression בנין *building* is traditionally
interpreted "the female," with reference to Gen. ii. 22 ויבן את הצלע כו'
and the rib *builded* he into woman, cf. Berakh. 61 a כבנין אוצר. Compare also Clem. *Hom.* XIX. 23 ἵνα τῷ ἐσομένῳ ἄρρενι αἰωνίως ἡ θήλεια τίκτῃ
δικαίους αἰωνίους υἱούς.

St Paul writes (2 Cor. v. 1) "For we know that if the earthly house of
our tabernacle be dissolved, we have a building from God, a house not
made with hands, eternal, in the heavens." This is not unlike a דרש upon
והתקין לו כו' in the benediction, which might be rendered "and didst
prepare for him *therefrom* [with especial reference to תבניתו from בנה
build] a perpetual building." Thus the בנין עדי עד would be οἰκοδομὴ ἐκ
θεοῦ...αἰώνιος, the image of God in man implying eternity. Cf. Wisdom
ii. 23 ἔκτισε τὸν ἄνθρωπον...εἰκόνα τῆς ἰδίας ἀϊδιότητος (v.l. ἰδιότητος), with
the critical note in Sanday and Headlam *Ep. to Romans* p. 51 (1895).
It is also possible that St Paul in 2 Cor. *l.c.* was allegorizing Eccl. xii.
3—5 "the keepers of the house shall tremble...because the man goeth to
his eternal house."

Philo on the *Cherubim* (Mangey I. 148) compares God to a "house."
From Jer. iii. 4 οὐχ ὡς οἶκόν με ἐκαλέσας καὶ πατέρα καὶ ἄνδρα τῆς παρθενίας
σου; he deduces ὅτι ὁ θεὸς καὶ οἶκός ἐστιν, ἀσωμάτων ἰδεῶν ἀσώματος χώρα
(cf. מקום τόπος, p. 67).

<hr/>

33.

p. 56, n. 36 *creation*] Whence was the world created? From snow
that was beneath the throne of glory, for *to the snow he saith* הוא ארץ
(Job xxxvii. 6), and the earth is his footstool. See Pirqé R. El. 3 with
Loria's commentary, and for Rambam's criticism of the statement see
Moreh Nebukhim II. 26 (vol. II. 121 ed. Friedländer 1885), Schechter
Studies in Judaism p. 83 (1896).   Jehudah b. Barzilai writes in
his commentary on *Sefer Yeçirah* p. 16 (מקיצי נרדמים Berl. 1885) that
God ברא תחלה לכל הבריות רוח הקדש להיות אות על אלהותו.

In Gen. i. 2 water is the material element, and is distinct from the
Spirit which "moved" [Deut. xxxii. 11 ירחף, Matt. iii. 16 ὡσεὶ περιστερὰν]
over it.   Compare Clem. Alex. *Ex Script. Proph. Ecl.* VII.
(Potter p. 990) αὐτίκα δι' ὕδατος καὶ πνεύματος ἡ ἀναγέννησις καθάπερ καὶ ἡ
πᾶσα γένεσις, Clem. *Hom.* XI. 24 τὰ πάντα τὸ ὕδωρ ποιεῖ τὸ δὲ ὕδωρ ὑπὸ
πνεύματος κινήσεως τὴν γένεσιν λαμβάνει...πρωτογόνῳ ἀναγεννηθεὶς ὕδατι
κ.τ.λ.   To be born ἐξ ὕδατος καὶ πνεύματος (Joh. iii. 5) should
accordingly mean, not of the one only but also of the other. In the new
birth however the material element is merged in and becomes a symbol of
the spiritual.

Ex. Rab. 15. 22 Three בריות or κτίσεις preceded the world, the water
and the wind or spirit and the fire, and they conceived and bare

respectively darkness, wisdom, and light.　See Freudenthal *Hellenistische Studien* Heft I. p. 71 (Breslau 1875).

34.

p. 59, III. 24 *everything is foreseen*]　*Everything* past, present and future *is* צפוי *seen* by God, as a watchman on his tower sees things in the distance coming and going as well as things close at hand.　This is also expressed by ראה, cf. Gen. i. 31 וירא א כו' *And God saw every thing that he had made*, Gen. Rab. 8. 4 When He was going to create the first man He *saw* righteous and wicked issuing from him (Wünsche p. 31).　　　　The point in the text is that God *foresees*, as it is said in *Apoc. Baruch* XXI. 5 (p. 37 ed. Charles) Thou...hast seen those things which are to be as those things which Thou art doing.

For illustrative uses of צפה see Gen. Rab. 4. 6 (Wünsche p. 17) At the beginning of the creation God *saw* Moses called good (Ex. ii. 2) &c., Aboth R. N. *B* VIII. (Schechter p. 23) It was צפוי *seen* before הקב"ה that the first man was going to make himself a βῆμα of wood to sit and judge upon it, Midr. Ps. lxxxiii. אדום אהלי David saw by the Holy Spirit that Edom THE WICKED was going to destroy the sanctuary (Buber p. 369), and see the passage cited below from the Jalqut.

And I also say unto thee, that thou art Peter, and upon this rock I will build my Church (Matt. xvi. 18).　Compare in Jalqut I. 766 (with ref. to ילמדנו) כי מראש צורים אראנו (Num. xxiii. 9), to let thee know the hatred of *otho rasha'* that wicked one...　*Aliter.* I see that they preceded the beginning of the creation of the world.　Parable of a king who wanted to build, and was digging down and trying to lay a foundation, but found only swamp.　When at length in one place he found פטרא *petra* underneath, בונה אני כאן אמר *he said here I build*, and he laid a foundation and built.　So when the Holy One wanted to create the world, He passed over the generations of Enoch and of the flood as unsound; but when He saw (צפה) Abraham who was going to arise He said, Lo, I have discovered a *petra* to build and to found the world upon.　Therefore He called Abraham צור *rock*, as it is said (Is. li. 1) *Look unto the rock whence ye were hewn.*　And He called Israel rocks.　And it is said (Ps. lxxiv. 2) *Remember thy congregation, which thou hast purchased of old.*　The idea of Israel is older than anything.　　　　See in Ex. Rab. 15. 7 (Wünsche p. 107) a presumably later form of this with צור for פטרא.

ib. *judged &c.*]　Cf. Ecclus. xvi. 12 As his mercy is great &c.

35.

p. 59, III. 25 *net* (Eccl. ix. 12)]　For parallels to Ecclesiastes in the New Testament see Rom. viii. 20 τῇ γὰρ ματαιότητι κ.τ.λ. (Eccl. i. 2 &c.), Rom. ii. 16 τὰ κρυπτὰ κ.τ.λ. & 2 Cor. v. 10 φανερωθῆναι κ.τ.λ. εἴτε ἀγαθὸν εἴτε φαῦλον (Eccl. xii. 14 כו' נעלם כל על במשפט).　See also Note 32.

36.

p. 60, n. 40 *the banquet*] Ps. xvi. 15 χορτασθήσομαι ἐν τῷ ὀφθῆναι τὴν δόξαν σου, Ecclus. xxiv. 21 οἱ ἐσθίοντές με...οἱ πίνοντές με (Joh. vi. 35), St Luke xiv. 15.

37.

p. 62, III. 28 *essentials*] See Chag. I. 8 (א 11) in *Crit. Note*, MISHNAH Surh. II. 416, *Chagigah* Streane p. 47 (1891) "Rules for dissolving vows fly in the air and have nothing to rest upon. Halakhoth for sabbath, festival-offerings, and trespasses are as mountains that hang by a hair, the Scripture little and the halakhoth multitudinous." With these are contrasted things which are *corpora legis*. Compare Col. ii. 16 "Let no man therefore judge you in meat, or in drink, or in respect of a feast or a new moon or *a sabbath* [σάββατα שבתא]: which are a shadow of the things to come; τὸ δὲ σῶμα τοῦ Χριστοῦ," noting that νόμος is a patristic name of Christ (Justin *Dial.* 11, p. 42 ed. Otto). Cf. Berak. 63 a and Lev. R. 24. 5 (גופי תורה), T. J. Ber. I. 3 c₃₀ (*The Decalogue* גופה של שמע), Buxt. 405, Kohut II. 334. The Rabbinic expression *fly in the air with nothing to rest upon* might have suggested ἀέρα κενεμβατεύων (*A Conjectural Emendation of Col.* ii. 18, Journ. of Philology VII. 130) to St Paul.

ib. *Aftercourses.* Clem. *Strom.* I. 20 (*l.c.* Note 2), having described Greek philosophy as φραγμὸς τοῦ ἀμπελῶνος, continues, καὶ ἡ μὲν ὡς ἄρτος ἀναγκαία πρὸς τὸ ζῆν, ἡ κατὰ τὴν πίστιν ἀληθεία· ἡ προπαιδεία δὲ προσοψήματι ἔοικεν καὶ τραγήματι. Δείπνου δὲ λήγοντος γλυκὺ τρωγάλιον, κατὰ τὸν Θηβαῖον Πίνδαρον. On פרפראות see also p. 164.

Gematria in this verse or *baba* should be taken, not in its usual exegetical sense as in the footnote (p. 62, n. 46), but in its "ursprüngliche Bedeutung Geometrie und Arithmetik," as in T. J. Terumoth v. 3 (43 c₄₇) עד שלמדנוה מחשבון גימטרי' until we learned כמה יהא בעיסה by *gematric* calculation (Zunz *G.V.* p. 326 n., 1832), which was wanted also for *tequfoth.* See Geiger on Aboth I.—III., Strack on Aboth, Kohut *A.C.*, Levy *Neuhebr. u. Chald. Wörterbuch*, Maim. *Hilk. Genebah* VIII. 1 with Maggid Mishnah, Tosafoth Yomtob. Thus Greek Science—or say with St Clement Philosophy—is ranked below חכמת האלוהות המקובלת. It may be a contradiction in terms to make προπαιδεία an aftercourse, but this best marks it as secondary to the one thing needful. On the meaning of חכמת יוונית in Sotah 49 b see Dr D. H. Joel's *Religionsphilosophie des Sohar* p. 338 (1849).

It has been thought that Gematria in Aboth includes a rudimentary form of what was afterwards called by the Arabic name Algebra. On Greek Algebra see Dr Heath's *Diophantos of Alexandria* (Camb. 1885). Notice in Levy *Nheb. Wbuch* I. 479 (1876) the word הנדסה for Mathematik und Algebra.

Rashi explains Gematria by נוטריקון (p. 100, n. 1) and חשבון אותיות
letter-reckoning. Sachs (quoted by Levy) identifies the word with
γραμματεία instead of γεωμετρία, and so Bacher (*Babl. Amoräer*). *Athbash*,
described below with some other cipher alphabets, is called Gematria by
Rab in Sanhedrin.

א״ת ב״ש. In this permutation the letters from א to ת are interchanged
with the letters in reverse order from ת to א respectively. St Jerome
writes on Jer. xxv. 26 "Sicut apud nos Graecum alphabetum usque ad
novissimam litteram per ordinem legitur, hoc est *Alpha, Betha*...rursumque
propter memoriam parvulorum solemus lectionis ordinem invertere et
primis extrema miscere, ut dicamus *Alpha, O, Betha, Psi*: sic et apud
Hebraeos...Legimus itaque *Aleph, Thau, Beth, Sin,* אתבש." He then
explains ששך as בבל disguised by Athbash.   In Jer. li. 1
ר' י' לב קמי is identified with כשדים by Athbash. See the מדות ל״ב of ר' י'
הנלילי *Mid.* 29.   On אפרא by Athbash for תונג (Prov. x. 1) see
Kohut I. 59.

According to Rab in Sanhedrin 22a the words מנא מנא תקל ופרסין
(Dan. v. 25) were written בגימטריא (that is in the Athbash cipher)
יטת יטם אדך פוגחמט, cf. Journ. of Philol. VII. 138.

Dr E. G. King in *Hebrew Words and Synonyms* p. 25 (1884) quotes
Rashbam as writing on Exodus iii. in Athbash "He calls Himself אהיה
and we call Him יהיה with *Vau* for *Yod* as in Eccl. ii. 22 כי מה הוה לאדם."

א״ל ב״ם. In this cipher the letters from א to כ are interchanged with
those from ל to ת respectively. Thus רמלא, for רמליה, becomes טבאל
(Is. vii. 6) by Albam. See Num. Rab. 18. 21 (Wünsche p. 454,
1885).   Notice in Num. R. *l.c.* the identification of *fear* with
Torah by Gematria, thus יראת בגמטריא תרי״א ותורה תרי״א ויראה ותורה
עמם הרי תרי״ג. That is to say, יראת and תורה are each numerically 611 :
add יראה and תורה, *counting each word as one*, and we get 613 the number
of the commandments in the Torah. Wünsche inadvertently omits ותורה
and writes "Und ויראה zusammen giebt sechshundertunddreizehn" (p. 452)
without note or comment.

א״ט ב״ח. *Atbach* is applied to the word מנון (Prov. xxix. 21) in Sukkah
52b and is thus explained, cf. Ex. Rab. 15. 7 (Wünsche p. 108, 1882).
Arrange the twenty-seven letters, including the five *finals*, as far as possible
in pairs, as ט״א, צ״י, ק״ץ, whereof each amounts numerically to ten, or a
hundred, or a thousand, thus

אבגדה	יכלמן	קרשתך
טחזו	צפעס	ץףןם

Using the tens and the hundreds only and putting the two isolated
letters together, by the interchanges ה״ה, נ״ה, ו״ו, נ״ה, מ״ם we turn מנון into
סהרה. Hence the evil יצר will *witness* in the world to come against those
whom he has led astray in this world, for it is said מפנק מנוער עבדו כו'

(Prov. *l.c.*). The evil *yeçer* is with a man מנעוריו "from a child," and is his "servant," for it is said that he may rule over it (Gen. iv. 7).

As the letters ה"ן stand alone in Atbach, so (Ex. R. *l.c.*) Israel are מפורשים and separate from the nations, for it is said הן עם לבדד ישכון כו' (Num. xxiii. 9). This הן is also explained as ἔν (Wünsche p. 108 n.).

When the days of the week in their order are arranged in pairs, the last day is left without a *ben zug*. Accordingly Israel becomes its σύζυγος*, and the Sabbath is called the Bride (Heb. Auth. P. B. p. 111).

On the alphabet אח"ס בט"ע see Shabbath 104 a, Kohut, Levy, Zunz *l.c.* The letters from א to ש arranged in three parallel columns would give seven triads of letters אח"ס, בט"ע, גי"ף, דכ"ץ, הל"ק, ומ"ר, and זנ"ש, but these last and the remaining letter are written in pairs ש"ת, ז"ן in order that ת may not be without a "yoke-fellow."

In Midr. Ps. xc. it is said on זרמתם שנה יהיו, These are the nine hundred and seventy four generations that were before the creation of the world. Said R. Jochanan, Why has *Bereshith* a large *beth*? In order that it may count as if made up of two : *aleph* changes to *lamed* by Albam, and *yod* to *mem* by Athbash : thus finally בראשית becomes בברלשמת, that is 974. Afterwards "God created the heavens and the earth" (p. 392 ed. Buber).

At the beginning of his book the רוקח (Ben Jacob's *Oçar* p. 551) R. El'azar b. Jehudah b. Qalonymus of Worms writes that רק̇ח is by Gematria his name אלעזר, and שמ̇ן is אלעזר בן יהודה. He adds that every man ought to stamp his name in his book, and gives as examples תנ̇א דב̇י אלי̇הו which begins וינג̇ש את האדם, Midrash תד̇שא which denotes זה רב̇י פינח̇ס ב̇ן יא̇יר, *Bereshith Rabbah* where ואה̇יה שעש̇ועים near the beginning amounts to זה רב̇י הוש̇עיה רב̇א, *Seder 'Olam* in which עם הכולל] מאד̇ם or with one for the whole word added to *eighty-five*, as תורה and יראה together count for *two* in Num. R. *l.c.*] is equivalent to יוס̇י. The writer does not explain this : nor does Buxtorf s.v. גמט explain "שפה אחת valet 794. *Totidem* לישון הקדש."

The evil *yeçer* is by Gematria הרשע ὁ πονηρός (Note 5) ; and Rabbenu Shimshon in his שפתי הכהן on the Pentateuch equates יצר הרע (sc. *'im ha-kolel*) to ורק רע (p. 24 Warsaw 1883). Satan has no power on the day of Atonement for השטן is only 364 (Nedar. 32 b Tos. & Num. R. *l.c.*). Elohim is הטבע *nature* (Joel *Sohar* p. 232 n.). The ציצית with 8 threads and 5 knots gives 613, the number of the commandments. See Num. R. *l.c.* and cf. St James ii. 10 (p. 86 Mayor ed. 1). The number 318 in Gen. xiv. 14 is the number of אליעזר of Damascus, and in its Greek form

---

* For the form σύνζυγος (p. 14 n.) see Thayer *N. T. Lex.*

IHT, according to the *Epistle of Barnabas*, it hints at Jesus and the Cross.   See also Mr P. H. Mason's work SHEMETS DAVAR *A Rabbinic Reading-Book* (Camb. 1880), in which interesting examples of Gematria are given and explained.

פרפראות לחכמה. For works so named see Ben Jacob's *Oçar ha-Sefarim* (p. 496, 1880).

In the periodical *Beth Talmud* (ed. Isaac H. Weiss, Wien) vol. II. 169 (1882) art. נתיבות האגדה by מא"ש (Friedmann) reference is made to a commentary on the Torah (abbreviated from that of Nachmanides) by R. Jacob baal ha-Turim (*Oçar* pp. 479, 547) containing פרפראות שלפני המזון, of which forty species are reckoned.

One of these (no. 27, *Beth Talm.* p. 208) is Gematria, under which head examples are given of the inclusive reckoning '*im ha-kolel* above mentioned. The author of '*Ittur Bikkurim* (it is said in a note) כייל כללים בשימוש הגמטריאות. His gematric license allows the insertion or omission of *matres lectionis*, the omission of epenthetic and servile letters, and the counting in of letters, words and sentences as units. Thus (1) בראשית with *one* added for the word is equated to שש סדרים, (2) והארץ היתה תהו ובהו (1152) with the addition of *one* for the whole sentence and *sixteen* for the number of its letters makes up אלפים שנה בלי תורה (1169). (3) ורוח אלהים מרחפת (1034) is said to amount to זו היא רוחו של מלך המשיח (1032) when the *letters* on both sides are counted in as units. The alleged equality may be made out by counting in the *words* instead of the letters of the two expressions, and adding *one* for the former or writing זה for זו or reading זו היא as one word. In the example (1) we may suppose שש to stand for שש׳, that is ששה.

Under no. 37 on letter-changes (p. 210 n.) notice the reversed alphabet תשר"ק, and the alphabet of twenty-seven letters (ending with the five finals) בכ"ר, אי"ק, &c., which in effect allows tens or hundreds to count as units.

Under no. 18 on the counting of letters (p. 206, cf. Midr. Rab., Jud. b. Barzilai on *Sefer Yeçirah*) it is said that the Decalogue has 620 letters, pointing to the 613 commandments to Moses [p. 108] and the 7 to the sons of Noah, and its σημεῖον is כתר תורה.

On the various kinds of צירוף האותיות (Buxt. 1945) see also the א"ב of R. 'Aqiba in Jellinek *Bet ha-Midrasch* III. 50 sq., and אור זרוע pages 5 sq. (Zitomir 1862).

38.

p. 63, n. 1 *Paradise*] The word פרדס (2 Cor. xii. 4 παράδεισος) was made an acrostic נוטריקון of the methods of interpretation פשט, רמז, דרש, סוד.

In Chagigah 14 b R. 'Aqiba says to the three who went with him into the *pardes*, When ye come nigh to stones of clear marble, say not *Water, water* (Gen. i. 7). It was not to be said that in the beginning the world was מים במים (T. J. Chag. II. 1, 77 c s.f.), as if formed from preexistent ὕλη. See Levy s.v. מים, Joel *Sohar* p. 322 (Leipz. 1849), Joel *Blicke* I. 166.

From Ps. civ. 2 it is deduced in Gen. Rab. 3. 1, Ex. R. 15. 22 that "there was light" already before the world was made. So the Zohar on Genesis (I. 16 b, Brody 1873) אוֹר דכבר הוה כו׳. This illustrates the exegetical rule that there is no regular *succession* in the Torah (Note 1).

Creation began from נקודה a *dot* or *point*; take the *yod* representing this from אויר *ἀήρ* and there remains אור *light* (Zohar *l.c.*). In *Midr. Shocher Tob* on Ps. civ. (Buber p. 440) it is asked, How did the Holy One create the light? He put on a white טלית and made the world resplendent with its אור.

On the *foundation stone* of the world see Buxt. 2541 s.v. שתייה, cf. Note 3 *cornerstone*. With the transparent stones like water in Chagigah *l.c.* compare Rev. iv. 6 ὡς θάλασσα ὑαλίνη ὁμοία κρυστάλλῳ, cf. xv. 2 "mingled with fire" (Ezek. i. 4 *amber*), xxi. 1 "and the sea is no more", and see Mr Streane's *Chagigah* p. 83, n. 6.

39.

p. 64, n. 2 *in whom the evil nature is strong*] Ecclus. xxviii. 10 As is the fuel of the fire, so will it burn...as is the strength of the man, so will be his wrath, Sukkah 52 a end כל הנדול מחבירו יצרו גדול הימנו the greater a man the greater his *yeçer*. A proof of God's might is שכובש יצרו, see Joma 69 b with comm. and *Variae Lectiones* (ד״ס IV. 202).

40.

p. 66, IV. 7 מאד מאד כו׳] Ecclus. vii. 17 Humble thy soul greatly; for the punishment of the ungodly man is fire and the worm, Syr. *Summopere* (טב טב) *deprime teipsum quia finis omnium hominum ad vermem est futurus*. In Ecclus. xxxix. 16 All the works of the Lord are καλὰ σφόδρα, the Hebrew (p. 169 n.) has כלם טובים without מאד *very* (Gen. i. 31).

41.

p. 67 n. הקב״ה *the Holy One blessed He*, Surh. IV. 465 *sanctus deus benedictus*] As ברוך אתה is naturally rendered "blessed art Thou" (Heb. Auth. P. B.), so ברוך הוא is most simply rendered as in דברי אבות העולם "blessed is (instead of *be*) He," and is thus distinguished from clearly optative forms of the ascription. Cf. Rom. i. 25 ὅς ἐστιν εὐλογητὸς εἰς τοὺς αἰῶνας, 2 Cor. xi. 31 ὁ ὢν εὐλογητὸς εἰς τοὺς αἰῶνας, and see Rom. ix. 5 R.V. marg. *be (is) blessed for ever* with Sanday and Headlam's note.

On the requirement to say (not write) a blessing at the mention of the Name of God see Gen. Rab. 49. 1, Jalqut II. 946 on Prov. x. 7 זכר צדיק לברכה. With the omission of ה״ב after הק׳ in some of the older Hebrew manuscripts compare in the New Testament the omission, that is to say in writing, of the Doxology to the Lord's Prayer, on which see *Lectures on Teaching of 12 Apost.* pp. 65—68. See also *The Jewish Quarterly Review* art. AMEN by Mr H. W. Hogg, vol. IX. 1—23 (Oct. 1896).

The practice of bowing "at [R.V. *in*] the name of Jesus" is perhaps an adaptation of the customary Jewish benediction of "the Name." On this point Dr Gifford refers me to the works of Jeremy Taylor. See *Holy Dying* Chap. IV. sect. VIII. *The Special Precepts of the Gospel* no. 69 "To worship the holy Jesus at the mention of His holy name; as of old God was at the mention of Jehovah" (Phil. ii. 10).   Compare MISHNAH Joma VI. 2 (Surh. II. 240) And the priests and the people when they heard the "nomen explicatum" uttered by the high priest were bowing and worshipping and falling upon their faces and saying *Benedictum nomen &c.*, T. J. Joma III. 7 (40 *d*) Those close by fell upon their faces, those at a distance said *Benedictum nomen &c.*, Eccl. Rab. iii. 11 end.

On the practice of bowing at the beginning or end of certain of the Eighteen Benedictions see BERAKHOTH T. B. 34 a & b, T. J. I. 8 (3 *c* & *d*. Schwab p. 21, cf. IV. 1 p. 72), Tosefta ed. Zuckermandel p. 1, Tur *Orach Chayim* §§ 113, 121. For the benedictions called אבות and הודאה or מודים (cf. Schoettgen on Phil. ii.) see Heb. Auth. P. B. pages 44, 51.

According to Shulkan 'Arukh *Orach Chayim* § 123 at the words *He who maketh peace &c.* (Heb. Auth. P. B. p. 54) כורע ופוסע כו' i.e. he takes three steps backwards with one בריעה, looks to his right at the words עושה כו' and to his left at the words הוא יעשה כו' while still כורע, and ends with an obeisance like a slave leaving the presence of his master.

JEREMY TAYLOR *The Life of our blessed Lord and Saviour Jesus Christ* Part I. *Ad* sect. v. 8 (*Works* ed. Heber vol. II. 72, 1822) "He hath changed the ineffable name into a name utterable by man, and desirable by all the world; the majesty is all arrayed in robes of mercy, the tetragrammaton [g] or adorable mystery of the patriarchs is made fit for pronunciation and expression, when it becometh the name of the Lord's Christ."

[g] Nomen enim Jesu Hebraicè prolatum nihil aliud est nisi Τετραγράμματον vocatum per Schin. Videat, cui animus est, multa de mysterio hujus nominis apud Galatinum. Ad eundem sensum fuit vaticinium Sibyllæ.

The oracle quoted runs thus in Rzach *Oracula Sibyllina* I. 324 sq. (Vindobonae 1891):

δὴ τότε καὶ μεγάλοιο θεοῦ πάις ἀνθρώποισιν
ἥξει σαρκοφόρος θνητοῖς ὁμοιούμενος ἐν γῆ·
τέσσαρα φωνήεντα φέρει, δύ' ἄφωνα δ' ἐν αὐτῷ
δισσὸν ἐν ἀγγέλλοντ'· ἀριθμὸν δ' ὅλον ἐξονομήνω·
ὀκτὼ γὰρ μονάδας κ.τ.λ.

Thus the name 'Ιησοῦς is described as a Tetragrammaton of vowels, attention is called to the duplication of its consonant *sigma*, and the number of the name (888) is given, as also by Irenaeus.

apud Galatinum. See lib. II. cap. 10 of Peter Galatin's *Opus de Arcanis Catholicae Veritatis &c.*

For cabalistic evidences of Christianity see Bartolocci *Bibliotheca Magna Rabbinica.* On the name JESUS and the TETRAGRAMMATON see

Pars IV. pp. 420, 533 &c. The Name יהוה of three different letters with one repeated adumbrates the Trinity and the Incarnation: Psalm xcvi. 12 יעלז שדי וכל־אשר־בו is an acrostic of ישׁו Jesu, as the preceding verse is of יהוה יהו: Shekhinah by an inclusive gematric reckoning, i.e. with *one* counted in for the whole word, amounts to 386, which is the number of the name ישׁוע Jesu.

The word בראשׁית expanded acrostically reveals d ctrines of Christianity, and its letters make באתי רשׁ *Ego veni pauper.*

Jewish cabalists have found the Name in Psalm xcvi. 11 and 1 Chron. xvi. 31—32, and have read Gen. i. 9 יקוו המים כו' as hinting cryptically at יהוה אחד. The opening words יסוד היסודות ועמוד החכמות of Rambam's *Yad ha-Chazaqah* are an acrostic of יהו.

There are Talmudic allusions to the use of Jesus as a name of power for healing, as in T. J. Abodah Zarah III. 40 d_{42} אתא חד ולחש ליה בשמיה דישׁו בן פנדרא. It has been suggested that Pandera is an Aramaic form for Pantheros, an anagram of the Greek *Parthenos* virgin.

The Incarnation *A Study of Philippians* ii. 5—11. See under this title Dr Gifford's thorough discussion of the passage Phil. ii. 5—11 in the *Expositor* (Sept. & Oct. 1896).* With "Christ Jesus...emptied (ἐκένωσεν) himself, taking the form of a servant...he humbled himself, becoming obedient *even* unto death, yea, the death of the cross. Wherefore also God highly exalted (ὑπερύψωσεν) him," we may compare Isaiah lii. 13, liii. 12 "Behold, my servant...shall be exalted and lifted up, and shall be very high...Therefore will I divide him a portion with the great, and he shall divide the spoil with the strong; because he poured out his soul unto death."

With ἑαυτὸν ἐκένωσεν...μέχρι θανάτου compare Is. liii. 12 הערה למות נפשׁו he emptied out his soul to death. Rashi on Isaiah refers to Gen. xxiv. 20 ותער כדה καὶ ἐξένωσε τὴν ὑδρίαν, and on ותער in the Torah *l. c.* (p. 41 ed. Berliner, Berlin 1866) he writes that this usage is common in the Mishnah, as המערה מכלי אל כלי he who empties from vessel to vessel, and is found in Isaiah *l.c.* and Psalm cxli. 8 אל תער נפשׁי, R.V. marg. *pour thou not out my life,* Field's *Origenis Hexaplorum Quae Supersunt* A. μὴ ἐκκενώσῃς, Σ. Θ. μὴ ἀποκενώσῃς.

With διὸ καὶ ὁ θεὸς αὐτὸν ὑπερύψωσεν compare Is. lii. 13 ירום ונשׂא וגבה מאד, on which see Jalqut II. 571 מי אתה הר הגדול with Dr E. G. King's notes in *The Yalkut on Zechariah* pp. 17—18 (Camb. 1882), and Isaiah *LIII. according to the Jewish Interpreters* ed. Neubauer & Driver with Intr. by Pusey (Oxford 1877).

The exaltation of the Son of God is expressed realistically in the *Shepherd of Hermas* by the figure of ἀνήρ τις ὑψηλὸς τῷ μεγέθει ὥστε τὸν πύργον ὑπερέχειν a man taller than the tower, cf. *Evang. Pet.* μέχρι τοῦ οὐρανοῦ κ.τ.λ. On the sons of Anak see Rashi & שׁפתי חכמים on Num. xiii. 33, Sotah 34 b, Num. Rab. 16. 11, and cf. Midr. Ps. xxii. on ומקרני רמים.

---

* Enlarged and published separately, 1897.

42.

p. 72, n. 21 *uniting man and wife*] Gen. Rab. 68. 3—4 (Wünsche p. 327) We find in Torah, Prophets and Kethubim that אין זיווגו של איש אלא מן הקב״ה "marriages are made in heaven." *In six days the Lord made the heavens and the earth* (Ex. xx. 11). What is His occupation עד עכשיו ἕως ἄρτι (Joh. v. 17)? He sits and couples couples, a work harder to Him than the rending of the Red Sea, cf. Lev. Rab. 8. 1, Sotah 2 a, Sanhedrin 22 a.

Ex. Rab. 30. 9 (Wünsche p. 219) God does not break the Sabbath by His work in nature, that is to say by the continued movement of things, as of the rain from heaven to earth, for this is done בתוך חצירו within His own precincts, the whole world being His (Joel *Blicke* II. 173).

Mishnah Berakh. VIII. 5 (Surh. I. 30) Beth Shammai say *Qui creavit facem ignis*, but Beth Hillel, regarding creation as still continuing, say *Qui creas faces ignis*, cf. Joel *Sohar* p. 187 (Leipz. 1849).

The Holy One created His world by the letters *Jod* and *He* of יה, which represent אבא ואמא the father and the mother respectively (Joel *Sohar* p. 237). Generally, in the mystic sense, συνουσία is γενέσεως ἀρχή (Clem. *Strom.* III. 3, Potter p. 519). Rab says in Baba Bathra 74 b that God created everything in His world male and female, including Leviathan and Behemoth (Bacher *Babl. Amoräer* p. 21).

On the formation of the woman from one of the two SIDES (Ex. xxvi. 26) of Adam see Gen. Rab. 17. 6 (Wünsche p. 76), and compare Clem. R. II. 12 (*Apost. Fathers* by Lightfoot & Harmer p. 90, 1891) "For the Lord Himself, being asked by a certain person when His kingdom would come, said, *When the two shall be one, and the outside as the inside, and the male with the female, neither male nor female.*"

43.

p. 74, IV. 25 *interrogate*] שאלת נדרים is the questioning of a person who has vowed a vow, especially by a Rabbi, in order to find a "door of repentance." See Lowe *Fragm. of T. B.* p. 62 note G, Schechter in Montefiore's *Hibbert Lectures* p. 560.

44.

p. 78, n. 1 *by ten things the world was created*] The ten things, for which Scripture proofs are given (Streane *Chagigah* p. 60), are חכמה תבונה דעת כח גבורה גערה צדק משפט חסד רחמים. Qiddushin 71 a mentions names of God of twelve and forty-two letters respectively, and Rashi writes that "they have not explained to us" what they are. See also Maimonides *Moreh Nebukhim* I. 62 (vol. I. 273—279, Munk 1856). Bacher conjectures in *Die Agada der Babylonischen Amoräer* (Budapest 1878) that the name of *forty-two* letters is made up of the Tetragrammaton יהוה and the thirty-eight letters of the above "ten things," "Der 42buchstabige

Name Gottes ist also nichts anderes als der Ausdruck für das Wesen Gottes und seine Attribute" (p. 18); and that the name of *twelve* letters is חכמה תבונה דעת (p. 19).

45.

p. 79, n. 1 *the chariot*] Ecclus. xlix. 8 ὅρασιν δόξης ἣν ὑπέδειξεν αὐτῷ ἐπὶ ἅρματος Χερουβίμ. A Talmudic interpretation of Cherub is *sicut puer* (Buxt. 1084).

Chagigah 13 a quotes from Ben Sira אין לך עסק בנסתרות Thou hast no business with the secret things (Deut. xxix. 29). The *Fragment of Ecclus.** in Hebrew lately identified and described by Mr Schechter (*Expositor* IV. 1—15, 1896) contains the Neo-Hebrew word עסק, for which the Greek of Ecclus. xl. 1 has ἀσχολία, partly perhaps because of the assonance. In Acts vi. 3 עסק might be used to render χρεία (Ecclus. iii. 22).

Rashi on Prov. xxv. 27, with reference to the matters of *bereshith* and *the chariot*, explains וחקר כבודם כבוד as meaning that one may however speculate בדברי חכמים אשר כבודם כבוד on words of the wise *whose glory is glory*. For the idiom כבודם כבוד, which is not uncommon, compare Prov. xiv. 24 the folly of fools is folly, Berak. 23 a his prayer is a prayer, Pesach. 113 b their life is not life, Rom. xi. 6 χάρις οὐκέτι χάρις, St James v. 12 &c. The verse in question might be rendered to the effect that, as to eat honey much is not good, so to pry into the inscrutable things " whose glory is glory " is *not good*.

Midrash Mishlé applies Prov. xxv. 16 דבש מצאת וכו' to Ben 'Azzai and Ben Zoma, who entered the *pardes* (p. 63).

46.

p. 80, v. 4 (cf. IV. 4) *was Abraham tempted*] Not "God did tempt Abraham" (Gen. xxii. 1). Compare Heb. xi. 17 πειραζόμενος, St James i. 13 μηδεὶς πειραζόμενος κ.τ.λ. ib. ver. 14 ὑπὸ τῆς ἰδίας ἐπιθυμίας κ.τ.λ., cf. Sukkah 52 b the evil *yeçer* מסית [1 Chron. xxi. 1] seduces a man in this world &c., Aboth IV. 32 let not thy *yeçer* give thee false assurance.

47.

p. 83, v. 8 *rains...Jerusalem*] Of rain it is said in Ta'anith 7 a גדול יום הגשמים מתחיית המתים the day of the rains is greater than that of the quickening of the dead, the one being for righteous and wicked alike (Matt. v. 45) and the other for the righteous only. Or it is as (or greater than) the day on which the Torah was given, see Midr. Ps. cxvii. 1 הללו את ה' כל גוים *For thou art great and doest wondrous things* (Ps. lxxxvi. 10)

---

* The recently published work *The Original Hebrew of Ecclus. XXXIX.* 15 to *XLIX.* 11 (ed. Cowley & Neubauer, Oxford 1897) contains the folio described by Mr Schechter and others following it which were afterwards discovered.

22

and נפלאות is naught but *rains* (Job v. 9—10). Said R. Tanchum bar Chiyah גדולה ירידת גשמים ממתן תורה, for the giving of the Torah was a joy to Israel, but the fall of the rains is a joy to the whole world. Sifré II. § 42 ונתתי מטר ארצכם (Deut. xi. 14) it is a blessing which includes all others, for it is said ויתרון ארץ בכל היא כו' (Eccl. v. 8, Schiffer p. 29). On drought see v. 11, Ta'anith 7 b. The Resurrection is placed in the month Nisan by R. Isaac ibn גיאת in his מאה שערים II. p. 106 (Fürth 1861).

A meaning of פגע רע *mishap* is possession by an evil spirit (Buxt. 1696, Kohut VI. 294). It is said in Aboth R. N. *A* & *B* (Schechter pp. 103—105) that no one was ever נפגע in Jerusalem, *A* adding that if any one so afflicted looked upon the walls of Jerusalem he was healed.

"The Evangelists mention no instance of possession at Jerusalem" (Westcott *Gosp. Miracles* p. 78, 1859). Sifré II. § 193 on Deut. xx. 4 "*For the Lord your God is he that goeth with you...to fight for you against your enemies, to save you* from serpents and scorpions and evil spirits." All these are מזיקין *nocentes,* and they belong to "the power of the enemy" (Mark xvi. 17—18, Luke x. 19). Midr. Ps. xci. 13—14 (Buber p. 400) Noah trod on serpents and scorpions ולא היו מזיקים אותו. How is it that Israel pray and are not heard in this world? It is because they have not the knowledge of *Shem ha-mephorash,* which they will have in the time to come (Is. lii. 6).

48.

p. 83, n. 12 *Sychar*] In Rab. Joseph Schwarz's *Das heilige Land* [Jerus. 1846] *Deutsch bearbeitet von Dr Israel Schwarz* (Fr. a. M. 1852) it is said that south-east from Sichem is a village Aschar, and not far from it on the Jerusalem road "ein groszer 100 Fusz tiefer Brunnen Jakobsbrunnen genannt...Es scheint mir nun dasz dieses Dorf Aschar kein anderes ist als das ehemalige Sechu, und der sogenannte Jakobsbrunnen nicht weit davon die grosze Grube ist, woselbst Saul [1 Sam. xix. 22 ויבא עד בור הגדול אשר בשכו] bei seiner Reise nach Ramah nach dem Aufenthalte von David und Samuel sich erkundigte" (pp. 124, 125). In his *Karme Schomron* Schwarz had suggested that Aschar was Sychar. See also Neubauer *La Géographie du Talmud* p. 171.

Schwarz supposes Aschar to be referred to in Gen. Rab. 98. 20 מעל זו אזכרות שבבעל (Gen. xlix. 25), and Mr Schechter supports this conjecture by a reading אַסְכָּרוֹת בַּבַעַל in the *Midrash ha-Gadol,* of which he is preparing an edition. The name in this form would be like Gur-baal (2 Chron. xxvi. 7), and would mean "Ascharoth im Thal" (*Das heil. Land* p. 128). It is said in *Mattanoth Kehunnah* (cf. תאר יפה) on Gen. R. *l.c.* that some place בגובה ההרים must be meant, and Schwarz remarks in his *Recension über* ערך מילין *des S. Rapoport* p. 5 (Wien 1853) that "die Gegend Salim und Askar ziemlich hoch liegt" in contrast with Beth Shean "that coucheth beneath" (Gen. Rab. *l.c.*). He wonders why Rapoport did not mention his *Heilige Land* "da er doch schon im Besitz meines Werkes war" (*Recension* l.c.). On בעל> (בית הבעל) see Buxt. 333, Bacher *Babl. Amoräer* p. 48, Prof. W. R. Smith *The Religion of the Semites* Lect. 3. Schwarz thinks that סוכר עין (Menach. 64 b) may be referred to in the name עין כושית in T. J. 'Abodah Zarah v. 4, 44 d_{31}.

It has also been suggested that ᾽Ισκαριώτης may be from אסכרות (Rap. '*Erekh Millin* p. 28). There is a form Iskar for Askar (Westcott on St John iv. 5). The Sadducees disagreed with the Pharisees about the '*omer*. See Obad. Bert. in Surh. *l.c.* p. 83 n.

49.

p. 84, v. 9 *the well*] Omit פי before הבאר. In the New Testament see St John vi. 51 " I am the living bread which came down from heaven," 1 Cor. x. 4 "that spiritual Rock that followed them…was Christ." Rashi on Ta'anith 9 a [not fol. 19. 1 as Schoettgen I. 623, 1733] writes "*The well of Miriam*, a rock with waters flowing from it, and it rolled and went along with Israel. And it was the rock that Moses struck, which would not let its waters flow for him because Miriam had died." Through Moses, Aaron, and Miriam three "good gifts" were given to Israel, באר וענן ומן the well, and the cloud, and the manna (Ta'an. *l.c.*). The same three things are brought together in 1 Cor. x. 2—4 " And were all baptized unto Moses in the cloud and in the sea; And did all eat the same spiritual meat; And did all drink the same spiritual drink." At the beginning of Aboth R. N. it is said that Moses was *sanctified in the cloud*. St Paul prefers " rock " to " well " as a symbol of Christ. That the rock or well was to continue with Israel in the wilderness is deduced from Ex. xvii. 6 הנני עומד לפניך כו', on which see Mekhilta (Fr. 52 b) and Targ. Jonathan.

St Paul seems to testify to the prevalence of Midrashic interpretation in his day by adopting the method and using it in an anti-Jewish sense (Gal. iv., Clem. *Hom.* II. 22). But it is not said that the things allegorized " are an allegory," for פשוטו מידי יוצא מקרא אין *Scriptura non egreditur ex simplicitate sua, id est, simplici & literali sensu* (Buxt. 1861), cf. Shabbath 63 a, Jebamoth 11 b & 24 a, Bacher *Babl. Amoräer* p. 113, Dobschütz *Die Einfache Bibelexegese der Tannaim* p. 14 (1893).

50.

p. 92, v. 21 *sponge*] Dr Swete on the Gospel of Peter p. 8₃ (1893) writes " Origen *Matt.* 137 may have had this in view when he compares the sponge to the writings of unbelievers filled *non de uerbo potabili…sed de aliquo contrario et nociuo et non potabili aceto intelligibili.*"

ib. n. 36 *sieve.* Cf. Ecclus. xxvii. 4 In the shaking of a sieve, the refuse remaineth ; so the filth of man in his reasoning, St Luke xxii. 31 ἐξῃτήσατο ὑμᾶς τοῦ σινιάσαι κ.τ.λ.

51.

p. 96, v. 32] Heb. Auth. P. B. p. 204 (cf. *Crit. Note*) Turn it (the Torah) and turn it over again, for everything is in it, and contemplate it, *and wax grey and old over it, and stir not from it*, for thou canst have no better rule than this. Mr Schechter compares Ecclus. xi. 20 Be stedfast in thy covenant, and be conversant therein, and wax old in thy work.

With Eccl. xii. 13 (p. 96 n.) compare Ecclus. xliii. 27 καὶ συντέλεια λόγων Τὸ πᾶν ἐστιν αὐτός [1 Cor. xv. 28 ἵνα ᾖ ὁ θεὸς πάντα ἐν πᾶσιν], on which it is remarked in the *Speaker's Commentary* "This clause is evidently a spurious Hellenistic addition by the younger Siracide."

The verse runs thus in the *Original Hebrew of Ecclus.* (p. 18 ed. Cowley & Neubauer):

עוד כאלה לא·נוסף   וקץ דבר הוא הכל :

52.

p. 99, vi. 1 *Thorah for its own sake...they reveal to him secrets of Thorah,* cf. Ecclus. xiv. 21] Mr Schechter suggests in explanation of Ecclus. vi. 22 "For wisdom is *according to her name;* and she is not manifest unto many" that κατὰ τὸ ὄνομα αὐτῆς may be a rendering of לשמה read כשמה, with the sense that she is not manifest to the many who do not seek her for her own sake, cf. Ecclus. xxxv. 5 χάριν ἐντολῆς which may be for לשם מצוה, St Matt. x. 41 εἰς ὄνομα προφήτου...δικαίου. For another suggestion see Note 55.

ib. וכנהר. See Note 16, and cf. Ecclus. xlvii. 14 "How wast thou wise in thy youth! and didst make instruction to overflow (or didst overflow with instruction) like the Nile" (Cowley & Neub. *Original Heb. of Ecclus.* p. 35).

ib. *and exalts him.* Compare Ecclus. iv. 11, xv. 5.

53.

p. 100, vi. 2 *read not*] " Die Litteratur über diese Formel ist angegeben in meinen Prolegomena critica in V. T. Hebraicum, Leipzig 1873, S. 68. 69. 122" (Strack *Die Sprüche der Väter*).　　"The formula אל תקרי is called by Jerome *Non debemus legere* or *Legi potest*" (Krauss in *J. Q. R.* vi. 252).

54.

p. 102, vi. 6 *in the name of him that said it*] "In Pesiqta [or *Pesiqatha* pl.] and other Agadoth" (Machsor Vitry) Moses is said to have found the Holy One studying the tract Red *Heifer* and quoting decisions of Rabbis in their names, as "R. Eliezer says *A calf of the* second year." See Mishnah Parah I. 1, Pesiqta פרה (Buber 40 a), Jalqut יתרו I. 268 in the name of פסיקתא. A scholar should "verify his citations."

55.

p. 102, VI. 7 *Great is Torah*] Sayings about Wisdom are applied to the Torah here and elsewhere. Bereshith Rabbah begins with Prov. viii. 30 ואהיה אצלו אמון ואהיה שעשועים יום יום "Then I was by him, *as* one brought up *with him* (R.V. *as* a master workman): and I was daily *his* delight, rejoicing always before him," and it explains אמון by the words רבתא, מוצנע, מכוסה, פדגוג. Torah is here identified with Wisdom, and is also made to say with reference to Prov. *l.c.* "I was כלי אומנתו של הקב״ה," the instrument [Aboth III. 23] by which He created the world. "He looked into the Torah and created the world," אמון being read as אומן. The Torah says בראשית ברא by *reshith*, which is Torah, He created.

So in Zohar פר׳ תרומה (II. 161 a Lublin) it is said אל תקרי אמון אלא אומן read not *amon* but *omen*, that is τεχνίτης. The אורייתא or Torah was not the actual creator but only אמון אצלו. She was "by Him" ages before the creation, for יום יום means 2000 years (Ps. xc. 4). He looked at the word שמים in the Torah and created the heavens, at the word אור and said "Let there be light," and so on. Compare Wisdom vii. 22 R.V. "For she that is the artificer of all things taught me, *even* wisdom," and in the New Testament 1 Cor. i. 24 "Christ...the wisdom of God," Heb. i. 2 "through whom also he made the worlds."

As פדגוג παιδαγωγός (Buxt. 1698) is made to be a meaning of אמון, which is Wisdom, who is the Torah, so St Paul writes "the law was our παιδαγωγός *to bring us* unto Christ" (Gal. iii. 24).

Wisdom is רבתא *great*, like the Torah, and is מכוסה *covered*, and מוצנע, cf. Buxt. 1928 on צנע *Abscondere, Occultare, ut ea quae reponuntur in thesaurum & asservantur quasi abscondita*, and see the commentaries on Gen. Rab. *l.c.* Thus the Midrash makes Wisdom ἀποκεκρυμμένην...πρὸ τῶν αἰώνων (1 Cor. ii. 7). If we may regard אמון in the sense סתים (Zohar אחרי מות III. 65 b, Brody 1873) as an ὄνομα of Wisdom, comparing Ex. xxxiv. 14 כי יהוה קנא שמו, we may say that she "is *according to her name*...not manifest" (Ecclus. vi. 22).

56.

p. 105 תורה] Meanings of ירה are "*iecit*...sortes, sagittas, *manum emisit*...inde monstravit indicavit" (Gesenius). Hence Torah was "pointing out what was to be done in some special case," or it was a response obtained by casting lots. See Mr Montefiore's *Hibbert Lectures* p. 68 n. (1892).   The Pentateuch, which contained several *torahs* or νόμοι (Lev. vi.—xv., Num. v. vi. xix.), was called the Torah κατ᾽ ἐξοχήν, but Prophets and Hagiographa were often grouped with it under that name, and the study of Torah might include anything in its religious aspect, for "everything is therein."

According to Rish (Heb. רי״ש), that is R. Iacob ben Shimshon, the author of the commentary on Aboth in "Machsor Vitry," Moses received the whole Torah.   If Rabbis decide differently, how is one to learn Torah? All the words of the wise *were given from one shepherd* (Eccl. xii. 11). One pastor Moses spake them from the mouth of the Lord of all. "These and those are words of the living God." See Chagigah 3 b (Streane p. 9), 'Erubin 13 b, Gittin 6 b.   Says R. 'Aqiba in Sifra (Weiss 112 c, cf. 105 a) The Torah was given with its *halakhoth, diqduqim* and *perushim* by the hand of Moses from Sinai.   See also Note 1.

It is written "the two tables of stone...*and* on them *according to* all *the* words" (Deut. ix. 10). Why not briefly "on them all words"? The three added letters ו, כ, ה cannot be superfluous, but must hint at something more than the Scripture. They teach that together with it *Mishnah, Talmud, Agadah* and the future discoveries of scholars were spoken to Moses on Sinai. "Is there a thing whereof men say, See, this is new? it hath been already, in the ages that were before us" (Eccl. i. 10). See T. J. Peah II. 6, Megillah IV. 1, Chagigah I. 8 (17 a, 74 d, 76 d). Midr. Rab. Ex. 47. 1, Lev. 22. 1, Eccl. i. 9. § 2 on מה שהיה, v. 8. § 2 on ארץ ויתרון.

Sundry sayings about the writing of Torah are hung upon Hosea viii. 12 "Though I wrote for him the great things of my Torah, they have (or would have) been accounted as a strange thing," and Ex. xxxiv. 27 (p. 105). See the passages last cited, Gittin 60 b with Rashi and Tos. ד"ה אתמוהי, Pesiqta Rabbathi ריש פ"ה (Friedm. 14 a), Tanchuma נח ג', וירא ה', תשא ל"ד (11 a, 25 a, 127 a Warsaw 1879), Buber Tanch. כי תשא II. 58 b, Jalqut I. 405.

Was the greater part (רובי) of the Torah in writing? No, but Scripture with the deductions from it by the thirteen *middoth* of R. Ishmael (Sifra *init.*) comes to more than the oral Torah. Or things proved by Scripture are of greater worth than mere traditions. If everything had been written, Israel would have had no advantage over a "strange" people, as the Christians (Frankel), who like themselves could produce their books and parchments. The oral Law was not written, lest the Gentiles should borrow it with the written Law and call themselves Israel. Or "should I write" the Mishnah, which is greater than the Miqra (Deut. Rab. 14. 10), to become "as a strange thing" by translation into the language of strangers?

Moses wanted the Mishnah to be in writing, but God kept it as His unwritten μυστήριον for Israel, to distinguish them from the nations of the world. What was oral was to be said, and what was written was to be read. The sayer of Targum in the Synagogue might not look at the roll of the Torah, and the reader of Torah might not take his eyes off from it.

But when the oral Law was in danger of being forgotten, the writing of it was justified by Psalm cxix. 126. "It was a time to do something for God, even if by such doings His law was apparently destroyed" (*Encycl. Brit.* art. MISHNAH, Berak. 63 a, Rish). Shemuel said that 3000 halakhoth were forgotten in the days of the mourning for Moses (Temurah 15 a). Rab Papa said that there were 600 Sedarim of the Mishnah and our Rabbis that there were 700 (Chagig. 14 a), in their days (Rashi).

57.

p. 114. § 4 (cf. p. 106) *words of Qabbalah*] Elias Levita near the end of Massoreth ha-Massoreth (p. 261 ed. Ginsburg, 1867) says that the Massorites call the Former Prophets אישלמתא קדמיתא and the Latter Prophets אישלמתא תנינא, he knows not why. Rapoport in a letter to Luzzatto (אגרות שי"ר p. 94 ed. Gräber, 1885) explains אישלמתא by Qabbalah, comparing Syr. משלמנותא *tradition* in St Matt. xv. and at the end of Genesis in נוסחת אוסשעריום *. See also Prof. Dr Ludwig Blau *Zur Einleitung in Die Heilige Schrift* pp. 24—26 (Budapest 1894), and in the same work notice *inter alia* p. 16 Eine vierte Bezeichnung für die ganze H. Schr. ist תורה &c.

Rapoport objects to the statement in Zunz *G. V.* p. 44 n. (cf. p. 353) that "Sämmtliche nichtmosaische Biblische Bücher heissen קבלה," apparently meaning to say that Qabbalah is used in Mishnah and Gemara for Nebiim only and not for Kethubim. But Job is quoted as Qabbalah in Niddah 25 a, Psalm lxix. in Sotah 37 a כי באו מים [p. 67 *init.*] ועליו מפרש בקבלה הושיעני אלקים עד נפש כו', Psalm cxxxix. in T. J. Niddah III. 50 d_{31} (p. 106), and on Baba Qamma 2 b וכי תימא דברי תורה מד"ק לא ילפינן Rashi explains "words of Qabbalah" by נביאים וכתובים. So in the Mattanoth Kehunnah on Num. Rab. 9. 7 "Thus far from Qabbalah (1 Chron. vii. 40), what is the proof from Torah?" we read *And all Scripture is called Qabbalah except the Torah of Moses.*

Qabbalah as a designation of books of Scripture has been taken to mean something received by direct inspiration from God.

Thus on Chullin 137 a it is said that the Torah of Moses is called Torah because it was given for all generations, and that of the prophets only Qabbalah because they received their prophecies from the Holy Spirit from time to time as they were wanted.

Again, whereas the Mishnah cites Jonah iii. 10 without calling it Qabbalah and then Joel ii. 13 as Qabbalah (p. 106), "Rashi" (Zunz *l.c.*) gives as the explanation of some Tosafist that Qabbalah is used of a prophet's message from above and not of mere narrative (Surh. II. 362). But books of the Former Prophets, which are רק סיפורים (Rapoport), are called אישלמתא Qabbalah.

The interpretation of Qabbalah in Excursus III. 4 (p. 114) as a tradition from Sinai agrees with the statements in Gemara and Midrash to the effect that the Torah of Moses comprised everything that was to be revealed. See Note 28, Tos. Bekhoroth 58 a ד"ה מפי, Sifra (end) "A prophet is not allowed henceforth לחדש דבר to innovate a word," Buxt. 2290 on רשאי, Weber *System der Altsyn. Palästinische Theologie* p. 79 (Leipz. 1880).

* Rapoport's quotation from Ussherius comes from Walton's *Polyglot* vol. VI. *Variae Lectiones Syriacae* p. 5 b, where the colophon to Genesis with משלמנותא is given (F. C. B.).

For Qabbalah used of Scripture see also Chagigah 10 b (Streane p. 51), Rosh ha-Shanah 19 a, Ta'anith 17 b, Niddah 23 a, T. J. Challah I. 1 (57 b_{16}), Mass. Soferim 18. 3. Tosefta Yoma & Niddah (Zuck. pp. 183$_{24}$, 186$_{17}$, 645$_1$). Gen. Rab. 7. 2, Eccl. Rab. vii. 23, Pesiqta פרה (Buber 36 a), Midr. Ps. lxviii. (Buber p. 318). Some references already given are included in Friedmann Mekhilta 5 a, 15 b, 27 a, 28 b (bis), 30 a, 44 b, 65 a, 72 a & Sifré 33 a (bis), 52 a, 83 b. See also Weiss Sifra 86 b, that is col. 2 of the last folio of אחרי מות. Rosh ha-Shanah 7 a quotes words of Ezra after Zech. i. 7 (p. 106), but not expressly as Qabbalah.

On the History of Jewish Tradition see Mr Schechter's *Studies in Judaism.*

ib. *they would have questioned the authority of the Prophet.* See in this connexion the comparison in T. J. Berakh. I. 7 (3 b) to two envoys of a king one of whom is and the other is not to be believed without credentials, with allusion doubtless to Christianity.

58.

p. 117 *thou destroyest the whole world*] See p. xxviii. of ספר תגין "SEPHER TAGHIN *Liber Coronularum*" ed. J. J. L. Bargès (Paris 1866).

59.

p. 120 § 4 *The division of the Decalogue*] See the essay *Ueber die ursprüngliche und richtige Eintheilung des Dekalogs* von Dr L. Heilbut (Berlin 1874), which includes an interesting account of modern discussions of the question.

60.

p. 124 THE LORD'S PRAYER] *Our Father which art in heaven.* The short reading Πάτερ without ἡμῶν κ.τ.λ. in St Luke xi. 2 raises the question of the original language of "The Prayer," as the Lord's Prayer was called in early Church writings. "Our Father" corresponds to the Hebrew ABINU, and "Father" without the pronoun to the Aramaic ABBA, as in Ἀββά ὁ πατήρ in St Mark xiv. 36, Rom. viii. 15 (see Sanday & Headlam's note), Gal. iv. 6. The fact that the pronoun in אבינו originally implied limitation to Israel is (so far as it goes) an indication of the priority of Πάτερ ἡμῶν to Πάτερ without ἡμῶν.

The Midrash on Ps. xiv. illustrates *The fool hath said in his heart* by the case of Esau. His plan is, not that I should slay *Abba* the father, but that Ishmael should do this; and when he has slain *Abi* my father, and I my brother, then I will slay him and have the world to myself. Here the Aramaic *Abba* "the father" is followed in the next line but one (Buber p. 112) by the Hebrew *Abi* "my father." So Πάτερ and Πάτερ ἡμῶν may be thought to point to Aramaic and Hebrew originals respectively.

In the Hebrew of Delitzsch St John xii. 27—28 " Father, save me from this hour...Father, glorify thy name" becomes אבי...אבי כו׳ My Father, save me from this hour...My Father, glorify thy name, and in St Luke xi. the Prayer commences (שבשמים) אבינו, *Our Father* (*which art in heaven*), the short reading being imperfectly indicated by the use of brackets.

[In all forms of post-Biblical Palestinian Aramaic except Samaritan *ab(b)â* and *immâ* are used for *my father* and *my mother*. Compare *Onk.* Gen xx 12 אימא בת לא בת אבא היא ברם בת אחתי; *syr. hier.* Lc viii 21 אבא ואבכון John xx 17 אימא ואחאי.

The only traces in Edessene Syriac of the use of ܐܒܐ for *my* (or *thy*) *father* are found in the Old Syriac Gospels (*crt.* Mt x 32, Lc ii 49, Joh vi 32; *sin.* Mt vi 4, xv 13). ܐܒܐ is found now and then even in the Peshitta for πάτερ (e.g. Joh xii 28) in place of the more usual ܐܒܝ, but it never occurs in the Peshitta where the Greek has μου. For "Abba, Father" the Old Syriac has the one word *My Father* in the Gospel, and according to S. Ephraim *our Father* in the Epistles. The Peshitta has the two words *Abba, My Father* in the Gospel, and *Abba, our Father* in the Epistles (F. C. B.).]

The Prayer may have been given in Aramaic or Greek or Hebrew, which last seems to have been the ordinary language for set forms of prayer (Hamburger *Real-Encycl.* art. *Gebetsprache*), or in a mixed dialect. Compare the passage cited from T. J. Sanhedrin vi. 3 (5) in the Introduction to Susanna in the *Speaker's Commentary*, where ABBA (Schwab p. 280 *Mon père*) is followed by a sentence in Hebrew, except its last word כאסקופה. For examples of prayers in Aramaic see Heb. Auth. P. B. p. 151 יקום פרקן כו', Wünsche *Erläuterung der Evangelien* Matt. vi. 13.

In the Hebrew New Testament we might read in St Luke xxiii. 46 אבא בידך אפקיד רוחי i.e. ABBA, into thine hand I commit [R.V. Ps. xxxi. 5 *commend*] my spirit. In the Authorised Hebrew Daily Prayer Book see in the Hymn אדון עולם אשר מלך Into thy hand I commend my spirit, when I sleep, and when I wake; And with my spirit, my body also: the Lord is with me, and I will not fear (pp. 3, 297). See also in the *Evening Service* (p. 101) Blessed be the Lord by day; blessed be the Lord by night; blessed be the Lord when we lie down; blessed be the Lord when we rise up. For in thy hands are the souls of the living and the dead, as it is said, In his hand is the soul of every living thing, and the spirit of all human flesh. Into thy hand I commend my spirit; thou hast redeemed me, O Lord God of truth. Our God who art in heaven, assert the unity of thy name, and establish thy kingdom continually, and reign over us for ever and ever. The book ends with NIGHT PRAYER FOR YOUNG CHILDREN... 2. Hear, O Israel &c.... 6. Into thy hand I commend my spirit: thou hast redeemed me, O Lord God of truth. 7. For thy salvation I hope, O Lord.

*** For infants 2, 6, 7.

In St John xix. 30 Τετέλεσται, καὶ κλίνας τὴν κεφαλὴν παρέδωκεν τὸ πνεῦμα
Dr Abbott in *The Spirit on the Waters* (p. 256, 1897) takes the rare
phrase "unfortunately translated" *bowed his head* to mean *laid his head
down* i.e. to rest (Matt. viii. 20, Luke ix. 58). The rendering of Delitzsch
ויט את ראשו ויפקד את רוחו (Heb. N. T. 1880) connects the saying with
Psalm xxxi. 5, but not with Matt. or Luke *l.c.* After the evening
AUDI a scholar should at least say one פסוקא דרחמי such as the verse *En
tes mains je recommande mon âme &c.* (Berak. 5 a *init.*, Schwab p. 234).
See also Num. Rab. 20. 20 (Wünsche p. 500), Mekhilta בשלח on the words
נטית ימינך (Fr. 42 a).

The Manna.

Wisdom xvi. 8—28 Yea, and in this thou didst persuade our enemies,
that thou art he that delivereth out of every evil...thou gavest thy people
angels' food to eat, and bread ready for their use didst thou provide for
them from heaven without their toil, bread having the virtue of every
pleasant savour, and agreeing to every taste; For thy nature manifested
thy sweetness toward thy children; while that bread, ministering to the
desire of the eater, tempered itself according to every man's choice... For
the creation, ministering to thee its maker,...converting itself into all forms,
it ministered to thine all-nourishing bounty, according to the desire of
them that made supplication; That thy sons, whom thou lovedst, O Lord,
might learn that it is not the growth of the earth's fruits that nourisheth
a man, but that thy word preserveth them that trust thee. For that which
was not marred by fire, when it was simply warmed by a faint sunbeam
melted away; That it might be known that we must rise before the sun to
give thee thanks, and must plead with thee at the dawning of the light.

Thus God is represented as the Father in heaven, who gives bread to
His children and delivers them from evil (ἐκ παντὸς κακοῦ).

By a curious אל תקרי or exegetic various reading the Psalmist's
"angels' food" here referred to is made to mean not *bread of* ABBIRIM
but *bread of* EBARIM, bread which preternaturally permeated and was
wholly consumed by the *members*. See Midr. Ps. lxxviii. (Buber p. 345),
Joma 75 b, Mekhilta & Sifré (Fr. 59 b, 24 a), Bacher *Die Agada der Tannaiten* I 254 (1884). So St Cyril of Jerusalem writes of the Bread
in the Prayer in his last *Catechetical Lecture*: "*Give us this day our substantial bread.* This common bread is not substantial bread, but this Holy
Bread is substantial, that is, appointed for the substance of the soul. For
this Bread *goeth* not *into the belly and is cast out into the draught,* but is
distributed into thy whole system for the benefit of body and soul. But
by *this day,* he means, 'each day,' as also Paul said, *While it is called
to-day.*" See Dr Gifford's translation and notes in *Nicene and post-Nicene
Fathers* ed. Wace and Schaff (Lect. XXIII. § 15 p. 155, 1894).

The manna is described in Rabbinic writings as bread of Wisdom (Prov. ix. 5, cf. Ecclus. xv. 1—3) and food for soul and spirit and as agreeing to every taste. See Ex. Rab. 21 & 25, Midr. Ps. xxiii. on לא אחסר, Zohar on הנני ממטיר (II. f. 61, Brody 1873), Wetstein on St John vi. 32, Gfrörer *Philo und die alexandrinische Theosophie* I. cap. 8, Deane on Wisdom *l.c.*   Pesiqta psq. 6 *init.* (Buber 57 a) deduces from Neh. ix. 6 ואתה מחיה *and Thou quickenest* that God is the מחיה or *sustenance* of the ministering angels.   In St Mark xii. 44 *all her living* is lit. כל מחיתה.

The gathering of the manna was to be as follows according to Ex. xvi. 4—5 (Sept. ed. Swete): εἶπεν δὲ Κύριος πρὸς Μωυσῆν Ἰδοὺ ἐγὼ ὕω ὑμῖν ἄρτους ἐκ τοῦ οὐρανοῦ, καὶ ἐξελεύσεται ὁ λαὸς καὶ συλλέξουσιν τὸ τῆς ἡμέρας εἰς ἡμέραν, ὅπως πειράσω αὐτοὺς εἰ πορεύσονται τῷ νόμῳ μου ἢ οὔ· καὶ ἔσται τῇ ἡμέρᾳ τῇ ἕκτῃ καὶ ἑτοιμάσουσιν ὃ ἐὰν εἰσενέγκωσιν, καὶ ἔσται διπλοῦν ο ἐὰν συναγάγωσιν τὸ καθ᾿ ἡμέραν εἰς ἡμέραν.

ἄρτους ἐκ τοῦ οὐρανοῦ. St John vi. 31, 34 Ἄρτον ἐκ τοῦ οὐρανοῦ ἔδωκεν αὐτοῖς φαγεῖν… Κύριε, πάντοτε δὸς ἡμῖν τὸν ἄρτον τοῦτον, cf. Ex. xvi. 15 Οὗτος ὁ ἄρτος ὃν ἔδωκεν Κύριος ὑμῖν φαγεῖν. Westcott and Hort *N.T.* under *Quotations from the Old Testament* "St John vi 31; Ex xvi 4, 15; Ps lxxviii (lxxvii) 24." The Didaché in the Prayer has Πάτερ ἡμῶν ὁ ἐν τῷ οὐρανῷ…ὡς ἐν οὐρανῷ, St Matt. τοῖς οὐρανοῖς…οὐρανῷ.

τὸ τῆς ἡμέρας εἰς ἡμέραν. Heb. דבר יום ביומו, Syr. מאכולתא דיומא ביומא the βρῶμα *of the day in the day,* A.V. *a certain rate every day* marg. *the portion of a day in his day,* R.V. *a day's portion every day.* Notice that Syr. and R.V. give no literal rendering of ביומו *in its day.*

ὅπως πειράσω αὐτούς, Heb. למען אנסנו, 1 Cor. x. 2, 12 καὶ πάντες [τὸ αὐτὸ] πνευματικὸν βρῶμα ἔφαγον…πειρασμὸς ὑμᾶς οὐκ εἴληφεν εἰ μὴ ἀνθρώπινος· πιστὸς δὲ ὁ θεός, ὃς οὐκ ἐάσει ὑμᾶς πειρασθῆναι ὑπὲρ ὃ δύνασθε κ.τ.λ.

τὸ καθ᾿ ἡμέραν εἰς ἡμέραν. Heb. יום יום *day day,* Syr. בכליום.

Shammai and Hillel. Beça 16 a records that Shammai used to eat " to the honour of sabbath" and provide choice food in advance for that day: Hillel did all things "to the name of heaven" and lived by the rule Ps. lxviii. 20 ברוך ה' יום יום *Benedictus Dominus die quotidie.*

The Prayer is fully discussed by Dr F. Chase on *The Lord's Prayer in the Early Church* (Camb. *Texts and Studies* vol. I. no. 3, 1891); and the work of the late Bishop of Durham (Dr Jos. B. Lightfoot) *On a Fresh Revision of the English New Testament* contains in its latest form (1891) Appendix I. *On the Words* ἐπιούσιος, περιούσιος, Appendix II. *The Last Petition of the Lord's Prayer* reprinted from the *Guardian* of Sept 7th, 14th, 21st 1881. This work is hereinafter quoted by page with the letter D prefixed.   The late Canon F. C. Cook of Exeter (D. 270) published two letters dated May 21 and Nov. 26, 1881 respectively to the Bishop of London on *Deliver us from Evil,* and after them a work on *The Revised Version of the First Three Gospels* (1882). The *Second Letter* was written "in answer to three letters of the Lord Bishop of Durham."

Our daily Bread.

The whole Prayer in St Luke xi. in the Revised Version is as follows:

...Father...Hallowed be thy name. Thy kingdom come...Give us day by day our daily bread. And forgive us our sins; for we ourselves also forgive every one that is indebted to us. And bring us not into temptation...

The dots indicate omissions from the text (but not from the margin) of the words given in the text of the A. V. "Our, which art in heaven, Thy will be done as in heaven so in earth, but deliver us from evil." The R. V. gives *day by day* without alternative, omitting the A.V. marg. Or *for the day*.   This last omission is noteworthy in connexion with the objection made (sometimes without due discrimination) to prayer for the morrow in the interminable discussion of the Greek word rendered *daily*. Omit this altogether, and what remains of St Luke xi. 3 *Our bread give us day by day* is a prayer for a succession of morrows. The objection is of force as against John Lightfoot *Hor. Hebr.* Matt. vi. 11 "*Our daily bread*. That is provide *to-morrow's bread*, and give it to us to-day, that we be not solicitous for to-morrow," rather than against prayer for the food of tomorrow to be gathered "in his day" (A.V. marg.).

The word ἐπιούσιος occurs in the petition for the Bread, and is not extant in any earlier writing. St Luke's form of the petition is τὸν ἄρτον ἡμῶν τὸν ἐπιούσιον δίδου ἡμῖν τὸ καθ' ἡμέραν, and St Matthew's τὸν ἄρτον ἡμῶν τὸν ἐπιούσιον δὸς ἡμῖν σήμερον (Origen *De Orat. Libell.* 27 end, Lommatzsch tom. XXVII.). St Cyril of Jerusalem (*l.c.* p. 178) judiciously identifies St Matthew's form with St Luke's*. There are different ways of approaching the question how the petition was or may be expressed in Hebrew or Jewish Aramaic. If it refers to Ex. xvi. 4, we may conjecture that there was an early Aramaic form of it like

ביומא	דיומא	לחמא	לן	הב
in-the-day	*of-the-day*	*the-bread*	*to-us*	*Give.*

As a rendering of τὸν ἄρτον τὸν ἐπιούσιον into Hebrew, Wünsche in *Erläut. der Evv.* Matt. vi. 11 suggests לחם יום ביומו *bread of a day in its day*. St Luke's τὸ καθ' ἡμέραν, which may have come from Ex. xvi. 5 Sept., may be expressed in Hebrew by יום יום. Or, comparing Is. lxvi. 23 מדי חדש בחדשו ומדי שבת בשבתו (1 Sam. vii. 16, Zech. xiv. 16, 2 Chron. xxiv. 5 מדי שנה בשנה), we may write מדי יום ביומו for *day by day*.

Delitzsch and others render St Luke's form of the petition in Hebrew by את־לחם חקנו תן־לנו יום יום *the bread of our portion give us day by day,*

---

* Learned Latin writers have inferred from the Vulgate that St Matthew's word ἐπιούσιον was not used by St Luke (D. 250). Mangey on the Lord's Prayer (ed. 3, 1721), connecting *quotidianum* with τὸ καθ' ἡμέραν, argues that "The true and antient reading may probably have been that of St Luke, where from the vulgar Latin the word ἐπιούσιος appears to have been wanting."

with reference to Prov. xxx. 8 (R.V. marg. *the bread of my portion*). The same sense of τὸν ἄρτον ἡμῶν τὸν ἐπιούσιον might be expressed by לחם דיינו *bread sufficient for us*, cf. Prov. xxv. 16 Hast thou found honey? eat דַּיֶּךָ *so much as is sufficient and not more than sufficient for thee*, lest thou be filled therewith, and vomit it. For uses of די *sufficient* in Jewish forms of prayer for food see Berakh. 29 b, Cant. Rab. vii. 2 מה יפו § 2.

A response דיינו *sat nobis* was used in connexion with blessings with reference to Mal. iii. 10 ברכה עד בלי די, cf. Shabbath 32 b, Makkoth 23 b, T. J. Berak. 14 c (last folio) & Ta'an. iii. 9 (66 d), Lev. Rab. 35 *sub fin.*, Friedmann סדר והגדה של לילי פסח (Wien 1895) where it is suggested (p. 107) that it was used in the Temple.

Dr Chase's working hypothesis (p. 45) is that the original form of the petition might be represented by four Syriac words meaning *Our-bread of-the-day give to-us*, and Ciasca's Arabic *Diatessaron* (Romae 1888) is quoted as rendering it in three words

Give-us the-bread of-our-day,

and shewing no trace of ἐπιούσιος. But this *Diatessaron*, when قوة *strength* [cf. Deut. xxxiii. 25] has been corrected into قوت, is found to read (cap. ix.):

اعطنا قوت يومنا

of-our-day QUT *Give-us,*

and it uses QUT in cap. xxi. to render St John iv. 8 τροφάς.

Hence and from the versions of St James ii. 15 λειπόμενοι τῆς ἐφημέρου τροφῆς I was led to think that the Arabic translator might have had before him a short Syriac form of the petition, with סיברתא *cibum* for the Peshito (or Peshîttâ) לחמא דסונקנא. But on reflexion I see no reason to doubt that he was translating as from the Peshito, and wrote قوت for לחמא דסונקנא *panem quo opus est*. On قوت, which implies *sufficiency*, see Lane's *Arabic-English Lexicon* I. 2572, and in Payne Smith's *Thesaurus Syriacus* col. 2680 see ܣܘܢܩܢܐ explained in terms of قوت. The Arabic word for *bread* in the Prayer is *ḥubz*, as in Lagarde's *Die vier Evv. Arabisch* (Leipz. 1864) خبزنا كفافنا *give us in the day* (Matt. & Luke).

Ciasca's Arabic and the Peshito have the same order of words, both beginning with a verb meaning *Give*, and both ending with יומנא, which (with suitable pointings) means in Syriac σήμερον and in Arabic *our-day*.

The explanations of ἐπιούσιος. The epithet of the Bread has been derived from εἶναι and from ἰέναι, and explained in a great variety of ways. See Mr J. B. McClellan's "The New Testament in Two Volumes," of which only vol. I. *The Four Gospels* (1875) has been published.

Origen tells us in *De Orat.* 27, I. p. 245 Delarue (D. 217) that the word ἐπιούσιος does not once occur in Greek literature and is not current in the colloquial language: "It seems to have been coined by the Evangelists. Matthew and Luke agree in using it without any difference. The same course has been taken in other cases also by persons translating from the Hebrew. For what Greek ever used either of the expressions ἐνωτίζου or ἀκουτίσθητι?...A similar expression to ἐπιούσιον occurs in Moses, being uttered by God, *But ye shall be to me a people περιούσιος.* And it seems to me that both words are formed from οὐσία." He continues "...*We pray therefore to be nourished with the Incarnate Word.* But some man will say that ἐπιούσιον is framed from ἐπιέναι *to come next after,* so that we are bidden to ask for the bread which is PROPER TO THE FUTURE WORLD... *to-day* being taken, as in many passages of Scripture, to signify the present world, *to-morrow* the future world" (McClellan pp. 636—7, D. 230).

When St Jerome (about A.D. 383) revised the Latin of the New Testament, he substituted *supersubstantialem* for *quotidianum* in the first Gospel only, thus leading the learned Abelard and others to surmise that ἐπιούσιον was not to be found in the third (D. 251). In his commentaries on the Epistle to Titus and on St Matthew's Gospel he is "apparently consistent with himself in connecting the word with οὐσία," but in later works he shews indecision and writes *Panem nostrum substantivum* sive *supercenturum...quotidianum* sive *super omnes substantias.* "In one point only is he consistent throughout. He insists on a spiritual as opposed to a literal interpretation of the bread" (D. 250).

Correct principles of philology point to one of the derivations of ἐπιούσιος from ἰέναι, and its derivation from οὐσία "if not impossible, is at least more difficult" (D. 223). But if the most learned of Patristic writers, as Origen and St Jerome, could liken it in structure to περιούσιος, this may have been done also by the earlier generation which made and gave currency to the new compound; and the form ἐπιούσιος may have been preferred to the more correct ἐπούσιος, to set over against περιούσιος, as ὁμοούσιος was chosen rather than ὁμόσιος (cf. ὁμέστιος) to contrast with ὁμοιούσιος. The more difficult derivation seemed possible to Beza (D. 257).

Dr W. Kay defends it in the *Journal of Philology* (vol. v. 48—51, 1874), contending that the participle ἐπιών belongs to ἐπεῖναι. Liddell and Scott's *Lexicon* connects ἐπιοῦσα first with ἐπεῖναι and then with ἐπιέναι (p. 518 ed. 7, 1883), quoting Herodotus III. 85 in both cases.

Mr Wratislaw in the *Churchman* for July 1888 replied to Dr Kay "But the real fact is that ἐπεῖναι does possess a participle ἐπών, well-known to Plato and Demosthenes, though unknown to the controversialists upon ἐπιούσιος. PLATO has it twice, in the *Lysis* 217 c οἷον τὸ ἐπόν, where ἐπόν is a certain correction of Heindorf's for ἔτι ὄν: and in the *Parmenides* 132 c ὃ ἐπὶ πᾶσιν ἐκεῖνο τὸ νόημα ἐπὸν νοεῖ. DEMOSTHENES has it in the *Oration against Meidias* p. 517, line 15 ἐπόντος τοῦ φόβου τούτου. I think the false analogy between περιούσιος and ἐπιούσιος may now be dropped, and the claims of ἐπὶ and εἶναι to have originated ἐπιούσιος set aside for ever." Mr Wratislaw then undertakes to prove as below by examples, including "the evidence which Dr Lightfoot has been the first to bring forward," that ἡ ἐπιοῦσα does not necessarily mean ἡ αὔριον.

1. "In the Ecclesiazusae of Aristophanes one of the speakers, after describing the time (ver. 20) καίτοι πρὸς ὄρθρον γ' ἐστίν 'tis close on day-break, exclaims (ver. 105) νὴ τὴν ἐπιοῦσαν ἡμέραν, where τὴν αὔριον would be quite out of place" (D. 226).

2. Plato *Crito* p. 44 A. Very early in the morning (ὄρθρος βαθύς) Crito informs Socrates that the fatal ship has arrived at Sunium, and that on the morrow Socrates must end his life. Socrates thinks that it will not arrive τήμερον to-day... not τῆς ἐπιούσης *on the on-coming day*, but τῆς ἑτέρας, for in a vision "Methought a lady...called to me and said, Socrates on the *third* day thou wilt come to fertile Phthia." Of the three days here mentioned "The first is termed both τήμερον and τῆς ἐπιούσης, the second τῆς ἑτέρας, and the third τῇ ὑστεραίᾳ [τῆς ἑτέρας]. Hence it is clear that in the early morning the day of which the major part is yet to come is represented by ἡ ἐπιοῦσα. This makes it manifest that ἡ ἐπιοῦσα is not in itself equivalent to ἡ αὔριον, although very often the context allows it to be so used."

3. It is argued that ἡ ἐπιοῦσα may possibly have the same meaning in Acts xx. 15 τῇ ἐπιούσῃ κατηντήσαμεν ἀντικρὺ Χίου κ.τ.λ., although the Revised Version reads "And sailing from thence, we came the *following* day over against Chios, and the next day we touched at Samos, and the day after we came to Miletus."

4. Prov. xxvii. 1 μὴ καυχῶ τὰ εἰς αὔριον, οὐ γὰρ γινώσκεις τί τέξεται ἡ ἐπιοῦσα (D. 222). The Greek of the LXX. is "an extremely vivid and correct gloss upon and paraphrase of the original Hebrew," ἡ ἐπιοῦσα standing for םוי A DAY, and the sense being, Thou knowest not what the space of a day, "between now and to-morrow," may bring forth. This is a doubtful interpretation, but αὔριον sometimes connotes a more distant future than ἡ ἐπιοῦσα.

5. Xenophon *Anabasis* I. 7. 1—2. Here "the two senses of ἐπιοῦσα appear to exhibit themselves in very close proximity." Cyrus holds a review at midnight, expecting the king to arrive εἰς τὴν ἐπιοῦσαν ἕω. After the review come deserters from the king's army, ἅμα τῇ ἐπιούσῃ ἡμέρᾳ. The same day is called ἡ ἐπιοῦσα before and at its commencement.

It is inferred that St Matthew's τὸν ἄρτον ἡμῶν τὸν ἐπιούσιον δὸς ἡμῖν σήμερον "is the proper formula for a *morning* prayer, or a prayer said at the beginning of or early in the day," while in using St Luke's form τὸ καθ' ἡμέραν κ.τ.λ. "we must be supposed to ask at any time for the bread of the on-coming space of a day, reckoning from the moment of using the prayer." The Didaché however, which reads τὸν ἄρτον ἡμῶν τὸν ἐπιούσιον δὸς ἡμῖν σήμερον, adds at the end of the Prayer τρὶς τῆς ἡμέρας οὕτω προσεύχεσθε. The days of *bereshith* begin in the evening.

"It is at least possible," as Dr Chase well remarks, "that the apparent analogy of περιούσιος, occurring in a group of passages (Ex. xix. 5, Deut. vii. 6, xiv. 2, xxvi. 18) which we know to have occupied an important place in Apostolic teaching (Tit. ii. 14, 1 Pet. ii. 9; comp. Acts xx. 28, Eph. i. 14), may have suggested or facilitated this representation of the original Aramaic word." It is assumed that this may have been דיומא *of-the-day*, the Hebrew יום *day*, Targ. יומא being rendered ἡ ἐπιοῦσα in Prov. xxvii. 1 Boast not thyself of to-morrow, οὐ γὰρ γινώσκεις τί τέξεται ἡ ἐπιοῦσα.

If דיומא stood in a primitive form of the petition and was first rendered τῆς ἐπιούσης, this might have led (1) to the MAHAR *quod dicitur crastinum* of the Gospel according to the Hebrews (D. 237), and (2) to the coining of ἐπιούσιος (from ἰέναι) with a side glance, under the attraction of a "false analogy," to the imperfectly understood περιούσιος (from εἶναι).

With this comprehensive derivation would agree the expositions of homilists as St Chrysostom, who "seems throughout to be wavering between the meanings *daily* and *necessary*, i.e. between the derivations from ἰέναι and εἶναι" (D. 236). If a word could be analysed in a variety of ways, the homilist, caring little for philology as such, was content to combine the religious lessons deducible from them all. He was like the Jewish Rabbi who would have said, read not ἐπ-ιούσιος but ἐπι-ούσιος, with intent to put new meanings into the word by a fresh derivation of it.

Origen may have "himself first started the derivation from εἶναι, οὐσία," with reference (after his manner) to *absolute being*, or "may have got it from one of his predecessors, Pantaenus or Clement" (D. 231). Mr McClellan on the New Testament (p. 636) quotes from St Clement of Alexandria *Paed.* I. 12 "The Divine Teacher prepares us for contentment and simplicity of life &c., for He saith *Be not careful for the morrow* [Matt. vi. 34], meaning that the Christian ought to enter upon a life of contentment and self-ministration, and only for the single day (ἐφήμερον)," as a passage "which, although perhaps not a direct interpretation, is of considerable importance as testifying to Clement's recognition of the Old Latin *quotidianus* [Matt. vi. 11], and consequently to the originality of his illustrious successor's theory of the derivation from οὐσία."

Various passages however in the works of Clement seem to me to shew that he may have taken the same view of the petition as Origen after him. He defines prayer as ὁμιλία *converse* with God. He writes in *Paed.* II. 1, according to Bishop Kaye's rendering, "It should be our aim to raise our eyes to the truth, firmly to lay hold of the Divine food from above, and to be filled with the inexhaustible contemplation of Him who really exists [τοῦ ὄντως ὄντος], tasting the unchangeable, enduring, pure pleasure. For the food of Christ signifies that we ought to look for this agape." In the same chapter, with a play upon the two senses of ἄριστον, he disparages the *ephemeral* meat and drink in comparison with the spiritual, and teaches that by partaking of the repast of "righteousness and peace and joy in the Holy Ghost" we become possessed of τὸ ἄριστον τῶν ὄντων, the choicest of the things that are. Judging from such words we may think that Clement would have said *Pray not* (very much as the Gospel says *Labour not*) *for the meat which perisheth*, or like St Jerome on the Epistle to

Titus, *Absit quippe ut nos, qui in crastinum cogitare prohibemur, de pane isto qui post paululum concoquendus et abjiciendus est in secessum in prece dominica rogare jubeamur* (D. 249).

He uses the expression Spiritual Food in *Paed. l.c.* (Potter p. 169, cf. p. 971) ἀλλ' οὐκ εὔλογον τραπέζης δαιμονίων μεταλαμβάνειν τοὺς θείας μετέχειν καὶ ΠΝΕΥΜΑΤΙΚΗΣ κατηξιωμένους ΤΡΟΦΗΣ, thinking perhaps of the Didaché, with which its expounders shew that he was acquainted. In its Eucharistic section and after the Lord's Prayer we read, "Thou, O Almighty Sovereign, didst create all things for Thy name's sake, and gavest men food and drink to enjoy, that they might give thanks unto Thee; but TO US Thou didst graciously give SPIRITUAL FOOD and drink and life eternal." The idea of spiritual food runs through the Bible, but the nearest approach in it to the expression is in St Paul's use of the terms spiritual meat and drink with reference to Manna and what is rabbinically called the Well. Philo identifies the λόγος with the "bread from heaven" (Ex. xvi. 4, Deut. viii. 3), cf. Gfrörer *l.c.* p. 179, Jowett on Philo and St Paul (*Epp. of St Paul* I. p. 484, 1859).

In Clem. *Strom.* VII. 13 (Potter p. 881) it is said of the gnostic διὸ καὶ δικαίως εὔχεται, "Ἄφες ἡμῖν λέγων· καὶ γὰρ ἡμεῖς ἀφίεμεν...καὶ ἐπὶ τῶν πενομένων ἀδελφῶν οὐκ αὐτὸς αἰτήσεται ὁ γνωστικὸς οὐ χρημάτων περιουσίαν εἰς μετάδοσιν κ.τ.λ., will not the gnostic not ask for superabundance to give away, but pray that others may have what they want? Canon Cook on *The Revised Version of the First Three Gospels* infers that Clement regarded ἐπιούσιος "as the proper antithesis to περιούσιος."

The Epistle of Barnabas. The writer quotes in chap. x. of his *Epistle* (pp. 101—103 ed. Cunningham 1877) the Mosaic prohibition of unclean meats "Ye shall not eat swine, nor eagle, nor falcon, nor raven, nor any fish that hath not scales upon him," and concludes that *there is no commandment of God to abstain from eating, but Moses spake in the spirit... but they after the desire of the flesh received his words as though they concerned meats.* An allegorist who explains away the obvious literal sense of the Levitical ordinance "Thou shalt not eat &c." would not improbably have spiritualised the "bread" in the Lord's Prayer.

Tertullian. In Tertull. *De Orat.* 6 Quanquam PANEM NOSTRUM QUOTIDIANUM DA NOBIS HODIE spiritaliter potius intelligamus, Christus enim panis noster est &c., the spiritual interpretation of the bread is independent of the epithet ἐπιούσιος.

Jacob of Serug (D. 241). Mr Burkitt gives me some extracts from the *Homilies* of Jacob of Serug, "who flourished in the 5th century, and wrote *inter alia* the accepted exposition of the Lord's Prayer in Syriac corresponding to S. Cyprian's in Latin, or to that of Evagrius in Egypt, using for his text the *Diatessaron.* He explains at great length (without hinting at any spiritualised interpretation of the clause) that לחמא אמינא דיומא means DAILY PROVISION, not gold, or silver or jewels; adding that the poor man prays for daily bread, that he may be contented with what he hath:

24

the rich man also prays for daily bread, that he may be ashamed that he hath ten thousand loaves, and that he may know that the superfluity which he has belongs not to him but to the poor outside."

Mangey on the Lord's Prayer (ed. 3, 1721) writes on ἐπιούσιον κ.τ.λ. "The *African* Fathers have chose the mystical sense, and have explain'd this daily Bread of Christ's Body. They observe, that *as he was the living Bread that came down from Heaven*, so this living Bread is here pray'd for ; and therefore suppos'd, that the spiritual food and nourishment, receiv'd in the holy Sacrament, were the subject of this petition. This interpretation seems partly owing to the primitive custom of receiving the Communion daily, which might give the name of *daily Bread* to the sacred Elements ; and partly to the pious mistake, that nothing temporal could be ask'd for in this Divine form. But most certainly this is neither a true nor an useful sense of the words. This mystical explication of Bread is the product of warm imaginations; and is neither agreeable to our Saviour's design, nor to the notions of his hearers. He cannot be thought to teach them to pray for that heavenly Bread, of which probably they had never yet heard. The literal interpretation of the words then is more probable, and *daily Bread* means no other than the necessaries of this life (pp. 126 sq.)." But see on *De Profugis* in Mangey's Philo I. p. 566 (1742) the note "οὐράνιος τροφή. Eadem fere scribuntur Joh. vi. 32—51. Philo λόγον esse docet cœleste alimentum, Dominus seipsum ; eundem mysticum sensum ex mannæ manducatione uterque deducit...nec mira nec nova visa est ista de pane cœlesti doctrina. Soli illi quibus hebetiores aures & animi erant, Christi dictis sunt offensi."

Libera nos a Malo.

On the petition ῥῦσαι ἡμᾶς ἀπὸ τοῦ πονηροῦ, lit. *deliver us from the evil* (Matt. vi. 13), see Canon Cook's *Second Letter* above mentioned (p. 179).

In Appendix II. (D. 319) Bp Lightfoot sums up thus, " *the earliest Latin Father and the earliest Greek Father, of whose opinions we have any knowledge, both take* τοῦ πονηροῦ *masculine. The masculine rendering seems to have been adopted universally by the Greek Fathers.* At least no authority, even of a late date, has been produced for the neuter. *In the Latin Church the earliest distinct testimony for the neuter is S. Augustine at the end of the fourth and the beginning of the fifth century.* From that time forward the neuter gained ground in the Western Church till it altogether supplanted the masculine." No reference however is made to St Clement of Rome, who perhaps alludes to the Prayer in the passage cited (1877) from the lost and found ending of his Epistle to the Corinthians at the end of Excursus V. (p. 130).

Jacob of Serug gives *Deliver me from Satan who contendeth against me* as a paraphrase of the petition *Deliver us from* BISHA.

On the hypothesis that the Prayer was given in ARAMAIC it has been said *, "The Aramaic original of ἀπὸ τοῦ πονηροῦ seems to have been *men bisho*...which can be translated *from evil*, and *from the evil*, but not *from the Evil One*"; and to this it is objected that, according to Dr Payne Smith's *Thesaurus*, the Syriac BISHA (or *bisho*) "Imprimis usurpatur de diabolo" (D. 293). But Dr Payne Smith's words do not apply to the Jewish Aramaic בישא. On this see Buxtorf, Kohut and Levy's Lexicons; and for the saying attributed to Ben Sira *Do not good to the evil* (ביש) *and evil* (ביש or בישא) *shall not befall thee* see also Schechter in *J. Q. R.* III. 694, and Cowley and Neubauer's *Original Heb. of Ecclus.* pp. xx, xxix. See also the various versions of Ecclus. vii. 1—2, comparing the Syriac ארחק מן בישא with Aboth I. 8 הרחק משכן רע. "The feminine in Syriac is the proper equivalent for the neuter in Greek, as any common Syriac grammar will show. The masculine however may be so used. Thus, in this particular word the masculine *bîsho* properly represents ὁ πονηρός, but may represent τὸ πονηρόν, though the proper representative of the latter is the feminine *bîshtho*" (D. 291). But the Targumic Jewish Aramaic sometimes has *bîsh* or *bîsho* where the Syriac has *bîshtho*, as for רע *evil* in Gen. ii. 9, Ps. vii. 10, Job i. 1, 8, ii. 3.

"So familiar was the word *bîsho*, 'the Evil One,' as a synonym for Satan to the ear of a Syrian, that in the Curetonian [and *sin.*] Syriac it appears in Matt. xiii. 39, where the original has ὁ διάβολος, and in the Peshito Syriac in Acts x. 38, where the original has τοῦ διαβόλου" (D. 292).

It was the New Testament itself which gave currency to the use of בישא for ὁ πονηρός "the Evil One" in Christian Syriac literature, and from this later usage we cannot safely infer that the Jewish Aramaic בישא had exactly the same sense and application. Compare the use of הרע as a rendering of ὁ πονηρός in the Parable of the Sower (p. 192).

"But the objection from the absence of this designation in the Talmudical and early Rabbinical writings still remains to be dealt with. What shall we say to this?" (D. 284). Then follow the passages from Ex. Rab., Deut. Rab., and Baba Bathra cited above in Note 5:

Ex. Rab. 21. 7 (Job xvi. 11) "it is also written *God hath delivered me over to the wicked one* i.e. He hath put me into the hand of Satan" (D. 286). Here however we have merely a casual application to Satan of an indefinite singular עויל "ungodly" (Sept. ἀδίκου), which stands in parallelism with the plural רשעים (Sept. ἀσεβεῖς), thus

יסגירני אֶל אֶל עויל   וְעל ידי רשעים ירטני.

Wünsche reads (p. 170) *Er überlieferte mich* EINEM VERKEHRTEN GOTTE [אֶל אֶל עויל] d. i. er gab mich in die Gewalt des Satans, damit die Israeliten, wenn Gericht über sie gehalten wird, nicht als Frevler hervorgehen.

---

* See Dr Neubauer's letter of the 18th June 1881 in the *Academy* (p. 455).

Darum stürtze er mich in seine Gewalt. Das wollen die Worte sagen Hi. 16. 11 *In die Hand der Frevler übergiebt er mich*.

Deut. Rab. 11. 11 (Ps. xxxvii. 32) "*The wicked one watcheth for the righteous one, and seeketh to slay him**. [Now] there is none so wicked among all the Satanim altogether as Samael... Thus also did Samael the Wicked One watch for the soul of Moses and say &c." (D. 286). Here רשע *wicked* is taken to mean Samael *the wicked*, and the epithet הרשע is applied to him in conjunction with his name, as it might be to Titus or Nebuchadnezzar. Notice that for רשע without the article the Septuagint has ὁ ἁμαρτωλός. So in Job xxi. 30 רע (Targ. בּישׁ, Syr. בּישׁא) is rendered ὁ πονηρός, thus ὅτι εἰς ἡμέραν ἀπωλείας κουφίζεται ὁ πονηρός, εἰς ἡμέραν ὀργῆς αὐτοῦ ἀπαχθήσονται. Conversely מרע *a malo* without the article (p. 128 n.) is a possible form of the original of ἀπὸ τοῦ πονηροῦ.

Baba Bathra 16 a (Job ix. 24) "*The earth is given into the hands of the wicked one*... Job meant in this phrase [the wicked one] none but Satan" (D. 286). Here again there is merely an application to Satan of רשע (Sept. ἀσεβοῦς), an indefinite or collective singular standing in parallelism with a plural "her judges" thus

ארץ נתנה ביד רשע   פני שפטיה יכסה.

Talm. Jerus. Shabbath ii. 6 Zit. (5 b § 3 ed. princ.) quotes Ps. cix. 7 בהשפטו יצא רשע (Sept. ἐν τῷ κρίνεσθαι αὐτὸν ἐξέλθοι καταδεδικασμένος) in proof that Satan accuses only in time of danger. When a man is on his trial רשע will come forth, comm. והוא המלאך הרע יבא ממקומו ללמד עליו קטגוריא i.e. the Evil Angel (Ps. lxxviii. 49 ἀγγέλων πονηρῶν) will emerge from his place to suggest a case against him.

In Aboth R. N. ed. Schechter *A* 1. & הוספה ב' (pp. 4, 151) the wicked serpent touches the tree with hands and feet, and shakes off its fruits to the ground. Or (some say) he did not touch it at all; but when the tree saw him it cried out Wicked One, Wicked One, touch me not, for it is said (Ps. xxxvi. 11) Let not the foot of pride come against me, and let not the hand of the wicked remove me.   This story is told of Samael the Wicked in *Sefer ha-Bahir* (Zohar בראשית 28 b ed. Cremona), quoted by Gill on St Matt. xiii. 19. Samael the Wicked is mentioned in Jellinek's *Bet ha-Midrasch* Midr. אלה אזכרה (ii. 66) and היכלות רבתי (iii. 87).

Origin of the term the Evil One. The New Testament is the earliest known authority for the expression the evil one, and Canon Cook suggests that the general use of the term ὁ πονηρός in that sense "may

* Ungodly men say *let us lie in wait for the righteous man...Let us condemn him to a shameful death* (Wisdom ii. 12, 20). There is a tract of Philo *De eo quod deterius potiori insidiari soleat* (Mangey i. 191). The title ὁ δίκαιος (Acts iii. 14, vii. 52, xxii. 14) "first appears in Enoch as a Messianic designation" (*Enoch* pp. 51, 112 ed. Charles). The New Testament expression the Evil One (Matt. xiii. 19, Eph. vi. 16, 1 Joh. ii. 13—14) may have been used in earlier writings now lost.

probably have originated in our Lord's exposition of the Parable of the Sower." The Greek ὁ πονηρός in St Matt. xiii. 19 and elsewhere may be thought to stand for some Hebrew or Aramaic expression having ὁ Σατανᾶς (Mark iv. 15) and ὁ διάβολος (Luke viii. 12) for synonyms (Note 20). Perhaps a Targumist in retranslating the Parable of the Sower would have rendered ὁ πονηρός by יצרא בישא, for the Evil Impulse occupies the heart (Note 21) and is the foe of Torah (Note 22), and it is said ἔρχεται ὁ πονηρὸς καὶ ἁρπάζει τὸ ἐσπαρμένον ἐν τῇ καρδίᾳ. BISHA may have been used sometimes as an abbreviation of יצרא בישא, in accordance with the saying that the evil yeçer has רע bish for one of its names. With Aboth iv. 2 compare ὅτι ἰσχυροί ἐστε...καὶ νενικήκατε τὸν πονηρόν (1 Joh. ii. 14).

The Septuagint uses πονηρός occasionally for רשע wicked (2 Sam. iv. 11, Is. liii. 9), but in the great majority of cases for רע evil. It uses ὁ πονηρός as an epithet of Haman (p. 128), but not as a name of the Evil One; nor is הרע so used except in Hebrew New Testaments. Such expressions as Ben Sira's πονηρὸν ἐνθύμημα (pp. 149, 152) may have led up to the use of ὁ πονηρός by itself as a name of Satan, cf. Tobit iii. 8, 17 Chald. & Heb. Asmodai the king of the demons, Sept. & Syr. the evil demon. Notice the LXX. rendering ἐγὼ γὰρ οἶδα τὴν ΠΟΝΗΡΙΑΝ αὐτῶν of Deut. xxxi. 21 for I know את יצרו their imagination.

2 TIM. iv. 18 ῥύσεταί με ὁ κύριος ἀπὸ παντὸς ἔργου πονηροῦ καὶ σώσει εἰς τὴν βασιλείαν αὐτοῦ τὴν ἐπουράνιον· ᾧ ἡ δόξα εἰς τοὺς αἰῶνας τῶν αἰώνων, ἀμήν. This is not improbably an application of words of the Lord's Prayer. The expression from every evil work, "from the sphere of evil in every form" (Ellicott), may be a paraphrase of men bisha or מרע, which in places of the Old Testament is freely rendered ἀπὸ παντὸς κακοῦ, ἀπὸ κακῶν, ἀπὸ ὁδοῦ κακῆς, ἀπὸ παντὸς πονηροῦ πράγματος (Prov. iii. 7, iv. 27, Job i. 1, 8, ii. 3, xxviii. 28).

1 ST JOHN ii. 12—14 ἀφέωνται ὑμῖν αἱ ἁμαρτίαι...ἐγνώκατε τὸν πατέρα...νενικήκατε τὸν πονηρόν may refer to ἄφες ἡμῖν τὰς ἁμαρτίας...πάτερ...ἀπὸ τοῦ πονηροῦ in the Prayer. The writer's preference for the masculine ὁ πονηρός would not necessarily exclude a neuter rendering of ἀπὸ τοῦ πονηροῦ. In favour of the masculine interpretation of ἐκ τοῦ πονηροῦ in St John xvii. 15 it is said that "whereas τὸ πονηρόν, 'the evil thing,' is never found in S. John's writings, ὁ πονηρός, 'the Evil One,' occurs many times" (D. 280). This suggests more than it was intended to prove. The neuter MALUM is made to mean the Evil One in an interpretation of a malo quoted by Bp Lightfoot, "Hoc est a diabolo, qui totius mali et auctor est et origo. Diabolus natura caelestis fuit, nunc est nequitia spiritalis; aetate major saeculo, nocendi usu tritus, laedendi arte peritissimus, unde non jam malus, sed malum dicitur, a quo est omne quod malum est" (D. 305). Compare the neuter χεῖρον in the title of Philo's De eo quod deterius &c. (p. 188 n.).

The Liturgies. The Liturgies contain petitions for deliverance from the crafts and assaults of the devil, "but all such prayers are, I believe, invariably connected with petitions to be delivered from evil, from all evil

and mischief, and specially from sin and wickedness, and, in comparison
with such petitions, occupy a secondary place" (Canon Cook in D. 306).
Thus the Book of Common Prayer reads in the *Litany* "FROM ALL EVIL
and mischief; from sin, from the crafts and assaults of the devil &c. *Good
Lord, deliver us*," and in the exposition of the Prayer in the *Catechism*
"and that it will please him to save and defend us in all dangers ghostly
and bodily; and that he will keep us from all sin and wickedness, and from
our ghostly enemy, and from everlasting death."   In the Eastern
Liturgies (Brightman, Oxford 1896) "The general result seems to be that
prominence is given to ὁ πονηρός, but combined with the larger reference to
all evil" (E. H. G.).   On the *Apostolic Constitutions* see Canon
Cook's *Second Letter*, and in the *Didaché* (ed. Bryennius 1883) compare φεῦγε ἀπὸ παντὸς πονηροῦ καὶ ἀπὸ παντὸς ὁμοίου αὐτοῦ, εἰς τὸ πονηρόν...
ῥυσθείητε τέκνα ἀπὸ τούτων ἁπάντων, ῥῦσαι ἡμᾶς ἀπὸ τοῦ πονηροῦ, τοῦ ῥύσασθαι
αὐτὴν ἀπὸ παντὸς πονηροῦ (chaps. 3, 5, 8, 10).

Conclusion.

τὸν ἄρτον ἡμῶν τὸν ἐπιούσιον] On the differences between the two Greek
forms of the Prayer see Mr T. E. Page's *Critical Notes on the Lord's
Prayer* in the *Expositor* 3rd series vol. VII. (1888), and see Thayer *N. T.
Lex.* on ἐπιούσιος. While it is scarcely credible that the perplexing new
compound belonged to the Prayer as first taught, it must have been current
in versions of it before the Greek Gospels were written. The word itself
is an indication that the original language of the Prayer was not Greek.
Nor is it likely that ἐπιούσιος was even the first Greek rendering of its
presumably simple Semitic archetype.

Supposing the petition for the bread to mean *Give us this day* (or *day
by day*) *our daily bread*, its two forms may have been derived from a
Semitic original meaning *Give us the bread of the day* IN THE DAY (p. 180),
as conversely in Lagarde's Arabic both σήμερον and τὸ καθ' ἡμέραν are
rendered *in the day* (p. 181).   Before ἐπιούσιος was thought of
simple Greek words meaning *daily* or *of the day* may have been in use
in the Prayer, cf. ἐφημέρου τροφῆς (Jas. ii. 15), τὴν τῆς ἡμέρας τροφήν
(D. 235).   The Old Latin* *panem quotidianum*, which has been
thought to represent τὸ καθ' ἡμέραν (p. 180 n., M°Clellan p. 644), may embody a true tradition of the original of ἄρτον ἐπιούσιον. Cureton remarks
that the Old Syriac "constant of the day" is an equivalent of *quotidianum*.

Some think that the original of "daily" bread was bread *of* מחר *to-
morrow* (p. 184): others that *of the day* may have been rendered ἐπιούσιον
because ἡ ἐπιοῦσα stands for "a day" in Prov. xxvii. 1. Possibly there was
a previous rendering τῆς ἐπιούσης.   A Rabbinic saying distinguishes

* Mr Burkitt in *Texts and Studies* vol. IV. no. 3 *The Old Latin and the Itala*
shews reason to think that *Itala* meant the Vulgate.

between the instant and the distant *morrow* (Kohut v. 115 *a*), in a note
on Ex. xiii. 14 וְהָיָה כִי יִשְׁאָלְךָ בִנְךָ מָחָר ἐὰν δὲ ἐρωτήσῃ σε ὁ υἱός σου μετὰ
ταῦτα *And it shall be when thy son asketh thee* IN TIME TO COME (Heb.
to-morrow). Although usually equivalent to ἡ αὔριον in its ordinary sense,
ἡ ἐπιοῦσα may denote the day present reckoned from its commencement.

Supposing ἐπιούσιος to be a derivative of εἶναι and to mean *sufficient*
(D. 228, 236), using the liturgical word דַּיֵּינוּ (p. 181) and borrowing from
Gen. xlvii. 15 *Give us bread* and Ex. xvi. 5 *daily*, we may express St Luke's
form of the petition in Hebrew thus

הָבָה־לָנוּ לֶחֶם דַּיֵּנוּ יוֹם יוֹם.

Compare St James ii. 16 τὰ ἐπιτήδεια τοῦ σώματος, the Peshito rendering
in the Prayer *the bread of our necessity* (D. 239), and Dr Chase's note
in *Texts and Studies l.c.* p. 52.

The epithet ἐπιούσιος "is not part of the original form of the petition,
and is due to liturgical use" (ib. p. 53). Nor is it quite clear why the new
word should have been constructed simply and solely to represent anything
that is likely to have stood in the Prayer in its original form. According
to the rules of philology it should be derived from ἐπιών or ἐπιοῦσα, and its
connexion with οὐσία "can only be maintained on the hypothesis that its
form was determined by false analogies, with a view to exhibiting its
component parts more clearly" (D. 225). A false analogy which com-
mended itself to erudite interpreters of the word may have had attractions
for those who coined it (p. 182).

Origen (p. 182) gives a choice of derivations for the epithet of the
bread, but has no doubt of its being ἄρτος ἀληθινός. Bread was understood
mystically before ἐπιούσιος came into existence, and the most curious interpretations of the "strange word" (D. 228) lead only to such results as
may be reached *more rabbinico* without it (p. 178).　　　Tertullian
makes *panem nostrum* QUOTIDIANUM mean Christ (p. 185).

The petition would doubtless soon have been spiritualised if nothing
had been left of it but *Give us bread*.　　　St James says that "wisdom"
should be prayed for (i. 5), but does not say this of daily food (ii. 15).

With reference to St John vi. 32 sq., notice the remark on Διψῶ (ib.
xix. 28) in *The Spirit on the Waters* p. 255 "Nowhere in Christ's doctrine
does the fourth Evangelist use *thirst* or kindred words (such as *bread,
water, life, flesh, blood*) in any but a spiritual sense."

The American Revisers write on St Matthew vi. 11 "Let the marg.
read Gr. *our bread for the coming day*, or *our needful bread*. So in Luke
xi. 3." The one may be a paraphrase, the other a more exact rendering of
the original which lies behind the Greek.

ἀπὸ τοῦ πονηροῦ] The obvious Biblical rendering of ἀπὸ τοῦ πονηροῦ is
מֵרָע *a malo* (p. 188), cf. Job i. 1, 8 Vulg. recedens *a malo*, Sept. ἀπὸ παντὸς
πονηροῦ πράγματος. A possible alternative is מֵרָשָׁע *ab impio*.　　　The

word רשע (it is said) occurs about 300 times and "the LXX. render it by κακός, ἀσεβής, ἄδικος, ἁμαρτωλός, παράνομος, &c., but never by πονηρός." Exceptions to this are 2 Sam. iv. 11 כו' אף כי אנשים רשעים ἀλλὰ καὶ νῦν ἄνδρες πονηροὶ ἀπέκτειναν ἄνδρα δίκαιον, Is. liii. 9 ויתן את רשעים קברו καὶ δώσω τοὺς πονηροὺς ἀντὶ τῆς ταφῆς αὐτοῦ, but as a rule πονηρός corresponds to רע evil and not to רשע wicked. Compare Ps. vii. 9 Oh let רע רשעים πονηρία ἁμαρτωλῶν the evil of the wicked come to an end, Ps. x. 15 Break thou the arm of רשע ורע ἁμαρτωλοῦ καὶ πονηροῦ the wicked and the evil, Ezek. xviii. 20 ורשעת רשע and the wickedness of the wicked impietas impii ἀνομία ἀνόμῳ.

The Hebrew for πονηρός being as a rule רע evil, it may be thought that St Matt. xiii. 19 ἔρχεται Ο ΠΟΝΗΡΟΣ (R.V. the evil one, A.V. the wicked one) καὶ ἁρπάζει τὸ ἐσπαρμένον ἐν τῇ καρδίᾳ αὐτοῦ should be rendered as by Delitzsch ובא הרע כו'. It does not however appear that הרע was ever used quite in this way for the Evil One until the Greek Testament was translated into Hebrew. On the other hand actual Rabbinic usage as far as it goes favours the use of רשע in the required sense (p. 188), thus

בא רשע וחטף הזרע הזרוע בלבבו.

A like expression would serve to render ὁ ἄνομος (cf. Ezek. l.c.) in 2 Thess. ii. 8, which Westcott and Hort connect with Is. xi. 4 ימית רשע.

The Syriac versions render ἀπὸ τοῦ πονηροῦ by מן בישא from the evil. This is also the most obvious expression for ἀπὸ τοῦ πονηροῦ in Jewish Aramaic, which may have been the original language of the Prayer; but it does not follow that in the earlier dialect it must have meant precisely the same as afterwards in Christian Syriac. By literal translation from the New Testament הרע is made to have a meaning which, so far as we know, it had not in genuine Hebrew, and the like may have happened to its Syriac synonym בישא (p. 187).

If the titles the Righteous One (p. 188 n.) and the Evil One are to be regarded as correlative, they are best accounted for as specialisations of the Biblical צדיק righteous and רשע wicked respectively. From this point of view the most natural Aramaic rendering of ὁ πονηρός is not בישא (D. 293) but רשיעא (p. 140).

But the best Hebrew rendering of the ambiguous ἀπὸ τοῦ πονηροῦ is מרע (Aram. מן בישא). This is found several times in the Bible in the phrase "depart from evil," רע may denote an evil person or spirit, it is a name of "the imagination of man's heart," which is also πονηρία and ὁ πονηρός (pp. 147, 189), and it describes the evil way to be shunned according to sayings of the Jewish Fathers (p. 35) and the things deprecated as evil in Jewish Prayers*.

* See p. 129. 1—3 with the Variae Lectiones in Rabbinovicz ד"ס vol. i., and Heb. Auth. P. B. p. 7.

HEBREW TEXT

OF THE

SIX PERAQIM.

ספר

דברי אבות העולם

ובו

מסכת אבות

מכ״י אחד ואין שני הכולל כל המשנה כולה כפי נוסחת התלמוד שלבני ארץ ישראל

עם חלופי גרסאות והגהות ועם פרוש בלשון אנגלית

ופרק רבי מאיר

כפי הנוסחא הנודעה עם פרוש קנר

חברו

כארולוס טילור

ראש לחברת יוחנן הקדוש המבשר

הוצאה שניה

קאנטאבריגיא

בבית הדפוס אשר למדרש החכמה

———

שנת תרנ״ז לפ״ק

האומר דבר בשם אומרו

מביא גאולה לעולם

מסכתא דאבות

פרק ראשון

א

משה קבל תורה מסיני ומסרה ליהושע ויהושע לזקנים
וזקנים לנביאים ונביאים מסרוה לאנשי כנסת הגדולה הן
אמרו שלשה דברים היו מתונים בדין והעמידו תלמידים
הרבה ועשו סייג לתורה :

ב

שמעון הצדיק היה משירי כנסת הגדולה הוא היה אומר
על שלשה דברים העולם עומד על התורה ועל העבודה ועל
גמילות חסדים :

ג

אנטיגנס איש סוכו קבל משמעון הצדיק הוא היה אומר
אל תהיו כעבדים המשמשים את הרב על מנת לקבל פרס
אלא היו כעבדים המשמשין את הרב על מנת שלא* לקבל
פרס ויהי מורא שמים עליכם :

א נ״א שלא על מנת

ד

יוסי בן יועזר איש צרדה ויוסי[א] בן יוחנן איש ירושלם
קבלו מהן יוסי בן יועזר איש צרידה[ב] אומר יהי ביתך בית
ועד לחכמים והוי מתאבק בעפר רגליהן ושותה בצמא[ג]
את דבריהם :

ה

יוסי בן יוחנן איש ירושלם אומר יהי ביתך פתוח לרוחה
ויהיו עניים בני ביתך ואל תרבה שיחה עם האשה :

ו

באשתו אמרו קל וחומר באשת חבירו מיכן[ד] אמרו
החכמים כל זמן שהאדם מרבה[ה] שיחה עם האשה גורם
רעה לעצמו ובוטל מדברי תורה וסופו יורש[י] גיהנם :

ז

יהושע בן פרחיא ומתאי[ז] הארבלי קבלו מהם יהושע בן
פרחיה אומר עשה לך רב וקנה לך חבר והוי דן את כל
האדם לכף זכות :

<hr />

א בנ״א נקרא כל אחד מב׳ התנאים האלה בשם יוסף

ב בנ״א חסר כאן איש צרידה. וי״ג לעיל קבלו ממנו

ג עיין ירמיה ב׳ כ״ה. וכ״א והוי שותה בצמא

ד כ״א מכאן   ה כ״א כל המרבה

י כ״א יורד ל׳ ויש עוד כ״א יורש ל׳

ז בכל הספרים מצינו כאן ולקמן מלת מתאי במקום מתי

ח

מתאי הארבלי אומר הרחק משכן רע ואל תתחבר
לרשע ואל תתיאש מן הפורענות:

ט

יהודה בן טבאי ושמעון בן שטח קבלו מהם יהודה בן
טבאי אומר אל תעש עצמך כעורכיᵃ הדיינים וכשהיו בעלי
הדיןᵇ עומדין לפניך יהיו בעיניך כרשעים וכשנפטרין מלפניך
יהיו בעיניך כצדיקיםᵍ שקיבלוᵈ עליהן את הדין:

י

שמעון בן שטח אומר הוי מרבה לחקור את העדים
והוי זהירᵉ בדבריך שמא מתוכן ילמדו לשקר:

י"א

שמעיה ואבטליון קבלו מהן שמעיה אומרי אהוב את
המלאכה ושנא את הרבנות ואל תתודע לרשותי ואל תתיאש
מן הפורענות:

א כ"א כעורכי   ב כ"א וכשיהיו בעלי דינין

ג כ"א כזכאין

ד כ"א כשקבלו ויש עוד כ"א לכשקבלו   ה כ"א זריז

ו בכ"א מנאתי גם כאן המאמר המיוחס לאבטליון חכמים הזהרו בדבריכם

ז ברוב הספרים חסר כאן ואל תתיאש וג' וזה הנכון עיין לעיל משנה ח'.
ואח"ת מ"ט נשנו התיבות הכ"ל וי"ל שאולי טעה המעתיק מפני קרוב המבטא
בין מלת לרשות ומלת לרשע ולפיכך נוסף כאן המאמר הנכתב סם אחר מלת
לרשע

י"ב

אבטליון אומר חכמי' הזהרו בדבריכם שמא תחובו
חובת גלות ותגלו למקום המים הרעים וישתו התלמידים
הבאים אחריכם וימותו ונמצא שם שמים מתחלל :

י"ג

הלל ושמאי קבלו מהן הלל אומר הוי מתלמידיו של
אהרן אוהב שלום ורודף שלום אוהב את הבריות ומקרבן
לתורה :

י"ד

הוא היה אומר נגד שמאיᵃ אבד שמאי די לא מוסיף
יסוףᵇ ודילא ילףᵍ קטלא חייב ודי אשתמש בתגאיᵈ חלף :

ט"ו

הוא היה אומר אם אין אני לי מי לי וכשאני לעצמי מה
אני אםᵉ לא עכשיו אמתי :

א נ"א שמיה

ב נ"א ודלא יוסיף יסיף

ג נ"א ודלא יליף

ד ואפשר לקרות בתאנא ל"ד הרמב"ס ז"ל: ונאמר עוד על דרך הסימן

(ס"י הסמוס) תלמיד אין גברא אחרינא לא עכ"ל

ה נ"א ואם

ט"ז

שמאי אומר עשה תורתך קבע אמור מעט ועשה הרבה
והוי מקבל את כל האדם בסבר פנים יפות :

י"ז

רבן גמליאל אומר עשה לך רב והסתלק מן הספק ואל
תרבה לעשר אומדות :

י"ח

שמעון בנו אומר כל ימי גדלתי בין החכמים ולא מצאתי
לגוף טוב אלא שתיקה[א] לא[ב] המדרש הוא העיקר אלא
המעשה וכל המרבה דברים מביא חטא :

י"ט

רבן שמעון בן גמליאל אומר על שלשה דברים העולם
קיים[ג] על הדין ועל האמת ועל השלום[ד] :

א ‏נ"א משתיקה תסת אלא שתיקה

ב ‏נ"א ולא ויס כן נ"א לא מדרש הוא עיקר אלא מעשה

ג ‏נ"א עומד עיין לעיל מ' ב'

ד ‏שנ' אמת ומשפט שלום שפטו בשעריכם. התיבות האלו נוספו לראיה
ברוב הספרים. אבל בפי' המיוחס לרש"י הנדפס עס ספר ד"ק למהר"ל
מפראג בקראקא בשנת סמ"ט לפ"ק מנאתי דברים הללו: ובמשנה **טברנית**
אין כתיב שם פסוק

פרק שני

א

רבי אומר אי זו היא דרך ישרה שיבור לו האדם כל
שהיא תפארת לעושה תפארתא לו מן האדם והוי זהיר
במצוה קלה כחמורהב שאין אתה יודע מתן שכרן של
מצות והוי מחשב הפסד מצוה כנגד שכרה ושכר עבירה
כנגד הפסדה והסתכל בשלשה דברים ואין אתה בא לידי
עבירה דע מהי למעלה ממך עין ראהד ואוזן שומעת וכל
מעשיך בספר נכתבים :

ב

רבן גמליאל בנו של ר׳ יהודה הנשיא אומר יפה תלמוד
תורה עם דרך ארץ שיגיעת שניהם משכחת עון וכלה תורה
שאין עמה מלאכה סופה בטלה לגוררי עון וכל העמלים

א כ״ח ותפארת   ב כ״ח בכחמורה

ג בכ״י אחד אחר ראיתי חסר מה ואולי זה הנכון עיין פרושי בלשון
אנגלית   ד חסר ויו

ה כתיב כאן עון וכל וכתיב להלן עון וכל וזו סבת ט״ס בכ״י הנ״ל
שהשמיאמר וכל תורה וכו׳ נסכח סם לגמרי   י כ״ח וגוררת

עם הציבור יהיו עמלים[א] עמהן לשם שמים שזכות אבותם
מסייעתן וצדקתן עומדת לעד ואתם מעלין[ב] עליכם שכר[ג]
כאילו עשיתם :

ג

הוו זהירים ברשות שאין מקרבין[ד] לאדם אלא לצורך
עצמן ונראין[ה] כאוהבין בשעת הנאתן ואין עומדין לאדם
בשעת דחקו :

ד

הוא היה אומר עשה רצונו כרצונך כדי שיעשה רצונך
כרצונו בטל רצונך מפני רצונו כדי שיבטל[ו] רצון אחרים
מפני רצונך :

ה

רי[ז] הלל אומר אל תפרוש עצמך[ז] מן הציבור ואל
תאמן בעצמך עד יום מותך ואל תדין את חבירך עד

א כ"ח עוסקים וכמ"ו כן לעיל העוסקים תחת העמלים

ב כ"ח מעלה אני

ג ל"ג שכר הרבה

ד בכ"ח נוספה מלת לו כאן ולהלן במשנה זו לפני מלת לאדם

ה כ"ח נראין

ו בכ"ח חסר ר אבל בכ"י הכ"ל נמצאת תיבת ר

ז בכ"ח חסר עצמך

שתגיע למקומו ואל תאמר דבר שאיפשר לו להשמע[א]
שסופו[ב] ואל תאמר כשאפנה[ג] אשנה שמא לא תפנה :

ו

הוא היה אומר אין בור ירא חטא ולא עם הארץ
חסיד ולא הביישן למד ולא הקפדן מלמד ולא כל המרבה
בסחורה מחכים ובמקום שאין אנשים השתדל להיות איש :

ז

אף הוא ראה גולגולת אחת שצפה על פני המים ואמר
לה אל[ד] דאטיפת אטיפוך וסוף מטיפיך יטופון :

ח

הוא היה אומר מרבה בשר מרבה רמה מרבה נכסים
מרבה דאגה[ה] מרבה שפחות מרבה זמה מרבה עבדים
מרבה גזל מרבה נשים מרבה כשפים מרבה תורה מרבה
חיים מרבה חכמה מרבה ישיבהי מרבה צדקה מרבה

א כ״א שאי אפשר לשמוע. אבל הפי׳ המיוחס לרש״י הנ״ל מסייע לגרסא
שלפנינו וז״ל : כלומר אל תאמר על דבר של תורה שאתה יכול לשמוע עכשיו
שתשמע לבסוף אלא לאלתר הט אזנך לשמוע עכ״ל

ב ואפשר לקרות וסופו. ומ״מ צריך להוסיף כאן מלת להשמע

ג כ״א לכשאפנה   ד כך הוא בכ״י

ה ברוב הספרים מצינו כאן התיבות הנכתבות להלן מרבה נשים
מרבה כשפים

י כ״א מרבה ישיבה מרבה חכמה. עוד מצאתי נוסף מרבה עצה מרבה
תבונה (כ״א תורה)

(8)

שלום קנה שם טוב קנה לעצמו קנה לו דברי תורה קנה
לו חיי העולם הבא :

ט

רבן יוחנן בן זכאי קבל מהלל ומשמאי הוא היה אומר
אם עשית[א] תורה הרבה אל תחזק טובה לעצמך כי לכך
נוצרתה :

'

חמשה תלמידים היו לו לרבן יוחנן בן זכאי ואילו הן
ר' ליעזר[ב] בן הורקנוס ור' יהושע בן חנניה ור' יוסי הכהן
ור' שמעון בן נתנאל ור' אלעזר בן ערך הוא היה מונה
שבחן אליעזר[ג] בן הורקנוס בור סיד שאינו מאבד טיפה
יהושע בן חנניה[ד] אשרי יולדתו יוסי הכהן[ה] חסיד שמעון
בן נתנאל ירא חטא אלעזר בן ערך מעין המתגבר :

י"א

הוא היה אומר אם יהיו כל חכמי ישראל בכף מאזנים
ואליעזר בן הורקנוס בכף שניה מכריע את כלן אבא שאול

א ל"ג כאן למדת עיין מ' י"ט. והרי יש גרסין טובה תחת תורה
ב לפי מיעוט ההפרש בין שם אלעזר לשם אליעזר תמצא זה תחת זה
במקומות הרבה
ג ל"ג כאן ר' קודם שמות ר' אליעזר וחבריו כי אפילו אם תאמר שכבר
נסמכו קס"ד שרבן יוחנן קרא לתלמידיו בשם ר'
ד בקנת הספרים חסר כאן שם אביו של ר' יהושע
ה כ"א יוסי בקסור כנוי הכהן
י כ"א כמעין

אומר משמו אם יהיו כל חכמי ישראל בכף מאזנים
ואליעזר בן הורקנוס עמהן[א] ואלעזר בן ערך בכף שניה מכריע
את כולם :

י"ב

אמר להם צאו וראו אי זו היא דרך טובה[ב] שידבק
בה אדם רבי ליעזר אומר עין טובה ר' יהושע אומר חבר
טוב ור' יוסי אומר שכן טוב ור' שמעון אומר הרואה את
הנולד ר' לעזר אומר לב טוב אמר להם רואה אני את
דברי אלעזר בן ערך מדבריכם[ג] שבכלל דבריו דבריכם :

י"ג

אמר להם צאו וראו אי זו היא דרך רעה שיתרחק ממנה
אדם ר' ליעזר אומר עין רעה ור' יהושע אומר חבר רע ור'
יוסי אומר שכן רע ור' שמעון אומר הלווה ואינו משלם אחד
לווה מן האדם כלווה מן המקום ברוך הוא[ד] שנ' לווה רשע
ולא ישלם וצדיק חונן ונותן ר' לעזר אומר לב רע אמר להם
רואה אני את דברי אלעזר בן ערך מדבריכם שבכלל דבריו
דבריכם :

א נ"א אף עמהם
ב נ"א ישרה עיין משנה ח' דפרק זה
נ בנ"א חסר' מלת מדבריכם כאן ולקמן במשנה י"ג
ד נ"א כאלו לוה מן המקום. וחסר ב' ה' כאן ונשאר מקומות

י"ד

והן^א אמרו שלשה דברים ר' ליעזר אומר יהי כבוד
חבירך חביב עליך כשלך ואל תהי נוח לכעוס ושוב יום
אחד לפני מיתתך והוי מתחמם כנגד אורן של חכמים^ב
והוי זהיר מגחלתן שמא תכוה שנשיכתן נשיכת שועל
ועקיצתן עקיצת עקרב ולחישתן לחישת שרף וכל דבריהם
כגחלי אש :

ט"ו

ר' יהושע אומר עין רעה^ג ויצר הרע ושנאת הבריות
מוציאין את האדם מן העולם :

ט"ז

ר' יוסי אומר יהי ממון חבירך חביב^ד עליך כשלך התקן^ה
עצמך ללמוד תורה שאינה ירושה לך וכל מעשיך יהיו לשם
שמים :

י"ז

ר' שמעון אומר הוי זהיר בקרית שמע ובתפלה וכשאתה
מתפלל אל תעש תפלתך קבע אלא תחנונים^י לפני המקום

א כ"א הן

ב כנ"ל אע"פ שבס"א חסר והוי מתחמם כנ' א' של חכמים. ועוד להלן
יס כ"א בנחלתן שלא תכוה

ג כ"א הרע   ד בנ"א חסר חביב

ה כ"א והתקן   י כ"א רחמים ותחנונים

ברוך הוא שנ' כי אל רחום וחנון הוא ארך אפים ורב חסד[א]
ואל תהי רשע בפני עצמך :

י"ח

ר' לעזר אומר הוי שקד[ב] ללמוד תורה[ג] מה שתשיב
לאפיקורוס ודע לפני מי אתה עמל ומי הוא בעל מלאכתך[ד] :

י"ט

ר' טרפון אומר היום קצר והמלאכה מרובה והפועלים
עצלים והשכר הרבה ובעל הבית דוחק הוא היה אומר לא
עליך המלאכה לגמור ולא אתה בן חורים לבטל[ה] אם
למדתה תורה הרבה נותנין לך שכר הרבה ונאמן הוא בעל
מלאכתך שישלם לך שכר פעולתך ודע מתן שכרן של
צדיקים לעתיד לבוא :

א נ"א כי (אל) חנון ורחום הוא ארך אפים ורב חסד ונחם על הרעה.

ב נ"א שקוד

ג בנ"א נוסף כאן ודע

ד נ"א ונאמן הוא בעל מלאכתך כדלקמן במשנה י"ט. ועוד ברוב הספרים
תמצא גם כאן התיבות הנכתבות שם שישלם לך שכר פעולתך

ה נ"א להבטל ממנה

פרק שלישי

א

עקביה בן מהללאל אומר הסתכל[א] בשלשה דברים ואין[ב]
אתה[ג] בא לידי עבירה דע מאין באתה ולאין[ד] אתה הולך
ולפני מי אתה עתיד ליתן דין וחשבון דע[ה] מאין באתה
מטיפה סרוחה ולאין[ד] אתה הולך לרמה ותולעה[י] ולפני מי
אתה עתיד ליתן דין וחשבון לפני מלך מלכי המלכים
ברוך הוא[י] :

ב

ר' חנניה[ח] סגן הכהנים אומר הוי מתפלל בשלומה של
מלכות שאילולי[ט] מוראה איש את רעהו חיים בלענו[י] :

[א] כ״א הסתכל	[ב] כ״א ואי
[ג] כך הוא בבמדבר י״א ט״ו	[ד] כ״א ולאן
[ה] בכ״א חסר דע	
[י] כ״א למקום (עפר) רמה (כ״א ורמה) ותולעה	
[ז] כ״א הקב״ה	
[ח] כ״א חנינא כאן ובשאר מקומות	
[ט] כ״א שאלמלא	
[י] בלעו בלשון נסתר	

(13)

3

ג

רׄ חנניה בן תרדיון אומר שנים שהיו יושבין ואין ביניהם
דברי תורה הרי זה מושב לצים שנׄ ובמושב לצים לא ישב
אבל שנים שהיו יושבין ועוסקין בדברי תורהא שכינה
ביניהםב שנׄ אז נדברו יראי ייׄ איש אל רעהו וגוׄ :

ד

אחד שיושב ושונה מעלה עליו הכתוב כאילו קיים
את כל התורה כולהג שנׄ ישב בדד וידום כי נטל
עליו :

ה

רׄ שמעון אומר שלשה שהיו אוכליןד על שלחן אחד
ולא אמרו עליו דברי תורה הריה כאילו אכלו מזבחי מתים
שנׄ כי כל שלחנות מלאו קיא צואה בלי מקום :

א כ״א ועוסקין בתורה כאן ולהלן במׄ טׄ ויש עוד כ״א ויש ביניהם דברי
תורה

ב כ״א עמהם ויש עוד כ״א שרויה ביניהם כאן ולהלן במׄ טׄ

ג כ״א אין לי אלא שנים מנין שאפילו אחד שיושב ועוסק בתורה שהקב״ה
קובע לו שכר ועיין ברכות דף וׄ ע״א

ד כ״א שאכלו ויש שנוים אחרים כזה במסניות אחרות

ה בכ״א חסר הרי

ו

אבל שלשה שהיו אוכלין על שלחן אחד ואמרו עליו
דברי תורה כאילו אכלו משלחנו של מקום ברוך הוא
שנ׳ וידבר אליוֹ* זה השלחן אשר לפני יוֹ :

ז

חנניה[ב] בן חכינאי אומר הניעוֹר בלילה והמהלך בדרך
יחידי ומפנה לבו לבטלה הרי זה מתחייב בנפשו :

ח

ר׳ נחונייה בן הקנה אומר כל המקבל עליו עול תורה
מעבירין ממנו עול מלכות ועול דרך ארץ וכל הפורק ממנו
עול תורה נותנין עליו עול מלכות ועול דרך ארץ :

ט

ר׳ חלפתא איש כפר חנניה אומר עשרה שהיו יושבין
ועוסקין בדברי תורה השכינה[ד] ביניהם שנ׳ אלהים נצב
בעדת אל ומנין אפי׳ חמשה[ה] שנ׳ בקרב אלהים ישפוט

א נ״ל אלי
ב נ״א רבי חנינא   ג נ״א שכינה כדלעיל מ׳ ג׳
ד דע כי בספרים הרבה נתחלף סדר הרחיות אשר הביא ר׳ חלפתא על הג׳
והה׳ כי השלשה נתיחדו פס לענין הדין והחמסה לענין האגודה ועיין היטב
תוספות דמסכת סוכה דף י״ג ע״א ד״ה בשלש. ובפ״ק דברכות זכרו
מהמנינים הנ״ל העשרה והשלשה והשנים והאחד ועוד הביאו הרחיות אשר
הביא כאן ר׳ חלפתא אבל לא זכרו מספר החמסה

ומנין אפילו שלשה שנ׳ ואגודתו על ארץ יסדה ומנין
אפילו שנים שנ׳ אז נדברו יראי ייָ איש את* רעהו
ומנין אפילו אחד שנ׳ בכל המקום אשר אזכיר את שמי
אבא אליך וברכתיך :

,

ר׳ לעזר בן יהודהᵇ איש ברתותה אומר תן לו משלו
שאתה ושלך שלו וכן הוא אומרᵈ כי ממך הכל
ומידך נתנו לך :

י״א

ר׳ יעקבᵈ אומר המהלך בדרך ושונה ומפסיק מִשְׁנָתוֹᵉ

ב בנ״א חסר בן יהודה	א ג״א אל ע׳ מלאכי ג׳ ט״ז
ד נ״א רבי שמעון	ג נ״א וכן בדוד הוא אומר

ה נ״א ממשנתו : וא״ת למה נורת הפתח תחת הכנון בכ״י שלפנינו וי״ל
שבס״י דומה נורת הקמן לפתח שתחתיה חירק אבל לפעמים הפתח בלבד
עומד במקום הקמן לגמרי . והרי דבר נפלא שראיתי בספר גור אריה (וזה
פרוש לפרוש רש״י על התורה להגאון מהר״ל מפראג) על הפסוק בראשית י״ח
ג׳ וז״ל : לגדול שבהם אמר וקראם כלם אדוני׳ פי׳ הא דכתי׳ הא דכתי׳ דמשמע
לשון רבים מדלא כתי׳ אדוני בחירק ואם״כ אמר אל נא תעבור דמשמע לשון
יחיד אלא האמירה היא לאחד וקראם כולם אדוני׳ לכך קאמר אדוני בלשון רבים.
וא״ת אי לשון רבים הוי למכתב אדני בפתח דמשמע לשון רבים וי״ל בקמן
משמע לשון יחיד וגם לשון רבים וכן מורה הנקודה שהוא קמן והוא מורכב מן
פתח שהוא לשון רבים ומן חירק שהוא לשון יחיד ולפיכך השם שהוא קדום
נקוד בקמן לפי שהקב״ה יחיד ודרך כבוד אומרים לו לשון רבים ומפני שכאן
הוא מדבר לגדול וקראם כולם אדונים לכן קאמר אדני בקמן שהו׳ ליחיד
ומדבר אותו בלשון רבים וזה שכיון רש״י לפרש על ויאמר ה׳ : לגדול שבהם
אמר וקראם כולם אדונים כדי לתרץ לשון אדני בקמן

ואומר מה נאה אילן זהא מה נאה אילן זה ומה נאה ניר
זהב מעלין עליוג כאילו מתחייב בנפשו :

י"ב

ר' דוסתי בר' ינאי אומר משם ר' מאיר אומרד תלמיד
חכם שהוא יושב ושונה ושכחה דבר אחד ממשנתו מעלין
עליו כאילו מתחייב בנפשו שנ' רק השמר לך ושמר
נפשך מאד פן תשכח את הדברים אשר ראו עיניך יכול
אפילו תקפה עליו משנתו תל' ופן יסורו מלבבך כל ימי
חייך הא אינו מתחייבו עד שישבח ויסירם מלבו :

י"ג

ר' חנניה בן דוסא אומר כל שיראת חטאו קודמת
לחכמתו חכמתו מתקיימת וכל שחכמתו קודמת ליראת
חטאו אין חכמתו מתקיימת :

א בכ"א נמצא מה נאה אילן זה פעם א' בלבד

ב כ"א ומה נאה נירא זו

ג כ"א מעלה עליו הכתוב

ד כך הוא בכ"י אשר לפנינו וכמו כן בכ"י הנ"ל (וגם זה שמור בבית
עקד הספרים אשר למדרש החכמה של קאמברידם וסימנו 667 .Add) ויש
לתמוה על ההתיחסות אשר ביניהם

ה כ"א ושוכח. וי"ג כל השוכח תחת תלמיד וכו'

ו כ"א תלמודו תחת דבר (אחד) ממשנתו

כך הוא בחסור מלת בנפשו

ח כ"א עד שישב לו

(יז)

י"ד

הוא היה אומ' כל שמעשיו מרובים מחכמתו חכמתו
מתקיימת וכל שהחכמתו מרובה ממעשיו אין חכמתו
מתקיימת :

ט"ו

הוא היה אומר כל שרוח הבריות נוחה ממנו‌א רוח
המקום נוחה הימנו וכל שאין רוח הבריות נוחה ממנו‌א
אי‌י רוח המקום נוחה הימנו :

ט"ז

ר' דוסא בן הרכינס אומר שינת‌ב שחרית ויין של
צהריים ושיחת הילדים וישיבת בתי כנסיות של עמי הארץ
מוציאין את האדם מן העולם :

י"ז

ר' ליעזר המודעי אומר המחלל את הקדשים והמבזה
את המועדות והמפר בריתו של אברהם אבינו והמגלה
פנים בתורה‌ג אף על פי שיש בידו מעשים טובים‌ד אין לו
חלק לעולם הבא :

א כ"א הימנו. ובכ"א חסר המאמר וכל שאין כו'

ב כ"א שינה של

ג בכ"א נוסף כאן שלא כהלכה ועוד נוסף בין כאן בין לעיל (לפני
המאמר והמפר כו') והמלבין פני חבירו ברבים

ד כ"א תורה ומעשים טובים

י"ח

ר' ישמעאל אומר הוי קל לראש ונוח תשחרותᵃ והוי
מקבל את כל האדם בשמחה :

י"ט

רבי עקיבה אומר שחוק וקלות ראש מרגילין את
האדם לערוהᵇ :

כ

הוא היה אומר מסורותᵍ סייג לתורהᵈ נדרים סייג
לפרישות סייג לחכמה שתיקה :

כ"א

הוא היה אומר חביב אדם שנברא בצלמᵉ שנ' כי
בצלם אלהים עשה את האדם :

ᵃ בכל הספרים מצינו כאן הוי קל לראש ונוח לתשחורת ויש פרושים
סונים על משנה זו ונ"ע

ᵇ נ"א מרגילין לערוה (ס"א לדבר עבירה)

ᵍ נ"א מסורת בלשון יקיד ועוד בחסור התיבות הוא היה אומר

ᵈ חסר כאן מעשרות סייג לעושר

ᵉ נ"א חיבה יתירה נודעת לו (שנברא בצלם אלהים).   וי"א שאין ראיה
מהמקרא שהקב"ה הודיע לאום אדם שנברא בצלמו עד שבא נח ונאמר לו שפך
דם האדם באדם דמו ישפך כי בצלם אלהים עשה את האדם ומ"מ לא נודעת
חנה זו לאדה"ר (עין דרך חיים למהר"ל מפראג)

כ"ב

חביבין ישראל שנקראו בנים למקום[א] חיבה יתירה
נודעת להם שנקראו בנים למקום[ב] שנ' בנים אתם לייָ
אלהיכם :

כ"ג

חביבין ישראל שניתן להם כלי[ג] שבו נברא העולם[ד]
חיבה יתירה נודעת להם שניתן להם כלי שבו נברא
העולם[ה] שנ' כי לקח טוב נתתי לכם תורתי אל תעזובו :

כ"ד

הכל צפוי והרשות נתונה ובטוב העולם נדון והכל
לפי המעשה[י] :

כ"ה

הוא היה אומר הכל נתון בעירבון והמצודה פרושה[ז]
על כל החיים החנות פתוחה והחנוני מקיף והפנקם פתוחה[ח]

א בנ"א חסר למקום

ב בנ"א חסר כאן שנקראו בנים (למקום)

ג נ"א כלי חמדה כאן ולהלן

ד בנ"א חסרו כאן התבות שבו נברא העולם

ה בנ"א חסר כאן המאמר שנתן להם כלי (חמדה) שבו נברא העולם

י נ"א לפי רוב המעשה. ובספר אחר מצינו לא הכל לפי רוב המעשה.

וי"ג אבל לא ע"פ המעשה

ז נ"א ומצודה פרוסה   ח נ"א פתוח

והיד כותבת וכל הרוצה ללוות בא ולוווהᵃ והגבאין מחזרין
תמידᵇ בכל יום ונפרעים מן האדם לדעתוᵍ ושלא לדעתוᵈ
ויש להם על מה שיסמכוᵈ והדין דין אמת והכל מותקןᵉ
לסעודה :

כ"ו

רᶜ לעזר בן עזריה אומר אם אין תורה אין דרך ארץ
אם אין דרך ארץ אין תורה אם אין חכמה אין
יראה אם אין יראה אין חכמה אם אין דעת אין בינה
אם אין בינה אין דעת אם אין קמח אין תורה אם אין
תורה אין קמח :

כ"ז

הוא היה אומר כל שחכמתו מרובה ממעשיו למה הוא
דומה לאילן שענפיו מרובין ושרשיו מעוטיםᵍ והרוח באתהᵸ

א נ' א יבא וילוה. וי"ג וכל הרוצה ליטול בא ונוטל. ובס"א חסר המאמר
לגמרי
ב נ"א מחזירין תדיר   ג נ"א מדעתו
ד ס"א שיסמוכו   ה נ"א מתוקן
י בס"א נתחלף סדר מאמרים של משנה זו· ובכ"י סנג' (Add. 667)
מנאתי : אם אין דרך ארץ אין תורה אם אין תורה אין חכמה אם אין חכמה
אין יראה אם אין יראה אין בינה אם אין בינה אין דעת אם אין דעת אין
קמח אם אין קמח אין תורה
ז נ"א מועטין   ח נ"ל באה

ועוקרתו והופכתו על פניו[א] וכל[ב] שמעשיו מרובים מחכמתו
למה הוא דומה לאילן שענפיו מעוטים[ג] ושרשיו מרובים
אפילו[ד] כל הרוחות באות עליו אינן מזיזות אותו ממקומו:

כ"ח

ר' לעזר הסמה[ה] אומר קינים ופתחי נדה הן הן גופי
תורה[ו] הלכות תקופות וגימטרייה[ז] פרפראות[ח] לחכמה:

[א] שנ' והיה כערער בערבה ולא יראה כי יבוא טוב ושכן חררים במדבר
ארץ מלחה ולא תשב: פסוק זה נוסף לרׁאיה בהרבה ספרים
[ב] נ"א אבל כל
[ג] נ"א מועטין
[ד] נ"א שאפילו כל הרוחות שבעולם באות ונושבות בו אין מזיזות (נ"א
מזיזים) אותו ממקומו שנ' והיה כעץ שתול על (פלגי) מים ועל יובל ישלח
שרשיו ולא יראה כי יבא חם והיה עלהו רענן ובשנת בצרת לא ידאג ולא ימיש
מעשות פרי
[ה] ר"ל חסמה וכך הוא במסכת תרומות פׁ"ג מ"ה ומפורסם טעם שם החכס
הזה בויקרׁא רבה אחרי מות פׁ כ"ג' ול"ג בן (נ"א בר') חסמא
[ו] בנ"א חסרה מלת תורה
[ז] נ"א וגימטריׁ(א)ות בלשון רבים
[ח] נ"א פרפריות. כן גרסת הערוך. וׁח"ב פׁ' בלשון יוני עגולה שׁׁאׁר
החכמות סובבות החכמה האׁמׁתית שהיׁׁא כמרכז ונקודה תוך העגולה

פרק רביעי

א

בן זומא אומר אי זה הוא* חכם הלמד מכל אדם*
שנ' מכל מלמדי השכלתי* :

ב

אי זה הוא גיבור הכובש את יצרו שנ' טוב ארך אפים
מגבור ומושל ברוחו מלוכד עיר :

ג

אי זה הוא עשיר השמח בחלקו שנ' יגיע כפיך כי
תאכל אשריך וטוב לך אשרי* בעולם הזה וטוב לך בעולם*
הבא :

א כ"א איזהו כאן ובמסניות האחרות   ב בנ"א חסר אדם
ג ל"ג כי עדותיך וג'   ד כך הוא בלא יוד
ה כ"א לעולם וכמו כן נתחלפו התבות ב' ול' בהרבה מקומות

ד

אי זה הוא מכובד המכבד את הבריות שנ׳ כי מכבדי
אכבד ובוזי יקלו :

ה

בן עזאי אומר הוי רץ למצוה קלה[א] ובורח[ב] מן העבירה
שמצוה גוררת מצוה ועבירה גוררת עבירה ששכר מצוה
מצוה ושכר עבירה עבירה :

ו

הוא היה אומר אל תהי בז לכל אדם ואל תהי מפליג
לכל דבר שאין לך אדם שאין לו שעה ואין לך דבר שאין
לו מקום :

ז

ר׳ לויטס איש יבנה[ג] אומר כל המחלל שם שמים בסתר
נפרעין ממנו בגלוי אחד שוגג ואחד מזיד בחילול השם[ד] :

א בכ״א נוסף כאן כנ(ב)חמורה וע׳ פ׳׳ב מ״א

ב כ״א וברח

ג בכל הספרים יש כאן שתי מסניות ואלו הן : ר׳ לויטס איש יבנה אומר
מאד (מאד) הוי שפל רוח (בפני כל האדם) שתקות אנוש רמה : ר׳ יוחנן בן
ברוקה אומר כל המחלל וכ׳ :

ד כ״א אחד בשוגג ואחד במזיד ולא נמצא בחילול השם

ח

ר׳ ישמעאל בנו[א] אומר הלמד על מנת ללמד מספיקין[ב]
בידו ללמוד וללמד הלמד על מנת לעשות מספיקין בידו
ללמוד וללמד[ג] ולעשות:

ט

ר׳ צדוק אומר[ד] אל תעשם[ה] עטרה להתגדל בהן ולא
קרדום לאכל[ו] מהן וכך היה הלל אומר ודי אשתמש בתגא
חלף הא כל הנאות[ז] מדברי תורה נטל חייו מן העולם:

י

ר׳ יוסי אומר כל המכבד את התורה גופו מכובד על
הבריות וכל המחלל את התורה גופו מחולל על הבריות:

א בנ״א חסר בנו
ב הנה מצינו בפרוש המיוחם לרמ״ו: : הכי גרסינן אין מספיקין בידו
ללמוד וללמד עכ״ל. ואולי זה הנכון כי המעיין אע״פ בלמד לאחרים ואינו
מבקש לעשות אין חכמתו מתקיימת
ג בנ״א נוסף כאן לשמור
ד בנ״א נוסף כאן תלמידי חכמים. וי״ג אל תפרוש מן הצבור כו׳
ה לפי קנת הספרים מדבר בלשון יחיד כאן ולקמן באומרו אל תעשה וג׳
ו כך הוא בלי וי״ו. ובנ״א נמצא לאכול ממנה. וי״ג לחפור בה(ם)
ז כ״א הא (למדת) כל הנהנה

י"א

רֹ ישמעאל אומר החושךֹֹֹֹֹֹֹֹֹֹֹֹ[א] עצמו מן הדין פורק ממנו
איבה וגזל ושבועת שוא והגם לבו בהוראה שוטה רשע
וגם רוח :

י"ב

הוא היה אומר אל תהי דן יחידי שאין דן יחידי אלא
אחד ואל תאמר קיבלוֹ[ב] דעתי שהן רשאין ולא אתה :

י"ג

רֹ יוחנןֹ[ג] אומר כל המקיים את התורה מעוני סופו
לקיימה מעושר וכל המבטל את התורה מעושר סופו
לבטלה מעוני :

י"ד

רֹ מאיר אומר הוי מעט עסקֹ[ד] ועסוק בתורה ותהיה[ה]
שפל רוח בפני כל אדם ואם ביטלתי מן התורה יש לך

א נ"א רֹ שמעון אומֹ כל החושך.   וי"ג רֹ ישמעאל בנו כוֹ
ב נ"א קבלו
ג נ"א (יו)נתן
ד נ"א ממעט בעסק
ה נ"א והוי   י נ"ל בטלת

בטילים הרבה[א] ואם עמלת בתורה יש לו[ב] שכר הרבה
ליתן לך :

ט״ו

ר׳ ליעזר בן יעקב אומר העושה מצוה אחת קנה[ג] לו
פרקליט אחד והעובר עבירה אחת קנה[ג] לו קטיגור אחד
תשובה ומעשים טובים כתרים לפני הפורענות :

ט״ז

ר׳ יוחנן הסנדלר אומר כל כניסה שהיא לשם מצוה[ד]
סופה להתקיים ושאינה לשם מצוה[ד] אין סופה להתקיים :

י״ז

ר׳ לעזר[ה] אומר יהי כבוד תלמידך חביב עליך ככבוד
חבירך[ו] וכבוד חבירך כמוראי רבך ומורא רבך כמורא
שמים :

א בכ״א נוסף כנגדך　　　ב בכ״א חסר לו
ג כ״א קונה　　　ד כ״א שמים
ה בכ״א נוסף בן שמוע
י בא ראה נקות לשון התנא במשנה זו שכל מאמר תלוי בשלפניו ואין הפסק
ביניהס ול״ג ככבוד עצמך (כ״א בשלך) כי לפי זה לא יהיה נרוף וקשור בין
כל מאמר ומאמר
י כ״א ככבוד

י"ח

ר' יהודה אומר הוי זהיר בתלמוד ששגגת תלמוד[א] עולה
זדון :

י"ט

ר' שמעון אומ' שלשה כתרים הן כתר תורה וכתר כהונה
וכתר מלכות וכתר שם טוב עולה על גביהן :

כ

ר' נהוראי[ב] אומר הוי גולה למקום תורה ואל תאמר היא
תבוא אחרי שהחבירין[ג] יקיימוה בידך ואל בינתך אל תשען :

כ"א

ר' ינאי אומר[ד] אין בידינו לא משלות הרשעים ואף לא
מיסורי הצדיקים[ה] :

א כ"ה בלמוד ששגגת למוד

ב גמרא בשבת דף קמ"ז ע"ב : תנא לא ר' **נהוראי** שמו אלא ר' נחמיה
שמו ואמרי ליה ר' אלעזר בן ערך שמו ולמה נקרא שמו ר' נהוראי שמנהיר
עיני חכמים בהלכה ע"כ. ועוד בערובין דף י"ג ע"ב : תנא לא ר' **מאיר**
שמו אלא ר' נהוראי שמו ולמה נקרא שמו ר"מ שהוא מאיר עיני חכמים בהלכה
ולא נהוראי שמו אלא ר' נחמיה שמו וג'

ג כ"ה שהיא תבא אחריך או (ש)חביריך כו'

ד כ"ה הוא היה אומר   ה כ"ה מייסורין של צדיקים

(28)

כ״ב

ר׳ מתיה[א] בן חרש אומר הוי מקדים לשלום כל האדם[ב]
והוי זנב לאריות ולא[ג] ראש לשועלים :

כ״ג

ר׳ יעקב אומר העולם הזה דומה לפרוזדור לפני העולם
הבא התקין עצמך לפרוזדור[ד] כדי שתכנס לטרקלין :

כ״ד

הוא היה אומר יפה שעה אחת בתשובה ומעשים טובים
בעולם הזה מכל חיי העולם הבא יפה[ה] שעה אחת של קורת
רוח בעולם הבא מכל חיי העולם הזה :

כ״ה

ר׳ שמעון בן אלעזר אומר אל תרצה את חבירך[ו] בשעת
כעסו ואל תנחמנו בשעה שמתו מוטל לפניו ואל תשאל לו
בשעת נדרו ואל תשתדל לראותו בשעת קלקלתו :

א נ״א ר׳ מתתיא
ב נ״א בשלום כל האדם ו[י]״ג שלום לכל א׳
ג נ״א ואל תהי
ד נ״א (ו)התקן עצמך בפרוסדור
ה נ״א ויפה
ו כך הגרסא גם כן בכ״י הנז׳ (המסומן Add. 667)
(29)   5

כ״ו

שמואל הקטן אומר בנפל אויבך אל תשמח ובהכשלו
אל יגל לבך א :

כ״ז

אלישע בן אביה ב אומר הלמד ג ילד למה הוא דומה
לדיו כתובה על נייר חדש והלמד ג זקן למה הוא דומה לדיו
כתובה על נייר מחוק :

כ״ח

ר׳ יוסי בן ד יהודה איש כפר הבבלי אומר הלמד מן
הקטנים למה הוא דומה לאוכל ענבים קהות ושותה יין מגתו
והלמד מן הזקנים למה הוא דומה לאוכל ענבים בשולות
ושותה יין ישן :

א ברוב הספרים כתיב פן יראה יי׳ ורע בעיניו והשיב מעליו אפו . ויש
דורסין בכאן חרון אפו לא נאמר אלא אפו מלמד שמוחלין לו כל עונותיו אבל
בספרי המשנה המדוייקים לא תמצא דבר מזה כי אם הפסוק כמו שהוא מבלי
דרשה כלל (ע׳ נחלת אבות לדון ינקק אברבנאל)
ב נ״א אבויה
ג נ״א הלומד תורה
ד נ״א בר וי״ג בר׳

כ״ט

ר״א אומר אל תסתכל בקנקן אלא במה שיש בו יש קנקן
חדש מלא ישן וישן שאפי׳ חדש אין בו :

ל

ר׳ ליעזר הקפר אומר הקנאה והתאוה והכבוד מוציאין
את האדם מן העולם :

ל״א

הוא היה אומר הילודים למות והמתים להחיות[ב] והחיים
לידון לידע להודיע ולהודיע ולהודע[ג] שהוא[ד] היוצר והוא
הבורא והוא המבין והוא הדיין והוא עד[ה] והוא בעל דין והוא
עתיד לידון[ו] שאין לפניו לא עולה לא שכחא לא משוא[ז]
פנים ולא מקח שוחד שהכל שלו[ח] ודע שהכל לפי חשבון[ט] :

א כ״א רבי מאיר . וי״ג להלן מלא יין ישן וישן אפילו כו׳

ב כ״א לחיות

ג ה״ג לידע ולהודיע ולהוו(ד)דע

ד כ״א שהוא אל הוא

ה כ״א הוא העד

ו כ״א ליתן דין תקת לדין . וי״ג לדון (ברוך הוא)

ז כ״א משא

ח בס״א חסר שהכל שלו

ט כ״א שהכל בא בחשבון (כ״א לידי חשבון)

ל״ב

אלא יבטיחך יצרך ששאול בית מנוס שעל כרחך אתה
נוצר ועל כרחך אתה נולד ועל כרחך אתה חי ועל כרחך
אתה מת ועל כרחך אתה עתיד ליתן דין וחשבון לפני מלך
מלכי המלכים הּקּבּהּ :

א בנ״א נמצא ואל ונכללו משנה זו והקודמת אליה בסוגיא אחת

ב נ״א שיש בשאול בית מנוס לך

ג י״ג בסדר הפוך וע״כ אתה מת וע״כ אתה חי

פרק חמישי

א

בעשרה מאמרות נברא העולם ומה תלמוד לומר והלא
במאמר אחד היה* יכול להבראות אלא להיפרע מן הרשעים
שמאבדין את העולם שנברא בעשרה מאמרות וליתן שכר טוב
לצדיקים שמקיימים את העולם שנברא בעשרה מאמרות :

ב

עשרה דורות מאדם ועד נח להודיע כמה ארך אפים
לפניו שכל הדורות היו מכעיסין לפניו* עד שהביא עליהם
את* המבול :

ג

עשרה דורות מנח ועד אברהם להודיע כמה ארך אפים
לפניו שכל הדורות היו מכעיסין לפניו* עד שבא אברהם
אבינו וקבל* שכר כולם :

<hr>

א בנ״א חסר היה
ב כ״א ובאין תחת לפניו
ג כ״א (את) מי המבול
ד כ״א וקבל עליו

ד

עשרה נסיונות נתנסה אברהם אבינו ועמד בכולם להודיע
כמה היא[א] חיבתו של אברהם אבינו :

ה

עשרה נסים נעשו לאבותינו במצרים ועשרה[ג] על הים :

ו

עשר מכות הביא הֻקָבָה[ב] על המצרים במצרים ועשר[ד] על
הים :

ז

עשרה[ג] נסיונות נסו אבותינו את המקום במדבר שנ׳ וינסו
אותי זה עשר פעמים ולא שמעו בקולי :

ח

עשרה נסים נעשו[ד] בבית המקרש[ה] לא הפילה[י] אשה

א בכ״ח חסר היא   ב כ״ח (ו)עשר תק׳ (ו)עשרה

ג כ״ח ועשרה ובקנת הספרים חסר׳ משנה זו

ד כך גרסו במסכת יומא דף כ״א ע״א אבל ברוב הספרים כתיב נעשו
לאבותינו כדלעיל

ה כ״ח במקדש

י הנה בכ״י הנ״ל (המסומן Add. 667) מצאתי דברים הללו כהויתן :
לא הפילה כ׳ כבר פרשתיו היטב במסכ׳ יומא בפר׳ ראשון עכ״ל. ויס
לסאול למי הפרום הנרמז כאן

מריח בשר הקדש ולא הסריח בשר קדש‎ מעולם‎ ולא אירע
קרי לכהן גדול ביום הכפורים ולא נראה זבוב בית המטבחיים
ולא נמצא פסול בעומר ובשתי הלחם ובלחם הפנים ולא
כיבו גשמים את המערכה‎ ולא ניצחה הרוח את עמוד
העשן עומדים צפופים ומשתחוים רווחים ולא הזיק נחש
ועקרב בירושלמי‎ ולא אמר אדם לחבירו צר לי המקום שָׁאלין
בירושלם :

ט

עשרה דברים נבראו‎ בין השמשותי פי הארץ ופי הבאר
ופי האתון והקשת והמן והמטה והשמיר והכתב והמכתב
והלוחות ויש אומרין אף המזיקים וקבורתו של משה ואילו
של אברהם אבינו ויש אומרים אף צבת בצבת עשוייה‎ :

י

שבעה דברים בגולם‎ ושבעה בחכם החכם אינו מדבר

<hr>

א כ״ח ולא התליע בשר הקדש
ב לפי רוב הספרים זה הוא מקום המאמר הג״ל ולא נראה זבוב (ב)בית
המטבחיים. ויש שנוייס אחריס בסדור הנסיס
ג יש שנוב בכאן כי הנה בפרק קמא דיומא קתני משנה זו ולא קתני בה
ב' הנסיס ולא כבו גשמים ולא נצחה הרוח אבל מוספינן להו מנרייתא ע״ם.
ויש כאן כ״ח אש של עצי (ס״ח שעל גבי) המערכה
ד כ״ח בירושלם מעולם כו' בשעולין לירושלם
ה ברוב הנוסחאות נוסף בערב שבת בין כאן בין להלן אחר מלת השמשות
ו בנ״ח נוסף (עם חשיכה) ואלו הן
ז כ״ח העשויה   ח כ״ח נאמרו בגולם

לפני מי שגדולא ממנו בחכמהב ואינו נכנס לתוך דברי חבירו
ואינו נבהל להשיב שואל כהלכה ומשיב כעניינג ואומר על
ראשון ראשון ועל אחרון אחרוןד על מה שלא שמע אומר לא
שמעתי ומודה על האמת וחלופיהן בגולם :

י"א

שבעה מיני פרעניות באיןד על שבעה גופי עבירותה מקצתן
מעשרין ומקצתן שאינו מעשריןו רעב של בצורת בא מקצתן
רעיבים ומקצתן שבעים גמרו שלא לעשר רעב של מהומה
ושל בצורה בא ושלא ליטול חלהז רעב של כלייה באח :

י"ב

דבר בא לעולם על מיתות האמורות בתורה שלא נמסרו
לבית דין ועל פירות שביעותט :

א נ"א בפני מי שהוא גדול

ב בחכמה ובמנין.   כך הגרסא ברוב הספרים אבל בקצתן חסרו התבות
האלו לגמרי

ג נ"א שואל בענין ומשיב כהלכה.   והנה בספר נחלת אבות לר"י אברבנאל
כתיב שואל ומשיב שומע ומוסיף שואל בענין ומשיב כהלכה

ד נ"א באין לעולם

ה נ"א עבירה   י נ"א אינן

ז נ"א בצורת באה (כאן ולעיל) ושלא ליטול את החלה

ח שבעה מיני פורענות באין על שבעה גופי עבירו' מקצתן רעבים ומקצתן
שבעים גמרו שלא לעשר רעב של כלייה באה: כך גרסת משנה זו בכ"י
המסומן Add. 667

ט נ"ל שביעית.   ע' מ' ט"ו דפרק זה

י"ג

חרב בא לעולם על ענוי הדין ועל עיוות הדין ועל המורים‎ᵃ
בתורה שלא כהלכה

י"ד

חיה רעה באה לעולם על שבועת שוא ועל חילול השם
גלות בא לעולם על עבודה זרה ועל גלוי עריות ועל שפיכות
דמים ועל השמט הארץ‎ᵇ :

ט"ו

בארבעה פרקים‎ᶜ הדבר מרובה‎ᵈ ברביעית בשביעית במוצאי
שביעית ובמוצאי החג שבכל שנה‎ᵉ ברביעית מפני מעשר עני
שבשלישית בשביעית מפני מעשר עני שבששית ובמוצאי
שביעית מפני פירות שביעית ובמוצאי החג שבכל שנה‎ᵉ מפני
גזל מתנות עניים :

א כ"א חרב באה כו' ועל המורים פנים כו' ע' פ"ג מ' י"ז. ועל סכוס
המסניות בדפוס זה ע' הקדמתי בלשון אנגלית
ב כ"א גלות בא לעולם על שפיכות דמים ועל שמיטת הארץ ועל גילוי
עריות וחסרו התבות על (עובדי) ע"ז ואולי זה הנכון כיון סענין ע"ז כבר נרמז
בכלל חילול השם
ג כ"א דברים
ד כ"א מתרבה
ה כ"א שנה ושנה   י כ"א שני

(37)   6

ט"ז

ארבע[א] מידות באדם האומר שלי שלי ושלך שלך[ב] מדה
בינונית ויש אומרי[ב] מדת סדום שלי שלך ושלך שלי[ד] עם
הארץ שלי ושלך[ד] חסיד שלך ושלי שלי רשע :

י"ז

ארבע[א] מדות בדיעות נוח לכעוס ונוח לרצות יצא שכרו
בהפסדו קשה לכעוס וקשה לרצות יצא הפסדו בשכרו קשה
לכעוס ונוח לרצות חסיד נוח לכעוס וקשה לרצות רשע :

י"ח

ארבע מידות בתלמידים ממהר[ה] לשמוע וממהר לאבד
יצא שכרו בהפסידו קשה לשמוע וקשה לאבד יצא הפסידו
בשכרו ממהר לשמוע וקשה לאבד חכמי קשה לשמוע וממהר
לאבד זה חלק רע[ו] :

א נ"א ארבעה

ב בנ"א נוסף זו

ג בנ"א נזכרה מדת עם הארץ בריש כל המדות

ד ר"ל שלי ושלך **שלך** בו' ואולי זה עיקר כיון סקנצור הלשון יורה ליוסן
הגרסא. אבל בכל הספרים נמצא כאן ישלי שלך ושלך שלך וכמו כן להלן נמצ'
שלך שלי ושלי שלי תחת **שלך ושלי שלי**

ה נ"א מהויר כאן ולקמן

ו נ"א זה (ס"א זו) חלק טוב

י"ט

ארבע מידות בנותני צדקה רוצה שיתן ואל‎ⁱ יתנו אחרים
עינו רעה בשל אחרים שיתנו‎ᵇ אחרים והוא לא יתן עינו רעה
בשלו יתן‎ᵍ ויתנו אחרים חסיד אל‎ⁱ יתן ואל‎ⁱ יתנו אחרים
רשע :

כ

ארבע מידות‎ᵉ בהולכי בית המדרש הולך ואינו עושה
שכר הליכה בידו הולך ועושה חסיד לא הולך ולא עושה
רשע :

כ"א

ארבע מידות ביושבי‎ⁱ לפני חכמים ספוג ומשפך משמרת
ונפה ספוג שהוא סופג את הכל משפך שהוא מכנים בזו
ומוציא בזו משמרת שהיא מוציאה‎ⁱ את היין וקולטת את
השמרים נפה שהיא מוציאה‎ⁱ את הקמח וקולטת את הסלת :

כ"ב

כל אהבה‎ʰ שהיא תלוייה בדבר בטל דבר ובטלה אהבה
ושאינה תלויה בדבר אינה בטלה לעולם‎ᵗ :

ב כ"א יתנו	א כ"א ולא
ד כ"א לא	ג כ"א שיתן

ה חסרה מדה אחת מן הד' וזו היא: עושה ואינו הולך שכר מעשה (כ"א
עשייה) בידו. וי"ג בהולכי(ם) לבית כו'

ז כ"א שמוציאה	י כ"א ביושבים

ח הנה בספר נחלת אבות הכ"ל נהפך סדר המשניות ונזכר ענין המחלוקת
קודם לענין האהבה

ט כ"א עולמית

אבות פרק חמישי בעשרה

כ"ג

אי זו היא אהבה שהיא תלויה בדבר זו אהבת אמנון
ותמר ושאינה תלויה בדבר זו אהבת דוד ויהונתן :

כ"ד

כל מחלוקת שהיא לשם שמים סופה להתקיים ושאינה
לשם שמים אין סופה להתקיים :

כ"ה

אי זו היא מחלוקת שהיא לשם שמים׳ מחלוקת שמאי
והללב ושאינה לשם שמים זו מחלקתו של קרחג :

כ"ו

כל המזכה את הרבים אין חטא בא על ידו וכל המחטיא
את הרבים איןד מספיקין בידו לעשות תשובה :

כ"ז

משה זכה וזיכה את הרבים וזכות הרבים תלויה בו שנ׳
צדקת יי׳ו עשה ומשפטיו עם ישראלה :

א בנ"א נוסף זו
ב נ"א מחלוקת הלל ושמאי
ג נ"א קרח וכל עדתו
ד נ"א חטא הרבים תלוי בו ואין
ה חסר ענין ירבעם וזה הוא : ירבעם חטא והחטיא את הרבים חטא הרבים
תלוי בו שנ׳ על חטאת ירבעם בן נבט אשר חטא ואשר החטיא את ישראל :

(40)

כ"ח

כל שיש בו שלשה דברים° תלמידו° של אברהם° ושלשה
דברים° תלמידו° של בלעם :

כ"ט

עין טובה ונפש שפלה ורוח נמוכה° תלמידו של אברהם
עין רעה ונפש רחבה° ורוח גבוהה תלמידו של בלעם ומה
בין תלמידיו של אברהם לתלמידיו של בלעם תלמידיו° של
בלעם יורדים לגהינם° שנ' ואתה אלהים תורידם לבאר
שחת° אבל תלמידיו של אברהם יורשין גן עדן' שנ' להנחיל
אוהבי יש ואוצרותיהם אמלא :

א   כ"ח כל מי שיש בידו ג' דברים הללו

ב   כ"ח מתלמידיו כאן ולהלן במ' כ"ט

ג   כ"ח אברהם אבינו כאן ולהלן וכמו כן נוסף כנוי הרשע לבלעם

ד   כ"ח וג' דברים אחרים

ה   בכ"א נמצא ענין הרוח קודם לענין הנפש

י   כ"א קצרה

ז   הנה אחר שהזכיר פס בלעם פתח במה דפייס וסמך לו לרשע ענין
קללתם של רשעים ואח"כ חזר וזכר ברכת הצדיקים כיון שאין רצונו לסיים אלא
בדברים טובים וזו הגרסא הנכונה אע"פ שבקרוב הספרים נזכר ענין בני
אברהם ברישא וענין בני בלעם בסיפא

ח   בכ"א נוסף ויורשין באר שחת ובספרים הרבה כתיב יורשין גיהנם ויורדין
לבאר שחת

ט   ל"ג אנשי דמים ומרמה לא יחצו ימיהם ואני אבטח בך

י   כ"א אוכלין בעולם הזה ונוחלין לעוה"ב תחת יורשין גן עדן

ל

ר׳ יהודה בן תימא אומר הוי עז כנמר וקל כנשר ורץ
כצבי וגבור כארי לעשות רצון אביך שבשמים :

ל״א

הוא היה אומר עז פנים לגהינם ובושׁ[ב] פנים לגן עדן יהי
רצון מלפניך י׳׳[ו] אלהינו ואלהי אבותינו שתבנה עירך[ג] בימינו
ותן חלקינו בתורתך :

ל״ב

בן בג בג אומר הפוך בה והפך[ד] בה דכולה בה והפוך
בה[ה] ומנה לא תזועי שאין לך מידה טובה ממנה :

ל״ג

בן הֵא הֵא אומר לפום צערה אגרה :

חסלת אבות פרקים ה׳ :

א בנ״א חסר ר׳

ב נ׳׳א ובושת

ג נ׳׳א שיבנה בית המקדש במהרה.   ובקנת הספרים חסר כל המאמר
יהי רצון כו׳

ד נ׳׳א והפיך ו׳׳ג והפוך

ה הכי גרסינן.   ע׳ פרושי בלשון אנגלית

ו נ׳׳א תזוז

הוא (נ"א שמואל הקטן) היה אומר בן חמש שנים למקרא
בן עשר שנים למשנה בן שלש עשרה למצות (נ"א למצוה)
בן חמש עשרה לתלמוד (נ"א לגמרא) בן שמנה עשרה לחפה
בן עשרים לרדוף בן שלשים לכח בן ארבעים לבינה בן
חמשים לעצה בן ששים לזקנה בן שבעים לשיבה בן שמונים
לגבורה בן תשעים לשוח (נ"א לשוחה) בן מאה כאלו מת ועבר
ובטל מן העולם :

המאמר הזה אע"פ שנכלל במסכת אבות ונמצא או קודם למאמר בן בג
בג או כאן נרוב הספרים איננו באמת מן המסנה. ובענין זה אמר אברבנאל
כפי מה שנמצא במשניות הישנות הספרדיות במאמרים האלה נישלמה (מסכתא)
ר"ל מאמר בן בג בג ומאמר בן הא הא לפום צערא אגרא אבל במשניות אשר
אתנו פה היום נמצא עוד מאמר בן חמש למקרא וכו' ע"כ. ואח"כ אמר הסכס
הזה ספרק ו' אינו הוא ממסכת אבות אבל מפני שנתפשט המנהג לקוראו
וגם לשלימות המלאכה התעסקתי ג"כ בפירושו. וגם אני הנעיר אעשה כמהו

פרק ששי

הוא פרק קנין התורה

כל ישראל וכו׳

א

שנו חכמים בלשון המשנה ברוך שבחר בהם ובמשנתם :
רבי מאיר אומר כל העוסק בתורה לשמה זוכה לדברים
הרבה ולא עוד אלא שכל העולם כלו כדי הוא לו נקרא
רע אהוב אוהב את המקום אוהב את הבריות משמח את
המקום משמח את הבריות ומלבשתו ענוה ויראה ומכשרתו
להיות צדיק חסיד ישר ונאמן ומרחקתו מן החטא ומקרבתו
לידי זכות ונהנין ממנו עצה ותושיה בינה וגבורה שנאמר לי
עצה ותושיה אני בינה לי גבורה ונותנת לו מלכות וממשלה
וחקור דין ומגלין לו^א רזי תורה ונעשה כמעין שאינו פוסק^ב
וכנהר שמתגבר והולך^ד והוה צנוע וארך^ד רוח ומוחל על
עלבונו ומגדלתו ומרוממתו על כל המעשים^ה :

<hr>

א נ״א ומגלין לו מן השמים

ב נ״א כמעין המתגבר (ע׳ פ׳ג מ״י) שאינו פוסק את מימיו

ג נ״א המתגבר בלי מלת והולך

ד נ״א ושפל. [וי״ג ויהא תחת והוה]

ה נ״א המעשים כולם

(44)

ב

אמר רבי יהושע בן לוי בכל יום ויום בת קול יוצאת מהר
חורב ומכרזת ואומרת אוי להם לבריות מעלבונה של תורה
שכל מי שאינו עוסק בתורה נקרא נזוף שנאמר נזם זהב
באף[א] חזיר אשה יפה וסרת טעם : ואומר והלחת מעשה
אלהים המה והמכתב מכתב אלהים הוא חרות על הלחת אל
תקרא חָרות אלא חֵרות שאין לך בן חורין אלא מי שעוסק
בתלמוד תורה וכל מי שעוסק בתלמוד תורה הרי זה מתעלה
שנאמר וממתנה נחליאל ומנחליאל במות ב :

ג

הלומד מחברו פרק אחד או הלכה אחת או פסוק אחד
או דבור אחד אפילו אות אחת[י] צריך לנהג בו כבוד שכן
מצינו בדוד מלך ישראל שלא למד מאחיתפל אלא שני
דברים בלבד קראו[ד] רבו אלופו ומידעו שנאמר ואתה אנוש
כערכי אלופי ומידעי : והלא דברים קל וחמר ומה דוד מלך
ישראל שלא למד מאחיתפל אלא שני דברים בלבד קראו[ד]
רבו אלופו ומידעו[ה] הלומד מחברו פרק אחד או הלכה אחת
או פסוק אחד או דבור אחד או אפילו אות אחת על אחת

א אֻמר מר נזוף הוא נוטריקון של נזם ואף

ב כ״א ואם הגים דעתו הקב״ה משפילו שנ׳ ומבמות הגיא

ג בס״א לא נמצא כאן או פסוק אחד או דבור אחד (או) אפילו אות אחת

ד כ״א עשאו

ה בס״א חסר והלא דברים ק״ו כו׳ עד מלת ומידעו

כמה וכמה שצריך לנהג בו כבוד ואין כבוד אלא תורה[א]
שנאמר כבוד חכמים ינחלו ותמימים ינחלו טוב : ואין טוב
אלא תורה שנאמר כי לקח טוב נתתי לכם תורתי אל
תעזבו :

ד

כך היא דרכה של תורה פת במלח תאכל ומים במשורה
תשתה ועל הארץ תישן וחיי צער תחיה ובתורה אתה[ב] עמל
אם אתה עשה כן אשריך וטוב לך אשריך בעולם הזה וטוב
לך לעולם הבא :

ה

אל תבקש גדלה לעצמך ואל תחמוד כבוד יותר מלמודך
עשה[ג] ואל תתאוה לשלחנם של מלכים ששלחנך גדול
משלחנם וכתרך גדול מכתרם ונאמן הוא בעל מלאכתך
שישלם לך שכר פעלתך

ו

גדולה תורה יותר מן הכהנה ומן המלכות :   שהמלכות
נקנית בשלשים מעלות והכהנה בעשרים וארבע והתורה

א כ"א אלא לחכמים ואולי זה הנכון. ובכ"י Add. 667 נמצא אלא חכמה
ב כ"א תהא
ג ס"י ואל תחמוד כבוד יותר מלמודך (וחסר' מלת עשה) ופי' בספר ד"ס
למהר"ל מפראג ואל תחמוד שום כבוד יותר כי בלמוד שלך יש לך כבוד די
שהוא עקר הכבוד כמו שאמר למעלה כבוד חכמים ינחלו.   ובכ"י Add. 667
חסרו ג' המלות יותר מלמודך עשה

נקנית בארבעים ושמונה דברים* : ואלו הן בתלמוד בשמיעת
האזן בעריכת שפתים בבינת הלב באימה ביראה בענוה
בשמחה בטהרה בשמוש חכמים בדקדוק חברים בפלפול
התלמידים בישוב במקרא במשנה במעוט סחורה במעוט דרך
ארץ במעוט תענוג במעוט שנה במעוט שיחה במעוט שחוק
בארך אפים בלב טוב באמונת חכמים בקבלת היסורין המכיר
את מקומו והשמח בחלקו והעושה סיג לדבריו ואינו מחזיק
טובה לעצמו אהוב אוהב את המקום אוהב את הבריות
אוהב את הצדקות אוהב את המישרים אוהב את התוכחות
ומתרחק מן הכבוד ולא מגיס לבו בתלמודו ואינו שמח
בהוראה נושא בעול עם חברו ומכריעו לכף זכות ומעמידו על
האמת ומעמידו על השלום ומתישב לבו בתלמודו שואל
ומשיב שומע ומוסיף הלומד על מנת ללמד והלומד על מנת
לעשות המחכים את רבו והמכון את שמעתו והאומר דבר
בשם אומרו הא למדת כל האומר דבר בשם אומרו מביא
גאלה לעולם שנאמר ותאמר אסתר למלך בשם מרדכי :

ז

גדולה תורה שהיא נותנת חיים לעושיה בעולם הזה

א יש סלופיס שונים בגרסת אלו מ"ח הדברים ובסדורן ויש ספריס שנמנ' בהס
הגרסאות בכונת הלב בשכלות הלב.   (וסהר' מלת בטהרה).   בדבוק חברים.
בישיבה. בדרך ארץ. אהוב אוהב משמח את המקום משמח את הבריות.
ואינו רודף אחר הכבוד. ולא מגיס לבו בהוראה. ומתישב בתלמודו. שואל
כענין ומשיב כהלכה. והלומד ע״מ לעסוק. המחכם (בענין הדגום). והמבין
את שמועתו. הא למדת שכל האומר דבר שלא שמע מפי רבו ע״ש רבו גורם
לשכינה שתסתלק מישראל והאומר כו'

ובעולם הבא שנאמר כי חיים הם למצאיהם ולכל בשרו
מרפא : ואומר רפאות תהי לשרך ושקוי לעצמותיך : ואומר
עץ חיים היא למחזיקים בה ותמכיה מאשר :   ואומר כי
לוית חן הם לראשך וענקים לגרגרתיך : ואומר תתן לראשך
לוית חן עטרת תפארת תמגנך : ואומר כי בי ירבו ימיך
ויוסיפו לך שנות חיים : ואומר ארך ימים בימינה בשמאולה
עשר וכבוד :   ואומר כי ארך ימים ושנות חיים ושלום יוסיפו
לך :

ח

רבי שמעון בן יהודה[א] משום רבי שמעון בן יוחאי אומר
הנוי והכח והעושר והכבוד והחכמה הזקנה והשיבה והבנים
נאה לצדיקים ונאה לעולם שנאמר עטרת תפארת שיבה
בדרך צדקה תמצא :   ואומר תפארת בחורים כחם והדר
זקנים שיבה :   ואומר עטרת זקנים בני בנים ותפארת בנים
אבותם :   ואומר וחפרה הלבנה ובושה החמה כי מלך יי'
צבאות בהר ציון ובירושלים ונגד זקניו כבוד :

ט

רבי שמעון בן מנסיא אומר אלו שבע[ב] מדות שמנו חכמים

<hr>

א נ"א בן מנסיא
ב קסיא סכנר הוזכרו ס' ולפיכך ים מוסקין ה' מהן

לצדיקים כלם נתקימו ברבי ובבניו : אמר רבי יוסי[א] בן קסמא
פעם אחת הייתי מהלך בדרך ופגע בי אדם אחד[ב] ונתן לי
שלום והחזרתי לו שלום אמר לי רבי מאיזה מקום אתה
אמרתי לו מעיר גדולה של חכמים ושל סופרים[ג] אני אמר לי
רבי רצונך שתדור עמנו במקומנו ואני אתן לך אלף אלפים
דינרי זהב[ד] ואבנים טובות ומרגליות אמרתי לו אם אתה
נותן לי כל כסף וזהב ואבנים טובות ומרגליות שבעולם איני
דר אלא במקום תורה וכן כתוב בספר תהלים על ידי דוד
מלך ישראל טוב לי תורת פיך מאלפי זהב וכסף : ולא
עוד שבשעת פטירתו של אדם אין מלוין לו לאדם לא כסף
ולא זהב ולא אבנים טובות ומרגליות אלא תורה ומעשים
טובים בלבד שנאמר בהתהלכך תנחה אתך בשכבך תשמור
עליך והקיצות היא תשיחך :　　בהתהלכך תנחה אתך בעולם
הזה בשכבך תשמור עליך בקבר והקיצות היא תשיחך לעולם
הבא : ואומר לי הכסף ולי הזהב נאם יי' צבאות :

א בנ״א נמצא תניא א״ר יוסי ולא הובא' ברייתא זו קודם לנאמר חמשה
קנינים כו' כדלעיל אלא לאחריו. ואמר החכם ר' ינסק יעבץ בפרושו חסדי אבות
שהוא ראה נסתאות חלוקות מהן מביאות ענין הקנינים שקנה הקב״ה ובלתי
מביאות ענין ר' יוסי בן קסמא ומהן עושות להפך ומהן מביאות שתיהן ומהן
מביאות המאמר כל מה שברא הקב״ה בעולמו כו' בסוף ענין ר' יוסי בן קסמא
ומהן מביאות בסוף הפרק מה שאמר ר' חנניא בן עקשיא ומהן אינן מביאות
רק פסוק ה' חפץ כו'

ב כ״א זקן אחד

ג בנ״א חסר ושל סופרים

ד ס״א ואני אתן לך כמה כסף וכמה זהב א״ל אם אתה נותן לי כל כסף
וכל זהב שבעולם איני דר אלא במקום תורה לפי שבשעת פטירתו כו'. וא״כ
הובא' ג' הפסוקים טוב לי כו' לי הכסף כו'

'

חמשה[א] קנינים קנה הקדוש ברוך הוא בעולמו ואלו הן
תורה קנין אחד שמים קנין אחד וארץ קנין אחד אברהם קנין אחד
ישראל קנין אחד בית המקדש קנין אחד : תורה מנין
דכתיב יי' קנני ראשית דרכו קדם מפעליו מאז : שמים
וארץ מנין דכתיב כה אמר יי' השמים כסאי והארץ הדם
רגלי אי זה בית אשר תבנו לי ואי זה מקום מנוחתי : ואומר
מה רבו מעשיך יי' כלם בחכמה עשית מלאה הארץ קנינך :
אברהם מנין דכתיב ויברכהו ויאמר ברוך אברם לאל עליון

א ג"ל ארבעה כדאיתא בכ"י הסמון Add. 667 ולזה הסכימה גרסת
התלמוד (פסחים דף פ"ז ע"ב) כך ישראל שהם בני בחוני בני אברהם
יצחק ויעקב ויעקב מארבעה קנינים שקניתי בעולמי תורה קנין אחד
דכתיב יי' קנני ראשית דרכו שמים וארץ קנין אחד דכתיב קונה שמים וארץ
בית המקדש קנין אחד דכתיב הר זה קנתה ימינו ישראל קנין אחד דכתיב עם
זו קנית. ובמכילתא ג'כ בפ' בשלח בפסוק עד יעבור עמך כו' נזכרו ד' קנינים
האלו. אבל בספרי בפ' האזינו בפסוק הלה' תגמלו זאת לא מנה רק ג' שנקראו
קנין למקום והם תורה וישראל ובית המקדש. ובענין זה כתב בעל הפרוש
המיוחס לרשב"ס ואני אומר כשם שהספרי והמכלתא חלוקים שזה אומר ג' וזה
אומר ד' כך אפשר שהגדה שלישית חולקת לומר חמשה. ואמר ג'כ חמשה
קנינים במחזורים וכן מצאתי בתנא דבי אליהו שהוא מחמש' קנינים
שקנה הקב"ה וראיתי במדרש של ר' שמעון (?) קרא בספר משלי שמוציא קנינו של
אברהם מדכתיב אלה תולדות השמים והארץ בהבראם אל תקרי בהבראם
אלא באברהם זהו שאמר הכתוב ברוך אברם וג' וכן פתרון המקרא ברוך
אברם לאל עליון הקונה אותו כדרך שקנה שמים וארץ עכ"ל. אבל ע"ד הפשט
אין ראיה מהמקרא זה רק לקנין שמים וארץ ואברם איננו מן הקנינים ובחופן
זה די להביא ד' הפסוקים הנז' במסכת פסחים

קונה שמים וארץ : ישראל מנין דכתיב עד יעבר עמך יי' עד
יעבר עם זו קנית : ואומר לקדושים אשר בארץ המה ואדירי
כל חפצי בם : בית המקדש מנין דכתיב מכון לשבתך פעלת
יי' מקדש אדני כוננו ידיך : ואומר ויביאם אל גבול קדשו
הר זה קנתה ימינו :

י"א

כל מה שברא× הקדוש ברוך הוא בעולמו לא בראו אלא
לכבודו שנאמר כל הנקרא בשמי ולכבודי בראתיו יצרתיו
אף עשיתיו : ואומר יי' ימלך לעולם ועד : רבי חנניא בן
עקשיא אומר רצה הקדוש ברוך הוא לזכות את ישראל
לפיכך הרבה להם תורה ומצוות שנאמר יי' חפץ למען צדקו
יגדיל תורה ויאדיר :

× נ"א וכולם לא בראם הקב"ה אלא לכבודו

סליק פרקא
דרבי מאיר

דברי אבות העולם

SAYINGS

OF

THE JEWISH FATHERS.

APPENDIX.

AN APPENDIX

TO

SAYINGS

OF

THE JEWISH FATHERS

CONTAINING

A CATALOGUE OF MANUSCRIPTS
AND NOTES ON THE TEXT OF ABOTH.

EDITED FOR THE SYNDICS OF THE CAMBRIDGE UNIVERSITY PRESS

BY

CHARLES TAYLOR D.D.

MASTER OF ST JOHN'S COLLEGE CAMBRIDGE.

REPRINT BY PERMISSION OF CAMBRIDGE UNIVERSITY PRESS

FIRST PUBLISHED 1900

PREFATORY NOTE.

Shortly after the first publication of *Sayings of the Jewish Fathers* (1877) this APPENDIX was announced as in preparation under the title, *A Catalogue of Manuscripts of the Text of Aboth and of Commentaries upon it with especial reference to Disputed Readings.* It contains an account of a number of such manuscripts; *Notes on the Text* replacing the "Critical Notes" which preceded the Translation in the First Edition of the *Sayings*; and an *Index* to the Second Edition (1897) made by Mr J. H. A. Hart, B.A., Naden Divinity Student and Scholar of St John's College.

The famous MS. described in No. 20 has now been edited for the Mekizé Nirdamim under the name "Machsor Vitry" claimed for it by S. D. Luzzatto, who even conjectured that the *perush* on Aboth in it is by R. Simchah of Vitri-le-Français. It is in reality a recension of the commentary of R. Jacob Shimshoni (רי״ש) or ben Shimshon, whose name is given acrostically in Oxford and Cambridge manuscripts (*App.* pp. 23, 93). "This name was first pointed out, no doubt from the acrostic, by Isaac Metz, in the notice of the Oppenheim MS. in his Catalogue of that collection (קהלת דוד, or *Collectio Davidis*, Hamburgi, 1826, 8vo.) p. 284, No. 627" (Sch.-Sz.).

A manuscript purchased for the Bodleian Library in 1875 is shewn to be a copy of R. Israel of Toledo's Arabic commentary on the Six Peraqim (No. 90). His descendant

R. Isaac's *perush* (Nos. 1, 115) having been collated for the First Edition of the *Sayings*, one of the passages of the commentary in No. 90 marked by a previous owner was identified as R. Israel's by means of R. Isaac's *perush*, from which it soon appeared that the said Arabic commentary was the "great and wide sea" from which R. Isaac had drawn.

The codex described in No. 170 was found to contain a mixed Rashi-Rambam commentary on Aboth with additional notes on a passage of Pereq III. quoted in the name of R. Meshullam ben Qalonymos, and not, as had been thought, a whole commentary by R. Meshullam.

Ample materials for a continuation of the *Catalogue* have been collected, but it seemed best to publish it as it has stood now for some years without further delay.

C. TAYLOR.

5th March 1900.

MANUSCRIPTS OF ABOTH.

The Manuscripts are indexed on pages 1, 25, 57, 105.
The *Index of the Mishnah* is on pages 64—65.

פרקי אבות

BRITISH MUSEUM MANUSCRIPTS

Nos. **1—22, 160—168***.

I. Commentaries on Aboth with or without the text

Name	Number
Rashi	19
Jacob ben Shimshon . . , .	4, 5, 14, 19—22
Maimonides (Hebrew)	3, 5, 6, 14, 16
Rabbenu Jonah	2
Isaac Israeli	1
Isaac ha-Cohen ben Chayim . . .	15
Eliezer Nachman Foa	18

II. The text alone

Nos. 7—13, 17.

* Nos. 160—168 are indexed on p. 105.

MANUSCRIPTS

OF THE TEXT OF ABOTH, AND OF
COMMENTARIES ON ABOTH.

No. 1.

BRITISH MUSEUM, Oriental 1003.

THIS is a very good copy of the valuable commentary on Aboth, six Peraqim, by

יצחק בר׳ שלמה בר׳ יצחק בר׳ שלמה בר׳ ישראל הסופר בן ישראל (תנצב״ה).

The commentary is founded upon that of the writer's ancestor R. ISRAEL, to whom he frequently alludes. He tells us that he wrote it at an early age, for his own improvement, כי כוונתי להועיל לעצמי; and that it was completed in the 28th *year of his age,* in 5128 A.M. = 1368 A.D., the date being given on the last page, thus :

שנת ח״י עלי מאה וחמש אלפים ליצירה.

He describes it as a *spicilegium* from the Arabic commentary of R. ISRAEL :

ולקטתיו מהים הגדול ורחב ידים פי׳ החכם הפילוסוף האלהי התורני הר׳ ישראל ז״ל אשר הרחיב בפי׳ מסכתא זו בלשון ערב כו׳.

This MS. is quoted as B in the *Critical Notes.* For further particulars see the notes on the Cambridge MS., "ST JOHN'S COLLEGE, K. 7."

No. 2.

BRITISH MUSEUM, Harley 269.

This contains *inter alia* a commentary on the five Peraqim of Aboth, fol. 137 a—182 b, by R. Jonah (of Gerona), which was transcribed in the year הריא ליצירה = 1451 A.D. See fol. 182 b.

He justifies the omission of וּבתפלה in II. 17 * as follows (154 a):

ר' שמעון אומ' הוי זהיר בק"ש והזהיר בק"ש יותר מן התפלה מפני שזמן תפלה
גדול ורחב הוא עד ד' שעות וזמן ק"ש קצר ומכוון עד הנץ החמה כותיקין וזהו
לשון הוי זהיר כי צריך זהירות גדולה ·

This note is cited by Isaac b. Shelomoh, who makes much use of
R. Jonah's commentary, and expressly states, at the beginning of QINYAN
THORAH, that it was on the FIVE PERAQIM only.

No. 3.

BRITISH MUSEUM, Harley 5686.

This contains *inter alia* the five Peraqim, pointed, with the commentary of Maimonides, followed by Pereq R. Meir, with a brief commentary,
fol. 359 a—377 b. The commentary is very neatly written in small characters. It was copied in the year 1464 A.D. by Leon b. Jehoshu'a de' Rossi of
Cesena, for R. Joab 'Immanuel of Reggio†, according to the statement at
the end of Pereq R. Meir:

תם ונשלם שבח לאלהי עולם כי הוא הנסתר ונעלם מידי ליאון בר' יהושע
ישר"ו מן האדמים איש ציסינה פה בארייו יום ו' ט"ו נובימ' רכ"ד לכמ"ר יואב
עמ' מארייו ישר"ו לברכה יהיה אמן ·

The MS. has some interesting historical notes, as that on the burning of
twenty-four cartloads of Hebrew books in France (cf. Graetz, *Geschichte
der Juden*, Vol. VII. Note 5), in year 1244 A.D. (fol. 33 b):

ובשנת חמשת אלפים ור' שנים לבריאת עולם... גרמו עונותינו ונשרפו כ"ד
קרונות מלאים ספרי תלמוד והלכות ואגדות בצרפת ...

No. 4.

BRITISH MUSEUM, Additional 11639.

A small MS., neatly written, and finely illuminated, containing *inter
alia* Aboth, with a brief commentary, to some extent resembling that
in No. 20. The date of the MS. as inferred from its calendar, which commences with the cycle רס"ו (fol. 563 b‡, 570 a), is about

$$265 \times 19 = 5035 \text{ A.M.} = 1275 \text{ A.D.}$$

---

* No. 20 has ותפילה in the text, but remarks upon it in the commentary, אין אנו גורסין
במשנה.

† See the Cambridge University *Catalogue of Hebrew MSS.*, by Dr S. M. Schiller-
Szinessy, Vol. I. pp. 75, 88, 93.

‡ There is a mistake in the pagination of this MS., fol. 560 following immediately upon
529.

On fol. 140 b is written in gold letters:

בנימן סופר קורא וקרא חזק ואמץ אל תערץ ואל תירא אמן סלה.

and on 304 b:

בנימן הסופר אומרה.

Fol. 194 a—200 a contain the five Peraqim, without points, in double columns, with the commentary in the margin. Pereq V ends thus:

.. .אביך שבשמים. בן בג בג או' הפוך בה והפיך בה דכולא בה ומינה כו'
הימינה. בן הא הא כו'. יהי רצון כו'.

סליק פרקא וחסלת מסכתא.

Then come the AGES, and ר' מאיר כו', ending on fol. 201 b with סליק,
the saying of בן בג בג (down to תזוז only) being *repeated*, and followed
by ר' חנינא בן עקש' כו', to which is appended the note, אחר כל פרק יאמר זה.

This MS. therefore supports the statement of No. 20 that ABOTH ends
at אביך שבשמים, by omitting the saying עז פנים כו', as above, and by
repeating בן בג בג כו', as if it were an *additamentum*, rather than an
integral part of the Masseketh.

The notes on the five Peraqim break off, for want of space, on the
pages:

194 b, 195 b, 197 b, 199 b, 201 b,

and are continued on fol. 669 a—672 b. Then follow notes on the AGES,
and on R. Meir &c., ending on fol. 674 b.

At fol. 667 a commences a סדר של חכמים, corresponding to that in
No. 20, Vol. II. 101 b.

Readings:

The text has the words ודמוסיף יוסיף, in I. 14: omits *the three clauses*
זו מחלוקת שמאי, in III. 21—3: reads של מהומה באה (v. 11): חבה יתרה כו'
והילל (v. 24): and agrees with 𝔄 in v. 28, having the introverted order, and
omitting the words אנשי דמים כו'.

No. 5.

BRITISH MUSEUM, Additional 16577.

A fine P. B., Italian rite, illuminated, containing Aboth, pointed, with
the commentary of Rambam (fol. 91 a—104 b), followed by Pereq R. Meir,
which is annotated,

כפי מה שפירש רבינו שלמה ז"ל.

Readings :

לפרוזדוד‏ +‏ .‏‏‏ 23, ‏‏‏ וכתר שם טוב על גביהן*‏ .‏ ‏‏ IV. 19,

סמא‡ דכולא בה ‏ v. 31,‏ .

Fol. 286 a contains verses with the acrostic of יצחק. The last page of the MS. contains illuminations, in the midst of which is written in gold letters :

לה׳ הארץ
ומלאה
שלי אברהם
יזײא בכ״ר
יעקב ז״ל

No. 6.

BRITISH MUSEUM, Additional 17057.

An incomplete text of Aboth, unpointed (except the first line), with Rambam's commentary, breaking off at Pereq IV. 5.

No. 7.

BRITISH MUSEUM, Additional 17058.

P. B., with Aboth, six Peraqim, pointed, fol. 236 a—241 b. Pereq VI. begins, as in some other copies, without the words שנו חכמים כו׳.

No. 8.

BRITISH MUSEUM, Additional 18229.

P. B., with Aboth and Pereq R. Meir, pointed, fol. 97 a—104 a. The words שנו חכמים כו׳ are wanting, as in No. 7.

Before משה קבל is written :

אומ׳ אותן מפסח עד עצרת ר״ל עד שבועות·

and at the end of R. Meir :

ואחר שאמרו האבות אומ׳ קדיש דרבנן וזהו· יתגדל ויתקדש שמיה רבא כו׳.

* This is the reading of No. 20 (fol. 121 b).

† See No. 20, fol. 122 b : פרוזדוד בדלת. ואולם לכסא מיתרגמ׳ ופרוזודרא.

‡ This reading is common in Italian Machazors.

No. 9.

A small P. B., with Aboth, six Peraqim, pointed, fol. 132 b—159 b. The name יוסף is marked on fol. 249 b.

Notice the reading of III. 9 :

... בעדת אל בקרב אלהים ישפוט ומנין אפי׳ חמשה שנ׳ ואגודתו כו׳.

‘ The margin here adds ומנין אפי׳ שלשה שנ׳. Thus the number THREE, having been omitted in the first instance, is inserted *before the number* FIVE. Compare No. 12.

No. 10.

A small P. B., with an unpointed text of Aboth, fol. 180 b—198 a, remarkable for its omissions, in which respect it resembles the Paris MS., 636.

It is further remarkable as giving SIX Peraqim, followed by Pereq R. MEIR, or altogether **Seven Peraqim.**

Readings :

II. 4 is omitted *in loc.*, and placed between IV. 19, 20.

III. 8 is followed by 13 (ור׳ חנינה בן זומא* כו׳), and 13 by 16 ; 9—12, 14, 15 being omitted. 17, תורה תשובה ומעשים טובים. 25, על מי. 26 ends, אם אין קמח אין תורה יש תורה ויש קמח.

IV. 8 is attributed to ר׳ יוסי. 9 is omitted. 14 ends at כנגדך, which is inserted after בטילים הרבה. 13 (with יוחנן for חנניה) *follows.* 23, לפרוזדוד. 25, בשעת אבלו, for בשעה שמתו כו׳. 28 (down to מגתו) follows, and then 30—32 ; 26, 27, 29 being omitted.

v. 9 is omitted. 23, 24 (מחלוקת שמאי והלל) come *before* 21, 22. 30, יהודה בן טבאי כו׳ שבשמים.

The Pereq ends with שמואל הקטן כו׳, and בן חמש כו׳ ; 30—32 not being included.

---

* This text has other variations in names besides those mentioned above.

Then follows :

פרק ששי

בן בג בג אומ׳ הפוך והפך בה דכולה בה סיב ובלה בה ומנה לא תזוע׃ בן
הא הא או׳ לפום צערא אגרא׃ תניא ר׳ נתן אומר הלמד תורה מן הקטנים כו׳.

The Pereq continues as in "PARIS, 636." It ends on fol. 194 b, and is
followed by

,פרק ר׳ מאיר

which concludes on fol. 198 a with the words :

סליקו להו מסכת אבות.

No. 11.

BRITISH MUSEUM, Additional 18691.

P. B., with pointed text of Aboth, and Pereq Rabbi Meir as far
as אלא תורה ומעשים טובים בלבד שנ׳ (VI. 9), fol. 133 a—154 b.

No. 12.

BRITISH MUSEUM, Additional 19666.

P. B., with pointed text of Aboth, six Peraqim, fol. 87 b—99 a, preceded
by the words :

פרקי אבות שקורין מפסח לשבועות.

The letters of אלעזר are marked on fol. 275 b.

Readings :

III. 9, ,בעדת אל ומניין אפילו שלשה שנ׳ בקרב ... חמשה שנ׳ ואגודתו כ׳ ...
the number THREE coming before FIVE. 17 is read as in 𝔄, except תורה
ומעשים טובים.

IV. 19, על גביהם, without עולה.

v. 31, בה (?) סמא דכולא בה ובה תחזה וסיב וכולה. Compare *Crit. Note*
on the origin of the reading ובלה בה.

No. 13.

BRITISH MUSEUM, Additional 19667.

A very small P. B., described as " Preces secundum ritum Hispanicum."

The five Peraqim, pointed, are written in the upper and lower margins of fol. 228 a—284 b, and upon fol. 285, which concludes the MS.

Reading, in v. 24, מחלוקת בית שמאי ובית הלל.

Ending of ABOTH :

After שבשמים אביך (fol. 283 a), come כו' בנפול אויבך, and בן חמש כו', followed by :

תניא ר' יהודה הנשיא אומ' עז פנים לגיהנם כו',

the saying עז פנים כו' being introduced only as *baraitha;* and after this, ר' חנינא בן עקשיא כו', and בן בג בג כו', *followed by* בן הא הא כו'.

No. 14.

BRITISH MUSEUM, Additional 19944—5.

A very fine P. B., Italian rite, with illuminations; written in Florence by יצחק סופר בן עובדיה, and dated* 5201 A.M. = 1441 A.D.

Vol. I. 117 b—136 b contains Aboth, pointed, with the commentaries of Maimonides, and " Rashi," in double columns. Pereq R. Meir follows, with the commentary of " Rashi;" for although this part of the commentary is said in Dukes' catalogue to be unnamed, the רש"י on fol. 136 b must be intended to be carried on.

The commentary here attributed to RASHI† agrees with that of the " Machazor Vitry." Its sixth Pereq is often used to supplement the commentary of Maimonides, which, according to an express statement of Isaac bar Shelomoh, was on the FIVE Peraqim only.

---

* See Vol. II. 169 b.

† Bar S. quotes it in the name of RASHBAM, and quotes a different commentary in the name of RASHI.

No. 15.

BRITISH MUSEUM, Additional 26960.

Contains *inter alia* a commentary, fol. 64 a—188 b, on the six Peraqim
by

יצחק הכהן בן חיים נ״ע (בן אברהם בן יצחק בן יוסף הכהן נ״ע).

The commentary is dáted at the end, עֶזְרָא (= 1518 A.D.).

No. 16.

BRITISH MUSEUM, Additional 27070.

P. B., containing Aboth, pointed, with the commentary of Rambam,
fol. 158 b—176 b, followed by Pereq R. Meir, without a commentary.

At the end of Pereq V is written :

חסלו פירוש ומסכת אבות להר״ם ב״מז״ל.

No. 17.

BRITISH MUSEUM, Additional 27072.

P. B., written in the year 1482 A.D. (fol. 309 b), by Abraham Farissol
b. Mordekai Farissol, of Avignon.

It contains a pointed text of Aboth, fol. 119 a—134 b, followed by Pereq
R. Meir.

At the end of Pereq V is written :

נשלמו פרקי אבות.

No. 18.

BRITISH MUSEUM, Additional 27115.

Aboth, six Peraqim, with the commentary of

אליעזר נחמן פואה

transcribed by one שלמה (fol. 114 b).

No. 19.

This MS., which is described by Luzzatto in *Kerem Chemed*, Vol. IV. p. 201, contains two commentaries on Aboth.

I. The first, which is ascribed to

רבינו ישעיהו ז״ל,

(and in a later hand to Rashi), agrees with that which Isaac bar Shelomoh quotes in the name of RASHI, and which is printed as his.

Readings:

I. 3 (fol. 3 b, line 2), ושמעתי שצדוק ובייתוס כו', without the reference to the 'Aruk which is found in some copies of this commentary.

IV. 8 (fol. 7 a, line 22), ה״ג אין מספיקין בידו ללמוד וללמד, a reading cited by Isaac bar Shelomoh as peculiar to " Rashi."

This commentary properly consists of five Chapters only, according to the statement of bar S.; but the MS. has additions which cause some confusion in the ending. Thus, after Aboth (fol. 11 b), comes:

פרק ר' מאיר. בן חמש כו'.

followed, at the end of the AGES (fol. 12 a), by

סליק מסכת אבות. וזהו פרק ר' מאיר. זוכה לדברים הרבה כו'.

At the commencement of fol. 13 b there is this note on the ה' קנינים:

נראה בעיניי שהברייתא לא נכתבה כתיקנה שהרי במסכת פסחים בפרק האשה
לא שנינו אלא שלשה...

after which comes a second interpretation of the AGES (fol. 13 b, line 12) followed, at the end of 14 a, by

נשלמו פירוש ממסכת אבות ופירוש מפרק ר' מאיר על ידי שלמה בר' משה.

II. On the same page is written:

פירוש ממסכת אבות ממ״ה רבינו שלמה ז״ל,

as the title of the second commentary, which accordingly follows, after five blank pages, on fol. 17 a—47 b, and is a recension of that in No. 20, the commencement of which is printed, *with collations from this MS.*, in *Kerem Chemed*, loc. cit.

Luzzatto concludes with the remark (p. 204) that the commentary on Aboth by " Qimchi" which de-Rossi claims to have seen in a printed Turin Siddur is a "a dream"; the Siddur containing only the well known commentary which is printed under the name of RASHI. On p. 201 he expresses the opinion that neither of the two commentaries in this MS. was the work of RASHI.

No. 20.

Two fine folio volumes, described as "the Machazor of R. Simchah
of Vitry, originally compiled about 1100 A.D." But they are in reality a
compilation of a century later (1210 A.D.), by Rabbi

יצחק בר' דורבלו,

who made use of R. Simchah's MACHAZOR VITRY *inter alia*. He also expressly cites the Machazor of R. Jacob ben Shimshon (Vol. I. 42 a, col. 1),
the author of the commentary on Aboth in Vol. II. This MS. is one of the
Almanzi collection.

On the celebrated Bodleian MS. which likewise goes by the name of
Machazor Vitry see below, under "BODLEIAN LIBRARY, 1100."

The genuine Machazor Vitry was described by Isaac de Lates in the
fourteenth century as,

המחזור הקטן הנקרא דיויטרי
The SMALL *Machazor called de Vitry;*

which points to a smaller compilation than No. 20. The above testimony of
de Lates — taken from a Bodleian MS. (No. 1298 in Neubauer's *Catalogue*,
fol. 10 β) of a work by that author, dated 5132 A.M. (= 1372 A.D.), and which
has also been printed in the Hebrew part (*Ozar Tob*) of Berliner and
Hoffmann's *Magazin für die Wissenschaft des Judenthums* for 1877
(see p. 073, line 29)—is cited in the *Histoire Littéraire de la France*,
Vol. XXVII. p. 474, where it is added in a note, that the reference may
perhaps be to "la petite rédaction que l'on trouve dans les bibliothèques de
Parme et de Rome (mal reconnue par de Rossi et Assémani) et dans la
bibliothèque Günzburg"; but on general grounds, and in accordance with
the statement of de Lates, the claim to priority must be decided in favour
of the smaller compilation as against the larger. The latter, as I am informed, consists mainly of the דינים.

In the שאלות ותשובות of ר' יוסף קלון (ed. Venice, רע"ט = 1519 A.D.), who
lived in the middle of the fifteenth century, the Machazor Vitry is referred
to in section קע"ו (by misprint קע"א), where it is said:

והנה דבר ידוע הוא כי מחזור ויטרי נתיסד על פי רבינו שלמה,

the reference in the context being to the דינים only. A reference to the
above work of R. Joseph Qolon is given in the שפתי ישנים of ר' שבתי בס
of Prag (§ 140) where the following account is given of the Machazor:

מחזור ויטרי ר' שמחה מעיר ויטר"י, תלמיד רש"י, והוא ממהלך הכוכבים
ומזלות, עיין (בשו"ת) מהרי"ק שורש קע"ו.

I am informed by Dr Neubauer that in the Bodleian MS. No. 692, § 12, containing casuistic responsa, the "Machazor Vitriac" is quoted (fol. 175, resp. 80) on the subject of הגדת פסח, thus:

וטעם המביאי' ראיה להיתר משום דכתיב במחזור ויטריך כו'.

In the above mentioned No. 692, resp. 131, fol. 194 b there is also a section headed, הועתק מן מחזור ויטרי, and commencing:

אומ' רבי' יצחק בר' אברהם דאסור לקרות בבה"כ בתוך החומ"ש היכא דאיכא ס"ת בעיר.

Thus the מחזור ויטרי is quoted for דינים in a MS. copied about 1303—7 A.D.

For another reference to the Machazor Vitry compare Steinschneider's recently published Munich *Catalogue*, Cod. 240, § 5 (מערכת האלהות), fol. 43 b:

מצאתי במחזור ויטרי שהוסד לפי רש"י כו'.

In all this (and more which might be added *) there is no evidence to shew what the genuine "Machazor Vitry" contained, except as regards the דינים. It is quite possible, however, that the greater part of it may be found embedded in this No. 20, of which we shall now proceed to give some account.

The Compiler.

1. The MS., whilst in the possession of Giuseppe Almanzi of Padua, was examined by S. D. Luzzatto, and described by him (*Kerem Chemed*, Vol. III. p. 200) as

מחזור ויטרי לרבנו שמחה תלמידו של רש"י,

the work of the actual compiler being inadequately described in the words:

ויש בו כה וכה דברים נוספים מר' יצחק ברבי דורבלו.

He remarks that he is unable to identify this ISAAC בר' דורבלו, but records a suggestion which was made to him by Rapoport that he was

ר' יצחק מאורבייללו בעל ספר המנהל.

This however does not account for the בר' which precedes דורבלו, nor does the latter resemble the transliteration of d'Orbeil so closely as might have been expected; to say nothing of the circumstance that it is the custom of our R. Isaac to use the Hebrew מן, in preference to the French *de*, as a prefix of locality, *e.g.* in מדנפירא, מברינא, מוישרי, מפריש.

---

* For example, Dr Neubauer favours me with several references to the מחזור ויטרי in the so-called Zürich glosses to the סמ"ק. See MS. Opp. Addit., No. 879 in Neubauer's *Catalogue*, folios 41, 82, 135, 171.

As the name of דון אברבנלו occurs both with and without the ו, so the
name of * ר' דורבלו is written both with the termination ו, as in this MS.
(Vol. I. 158 b, 159 a, 161 b ; Vol. II. 38 a, 40 b, 53 b, &c.), and without it, as
on p. 8 of the חופש מטמונים of Berl Goldberg (Berlin, 1845), where (in
No. י"ב of the תשובות of רש"י) there occurs the passage :

מי אנכי חדל אישים וישפל להכנים ראש אצל הר גבותה ותלול המחלק שלל
לאנפיו בשורות ענף ועשית פרי ומה עלתה על לב רבינו הזקן ראש נדיבי פאתי
יעקב ר' דורכל (צ"ל דורבל) להזקיק צעיר לימים לענות על ריב אמר לי
לבי מאשר יקרתי בעיניו מאז חבבני ובא להתפנג בבנו וקטנו לתהות בקנקן
ריקן אולי לחכמה להשיב נכוחה ויקרא מרי עלי חכם בני ישמח לבי על הדברים
הכתובים אני כותב לפניהם מה דעתי נוטה·

The "R. Durbal" spoken of in this passage, which is referred by Grätz
(*Gesch. der Juden*, VI. 78), was a זקן when Rashi was young, and may have
been a great-grandfather, or more remote ancestor, of our יצחק בר' דורבלו,
who was a younger, perhaps much younger, contemporary of Rashi's grandsons. He is referred to by Zunz in his *Literaturgeschichte der Synagogalen Poesie*, p. 252, where it is said that " R. Salomo... stand mit
Durbel, &c. in brieflicher Verbindung." A later Durbel is doubtfully
referred to on p. 484 of the same work : " Daniel [oder Durbel ?] b. Jacob,
vermuthlich unfern den Jahren 1200—1240. '

I have seen a volume of Lent Sermons by one Petrus DORBELLUS ande-
gauensis, which was published in Paris in the year 1518 A.D. ; and there
was a Nicolas Dorbellus, a professor at Poitiers, who died in the year
1455 A.D. The name of the latter is indeed explained by *de Orbellis* in
Zedler's *Universal Lexicon*, Vol. xxv., Col. 1743 : "Orbellis (Nicolas von),
sonsten auch Dorbellus genannt, ein minorit von Angers," &c. ; but this
explanation may perhaps have been given conjecturally, since the name in
question was already of some antiquity, the elder דורבל, mentioned above
in connexion with Rashi, having been born if not in the *tenth* at any rate
early in the *eleventh* century.

It may be worth while to compare the diverse interpretations of the
second name of ר' שבתי דונולו בן אברהם, which Zunz explains as a
designation of locality : "Vermuthlich war er in *Nola* ansässig (*Gottesdienstl. Vorträge*, p. 362); whilst Grätz identifies it with Δόμνουλος
(*Gesch. der Juden*, v. 352). Cf. Steinschneider's Bodleian *Catalogue of
Hebrew Books*, No. 6864.

The compiler, whatever may have been his nationality, had at least
visited RUSSIA, as we gather from his statement (Vol. I. 158 b, col. 2) :

ואני נשאלתי ברוסייא כו'·

---

* We should perhaps read דון דורבלו in place of דון דייבלו, "Don Diavolo," which is
given as a reading of a manifestly corrupt signature in the *Hist. Littéraire de la France*,
Vol. XXVII. p. 665. For the form Abarbanelo see Schiller-Szinessy's *Catalogue*, Vol. I. 112.

It has even been suggested that he is to be identified with the ISAAC OF RUSSIA mentioned in Schiller-Szinessy's *Catalogue**, Vol. I. 54, 163, 164, &c.

He records a subsequent meeting with R. Isaac ha-Laban at PRAG (Vol. I. 159 a, col. 1) :

כשבאתי אצל הרב רב יצחק בר׳ יעקב הלבן בבהם בעיר פרגא נומיתי לו שכן שאלוני ברוסייא וכן השבתי כו׳.

The MS. is full of allusions to Rashi, who was no longer living. Cf. I. 138 a:

בימי רבינו שלמה שאלו דבר זה ...

Rashi's grandson רבינו תם, or יעקב בן מאיר, is frequently cited.

Still later generations are referred to. Cf. Vol. I. 158 b, col. 2 :

ואני יצחק בר׳ דורבלו ראיתי ברמרו† דאתרייא (sic) ביה מילתא בר׳ יוסף בנו של רבינו יעקב בן רבנא מאיר מבנו. ואחר שהתפללו מנחה בערב שבת בבית הכנסת ישב לו ר׳ שלמה אחי רבינו שהיה מתפלל. וא׳ לו רבינו יעקב אחיו לך להביא יוסף בני לבית הכנסת. שלח עמו החבר ר׳ יצחק בן רבינו שמואל ואחרים עמו. כיון שבא לבית הכנסת ירד הרב ר׳ שלמה לפני הארון וא׳ ברכו.

From this we gather that he was present at Rameru on the occasion of the death of a grandson of Jacob ben Meir, and it may be inferred with probability that he was himself a *younger* contemporary of the grandsons of Rashi.

In immediate sequence upon the above he speaks as an eyewitness of the practice in Bourgogne on such occasions :

תמהתי מה טעם איחרו להביאו עד אחר המנחה כי ראיתי במלכות ברנוויינא שנהגו כו׳.

Lower down in the same column are the words (already quoted) ואני נשאלתי ברוסייא כו׳.

The above passages in which the name of בר׳ דורבלו occurs are found in the latter half of הילכות אבל. The same section contains the passage referring to the Machazor Vitry (which we shall notice again lower down), as also the following two passages of interest, in all of which the name of our R. Isaac occurs.

---

* In Vol. II. p. 66 of the same *Catalogue* (MS. No. 92), which was not printed until the above had been for a long time in type, it is expressly stated that our Isaac בר׳ דורבלו was none other than this Isaac of Russia. It is added that this No. 20 doubtless contains large and important portions of the Machazor of ר׳ תם, a work which R. Meir of Rothenburg distinctly cites. Our R. Isaac is further identified as the editor of Rabbenu Tam's ספר הישר.

† Rameru (Ramerupt), in N. France, where ר׳ תם resided.

The former of the two passages refers to an accusation of sorcery brought against the Jews in Paris in consequence of their practice of throwing earth [with *herbs*, according to (ד) שע״ו. ס׳ יורה דעה. שלחן ערוך] behind them on the return from a funeral. It is found in Vol. I. 161 a and 161 b.

בפריש הלשינו פעם אחת משומדים אל המלך על כל ישר׳ שהיו משליבין עפר אחריהם בשעה שחוזרין מאחרי המת להטיל כשפים על הגוים להמיתם, קיבל לשון הרע, וקרא אל הרב ר׳ משה בר׳ יחיאל בן הרב ר׳ מתתיה הגדול מפריש וא׳ לו כו׳ ... הוספתי זה לספר בשבחו של מקום כו׳. יצחק בר׳ דורבלו :

The latter of the two passages (Vol. I. 162 a, col. 1) shews that our R. Isaac was present at Rameru on the occasion of the wedding of R. Jacob ben Meir's daughter.

ונמצא במדרש אין אומרי׳ החי אלא בבית האבל, אבל שמעתי רבינו יעקב בחתונת בתו ברמרו ואמר החי ושאלו ממנו למה אמרו, והשיב שהרבה טרח למצוא אותו מדרש ולא מצאו לא בתלמוד שלנו ולא באבל רבתי ולא במסכת שמחות, לפיכך אינו נמנע מלאומרו בכל עת תמיד. יצחק בר׳ דורבלו· ת׳ * :

The section הילכות אבל ends in the next column.

The name of בר׳ דורבלו occurs again in several passages of הילכות ראש השנה, which commences at Vol. II. 35 a (סימן שט״ו) and extends to fol. 45 a, col. 2. One such passage will be cited below in § 3, from Vol. II. 38 a, col. 2. Some pages later (II. 40 b, col. 2) is the section :

ואני או׳ דודאי מן הזמנים הוא ... וקא חשיב נמי ראש השנה. יצחק בר׳ דורבלו † :

At the end of תפילות ראש השנה (II. 53 a, col. 1, סימן ש״ג) comes a short quotation from רבינו ניסים, which is signed :

כ״ש באלמיינא אני יצחק בר׳ דורבלו· ת׳ :

and this signature is also found once again in the next column (סימן שנ״א).

Now to return to the above mentioned passage in which the MACHAZOR VITRY is expressly mentioned—in Vol. I. 159 a, col. 2, at the conclusion of a section signed יצחק בר׳ דורבלו, is a fresh section commencing :

ומיפירושי רבינו חננאל בר׳ חושיאל איש רומי העתקתי כו׳,

---

* The abbreviations ת׳ and תו׳ denote תוספת.

† This is followed immediately by a paragraph signed א׳ב׳ן׳. This denotes the celebrated Eliezer ben Nathan of Mainz, who is quoted as in correspondence with R. Jacob ben Meir in the ספר הישר [see for example, סימן תרט׳ו], of which our R. Isaac was the editor. See above, p. 15 note *.

and ending :

עד כאן הוספתי לפרש אני יצחק בר' דורבלו על פי אשר ראיתי מעשה, והבא
לידי, ושפירשתי ושקיבלתי. ת'. **מכאן ואילך ממחזור ר' שמחה
מויטרי.**

But this מכאן ואילך, from which Luzzatto seems to have inferred that
he had a veritable MACHAZOR VITRY before him, applies only to the immediate context, for (i) only two leaves later (161 b) there is another signature
of יצחק בר' דורבלו, and (ii) one page earlier (158 b) the same form of
expression is used with reference to another authority :

‎**מכאן ואילך** ליקוטין מדברי רבינו שלמה כו'. . .

For other examples of the same formula compare :

I. 53 b, col. 1 (סימן ק"ל). **מיכן ואילך** פרש"י בסוטה. עד כאן ה"ג.

‎**מכאן ואילך** יסד ר' מאיר שליח ציבור. II. 29 b, col. 2 (סימן ש'ג).

עד כאן תוספת. **מיכן ואילך** יסוד העמרמי. II. 46 a, col. 2 (סימן שמ"ד).

From the way in which בר' דורבלו here refers to R. Simchah's Machazor it
would seem that he regarded it as merely one of several sources from
which his materials were drawn. Luzzatto himself (*loc. cit.*) calls attention
to the occurrence of later literature in the MS., thus:

ובסימן קמ"ד נמצא... קצור הלכות שבת **מס' התרומה** אולי ר' יצחק בר'
דורבלו הכנים אותו בספר רבנו שמחה שהיה קודם בעל התרומה, או המעתיק
הוסיף אותו.

But this is by no means a solitary instance. The work contains so much
comparatively late literature, including for example poems which are
ascribed, as below, to IBN EZRA, that its compilation as a whole must
be attributed, not to R. Simchah, but to R. Isaac b. R. דורבלו. The use
made of the MACHAZOR VITRY by our MS. is in itself an evidence that it
claims to be something different therefrom.

The following notices from other sources of Isaac b. דורבלו may be
added to those already given from the MS. before us.

a. In Brüll's *Jahrbücher für Jüdische Geschichte und Literatur*,
II. 77 the annexed citation is given from Mannheimer's *Geschichte der
Juden in Worms*, p. 27 (Frankfurt, 1842).

אני יצחק בר' דרבלו ראיתי בוורמשא כתב ששלחו אנשי רינוס לארץ
ישראל שנת תש"ך לפרט, שאלי את קהלות ארץ ישראל על שמועה ששמענו
על ביאת המשיח, וגם סירכא דלבא מה אתון ביה.

b. For the next passage I am indebted to Herr S. J. Halberstam. It
occurs in his MS., No. 115, of the האסופות ס', fol. 41 a.

וְאֲנִי יִצְחֲק בר׳ דוֹרְבֵלוֹ אומר כיון שאין בקיאין במראה כראשונים יש לנו
לנדור בעצמינו פן ירגילו להתעצל ולהקל, כאשר ראיתי במלכות פּוֹלִין בסוחרים
ההולכים בדרך.*

c. The following passage also is supplied by Herr Halberstam from the
same MS., fol. 101 c.

יִצְחֲק בֶּן דוֹרְבֵלוֹ„ אין מונין האבל במניין העשרה להתפלל עמו ביום
ראשון ולא לגבי ברכת המזון ולא לעשרה ולא לשלשה אבל מכאן ואילך מונין
אותו למנין להתפלל ולברך עמו וכן הלכה.

Thus we have traced the name of DORBEL as far back as, perhaps, the
tenth century, and on the other hand down to the *sixteenth*. Moreover,
our R. Isaac of that name has been found in Russia, Prag, Poland, Worms
and Burgundy; and he has been found on two occasions at Rameru in
N. France in the lifetime of Rashi's famous grandson Jacob ben Meir, of
whom he was clearly a disciple. A man of his varied experience may well
have been the compiler of a Machazor such as this, in which so many
authorities are quoted, and the ritual uses of various countries are compared one with another. But in any case no sufficient reason has yet been
shewn for regarding so comprehensive a work as a mere edition of the
Machazor Vitry, however much of the latter it may hereafter be proved to
contain.

Dates of Compilation and Transcription.

2. Of the later literature contained in the compilation, notice the
poems :

I. 90 a (סימן קצ״ז)   אחר לר׳ אברהם אבן עזרא „
כי אשמרה שבת אל ישמרני,
אות היא לעולמי עד בינו וביני, כו׳.

II. 92 b (סימן תכ״ג).   פיוט לר׳ אברהם אבן עזרא „
אשריך הר העברים על ההרים הגבוהים, כו׳.

II. 167 b (סימן תצ״ב).   זמר אחר לר׳ יוסי קמחי „
יחיד וזולתו עזרי מאין, ונראה בלבבות ונעלם מעין, כו׳.

II. 226 (סימן רנ״ד).   אחר לר׳ אברהם אבן עזרא „
קוראי מגילה הם ירננו אל אל, כו׳.

On the next folio (227 b, col. 1) one " R. Abraham " is referred to as no
longer living, thus, מפי ר׳ אברהם נ״ע. The proper place of the last mentioned poem, as appears from its paragraph mark, is before the poem,
אשריך כו׳; and it is through the misplacement of some portions of the MS.,

* This passage is to be found in the Bodleian MS. No. 1101, fol. 210 b (Neubauer's
Catalogue), with the difference that it is there in the third person, and that the name
דורבלו is missing, thus ...אום׳ בר׳ יצחק ור׳.

on which see below (§ 4), that it is found in the second volume, instead of the first.

At the end of Vol. II. are several pages on the calendar—כך תיקון בצרפת (fol. 263 b). Fol. 264 b, col. 1 indicates the date of the *compilation* (1210 A.D.) :

ויש לנו ד׳ אלפים וט׳ מאות וע׳ שנה מבריאת עולם.

At the end of fol. 267 a is written :

נשלם :　　חזק :
והא לך סדר התקופות
והמולדות ושאלה :

and fol. 267 b commences :

תקע״ט למניין שנת ה׳ אלפים ושנים לבריאת שלם. ושנת ה׳ למחזור רס״ד …

whence it may be inferred that the *transcription* was completed not before 1242 A.D. On fol. 268 b, col. 1, is written, השלמתי מחזור רס״ד.

The Scribe.

3. The name of the principal scribe, שמעיה, is indicated in several places. Immediately before Aboth (II. 92 b) is written :

סליקו הילכות סכות.　　חזק שמעיה לא יוזק.

Cf. Vol. I. 122 a, 173 b ; II. 92 a, 93 b, 97 b, 101 a, 101 b.

The expression הכותב, which occurs in several places, denotes not the scribe, but the compiler יצחק בר׳ דורבלו. Compare :

(I. 99 a) ואני הכותב שאלתי זה כמה שנים על זה לר׳ אשר בר׳ משולם מלוניי״ל, והא לך תשובתו כו׳.

(I. 111 b) ולי אני הכותב הראה מורי ראיה מפורשת ממסכת שמחות כו׳.

(II. 38 a) עזריאל בר׳ נתן ז״ל. ואני יצחק בר׳ דורבלו מצאתי תשובה זו מרבינו עזריאל וכתבתיה כאן למען תמצא. ואחריה אכתוב תשובת רבינו יעקב על דבר זה שהשיב לשזנא לר׳ שמעון בר׳ נתנאל.

(II. 117 b) ואני הכותב תמה עלה דההיא דאמרי׳ כו׳.

(II. 144 a) שמעתי אני הכותב דבן בג ובן הא הא גרים היו כו׳.

(II. 175 b) ואני הכותב מצ׳ בה̇ג̇ דרב יהודאי גאון כו׳.

Index of the Manuscript.

4. The MS. is in some confusion. Thus, מסכת דרך ארץ (סימן תקל״א) begins at Vol. II. fol. 231 b, and ends, with the words, סליק מסכת דרך ארץ

פרקים י׳, at Vol. I. fol. 120 b. It is followed by other matter (as far as
(סימן תקע׳ו belonging to Vol. II., all of which is placed between ר׳ע סימן
and ס׳ רע׳א, and ends at Vol. I. 153 b, with the words :

עד כאן העתקתי מכתיבת יד החבר ר׳ משה מברינא*. ועוד
אומרי׳ כי יש חרם שלא לבטל תפילה בשבת ויום טוב בשום דבר אם לא
ביטל כבר ג׳ תפילות ואם בשביל תקנת הקהל אף לכתחילה מותר. סליק.

The above-mentioned tract דרך ארץ is divided in this MS. into *ten*
chapters, the second of which chapters includes what is elsewhere given,
under the title of פרק בן עזאי, as a chapter by itself; and in this respect
the reading of our MS. differs from that of the "Machazor Vitry," as
quoted in some editions of the Talmud Babli. Portions of the first and
second chapters are missing, viz. between איסור ערוה ובא (Vol. II. 231 b),
and הכת׳ אום׳ אמרו צדיק כי טוב (Vol. I. 116 a). The tract is preceded by
two fragments from the beginning and the end of הילכות דרכן של תלמידי
חכמים (Vol. II. 230, 231), now better known under the name of דרך
ארץ זוטא.

The order of the סימנים in the MS. as at present † arranged may be
gathered approximately from the annexed table, which indicates its chief
omissions and transpositions. It is defective at the beginning, the first
paragraph mark being ז׳. The second volume contains the *twenty-one*
chapters of מסכת סופרים (fol. 215—223, 233—238, 228 a) and not chapters
I—XIV. only, as Luzzatto was led by the disorder of the MS. to remark.

VOL. I.			VOL. II.		
ז׳	to	רמ׳ט	רפ׳ה	to	תקכ׳ז
(1 a)		(109 a)	(12 a)		(222 b)
רע׳ה					
(111 a)					
רס׳ב	to	ר׳ע	ר׳נ	to	רס׳א
(112 a)		(115 a)	(225 a)		(227 b)
תקל׳ב	to	תקע׳ו	תקכ׳ח	to	תקל׳א
(120 b)		(152 b)	(229 a)		(231 b)
רע׳א	to	רע׳ד	Folios 239 a—260 b contain poems		
(154 a)		(156 b)	not marked with any סימן‡.		
רע׳ו	to	רפ׳ד	תקע׳ה	to	תק׳ף
(159 b)		(163 a)	(263 b)		(268 b).

* This ברינא may denote *Brünn* the capital of Moravia, or possibly *Brienne* in France.
† August, 1882.
‡ Observe that a number of folios have been transposed from this their proper place to
Vol. I. 120—152.

Some of the main sections are divided into subsections, as below :

קנ"ה] This contains הלכות שבת, extracted from the ספר התרומה of ר' ברוך בר' יצחק, with the numerals from א' to נ"ג (I. 60 a—70 a).

תק"ם] This contains הלכות שחיטה, extracted from the same work, and numbered from א to קל"ח (I. 129 b—143 b).

רפ"ד] In this section, which contains *inter alia*,

הילכות פסח מבוארות מבית מדרשו של רבינו שלמה בר' יצחק צרפתי ז"ל, there is a numbering from א' to ק"ט (I. 163 b—II. 11 b). The folios I. 178—181 are out of order.

תצ"ט] This section contains הילכות נידה, numbered from א' to כ"ד (II. 176 a—177 b), from the above-mentioned ספר התרומה.

The Commentary on אבות.

5. In Vol. II., fol. 93 a—144 a, סימן תכ"ד to תכ"ט ס', is an unpointed text of the six Peraqim, accompanied by a very copious and valuable commentary, of which many copies—more or less complete—are extant, especially in Prayer-Books of the Franco-German rite. French words are used in several places. Cf. fol. 118 b :

שָׂא דוֹלוּר שָׂרַא פּוֹר לוּיּ

Sa douleur sera pour lui,

where, as elsewhere, the לע"ז has been explained by a possessor of the MS.

The Six Peraqim commence on the following pages respectively

93 a,	102 b,	109 b,	117 b,	125 b,	136 b.
(I.)	(II.)	(III.)	(IV.)	(V.)	(VI.)

On fol. 101 a, &c. there is סדר מקבלי התורה, introduced by the words,

שכחתי לעיל בריש פירקי'.

Before משה קבל is written :

פירקי אבות דר' נתן· ודין סימנהון· כשאום' בבקר· בראשית ויצא· שמות ויקחו·

The commentary borrows freely from the אבות, or משנה, or ברייתא, of רבי נתן, which is commonly designated by the one word ברייתא.

The following references in the commentary deserve notice :

fol. 96 b.   כפרש"י בוזאת תהיה כו'·
(I. 8).

fol. 105 a. (II. 5).	הילל כת' במשנת רבינו גרשום ור' אפרים* בלא ר'.
fol. 109 a. (II. 17).	ואני שמעתי בשם ר֒ת אל תהי רשע כ'.
fol. 115 b. (III. 25).	ור' משולם בר' קלונימוס איש רומי פ' לסעודה ליום המיתה כמו שמפורש בפ' גן עדן שיסד ר' יהושע בן לוי כו'. . .
fol. 117 b (III. 25).	ורב נתן הבבלי שסידר את הערוך פי' כו'. . .ובלשון **ערבי** קרוי פורפאורא, ואני הכותב תמה עלה דההיא דאמרי' כו'.
fol. 128 b. (v. 9).	כמו שמצינו באגדת השכם†, ודברי הימים של משה.
fol. 143 b. (VI. 10).	וראיתי מדרשו של ר' שמעון (נ"א שמשון) קרא בכפר משלי כו'.

The Note on the "*Five Possessions*", which this last reference introduces, *is one of the distinctive passages of this commentary*. Its contents
are given in the Rabbinic foot note on the words חמשה קנינים.

Compare also the note on הלל ר' (II. 5), where the title ר' is said to be
a corruption of the numeral ד; the note on the form of the word פרוזדור
(IV. 23), which is to be written בשני דלתין, that is to say, with a *Daleth*
at the end, and not with a *Resh*, פרוזדור; and the notes, in the introductory portion of the commentary, on the different systems of vowel points
(fol. 93 b, lines 9, 10):

ולפיכך אין ניקוד נוברני‡ (נ"א טבריני) דומה לניקוד שלנו ולא שניהם דומים
לניקוד ארץ ישר',

and on the unlawfulness of pointing the Thorah (fol. 93 b, lines 11, 12):

ולפיכך לא ניתן ספר תורה לינקד כו',

with which compare the similar sayings from תשובות הגאונים, in סימן ק״כ
(Vol. I. 49 a):

ספר תורה שניתן למשה בסיני לא שמענו בו ניקוד ולא ניתן ניקוד בסיני כי
החכמי' ציינוהו לסימן ואסור לנו להוסיף מדעתינו פן נעבור בבל תוסיף,
לפיכך אין נוקדין ספר תורה.

The Ending of אבות.

6. In this commentary it is expressly asserted (Vol. II. fol. 134 b) that
מסכת אבות ends at the words

לעשות רצון אביך שבשמים.

But the customary additions are given immediately afterwards, thus:

יהודה בן תימא אומ' הוי עז כנמר וקל כנשר ורץ כצבי
וגיבור כארי לעשות רצון אביך שבשמים.

עז כנמר, אנגריש* ב', כדא' בביצה שלשה עזין הן יהר' באומות, הוי בעל זרוע
לעסוק בתורה בכל כחך. וקל כנשר, שהוא חש לאכול ומגביה לטום מכל
העופות. וגבור כארי, מלשון המקרא הוא, כמו שא' דוד בשאול ויהונתן,
מנשרים קלו מאריות גברו. חסלת מסכת אבות.

שמואל הקטן אומ' בן חמש שנים למקרא כו' בן מאה כאילו
מת עבר ובטל מן העולם. ברוב המחזורים שנינו ההיא דשמואל הקטן
אומ' בנפל אויביך אל תשמח בסוף בי' מאמרות, ואעפ' ששנויה למעלה בפ' בן
זומא, כדי לסמוך עליה הוא היה או' בן חמש שנים למקרא, ויש שאין כת' למעלה
לדשמואל הקטן וכת' הכא ...

†תניא ר' נתן אומ' עז פנים לגהינם כו'.

The sayings of בן בג בג and בן הא הא are not given as part of
the genuine Five Peraqim, but are placed at the end of Pereq VI. (143 a).

The Authorship of the Commentary.

7. We have already intimated (p. 12) that the name of the author of
the commentary on Aboth in this manuscript is

ר' יעקב ברבי שמשון.

This is inferred from the acrostic verses prefixed to its fifth Pereq in
the Cambridge University MS. Addit. 1213,—No. 92 as described in
Schiller-Szinessy's *Catalogue* (Vol. II. pp. 61—72), and to its fourth and
fifth Peraqim in the Bodleian MS. Opp. 317. The acrostic in the former
MS. gives the name יעקב simply, whilst those in the latter give the full
name יעקב ברבי שמשון. He was the teacher of Rashi's grandson Rabbenu
Tam; and, as we gather from the above mentioned MS. No. 92 (fol. 27 b,
line 15), the name of his own teacher was R. Shemuel Hallevi. For an
allusion to him in this MS. see Vol. I. fol. 76 a, col. 2:

פי' הרב ר' יעקב בר' שמשון כו' ... ואני שמעתי מפי הרב חוטב דט"ו
שבחות יש בו כו'.

In Vol. I. fol. 42 a, col. 1, he is named as the compiler of a MACHAZOR.

---

* "ENGRI (an-gri), *s. m.* Espèce de léopard du Congo. On trouve aussi engroi." See the
French Dictionaries of Littré and of the *Académie Française*.

† For the remainder of this ברייתא see *Critical Notes*.

His commentary on Aboth is frequently given anonymously; and it has also been ascribed to or cited in the names of Rashi, R. Isaiah, Rashbam and R. Ephraim*. Luzzatto attributed it conjecturally to R. Simchah, whom (as we have seen) he regarded as the compiler of the Machazor of which it here forms part.

When the name of the author of the commentary was once forgotten, it is not to be wondered at that it should have been ascribed to the famous Rashi or one of his school; but it may be remarked that the abbreviation רי״ש, for R. Jacob Shimshoni, would readily have been corrupted into רש״י. The same might have been mistaken for an abbreviation of ר׳ ישעיה. Notice the confusion between the names of R. Isaiah and Rashi in the heading of the first commentary in the MS. No. 19 described above.

No. 21.

BRITISH MUSEUM, Additional 27208.

A very small P. B., containing Aboth, six Peraqim, pointed, fol. 177 b—227 b, with a marginal commentary, agreeing, on the whole, with No. 20.

No. 22.

BRITISH MUSEUM, Additional 27556.

P. B., with the commentary of Eleazar of Worms. The name אלעזר is marked on fol. 164 b, 166 a, 168 b, 170 b, 186 a.

Aboth, six Peraqim, pointed, is found on fol. 160 b—185 a, accompanied by a marginal commentary agreeing with No. 20.

Reading of III. 9 (fol. 167 b):

‎... בעדת אל בקרב אלהים ישפוט מניין שאפילו חמשה שנ׳ ואגודתו...שלשה
שנ׳ בקרב אלהים ישפוט כו׳.

where the clause בקרב ונו׳ is repeated.

But the commentary is upon the reading of 𝔄, thus:

‎וסתם דיינין חמשה כדברי ר׳ שהיה אומ׳ דייני׳ בחמשה...וי״מ מניין אפי׳ חמשה
שנ׳ אלהים נצב בעדת אל שהיא׳ עשרה ונם בקרב בתוך העד׳ שהיא חציה
המשה אלהי׳ ישפוט כי בקרב כמו בתוך...כך פי׳ רבי׳ נחמיה·

* R. Shemuel of Uceda, the author of the commentary on Aboth called MIDRASH SHEMUEL, refers to it in the preface to his own work as a commentary which was variously attributed to רשב״ם and ר׳ אפרים. See *Critical Notes*, on III. 24.

פרקי אבות

Nos. 23—90.

BODLEIAN LIBRARY MANUSCRIPTS

I. Commentaries with or without the text

Name	Number
Rashi	29, 37, 54, 55
Jacob ben Shimshon .	24–27, 42, 44, 46, 47, 56–58, 85
Maimonides (Arabic) . . .	23, 28, 39
,, (Hebrew) . .	24, 40, 41, 44–47, 66, 88
El'azar ben Shelomoh . . .	36
Rabbenu Jonah	29, 30
Israel of Toledo (Arabic) . .	90
Joseph ibn Shoshan . . .	33
Isaac Israeli	31
R. Shelomoh (Arabic) . . .	28
Joseph Ja'betz	33
Mosheh Al'asqar	32
Gabriel of Nikolsburg . . .	34
Mosheh ben Israel . . .	35
Anonymous	38, 87
Translation	86

II. The text alone

Nos. 43, 48–53, 59–65, 67–84, 89.

3

In the following list of manuscripts of Aboth in the Bodleian Library the numbers according to Neubauer's as yet unpublished *Catalogue* of Hebrew Manuscripts are given. That is to say, the heading "BODLEIAN LIBRARY, 120", for example, designates the manuscript numbered 120 in Neubauer's *Catalogue*.

No. 23.

BODLEIAN LIBRARY, 120.

Poc. 285 (Uri 66).

This contains a good text of the five Peraqim (pointed for the most part), with the Arabic commentary of Maimonides, in Hebrew characters, fol. 97 b—192 b; followed by some extraneous matter as far as fol. 193 b, which ends with the words :

ואיצֵא מן מסכת אבות.

These words are repeated on the following page, and serve to introduce שמואל הקטן כו׳, the AGES*, and the ברייתא on עז פנים לגהינם כו׳ ; all of which—as also a few leaves of the five Peraqim—have been supplied by a later hand.

At the end of Aboth is written :

וכתב ישמעאל בן יוסף הסופר בר׳ שמואל המלמד תנצב״ה.

Readings :

I. 4, ממנו (for מהן). בצמאה. 6, באשת חבירו קל וחומר. 14, נגד שמא אבד שמא, as 𝔄. 15, אם ‡ואני לי. 18, אלא שתיקה. 19. The margin, not the text, has שנ׳ אמת כו׳.

II. 1, מרבה חכמה מרבה. 5, שאי אפשר להשמע. 8, ועונשן של עבירה אם עשיתה תורה, the margin adding, ישיבה. 9, מרבה עצה מרבה תבונה. *omitting* תורה. 10, בור סוד. 15, עין רעה. 18, ללמוד מה שתשיב. הרבה 19, למדתה תורה הרבה נותן לך...לבּטַל אבל אם.

III. 1, בלעונו. 2, למקום. לרימה ותולעה ולאין, as 𝔄. The margin adds, 7, ומפנה. 9, as 𝔄. 17, as 𝔄, except תורה ומעשים טובים. The margin adds, מעשרות סייג לעושר. 20, om. הוא היה אומר. 23, the text omits והמלבין כו׳. 24, חיבה יתירה כו׳. לפי רוב המעשה אבל לא על פי המעשה. 28, וגֵימַטְרִיָא חַסְמָא.

---

* These are given as part of Rambam's text in many Italian Prayer Books, but he does not comment upon them.

† The negative is also omitted, by a clerical error, in a few other MSS.

IV. 8, in margin, not in text, 'וכל הלמד ע״מ לעשות כו'.   19, om. עולה.

prima manu.   23, לְפָרוֹזְדוֹר. בְּפָרוֹזְדוֹר.   31, לָמָוֶת. לִחְיוֹת.

V. 10, 'שואל כהלכה כו.   15, שלך ושלך שלך. ...שלי ושלי שלי...שלך ושלי שלי, as 𝔄. The margin adds, (1) שלך, and (2) שלי.   31, (*sic*) דכולא בה ובה, with marginal additions.

No. 24.

BODLEIAN LIBRARY, 376.

Mich. 507 (ol. 665).

A very carefully written MS., containing:

I. A commentary on the six Peraqim, fol. 1 b—35 b, agreeing with No. 20.

II. The five Peraqim, pointed, with the commentary of Maimonides in Hebrew, fol. 54 a—77 a; followed by an unpointed text of Pereq R. Meir.

At the end of the MS. the scribe, Mordekai ben Levi חלפן states that it was finished in 5237 A.M. = 1477 A.D., and that it was written for R. Noah ben Immanuel of Norzi.

No. 25.

BODLEIAN LIBRARY, 377.

Mich. 311 (ol. 666).

At the beginning is an indifferently written commentary on the six Peraqim, agreeing with No. 20. Fol. 51 a gives the date ק״צג = 1433 A.D., and the scribe's name,

אביגדור בר' יוסף הכהן.

No. 26.

BODLEIAN LIBRARY, 378.

Can. Or. 83.

Folio, three columns to the page, well written. It begins (fol. 1 a—17 b) with another copy of the same commentary.

No. 27.

Bodl. 145 (Uri 204).

Another copy of the same commentary, breaking off abruptly at the end of the fifth chapter with the words, סליק פרק חמישי, the remainder of the leaf on which they are written having been cut off. Folio, double columns, well written.

No. 28.

BODLEIAN LIBRARY, 380.

Poc. 43 (Uri 238).

Rambam on the five Peraqim: Arabic in Hebrew characters, followed by קנין תורה, with a commentary by

ר׳ שלמה אלסגֿלמאסי.

No. 29.

BODLEIAN LIBRARY, 381.

Bodl. Or. 598.

This MS. contains two commentaries on the five Peraqim, viz. by

I. R. JONAH, fol. 1 a—53 b.

II. "RASHI," fol. 54 a—62 b.

The margin of I. contains the text.

No. 30.

BODLEIAN LIBRARY, 382.

Opp. Add. 4to, 59.

Another copy of the commentary of R. JONAH on the five Peraqim.

No. 31.

BODLEIAN LIBRARY, 383.

Poc. 202 (Uri 220).

The commentary of ISAAC b. R. SHELOMOH, followed by a commentary on Job by R. Isaac Israel.

Near the beginning of תורה קנין this copy reads :

ורמב״ם ורמ״ה ורבי׳ יונה ז״ל לא פי׳ פרק זה לפי שאינו ממסכת׳ זו·

In other copies, רש״י also is classed with those who commented on the five Peraqim only; but his name is here omitted, probably by a clerical error.

No. 32.

BODLEIAN LIBRARY, 384.

Opp. 244 (ol. 421).

A copious commentary on the six Peraqim, headed :

ספר מרכבת המשנה שחבר החכם השלם הה״ר יוסף בכ״ר החכם השלם
הה״ר משה אלאשקר זלה״ה·

The writer quotes רמב״ם, רשב״ם (fol. 48 a), and רש״י, &c.

No. 33.

BODLEIAN LIBRARY, 385.

Mich. 265.

This MS. contains the commentaries of

    I.   יוסף יעב״ץ, on the six Peraqim, fol. 1 a—40 b.

    II.   יוסף ן׳ שושאן, on the five Peraqim, fol. 41 a—89 b.

No. 34.

BODLEIAN LIBRARY, 386.

Mich. 94.

The commentary of R. GABRIEL of Nikolsburg, fol. 1 a—56 b, as far as IV. 19. The notes on Pereq III., which break off at § 11, are in a later hand (fol. 30 a—45 b).

No. 35.

BODLEIAN LIBRARY, 387.

Opp. 243 (ol. 420).

At the beginning is בית אבות, the commentary of R. Moses ben Israel on the six Peraqim. This ends on fol. 88 a. At the end of Pereq v. (fol. 75 a), רשב"ם is quoted on the names בן הא הא, and בן בג בג.

No. 36.

BODLEIAN LIBRARY, 388.

Opp. 246 (ol. 423).

"Commentary (Agadic and mystical) on Abhoth (beg. i. 5*, and has also the sixth chapter) by a French or Rhenish Rabbi, the son of R. Sh'lomoh...The author composed his comm. before 5009 = 1249 (fol. 84 b)". See Neubauer's *Catalogue*.

No. 37.

BODLEIAN LIBRARY, 389.

Opp. 378 (ol. 800).

On fol. 2 a—13 b is a commentary on the six Peraqim. The date of transcription שכ"ז = 1567 A.D. is given at the end. As far as the end of Pereq v. it agrees with the "RASHI" of Isaac b. R. Shelomoh.

No. 38.

BODLEIAN LIBRARY, 390.

Opp. 245 (ol. 422).

A lengthy commentary on the six Peraqim, beginning with a reference to the MIDRASH SHEMUEL on the saying, כל ישראל יש להם חלק כו'.

* וסופו יורד לגיהנם.

No. 39.

Poc. 68 (Uri 215).

Maimonides on Sanhedrin : Arabic in Hebrew characters. The five Peraqim begin on fol. 10 b. At their conclusion the date 1488 A.D. is given thus :

שנת הרמ״ח ליצירה דהיא שנת אתשצ״ט לשטרות.

The scribe's name was

יוסף בר ידיד המכונה גֿרֿאֿוֿיֿ נב׳ע בר יצחק בר משה בר יוסף.

Readings :

II. 18, תורה *omitting*, ללמוד מה שתשיב.

III. 9, om. ׳ג שלשה ׳שנ. ומניין אפי׳ ‎17, שיש לו בידו מעשים טובים. om. שלא כהלכה.

v. 24, שמאי והלל. ‎29, after שבשמים is written :

‫[שמואל הק׳ כו׳‎...‫ר׳ יהודה הנשיא] אומ׳ עז פנים לגיהנם ...‬

but the sayings in brackets are marked for omission, and replaced by the words הוא היה.

Pereq VI. follows (fol. 50 a), with short Hebrew notes.

No. 40.

Opp. 95 (ol. 850).

Maimonides on the Mishnah, three Sedarim :

ביאור הרמב״ם על משניות נזיקין וסדר קדשים וסדר טהרות שהתחיל לחברם בהיותו בן עשרים ושלשה שנים.

The commentary on the five Peraqim, fol. 60 b—68 b, is followed by

אבות מר׳ נתן.

No. 41.

Can. Or. 14.

Maimonides on the Mishnah, קדשים and זרעים, and on the five Peraqim, fol. 297 a—313 a.

No. 42

BODLEIAN LIBRARY, 692.

Opp. 317 (ol. 627).

This contains *inter alia* a commentary on the six Peraqim, fol. 114 b ⋯ 130 b, agreeing with No. 20. Before Pereq IV. (fol. 124 a), and also before Pereq V. (fol. 127 a), is found an acrostic of

יעקב ברבי שמשון,

who is accordingly described in the *Catalogue* as PROBABLY THE AUTHOR OF THE COMMENTARY. His name is given again acrostically in an astronomical treatise, ספר האלקושי, of date 1123 A.D., which is bound up in the same volume. See fol. 91 b.

In the middle of Pereq V., on the margin of fol. 129 b, is written:

עד הנה כתבתי בשנת ע״ה לפרט (1315 A.D.)

and on the following page, 125* a:

פה התחלתי צ״ו לפרט (1336 A.D.)

In the margin of fol. 126* b is written, after בן הא הא כו׳, and before the AGES:

חסלת מסכת אבות פרקים חמשה.

The name of the scribe, שמואל, is marked in several places.

No. 43.

BODLEIAN LIBRARY, 1057.

Opp. Add. fol. 11.

P. B., with the six Peraqim, pointed, fol. 215 b—221 b.

No. 44.

BODLEIAN LIBRARY, 1059.

Mich. 610 (ol. 434).

P. B., containing Aboth, pointed, with the commentary of Rambam, fol. 126 b—144 a, followed by:

פרק ר׳ מאיר כפי מה שפירש רבינו שלמה זצ״ל.

* The number 125 occurs twice in the pagination of the MS., and is marked with an ASTERISK upon its second occurrence.

No. 45.

Can. Or. 49 B.

P. B., containing Aboth, pointed, with the commentary of Rambam, fol. 69 b—82 a; followed by Pereq R. Meir, with a commentary which is written as if it were a continuation of that of Rambam.

No. 46.

Can. Or. 18.

P. B., containing Aboth, pointed at the beginning, with Rambam's commentary in the margin, fol. 395 a—403 a; followed by Pereq R. Meir, with a commentary (= No. 20), which is attributed to רש״י, with the remark :

כי הרמב״ם לא פירש דבר ע׳ז.

No. 47.

Mich. 525 (ol. 446).

P. B., with Aboth, pointed, and Rambam's commentary, fol. 89 b—107 b ; followed by פרק של ר׳ מאיר, with פי׳ רבי שלמה ז״ל.

No. 48.

Mich. Add. 64.

P. B., with a pointed text of Aboth and Pereq R. Meir, fol. 32 b—39 a.
Before חמשה קניינין כו׳ (fol. 38 b), is written :

ויש מקומות שמתפללין מנחה כשאמרו עד כאן ואחר כך אומ׳ אילו חמשה
קניינין שהרי אנו אומרין קודם מנחה אילו פירקי אבות ואין חובה אלא
מנהג.

No. 49.

BODLEIAN LIBRARY, 1065.

Opp. Add. 4to, 62.

P. B., with pointed text of Aboth and ר' מאיר כו', fol. 106 a—117 b. At the end of Pereq v. is written, תם פרקי אבות (fol. 115 a).

No. 50.

BODLEIAN LIBRARY, 1067.

Mich. 360 (ol. 447).

P. B., with fragments of Aboth, pointed, in the margins of fol. 198, 199:

(1) From ובורח מן העברה, to לצדיקים שמקיימים (iv. 5—v. 1).

(2) From ומכריעו לכף זכות (vi. 6), to the end of the chapter.

No. 51.

BODLEIAN LIBRARY, 1071.

Can. Or. 27.

"Compendium of מחזור," with the six Peraqim, pointed, fol. 132 a—145 a.

No. 52.

BODLEIAN LIBRARY, 1081.

Reggio 63.

P. B., with Aboth and קנין תורה, unpointed, fol. 141 b—159 b.

Here and in No. 53 the fifth Pereq ends:

בן בג בג אומר הפוך בה דכלא בה כו'...בן ההא אומר כו'...בן חמש שנים מן העולם...

No. 53.

BODLEIAN LIBRARY, 1094.

Mich. 290 (ol. 443).

Fragment of a Machazor, with Aboth, pointed—ending, נגמרה מסכת אבות; followed, after a blank page, by פרק ששי, fol. 14 b—23 b.

No. 54.

Opp. Add. 4to, 28.

"Siddur, according to R. 'Amram Gaon," transcribed by Moses b. Isaac גרסיאן, at עיר רודום, and dated (fol. 90 a), הקפ״ו = 1426 A.D.

On fol. 91 a commences

פירוש פרקי אבות לרש״י ז״ל.

Readings :

II. 17 (fol. 98 b). הוי זהיר בק״ש לקרותו בשעתו ובתפילין לא גרסינ'

IV. 8 (fol. 102 b). אין מספיקין בידו כו'

IV. 19 (fol. 103 a). וכתר שם טוב על גביהן

At the end of Pereq v. is written, סליקו להו פרקי אבות ה'. Then follow the AGES, and שנו חכמים כו'.

No. 55.

Mich. 571 (ol. 533).

P. B., containing Aboth, pointed, with the commentary of "RASHI" in the margin, fol. 85 b—99 b ; followed by Pereq VI., with a marginal commentary, fol. 100 a—102 b.

It has the following note on IV. 8 (fol. 93 b):

הכי גרסינן אין מספיקין בידו ללמוד וללמד.

No. 56.

Opp. 59 (ol. 668).

This, which is described as a copy of the MACHAZOR VITRY, contains a commentary on the six Peraqim, fol. 285 b—294 b, agreeing with No. 20.

Reading, in the note on the ה' קנינים (fol. 294 a) :

וראיתי במדרש ר' שמ'עון שמשון קרא בספר משלי...

the name שמעון being marked for omission, and replaced by שמשון.

No. 57.

BODLEIAN LIBRARY, 1101.

Opp. Add. fol. 14.

" A fragment of the preceding," that is of another copy of the so-called MACHAZOR VITRY. See No. 20.

fol. 195 b.   פיסקי של ביצים מן הרב יעקב בר׳ שמשון

At the beginning of fol. 90, after a lacuna, comes, ר׳ חנניה בן עקשיא כו׳, but Aboth has disappeared.

No. 58.

BODLEIAN LIBRARY, 1102.

Opp. 649 (ol. 1483).

P. B., with a pointed text of the six Peraqim, and marginal commentary (= No. 20), fol. קס״ב to קל״ז.

The commentary from IV. 8 to the end is in a comparatively late hand (שו״ב = 1548 A.D.).

No. 59.

BODLEIAN LIBRARY, 1103.

Can. Or. 86.

P. B., with pointed text of Aboth, fol. 36 a—46 a; followed by שנו חכמים כו׳, before which is written :

סליקא לה מסכת אבות

מכאן ואילך אינו מפרקי אבות.

No. 60.

BODLEIAN LIBRARY, 1105.

Opp. 758 (ol. 653).

P. B., with the six Peraqim, pointed, fol. 145 a—162 a

No. 61.

BODLEIAN LIBRARY, 1106.

Opp. 642 (ol. 1476).

P. B., with the six Peraqim, pointed, fol. 54 b—67 a.

The תקופות begin (fol. 316 b) with the year צ"ז = 1337 A.D.

No. 62.

BODLEIAN LIBRARY, 1109.

Opp. 643 (ol. 1477).

P. B., with the six Peraqim, pointed, fol. 102 a—114 b.

The calendar begins (fol. 237 a) with the year:

ק"ט י"ז למחזור רס"ט = 1349 A.D.

No. 63.

BODLEIAN LIBRARY, 1110.

Mich. 162 (ol. 543).

P. B., ending with the six Peraqim, pointed.

No. 64.

BODLEIAN LIBRARY, 1112.

Opp. 157 (ol. 1007).

P. B., with the six Peraqim, pointed, fol. מ"ד to מ"ט. Dated, on the title page, ונדיב על נדבתו יקום, and, on fol. ק"ח :

ואתם הדבקים בה' אלהיכם חיים = 1698 A.D.

Transcribed by :

צבי הירש בלא"א דוד כ"ץ הסופר פה ק"ק לאשיץ.

No. 65.

BODLEIAN LIBRARY, 1113.

Opp. 158 (ol. 1008).

P. B., with the six Peraqim, unpointed, fol. נ"א to נ"ה. Dated at the beginning, קדוש = 1650 A.D.

No. 66.

BODLEIAN LIBRARY, 1114.

Opp. 156 (ol. 1006).

P. B., containing Aboth and Pereq R. Meir, pointed, with Rambam on Aboth, in the margin, fol. ל״א to ל׳ח. The commentary is abbreviated *in loc.* for want of space, and is supplemented on fol. קט׳ו—קק״ב.

No. 67.

BODLEIAN LIBRARY, 1115.

Mich. 73 (ol. 542).

P. B., with the six Peraqim, pointed, fol. 104 a—115 b.

No. 68.

BODLEIAN LIBRARY, 1116.

Opp. 645 (ol. 1459).

P. B., with the six Peraqim, written in large square characters, and pointed, fol. 79 a—97 b.

Reading : III. 9, omits שני חמשה שאף. ומנין. A late hand has supplied the omitted words in the margin (fol. 84 b).

No. 69.

BODLEIAN LIBRARY, 1117.

Can. Or. 44.

P. B., incomplete, beginning with the six Peraqim, pointed, from שנים אלא לי אין (III. 4), to the end of the sixth chapter (fol. 19 a).

No. 70.

BODLEIAN LIBRARY, 1119.

Mich. Add. 41.

P. B., with the six Peraqim, unpointed, fol. 76 b—89 a.

No. 71.

Can. Or. 102.

P. B., with the six Peraqim, unpointed (for the most part), fol. 72 b—
91 a. Dated on the last page, ק״פל יוד שׁין = 1550 A.D.

No. 72.

Mich. 200 (ol. 541).

P. B., with the six Peraqim, unpointed, fol. 93 b—120 b.

No. 73.

Bodl. 24 (Uri 300).

P. B., ending with the text of Aboth, unpointed (for the most part), as
far as v. 26 : ישׁר׳ את והחטיא חטא ירבעם.

Readings :

II. 18, תשׁיב כדי. III. 9, ישׁפט אלהים בקרב אל בעדת omitting ומנין
28, תורה גופי, with הלכות added in the text as a שׁנ׳ חמשׁה אפי׳.
correction. v. 8, בירושׁלים שׁאלין. v. 9 is omitted.

No. 74.

Opp. 646 (ol. 1480).

P. B., with the six Peraqim, pointed, fol. 96 b—116 b.

No. 75.

Can. Or. 110.

P. B., with the six Peraqim, unpointed, fol. 113 b—140 b.

The Mishnioth, up to fol. 122 a, have rubricated initial words. From
fol. 122 b to the end blank spaces are left at the beginnings, the rubrication
not having been completed.

Dated at the end, ק״פל רנ״ב = 1492 A.D.

No. 76.

BODLEIAN LIBRARY, 1126.

Opp. 776 (ol. 268).

A small illuminated Siddur, containing the six Peraqim, unpointed, fol. 40 b—27 a (numbered *from the end of the MS.*).

Dated on fol. 1 b, רל״א = 1471 A.D.

No. 77.

BODLEIAN LIBRARY, 1129.

Opp. 336 (ol. 723).

P. B., with the six Peraqim, unpointed, fol. 25 a—32 b.

The date 1394 A.D. is given at the end of fol. 65 a, thus:

היום אנו לבריאת עולם לה׳ אלפים ומאה וחמשים וארבעה נמצא יש לנו
מבריאת עולם ער״א מחזורים וה׳ שנים ממחזור ער״ב.

Ending of Pereq v.:

‎..אביך שבשמים. בן בג בג כו׳. בן הא הא כו׳. בן חמש כו׳. ר׳ יהודה
הנשיא אומ׳ עז פנים לגהינם ובוש פנים לגן עדן. עז פנים ר׳ אליעזר או׳ כו׳:

No. 78.

BODLEIAN LIBRARY, 1132.

Can. Or. 108.

P. B., with Aboth and קנין תורה, pointed, 247 a—275 a. In II. 17, ובתפלה is omitted (fol. 253 b).

No. 79.

BODLEIAN LIBRARY, 1133.

Opp. Add. 8vo, 18.

P. B., with the six Peraqim, pointed, fol. 224 a—247 a.

The sixth Pereq begins:

פרק מִשֶּׁנָה. שנו חכמים כו׳.

No. 80.

BODLEIAN LIBRARY, 1135.

Opp. Add. 8vo, 17.

A miniature סידור, "Spanish rite," containing, near the end, the six Peraqim, pointed.

Chapters III. and IV. are headed respectively פרק ב and פרק ג.

The ending of Chapter v. (Jehudah ben Thema's saying הוי עז כנמר כו' being omitted by a clerical error) is as follows :

‎...לא יחצו ימיהם ואני אבטח בך" יהודה בן תימא או' בן חמש שנים כו' מן העולם.

Then comes a separate section headed פרק, commencing with בן בג בג כו' and continuing as in No. 81.

No. 81.

BODLEIAN LIBRARY, 1137.

Can. Or. 24.

"Common Prayers (Catalan rite ?)," with the six Peraqim, pointed, fol. 93 a—106 a.

Readings :

III. 8 is followed by 10, which is ascribed to ר' חלפתא איש כפר חנניה.

IV. 8, אין is written before the first מספיקין, but is crossed out by a later hand. 23, לפרוזדוד.

Pereq v. ends thus :

‎...שבשמים. שמואל הקטן או' בנפול אויבך כו'. הוא היה או' בן חמש כו'.

Then follows (fol. 105 b) :

פרק ששי

בן בג בג או' הֲפוֹךְ וְהַפֵּךְ בָּה דְּכוֹלָא בָה ומינה לָא תָזוּז.

בן הא הא או' לפום צערא אנרא.

‎*תניא ר' נתן אומר הלומד תורה מן הקטנים כאלו אוכל ענבים כהות ושותה יין מנתו, והלומד תורה מן הגדולים למה הוא דומה כאלו אוכל ענבים בשולות ושותה יין ישן.

---

* This saying is omitted at the place (IV. 28) where it is usually found.

תניא ר' יהודה הנשיא או' עז פנים לגיהנם ובוש פנים לגן עדן.

ר' אליעזר אומר ממזר, ר' יהושע או' בן הנדה, ר' אליעזר או' אף לא עמדו
אבותיו על הר סיני, ועל כלם אליהו כותב והקב״ה חותם ואו' אוי לו למי
שפוסל את זרעו ופוגם את משפחתו ולנושא אשה שאינה הוגנת לו שכל הנושא
אשה שאינה הוגנת לו אליהו כופתו, והקב״ה רוצעו, וכל הפוסל פסול ואינו מדבר
בשבחו לעולם.

ואמר שמואל ובמומו פוסל, סוף אדם למות וסוף בהמה לשחיטה, הכל למיתה
הן עומדים.

תניא ר' אבא או' מי שגדול בחכמה ועמלו בתורה עושה נחת רוח ליוצרו גדל
בשם טוב ונפטר בשם טוב ועליו אמר שלמה בחכמתו טוב שם משמן טוב ויום
המות מיום הולדו.

למוד תורה הרבה כדי שיתנו לך שכר הרבה ודע מתן שכרן לצדיקים לעתיד
לבא.

ר' חנניא בן עקשיא או' רצה המקום לזכות את ישראל לפיכך הרבה להם תורה
ומצות שנא' חפץ למען צדקו ינדיל תורה ויאדיר.

No. 82.

BODLEIAN LIBRARY, 1139.

Mich. 2 (ol. 546).

P. B., commencing with the six Peraqim, pointed. Transcribed by
מרדכי בר' אליה (fol. 76 a), and dated יִרְאוּ עינינו וישמח לבנו = 1457 A.D.

Pereq III. 9—12, 15 are omitted.

Pereq VI., which is headed פרק, commences, בן בג בג כו', and continues as in No. 81.

No. 83.

BODLEIAN LIBRARY, 1142.

Opp. Add. 8vo, 14.

"Common Prayers (Provençal rite?)" with Aboth, **Seven Peraqim,**
pointed, fol. 133 a—153 a.

The fifth Chapter ends:

...שבשמים. הוא היה אומ' עז פנים לגיהנם ובוש פנים לגן עדן.

The sixth begins (fol. 148 a) :

בן בג בג ...

and continues as in No. 81, except that it repeats 'בנפול אויבך כו from IV. 26, but with the addition of מלמד שמוחלין לו כל עונותיו, and then adds the saying 'בן חמש שנים כו.

Then follows (fol. 149 b) what is commonly called the sixth Chapter under the name of the seventh, thus :

פרק שביעי

'ר' מאיר אומ' כל העוסק בתורה לשמה זוכה לדברים הרבה כו.

Readings :

III. 9, THREE before FIVE.   VI. 10, ·ארבעה קנינין.

No. 84.

BODLEIAN LIBRARY, 1145.

Opp. Add. 4to, 96.

P. B., rite of Yemen, with the Assyrian, or Babylonian, vocalisation, containing Aboth, unpointed (except at the beginning), and קנין תורה, fol. 11 b—16 a.   The date 5233 A.M. (=1473 A.D.) occurs on fol. 84 b.

The sixth Chapter here departs widely from its usual form, and is read as follows.   After בשם מרדכי (VI. 6) comes :

גדולה יראה שהיא מביאה לכל המדות האלו· וכן הוא אומ' תחלת חכמה יראת יי' ואמרו חכמים הכל בידי שמים חוץ מיראת שמים·

אשרי מי שיכול לשום את עצמו אלם ולא אלם ממש שלא יחטא ויחייב את עצמו· חרש ולא חרש ממש· חגר ולא חגר ממש· וכל כך למה שלא יחטא ויחייב את עצמו ואת איבריו) לגיהנם· יהי עז כנמר וקל כנשר ורץ כצבי וגבור כארי לעשות רצון* כדי שיזכה להיות מיורשי גן עדן·

אשרי אדם שישים עצמו כשור לעול וכחמור למשוי...

And so on, with a long series of BEATITUDES, ending with the saying on the " 310 æons " which each צדיק is destined to inherit :

שנ' להנחיל אוהבי יש ואוצרותיהם אמלא·

* A later hand has written יוצרו above the line.

No. 85.

BODLEIAN LIBRARY, 1204.

Opp. 160 (ol. 1010).

" R. Ele'azar of Worms' commentary on the common prayers," &c. From fol. 275 a to the end, there is a commentary on Aboth (= No. 20), breaking off in the middle of the AGES.

No. 86.

BODLEIAN LIBRARY, 1217.

Can. Or. 12.

On fol. 216 a—241 a is a Hebrew-German translation of the six Peraqim.

No. 87.

BODLEIAN LIBRARY, 2252.

Mich. 125.

On fol. 151 a—186 a is a " philosophical" commentary on the six Peraqim, written in an Italian cursive hand, of the latter part of the 16th century.

No. 88.

BODLEIAN LIBRARY, 2282.

Opp. 572 (ol. 1159).

On fol. 25 a—38 a is Rambam's commentary on ABOTH.

No. 89.

BODLEIAN LIBRARY, 2284.

Mich. 548.

Fol. 49 a—61 b (numbered from the commencement of the *second part of the MS.*) contains a pointed text of the six Peraqim.

No. 90.

Bodleian Library, 2354.

Opp. Addit. Qto. 126.

This proves to be the lost Arabic commentary of R. Israel of Toledo (cent. XII—XIII), upon which the commentary of his descendant Isaac b. R. Shelomoh* on the six Peraqim (1368 A.D.) is founded.

1. The MS., which is probably of the latter part of the sixteenth century, is "in mixed (Rabbinic and current) oriental Sephardic hand-writing." It is defective at both ends, and at two places in the middle. At present there remain 191 leaves. The page generally contains 19 lines, of about 13 words; but some pages (69 a—76 b) are more closely written. Its six Peraqim, or portions of Peraqim, commence on the following pages:

1 a;	21 b;	67 b;	99 a;	136 a;	185 b.
(I. 8)	(II. 1)	(III. 1)	(IV. 3)	(V. 1)	(VI. 1)

Fol. 25 ends upon ושכר עבירה in II. 1, with the words ובלבד שבא (=𝔅 26 a₁₈†); and fol. 26 begins upon כאילו עשיתם in II. 2 (=𝔅 27 b₂₃):

תלך אל מצוה בל יחסב להום כאנהום עמלוהא ורבי מאיר הלוי ז"ל פסר ...

Fol. 27, which is misplaced, should follow 98. It ends with the catch-word וגימטריאות (III. 28), and the remainder of the third chapter is missing.

Fol. 99 begins with אֵיזֶהֶן עשיר (IV. 3). The commencement of the fourth chapter is missing.

Fol. 190 ends on VI. 3, with the words, רהיט ואזיל דכתיב בית אלהים נהלך (=𝔅 122 b₁).

Fol. 191, the last leaf of the MS., contains a fragment of the commentary on VI. 6, beginning a little before בשמחה, and breaking off at the clause

בפלפול התלמידין.

The commentary is very rich in illustrations from the ancient Jewish literature, and also contains many allusions to medieval works on ABOTH and on other subjects. The writer was evidently a philosopher, as well as a man of letters. He goes fully into discussion of ethical points. Notice in particular the Excursus of 26 pages on the principles of almsgiving (160 a—172 b) appended to his comments on v. 19.

---

* The references to R. Isaac's commentary in this article are taken (with one exception) from the manuscript K 7 in the library of St John's College Cambridge, which was quoted as 𝔅 in the *Critical Notes* to the *Sayings of the Jewish Fathers* (1877).

† The suffix denotes the line of the page. Thus the above reference is to line 18 of fol. 26 a, where fol. 26 denotes the original fol. 27 (כ"ז), the eleventh folio having been lost.

2. The following References occur in the Manuscript.

(1) רבינו שמואל 7 b_9, 11 b_{10}, 32 b_7*, 33 a_1, 46 b_2, 53 a_9*, 53 b_4, 55 b_{18}, 62 b_{13}.

(2) רבינו יונה 17 b_9, 22 a_{19}, 26 a_3, 39 b_{18}, 42 b_{14}, 45 a_{19}, 53 b_8, 77 b_{18}, 138 a_7.

(3) ר' מאיר (הלוי) 22 a_{11}*, 26 a_1, 53 b_7, 53 b_{11}*, 64 b_5, 82 a_{13}, 83 a_{12}, 93 b_2*, 141 a_{13}, 145 a_7, 152 a_2.

(4) רבינו משה 14 b_{15}, 55 b_{16}, (114 b_8*), 150 b_{17}.

(5) רש"י 143 b_{19}, 147 a_7.

(6) ר' יצחק בן גיאת 23 a_2, 148 a_{18}.

(7) רבינו סעדיה 146 b_7, 190 a_1.

(8) ראב"ד 16 a_{14}.

(9) רבינו האיי 149 a_{12}.

(10) רבינו חננאל 149 a_{19}.

(11) ר' שמעון 53 a_8.

(12) צאחב הלכות גדולות 169 a_{15}.

(13) אפלאטון 77 a_5.

(14) אל פילוסוף* 15 a_7, 17 a_{17}, 87 b_{19}.

(15) ארסטטאלים 104 b_8.

(16) גאליא(א)נוס 48 b_{10}, 48 b_{18}, 98 a_4, 180 a_{10}.

(17) אל שאער 67 b_{13}.

(18) ר' שלמה בן חרמת 23 a_1.

3. Notes on the above References.

(1). 32 b_7*.
II. 5.
The scribe here, interpolating אי, gives שׂ(אי) איפשר לשמוע as the reading of R. Shemuel; but his comments are rightly rendered : יקול אדא אמכנך אן תסמע כו'.

(1). 53 a_9*.
II. 14.
ר' שמעון (sic) ור' שמואל עָֿאֹם יקרו שנשיכתן נשיכת שועל. Here 𝕭 (40 b_7) reads : ורש"י ורשב"ג גורסין כו', but doubtless by a clerical error for ורש"י ורשב"ם, which is the reading of No. 1.

The citations from R. Shemuel will be given *in extenso* at the conclusion of this article. We have given them the first place in our list on account of their relation to the vexed question of the authorship of the great commentary in No. 20.

(3). 22 a_{11}*.
II. 1.
For ר' מאיר, who is quoted as recommending the *via media*, 𝕭 (24 b_{15}) substitutes רמב"ם.

* There is no distinctive form for final פ in this manuscript.

(3). 53 b₁₁*. רבי מאיר הלוי ז"ל יקרא עין הרע יריד אל רגבה ואל טמאעה

II. 15. ואל חסד והו אל צדיח מן אל וגהיין אחדהמא אן אל

עיין תווה (sic) עלא אב אגלב· ואל תאני כו'·

𝔅 (41 a₁₇) here reads: ... והרמ"ה גורם עין רֶעָה, which is also the true reading in the first line of the above quotation from No. 90, although the scribe has written הרע. In the last line read תונת כו', or in Arabic

characters الاغلب على تونت · 𝔅 (41 a₁₈) con-

tinues, citing our author's argument: וכת' הר' ישראל

ז"ל זו היא הגירסה הנכונה לפי שעין לשון נקבה על
הרוב·

(3). 93 b₂*. ורבי מאיר ז"ל יקרא והכל לפי רוב המעשה אבל לא על פי

III. 24. המעשה. [MS. לפי]·

Here 𝔅 (65 b₁₉) has: והרמב"ם והרמ"ה ז"ל גורסין כו'·

(4). 114 b₈*. R. Israel quotes, ריים אל מפסרין ז"ל, a title which 𝔅

IV. 9. (79 b₂₄) replaces by the name of רמב"ם. R. Israel then proceeds (114 b₁₁) to introduce his own opinion as follows:

ואני בער ולא אדע קטן השועלים תולעת ולא איש... פֿאקול
וכבוד הרב ז"ל עומד במקומו אן כו'·

and these words also are cited by R. Isaac (𝔅 80 a₂).

4. R. Isaac's use of this commentary.

A comparison of R. Isaac's citations with those of our author fully suffices for the identification of the latter with "R. Israel." The following examples will serve to indicate the *extent* to which he is indebted to the writer of this commentary.

A.

The MS. commences abruptly at I. 8 (הרחק משכן רע), with the words:

(סו)תרין כותלו של צדיק ופֿי כתאב אל חק אשאר אלא אבעאד מנّאורת אל
(ט)אלמין כקו' סורו נא מעל אהלי האנשים הרשעים האלה·

Then follow allusions to Lot, the Canaanites (Ex. xxiii. 33), and Nehemiah, in which 𝔅 follows our commentator, but without expressly quoting from him until the following clause, ואל תתחבר לרשע, upon which "R. Israel" remarks (1 b₁₂), and is quoted as remarking (𝔅 12 a₉), that a man should avoid the extremes of too great reserve and too great freedom in his intercourse with his fellows:

פֿינבני לאל אנסאן אן יכון מעא אל נאס ביין מנקבّץ וביין מנבסّט...

he must neither be חדל אי"שים, on the one hand, nor איש רעים, on the other.

B.

On I. 18 (שמעון בנו כו') R. Israel has a note extending from 13 b₁₂ to 18 a₁. There is apparently some omission at 14 b₁₅, where, after explaining the expression לְגוּף טוב, he concludes :

‎. . . ואמא בדברי תורה מחמוד אל כלאם פֿיהא ורבי' משה ז"ל . . . תגֹדה
‎פֿי מא הו מכתוב בעד פרק בעשרה מאמרות.

B gives an abstract of R. Israel's note up to this point, adopting his remarks freely, but without acknowledgment. Then comes a quotation of 36 lines (B 21 b₅—22 a₁₅)—*not found in its place in* No. 90—commencing :

‎וכת' הרב ישראל ז"ל כי הדיבור מתחלק לד' חלקים יש שכולו מועיל והוא דברי
‎תורה . . .

This is followed (1) by a quotation from R. Jonah, *which itself contains a reference to* רמב"ם, and (2) by אמר המחבר כו' (22 a₂₅). B then summarises the remaining 119 lines of R. Israel in 23 lines (B 22 b₇—23 a₄), somewhat as follows :

ולא המדרש כו'] R. Shim‘eon, having first given a caution against wordiness בדברי הגוף, now gives a like caution even with regard to דברי תורה. What is required is that a man should act up to his knowledge, as it is said, נאה דורש ונאה מקיים (= No. 90, 15 a₂). The prophet says, איכה תאמרו חכמים אנחנו כו' (= 15 a₁₁). And Sh. ben Chalaftha says that he who has learned Thorah, and does not practise it, is more severely punished than אותו שלא למד כל עיקר (= 15 b₁₄). A parable of a king who had a garden, and put two gardeners into it : one of them planted trees ; the other did not, &c. (= 15 b₁₅). But Doctrine is prior to Practice, . . . שהתלמוד מביא לידי מעשה (= 16 a₇). R. Jonah says that וכל המרבה דברים כו' refers to דברי תורה (= 17 b₉) ; and " R. Israel " approves of this interpretation, which is in accordance with the saying (= 18 a₁) :

לעולם ישנה אדם לתלמידיו דרך קצרה.

C.

R. Israel's note on II. 1 (רבי אומר כו') is interesting for several reasons. After giving an account of Rabbi, the son of the R. Shim‘eon אלדי כתם בה אל פרק אל מתקדם (21b₃), he states (1) the usual interpretation of איזו היא דרך ישרה כו', and (2) the view of Rambam*(?) viz. that it is the *via media*, אל אפֿעאל אל מתואססטה, with the remark (22 a₁₂) that, " by my life " they are charming renderings, only the words will not bear the senses put upon them. He quotes R. Jonah, whose interpretation is characterised as inconsistent and unintelligible (22 b₂) ; and then, referring

---

* See above, § 3. (3).

to the use which is made of this Mishnah in Nedarim * 22 b, he concludes
as follows (22 b₇—2 ३ a₄) :

מכאן ראיה שאין פירוש המשנה הזו וגרסנה (sic) כדברי המפרש הזה "

בל שהיא תפארת לעושיהו תפארת לו מן האדם "
פֿאניירו אל קראיון אל נירסא ונקלו אל ואו מן לעושיהו ונצֿמוהא אלא תפארת
פֿי ינחצֿם אל מענא באן יכון לעושיהו כנאיה לאלאה תעׄ ואל ואו צֿמיר האדם
והוא עבראני פֿציח אם מעושיהו יטהר נבר תֿם זאד שרחאׄ וקאל תפארת לו
מן האדם וצֿמיר לו עאייד לעושיהו אל מדכור יריד אן האדם הבורא גורם
לעושיהו התפארת עלא סביל ואמר לי עבדי אתה ישראל אשר בך אתפאר ולם
תסאמח אל כטאבה אכתר ממא כהאדה אן יכון אל כאלק גל גלאלהו יפתבׄר
באל מבלוק פֿי יכון חאצֿל האדאל קול עלא האדאל תאויל עבס‡ מא קצֿדוה אל
מפֿסרון יעני אן לא יקתצר אל אנסאן פֿי אפֿעאלהׄ עלא מא יכון בה מחמודאׄ
ענד אל נאס פֿקט אלא ובמא יכון מחמודאׄ ענד רבהו [רבהי] פֿי יכון עמלהו
כאלץ ואין שית קולת אן צֿמיר תפארת לו לאל אנסאן פֿיקול אן כל דרך
שהיא תפארת לעושיהו פֿאל נאס יחמדוה עליהא ותצֿ לו תפארת מן האדם
הבא "   וראית פֿי נסכֿה קדימה לרׄ שלמה בן חרמת שליח ציבור יזעם
אנהא ירושלמית תפארת מן האדם בחרף אל ואו והאדה מא אידני עלא
האדא אל תאויל והאכדא אלפֿינֿתהו פֿי גרסת רבי יצחק בן גיאת ז"ל
ולאסתחתם באנהא צחיחה ולא קנעת בהא אלא אנהא אליק וגֿהא אנכשפֿ לי
פֿיה אלא האדאל גאיה ומן שא פֿידוק אל מדאהב ויתכֿיר מא יואפֿקהו כי
אוז מילין תבחן וחיך אוכל יטעם לו :

Here again R. Isaac borrows freely, partly with and partly without
acknowledgement, from our author.

---

* The MS. has פׄ׳ ד׳ נדרים, that is to say, Pereq III, which commences with the words,
ארבעה נדרים.

† That is وغَيرُوا (فغَيرُوا). The א may be supposed to stand for a vowel, as in מעא (for مَعَ)
in the penultimate line of p. 48. In lines 4, 9 and 11—but not in lines 12 and 18—of the
above extract ف is written פֿ and detached from its following verb. On the other hand
האדה אל is several times, but not invariably, written as a single word. In lines 5 and 10
א... stands for "א..., with tenwin. In line 12 for כאלץ read "כאלצא.

‡ The word wanted in place of עבס is عكس, corresponding to which ॐ (25 a₈) has,
הפך כוונת המפשרים ז"ל.

§ For ולאסתחתם we should perhaps read ולאם אחתם, that is ولم أَحتِم.

First he sums up in eleven lines (ℬ 24 b₂—24 b₁₂) all the points in R. Israel's account in twenty-six lines (No. 90, 21 b₁—22 ᵃ₆) of Rabbi and his compilation of the Mishnah.

Next he gives the usual interpretation, and also cites Rambam for the opinion that :

דרך ישרה היא המדות הממוצעות כו'.

Then comes a long citation (ℬ 24 b₁₇—25 a₁₆) in the name of R. Israel, corresponding to the passage No. 90, 22 ᵃ₆—23 a₄, to the following effect :

The received interpretations, however plausible in themselves, do not suit the expressions used, (1) because when תפארת comes to anyone it is of course from others and not from himself, so that it is superfluous to add מן האדם, and (2) because עישה does not correspond to דרך but מצוה, the expression wanted being הלך. R. Jonah's interpretation is stated and criticised. The writer then suggests the reading תפארת לעושיהו, and the remainder of the citation is a somewhat abbreviated rendering of the passage given above from No. 90, ending with the words,

כי אוזן מילין תבחן וחך יטעם לאבול ע"כ.

It should be noticed that the reading תפארת לעושה of the copy described above as probably JERUSHALMITH is found also in the Cambridge University manuscript Addit. 470. 1 (fol. 144 b₃) of the Mishnah, from which the text of ABOTH referred to in this *Catalogue* is taken*.

R. Isaac, on the contrary, remarks (ℬ 25 a₁₆) : "but I myself have two corrected and pointed copies of the six Sedarim of the Mishnah which were written in Jerusalem the Holy City, and it is written in them תפארת לעושה ותפארת as it is written in all the books of ספרד and צרפת."

The specimens which we have given shew that the commentary in this manuscript tallies with that of R. ISRAEL as described in the passage cited on p. 3, in which R. Isaac remarks that he has culled his own from the "great and wide sea" of R. Israel's commentary in Arabic upon the Masseketh.

5. Readings of passages in Aboth.

Amongst the readings of R. ISRAEL, including some which have been already noticed, are the following :

I. 9, בעלי הדין (3 b₁₇).

II. 1, תפארת (*sic*) תפארת לעושיהו (22 b₉), conjecturally.

II. 5, דבר שאפשר לשמוע (32 a₄). The scribe has crossed out שאפשר and written over it שאי אפשר לו, but it is clear from the commentary

---

* This manuscript was cited as 𝔄 in the *Critical Notes*, and it has since been edited (1883) by the Rev. W. H. Lowe for the Syndics of the Cambridge University Press, under the name of "The Mishnah on which the Palestinian Talmud rests."

(32 b$_6$) that R. Israel approves the former reading, which he attributes to
R. Shemuel.

II. 7, על דאטפת אטפוך (36 a$_{18}$).

II. 8. He places the clause מרבה עבדים כו' (39 a$_{19}$) before מרבה
מרבה ישיבה מרבה חכמה (39 b$_{16}$), and reads שפחות כו'.

II. 15, עין רעה (53 b$_{11}$), although the scribe has written עין הרע.

II. 16, התקן, without ו (56 a$_7$).

III. 9, חמשה שנא' ואגודתו כו' (74 a$_{19}$), with the remark :

וישרח אגודה בחסב האדאל גירסא קבצת אל יד.

III. 24, לפי רוב המעשה (93 a$_{18}$)

IV. 14, הוי ממעט בעסק (119 a$_{19}$).

IV. 17, ככבוד חבירך (122 a$_{14}$).

IV. 23, פרוסדור (126 a$_6$). It is clear from the commentary that this is
R. Israel's reading, although the scribe has here again gone astray and
written

פרוזדור (sic) יקרא באל סין ולאליין.

v. 8, שאלין בירושלים (147 a$_{10}$). This reading is given as Rashi's.

As regards the ending of ABOTH according to this commentary, after
אביך שבשמים (v. 30) comes (179 b$_{13}$) :

הוא היה אומר עז כנים וגו'. רבי אליעור אומר עז פנים ממזר ..... סוף אדם
למות וכו'.

The writer then adds (179 b$_{18}$) :

ופי פרקי אבות יתלו האדה ר' יהודה אומר אשרי מי שעמלו בתורה יגדיל
תורה ויאדיר " שמואל הקטן קד כתבתהו פי כרק בן זומא " יהי רצון מלפניך
במהרה בימינו ...

But after commenting upon ובועת פנים לגן עדן and יהי רצון וגו', he
remarks (180 b$_{19}$) :

הונא תמת אל משנה " לאבן אפתן אל נאם אן יוצלון בהא מא ליס מן אל
מסכתא ולא היא משנה ואנכא היא ברייתא פי מסכת חלה וצ"ל כלה[והאדה
נצהא תניא רבי נתן אומר עז פנים לנהינם עז פנים " רבי אליעזר אומר
ממזר ...

The saying בן חמש שנים כו' is added, but with the remark that it is
not מן אל מסכתא (181 b$_{15}$), and it is followed by the sayings of בן בג בג
(183 b$_{13}$) and בן הא הא (184 a$_2$).

6. R. Israel's citations from R. Shemuel.

R. Israel's citations from R. Shemuel have to be taken into account
in connexion with the controversy as to the authorship of the commentary

in No. 20, which we have seen reason to ascribe to R. Jacob ben Shimshon (p. 23). R. Shemuel is cited on the following passages:

A.

(I. 12) אבטליון אומר הכמים הזהרו בדבריכם כו'.

ורבי שמואל ז"ל פ֗סר פ֗יה שלא תקלו בדברי תורה ואפילו אתם עכשו עומדים במקום בני תורה" שֶׁמָּא תחובו חובת גלות ותגלו למקום עמי הארץ [וייסיפו] להקל בדברי תורה וימותו ונמצא שם שמים מתחלל שאומרים אוי לו לפלוני שלמד תורה ראו מה אירע לו וזהו שמצינו רב בקעה (כי רב היה גודר גדרות למצות במקום עמי הארץ שהבקעה היא מ֗של למקום עמי הארץ והיה רב גודר להם גדרות וזהו בקעה) מצא וגדר בה גדר.

In this extract from No. 90, 7 b_9 the word וייסיפו has to be supplied, whilst on the other hand the words from כי רב to בקעה are evidently a gloss. The passage is found also in B 16 a_{16} in the name of Rashbam, and it is slightly abbreviated from a passage in No. 20, 98 a_9, where the writer introduces it as his own, viz. with the words וַאֲנִי אֹו'.

B.

(I. 15) הוא היה אומר אם אין אני לי מי לי כו'.

וכדאלך פ֗סר רבינו שמואל ז"ל אם אין אני לי מי לי אן לם אעמל פ֗י האדאל דונייא מא ינפֿעני פ֗י אל אכ֗ירה פ֗מן יכון מן יעינני פ֗י אל אכ֗ירה.

See No. 90, 11 b_{10}. This gives the general sense of the interpretation adopted in No. 20, 99 a_{18} (מפורש בברייתׁ כו') from the Aboth of R. Nathan, cap. XII. In this case B 19 a has no reference to Rashbam, which is explained by the fact that the commentary in No. 20 here gives a traditional interpretation only and not one which the writer claims as his own.

C.

(II. 5) ואל תאמר דבר ש(אי) אפשר לשמוע כו'.

ואל אליק ענדי גירסת רבינו שמואל ז"ל ותפסירהו ואל תאמר דבר שאי איפשר וצ"ל שאיפשר] לשמוע שסופו להשמע יקול אדא אמכנך אן תסמע דברי תורה ויכון מעך מהלא' לסמעהא לא תקול האדא לם יפותני וקד ימכננו סמעה פ֗י וקת אכ֗ור פֿאינך ליס תדרי מא יחדם * ולעל יעוקך עאיקין סמעה פ֗י וקת מתא טלבת דאלך.

---

* That is وَاَكَدَث . In the same line אכ֗ור is written for اَخَر, and יעוקך should be followed by the preposition عن before סמעה. The reader will detect further minor inaccuracies which we need not here specify in the extracts from No. 90.

See No. 90, $32\,b_6$ and $33\,a_1$. The passage is cited as Rashbam's in
ẞ $30\,a_{20}$, and corresponds to No. 20, $105\,b_7$, where the form of expression

ואל תאמר שאי איפשר לשמוע, אם אינך טרוד ועסוק במלאכה ואיפשר לך
לשמוע דבר תורה עכשיו כו'

is such as would almost certainly mislead an unwary scribe accustomed to
the usual reading.

D.

(II. 13) **אחד לווה מן האדם כלווה מן המקום כו'.**

ורבינו שמואל ז"ל פסר פי כאלו לוה מן המקום פאן אל מלוה ענד מא יסלף
מאלה לאל לוה פאנהו אמן באל תאלת אלדי חצר בינהם והו אל אללהו תע'
אלדי אוצאה וקאל אם כסף תלוה את עמי את העני עמך.

See No. 90, $46\,b_2$ and No. 20, $107\,b_{18}$, where the passage is introduced
with the words **ואני כך קיבלתי.** It is cited as Rashbam's own, with the
same prefatory words, in ẞ $38\,a_8$.

E.

(II. 14) **הם אמרו שלשה שלשה* דברים כו'.**

(a) פרבי שמואל יחסב יהי כבוד חבירך חביב עליך כשלך מע' ואל תהי
נח לכעוס קוולא' ואחדא' לאן אחדהומא סבבא' לאל אכׄר.

This is found in No. 90, $53\,b_4$ and No. 20, $108\,a_5$, and it is given in
ẞ $39\,a_{12}$ and $39\,b_{19}$ in the name of Rashbam.

(β) **שנשיכתן** נשיכת נחש ר' שמעון ור' שמואל ע̇א̇ם יכרו שנשיכתן
נשיכת שועל פאן אסנאן אל תעלב דקה והיא מעוׄגה.

This is found in No. 90, $53\,a_8$ and No. 20, $108\,a_{15}$, and is given as Rashbam's by R. Isaac, according to the carefully written copy No. 1 ($41\,b_{17}$).
thus:

ורש"י ורש"ב"ם† ז"ל גורסי' נשיכת שועל.

F.

(II. 15) **עין רעה ויצר הרע ושנאת הבריות כו'.**

ורבינו שמואל ז"ל פסר פי ושנאת הבריות אן יבגצׄוה אל נאס לקבח אפעאלה
פי ידמוה ויסבוה חתא תנפׄד פיה לענתהם.

See No 90, $55\,b_{18}$; ẞ $41\,b_5$; No. 20, $108\,a_{25}$.

---

* This is the reading of No. 20 (107 b).

† Here ẞ ($40\,b_7$) reads רשב"נ for רשב"ם, by a clerical error

G.

(II. 17) ‏ואל תהי רשע בפני עצמך.‏

‏ורבינו שמואל ז"ל פסר פיה לא תנפרד עז מואדת אל נאם ותנקבץ עז‏
‏מצאחבתהם פתציר עומד בפני עצמך חדל אישים כאילו עצמך יחיד בעולם.‏

See No. 90, 62 b$_{13}$; B 44 a$_{14}$; No. 20, 109 a$_8$. This passage is introduced in
No. 20 with the words ‏ולי נראה‏ ‏כך קיבלתי‏. Two lines later comes a
reference to ‏ר"ת‏, doubtless inserted by R. Isaac ben Dorbelo.

In all of these cases except B the interpretation cited by R. Israel in
the name of ‏ר' שמואל‏ is cited by R. Isaac in the name of Rashbam.
R. Isaac's citations are the more literally exact, and he has many more
than are to be found in No. 90. The commentary which they cite apparently agreeing with R. Jacob ben Shimshon's (No. 20), how are we to
account for the fact that they cite it as Rashbam's? We shall return to
this question in the section on the Cambridge University manuscript,
Additional 1213.

פרקי אבות

CAMBRIDGE MANUSCRIPTS.

Nos. 91—115.

I. Commentaries with or without the text

Name	Number
Anonymous	104, 114
Jacob ben Shimshon	99, 101, 108, 111
Maimonides (Arabic)	94
,, (Hebrew) . . .	99
Isaac Israeli	115
Joseph Ja'betz	102
מגן אלהים	106
פרח שושן	91

II. The text alone

Nos. 92, 93, 95—98, 100, 103, 105, 107, 109, 110, 112, 113.

For a general account of the Cambridge University codices from No. 91 onwards, here described in so far as they relate to אבות, see the unpublished part of Dr Schiller-Szinessy's *Catalogue*, which at present exists only in manuscript.

No. 91.

CAMBRIDGE UNIVERSITY, Dd. 5. 63.

A manuscript of 226 folios, of size $7 \times 5\frac{7}{8}$ inches, containing (fol. 221 a)

פרח שושן.

This consists of the six Peraqim, unpointed, commencing at folios 2 a, 40 a, 102 b, 140 b, 167 a, 212 a, respectively, with a discursive commentary in two parts, the one על דרך הפשט, the other (cabbalistic) ע׳ד הסוד or, as it is styled from fol. 105 a onward, ע״ד האמת.

It is written in African Rabbinic, except the initial words, which are in square character.

It was composed in the year עשה (= 1615 A.D.), at אקא (fol. 221 a), which is in תארודנת (Tarudant), a province of Morocco, by

יעקב הצורף בכ״מ יצחק המכונה פרנאן ממדינת תארודנת,

and transcribed two years later for R. Jacob bar Isaac ibn Abraham ha-Kohen (226 a).

No. 92.

CAMBRIDGE UNIVERSITY, Dd. 13. 7.

A manuscript of 166 leaves folio, containing an Ashkenazic Siddur in a Franco-Ashkenazic hand, in two volumes bound in one.

At the end of the first volume (fol. 36 b) the scribe, ישראל בר׳ משה זצ״ל, states that he completed it in the year 5147 A.M. (= 1387 A.D.).

It contains a good text of the six Peraqim, pointed (fol. 20 a—25 b), which has remarkable coincidences with the text of Aboth in the Cambridge MS. of the Mishnah, No. 98 in this Catalogue, and is on the whole a very good one, but has been much tampered with by a later hand.

Readings *prima manu*:

Pereq I. 3, על מנת שלא. 7, ומתאי. 8, מתאי. תחבר for תתחבר. 9, בעלי הדין. כזכאין probably, but the original reading has been erased and replaced by כצדיקים. אֶת הַדִּין* פְּשֶׁיִּקְבְּלוּ* (*sic*), with *עליהם added in the margin. 12, הבאי׳ אחריהם.

Pereq ɪɪ. 1, תפארת לְעוֹשָׂהָ תפארת. 17, ובתפלה is omitted in the text.

... בעדת אל מניין שאפי, 9. שאכלו, 5 and 6, מליחה סרוחה .Pereq ɪɪɪ. 1, שלשה שנ' ואגודתו, the clause on the number *five* being omitted, *prima manu.* 14, this mishnah omitted by error, but afterwards inserted by the original scribe. 22 and 23, חיבה יתירה כו' is omitted in the text.

Pereq ɪv. 9, לאכול מהם. 13, (?) אומ' ר' יהונתן. 14, מעט עסק is doubtless the original reading of the manuscript, but it has been altered into דומה לְפָרוֹסדּוֹד. 23, ולא ראש. 22, מְשַׁלֶוַת רשעים. 21, יש לו. ממעט בעסק והתקן עצמך בפרוסדוד. In both cases the ס has been roughly altered into ז. 24, בעולם הבא. בעולם הזה (?) לחיי העולם הבא. של קורת רוח לעולם הבא 29, אפילו without שֶ. 32, מנום without לך.

Pereq v. 8, שֶׁאֱלִין. 9, בין השמשות without בערב שבת. 10, the text omits ובמנין. ומשיב בעניין. 17, יצא הפסדו בשכרו is written of the נח, *prima manu.* 18, מָהַר. 32,

הֲפֹוֹךְ בָּהּ וַהֲפֵךְ בָּהּ דְּכָוֹּלָהּ בָּהּ **וכולך בה** וּבָהּ תֶּחֱזֵי כו'

the words וכולך בה being unpointed and marked for omission. 33, after אגרא ... comes the saying of Shemuel ha-Qatan בנפול אויבך כו', and the section concludes with the saying on the AGES, which is here attributed to him.

No. 93.

CAMBRIDGE UNIVERSITY, Dd. 15. 5.

A small Sepharadic* Prayer-Book in Rabbinic character, with the six Peraqim (fol. 229 a—266 b), pointed to the end of fol. 264.

No. 94.

CAMBRIDGE UNIVERSITY, Additional 271 (3).

Some loose tattered leaves of paper containing fragments of Rambam's commentary on ABOTH up to the third Pereq inclusive, in the original Arabic, written in or near Damascus.

The writing is of the 14th century, and resembles that of the codex Ff. 2. 7.

---

* Popularly written Sephardic. But cf. סְפָרָד in Obadiah 20, and ספרדי, which must be read *Sepharadi*, in the couplet at the commencement of the Haqdamah to Ibn Ezra's יסוד מורא.

No. 95.

CAMBRIDGE UNIVERSITY, Additional 375.

A thick manuscript on vellum, of medium quarto size, 13th century, square character, Ashkenazic hand, the folios as yet not numbered.

It contains the "order of the prayers of the whole year, according to the custom of the Jews of Rome and other towns of Italy."

Just beyond the middle of the manuscript, between פסח and שבועות, is a pointed text of the six Peraqim.

At the end of פסח is a note on the observance, by some persons, of the days between Passover and Pentecost as the days in which the disciples of R. Aqiba died and as days when the wicked are judged in Gehinnom, concluding with the saying,

ואל ישנה אדם מנהג מקומו להקל.

Then follows the remark on the recital of ABOTH,

וכן נהגו בין פסח לעצרת בכל שבת ושבת לשנות מסכת אבות תכף לתפילת
המנחה,

which is repeated, with a trifling variation, on the next page, on which מסכת אבות commences.

Readings:

Pereq I. 3, על מנת שלא. 4 and 5, יוסף, with marks (as elsewhere in the MS.) to indicate that it is the name of the scribe. 8, ואל תהי חבר. 12, הבאים אחריהם, *prima manu*. 14, יֵאָסֵף.

Pereq II. 2, מעלה אני. 6, הַבּוֹיִישָׁן. 9, מְהֻלָּל. תורתך. 14, by the addition of שלשה in the margin the reading is corrected into, הם אמרו בעל בריתך. תורה מה שתשיב. 18, שלשה שלשה דברים.

Pereq III. 9, ר' חֲלַפְתָּא כו'. The proof for לחמשה is שנ' בקרב כו', and the phrase שיושבין כו' is repeated after the several numbers. 12, כל השוכח בתי. בן אַרְפִּינָס. 15, הַבְּרִיוֹת. 16, דבר אחד מתלמודו חייב מיתה omitted. 20, מָסורוֹת. 24, לפי רוב המעשה אבל לא על פי המעשה. 25, וְגִימַטְרָיָא פַּרְפְּרָיוֹת. נופי הלכות. חֲסָמָא. 28, ומצודה.

Pereq ɪv. 19, ‏וכתר שם טוב על גביהן‎ 29, ‏בָּקַנְקַן‎. ‏קַנְקַן‎.

Pereq v. 13, ‏הַשְׁמַטַּת‎. 14, ‏בכל שנה ושנה‎ 17, ‏בַּלְמֵדִים‎. 27, ‏דברים‎
‏דברים רעים הַלָּלוּ‎. ‏טובים הַלָּלוּ‎.

Ending:

After ‏בתורתך‎ (v. 30) come the saying of Shemuel ha-Qatan, the AGES
(in his name), ben Bag Bag (with the reading, ‏...),‎ ‏והפך בה סַמָּא דָבוֹלָא בָהּ‎
and the saying of ben He-he.

At the end of Pereq v. is written,

‏סליק פירקי מסכת אבות.‎

and at the end of "Pereq R. Meir,"

‏סליק להו מסכת אבות‎
‏שבח לדר בערבות.‎

No. 96.

CAMBRIDGE UNIVERSITY, Additional 437.

An illuminated copy of the ‏תפלות‎ for the whole year, according to the
Italian rite, on 332 leaves of vellum, of which the three from 18 to 20 are
missing: "a most beautiful specimen of a pocket prayer book", and in good
preservation.

It was written by Isaac Zaraq for his children (fol. 3 a), and finished at
Ferrara in the year 1456 A.D. (fol. 332 a).

The six Peraqim, pointed, extend from fol. 189 b to 214 b.

This text supports several of the better readings. Notice in ɪ. 19,
‏קַיָּם‎ for ‏עומד‎; in v. 8, the composite reading ‏כִּשְׁאָלִין‎; and the spelling
‏בֶּן הָיְהֵי‎ in v. 32.

No. 97.

CAMBRIDGE UNIVERSITY, Additional 438.

A small thick volume containing a very old copy of the ‏תפלות‎ according to the Sepharadic rite.

In the latter half of the MS., the folios of which are not numbered, there
is a pointed text of Aboth, in six Peraqim, followed by Pereq R. Meir,
making in all **Seven Peraqim**, as in Nos. 10 and 83.

No. 98.

CAMBRIDGE UNIVERSITY, Additional 470. 1.

A manuscript on 250 leaves of paper, folio, $11\frac{5}{8} \times 8\frac{5}{8}$ inches, in Rabbinic character, Greek Sepharadic handwriting of the 14th century.

It contains the whole MISHNAH according to the recension of the Palestinian Talmud.

It is described in the unpublished part of Schiller-Szinessy's *Catalogue*, where it is numbered 73, and stands at the commencement of the section on TALMUDIC LITERATURE, to which the second volume is devoted.

It has since been edited by the Rev. W. H. Lowe, M.A., Hebrew Lecturer at Christ's College (Cambridge, 1883), under the title,

מתניתא דתלמודא דבני מערבא "

or in English,

"The Mishnah on which the Palestinian Talmud rests, edited for the Syndics of the University Press, from the unique manuscript preserved in the University Library of Cambridge, Add. 470. 1."

We have given below (1) a comparative index of the Mishnah, (2) specimen pages fol. 1 a and fol. 249 a and a page of shorter extracts *, and (3) the complete text of Aboth according to our manuscript.

The scribe's name seems to have been צדיק, צדקיה, or some other commencing with צ, as the lines are frequently filled up with that letter. See fol. 1 a line 20 and fol. 249 a line 24. Dr Schiller-Szinessy continues:

"The hand is a very distinct one and full of character. To judge from the nature of some of the mistakes to be met with here, the scribe must have been a faithful copyist, albeit not a very intelligent one. He apparently copied right and wrong with equal zeal; and in the *pointed* words, which frequently occur in the Mishnah, he has occasionally impossibilities of pronunciation. But these facts, so far from detracting from the value of this MS., are in our estimation an absolute advantage to it, providing it as they do with the guarantee that our scribe merely copied what was before him, but invented nothing that was his own. Of course, some deviations from the ordinary text in the shape of misspellings or omissions may be his; but consistently different wordings, or even spellings, cannot be his, but must be older. The same we must particularly assume to be the case with respect to the consistent forms of names of certain Mishnah-teachers, as also to the division of each Pereq into Halakhoth, which here frequently and widely differs from that of all three principal recensions, and lastly and above all, to the various readings headed נ״א, i.e. נסחא אחריתא."

COMPARATIVE INDEX OF THE MISHNAH,

shewing the title of each מסכת and the number of its פרקים according to the Cambridge University MS. *Additional* 470, and its positions in that MS. and in the edition of Surenhuis (1698—1703) respectively.

סדר זרעים

Sur. I.	p. in MS.	פרקים	מסכת	Sur. I.	p. in MS.	פרקים	מסכת
263	22 a	5	מעשר שיני	1	1 a	9	ברכות
245	25 b	5	מעשר ראשון	37	3 b	8	פיאה
289	27 b	4	חלה	76	7 a	7	דמיי
306	29 a	3	ערלה	109	9 a	9	כלאים
320	30 b	3	ביכורים	155	13 a	10	שביעית
				200	17 b	11	תרומות

סדר מועד

Sur. II.	p. in MS.	פרקים	מסכת	Sur. II.	p. in MS.	פרקים	מסכת
282	58 b	5	ביצה	1	32 b	24	שבת
300	60 b	4	ראש השנה	78	39 b	10	עירובין
355	62 b	4	תעניות	134	44 b	10	פסח
387	65 a	4	מגילה	206	49 a	8	כיפורים
413	67 a	3	חגיגה	176	52 b	8	שקלים
403	68 a	3	משקין	259	56 a	5	סוכה

סדר נשים

Sur. III.	p. in MS.	פרקים	מסכת	Sur. III.	p. in MS.	פרקים	מסכת
322	94 a	9	גיטין	1	69 a	16	נשים
359	98 b	7	קידושין	56	77 b	13	כתובות
178	100 b	9	סוטא	104	84 b	11	נדרים
				146	90 a	9	נזיר

סדר נזיקים

Sur. iv.	p. in MS.	פרקים	מסכת	Sur. iv.	p. in MS.	פרקים	מסכת
292	131 *b*	8	שבועות	1	106 *a*		נזיקין ⎧
322	136 *a*	8	עדיות	107	111 *a*	30	(באבא תינינא) ⎨
364	140 *b*	5	עבודה זרה	157	117 *a*		(באבא בתרא) ⎩
409	143 *b*	5	אבות	207	123 *a*	11	סנהדרין
492	148 *a*	3	הוריות	269	129 *a*	3	מכות

סדר קדשים

Sur. v.	p. in MS.	פרקים	מסכת	Sur. v.	p. in MS.	פרקים	מסכת
236	179 *a*	6	כריתות	7	149 *b*	14	זבחים
266	182 *b*	6	מעילה	65	156 *a*	13	מנחות
323	185 *a*	5	מידות	114	163 *a*	12	שחיטת חולין
284	188 *a*	6	תמיד	155	168 *a*	9	בכורות
383	191 *a*	3	קנים	192	173 *a*	9	ערכים
				218	176 *b*	7	תמורה

סדר טהרות

Sur. vi.	p. in MS.	פרקים	מסכת	Sur. vi.	p. in MS.	פרקים	מסכת
389	236 *b*	10	נדה	15	192 *a*	30	כלים
427	240 *b*	6	מכשירים	146	206 *a*	18	אהלות
450	243 *b*	5	זבים	213	214 *b*	14	נגעים
469	245 *b*	4	טבול יום	269	221 *b*	12	פרה
480	247 *a*	4	ידים	313	227 *a*	10	טהרות
492	249 *a*	3	עקצין	356	232 *a*	10	מקוות

Annexed are specimens from the above-mentioned MS. *Additional* 470.

איהן   איהן

מאמתי קורין את שמע בערבים משעה שהכהנים נכנסים לאכל בתרומתן עד

I a

סוף האשמורת הראשונה דברי ר׳ אליעזר וחכמים אומרים עד חצות רבן

ב מעשה שבאו בניו מבית המשתה   גמליאל אומר עד שיעלה עמוד השחר

אמרו לו לא קרינו את שמע אמר להם   אם לא עלה עמוד השחר חייבין

ג ולא זו בלבד אלא כל שאמרו חכמים עד חצות מצותן   אתם לקרות ״

עד שיעלה <u>עמוד השחר הקטר חלבים ואיברים ואכילת</u>

פסחים מצותן עד שיעלה עמוד השחר׳ כל הנאכלים ליום אחד מצותן עד שיעלה

עמוד׳ אם כן למה אמרו חכמים עד חצות אלא להרחיק את האדם מן העבירה

ב מאמתי קורין את שמע בשחרים משיכירו בין תכלת ללבן ר׳ אליעזר אומר

בין תכלת לכרתן עד הנץ החמה ר׳ יושע אומר עד שלש שעות שכן דרך

בני מלכים לעמוד בשלש שעות הקורא מיכן ואילך לא הפסיד כאדם שהוא קורא

ה בית שמאי אומרי׳ בערב כל אדם יטו ויקרו ובבוקר יעמדו שנ׳   בתורה ״

ובקומך בית הלל אומרי׳ כל אד(ם) ק(ו)רין כדרכן שנ׳   בשכבך

בדרך אם כן למה נאמר בשכבך ובקומך אלא בשעה (שד)רך בני אדם שוכבין ובשעה

ו אמר ר׳ טרפון אנ(י) הייתי בא בדרך והטיתי   שדרך בני אדם עומדין ״

לקרות כדברי בית שמיי   וסכנתי עצמי מ(פני) הלסטין אמרו כדיי הייתה

ז בשחר מברך שתים לפניה   לחוב בעצמך שעברת על דברי בית הלל ״

ואחת לאחריה בערב מברך שתים לפניה   ואחת לאחריה בערב מברך

שתים לפניה ושתים לאחריה אחת ארוכה ואחת קצ(רה) מקום שאמרו להאריך אינו

לקצר

ג רשאי לקצר אינו רשאי להאריך לחתום אינו רשאי (של)א לחתום שלא לחתום אינו צ

ח מזכירין יציאת מצרים (בלי)לות אמר ר׳ לע(ז)ר בן עזריה   רשאי לחתום ״

הרי אני כבן   שבעים שנה לא זכיתי (שת)אמר יציאת מצרים בלילות עד

שדרשה בן זומא שנ׳ למען תזכור את יום צאתך מ(אר)ץ מצרים כל ימי חייך ימי חייך

הימים כל ימי חייך הלילות וחכמים אומרי׳ ימי ח(יי)ך בעולם הזה כל ימי חייך להביא

הל ח (פרק) **ב** היה קורא בתורה   את ימות המשיח ״

והגיע זמן המקרא   אם כיון אל לבו יצא

ואם לאו לא יצא ובפרקים שואל מפני הכבוד ו(משיב) ובאמצע שואל מפני היראה ומשיב

דברי ר׳ מאיר ר׳ יודה אומר באמצע שואל מ(פני) הי(ר)אה ומשיב מפני הכבוד ובפרקין

ב אילו הן בין הפרקים בין ברכה   שואל מפני הכבוד ומשיב שלום כל האדם

ג ראשונה לשנייה ובין שנייה לשמע ובין שמע   לוהיה אם שמוע ובין והיה אם שמוע

149ᵃ

מטמין את הידים ספרי המירם אינן מטמאין את הידים אמ' רבן יוחנן בן זכיי וכי
אין לנו על הפרושין אלא זו בלבד והרי הן אומ' עצמות חמור טהורים ועצמות יוחנן
כהן גדול טמאים אמרו לו לפי חיבתן היא טומאתן שלא יעשה אדם עצמות אביו ואמו
תרוודות אמר להן אף כתבי הקדש לפי חיבתן היא טומאתן שלא יעשה אדם סיפרי
המירם שאינן חביבין אינן מטמאין את הידים " מֶ‍ה ‏ אומרין צדוקין קובלין אנו
עליכם פרושים שאתם מטהרין את הנצוק   אומרין פרושים קובלין אנו
עליכם צדוקין שאתם מטהרין את אמת המים הבאה בין הקברות אומרין צדוקין
קובלים אנו עליכם פרושים שאתם אומרי' מה אם שורי וחמורי שאיני חייב בהן מצות
הרי אני חייב בנזקן עבדי ואמתי שאיני חייב בהן מצות אינו דין שאהא חייב בנזקן
יאמרו להן לא אם אמרתם בשורי ובחמורי שאין בהן דעת תאמרו בעבדי ובאמתי
שיש בהן דעת שאם אקניטנו ילך וידליק גדישו של אחד ואהי חייב לשלם "   זֹן ‏ אמר
מין גלילי קובל אני עליכם פרושין שאתם כותבין את המושל עם משה בגט אומרי'   פרושין
קובלים אנו עליך מין גלילי שאתם כותבין את המושל עם היםב בדף ולא עוד אלא
שאתם כותבין את המושל מלמעלן ואת היםב מלמטן שנ' ויאמר פרעה מי יֹן אשר אישמע
בקולו לשלח את ישראל וכישלקה מה הוא אומ' יֹן הצדיק ופרעה ועמו הרשעים "   הל‍ז זֹ

מסכת עקצין   תפילה מסכתא "

פרק ראשון   כל שהוא יד ולא שומר מיטמא ומטמא ולא מצטרף שומר אף על
פי שאינו יד מיטמא ומטמא ומצטרף לא שומר ולא יֹ)ד לא מיטמא
ולא מטמא "   בֹ ‏ אלו מיטמין ומטמין ולא מצטרפין שורשי השום והבצלים והקלופות
בזמן שהן   לחים והפיטמה שלהם בין לחה בין יבישה העמוד שהוא מכוון כנגד
האוכל שורשי החזירין והצנון והנטם דברי ר' מאיר ר' יהודה אום' שורש צנון גדול
מצטרף והסיב שלו אין מצטרף שורשי המינתה והפוגם ירקות שדה וירקות גנה שעקרן
לשתלין והשיזרה של שבולת והלבינין שלה ר' לעזר אום' אף הסוג של רצפית הרי אלו מיטמין
ומטמין ולא מצטרפין "   גֹ ‏ אילו מיטמין ומטמין ומצטרפין שורשי השום והבצלין צ
והקפלוטות בזמן שהן   יבשין והעמוד שאינו מכוון כנגד האוכל יד הפרכיר טפח
מיכן וטפח מיכן יד האשכול כל שהוא וזנב של אשכול שריקנה ויד מכבר של תמרה
ארבעה טפחים וקנה של שבולת שלשה טפחים ויד כל הנקצרין שלשה דרכן להקצר
ידיהן ושורשיהן כל שהן ומלעין של שהן הרי אלו מיטמין ומטמין ולא מצטרפין "
דֹ ‏ אילו לא מיטמאין ולא מטמאין ולא מצטרפין שורשי קולסי אכרוב וחליפות תמרין
ל   והלפת את שדרכן להגזז ונעקרו ר' יוסי מטמא בכולם ומטהר בשורשו קולסי אכרוב

פסח   פרק עשירי   הלכה ד'

43 b   רבן גמליאל אומר כל שלא אמר שלשה דברים אלו בפסח לא יצא ידי חובתו
פסח מצה ומרורים פסח על שם שפסח המקום על בתי אבותינו במצרים מרורים על
שם שמררו המצרים את חיי אבותינו במצרים מצה על שם שנגאלו לפיכך אנו חייבין
להודות להלל לשבח לפאר לרומם לגדל לנצח למי שעשה לנו את כל הנסים האלו
והוציאנו מעבדות לחירות ונאמר לפניו הללויה "

סוכה   פרק רביעי   הלכה ד'

57 b   מצות ערבה כיצד מקום היה למטה מירושלם נקרא מוצא יורדין לשם ומלקטין
משם מורביות של ערבה ובאים וזוקפים אתם לצדדי המזבח וראשיהם כפופים על
גבי המזבח תקעו והריעו ותקעו בכל יום מקיפין את המזבח פעם אחת ואומרים
אנא יי' הושיעה נא אנא יי' הושיעה נא ר' יודה אום' אני והוא והושיעה נא אני
והוא והושיעה נא אותו היום מקיפין את המזבח שבע פעמים "

ביצה   פרק ראשון   הלכה ב'

58 b   *בהמה שנולדה ביום טוב הכל מודים שהיא מותרת ואפרוח היוצא מן הביצה
הכל מודים שהוא אסור "

סנהדרין   פרק עשירי   הלכה א'

128 a   אלו שאין להם חלק לעולם הבא האומ' אין תחיית המתים ואין תורה מן השמים
ואפיקורוס ר' עקיבה אום' אף הקורא בספרים החיצונים והלוחש על המכה ואומ' כל
המחלה אשר שמתי במצרים לא אשים עליך וגו' אבא שאול אום' אף ההוגה את
השם באותיותיו "

תמיד   פרק ששי   הלכה ח'

191 a   ...שיר ליום השבת מזמור שיר לעתיד לבוא לעולם שכולו שבת מנוחה לחיי
העולמים"† תוס' ביום הראשון ברא הקב"ה את עולמו בשני הכל מקלסין אותו בשלישי ישב
עליהם בדין ברביעי פרע מן הרשעים בחמישי נתן שכר טוב לצדיקים בששי מלך על
עולמו בשביעי הכל מקלסין לכבודו ואומ' מזמור שיר ליום השבת

טוב להודות ליי' ולומר
לשמך עליון "

* See T. B. Beçah 6 b. But cf. תוספתא, Yom Tob I. 1.
† See Aboth de-R. Nathan cap. I.

סדר נזיקין   אבות   פרק ראשון

The foregoing specimen pages and extracts have been chosen in each case with reference to some characteristic reading or readings which they contain, and the words to which it is desired to call attention have been in some cases underlined.

We conclude by giving the complete text of ABOTH, which was taken as the standard text in the writer's *Sayings of the Jewish Fathers* (Cambridge, 1877). It is here printed page for page and line for line according to the manuscript.

The mishnioth are not numbered in the manuscript, but we have added numbers in the margin corresponding to its punctuation and solely with reference thereto, a fresh mishnah being reckoned as commencing after every stop. The stop usually consists of a pair of dashes placed in a horizontal line, but the pair after בלעם in v. 27 are in a *vertical* line, and no extra space is left between it and the following word עין, the scribe having doubtless omitted this stop in the first instance.

The following selection of readings may serve to indicate the essential character of this text, and the merits and defects of its scribe.

Pereq I. 7 and 8, מתאי for נתאי or ניתאי. 11, the words ואל תתיאש מן הפורענות are repeated from 8. 19, the proof-text שנ' אמת ומשפט שלום כו' is omitted.

Pereq II. 5, דבר שאיפשר לו להשמע. 9, אם עשית. 10—13 and throughout the codex, לעזר and ליעזר often without א. 15, עין רעה.

Pereq III. 9, תורה after שלא כהלכה. 17, it omits חמשה שנ' בקרב כו', and likewise שנברא בצלם שנ' כי בצלם כו'... 21, מעשים טובים before תורה ו' 28, גופי תורה.

Pereq IV. 7, after אומר the scribe has omitted,

מאד מאד הוי שפל רוח כו'. ר' יוחנן בן ברוקה אומר.

Pereq v. 32,

הפוך בה והפך בה דכולה בה וכולך בה:

43 b ₁ מסכתא דאבות ° פרק ראשון '   משה קבל תורה מסיני ומסרה ליהושע ויהושע

לזקנים וזקנים לנביאים ונביאים מסרוה לאנשי כנסת הגדולה הן אמרו שלשה דברים

₂ היו מתונים בדין והעמידו תלמידים הרבה ועשו סייג לתורה " שמעון הצדיק

היה משירי כנסת הגדולה הוא היה אומר על שלשה דברים העולם עומד על   *144 a*

3 התורה ועל העבודה ועל גמילות חסדים" **אנטיגנס** איש סוכו קיבל משמעון

הצדיק הוא היה אומר אל תהיו כעבדים המשמשים   את הרב לק על מנת

לקבל פרס אלא היו כעבדים המשמשין את הרב על מנת שלא לקבל פרס ויהי

4 מורא שמים עליכם"   יוסי בן יועזר איש צרדה ויוסי בן יוחנן איש ירושלם

קבלו מהן יוסי בן יועזר איש צרידה אומר יהי ביתך בית ועד לחכמים והוי מתאבק

5 בעפר רגליהן ושותה בצמאה את דבריהם"   יוסי בן יוחנן איש ירושלם אומר

יהי ביתך פתוח לרוחה ויהיו עניים בני ביתך ואל תרבה שיחה עם האשה"

6 באשתו אמרו קל וחומר באשת חבירו מיכן אמרו החכמים כל זמן שהאדם מ/

מרבה שיחה עם האשה גורם רעה לעצמו ובוטל מדברי תורה וסופו יורש גיהנם"

7 יהושע בן פרחיא ומתאי הארבלי קבלו מהם יהושע בן פרחיה אומר עשה

8 לך רב וקנה לך חבר והוי דן את כל האדם לכף זכות"   מתאי הארבלי אומר

9 הרחק משכן רע ואל תתחבר לרשע ואל תתיא'ש מן הפורענות"   יהודה

בן טבאי ושמעון בן שטח קבלו מהם יהודה בן טבאי אומר אל תעש עצמך כערכי

הדיינים וכשהיו בעלי הדין עומדין לפניך יהיו בעיניך כרשעים וכשנפטרין מל/

10 מלפניך יהיו בעיניך כצדיקים שקיבלו עליהן את הדין"   שמעון בן שטח אומר

הוי מרבה לחקור את העדים והוי זהיר בדבריך שמא מתוכן ילמדו לשקר"

11 שמעיה ואבטליון קבלו מהן שמעיה אומר אהוב את המלאכה ושנא את

12 הרבנות ואל תתודע לרשות ואל תתיאש מן הפורענות"   אבטליון אומר חכמי'

הזהרו בדבריכם שמא תחובו חובת גלות ותגלו למקום המים הרעים וישתו התלמידים

13 הבאים אחריכם וימותו ונמצא שם שמים מתחלל"   הלל ושמאי קיבלו מהן

הלל אומר הוי מתלמידיו של אהרן אוהב שלום ורודף שלום אוהב את הבריות

14 ומקרבן לתורה"   הוא היה אומר נגד שמא אבד שמא די לא מוסיף יסוף ודילא

15 ילף קטלא חייב ודי אשתמש בתגא חלף"   הוא היה אומר אם אין אני לי מי

16 לי וכשאני לעצמי מה אני אם לא עכשיו אמתי"   שמאי אומר עשה תורתך

קבע אמור מעט ועשה הרבה והוי מקבל את כל האדם בסבר פנים יפות"

17 רבן גמליאל אומר עשה לך רב והסתלק מן הספק ואל תרבה לעשר אומדות"

18 שמעון בנו אומר כל ימי גדלתי בין החכמים ולא מצאתי לגוף טוב אלא שתיקה

לא המדרש הוא העיקר אלא המעשה וכל המרבה דברים מביא חטא"

19 רבן שמעון בן גמליאל אומר על שלשה דברים העולם קיים על הדין ועל האמת

1 וְעַל הַשָּׁלוֹם "   **פרק שני**   רבי אומר אי זו היא דרך ישרה 44b
שיבור לו   האדם כל שהיא תפארת לעושה
תפארת לו מן האדם והוי זהיר במצוה קלה כחמורה שאין אתה יודע מתן שכרן
של מצות והוי מחשב הפסד מצוה כנגד שכרה ושכר עבירה כנגד הפסדה
והסתכל בשלשה דברים ואין אתה בא לידי עבירה דע מה למעלה ממך עין ראה

2 ואוזן שומעת וכל מעשיך בספר נכתבים "   רבן גמליאל בנו של ר' יהודה
הנשיא אומר יפה תלמוד תורה עם דרך ארץ שיגיעת שניהם משכחת עון וכל
תורה שאין עמה מלאכה סופה בטלה לגרור עון וכל העמלים עם הציבור יהיו
עמלים עמהן לשם שמים שזכות אבותם מסייעתן וצדקתן עומדת לעד ואתם

3 מעלין עליכם שכר כאילו עשיתם "   הוו זהירין ברשות שאין מקרבין לאדם
אלא לצורך עצמן ונראין כאוהבין בשעת הנאתן ואין עומדין לאדם בשעת

4 דחקו "   הוא היה אומר עשה רצונו כרצונך כדי שיעשה רצונך כרצונו בטל

5 רצונך מפני רצונו כדי שיבטל רצון אחרים מפני רצונך "   ר' הלל אומר אל
תפרוש עצמך מן הציבור ואל תאמן בעצמך עד יום מותך ואל תדין את חבירך
עד שתגיע למקומו ואל תאמר דבר שאיפשר לו להשמע שסופו ואל תאמר

6 כשאפנה אשנה שמא לא תפנה "   הוא היה אומר אין בור ירא חטא ולא עם
הארץ חסיד ולא הביישן למד ולא הקפדן מלמד· ולא כל המרבה בסחורה מחכים

7 ובמקום שאין אנשים השתדל להיות איש "   אף הוא ראה גולגולת אחת שצפה

8 על פני המים ואמר לה אל דאטיפת אטיפוך וסוף מטיפיך יטופון "   הוא היה
אומר מרבה בשר מרבה רמה מרבה נכסים מרבה דאגה מרבה שפחות מרבה
זמה מרבה עבדים מרבה גזל מרבה נשים מרבה כשפים מרבה תורה מרבה חיים
מרבה חכמה מרבה ישיבה מרבה צדקה מרבה שלום קנה שם טוב קנה לעצמו

9 קנה לו דברי תורה קנה לו חיי העולם הבא "   רבן יוחנן בן זכאי קבל מהלל ומשמאי
הוא היה אומר אם עשית תורה הרבה אל תחזק טובה לעצמך כי לכך נוצרתה "

10 חמשה תלמידים היו לו לרבן יוחנן בן זכאי ואילו הן ר' ליעזר בן הורקנוס
ור' יהושע בן חנניה ור' יוסי הכהן ור' שמעון בן נתנאל ור' אלעזר בן ערך הוא היה
מונה שבחן אליעזר בן הורקנוס בור סיד שאינו מאבד טיפה יהושע בן חנניה אשרי
יולדתו יוסי הכהן חסיד שמעון בן נתנאל ירא חטא אלעזר בן ערך מעין המתגבר "

11 הוא היה אומר אם יהיו כל חכמי ישראל בכף מאזנים ואליעזר בן הורקנוס
בכף שניה מכריע את כולן אבא שאול אומר משמו אם יהיו כל חכמי ישראל בכף

145 *a*

מאזנים ואליעזר בן הורקנום עמהן ואלעזר בן ערך בכף שניה מכריע את כולם ״

12 אמר להם צאו וראו אי זו היא דרך טובה שידבק בה אדם רבי ליעזר אומר עין טובה ר׳
יהושע אומר חבר טוב ור׳ יוסי אומר שכן טוב ור׳ שמעון אומר הרואה את הנולד ר׳
לעזר אומר לב טוב אמר להם רואה אני את דברי אלעזר בן ערך מדבריכם שבכלל

13 דבריו דבריכם ״   אמר להם צאו וראו אי זו היא דרך רעה שיתרחק ממנה אדם
ר׳ ליעזר אומר עין רעה ור׳ יהושע אומר חבר רע ור׳ יוסי אומר שכן רע ור׳ שמעון
אומר הלווה ואינו משלם אחד לווה מן האדם כלווה מן המקום ברוך הוא שנ׳ לווה רשע
ולא ישלם וצדיק חונן ונותן ר׳ לעזר אומר לב רע אמר להם רואה אני את דברי אלעזר

14 בן ערך מדבריכם שבכלל דבריו דבריכם ״   והן אמרו שלשה דברים ר׳ ליעזר
אומר יהי כבוד חבירך חביב עליך כשלך ואל תהי נוח לכעוס ושוב יום אחד לפני מי/
מיתתך והוי מתחמם כנגד אורן של חכמים והוי זהיר מגחלתן שמא תכווה תכוה שנשיכתן
נשיכת שועל ועקיצתן עקיצת עקרב ולחישתן לחישת שרף וכל דבריהם כגחלי אש ״

15 ר׳ יהושע אומר עין רעה ויצר הרע ושנאת הבריות מוציאין את האדם מן העולם ״

16 ר׳ יוסי אומר יהי ממון חבירך חביב עליך כשלך התקין עצמך ללמוד תורה

17 שאינה ירושה לך וכל מעשיך יהיו לשם שמים ״   ר׳ שמעון אומר הוי זהיר בקרית
שמע ובתפלה וכשאתה מתפלל אל תעש תפלתך קבע אלא תחנונים לפני המקום
ברוך הוא שנ׳ כי אל רחום וחנון הוא ארך אפים ורב חסד ואל תהי רשע בפני עצמך ״

18 ר׳ לעזר אומר הוי שקד ללמוד תורה מה שתשיב לאפיקורוס ודע לפני מי אתה

19 עמל ומי הוא בעל מלאכתך ׳   ר׳ טרפון אומר היום קצר והמלאכה מרובה והפועלים
עצלים והשכר הרבה ובעל הבית דוחק הוא היה אומר לא עליך המלאכה לגמור ולא
אתה בן חורים ללמֹל לבטל אם למדתה תורה הרבה נותנין לך שכר הרבה ונאמן
הוא בעל מלאכתך שישלם לך שכר פעולתך ודע מתן שכרן של צדיקים לעתיד לבוא ״

1 **פרק שלישי**   עקביה בן מהללאל אומר השתכל בשלשה דברים
ואין את בא לידי עבירה דע מאין באתה ולאין
אתה הולך ולפני מי אתה עתיד ליתן דין וחשבון דע מאין באתה מטיפה סרוחה ולאין
אתה הולך לרמה ותולעה ולפני מי אתה עתיד ליתן דין וחשבון לפני מלך מלכי המלכים

2 ברוך הוא ״   ר׳ חנניה סגן הכהנים אומר הוי מתפלל בשלומה של מלכות שאילולי

3 מוראה איש את רעהו חיים בלענו ״   ר׳ חנניה בן תרדיון אומר שנים שהיו יושבין צ
ואין ביניהם דברי תורה הרי זה מושב לצים שנ׳ ובמושב לצים לא ישב אבל שנים שהיו
יושבין ועוסקין בדברי תורה שכינה ביניהם שנ׳ אז נדברו יראי יי׳ איש אל רעהו וגו׳ ״

4 אחד שיושב ושונה מעלה עליו הכתוב כאילו קיים את כל התורה כולה שנ' ישב בדד

5 וידום כי נטל עליו "   ר' שמעון אומר שלשה שהיו אוכלין על שלחן אחד ולא אמרו עליו דברי תורה הרי כאילו אכלו מזבחי מתים שנ' כי כל שלחנות מלאו קיא צואה

6 בלי מקום "   אבל שלשה שהיו אוכלין על שלחן אחד ואמרו עליו דברי תורה כ/ כאילו אכלו משלחנו של מקום ברוך הוא שנ' וידבר אלי זה השלחן אשר לפני יי' "

7 חננייה בן חכינאי אומר הניעור בלילה והמהלך בדרך יחידי ומפנה לבו לבטלה

8 הרי זה מתחייב בנפשו "   ר' נחונייה בן הקנה אומר כל המקבל עליו עול תורה מעבירין ממנו עול מלכות ועול דרך ארץ וכל הפורק ממנו עול תורה נותנין עליו

9 עול מלכות ועול דרך ארץ "   ר' חלפתא איש כפר חנניא אומר עשרה שהיו יוש/ יושבין ועוסקין בדברי תורה השכינה ביניהם שנ' אלהים נצב בעדת אל ומנין אפי' חמשה שנ' בקרב אלהים ישפוט ומנין אפילו שלשה שי' ואגודתו על ארץ יסדה /ומנין אפילו שנים שנ' אז נדברו יראי יי' איש את רעהו ומנין אפילו אחד שנ' בכל

10 המקום אשר אזכיר את שמי אבוא אליך וברכתיך "   ר' לעזר בן יהודה איש ברתותה אומר תן לו משלו שאתה ושלך שלו וכן הוא אומר כי ממך הכל

11 ומידך נתנו לך "   ר' יעקב אומר המהלך בדרך ושונה ומפסיק משנתו ואומר מה נאה אילן זה מה נאה אילן זה ומה נאה ניר זה מעלין עליו כאילו מתחייב צ

12 בנפשו "   ר' דוסתי בר' ינאי אומר משם ר' מאיר אומר תלמיד חכם שהוא יושב ושונה ושכח דבר אחד ממשנתו מעלין עליו כאילו מתחייב בנפשו שנ' רק השמר לך ושמור נפשך מאד פן תשכח את הדברים אשר ראו עיניך יכול אפילו תקפה עליו משנתו ת'ל ופן יסורו מלבבך כל ימי חייך הא אינו מתחייב עד שישב ויסירם מלבו "

13 ר' חנניה בן דוסא אומר כל שיראת חטאו קודמת לחכמתו חכמתו מתקיימת

14 וכל שחכמתו קודמת ליראת חטאו אין חכמתו מתקיימת "   הוא היה אומ' כל שמעשיו מרובים מחכמתו חכמתו מתקיימת וכל שחכמתו מרובה ממעשיו

15 אין חכמתו מתקיימת "   הוא היה אומר כל שרוח הבריות נוחה הימנו רוח המקום נוחה הימנו וכל שאין רוח הבריות נוחה הימנו אין רוח המקום נוחה הימנו "

16 ר' דוסא בן הרכינס אומר שינת שחרית ויין של צהריים ושיחת הילדים

17 וישיבת בתי כנסיות של עמי הארץ מוציאין את האדם מן העולם "   ר' ליעזר המודעי אומר המחלל את הקדשים והמבזה את המועדות והמפר בריתו של אברהם אבינו והמגלה פנים בתורה אף על פי שיש בידו מעשים טובים אין לו חלק

18 לעולם הבא "   ר' ישמעאל אומר הוי קל ראש וגוח תשחרות והוי מקבל את כל

146 a

19 האדם בשמחה "   ר׳ עקיבה אומר שחוק וקלות ראש מרגילין את האדם לע

20 לערוה "   הוא היה אומר מסורות סייג לתורה נדרים סייג לפרישות סייג

21 לחכמה שתיקה "   הוא היה אומר חביב אדם שנברא בצלם שנ׳ כי בצלם

22 אלהים עשה את האדם "   חביבין ישראל שנקראו בנים למקום חיבה יתירה נודעת

23 להם שנקראו בנים למקום שנ׳ בנים אתם לי׳ אלהיכם "   חביבין ישראל שניתן להם

כלי שבו נברא העולם חיבה יתירה נודעת להם שניתן להם כלי שבו נברא העולם

24 שנ׳ כי לקח טוב נתתי לכם תורתי אל תעזובו "   הכל צפוי והרשות נתונה ובטוב

25 העולם נדון והכל לפי המעשה "   הוא היה אומר הכל נתן בעירבון והמצודה

פרושה על כל החיים החנות פתוחה והחנוני מקיף והפנקס פתוחה והיד כותבת

וכל הרוצה ללוות בא ולווה והגבאין מחזרין תמיד בכל יום ונפרעים מן האדם

לדעתו ושלא לדעתו ויש להם על מה שיסמכו והדין דין אמת והכל מותקן לסעודה "

26 ר׳ לעזר בן עזריה אומר אם אין תורה אין דרך ארץ אם אין דרך ארץ אין תורה

אם אין חכמה אין יראה אם אין יראה אין חכמה אם אין דעת אין בינה אם אין בינה

27 אין דעת אם אין קמח אין תורה אם אין תורה אין קמח "   הוא היה אומר כל צ

שחכמתו מרובה ממעשיו למה הוא דומה לאילן שעינפיו מרובין ושרשיו מעוטים

והרוח באתה ועוקרתו והופכתו על פניו וכל שמעשיו מרובים מחכמתו למה הוא

דומה לאילן שעינפיו מעוטים ושרשיו מרובים אפילו כל הרוחות באות עליו אינן

28 מזיזות אותו ממקומו "   ר׳ לעזר הסמא אומר קינים ופתחי נדה הן הן גופי צ

תורה הלכות תקופות וגימטרייה פרפראות לחכמה "

פרק רביעי

1   בן זומא אומר אי זה הוא חכם הלמד מכל אדם

שנ׳ מכל מלמדי השכלתי "   אי זה הוא גיבור

2 הכובש את יצרו שנ׳ טוב ארך אפים מגבור ומושל ברוחו מלוכד עיר "   אי זה

3 הוא עשיר השמח בחלקו שנ׳ יגיע כפיך כי תאכל אשריך וטוב לך אשריך בעולם

4 הזה וטוב לך בעולם הבא "   אי זה הוא מכובד המכבד את הבריות שנ׳ כי מ׳

5 מכבדי אכבד ובוזי יקלו "   בן עזאי אומר הוי רץ למצוה קלה ובורח מן

6 העבירה שמצוה גוררת מצוה ועבירה גוררת עבירה ששכר מצוה מצוה ושכר

7 עבירה עבירה "   הוא היה אומר אל תהי בז לכל אדם ואל תהי מפליג לכל דבר

שאין לך אדם שאין לו שעה ואין לך דבר שאין לו מקום "   ר׳ לויטס איש יבנה

8 אומר כל המחלל שם שמים בסתר נפרעין ממנו בגלוי אחד שוגג ואחד מזיד

בחילול השם "   ר׳ ישמעאל בנו אומר הלמד על מנת ללמד מספיקין בידו

ללמוד וללמד הלמד על מנת לעשות מספיקין בידו ללמוד וללמד ולעשות"   46b

9   ר' צדוק אומר אל תעשם עטרה להתגדל בהן ולא קרדום לאכל מהן וכך
היה הלל אומר ודי אשתמש בתגא חלף הא כל הנאות מדברי תורה נטל חייו מן

10   העולם"   ר' יוסי אומר כל המכבד את התורה גופו מכובד על הבריות וכל

11   המחלל את התורה גופו מחולל על הבריות"   ר' ישמעאל אומר החושך עצמו
מן הדין פורק ממנו איבה וגזל ושבועת שוא והגס לבו בהוראה שוטה רשע וגס

12   רוח"   הוא היה אומר אל תהי דן יחידי שאין דן יחידי אלא אחד ואל תאמר

13   קבלו דעתי שהן רשאין ולא אתה"   ר' יוחנן אומר כל המקיים את התורה
מעוני סופו לקיימה מעושר וכל המבטל את התורה מעושר סופו לבטלה מעוני"

14   ר' מאיר אומר הוי ממעט עסק ועסוק בתורה ותהיה שפל רוח בפני כל אדם
ואם ביטלת מן התורה יש לך בטילים הרבה ואם עמלת בתורה יש לו שכר הרבה

15   ליתן לך"   ר' ליעזר בן יעקב אומר העושה מצוה אחת קנה לו פרקליט אחד
והעובר עבירה אחת קנה לו קטיגור אחד תשובה ומעשים טובים כתרים לפני

16   הפורענות"   ר' יוחנן הסנדלר אומר כל כניסה שהיא לשם מצוה סופה להתקיים

17   ושאינה לשם מצוה אין סופה להתקיים"   ר' לעזר אומר יהי כבוד תלמידך חביב
עליך ככבוד חבירך וכבוד חבירך כמורא רבך ומורא רבך כמורא שמים"

18, 19   ר' יהודה אומר הוי זהיר בתלמוד ששגגת תלמוד עולה זדון"   ר' שמעון אומ'
שלשה כתרים הן כתר תורה וכתר כהונה וכתר מלכות וכתר שם טוב עולה על

20   גביהן"   ר' נהראי אומר הוי גולה למקום תורה ואל תאמר היא תבוא אחרי

21   שחביריך יקיימוה בידך ואל בינתך אל תשען"   ר' ינאי אומר אין בידינו

22   לא משלות הרשעים ואף לא מיסורי הצדיקים"   ר' מתיה בן חרש אומר

23   הוי מקדים לשלום כל האדם והוי זנב לאריות ולא ראש לשועלים"   ר' יעקב
אומר העולם הזה דומה לפרוזדוד לפני העולם הבא התקין עצמך לפרוזדוד

24   כדי שתכנס לטרקלין"   הוא היה אומר יפה שעה אחת בתשובה ומעשים
טובים בעולם הזה מכל חיי העולם הבא יפה שעה אחת של קורת רוח בעולם

25   הבא מכל חיי העולם הזה"   ר' שמעון בן אלעזר אומר אל תרצה את חבירך
בשעת כעסו ואל תנחמנו בשעה שמתו מוטל לפניו ואל תשאל לו בשעת נדרו

26   ואל תשתדל לראותו בשעת קלקלתו"   שמואל הקטן אומר בנפל אויבך אל תשמח

27   ובהכשלו אל יגל לבך"   אלישע בן אביה אומר הלמד ילד למה הוא דומה לדיו
כתובה על נייר חדש והלמד זקן למה הוא דומה לדיו כתובה על נייר מחוק"

147 a

28 ר׳ יוסי בן יהודה איש כפר הבבלי אומר הלמד מן הקטנים למה הוא דומה
לאוכל ענבים קהות ושותה יין מגתו והלמד מן הזקנים למה הוא דומה לאוכל

29 ענבים בשולות ושותה יין ישן ״   ר׳ אומר אל תסתכל בקנקן אלא במה שיש בו

30 יש קנקן חדש מלא ישן וישן שאפי׳ חדש אין בו ״   ר׳ ליעזר הקפר אומר הקנאה

31 והתאוה והכבוד מוציאין את האדם מן העולם ״   הוא היה אומר הילודים למות
והמתים להחיות והחיים לידון להודיע ולהודיע ולהודע שהוא היוצר והוא
הבורא והוא המבין והוא הדיין והוא עד והוא בעל דין והוא עתיד לדין לדין שאין לפניו
לא עולה לא שכחה לא משוא פנים ולא מקח שוחד שהכל שלו ודע שהכל לפי חשבון ״

32 אל יבטיחך יצרך ששאול בית מנוס שעל כרחך אתה נוצר ועל כרחך אתה
נולד ועל כרחך אתה חי ועל כרחך אתה מת ועל כרחך אתה עתיד ליתן דין ח/
וחשבון לפני מלך מלכי המלכים הקּבּה ״

פרק חמישי

1 בעשרה מאמרות נברא העולם ומה
תלמוד לומר והלא במאמר אחד היה יכול להבראות אלא להיפרע מן הרשעים
שמאבדין את העולם שנברא בעשרה מאמרות וליתן שכר טוב לצדיקים שמ/

2 שמקיימים את העולם שנברא בעשרה מאמרות ״   עשרה דורות מאדם
ועד נח להודיע כמה ארך אפים לפניו שכל הדורות היו מכעיסין לפניו עד

3 שהביא עליהם את המבול ״   עשרה דורות מנח ועד אברהם להודיע כמה ארך
אפים לפניו שכל הדורות היו מכעיסין לפניו עד שבא אברהם אבינו וקבל שכר

4 כולם ״   עשרה נסיונות נתנסה אברהם אבינו ועמד בכולם להודיע כמה

5 היא חיבתו של אברהם אבינו ״   עשרה נסים נעשו לאבותינו במצרים ועשרה

6 על הים ״   עשר מכות הביא הקּבּה על המצרים במצרים ועשר על הים ״

7 עשרה נסיונות ניסו אבותינו את המקום במדבר שנ׳ וינסו אותי זה עשר פעמים ולא

8 שמעו בקולי ״   עשרה נסים נעשו בבית המקדש לא הפילה אשה מריח בשר הקדש
ולא הסריח בשר קדש מעולם ולא אירע קרי לכהן גדול ביום הכפורים ולא נראה זבוב
בית המטבחיים ולא נמצא פסול בעומר ובשתי הלחם ובלחם הפנים ולא כיבו גשמים
את המערכה ולא ניצחה הרוח את עמוד העשן עומדים צפופים ומשתחוים רווחים
ולא הזיק נחש ועקרב בירושלם ולא אמר אדם לחבירו צר לי המקום שאלין בירושלם ״

9 עשרה דברים נבראו בין השמשות פי הארץ ופי הבאר ופי האתון והקשת והמן
והמטה והשמיר והכתב והמכתב והלוחות ויש אומרים אף המזיקים וקבורתו של משה

10 ואילו של אברהם אבינו ויש אומרים אף צבת בצבת עשוייה ״   שבעה דברים בגולם

ושבעה בחכם החכם אינו מדבר לפני מי שגדול ממנו בחכמה ואינו נכנס לתוך דברי
חבירו ואינו נבהל להשיב שואל כהלכה ומשיב כעניין ואומר על ראשון ראשון ועל
אחרון אחרון על מה שלא שמע אומר לא שמעתי ומודה על האמת וחלופיהן בגולם "

11   שבעה מיני פרעניות באין על שבעה גופי עבירות מקצתן מעשרין ומקצתן
שאינן מעשרין רעב של בצורת בא מקצתן רעיבים ומקצתן שבעים גמרו שלא לעשר

12 רעב של מהומה ושל בצורת בא ושלא ליטול חלה רעב של כלייה בא "   דבר בא
לעולם על מיתות האמורות בתורה שלא נמסרו לבית דין ועל פירות שביעיות "

13   חרב בא לעולם על ענוי הדין ועל עיוות הדין ועל המורים בתורה שלא כהלכה
חיה רעה באה לעולם על שבועת שוא ועל חילול השם גלות בא לעולם על עבודה

14 זרה ועל גלוי עריות ועל שפיכות דמים ועל השמט הארץ "   בארבעה פרקים
הדבר מרובה ברביעית בשביעית במוצאי שביעית ובמוצאי החג שבכל שנה
ברביעית מפני מעשר עני שבשלישית בשביעית מפני מעשר עני שבששית וב/
ובמוצאי שבעת מפני פירות שביעית ובמוצאי החג שבכל שנה מפני גזל מתנות

15 עניים "   ארבע מידות באדם האומר שלי שלי ושלך שלך מדה בינונית ויש אומרי
מדת סדום שלי שלך ושלך שלי עם הארץ שלי שלך ושלך שלי חסיד שלך שלך ושלי שלי רשע "

16   ארבע מדות בדיעות נוח לכעוס ונוח לרצות יצא שכרו בהפסדו קשה לכעוס
וקשה לרצות יצא הפסדו בשכרו קשה לכעוס ונוח לרצות חסיד נוח לכעוס וקשה

17 לרצות רשע "   ארבע מידות בתלמידים ממהר לשמוע וממהר לאבד יצא
שכרו בהפסדו קשה לשמוע וקשה לאבד יצא הפסדו בשכרו ממהר לשמוע וקשה

18 לאבד חכם קשה לשמוע וממהר לאבד זה חלק רע "   ארבע מידות בנותני צדקה
רוצה שיתן ואל יתנו אחרים עינו רעה בשל אחרים שיתנו אחרים והוא לא יתן עינו

19 רעה בשלו יתן ויתנו אחרים חסיד אל יתן ואל יתנו אחרים רשע "   ארבע מידות
בהולכי בית המדרש הולך ואינו עושה שכר הליכה בידו הולך ועושה חסיד לא הולך

20 ולא עושה רשע "   ארבע מידות ביושבי לפני חכמים ספוג ומשפך משמרת
ונפה ספוג שהוא סופג את הכל משפך שהוא מכניס בזו ומוציא בזו משמרת שהיא
מוציאה את היין וקולטת את השמרים נפה שהיא מוציאה את הקמח וקולטת את

21 הסלת "   כל אהבה שהיא תלוייה בדבר בטל דבר ובטלה אהבה ושאינה תלויה בדבר

22 אינה בטלה לעולם "   אי זו היא אהבה שהיא תלויה בדבר זו אהבת אמנון ותמר

23 ושאינה תלויה בדבר זו אהבת דוד ויהונתן "   כל מחלוקת שהיא לשם שמים סופה

24 להתקיים ושאינה לשם שמים אין סופה להתקיים "   אי זו היא מחלוקת שהיא לשם

148 *a*

25 שמים מחלוקת שמאי והלל ושאינה לשם שמים זו מחלקתו של קרח "   כל המזכה
את הרבים אין חטא בא על ידו וכל המחטיא את הרבים אין מספיקין בידו לעשות

26 תשובה "   משה זכה וזיכה את הרבים וזכות הרבים תלויה בו שנ׳ צדקת יי׳ עשה

27 ומשפטיו עם ישראל "   כל שיש בו שלשה דברים תלמידו של אברהם ושלשה

28 דברים תלמידיו של בלעם"   עין טובה ונפש שפלה ורוח נמוכה תלמידיו של אברהם
עין רעה ונפש רחבה ורוח גבוהה תלמידו של בלעם ומה בין תלמידיו של אברהם
לתלמידיו של בלעם תלמידיו של בלעם יורדים לגהינם שנ׳ ואתה אלהים תורידם
לבאר שחת אבל תלמידיו של אברהם יורשין גן עדן שנ׳ להנחיל אוהבי יש ואוצרותיהם

29 אמלא "   ר יהודה בן תימא אומר הוי עז כנמר וקל כנשר ורץ כצבי וגבור כארי

30 לעשות רצון אביך שבשמים "   הוא היה אומר עז פנים לגהינם ובוש פנים לגן
עדן יהי רצון מלפניך יי׳ אלהינו ואלהי אבותינו שתבנה עירך בימינו ותן חלקינו

31 בתורתך "   בן בג בג אומר הפוך בה והפך בה דכולה בה וכולך בה ומנה לא

32 תזוע שאין לך מידה טובה ממנה "   בן הא הא אומר לפום צערה אגרה "

חסלת אבות פרקים ה׳

Although this is not the place to discuss the true form of the text of
Aboth, we must not omit to notice the reading in Pereq IV. 23:

העולם הזה דומה ל**פרוזדוד** לפני העולם הבא התקן עצמך ל**פרוזדוד** כדי
שתכנס לטרקלין.

It will be seen that there is good authority for reading פרוזדוד (or פרוסדוד)
with two *Daleths*, as in our manuscript, in preference to פרוזדור.

An estimate of the character of the manuscript as a whole may be formed
from the footnotes to Mr Lowe's edition of it, in which erroneous, doubtful or
peculiar readings are briefly discussed, or are marked with asterisks and have
attention called to them by the frequently recurring observation:

כן הוא בכתיבת היד.

No. 99.

CAMBRIDGE UNIVERSITY, Additional 491.

A fine copy of the first volume of the Machazor according to the Italian (Neapolitan ?) rite, on parchment, folio, with about 37 lines to the page.

Not dated, but of the first half of the 15th century, and written in an Italian Rabbinic hand by Shelomoh, son of a Shemuel צרפתי (fol. 84 a, 94 b), who was קדוש (fol. 138 a), that is *a martyr*.

It contains the five Peraqim and Pereq R. Meir, pointed, the former with Ibn Tibbon's rendering of Rambam's commentary (preceded by the Shemonah Peraqim), and the latter with an abridgment of R. Jacob ben Shimshon's commentary (No. 20), which is here, as elsewhere, attributed to Rashi (fol. 85 a—110 b).

It has the readings cited under No. 5, and likewise those in Pereq III. 9 and 17 cited under No. 12, and speaking generally it furnishes a good specimen of an Italian type of the text of ABOTH.

No. 100.

CAMBRIDGE UNIVERSITY, Additional 541.

An illuminated pocket Prayer-Book, of the Sepharadic rite, fourteenth century, Rabbinic character, on parchment, consisting originally of probably 210 leaves, of which all after fol. 190 are missing.

A text of the six Peraqim, pointed, commences on fol. 169 a, and breaks off with the words, וכוחל על עלבונו (VI. 1), at the end of the last remaining folio.

No. 101.

CAMBRIDGE UNIVERSITY, Additional 561.

A small codex of 228 leaves, parchment (except fol. 3, which is of paper attached to fol. 4), French Rabbinic character, with occasional illuminations.

The text of the manuscript is of the early part of cent. 14, the name of the original scribe פרץ (fol. 98 b), and the date of the marginal literature which has been added cent. 14—15.

On fol. 3 a is a statement in Italian, in Luzzatto's hand, to the effect that the date of the codex is 1329 A.D.

It contains on fol. 7 b—136 b a copy of the תפלות according to the Franco-Ashkenazic rite, in which is a text of the six Peraqim (85 b—94 a), with a marginal commentary abbreviated from R. Jacob ben Shimshon's (No. 20). Fol. 95, the next after ABOTH, is missing.

This text contains substantially the same baraithic matter as No. 20 at the end of Pereq v., and places the sayings of Ben He-he and Ben Bag-bag at the end of Pereq VI., but they have likewise been added in the margin of the preceding chapter (fol. 92 a).

No. 102.

CAMBRIDGE UNIVERSITY, Additional 655.

A small codex consisting of 60 leaves of paper, with 39 or 40 lines to the page, containing a commentary on the six Peraqim, written in a Sepharadic hand and in "Rashi" characters. It commences:

משה קבל תורה היה ראוי שיאמ׳ הקב״ה נתן תורה למשה ומשה מסרה

וכו׳. וי״ל שרצה להודיענו ב׳ עניינים גדולים הא׳ מהם מעלת התורה, הב׳

מעלת אדון הנביאים ע״ה :

The author is not named in the manuscript, but was in reality

ר׳ יוסף יעב״ץ

whose commentary has been printed in Adrianople (יקרה=1555 A.D.), and recently in Warsaw (1880).

The transcription was completed at Bologna, in the year רס״ד (=1504 A.D.). See fol. 59 a.

The author quotes, R. Joseph ibn Shoshan, Ralbag, R. Jonah, Ramban, R. Abr. ibn Ezra, Rambam, Rashi, R. Jacob (ben Asher ben Jechiel), author of the Turim. See pages 3 b, 5 b, 9 a, 9 b, 11 b, 19 a, 26 a, 46 b.

He has also frequent references to the great ISRAELI family of Toledo (fol. 3 b, 11 b, 51 b, 57 b, etc.).

In Pereq VI. (fol. 57 b) occurs the remark :

וכת׳ ר׳ ישראל הזקן ז״ל כי הז׳ הם בכלל הה׳ כי הכבוד בכלל העושר.

On this the scribe, who appears to have been one of the exiles from Spain or Portugal, writes in the margin, וכ״ש בארץ הזאת.

Another copy of the same is to be found in the "Imperial" Library of Paris (New Catalogue, No. 452).

No. 103.

CAMBRIDGE UNIVERSITY, Additional 662.

A Machazor, or the first volume of one, written originally on 246 or more leaves of parchment (of which some fifty at least are now missing from one place or other), folio, about twenty-two lines to the page, Ashkenazic "square" character of the 14th century.

It has numerous ציורים, or drawings.

From fol. 53 b to fol. 64 b is a pointed text of the six Peraqim.

1. *The different pronunciations of* רַב *and* רִבִּי.

Notice the remarkable pointing of רְבִּי in Pereq II. 1, and likewise of רְ (II. 15—19), corresponding to the current colloquial Jewish German pronunciation *Reb* for Rab.

Elias Levita in his ספר התשבי writes that this irregular pointing רְבִּי is found in many prayer books. He is at a loss to account for it; but thinks that it may have sprung out of the previous use of the abbreviation רְ, in which the Shva may have been used merely to denote the absence of a vowel. He continues,

‏...אך קשה לי שאנחנו האשכנזים קוראים הברת הריש בקמץ חטוף ונאמר רָבִּי‏
‏על משקל חָלִי עָנִי ולעולם לא מצאתיה כן.‏

In T. B. Sanhedrin 18 b and 36 a the words לא תענה על רִיב (Exod. xxiii. 2) are taken to mean, Thou shalt not gainsay a scholar greater than thyself. This is evidence of a practice of pronouncing רב as רִיב in former times, as is still done in the compound בִירִיבִי, "son of Ribbi."

In one of the inscriptions discovered by Professor Julius Euting in the course of his travels in Syria and Arabia in the years 1883-4, and which is quoted in the *Athenaeum* for the 26th September, 1885, from the last number of the *Sitzungsberichte* of the Academy of Berlin, Βηρεβί is found as a transliteration of בִירִיבִי, thus :

Σαμου|ήλ Γάλ|λου Βηρ|εβί שלום.

2. *Readings in the text of* ABOTH.

Pereq I. 4, מתאבק בעפר רגליהן ו' is omitted. 12, הבאים אחריהם. 19, קַיָּם.

Pereq II. 4, עשה רצונך כרצונו. The saying is repeated in its usual form after IV. 19. 17, בִּקְרִיאַת שמע.

Pereq III. 1, לתן את החשבון (twice), and so in IV. 32. 2, מורא מלכות.
בצלם 21, after חמשה שנ' ואגדתו כו', followed by שלשה שנ' בקרב כו', 9,
the clause חבה יתירה כו' is marked for omission. 25, om. ‏.‏ההנות פתוחה
תדיר בכל יום 26, אם אין חכמה אין דעת is marked for omission.

Pereq IV. 9, ‏.‏שאין רשאין הם 12, אל תַּעַשׂ. And on ולא אתה there is a
marginal note, אלא אתה‏.‏

Pereq v. 8, שְׁאָלִין‏.‏ 9, ופי הבאר is omitted. 31, דכלה, with the marginal note, ‏.‏ס"א דכולה It is from כלה written defectively that the reading
סיב ובלה not improbably arose.

3. *The censorship of Jewish writings.*

This manuscript is remarkable for the extent to which it has been
tampered with by the censors. See from fol. 183 b onward, where whole
sections and entire pages have been blotted out. The censorship of Jewish
writings dates from 1263 A.D., and has usually been conducted by converted
Jews. PABLO (Paul) CHRISTIANI directed the first censors, who held their
commission from JAYME (James) the First of Aragon. See TOURON's *Histoire
des hommes illustres de l'ordre de Saint Dominique* vol. I., pp. 486, 492
(Paris, 1743). The same king established the Inquisition in his dominions, as
TOURON relates (pp. 40—1) on the authority of the *Lettres Apostoliques* of
Gregory IX. and his successors, from 1236 to 1274 A.D.

No. 104.

CAMBRIDGE UNIVERSITY, Additional 667.

A codex of 228 leaves of vellum, quarto, double columns of thirty-nine
lines each, elegantly written in Rabbinic character in a French Ashkenazic
hand.

The main part of it, to folio 192, consists of a Machazor, compiled
apparently by

נתנאל בן יוסף,

who is named in a poem on fol. 190 a, line 10.

From the calendar, which commences with the cycle רס"ג (fol. 185 b), it
may be inferred that the codex is of the earlier part of the 13th century, a
little later than 262×19 ($=4978$) A.M., or 1218 A.D. Say about 1220 A.D.

The compiler must therefore have been R. Nathanael ben Joseph *ha-
Zaqen*, grandfather of the martyr, "Natanel (der heilige) de Chinon b.
Joseph b. Natanel, abbrev. הקר"ן " (Zunz *Literaturgeschichte der synago-*

galen Poesie p. 363). Notice the reference to a R. Jose מקינון in No. 20,
סימן שפ"ד.

The letters forming the word יעקב are marked on fol. 124 a, col. 1, to
indicate the name of the scribe.

In the Machazor is an unpointed text of the six Peraqim (fol. 82 a—
86 b), and also a commentary upon them (not always in agreement with the
reading of the text), whose six sections commence at the pages
102 b, 104 a, 104 b, 106 a, 107 b, 110 a,
respectively.

The commentary stands next after the poem :

אשריך הר העברים על ההרים הגבוהים כו',

which is signed acrostically אברהם, and is attributed in No. 20 to
Abraham Ibn Ezra.

The editor identifies himself with one of the Talmud commentators who
wrote on יומא, by his short note on Pereq v. 8 (fol. 108 a, col. 2, line 2) :

לא הפילה כו'. כבר פרשתיו היטב במסכ' יומא בפר' ראשון.

He must have been, like R. Isaac b. Dorbelo, a younger contemporary
of the grandsons of Rashi, who are expressly referred to in other parts of
the manuscript, thus :

fol. 66 a, col. 1,   נשלמו דברי רבינו תם זכר צדיק לברכה.
fol. 91 a, col. 2.   ואומר מורי רבינו שמואל...

Notice the reference to Rashi's son-in-law R. Simchah of Vitry :

בהילכות נידה תלמידי רש"י הרב ר' שמחה מויטרי סידר כו',

which occurs (fol. 169 b, col. 1) in the course of a section signed with the
name of Isaac b. R. Shemuel, who was nephew of R. Tham and grandson of
R. Simchah.

The commentary agrees and disagrees with the longer commentary in
No. 20 ; and also with that cited as Rashi's by R. Isaac Israeli (No. 1), and
printed as his in the דרך חיים of R. Löwe ben Beçaleel and elsewhere. But
"Rashi" commented on the five Peraqim only, according to the express
statement of R. Isaac Israeli on Pereq VI. 1 :

רש"י ורמב"ם ורי"זל ורמ"ה לא פירשו פרק זו לפי שאינו ממסכתא זו.

It commences thus (fol. 102 b) :

אתחיל פירושי אבות. מסרה, לימדה. ולא לזקנים שהיו בימי משה אלא
זקנים שהיו בימי יהושע. שהיו רודים ושוטרים על ישר' עם יהושע כדכת'
ויעבדו בני ישר' את יי' כל ימי יהושע וכל ימי הזקנים אשר האריכו ימים אחרי
יהושע,

and it continues in agreement with the "Rashi" of the *Derek Chayim.*

In the last mishnah of Pereq I. the text (82 b) reads עוֹמֵד, thus:

על שלשה דברים העולם עוֹמֵד (sic) על התורה ועל הדין ועל האמת ועל
השלום שנ' אמת כו',

but the commentary runs as follows (103 b, col. 2):

על שלשה דברים העולם קיים, ולא דמי לג' דברים העולם עומד דריש פירקין
דהתם ה"פ שהק' מעמידן (sic) בהם והכי קאמ' שבני העולם קיימים ביניהם
שאינם אוכלין זה את זה בדין שדנין את המעוות את חבירו, על האמת שמתוך
כך מאמינים זה את זה דמלוה איש ומרויח, גם על השלום. שפטו בשעריכם,
וכת' בתריה (?) אולי יחנן יי' צבאות שארית יוסף.

The note on Pereq II. 2 is as follows (104 a, col. 1):

וכל העוסק גרסי', ואתם מעלה כו', עתה מדבר כלשון התלמוד כשליח לפני
המקום אותן העסוקין לשם שמים אעפי שזכות אבותם מסייעתן מעלה אני
עליכם כאילו היא זכות עצמיכם, אינמי אפי' אין אתם מעלה אני וכו', אינמי
אעפי שאני בעצמי עושה התשועה הואיל ולשם שמים אתם עסוקין מעלה אני
כו' כך שמעתי.

In Pereq III. 9 the number *five* is connected with the clause ואנודתו כו'
(105 a, col. 1), on the ground that

איגוד של אצבעות של אדם חמשה.

RASHI on the contrary, according to R. Isaac Israeli, connects the *five*
with בקרב אלהים ישפט, explaining it as made up of

ג' דיינין וב' בעלי דין.

On מסורת in Pereq III. 20 (105 a, col. 2) the commentary has the short
note:

מסורות, מסורת הגדולה, סייג גדר וחיזוק לידע בירור של מקראות.

Here R. Isaac Israeli writes:

סינ פרש"י גדר וחיזוק ויא' כי מסורת היא תורה שבעל פה והיא סינ לתורה
שבכתב.

The note on Pereq III. 21 (105 b, col. 1) is directed against the forced
rendering of Gen. ix. 26 "God made man *in imagine*" (Ps. xxxix. 7):

..שנ' כי בצלם אלהים עשה את האדם, בצלם אלהים נברא האדם, וכל
המפטפט ודורש פני המקרא בדופי· כי בצלם אלהים עשה את האדם, חיישי'
שמא מין הוא.

This agrees with the note in No. 20 (vol. II. 114 b, end), of which it is
apparently an *earlier* form.

The midrashic note on Pereq III. 25 (105 b, col. 1),

ר' עקיבא קאמ' להו, הכל נתון בערבון, אינמי בערבין, נשמתו של אדם ערב על
כל האיברים, זכו זכתה היא לא זכו נידונת היא,

is quoted by R. Isaac Isr. as Rashbam's; and it is found in No. 20 (vol. II.
115 a).

In the short note on Pereq IV. 8 (106 b, col. 1, line 12),

על מנת לעשות, גדול הוא מהלמד על מנת ללמד,

there is *no mention of the peculiar reading which R. Isaac Israeli attributes to* RASHI,

רש"י ז"ל גורס ע"מ ללמד **אין** מספיקין בידו ללמוד וללמד וכו',

with the remark that Rashbam on the contrary reads מספיקין (without the
negative),

וכן גרסת כל הספרים.

On Pereq IV. 10 (106 b, col. 1) the writer has a reference to his TEACHER:

המכבד את התורה, שמלמדה לתלמיד הגון ומחבב דברי תורה לבני אדם.
לי'א מכבד שמשמר ספר תורה בכבודו, ואינו מניחו לא על גבי מיטה ולא על
גבי ספסל. **ואין ר' מודה.**

See below on Pereq IV. 19; and fol. 108 a, col. 1, line 8; 109 a, col. 2,
line 1, &c.

In the last clause of Pereq IV. 19, on the Three Crowns, the text (84 b,
col. 1) reads עוֹלָה על גביהן. The commentator, omitting עולה, writes
(106 b, col. 2):

...וכתר שם טוב עַל גביהן על ידיהן בא שם טוב לאדם כו'.

An alternative rendering is then dismissed as follows:

(*sic*) לא נר' ג' כתרים הן כמשמעו וכתר שם טוב על גביהן כלומ' גדול על
כולם, **ואין ר' מודה.** דא"כ הכי הוה ליה למיתני ארבעה כתרים הם.

In No. 20 (vol. II. 122 a) on the contrary the latter interpretation is
adopted, thus:

...כך קיבלתי ולי נר' על גביהן למעלה מכולן כו'.

The ten temptations of Abraham are enumerated in their place in the
note on Pereq V. 4 (107 b, col. 2); but the subject is resumed after the
conclusion of the chapter, in the form of an extract from *Midrash Tillim*
(109 b, col. 2). See on Psalm xviii. 31. In the former place references are
also given to Pirqe R. Eliezer [chaps. 26—31], and the קרובה of Rosh
ha-Shanah. See the סלוק for the second day in Ashkenazic Machazors.

Amongst the foreign words transcribed in this commentary notice, on
Pereq V. 30 (109 a, col. 1, line 25), as in No. 20, איננריש, thus:

הוי עז, **אינגריש**, אדוק ולהוט במצות.

There is a reading למצות [for בן י״ב], בן י״ג, in the course of the notes upon the AGES. After them is written (109 a, col. 1, line 6),

סליק מסכת אבות פירקין חמשא,

and after this,

תניא ר׳ נתן כו׳.

But the AGES are discussed over again in the sixth Pereq, and there the usual reading is given distinctly, thus (fol. 111 a, end of col. 1),

בן שלש עשרה למצות.

From the specimens given above it is evident that this commentary, while agreeing in style and more or less in subject-matter with the work commonly ascribed to RASHI is not identical therewith. It is a selection of notes from ancient sources by a compiler who added but little of his own. Some such collection of traditional interpretations must have formed the basis of the more extensive and more original treatise of R. JACOB BEN SHIMSHON (No. 20).

No. 105.

CAMBRIDGE UNIVERSITY, Additional 1176.

A defective Ashkenazic Siddur, of the 13th century, quarto, containing on the last leaf of its fourth remaining quire a fragment (Pereq I. 1—12) of a pointed text of ABOTH, which is called simply הפרקים.

Readings :

Pereq I. 3 על מנת שלא. 4 and 5, יוסף. 8, om. ואל תתחבר לרשע. 9, וּבְׂשֶׁיְקַבְּלוּ 12, כזכאין. הבאים אחריהם, with which words the fragment ends.

Notice the pointings ךְ׳ and ךְ׳, on the first and other folios of the codex, comparing No. 103, § 1 (p. 81).

No. 106.

CAMBRIDGE UNIVERSITY, Additional 1180.

A manuscript of the early part of the 15th century, excellently written in an oriental Sepharadic hand, in Rabbinic character. Quarto, double columns of 28 lines each. The folios are not yet numbered.

The codex contains *inter alia* a lengthy commentary on ABOTH, entitled

מגן אלהים,

which breaks off at Pereq v. 7 (··· עשרה נסיונות), at the end of the third column of fol. 92 from the commencement of the commentary.

The next part of the manuscript begins with a philosophico-cabbalistic letter, of not quite nine pages, by Moses of Narbonne (fol. 2 a, 6 a), on the שעור קומה (fol. 2 a, col. 1, line 2), a tract printed in רזיאל, fol. 37 sq., Amsterdam 1701. The letter commences, כל הנקרא בשמי, but is distinct from the commentary on ABOTH, although not unlike it in style.

Many lines in the manuscript end with the upper part of a ש, which may accordingly be assumed to be the initial letter of the scribe's name.

Each Pereq of the commentary is preceded by an introduction. The introduction to Pereq I. begins thus:

פי' מס' אבות הנקרא מגן אלהים" ויהי ביום השמיני. דרש לפרק ראשון ממסכת אבות· זה הדבר אשר צוה יי' תעשו וירא אליכם כבוד יי'· ת"ר בשעה שירד מ'שה ול,חות בידו בא שטן לפני הב"ה א"ל תורה היכן היא כו'·

Reckoning from this folio, the portions of the commentary on the five Peraqim (not counting the introductions to them) commence severally on the pages specified below, viz.,

Pereq I.	משה קבל	on fol. 4 b.
Pereq II.	ר' אומר	on fol. 18 b.
Pereq III.	עקביה	on fol. 43 b.
Pereq IV. 6, 7	...ר' לויטס איש יבנה	on fol. 67 a.
Pereq V.	בעשרה מאמרות	on fol. 85 a.

At the end of fol. 3 b is written,

ורבינו נסים מביא בענין אחר כבר ידוע שכל התורה שבכתב ושבע"פ נמסרה למשה כמו שדרשו ז"ל במגלה כו'·

The commentary on משה קבל begins with some very fanciful Gematria. Then follows a note on the difference between קבל and מסר. It is asked why it was said (fol. 5 a, col. 1, line 19),

משה קבל תורה מסיני ומסרה ליהושע ... אנטיגנוס קבל כו'·

And the answer is:

מוכרח היה לומר במשה קבל ולא לשון מסר ' כי לשון מכר משמע כל סודותיה ופירושיה ולא הניח לו כלום אלו אמ' מסר הש' תורה למשה היה משמ' שהש' לא עכב לעצמו כלום ואין בתורה יותר אלא מה שמסר למשה. וזה לא יתכן שהרי לא נמסרו למשה כל נ' שערי בינה שהרי כתי' ותחסרהו מעט מאלהים ' ועוד כי לא תוכל לראות את פני כי לא יראני האדם וחי ' שהרי כל התורה שמותיו של הב"ה ... ולפי' לא כת' במשה מסר אלא קבל ר"ל קבל כל מה שבכח אנוש ליגע כו'· אבל משה כשמכרה

ליהושע משה לא עכב לעצמו מכל מה שקבל דבר אלא הכל מסר ליהושע...אבל
באנטיגנוס ואילך כתי' קבל.... קבל משמעון הצדיק מה שקבל כלומ' מה
שהיה בכח שכלו לקבל ולפי' מימיו ואילך התחיל המחלוקת כו'.

The saying, כל התורה שמותיו של הב"ה, is also cited by Ramban.
See the introduction to his commentary on Genesis. Compare in the Zohar,
on Exod. xx. 12 (fol. 90 b, Lublin), דהא אורייתא שמא דקב"ה הוי.

The author shews an acquaintance with the work of בעל הטורים (Exod.
xxi. 1), when he writes near the end of fol. 7 b,

וכן הדין מצוה שיעשה פשרה טרם ישמע מדברים.

He names the *Sepher ha-Iqqarim* at the end of fol. 9 b.

He quotes RASHI near the end of fol. 20 a, col. 1 ; RAMBAM on the next
page and elsewhere; the ZOHAR on fol. 39 a, col. 1, line 13 ; and gives
cabbalistic interpretations in various other places. Notice his Gematria on
the Tetragrammaton, which he calls שם השם (fol. 20 a, col. 1, line 11) ;
and his express references to קבלה and חכמי קבלה (fol. 19 a, col. 2, line 3 ;
46 a, col. 2, line 20, &c.).

At the end of fol. 15 a notice the Gematria, which as it stands is inexact,

ואל תתחבר לרשע לרשע בגמ' ליצר הרע.

But לרשע may be written להרשע, and הרשע, ὁ πονηρός, is the gematric equivalent of יצר הרע.

The writer omits no opportunity of illustrating the strife between the
two principles in man. Witness his extraordinary interpretation of the
case stated at the beginning of Baba Meçia, *If two persons have hold of a
cloak, and both claim it, &c.* The cloak (he says) is man, and the two
persons are the spirit and the flesh (fol. 16 a, col. 2, line 6):

ומימרא בריש בבא מציעא שנים אוחזין בטלית...הם הצורה והחומר, או אם
תרצה לומ' הנשמה והגוף, או אם תרצה לומ' יצר טוב ויצר רע, זה אומר
הנשמה אומרת וכו'.

A peculiar reading of Pereq II. 4 is mentioned on fol. 23 b, col. 2, line 17:

יש שגורסין עשה רצונו כרצונך כדי שיעשה רצונו כרצונך.

The saying is repeated on fol. 74 b, col. 2, line 3, after the saying on the
Three Crowns (Pereq IV. 19), thus:

הוא היה אומר עשה רצונו כרצונך, נ"ל שכתבתיה למעלה.

On the next mishnah (fol. 25 a, col. 1) he raises the question whether
Hillel ha-Zaqen or some other Hillel is the speaker. This discussion illustrates his practice of attempting to account for the sequence and arrangement of the mishnioth throughout the masseketh.

In Pereq II. 15 he reads (fol. 30 b) :

‏צאו וראו אי זו היא דרך **ישרה** שידבק בה האדם.‏...

And two columns later he writes, that R. Eleazar identifies the ‏דרך ישרה‏ with ‏עין טובה‏, the quality of contentment, the lack of which is ‏מדה רעה עד מאד‏, and makes the enjoyment of the world like drinking salt water, which only increases thirst.

On Pereq II. 18, ‏ודע מה שתשיב כו׳‏, he writes that ‏אפיקורוס‏ may denote any man (whether a heathen, or a sceptical Jew), who does not believe in the oral Thorah. And he remarks on the words following that ‏עמל כו׳‏ refers to a service that springs ‏מיראה‏, and ‏בעל מלאכתך‏ to a service ‏מאהבה‏ (fol. 35 a, end).

In the introduction to Pereq v. (82 b) the ten ‏מאמרות‏ are compared severally with the ten ‏דברות‏.

No. 107.

CAMBRIDGE UNIVERSITY, Additional 1200.

Yemen Machazor, folio, written near the end of the 16th century (fol. 166 b), on paper, in S. Arabian Rabbinic character, with the so-called Babylonian vowel points ; on which see in the Palæographical Society's *Oriental Series*, Plate 91, with Schiller-Szinessy's description (1882). At fol. 18 b commences a text of the six Peraqim, of which the first only is pointed ; except that in the remaining five a few words, here and there, are pointed *in the ordinary way*, and not uniformly with the rest of the codex. Folios 1—17 are missing ; but their contents have been added in a modern hand, and with the ordinary vowel points, at the end of the codex.

The following readings will serve to shew the character of the text of ABOTH :

Pereq I. 2, ‏יוסי‏ 4 and 5, ‏על מנת שלא‏ 3, ‏משירי אנשי׳ כנסת הגדולה‏.

‏בני ביתך ולמד את כל בני ביתך ענוה‏ 5, ‏יוסף בן יוחנן‏, but ‏בן יעזר‏...

‏קיים‏ 19, ‏משתיקה‏ 15.

Pereq II. 2, ‏אם עשית טובה הרבה‏ 9, ‏שכר כאלו עשיתם‏.

Pereq III. 21, ‏בצלם‏ (without ‏אלהים‏) in both places. 24, ‏לפי רוב המעשה‏.

IV. 15, ‏פרקלט‏, without *yod*. 23, ‏לפרוזדוד‏ ‏בפרוזדוד‏. 26, ‏והשיב מעליו‏

‏שבשאול‏ 32, ‏חרון אפו לא נאמר אלא אפו מלמ׳ שמוחלין כו׳‏.

v. 8, ‏וקשה לאבד חלק טוב‏ 18, ‏שאלין‏ ‏אש של עצי‏ ‏נעשו לאבותינו‏.

7

No. 108.

Cambridge University, Additional 1213.

A codex of 80 leaves of paper, 8¼ by 5⅝ inches, containing the commentary of R. Jacob ben Shimshon on the six Peraqim, somewhat abbreviated, and defective at the end, written in three Greek Sepharadic hands, in rabbinic character, of cent. 15—16. The second hand begins at fol. 60 b, and the third at fol. 69 a.

The six chapters commence severally on the pages,

2 a, 18 b, 27 b, 39 b, 53 a, 72 b,

the first opening with an introduction,

משה קבל ת(ורה מסי)ני ומסרה לי(הושע וכו'. כך היא תחלת)המשנה
ומסכתא זו מסדר ישועות וסידרה אחר מסכת ע'ז למעלה מהוריות כו'.

The manuscript breaks off on Percq VI. 6, thus:

...והעושה סייג לדבריו כשמורה דברי תורה נזהר לעשות סייג לדבריו כדי
שלא יכשלו בו בני אדם ואף נזהר בתשובתו כמו שאמרו בפרק ראשון חכמי'
הזהרו

1. R. Isaac Israeli's citations.

It has been shewn above, under No. 90 § 6 (pp. 52—5), that the passages cited by R. Israel from " R. Shemuel," and by R. Isaac Israeli after him from " Rashbam," agree with the commentary in No. 20. The last we took to be a recension (by R. Isaac ben Dorbelo) of the commentary of R. Jacob ben Shimshon, which is also contained in this manuscript. A few more examples of R. Isaac's citations from " Rashbam " will serve to complete the identification of the commentary which he cites with that in No. 20 and No. 108.

A.

On Pereq II. 5, '(ר') הלל אומר אל תפרוש כו, we read in 𝔅 28 b₁₄ (see p. 46, note):

כת' רשב"ם כי זה הוא הלל הזקן אבל המעתיק טעה בדלת מנין הבבות
ונתחלפה לו ברי"ש וכת' ר' הלל ע"כ.

and in No. 108, fol. 21 a:

הלל כתוב במשנת ר' גרשום ור' אפרים בלא רי"ש והוא הלל הזקן.

The latter is an incomplete form of the note referred to by R. Isaac, which is found in its entirety in No. 20, fol. 105 a :

הילל כת' במשנת רבינו גרשום ור' אפרים בלא ר', והוא הילל הזקן. אבל
המעתיקים קלקלו השורה וטעו בד' של מניין הבבות ונתחלפה להם ד' ברייש,
וכתבו ר' הילל.

Thus we see that in No. 108 we have only an *abbreviation* of the commentary which R. Isaac cites as Rashbam's.

B.

On Pereq III. 4 we read in No. 108, fol. 28 b :

ומנין לאחד שיושב ...   אין אנו גורסין זו במשנת ר' אפרים ושאר כל
המשניות המדוייקות אבל מסיים הבבא ליראי ה' ולחושבי שמו,

and in ℬ 50 a$_{21}$:

וכן כת' רשב"ם ז"ל אין גורסין זה במשנאות אלא מסיים הבבא ליראי יי'
ולחושבי שמו ע"כ.

C.

On Pereq III. 9 Rashbam is quoted in ℬ 54 a$_5$ as saying that מנין without ו should be read in each case for ומנין, thus :

כת' רשב"ם כל מנין הכתובי' כאן אין כתי' בהן ו"ו במשניות ע"כ.

This is wanting in No. 20 and No. 108, but is found in another copy of the commentary, the property of the *Beth ha-Midrash* of the Ashkenazic Jews in London (fol. 112 b) :

...יצאו יהושע וכלב הרי עשרה. כל מנין השנויין כאן בלא יוד כתובים
במשניות. בקרב אלהים ישפוט כו'.

D.

On Pereq III. 17 compare the following extract from ℬ 60 a$_8$:

ורשב"ם ז"ל גורס והמאדים פני חבירו ברבים... וכן מצאתי בשית' סדרי
משנה שלי שכתו' מבחוץ והמאדים וכו',

with what is written in No. 108, fol. 31 b :

...והמאדים פני חבירו ברבים גרסין.

E.

On Pereq III. 24 Rashbam is quoted as below in ℬ 65 b$_{13}$:

רשב״ם ז״ל כת׳ שקבל מרבותיו שכך היא הגרסה ובטוב העולם נידון **אבל**
לא לפי רוב המעשה... והוא ז״ל כת׳ שמצא במשניות **והכל לפי**
רוב המעשה כו׳.

This is found in No. 20, fol. 115 a, and with some clerical errors in
No. 108, fol. 34 b, thus:

...(sic) **אלא** לפי רוב המעשה... כך קבלתי ואני מצאתי במשניות והכל (sic)
רוב המעשה כו׳.

F.

On Pereq IV. 15 the reading **תורה** ומעשים טובים is cited in ℬ 85 a$_7$ as
the reading of Rashbam against כל הספרים, and in No. 108, fol. 45 b, we
read accordingly:

תורה ומעשים טובים עומדין לו לאדם למגן כו׳.

Here No. 20 (vol. II. fol. 121 a) gives only the usual reading תשובה כו׳,
and makes no mention of the reading תורה כו׳.

G.

On the verse, *Rejoice not &c.* (Prov. xxiv. 17), which is put into the
mouth of Shemuel ha-Qatan in Pereq IV. 26, it is suggested in No. 108,
fol. 50 a, that he meant it to be applied to the case of scholars engaged
in controversy; and Rashbam is cited in ℬ 92 b$_{11}$ as explaining the saying
of Shemuel in this way, a part of the citation being written in the margin,
but by the original scribe.

H.

In No. 108, fol. 27 b, there is a quotation in the name of the author's
TEACHER, not found in any of the other copies which I have collated:

(Pereq III. 1)... מליחה סרוחה, וא״ת מה בכך מכל מקום הריני עתה חשוב
בנוי ובכח ובקומה לכך דע לאן אתה הולך, וא״ת מה בכך שתמות ותנוח
בקבר לכך דע לפני מי אתה עתיד ליתן החשבון, **מפי מורי ה״ר שמואל**
הלוי ז״ל.

Thus we are led to infer that even No. 20, whatever later additions it
may include, does not contain everything that was to be found in the
original text of the commentary. Notice its omissions mentioned under
§§ C and F.

2. The Author of the commentary.

Prefixed to Pereq v. in this manuscript are the acrostic verses :

יותן לי לבב להורות עמוקים דלות ראות קושט יושר הגיד בצוואת וגלות
ברב כח בקע בצרות יאורי מים ויבלי נהרות שם קודש קורא דורות. צוררי
ימגר ביום עברות נמוג והלום יסוד ערות בעלי עין בעשרה מאמרות,

From the verses even in this corrupt form one can gather that the
name of the writer was יעקב. They are given more correctly in No. 42,
thus :

יותן לי לבב להורות. עמוקים דלות ראות זרות. קושט יושר הגיד בצרות.
בּאר וגלות אמרות טהורות. בּרֹב כח בקע בצרות. יֿאורי מים יבלי נהרות.
שֵׁם קדוש קורא דורות. שֿוררי ימגר ביום עברות. נֿמוג והלום יסוד ערות.
בֿגילי עין ביוד מאמרות,

and the preceding chapter is introduced in No. 42 by the verses :

יֿונתי בהסתר בנקרות הצורים. עֿמודים תיכן בעשרת הדברים. קֿפאון לי ישית
יקרים וקדורים. בֿעליל הוציא תעלומות לאורים. בֿאמונת עתים וחוסן ישועות.
רֿב חכמה ורב דעת. בֿלתי סור ובלתי תעות. יֿסעד לי הבין שמועות. שֿמוע
מֿוסר שֿמוע מזמה. וֿנתן לי השכל והחכמה. וֿלבי גם יהגה אימה. בֿמושכי
שבט כבן זומֿא.

Thus the full name of the author is clearly given as,

יעקב ברבי שמשון.

On this R. Jacob see in vol. II. of Schiller-Szinessy's *Catalogue* under
No. 92, where our MS. No. 108 is described. He was a man of great
learning, who lived in the 11th and 12th centuries. From the Oxford MS.
Opp. 317, No. 42 in this *Catalogue* (p. 33), we learn that he was engaged in
writing his ספר האלקושי in the year 1123 A.D.

We have seen that he names as his teacher one R. Shemuel ha-Levi
(p. 92). From the כתב תמים*, as printed in אוצר נחמד, vol. III. 59, we
learn that he was also a disciple of Rashi, and that he was a teacher of
Rashi's grandson Rabbenu Tham, and a commentator on ABOTH, it being
there written, on the creation of man בצלם כו' (Pereq III. 21) :

והר' יעקב בר שמשון ׳׳פירש מס' אבות כתוב (sic) שם שמי שמפרש בצלמו
בצלם אלהים ברא אותו חיישינן שמא מין הוא... והוא היה תלמידו של
רבינו שלמה זצ"ל ורבו של רבינו יעקב זצ"ל.

---

* A work of R. Mosheh תקן, who lived in cent. 13—14.

This note on בצלם כו' is found in our copies of R. Jacob's commentary. In No. 108 it appears in the mutilated form :

כי בצלם אלהים עשה את האדם חוששין הוא לומר מין הוא.

Granted that the commentary emanated from the school of Rashi, it
would be a natural mistake to ascribe an anonymous copy of it to Rashi
himself. But the most tempting explanation is that the name of its proper
author רי"ש was corrupted into רש"י (p. 24). The former abbreviation is
actually used in R. Isaac ben Dorbelo's Machazor (No. 20)*. It is suggested
in Schiller-Szinessy's *Catalogue*, that this mistake of writing רש"י for
רי"ש has been made in the דעת זקנים, fol. 23 b, col. 2 (Livorno 1783,
folio), where an explanation of a clause in the Ages (בן י"ג למצות), found in
our R. Jacob's commentary, is given in the name of Rashi. We have seen
that its sixth Pereq is ascribed to Rashi in a number of Italian Machazors,
where it is used to supplement Rambam's treatise on the five Peraqim.

R. Isaac Israeli, who (on VI. 1) expressly states that Rashi commented
on the five Peraqim only, follows his ancestor R. Israel of Toledo (No. 90) in
attributing the commentary to one R. Shemuel, or Rashbam, whom we may
suppose to have been the grandson of Rashi of that name. The author
being presumably known to be of the school of Rashi and yet not Rashi
himself, and his grandson Rashbam being so famous as a Talmud commentator, the latter might easily come to be regarded by a Spanish rabbi
as the writer of the commentary. But we have good evidence to the
contrary in the acrostics which name Rashbam's elder contemporary
R. Jacob ben Shimshon as the true author, not to mention the independent
testimony of the כתב תמים to the effect that he was actually a commentator on אבות.

No. 109.

Cambridge University, Additional 1490. 1.

A French Ashkenazic Siddur, quarto, of the early part of the 14th
century, written on vellum in a south German rabbinic hand, and containing an unpointed text of the six Peraqim (fol. 25 a—30 b).

The following are specimens of its readings, including some obvious
clerical errors :

Pereq I. 1, הזהרו מדבריכם 12, כל המרבה שיחה 6, נתונין בדין .
רב וקנה לך חבר 17,...

---

* In vol. II. fol. 69 a, col. 2 (סימן שס"ג), a section ends עד כאן ת'. רי"ש. מ"ר.
A possible explanation of the confusion of names in the two commentaries in No. 19 is that
רש"י and רי"ש were first interchanged, and the latter (an unfamiliar abbreviation), perhaps
with the addition of ע"ה, was then read as ר' ישעיה.

Pereq II. 1, ‏הוי זהיר‎ (for ‏והוי‎). 2, ‏סוף בטילה‎.

Pereq III. 9, ‏בעדת אל ✻בקרב אלהים ישפוט, מניין אפי׳ שלשה שנאמ׳‎ ...
16, om. ‏ויין‎. ‏ר׳ דוסתאי ב״ר ינאי (אומ׳ר) משום ר׳ מאיר אומר‎ 12, ‏ואגודתו‎.
22 and 23 (but not 21), om. ‏תורה ומעשים (טובים‎ 17, (om. ‏של צהרים‎.
28, ‏והפנקם פתוחה‎ 25, om. ‏הכל צפוי בערבון‎ 24, ‏חבה יתירה כו׳‎
‏גופי תורה‎.

Pereq IV. 23, ‏לזקן‎. ‏הלומד תורה לילד‎ 27, ‏בפרוסדור‎. ‏לפרוסדור‎.
28, ‏שיש בשאול‎ 31, ‏והלומד מן הגדולים‎.

Pereq v. 8, ‏נעשו לאבותינו בבית המקדש‎. The chapter ends with the
baraithic additions found in No. 20 and elsewhere.

No. 110.

CAMBRIDGE UNIVERSITY, Additional 1495.

A small Prayer Book, vellum, written in an Italian rabbinic hand, of the
15th century. It contains a text of the six Peraqim, of which a few words
only, here and there, are pointed.

Its reading of Pereq II. 18 is as follows (fol. ‏קפ״ג‎, end) :

‏ר׳ אלעזר אומ׳ הוי שקוד ללמוד תורה מה שתשיב לאפיקורוס. ודע לפני מי‎
‏אתה עמל ומי הוא בעל בריתך, ונאמן הוא בעל מלאכתך שישלם לך שכר‎
‏פעולתך‎.

No. 111.

CAMBRIDGE UNIVERSITY, Additional 1523.

Five leaves of an Ashkenazic Siddur, of the early part of the 14th
century, parchment folio, rabbinic hand, two columns to the page.

Two leaves, not consecutive, contain portions of R. Jacob ben Shimshon's commentary on ABOTH. The former of these has the conclusion of
the fifth and the beginning of the sixth chapter ; and the latter a portion of
the sixth, ending (on § 9) with the words,

‏מלוין, לשון לויה‎.

These words are on the fourth page from the end of the commentary in
No. 20 (fol. 142 a).

✻ No mention is here made of the number *five*.

No. 112.

CAMBRIDGE UNIVERSITY, Additional 1729.

A Yemen Machazor, folio, written before 1644 A.D., but with some parts
supplied in a later hand. It contains, after the Sabbath *Minchah*, a text
of the six Peraqim, of which the first Pereq and a few words besides are
pointed, viz. with the Babylonian vowel-points, or ניקוד העליון, as in
No. 107.

Readings :

Pereq III. 1, סרוחה מֶלְחָה .24, והכל לפי רוב המעשה אבל לא על פי
המעשה.

Pereq IV. 17, חֲבִירְךָ ככבוד עליך חביב. 23, לפרוזדוד. בפרוזדוד...
כדי שתעלה לטרקלין.

No. 113.

CAMBRIDGE UNIVERSITY, Additional 1752.

A Provençal Machazor, defective, on parchment, quarto, well written in
square characters, with some letters and sentences rubricated, of the 14th
century.

It contains (at the end) an unpointed text of portions of ABOTH. The
second, third, and fourth chapters are here reckoned the *first, second* and
third respectively, the Pereq משה כו' being regarded as an Introduction.
Compare No. 80.

Before משה קבל is written,

ממתן תורה ועד משנה תורה משה קבל תורה.

In this Pereq our manuscript reads briefly, וישתו התלמידים וימותו (12),
and לא מדרש הוא עקר אלא מעשה, without the article (18). The *third*
folio from the beginning of ABOTH ends at Pereq II. 8,

...מרבה עבדים מרבה גזל מרבה תור'.

After this a leaf is missing, and the next begins, תורה שאינה ירושה לך (II.16).
In II. 18 the text agrees with No. 110, reading

...תורה מה שתשיב...ומי הוא בעל בריתך כו'.

The chapter ends :

...ופועלים עצלים ושכר הרבה ובעל הבית דוחק ודע מתן שכרן של צדיקים
לעתיד לבא.

Pereq III. (here called '‍ב). 1, ‏(sic)‎ ‏ולפני‎ ‏אתה עתיד לתת את החשבון‎.
‏גוזרין עליו‎ (sic) ‏מלכות ועול דרך ארץ‎, 8. ‏אבל שלשה‎ (sic) ‏על שלחן אחד‎, 5. This mishnah is given in the name of ‏ר' חנינא בן חקנה‎, next come ‏ר' דוסא כו'‎ (16), the (13—14), and after these, ‏ר' חנינא בן דוסא כו'‎ mishnioth 9—12 and 15 being omitted. 24, ‏אבל לא על פי רב המעשה‎. ‏הכל נתון בערבין‎, 25.

The last page of the codex has the beginning of Pereq ‏בן זומא‎, down to ‏הלומד על מנת ללמד אין‎ (8), the ‏אין‎ being written in the margin in rabbinic character.

No. 114.

CAMBRIDGE UNIVERSITY, Additional 1754.

Another Yemen Machazor, of the same character and date as No. 112. It contains the six Peraqim, pointed throughout with the Babylonian vowel-points, and accompanied by a marginal *Perush* running beyond the pages which contain the text.

The following are some of the readings of the text, which is on the whole a good one:

Pereq I. 4, ‏בצמאה‎. 6, ‏יירש גהנום‎. 9, ‏כרשעים שלא קבלו עליהם‎...
‏את הדין‎. 14, (*prima manu*) ‏נגד שמא אבד שמא‎.

Pereq II. 3, ‏שאין מקבלין לו לאדם‎. 14, ‏שלשה שלשה דברים‎. 15, ‏עין רעה‎.

Pereq III. 1, ‏מלחה סרוחה‎. 2, ‏חיים בלעו‎. 3 and 9, ‏שכינה עמהן‎. 9, om.
‏מרגילין לערוה‎. 19, ‏שלא כהלכה‎. om. ‏פנים בתורה‎. 17, ‏שמי‎, after ‏אבוא כו'‎.
‏והכל לפי רוב המעשה אבל לא על פי המעשה‎, 24.

Pereq IV. 3, ‏לעולם הבא‎. 17, ‏ככבוד חבירך‎. 23, ‏לפרוזדוד‎. ‏כפרוזדוד‎.
‏מכל חיי כו'‎ for ‏כחיי העולם הבא‎, 24.

Pereq V. 8, ‏שאלין‎. 24, ‏שמאי והלל‎. 26, ‏וחטאת הרבים תלויה בו‎.

The commentary cites R. JONAH on the last mishnah of Pereq I. On Pereq III. 7, it has the note:

‏הניעור כמו הניחור בחלוף העין מאותיות אהֹהֹעֹ והוא קול שמוציא האדם‎
‏כשהוא ישן כמו נחרת סוסיו וזה למה ששומעין אותו לסטים וחיות רעות‎
‏ובאות עליו‎.

No. 115.

A codex of 132 leaves of paper, of which the eleventh is lost, quarto,
usually twenty-five lines to the page, except when it contains portions of
the text, which is written large. Presented to St John's College, Cambridge, in the year 1684 A.D., by EDMUNDUS CASTELLUS, Professor of Arabic
in the University.

It consists (like No. 1) of a copy (but not so carefully written) of the
commentary on the Six Peraqim by R. ISAAC ISRAELI,

יצחק ס״ט בר׳ שלמה בר׳ יצחק בר׳ שלמה בר׳ יצחק * בר׳ ישראל הסופר בר׳
[צ״ל בן] ישראל ז״ל.

The six chapters commence severally on the pages,

1 b, 24 a, 47 a, 71 a, 97 a, 119 a.

The work was completed by the author (as he tells us) in the year
1368 A.D., in the 28th year of his age.   On fol. 115 b₁₄† he refers to,

הר׳ יעקב בן הרא״ש ז״ל,

that is to say, to Rabbenu Jacob ben Asher ben Jechiel, who died after
1340 A.D.

The transcription, which is in a Sepharadic rabbinic hand, was finished
on Tuesday, the 28th Elul, 5277 A.M., that is, 1517 A D. The place of writing
was אספי, and the name of the scribe,

משה בן יהודה בן אבי זמרא ס״ט.

A full and excellent description of another copy of this commentary is
given by Herr S. Sachs in his as yet unfinished catalogue (written in
Hebrew) of manuscripts in the Günzburg Library, now in St Petersburg.

1. The sources of R. Isaac Israeli's commentary.

The relation of this *Perush* to that of R. Israel may be gathered from
our description of the latter (No. 90). It uses most of the authorities
there named (p. 47), drawing especially from the commentaries of (or
attributed to) Rashi, Rashbam, Rambam, R. Meir ha-Levi, and R. Jonah,
as well as from R. Israel's own.

It also supplies a reference to R. JOSEPH IBN עבנין (or עקנין), a disciple
of Rambam, which No. 90, being defective at the beginning, omits. This

---

* In the description of No. 1 a בר׳ יצחק has fallen out before בר׳ ישראל.

† In explanation of this mode of reference see above, p. 46, note.

R. Joseph is cited on Pereq I. 7, 'והוי דן כו, immediately after Rambam,
thus :

‏...וכן לאדם חסיד (וישר ונאמן אין לדונו לחובה ואף כי כל דבריו נוטים
לחובה), כן כתב הרמ"בם וצ"ל וכן כת' הרמ"ה] ז"ל, והחכם ר' יוסף בן
עכנין ו"ל] תפש עליו וכת' כי דין זה שוה לכל ונ"א בכל] אדם בין צדיק
בין רשע, וכת' הר' ישראל ז"ל לשון משנתנו מסייע לר' יוסי בין (sic)
עכנין ז"ל והשכל מסייע להרמ"בם.

This is found in No. 115 at the end of fol. 11 a, a few lines only before the
passage, at which No. 90 commences,

‏...כמו שנא' סורו נא מעל אהלי האנשים הרשעים והאלה] ואמרו עונותיו של
רשע גרמו לסתור כותלו של צדיק (11 b_{10}).

The readings in square brackets are from No. 1. This codex, which is
in general superior to No. 115, omits the reference to R. ISRAEL in the
above passage [13 a_{17}]. But it is found in the Günzburg manuscript, as
described by Sachs, as well as in No. 115.

In No. 1, fol. 12 a, and in the Günzburg manuscript, but not in No. 115,
which has lost a folio at this place, there is a citation, also on Pereq I. 7,
from R. JOSEPH IBN GIQATILLA :

‏וקנה לך חבר...ובמשלי ר' יוסי ן' גיקטיליא ז"ל למה חברים העוסקין
בתורה דומים למדורה של עצים הא' מדליק את חבירו כך החבירים הלומדי'
זה שואל וזה משיב זה מקשה וזה מתרץ נמצאי' כלם דולקין ' אבל הלומד
יחידי דומה לעץ יחידי דולק שאין האור מתאחזת בו ע"כ.

The RABBENU MESHULLAM quoted on Pereq III. 25 (67 b_{10}), whom Sachs
inclines on the whole to regard as a צרפתי, proves on the contrary to be
a רומי, his note on the סעודה, which our R. Isaac cites, being introduced
thus in the earlier commentary of רי"ש, according to No. 20 (vol. I. 115 b_{19}):

‏ור' משולם בר' קלונימוס איש רומי פי' לסעודה ליום המיתה ...
On Meshullam see in Schiller-Szinessy's *Catalogue*, under No. 53 (vol. I.
p. 161).

Lastly, our R. Isaac quotes his father, א"א ז"ל (3 a_{22}, 19 b_5, &c.), and
his grandfather ISAAC (126 b_{17}, 127 a_{24}, &c.), whom he also calls זקני הר'
יצחק ישראל (122 a_5, &c.), at times with and at times without the
addition of ז"ל.

On Pereq II. 13 we read in this codex (38 a_{13}):

‏כאלו לוה מן המקום (ב"ה) מפרש בספר בן סירא לכך קורא מקום להק"בה
לפי שהוא מקומו של עולם ואין העולם מקומו ומצאתי בפי' ההגדה שחבר

הר' ישראל זקני (sic) ז"ל שכת' על ברוך המקום שנתן תורה לישראל
וכו' כשתמנה שם של ד' אותיות תמצא מניינו עולה למנין מקום כיצד וכו'*
ע"כ. וכת' הר' ישראל ז"ל...

But instead of הר' ישראל זקני we must read with No. 1 (39 a$_{20}$),

זקני הר' יצחק ישראל,

a reading further attested by the Günzburg manuscript (Sachs, *Catalogue*,
col. 42), and by the context of this very passage, in which a genuine citation
from R. ISRAEL immediately follows.

For some of our author's citations from the pseudo-Rashbam see on
No. 108, comparing No. 90 § 6. Examples of comments cited by him as
from RASHI on passages of ABOTH are given below.

2. R. Isaac Israeli's citations as from Rashi.

At the commencement of Pereq VI. (119 b$_4$) R. Isaac remarks:

רש"י ורמב"ם וריז"ל ורמ"ה לא פירשו פרק זו לפי שאינו ממסכתא זו.

On the earlier chapters RASHI is not unfrequently quoted. For
example:

A.

On Pereq III. 4 (50 a$_{20}$) he is quoted as follows:

כת' רש"י ז"ל ולא מצינו במשנה כתי' ישב בדד וידום אבל רגילין העם
לאומרו ע"כ.

This is a remark of some critical importance. It reveals the source of
not a few interpolations in the written text.

B.

On the reading of Pereq III. 9 (54 a$_{7, 19}$) he is quoted to the following
effect:

ורש"י ז"ל נורם מנין שאפי' ה' שנא' בקרב אלהים ישפוט, ופי' אלהים לשון
דיינים [ג' דיינים] וב' בעלי הדין הרי בכאן חמשה. מנין שאפי' ג' שנא' ואגודתו
על ארץ יסדה ומצינו ג' שסרויים אגודה שאגודת אזוב ג' קלחים בו ע"כ.

---

* The explanation given is that the squares of the numbers represented by the letters of
יהוה ($10^2 + 5^2 + 6^2 + 5^2$) together make up the numerical value of מקום ($40 + 100 + 6 + 40$).

C.

On Pereq III. 18 (60 b$_5$) we read :

פרש״י ז״ל קל הוי קל לראש כשאתה בחור הוי קל כנגד היוצר ונוח לתשחורת וגם
בעת זקנתך תהא נוח לו תשחורת מלשון זקנה כמו כי הילדות והשחרות. וי״א
הוי קל לראש לשר הבירה וכו׳.

D.

On Pereq III. 25 (67 b$_9$) a remarkable note is given in the name of
RASHI :

...והכל פרש״י אע״פ שהדין דין אמת ״ הכל מתוקן לסעודה א׳ רשעי׳ וא׳
צדיקי׳ יש להם חלק לעולם הבא לבירה הגדולה ע״כ.

E.

On Pereq IV. 8 (78 b$_{17}$),

רבי ישמעאל בנו אומר הלמד על מנת ללמד **מספיקין** בידו ללמוד וללמד,

a reading **אין** מספיקין is given as RASHI's, and as peculiar to him, thus :

רש״י ז״ל גורס ע״מ ללמד אין מספיקי׳ בידו ללמוד וללמד וכו׳, ופי׳ הלומד ע״מ
ללמד לקרותו רב או׳ ר׳ אין מספיקי׳ וכו׳. ורשב״ם גורם מספיקי׳ וכן גרס׳ כל
הספרי׳.

And it is written in the margin of the text,

רש״י גורם על מנת ללמד אין מספיקי׳ בידו וכו׳ ובכל הספרי׳ כתו׳ מספיקי׳.

F.

In Pereq IV. 17 (85 b$_{17}$) the reading ככבוד **חבירך** has the support of
the commentary quoted as RASHI's, thus :

פרש״י ז״ל ככבוד חבירך משמע קרוב לכבוד חבירך וכן במורא רבך קרוב
למורא רבך וכן וכבוד רבך קרוב לכבוד שמים ע״כ.

Over against this reading, which R. Isaac himself gives in his text, it is
written in the margin of the codex, י״ג חביב עליך כשלך.

G.

On Pereq V. 8 two passages are quoted as from Rashi :

(102 b$_{16}$) וכת׳ רש״י ולא כבו הגשמים ולא נצח׳ הרוח כמדומה (שהוא) שיבוש
דהא ביומא אמרי׳ הא משנה אנב גררה ולא קתני בה הני תרתי ומוסיפי׳ להו
בברית׳ והנך תלתא עומר ובשתי הלחם ובלחם הפנים בתלתא קא חשיב להו
והוו להו נמי י׳ ע״כ.

(102 b$_{24}$) ולא אמ' אדם לחבירו וכו'. פרש"י לפי שכל הדרים בתוכו היה
מזמין להם שהם (השם .marg) פרנסתן ולא הוצרך א' מהם לצאת משם
וכת' הר' ישראל ולפי זה יש לגרוס שָׁאֲלָין בירושלם ופי' שאתקיי' ואדור
כמו נפשו בטוב תלין ע"כ.

But R. Isaac himself, after "Rashbam" and R. Jonah (103 a$_4$), reads
כשעולין לירושלם.

II.

On Pereq v. 29,

יהודה בן תימא אומר הוי עז כנמר כו',

"RASHI" is quoted to the following effect (115 b$_7$) :

פרש"י ז"ל משנה זו שנויה (להלן) בזבחי' (sic) בפרק מקום שנהגו תכף לאות'
של ר' עקיבה שהיה אומ' עשה שבתך חול ואל תצטרך לבריו' ובא ללמדנו שלא
דבר ר' עקיבה אלא במי שהשעה דחוקה לו ביותר אבל צריך אדם לעשות
עצמו עז כנמר וקל כנשר לעשות רצון אביו שבשמים לקבל שבתות וימים
טובים ע"כ.

See also fol. 4 a$_{12}$, 40 b$_{7, 11}$, 50 a$_{24}$, 61 b$_{10}$, 66 b$_{20}$, 68 a$_{21}$, 70 b$_9$, 81 b$_3$, 96 b$_{26}$,
100 a$_{15}$, 103 a$_{16}$, 103 b$_{7, 9}$, &c.

These comments, or some of them, may perhaps be rightly attributed
to Rashi. They are more or less in his style, and one cannot doubt that he
expounded the tract ABOTH in his lectures, although he may not himself
have written down his notes upon it. In copies of R. Jacob ben Shimshon's
commentary (Nos. 20, 108, &c.), which (as we have seen) our R. Isaac quotes
as Rashbam's, sundry references are given to RASHI, but not as a writer on
ABOTH.

Thus much will suffice to indicate the character of R. Isaac's *Perush;*
but full justice could not be done to it without collating it in detail. It
is indispensable to any critical commentator on ABOTH, and would itself
amply repay the labour of careful editing.

3. The date of R. Israel's commentary.

R. Isaac Israeli, who was born in 1340 A.D., being of the sixth generation in descent from and including

ר' ישראל הסופר בן ישראל,

that is, R. Israel ha-Sopher ISRAELI, the latter would have been born in
the 12th or the 13th century according as we reckon on an average more or
less than 28 years to a generation. If he was the R. ISRAEL whose Arabic

commentary our R. Isaac cites, the author of this, as we assumed in our description of it (p. 46), may have been born late in the 12th century or early in the 13th. In either case his commentary might have been written not later than the middle of the 13th century ; nor is there apparently any internal evidence to the contrary, according to No. 90, the latest author of ascertained date quoted therein being RABBENU JONAH (p. 47), who died about 1230 A.D.

Sachs, however, in his *Catalogue* takes the author to be a different R. Israel, who died in 1317, or possibly 1322 A.D. He was without doubt (writes he) the R. Israel of Toledo (col. 26) who was engaged in controversy with R. Asher ben Jechiel (ט׳ סי׳ נ״ה כלל נ״ה כלל שו״ת הרא״ש). But the reasons assigned are, as they stand, not quite conclusive. They are to the effect that the R. Israel last named was a great scholar, who composed works in Arabic, and is styled "R. ISRAEL" simply by HA-ROSH ; and that the R. ISRAEL cited by our R. Isaac was a scholar of like calibre, who wrote in Arabic, and is referred to always as R. Israel, without further specification, *if* we assume him to be a different person from R. ISRAEL HA-SOPHER ISRAELI. But one's first impression from our R. Isaac's preface is that the R. Israel ha-Sopher named in his pedigree is the R. Israel whose work on ABOTH he cites ; and so perhaps thought the careful scribe of No. 1, when he copied as far only as the name of ישראל ר׳ in large letters, as below :

פי׳ מסכת אבות חברו יצחק בר׳ שלמה בר׳ יצחק בר׳ שלמה
בר׳ יצחק בר׳ ישראל הסופר בן ישראל תנצ״בה. תחלת דברי וראשית
אמרי כו׳... (2 a₆) ולקטתיו מהים הגדול ורחב ידים פי׳ החכם הפילוסוף
האלהי התורניי הר׳ ישראל ז״ל אשר הרחיב בפי׳ מסכתא זו בלשון ערב ...
ועוד לקטתיו משאר חיבורי המפרשי׳ ז״ל והוספתי אני מאשר חננוני מן
השמים לקשר דברי כל תנא ותנא כפי השגת שכלי׳ ועוד סיימתי כל משנה
ומשנה בפסוק לפי שכך הורגלתי להגידה ברבים ...

On either hypothesis, R. Israel's commentary on ABOTH may have been written within the half century 1250—1300 A.D., and on neither can it have been written much before or much after.

פרקי אבות

Nos. 116—170.

(Paris, 116—136. Hamburg, 137—150. Berlin, 151—155.
St Petersburg, 156, 157. London, 158—168. Parma, 170.)

I. Commentaries with or without the text

Name	Number
Rashi	116, 117, 170
Jacob ben Shimshon . .	118–121, 151, 152, 158, 161
Maimonides (Hebrew) . .	121, 122, 152, 153
Bachja ha-Dayyan . . .	160
Joseph ibn Shoshan . . .	129, 130, 160
R. David (Arabic) . . .	126
Isaac Israeli	123–125, (130)
Shem Tob ben Shem Tob . .	128, 160
Shim'on ben Tsemach Duran .	127
Joseph Ja'betz	131
Shabbethai ha-Sofer . . .	159
Aharon de Shelomoh Antones .	169
Abraham Taussig . . .	158
Anonymous	117, 132, 141
Translations	132, 144

II. The text alone

Nos. 133–140, 142, 143, 145–150, 154–157, 162–168.

The codices in the Imperial or as it is now called National
Library of PARIS numbered respectively in the new
Catalogue of Hebrew and Samaritan manuscripts,

152, 169, 306, 327, 328, 330, 387, 448, 452, 455, 583, 589,
636, 643, 644, 646, 719, 739, 769,

contain manuscripts of the text of ABOTH or of commentaries upon it as below, where the PARIS *Catalogue*
numbers are given in brackets.

Nos. 116, 117.

(PARIS 644, 769.)

Each of these contains a copy of the commentary having the unique
reading in Pereq IV. 8,

אֵין מספיקין בידו ללמוד וללמד,

which R. Isaac Israeli quotes as RASHI's (p. 101 E).

No. 116, which is a fine Machazor transcribed shortly before 1264 A.D.
by one Eliezer, contains also the text of the Six Peraqim separately (fol.
78 a—89 b). It reads in Pereq III. 9,

...שנ׳ אלהים נצב בעדת אל בקרב אלהים
ישפוט מניין שאפילו חמשה שנ׳ ואנודתו על ארץ יסדה מניין שאפילו שלשה
שנ׳ בקרב אלהים ישפוט.

In Pereq IV. 23 it has בִּפְרוֹזְדּוֹד, לִפְרוֹזְדּוֹד; and it places רב׳ אומר עשה
רצונו כו׳ (II. 4) after IV. 19.

The commentary (fol. 237 a—266 a) reads, on Pereq I. 3,

וּשְׁמַעְתִּי שצדוק וביתוס תלמידיו היו,

instead of referring (as some copies here do) to the עָרוּךְ, which would limit
its age.

Pereq VI. is also commented upon, and it is remarked that for "FIVE
possessions" the reading should be THREE.

No. 117 contains two commentaries, of which the former is that attributed to RASHI (fol. 91 a—95 b). See also under No. 130.

Nos. 118—120.

(PARIS 327, 387, 646.)

These contain copies of the commentary of R. JACOB BEN SHIMSHON, or רי״ש. See above pp. 90, 94.

No. 118 reads on Pereq v. 9, marking שנתגל for omission

ופי הבאר ‹שנתגל› פי׳ הבאר שהיה מגלגל עם ישר׳ במדבר מנחליאל כו׳.

In this mishnah the true reading may perhaps be והבאר, the interpolation of פי mouth being due in part to a misreading of the abbreviation פי׳ in some ancient *Perush*.

No. 119 contains Rashi's *Sepher ha-Pardes*, followed by the commentary of רי״ש on ABOTH. Notice in this the reading in the introductory part (fol. 202 a, line 4),

אין ניקוד טברני דומה לניקוד שלנו׳

and the reading on Pereq III. 18,

ויש מפרשין הוי קל ראש הקל את ראשך כלומר הוי זריז במלאכתך בבחורות׳
כדי שתנוח בזקנתך. וי״א הוי קל לראש לשר הבירה.

No. 120 is a fine Machazor transcribed a little before 1396 A.D. In the commentary we miss such critical notes as ובתפלה ל״נ (II. 17). In Pereq II. 1 it reads לעוֹשֵׂה תפארת.

Nos. 121, 122.

(PARIS 328—9, 330.)

These contain RAMBAM in Hebrew on ABOTH, in its place as a tract of the Mishnah ; and the former adds the commentary of רי״ש on Pereq VI., but under the name of Rashi.

Nos. 123—125.

(PARIS 152, 169, 448.)

The commentary of R. ISAAC ISRAELI on the Six Peraqim.

No. 124, which contains a roughly written copy of the commentary (fol. 119 a—196 b), breaks off on Pereq IV. 31 with the words

ומהו השחד אלא שהכוונה בזה׳

No. 125 begins on the *Great Synagogue*, and a leaf is missing before fol. 29, which commences at Pereq II. 5 with the words צבור שמעשיהם כעורים.

The copy of the same commentary which should be in No. 130 is missing

No. 126.

(Paris 583.)

At the beginning and up to fol. 134 a is a commentary in Arabic "attribué à R. David... Le ms. a été exécuté au Caire à une époque récente." If the author is R. David (ben Jehoshua) ben Abraham ben Mosheh ben Maimon, it may be put down to the middle of the 14th century.

No. 127.

(Paris 739.)

The work מגן אבות of R. Shim'on ben Tsemach Duran, completed in 1559—60 A.D., including a commentary on Aboth (fol. 199 b—269 a), first printed at Livorno in 1763 A.D.

No. 128.

(Paris 719.)

This includes a copy of R. Shem Tob ben Shem Tob's commentary on the Six Peraqim, defective at the end.

The Peraqim begin respectively on the pages,

107 a, 123 b, 128 a, 133 b, 135 b, 139 b.

Nos. 129, 130.

(Paris 455, 769.)

No. 129 is an excellent copy (but with three pages in a later hand) of the commentary of R. Joseph ibn Shoshan on Aboth, dated (?) 5148 A.M. (=1388 A.D.). He sometimes gives Arabic equivalents for Hebrew words, as for ספוג and משמרת in Pereq v. 21.

No. 130 is a defective copy of the same, dated 1496 A.D., commencing near the beginning of Pereq II. with the words,

וחוזר אותו הכח ומתצמצם בו׳,

which are found at fol. 24 a, line 14 in No. 129, so that the contents of 23 out of the 91 folios of that copy are missing in this.

The scribe Isaac ibn Shoshan writes that he transcribed "these commentaries of R. Isaac Israel and R. Joseph Shoshan at גוליטא on the coast of Tunis." The former of these is not in the codex.

No. 131.

(Paris 452.)

An unnamed commentary, which proves to be that of

ר׳ יוסף יעבץ

described above on p. 80.

No. 132.

(Paris 589.)

The volume begins with a German translation and commentary on ABOTH in Hebrew characters. On a fly leaf is written,

295. Liber Cabbalisticus. Lingua Theutonica.

Nos. 133—136.

(Paris 306, 636, 643, 647.)

Codices containing the text of ABOTH without commentary.

No. 133 has some remarkable correspondences with the text in the Cambridge Manuscript of the Mishnah, No. 98 (pp. 69—78). The following are specimens of its readings:

Pereq II. 5, שְׁלֹשָׁה שלשה ,14 שאיפשר לשמוע שסופו להשמע .18 מה without ודע.

Pereq III. 9, as in No. 98. 18, הוי קל ראש, with a small ל inserted above the line before ראש, in brown ink like the points, the letters of the text being black.

Pereq v. 9, ופי הבאר omitted. 28, the order as in No. 98, and שנ׳ אתה is omitted. 31, omitting שאין לך כו׳,

...הפוך בה וַהֲפֵךְ בה דכולה בה ומלך בה ובה תהוי ומנה לא תזוע.

The reading ומלך is clearly a corruption of וכולך (No. 98).

Nos. 137—150.

These are the codices of the Stadtbibliothek of HAMBURG numbered respectively,

34, 42, 89, 105, 109, 116, 129, 171, 200, 205, 208, 212, 234, 243 ;

and consisting mostly of Prayer Books which were examined by the writer in the year 1876. The corresponding numbers in the *Catalogue* of 1878 by Steinschneider are given below in brackets, with the letter S prefixed.

No. 137 (S. 85) contains portions of ABOTH, pointed, on seven folios, not arranged in their true order, namely,

From Pereq II. 13 to III. 17 on folios 36, 43 ;

From Pereq v. 3 to כל מה שנברא, in VI. on folios 2, 3, 8, 4, 5.

In Pereq III. 9 it reads, but with בקרב אלהים unpointed and marked for omission,

...בעדת אל (בקרב אלהים) מניין שאפילו שלשה שנ׳ ואגודתו כו׳,

thus deliberately omitting the number FIVE.

No. 138 (S. 87) contains a pointed text of ABOTH (fol. 60 a—7 b), with several omissions, some of which are supplied in a later hand.

Pereq II. 4 is omitted, but added below in the margin. In the text it stands after Pereq IV. 19, with the reading שיבטל רצונן. It is remarked by commentators on the received text that רצונו was to have been expected here, but רצון אחרים was put for it by way of euphemism.

No. 139 (S. 88) contains the Six Peraqim unpointed (fol. 38 b—48 b). It reads in inverted order,

ר׳ א׳ עשה רצונך כרצונו,

and places the saying after Pereq IV. 19, instead of at II. 4.

No. 140 (S. 89) has the Six Peraqim, pointed (fol. 74 a—93 b). It omits Pereq IV. 20, and in its place gives a short reading of II. 4,

ר׳ אומר עשה רצונך כרצונו בטל רצונך כו׳.

No. 141 (S. 56) consists of ten folios, modern, and has the beginning of a commentary on Job, followed by fragments on ABOTH (fol. 7—10).

No. 142 (S. 84) is a "Thephillah" of date 1459 A.D. in which Pereq VI. ends thus,

אַרְבָעָה קנינים...בן בג בג...בן הא הא...יהי רצון כו'.

No. 144 (S. 157) contains a Latin translation of ABOTH, written in an interleaved copy of a printed edition, by L. JOH. AD. SCHERZIUS, Leipsiae, 1664.

Nos. 143, 145—9 (S. 90, 93, 101, 94, 95, 97), contain the Six Peraqim, pointed or unpointed.

No. 150 (S. 98) has the Six Peraqim, pointed. It reads in

Pereq III. 9, repeating בקרב כו',

...בעדת אל בקרב אלהים ישפוט...חמשה שנ' בקרב...שלשה שנ' ואגודתו כו'.

שנברא **בצלמו** חבה יתירה לו שנברא בצלם כו' 22,

Pereq v. 31, הפוך בה והפך בה ובה תהוי ומנה כו'.

Nos. 151—155.

These manuscripts of the Royal Library of BERLIN, numbered respectively in the Oriental Collection,

361, 498, 567, 627, 629,

were collated in 1876. Their numbers in the *Verzeichniss* of Hebrew Manuscripts by Steinschneider forming Part II. of the general catalogue of manuscripts belonging to the above-mentioned Library and published in 1878 are given below in brackets.

No. 151 (S. 51) is a small German Machazor with marginal "Scholien," which "erklären den Inhalt und behandeln das Ritual häufig nach **ויטרי**." The commentary occasionally takes fantastic shapes, as of an ape, or a flamingo. On fol. 94 b (cf. 114) it forms the name of the scribe בנימן **הלבלר**, and on fol. 95 a that of his patron יצחק בן חננאל.

It has the Six Peraqim, pointed by a later hand, and accompanied by the commentary of **רש"י** (fol. 70 a—95 a). It omits ובתפלה in Pereq II. 17; תורה in II. 18; and חבה יתרה כו' in III. 22; reads גופיה תורה in the text of III. 28, with הֲלָכוֹת in the margin; and reads on III. 18, in the commentary,

הקל את ראשך והוי כקנה שהולך כו'.

No. 152 (S. 60) has the Five Peraqim with RAMBAM's commentary, in Hebrew, followed by Pereq VI. with that of רש"י.

No. 153 (S. 24) has ABOTH in its place in the Mishnah, with the commentary of RAMBAM in Hebrew (fol. 166 a—176 b).

No. 154 (S. 89) is a Yemen Siddur, containing the Six Peraqim with the נקוד העליון (fol. 16 b); the sixth Pereq is here of peculiar form, like that of No. 84. After בשם מרדכי it adds דבר בשם אומרו כו' ושאינו או'. Then come a number of BEATITUDES, and lastly the saying on the יש עולמות (T. B. Sanh. 100 a), and ר' חנניה בן עקשיא כו'. This chapter is named קנין תורה, and is expressly said to be ברייתא and no part of the genuine ABOTH.

In the Five Peraqim this manuscript, like No. 98, reads בצמאה (I. 4); עמלים כו' (II. 2); ככבוד חברך (IV. 7); פרוזדוד, with two *Daleths* (IV. 23); שמאי והלל (V. 25). It omits תורה in II. 18, and חבה יתרה כו' in III. 22 and 23.

No. 155 (S. 91) is another Yemen Prayer Book, folio, having the Six Peraqim, with occasional points (fol. 12 b—17 b). Twelve folios from the end of the full-sized pages is a calendar beginning at 1654 A.D.

Nos. 156, 157.

These are the manuscripts 147 and 148 in the first Firkowitz collection which I collated in the course of a visit to the Imperial Library of St PETERSBURG one day in September 1876. They are Prayer Books with the text of ABOTH, both incomplete.

No. 157 reads עין רעה (II. 15); לְפְּרוֹזְדוֹ כו' (IV. 23); אָבִיהָ (IV. 27); שמאי והלל (V. 25); שלי ושלך שלך כו' (V. 16).

No. 158.

This is the copy of the commentary of רש"י referred to above on p. 91 as belonging to the Ashkenazic Jews' College in LONDON. See under No. 6 in Neubauer's *Catalogue* of the Hebrew manuscripts belonging to the College (1886). No. 9 in the same collection is described as ספר עץ אבות, a commentary on Aboth by Naphtali ben R. Abraham Taussig "Neun Greschel," a descendant of Judah Löwe of Prague. The commentary in No. 6 (fol. 90 a—147 b)

is written for the most part in a "Magna-Graecian" hand
of from 1275 to 1325 A.D. The following account of it
is from a transcript of the commentary made for me by
Dr Schiller-Szinessy.

The scribe wrote from a copy which was defective in Pereq v., and
used another commentary to supplement it.

Passing over the gap inadvertently in the first instance, he goes on at
once from עם הארץ in v. 15 to עין טובה כו' (v. 28). But on perceiving the
omission he writes in the margin at the end of v. 15, "see on the next
folio," עיין בדף שני (fol. 136 b).

On the next page (fol. 137 a), after v. 28, he writes (with reference to
what he is about to insert to supply the omission) :

מכאן עד יהודה בן תימא אומ' הוי עז כנמר לא מצאתי בהעתק
והעתקתיו מפי' אחר ושכחתי מלכותבו במקומו לפיכך כתבתיו הנה,

and he accordingly gives notes extracted from this "other commentary" on
the omitted sayings, from ארבע מידות בדיעות כו' (v. 16) onward, on a
smaller scale and not quite covering the whole ground. These extracts
reach to the beginning of fol. 138 a. The saying of יהודה בן תימא (v. 29)
is then commented upon from the original manuscript.

Many of the Rabbinic commentaries on ABOTH are of this composite
character; but this note explaining how a part of one has come to be
embodied in another is quite exceptional, and of great interest. In other
cases, especially in short marginal commentaries, the writer, while following one *perush* on the whole, will frequently work into it notes from
another which seem to him more edifying or to the point, till the distinctive features of the original are more or less completely obliterated.

The sayings of בן הא הא and בן בג בג are commented upon in this
manuscript as part of Pereq v., whereas in No. 20 they are placed at the
end of Pereq R. MEIR. See above, p. 23.

No. 159.

This belongs to the same collection as No. 158, and is No. 37
in Neubauer's *Catalogue* of it. It is a Siddur, of "about
1610," including a pointed text of the Six Peraqim, and
with a grammatical commentary by one Shabbethai ha-
Sofer. The text of Aboth has the accented syllables
marked and Scripture passages accentuated. It is a
feature of the commentary on Aboth that it discusses
the pointing of words in the text.

Nos. 160—168.

The BRITISH MUSEUM manuscripts, Additional 26922, and
Oriental 2389, 2390, 2417, 2418, 2673, 2735, 2736, 2772.

No. 160 (Additional 26922, Almanzi collection), which is in a Sepharadic
Rabbinic hand, contains

(1) A commentary on the Five Peraqim by דון יוסף בן שושן (fol.
99 a—190 a), followed by a commentary on Pereq VI. by

ר׳ שם טוב ן׳ שם טוב·

(2) A commentary on the Six Peraqim by רבי׳ בחיי הדיין (fol.
217 a—285 b), copied by David Hassoun in the year 1534 A.D. (fol. 286 a),
for ר׳ משה הלוי בן אלקאבץ. It begins, ר׳ שלמה הלוי בכֹּר החכם השלם

ראשית חכמה יראת ה׳· עליון הנמצא הקדמון השוכן ברום חביון·

The author, who lived in the 13th century, quotes his teacher, the
famous Shelomoh ibn Addereth, וכן כתב מורי ר׳ שלמה נֹר (236 b), and
Rashi, Redaq and Rambam (229 a). On "Bachja" and his other works
see Dr Bela Bernstein's *Die Schrifterklärung des* Bachja b. Asher ibn
Chalâwa *und seine Quellen* (Berlin, 1891), an extract from the *Mag. f. d.
Wiss. des Judenthums*. Dr Bernstein does not notice this *Perush*. See
also Luzzatto in Steinschneider's המזכיר, vol. IV. 56 (Berlin, 1861).

Pereq v. ends with יהודה בן תימא··· הוא היה אום׳ עז פנים כו׳.

Pereq VI. is headed

פרק ששי , בן בג בג,

and contains comments on the sayings:

בן בג בג אום׳ הפוך בה והפך בה כו׳. לפום צערא אגרא· שמואל הקטן
אום׳ בן חמש כו׳. ר׳ אבא אום׳ אשרי מי שגדל בתורה כו׳. ר׳ חנניה כו׳.

No. 161 (Oriental 2735) is an Ashkenazic Machazor, of the 14th century,
on vellum, containing the Six Peraqim in square character, pointed (fol.
51 a—78 a), with the commentary of רי״ש in the margin of the text and
on the whole of the page preceding it. It shews a transitional state of
the ending of Pereq v. where, after שבשמים, come the sayings:

שמואל הקטן כו׳. בן חמש כו׳. עז פנים כו׳. (with *baraitha*). אשרי מי שגדל
בתורה כו׳.

These are followed by :

סליק פירקא, מכאן ואילך היא תוספת העולם,

and the sayings of בן הא הא and בן בג בג are not contained in this chapter, but come at the end of the next.

In the margin, however, after שֶׁבַּשָּׁמַיִם (fol. 71 b), is written, on the right hand,

הוא היה אומ' עז פנים כו'. בן הא הא כו'. בן בג בג כו',

and on the left hand,

סליקו לך מסכת אבות,

and the saying of בן בג בג is commented upon at the end of Pereq v., and not in its place in Pereq vi., where it stands in the text.

No. 162 (Or. 2736) is an Italian Siddur in Sepharadic handwriting, dated on the last page but one (fol. 479 a), Bertinoro, 5150 A.M., or 1390 A.D. It contains the six Peraqim, in square characters and with points (fol. 280 b —314 a).

No. 163 (Or. 2772) is an Ashkenazic Machazor, written a little before the year 1314 A.D., with which its calendar begins (fol. 297 a), and containing the Six Peraqim, in square characters and with points (fol. 92 a—122 a).

Nos. 164—168 are Prayer Books of the rite of Yemen.

No. 164 (Or. 2389) contains the Six Peraqim unpointed (fol. 16 b—22 a).

No. 165 (Or. 2390) the Six Peraqim with the נקוד העליון, except in the sixth and part of the fifth (fol. 18 a—24 a). Pereq vi. begins in the usual way, but ends with a series of BEATITUDES, like No. 84.

No. 166 (Or. 2417) the Six Peraqim unpointed (fol. 44 a—48 b), with here and there a short marginal note.

No. 167 (Or. 2418) the Six Peraqim with the נקוד העליון (fol. 12 a—17a).

No. 168 (Or. 2673) the Five Peraqim with the נקוד העליון (fol. 15 a—19 a).

No. 169.

Among Aboth manuscripts in the possession of the writer may be mentioned an autograph eclectic commentary of date 5423 A.M. by Aharon de Shelomoh Antones, a Sepharadi living in the neighbourhood of Amsterdam.

No. 170.

This is Codex 184 of the de-Rossi collection, now in the Royal Library of PARMA. It contains a commentary on the Five Peraqim followed by two fragments inserted to fill blank spaces ; additional notes on Pereq III. 24, 25 ending כך פי' ר' משולם בר' קלונימוס מרומי ; and a short Hebrew Lexicon from אבל to תפוח. De-Rossi ascribed the commentary to R. Meshullam ; but it is clearly of different authorship from the detached notes above mentioned, and it proves to be a recension of a well known work attributed to Rashi with additions from Maimonides. The notes by R. Meshullam are from the *Aruch*, which is also referred to by name on fol. 8 b.

The codex contains 108 leaves of paper, now measuring about 5½ by 4¼ inches. The writing is Spanish rabbinic, of about cent. xv. The volume is described as follows by Joh. Bern. de-Rossi in the published catalogue of his *MSS. Codices Hebraici &c.*, vol. I. p. 120 (Parma, 1803):

COD. 184

1. PIRKE AVOTH seu *Capitula patrum* cum *Comm.* R. Mescullam fil. Kalonymi de Roma.

2. ANON. *Lexicon breve heb.* chart. rabb. in 12 sec. xv.

Commentarii auctor colligitur ex verbis, quibus explicit, si ea quidem, ut videntur, de expositione integri libri sunt intelligenda, *Sic exposuit R. Mescullam fil. R. Kalonymi de Roma. Finitus et absolutus.* Hunc scriptorem vix memorat Wolfius T. I p. 102, de hoc autem opere silet profunde.

BENIACOB in his אוצר הספרים, No. 102 p. 458 (Wilna, 1880), follows de-Rossi in ascribing the commentary to R. Meshullam, without mention of his expression of doubt, "si ea quidem, ut videntur &c."

RAPOPORT accepted de-Rossi's conclusion, and even imagined that he had confirmed it. Finding the detached notes from R. Meshullam (fol. 68 a—69 b) in the *Aruch*, and not doubting that they belonged to the commentary, he called it R. Meshullam's, and added ומובא ממנו כבר מן הערוך (ערך סער). See letter I. p. 16 in *S. L. Rappoport's Heb. Briefe an S. D. Luzzatto*, ed. Eisig Gräber (Przemysl, 1885).

De-Rossi's "PIRKE AVOTH cum *Comm.*" comprises the commentary, two minor fragments written to fill up its last folio, and the detached notes from R. Meshullam.

1. Perush Rashi-Rambam.

A collation of the *Perush* in the manuscript with an edition of "Rashi" and Rambam's commentaries on the Five Peraqim (Mantua, 1560 A.D.) shews that it is a recension of the former with considerable additions from the latter, its longer notes in particular being more or less compounded of Rambam's.

Fol. 1 a—5 a. The Peraqim have for preface an expansion of כל ישראל יש להם חלק כו׳ with Rambam's enumeration of the thirteen foundations of the Law. See on Mishn. *Sanh.* XI (*al.* x) 1.

The Peraqim begin severally on

fol. 5 b, 15 b, 26 a, 36 a, 50 a.

The following extracts are given partly for the sake of their readings in the text of ABOTH, and partly as specimens of the *Perush.* Passages in **Rabbinic** type are from Rambam.

צדוק וביתום For the story of .עַל מְנָת שֶׁלֹא לקבל פרס PEREQ I. 3, the עָרוּךְ is referred to (8 b₄).

.וישותה בצמאה 4—5, יוסף. 6, יורש. 4,

ובאבות דר׳ נתן מוקים לה באשתו נדה…ואנן גרסי׳ ואפי׳ באשתו 6, טהורה ומפני שמתבטל מדברי תורה.

.וקנה לך חבר, ספרים. ואמרי לה חבר ממש 7, מתאי, 7—8.

.רחק, התחבק (*marg.* רְחֵק), and afterwards (*sic*) הרחק 8,

19. The Pereq ends thus,

שפטו בשעריכם וסמיך ליה אולי יחנן ובמשנה אין כתי׳ מקרא זה. והדין הוא הכהגת המדינה ביושר… והשלום מעלות המדות.

The edition reads ובמשנה טברנית אין כתיב שם פסוק, and adds the note that סמוך לשפטו בשעריכם is not אולי יחנן כו׳, the one verse being in Amos and the other in Zechariah.

PEREQ II. On 1, 3, 6, 10, 15 there are extracts from Rambam. The note on § 1 gives his enumeration of the eight gradations of negative commandments with the penalties attached.

.ואל תאמר דבר שאפשר לשמוע שסופו להשמע 5,

השתדר כמו השתדל ותעסוק בצרכי צבור…תרגו׳ ויאבק א׳ס ואסתדל 6,

(למדת .marg).   9, **עָשִׂית** (for שצפה).   צפה 7,

שְׁלֹשָׁה שְׁלֹשָׁה דברים...כל אחד אמ' שלשה...ונחש שרף לוחש בפיו 14,
שִׁיבְלֵייר כדרך שהאווזין שורקין זה לזה.

שִׁיבְלֵייר] *Siffler.* The לע"ז of the edition agrees generally with that of
the MS.

הוי זהיר בק"ש לקרותו בשעתו.   ותפלה ותפילין לא גר' 17,

The scribe has interpolated ובתפלה in his text ; and in the same saying
אלֹא תחנונים, where רחמים ו' is the true reading of the *Perush.*

PEREQ III. On 1, 4, 9, 17, 18, 19, 24 &c. there are extracts from
Rambam.

ודורש שיושב אחד 4,.   The compiler has recourse to Rambam for the
note,

ופי' וידוס מן הדבור... כאלו נתינת התורה כלה היתה בעבורו לבד,

having (we need not doubt) in his "Rashi" the note quoted as from Rashi
by R. Isaac Isr. (p. 100, A),

ולא מצינו במשנה כתי' ייצב בדד וידום אבל רגילין העם לאומרו.

הנעור, הצועק 7,   הרי אלו כאוכלי זבחי מתים 5,.

9. R. Isaac Isr. quotes Rashi for the reading **חמשה שנ' בקרב כו'**
and its interpretation (p. 100, B). The MS. gives this, and after it, with a
ויש גורסין, the view of Rambam.

13. Fol. 30 ends on **ר' חנינה בן דוסא כו'** with the line,
שמתרחק מן האסור והחטא,

and, *a leaf having been lost,* fol. 31 begins on § 17,
את המועדות והמלבין כו'.

והמגלה פנים בתורה אע"פ שיש בידו תורה ומעשים טובים 17,.

The *Perush* combines "Rashi" and Rambam thus,

מלבין הוא סמביים קבירו.   וי"א מאדים כו'.

מגלה פנים בתורה, דורש אגדות של דופי.   וי"א שעובר על מצות התורה
בפרהסיא...כיהויקים בן יושיהו.

והמפר בריתו, שלא מל.   וי"א המושך לו ערלה.

הֱוֵי קַל לָרֹאשׁ, בראשיתך (*sic*) בחור הוי קל כנגד היוצר... תשחורת 18,

לשון זקנה ... וי"א הוי קל לראש לשר הבירה ... **לתשחורת** לנזברו

מְנַשְׁטֵרֵיל... וי"א קָלוּת [קל ?] ידוע, ונח הוא הישוב והנחת.

The beginning of this agrees with R. Isaac Israeli's "Rashi" (p. 101, C);
the לע"ז with the edition ; and the end with Rambam.

25. The *Perush* quotes from Rambam הוא משל על המות, and continues
according to Rashi as quoted by R. Isaac Isr. (p. 101, D).

27. The Scripture proofs said to be not במשנה.   28, **וגימטריא**.

PEREQ IV. 7. Story from Rambam to illustrate מאד מאד הוי שפל רוח.

ib., ה"ג אחד בשוגג ואחד במזיד בחילול השם.   *No. 98 is defective here.*

8. R. Isaac Isr. quotes as distinctive of Rashi the negative reading
ה"ג אין מספיקין (p. 101, E); and the MS. reads אין מספיקין בידו ללמוד
וללמד (40 a₅).

9, וכך היה הלל **דורש**.   Note from Rambam.

11, בפני.   15,   14, ממעט בעסק.   ה"ג ר' ישמעאל **בנו**.

17, R. Isaac Isr. quotes Rashi as reading ככבוד הבירך (p. 101, F).
And this is the true reading of the MS., which, after some clerical errors,
concludes thus (44 a₁),

משמע קרוב לכבוד הבירך , וכן כבוד חבירך קרוב למורא רבך...

פרוזדור, פורקא בל'... שכל מי שטרח בערב שבת יאכל בשבת וי"מ 23,
טרקלין הסיכל ופרוזדור בית סער.

27, **אֲבִיָה**.   28, אגרייש בלעז.   קהות...

PEREQ V. 2, מי המבול ... לפניו ... **שבכל** הדורות.

5—6, ... ועשרה על הים הס קבלה... ומלינו בקבלה ג"כ... (53 a₁).

8. The MS. has the note וכמדומה לי שהוא שבוש... on the two sayings
צר לי המקום ללון **בתוכו**, ; and a note beginning לא כבו כו' ולא נצחה כו'
pointing to the reading שאלין בירושלם; both of which are quoted as
Rashi's by R. Isaac Isr. (p. 101, G).

9, נ"א צבתא בצבתא מתעבדא צבתא קמייתא במאי עבדא.

29, **יהודה בן תימא**... תכפה לאותה שלר' עקי'...עשה שבתך חול כו'.
This note is quoted as Rashi's by R. Isaac Isr. (p. 102, H).

עז פנים ...בימינו ... **עַד כאן כת' במשנה**, ומוסיפין בו עז פנים. 30,

ר' אליעזר אומ' ממזר... ושנינו במס' כלה... **ר' חנינא בן עקשיא**
אומ'. אינו לא מן המשנה ולא מן הברייתא אלא סיום יפה הוא ונהגו העם לאמרו
בסיום הפרקים לפי שאין אומ' על המשנה קדיש אלא על ההגדה כדאמ' מר
ואמ' יהא שמיה באגדתא.

.הפוך בה והפך בה ... ואל תתמה במשנה זו שהיא בלשון ארמי ... 31,

The *Perush* ends on fol. 67 a thus,

בן בג בג פי' בן גיורת בן גיורת שלא רצו חכמי' להלבין פניהם לפי שהיו
גרים ורמזוהו בזה הלשון. ג"כ **בן הא הא** ר"ל אל'ף מאברהם וה"א משרה
כמו שהיו מגיירין לאנשים ולנשים זיכת' ואת הנפש אשר עשו.

2. Minor Fragments.

1. The lower half of fol. 67 a is filled up with the fable of the Ant and
the Grasshopper, written in four lines, thus:

אמ' ליה שושפויי לאנמלתוי · הב לי מן
הטוי · אמ' ליה ואת בקייטא מאי עבדת'
אמ' ליה זמירנא · אמ' ליה השתא זיל
רקוד דלא אכלת מן חטוי דאגירנא בקיטוי.

שושפויי] See in Buxtorf שׁוֹשִׁיבָא, under שׁׁׁׁׁׁׁשׁׁב. The title of the fable
in Landsberger's *Fabulae aliquot Aram.* p. 28 (Berol. 1846) is שושמנא
וטיטיכום. Lewysohn, in *Zool. des Talm.* § 391 n, p. 294 (Frankf. a. M. 1858),
wrote conjecturally "שושיבא mag mit שושיפא verwandt sein," apparently
not knowing that שׁוּשִׁיפָא was in actual use for a kind of *locust.* But it
is so used in *Tosaphoth Chullin* 65 b, ד"ה ואלו כללי, where it is defined
as מין חגב. See Kohut's *Aruch Completum* under סוסבל (1890). On
the authority of Cod. de-Rossi 184 we may now add the form שׁוּשְׁפָא for
מין חגב, a kind of *locust* which says זמירנא, *I was singing,* or the Greek
טיטכום*. On the "locust" or "bird" פְּרַזֵי see *Aruch Compl.* and *Zool. des
Talmud* § 393, noting that the τέττιξ was often classed with birds, as by
the authorities named in the writer's *Dirge of Coheleth,* p. 35 (1874). It is
called טיטכום ציפרא in Landsberger's text of the fable.

* Thus the τέττιξ is מין חגב. This is of interest to commentators on Ecclesiastes, since
in ויסתבל החגב (xii. 5) it has been suggested that the חגב is the τέττιξ, and the objection
has been made that חגב could not have that meaning.

2. The spare page fol. 67 b is filled with Rambam's explanations of some ABOTH words in Arabic, beginning,

פרוזדור הו אל דהליז.   טרקלין הו אל קצר.
בור ועם הארץ וגולם וחסיד וחכם.

This fragment is written in a comparatively small hand, so as to fit into the blank space which marked the conclusion of the *Perush*. For the substance of line 1 in Hebrew see above under Pereq IV. 23 in Rabbinic type. The explanations of the words in line 2, which fill the remainder of the page, are from Rambam on שבעה דברים בגולם כו' (v. 10).

3. R. Meshullam ben Qalonymos.

Fol. 68 a—69 b. Four pages of additional notes on Pereq III. 24, 25, to which rather more than three pages had been given in the *Perush* (fol. 33 a—34 b).

In the upper margin of fol. 68 a is written ורצוני לפרש, and then follow notes commencing הכל צפוי ואית דאמרי הכל צפון, and ending,

והכל מתוקן לסעודה, זה כינוי של מיתה... ולמה נקראת מיתה סעודה
ללמדך כשנקראין בני אדם לסעודה הכל נכנסין בפתח אחד אבל ביושבין אין
יושבין אלא כל אחד ואחד לפי כבודו אף בשעת פטירתו מקרה אחד לצדיק
ולרשע ולעניין כבוד כל אחד כפי מעשיו. כך פי' ר' משולם בר' קלונימוס
מרומי.

A later hand has added תם ונשלם.

These notes are from the Art. סעד in the *Aruch*.

No. 20 quotes R. Meshullam on the סעודה (p. 22), and has on the preceding page (fol. 115 a),

ואית דאמרי הכל צפון מלמד שכל מעשיהם של בני אדם צפונין הן אצל
הק' שנ' הלא הוא כמוס עמדי.

The *Magen Aboth* gives הכל צפון as a reading of some of the גאונים, without mention of the name of R. Meshullam.

R. ISAAC ISRAELI quotes R. Meshullam on the סעודה (p. 99).

THE TALMUD TRACTS.

THE TALMUD TRACTS.

A. TALMUD JERUSHALMI.

This Index shews where the several Tracts begin in the Editio Princeps.

The Editio Princeps (Venez. 1523—4) of what remains of the Palestinian Talmud, or Talmud Jerushalmi (abbrev. T. J.), makes one volume consisting of four parts, in which the folios of the text are numbered 1—65, 1—83, 1—66, 1—51 respectively, and each folio has four columns, which we call (in italics) *a, b, c, d.* Frankel numbers them א' ב' ג' ד' in his edition of T. J. Berakhoth, Peah and Demai (1874—5). The same order and pagination are kept in the editions of Cracow (1609) and Krotoschin (1866). These are furnished with short marginal comments, and the latter has הגהות and מראה מקום by Mordecai Weissmann Chayoth.

There is a Zitomir edition of the T. J. with commentaries in four volumes, dated in their order 1866, 1860, 1867, 1865. It pages the tracts separately, but places them in the order of the Editio Princeps, except that it puts מכות after עבודה זרה.

Raphael Kirchheim first edited (Frankf. a. M. 1851) שבע מסכתות קטנות ירושלמיות, from MS. Carmoly, namely 1 מס' ספר תורה. 2 מס' מזוזה. מס' 7 . מס' כותים 6 . מס' עבדים 5 . מס' ציצית 4 . מס' תפילין 3 גרים. They have been reprinted in the new Wilna edition of the Talmud Babli (1883), in the order 7, 6, 5, 1, 3, 4, 2.

B. MISHNAH. TALMUD BABLI. TOSEFTA.

This Index gives the names of the Mishnah Tracts in the order of the editions of
Surenhusius (p. 64), Rabe (Snolzbach, 1760—2) and Jost (Berl. 1832—4).
Rabbinic type indicates that a Tract has no Babylonian Gemara.

ı סדר זרעים. ¹ברכות· ²פאה· ³דמאי· ⁴כלאים· ⁵שביעית· ⁶תרומות·
⁷מעשרות· ⁸מעשר סני· ⁹חלה· ¹⁰ערלה· ¹¹בכורים:

ıı סדר מועד. ¹שבת· ²ערובין· ³פסחים· ⁴שקלים· ⁵יומא· ⁶סוכה·
⁷ביצה· ⁸ראש השנה· ⁹תענית· ¹⁰מגילה· ¹¹מועד קטן· ¹²חגיגה:

ııı סדר נשים. ¹יבמות· ²כתובות· ³נדרים· ⁴נזיר· ⁵סוטה· ⁶גיטין·
⁷קדושין:

ıv סדר נזיקין. ¹בבא קמא· ²בבא מציעא· ³בבא בתרא· ⁴סנהדרין·
⁵מכות· ⁶שבועות· ⁷עדיות· ⁸עבודה זרה· ⁹אבות· ¹⁰הוריות:

v סדר קדשים. ¹זבחים· ²מנחות· ³חולין· ⁴בכורות· ⁵ערכין· ⁶תמורה·
⁷כריתות· ⁸מעילה· ⁹תמיד· ¹⁰מדות· ¹¹קנים:

vı סדר טהרות. ¹כלים· ²אהלות· ³נגעים· ⁴פרה· ⁵טהרות·
⁶מקואות· ⁷נדה· ⁸מכשירין· ⁹זבים· ¹⁰טבול יוס· ¹¹ידיס·
¹²עוקלין:

For a good comparative Index of the Tracts in MSS. and editions of the
Mishnah and the Talmudim see Strack's *Einleitung in den Thalmud.*
It is not possible to make a compendious Index which will suit all editions
of the Talmud Babli (abbrev. T. B.), but it is easy to index an edition for
private use. Thus, if a *Massekheth* be denoted by the number of its
SEDER with its own number in it as above, Berakhoth being I. 1 and so on,
the order of the מסכתות or מסכות (No. 98, f. 69 a) in the Amsterdam edition of 1644—7 (as I have it in an old binding) may be expressed by

    I. 1—11 [vol. 1]. ıı. 1. 2 [vol. 2]. 3. 12. 7. 11 [vol. 3]. 8. 5. 6. 9. 4.
10 [vol. 4]. ııı. 1. 2. 7 [vol. 5]. 6. 3. 5. 4 [vol. 6]. ıv. 1. 2 [vol. 7]. 3.
4 [vol. 8]. 5. 6. 9. 10. 7. 8 [vol. 9]. v. 1. 3 [vol. 10]. 2. 4. 5. 8. 11. 9. 10.
7. 6 [vol. 11]. vı. 7. 1—6. 8—12 [vol. 12].

In the Tosefta (which omits ıv. 9 and v. 9—11) the order in Dr M. S.
Zuckermandel's edition (Trier, 1882) is

    I. 1. 2. 6. 10. 3. 5. 4. 7—9. 11. ıı. ııı. ıv. 1—8. 10—12. v. 1. 3.
2. 4—6. 8. 7. vı. 1—4. 7. 6. 5. 8. 9. 11. 10. 12.

C. TALMUD CITATIONS.

The Mishnah is cited by *pereq* and *halakhah*, as Shabbath II. 3, with or without the word Mishnah.

The Talmud Babli is cited by the *folio* and *'ammud* of the tract referred to, as Berakhoth 6 a, with or without the prefix T. B.

We shall cite the תלמוד ארץ ישראל or Talmud Jerushalmi by *folio* and *column*, as in the Krotoschin edition, calling the two columns on the one side of a folio *a, b* and the two on the other side *c, d*, thus T. J. Nazir 52 *c*, and sometimes giving the *line* also. The folio number 52 belongs to Seder III., the division of the volume in which the tract Nazir is found. The T. J. will also be cited by *pereq* and *halakhah*. It would be convenient if it were customary to refer to the Zitomir edition, which numbers the *halakhoth* clearly and has less of the text in a page than ed. princ. in the 75 lines or thereabout of a column.

Before the age of printing, the *peraqim* in Talmud citations were indicated by their initial words, as we still speak of the *Te Deum* from its commencement in the Latin. Thus רש"י, near the beginning of his *perush* on Aboth, writes במאימתי קורין, meaning *In Berakhoth cap.* I, which commences מאימתי קורין את שמע בערבין. A chapter cited in this way, without mention of the tract to which it belongs, may be found with the help of the alphabetical list of the 524 פרקים of the Mishnah in Mr Lowe's *Fragment of T. B. Pesachim*, pp. 50 sq (Camb. 1879).

In Shabbath 31 a the words of Is. xxxiii. 6 אמונת עתיך חוסן ישועות חכמה ודעת are made to correspond to the names of the six *Sedarim* in their customary order. Thus the fourth becomes ישועות, as נזיקין is euphemistically named in editions of the T. J. and elsewhere. In Bemidb. R. XIII. 16 and Midr. Tillim, on תמימה כו' (ה' תורת (Ps. xix. 8—10), the six are named in the order III. I. VI. II. V. IV. An authority for the order I. II. III. V. VI. IV. is given by Neubauer in ANECD. OXON. *Mediaev. Jewish Chronicles* p. 3 (1887).

The Mishnah tracts are 60 in number according to Midr. R. on Cant. vi. 9 אחת היא יונתי, where it is said of verse 8 ששים המה מלכות [מ' הלכות] המה ששים מסכתיות של הלכות. The usual reckoning makes 63, but the three בבות (IV. 1—3) are merely subdivisions of נזיקין מס' (p. 65). Thus the number is reduced to 61. The further reduction to 60 is effected in various ways, as by omitting Aboth, which does not consist of הלכות, or by counting Shabbath and 'Erubin as one, or Sanhedrin and Makkoth as one. The question is fully discussed by Chaim M. Horowitz in *Uralte Tosefta's Abth.* I. (Frankf. a. M. 1889).

T. J. Niddah and other tracts mentioned by Strack have an incomplete Gemara. Sheqalim in the T. B. has a Gemara borrowed from the T. J., and Horaioth there has usually both T. B. and T. J. Gemara. Mr Lowe's alphabetical list shews by the use of small type when a chapter of the Mishnah has no Gemara.

The tracts in the Babli are paged separately* and arranged more or less arbitrarily in volumes, there being no complete tradition as to their order. The relative order of Rosh ha-shanah and Ta'anith is determined by Ta'an. 2 a, תנא מר"ה סליק: of Nazir and Sotah by Sot. 2 a: and of Shebu'oth, Makkoth by Makk. 2 b, end. Aboth is said by רי"ש to belong to סדר ישועות, its place in that Seder being said to be after 'Abodah Zarah and before Horaioth.

There are some variations in the names of the tracts, as below :

I. 7 מעשרות or מעשר ראשון.

II. 3 פסחים or פסח. 5 יומא or יום הכפורים or ביפורים (p. 64). 9 תענית. ביצה שנולדה ביום טוב the tract beginning יום טוב or ביצה 7 or תעניות. 11 מועד קטן or משקין. 12 חגיגה or ראייה (Tosefta).

III. 1 יבמות or נשים (No. 98, f. 77 b). 4 נזיר or נזירות (Tos.).

IV. 1—3 are parts of one tract נזיקין (p. 64). In the Tosefta כלים also is divided into three *Baboth.* 7 עדיות or עדויות. 8 עבודה זרה or עכו"ם or עבודת אלילים, but this is "lediglich Erfindung der Censur" (Strack).

V. 1 זבחים or שחיטת קדשים. 3 חלין or חולין or שחיטת חולין. (p. 65).

VI. 2 אהלות or אהילות (Tos.). 8 מכשירין or משקין.

Editions of the T. B. contain, usually at the end of the fourth Seder, certain so-called מסכתות קטנות, which however are not Mishnah Tracts. These minor tracts are אבות דרבי נתן (called also as by רי"ש the ברייתא or מישנה of R. Nathan), מס' סופרים, מס' אבל רבתי (or euphemistically מס' שמחות), מס' כלה, מס' דרך ארץ רבה, מס' דרך ארץ זוטא and פרק השלום. The new Wilna edition has also מס' כלה רבתי והברייתא. For the seven מס' קטנות ירושלמיות see p. 125.

---

* Except the tracts without Gemara and the short tract Tamid, and except the tracts v. 5. 8. 11. 9. 10. 7. 6 in ed. Amst. above mentioned. Note that this is not always bound in twelve volumes, and that the volumes of the copy indexed on p. 126 are not numbered. The MISHNAH as contained in editions thereof is sometimes called המשנה שבבמשניות.

ABOTH.

NOTES ON THE TEXT.

ABOTH.

NOTES ON THE TEXT.

CHAPTER I.

The manuscripts described above are hereinafter referred to by their numbers, except that the letters 𝔄 𝔅 ℭ 𝔇 𝔖 are used as below, namely

𝔄 for No. 98, which contains the text of Aboth, pp. 69—78.

𝔅 for No. 115, a copy of the commentary of R. Isaac Israeli or "Bar Shelomoh".

ℭ for No. 104, the Machazor of R. Nathanael ben Joseph, grandfather of "Natanel der heilige de Chinon."

𝔇 for No. 20, which contains a recension of the commentary of רי״ש (p. 24) by R. Isaac Dorbel. For the *Notes* I have used a transcript of this commentary made for me by the late Dr Schiller-Szinessy.

𝔖 for No. 159, which contains the commentary of Shabbethai ha-Sofer.

A few printed works on Aboth may be briefly mentioned here

R. Jonah (Berl. 1848). מלאכת שלמה (abbrev. M. Shelom.) printed with ha-Meiri's בית הבחירה (Wien, 1854): it consists of notes on the text cited mostly from יהוֹסֵ,ף אׁשׁכנזי (Ashk.). מנן אבות by Duran (Leipz. 1855). See No. 127*. מדרש שמואל (Midr. Shem.) by ש׳ די אוזידא (Wars. 1876). עץ אבות by Jacob Emden (Amst. 1741). S. Baer in the Siddur עבודת ישׁראל, pp. 271—294 (Rödelheim, 1868). Geiger on Aboth I. II. III. in *Nachgelassene Schriften*, bd. IV. (Berl. 1877). Cahn on Aboth I. (Berl. 1875). Strack *Die Sprüche der Väter* (ed. 2 Berl. 1888). In the Jewish *Authorised Daily Prayer Book* the six Peraqim are accompanied by a translation into English, pp. 184—209 (ed. 2 Lond. 1891).

---

* The date of transcription only is given on p. 109. Add that Dur. lived 1361—1444 A.D.

The Midrash Rabbah on the Pentateuch is cited by section *and subsection* according to the Wilna edition of 1878.

The Aboth de Rabbi Nathan should be read along with Aboth. The best edition, to which we shall sometimes refer by *pages*, is Mr Schechter's (Wien, 1887). This contains two parallel texts *A* and *B*, consisting of 41 and 48 chapters respectively, of which the former only had been printed previously.

The Baboth in Aboth.

Mr Schechter has transcribed from the Bodleian MS. Opp. 497, No. 1575 in Neubauer's *Catalogue*, a statement by R. El'azar of Worms of the number of בבות or (so to say) "verses", in the chapters of Aboth, elaborately illustrated with Scripture parallels for each number. He gives the numbers for the six chapters as 16, 13, 18, 25, 32, 11, and adds that the total for chaps. I—v. is 103, the number expressed by the initials of the words quoted above from Is. xxxiii. 6, namely א' ע' ח' ח' י' ו' (p. 127), whereas the sum of 16, 13, 18, 25, 32 is 104. It does not at once appear how the discrepancy is to be accounted for; but possibly the number 103 should be altered to 104, there being a species of Gematria called הכולל, which allows a word to count as *one* in addition to the number otherwise obtained. Buxtorf under גמט writes on Gen. xi. 1, "Hic שָׂפָה אַחַת valet 794. Totidem לְשׁוֹן הַקֹּדֶשׁ," although this amounts to 795.

In רי"ש on Aboth the saying *All Israel have a portion in the world to come &c.* is called בבא, and the word is used again in this way in the remarkable note on ר' הלל in II. 5. Cf. בבא דרישא and בבא דסיפא in Shabb. 3 a. The word מִישְׁנָה is also used for *baba* or *halakhah*.

The clause כל ישראל יש להם חלק לעולם הבא of the בבא above mentioned is found in Mishn. Sanh. XI. (א x.) 1, but is perhaps only a תוספת. Sanh. x. in א omits it and begins (p. 68),

אֵלּוּ [ואלו not] שׁאין להם חלק לעולם הבא.

1. קִבֵּל is used in the Kethubim.   תּוֹרָה, for התורה or את

התורה, means here, according to רש"י and others, *the whole Torah* שבכתב ושבעל פה. Torah, which is sometimes personified, may be used without the article "like proper names" (Geig.), but its omission here may be regarded as an abbreviation, the result of frequent repetition. Cf. in the *Didaché* (chap. 7) εἰς ὄνομα Πατρὸς καὶ Υἱοῦ καὶ ἁγίου Πνεύματος, following the full form εἰς τὸ ὄνομα τοῦ Πατρὸς καὶ τοῦ Υἱοῦ καὶ τοῦ ἁγίου Πνεύματος. Ecclus. xxiv. 23, νόμον ὃν ἐνετείλατο Μωυσῆς, takes תורה for התורה in Deut. xxxiii. 4 תורה צוה לנו משה. But Torah is something less than *the* Torah in Makkoth 23 b (end): 613 commandments were spoken to Moses, 365 negative, according to the days of the year, and 248 positive, according to the mem-l,ers of the human body. What then means, Moses commanded us תורה? This by Gematria is 611 only. The two אנכי and לא יהיה לך we heard מפי הגבורה. וּמְסֵרָה. מסר twice in the Bible, Numb. xxxi. 5, 16.

On מסורת, *traditio*, see chap. III. 20. Tradition from the point of view of reception is קַבָּלָה, doctrine received. Cf. ὁ καὶ παρέλαβον (1 Cor. xv. 3), τὴν παράδοσιν τῶν πρεσβυτέρων (Matt. xv. 2). Rabbinic commentators some-times introduce interpretations with a כך קיבלתי (p. 54). לַזְּקֵנִים

(ﭏ) is explained by Josh. xxiv. 31 (Jud. ii. 7) וכל ימי הזקנים כו'. The usual pointing is לִזְקֵנִים, to correspond to the following וזקנים; but we may regard this too as an abbreviation, like תורה for הַתּוֹרָה. On the same principle we should then read לַנְּבִיאִים וּנְבִיאִים. The chain of קבלה is traced backwards in Tosefta Yad. II. 16 (p. 683) ר' אליעזר אמר ... מקובלני מרבן יוחנן בן זכאי שקיבל מן הזוגות והזוגות מן הנָּבִיאים וּנְבִיאִים ממשה מסיני הלכה למשה מסיני. On משה קבל ומסרה see also No. 106 (p. 87). הָיוּ.

הֲיוּ ﭏ, Geig. *oder* הֲוֵיִ. ﬡ in I. 1, 3 היו. ﭏ remarks that the ע"ו form הֲוֶה sing. (but not הֲוֵו pl.) is Biblical. See Gen. xxvii. 29 הוה גביר לאחיך, and cf. Is. xvi. 4. Job xxxvii. 6. מְתוּנִים. מתן for חִכָּה in Targ. Job xxxii. 4 הוה מתן ית איוב. תַּלְמִידִים 1 Chron. xxv. 8 תלמיד. דסיינו להון...אנשי Targ. סייג. al. סייג. Baer סְיָג. סְיָג (ﭏ). סוגה בשושנים for Cant. vii. 3 כנשתא רבתא.

2. שִׁמְעוֹן, Greek Συμεών. There is a short form סימון, Σιμών.

מִשִּׁירִי (Baer Strack Auth. P. B.), from מֵן and a form of שאר with *yod* for *aleph*, but the pointing is doubtful. See Weiss משפט לשון המשנה p. 81 (Wien, 1867) and Mich. Cahn on Aboth, p. 8. Geig. שִׁירֵי. ﭏ here מִשִּׁירֵי, the *shin* followed by *yod* with dagesh and shva, and that by *yod* unpointed; and with single *yod* in the Mishnah Lesson איזהו מקומן (f. 10 b. Cf. Auth. P. B. p. 11), מעכבת שְׁיָרֵי הדם; giving the *diqduq* of the word as pl. from שִׁיּוּר. For a pl. שיורים see Kohut's *Aruch Completum* VIII. 69 שיצאו ממצרים * שִׁיּוּרִים אותם פי"ט במד"ר והקבוץ. ﬡ כְּנֶסֶת הַגְּדוֹלָה, the adj. with, the משירי לשון שירים 102. 4 substantive without the article, as in § 1. Cf. Ab. I. 12 (?), II. 15 יצר הרע.

---

* But the true reading in Bemidb. R. XIX. 21 seems to be as in ed. Wilna שיירות, *caravans*, on which Loria remarks כ"ה בתנחומא. With Kohut agrees Midr. ed. Frankf. 1705 A.D., while Jalq. I. 764 and Buber's Tanchuma read שיריים.

Gen. i. 31 יוֹם הַשִּׁשִּׁי, ii. 3 אֶת־יוֹם הַשְּׁבִיעִי, xli. 26 פְּרוֹת הַטּוֹבוֹת. Ps. civ. 18 הֶהָרִים הַגְּבֹהִים. Shabb. ix. 3 שֵׂעִיר הַמִּשְׁתַּלֵּחַ. הָעֲבוֹדָה,

ἡ λατρεία (Rom. ix. 4), the Temple service, for which a substitute had to be found בִּזְמַן שֶׁאֵין בֵּית הַמִּקְדָּשׁ קַיָּם (Megil. 31 b, Ta‘an. 27 b). Cf. Baba Q. 82 b כָּל זְמַן שֶׁעוֹסְקִין בַּעֲבוֹדָה. Sifré II. § 41 on Deut. xi. 13 gives prayer as a meaning of ‘abodah, וּלְעָבְדוֹ בְּכָל לְבַבְכֶם זוֹ תְּפִלָּה, comparing Ps. cxli. 2, although תְּפִלָּה אֵינָהּ דְּבַר תּוֹרָה (T. J. Berak. 3 b₆).

גְּמִילוּת חֲסָדִים. Is. lxiii. 7 גְּמָלָנוּ אֲשֶׁר כָּל כְּעַל...אַזְכִּיר יְהוָה חַסְדֵי. al. הח'.

Targ. גמלי חיסדא in Hos. iv. 1. T. J. Ta‘an. 68 a recites Ab. I. 2 and finds the Three Things in Is. li. 16 תּוֹרָה זוֹ בְּפִיךְ דְּבָרַי וְאָשִׂים אֶחָד בְּפָסוּק וּשִׁלָּשְׁתָּן וּבְצֵל יָדִי כִּסִּיתִיךָ...גְּמִילוּת חֲסָדִים זוֹ לִנְטוֹעַ שָׁמַיִם וְלִיסוֹד אֶרֶץ אֵלּוּ הַקָּרְבָּנוֹת. Here again תּוֹרָה stands for הַתּוֹרָה as in § 1.

3. אַנְטִיגְנוֹס, Gk. Ἀντίγονος. 𝔖 אַנְטִיגְנוֹס, Lat. Antigonus. 𝔄 וְהַגִּירְסָא אנטיגנס here and in Bekor. VI. 3, 4, 11, 12, VII. 2, 6. Duran הַקְּדוּמָה אנטיגנס הַנּוּ'ן פְּתוּחָה, and see Baer. But *Antignas* is a degenerate form, perhaps from a primitive אַנְטִיגְנוֹס. Cf. for the termination 𝔄 in Ab. II. 10, 11 הוֹרְקְנוֹס, 18 אפיקורוס, Baba M. xvi. 6 סוֹמְכוֹס, Bekor. VI. 13 אנדרוגינס. אִישׁ סוֹכוֹ. 𝔄 ℭ 𝔇 𝔖 (comm.) סוֹכוֹ. Others וסוכו הִיא עִיר בְּאֶרֶץ יִשְׂרָאֵל...כְּמוֹ שֶׁנִּזְכַּר. Dur. שׁוֹכוֹ, שׁוֹכָה. .בְּסֵפֶר יְהוֹשֻׁעַ...שׂוֹכוֹ וַעֲזֵקָה וְהוּא כָתוּב בְּסֵין וְיֵשׁ בַּשּׁוֹפְטִים פָּסוּק אִישׁ שׂוֹכוֹ For the use of אִישׁ see Ab. I. 4, 5, III. 9, 10, IV. 7, 28. Challah IV. 10. ‘Orl. II. 5, 12. Gitt. vi. 7. ‘Ed. vi. 2. Midd. I. 2. Dur. explains גָּדוֹל גָּדוֹל שֶׁבִּישִׁיבָה 𝔖 הַחֲכָמִים בְּאוֹתוֹ מָקוֹם. Geig. merely *abstammend aus*, and Bibl. אִישׁ אֶפְרָיִם, אִישׁ יִשְׂרָאֵל *von sämmtlichen Bewohnern.* פְּרֹס הַמְּשַׁמְּשִׁים, followed by יִן—(𝔄). Dan. vii. 10 יְשַׁמְּשׁוּנֵּהּ.

pause-form from פְּרַס. 𝔖 הַפֵּ"א בְּשָׁבָא וְהָרֵי"שׁ בְּפַתָּח. Jacob Emden וּבַהֶפְסֵק קָמוֹץ. Levy compares φόρος, but it is perhaps from פְּרֹס, to *divide.* Hence *ration,* פ פְּרוֶנְדָּא, provianda, provende; with the alternative אוֹ שְׁמָא לָשׁוֹן מַשְׂאַת הוּא בְּאַחַת הַלְּשׁוֹנוֹת. See also on פְּרַס, פַּרְסִין in Prof. Bevan's *Daniel,* p. 106 (Camb. 1892). Targ. 1 Chron. xviii. 2 6* נָטְלֵי פְּרַס מַסְּקֵי מִסְּין (ed. Dav. Wilkins, Amst. 1715, from MS. Cant.). Baer פְּרַס מַתָּנָה וּמִנְחָה 𝔖 פֵּירוּשׁוּ לְשׁוֹן. שָׂכָר, but Maim. חִילַּק בֵּין פְּרַס לְשָׂכָר (𝔅). The scribe in 𝔄 144 a₃ has written the letters לק prematurely and marked them for omission. עַל מְנָת הַמַּכְנִיס (𝔄) חַלּוֹת עַל מְנָת שֶׁלֹּא Teb. Yom. I. 2 מְנָת Baer מְנָת 𝔖 מְנָת. שֶׁלֹּא

---

* Quoted by Geig. p. 287. But the MS. (414 b) has מָיסַק, probably for מִיסִין, cf. Levy *Chald. Wörterbuch* s.v. נסא (S. S.).

שלא P. B. Auth. ‏ﬡ‎. ‏עַל מְנָת שלא לעשות קפנדריא‎ Megil. 29 a. ‏להפרייﬡ‎.
‏והר׳ ישראל ז״ל כת׳‎ on text ﬡ ,but the emendation is not wanted. ‏עַל מְנָת‎
Dur. ‏כִּי גִרסַת הַסְּפָרִים הִיא הַנְּכוֹנָה‎, but No. 90 (R. Isr.) begins on l. 8.
‏זאת היא גירסת המשנה ויש משנין אותה וגורסין שלא על מנת...ואין ראוי‎
‏לשנות הגירסא‎. Joseph Ja'betz (No. 102, f. 4 b) ‏ועוד אחרת הוקשה להם‎
‏גרסת הספרים...ע״מ שלא לקבל פרס...והוצרכו לשנות הגרסא מפני זה‎
‏Nos. 92, 95, 105, 107, 170 ﬠ ﬤ‎ (‏שלא ע״מ‎ marg.) ﬠ ﬡ Text. ‏...ואני אומ׳‎
(Rashi), R. Ephraim in Midr. Shemuel, ‏חובות הלבבות שער הבטחון‎
cap. 4 *sub fin.* (c. 1050 A.D.), Geig. (p. 287) Cahn. The received text of
'Abod. Zar. 19 a quotes Ab. I. 3 ending ‏שלא על מנת לקבל פרס כי אם‎
‏ע״מ שלא‎, but Rashi in comm. has preserved the true reading ‏בתורת ה׳ חפצו‎
‏לקבל פרס‎. **‏וִיהִי מוֹרָא‎** ﬡ ‏וִיהֵא‎. 'Abod. Zar. omits ‏ויהי מורא‎

‏שמים עליכם‎. ﬡ conjectures that it was added by Antigonus to explain
his former words, lest others should be led astray by them like ‏צדוק‎ and
‏ביתוס‎. No. 101 omits the preceding clause ‏אלא כו׳ פרס‎ doubtless through
homœoteleuton, but the original saying may have consisted of the ‏אל תהיו‎
clause only. **‏שָׁמַיִם‎**, to avoid saying GOD, as in § 12 ‏שם שמים‎. See

Chagigah 12 a in Mr Streane's edition (Camb. 1891). Nachum ‏זו גם איש‎
says on Gen. i. 1 that, but for the preceding ‏את‎, he would have taken ‏שמים‎
there to be ‏שמו של הקב״ה‎. *Shamayim* is Rabbinically resolved into ‏מַיִם שָׁ‎
and ‏אֵשׁ וָמַיִם‎. That to Heaven, or GOD, is a journey of 500 years comes
out of ‏שַׁדַּי‎ (Aq. Sym. ἱκανός Ezek. i. 24), a name of Him ‏שֶׁאמר דִּי‎, *who*
limited the extension of the world by saying *enough*; for the name spelt
out would be ‏יִ״ן לִ״ת וִ״ד‎ שי״ן דלי״ת יו״ד, and the "concealed" letters ‏יו״ד‎
amount by Gematria to 500. See Tosafoth Chag. 12 a ‏ד״ה מסוף העולם‎,
where this is given in the name of ‏ר׳ מנחם בר׳ עזריאל‎. Nestle well suggests that ‏שִׁקּוּץ שֹׁמֵם‎ (Dan. xii. 11) is for ‏בַּעַל שָׁמַיִם‎. With ‏שמם‎ cf. ‏ירושלם‎
for ‏־ים‎. Prof. Bevan illustrates the word-play from Gen. Rab. IV. 7
‏שמים שהבריות משתוממים עליהן‎ [Jer. ii. 12 ‏שֹׁמּוּ שָׁמַיִם‎].

4. ‏יוסי‎ ‏יְהוֹסֵף‎. ﬤﬥ Ashk. Nos. 95, 101, 105, 170. Ps. lxxxi. 6 ‏יְהוֹסֵף‎, ‏יוֹסֵף‎
(ﬡﬥ Baer) is an abbreviation frequent in Talm. See the forms ‏יוֹסִי‎,
‏יוסה‎ (ﬡ 1 b₆, 170 b₁₀), ‏יסא‎ in T. J. Berak. 3 c, lines 1—27 from end. No.
107 ‏יוסי בן יועזר‎ but ‏יוסף בן יוחנן‎, and so Ab. R. N. (pp. 27, 33), Mishn.
Chag. II. 2 in T. B. 16 a, with ‏יוסף‎ for ‏יוסי‎ in the margin, but ‏יוסי‎ in
Tosafoth. ‏יְרוּשָׁלֵים‎ (ﬥ). ﬡﬠﬤﬥ ‏ירושלם‎. ‏מֵהֶם‎ or ‏מהן‎, ﬡﬠﬤﬥ
Baer Strack. ‏מֵמֶּנּוּ‎ ﬥ (ref. to Midr. Shem.) Ashk. No. 23. The pl. would
mean from Shim'on and Antigonus (ﬡ), or ‏מישירי כנסת הגדולה‎ (ﬠ), or
‏ובית מועד לכל‎ (ﬤ). ‏בֵּית וַעַד‎ or ‏בית ווﬠד‎. Job xxx. 23 ‏מאנשי פ״ה‎ (ﬥ).

מתאבק בעפר רגליהם ו'. No. 103 omits מִתְאַבֵּק, Baer בַּק. —חי.

והוי שותה or וְשׁוֹתֶה (niph.) ויאבק איש עמו Gen. xxxii. 25.

בַּצְמָא (ƽ) or בַּצָּמָא [Jud. xv. 18], BCD Baer Strack Auth. P. B. ƽ Nos.
23, 114, 170, בצמאה, Jer. ii. 25 וגרונך מצמאה. Ashk. בְּצָמְאָה. There is a
reading כְּצָמֵא with *caph*, which may have come out of Rashi's comment
כאדם שהוא צמא.

5. (ƽ), בֵּיתְךָ. לָרְוָחָה. Ex. viii. 11 (15) כי היתה הָרְוָחָה.

שִׂיחָה. No. 107 adds (cf. Ab. R. N.) ולמד את כל בני ביתך ענוה.

עִם הָאִשָּׁה. Cf. Nedarim 20 a, Ab. שיחת הילדים Ab. III. 16.

R. N. VII. (p. 35). Ecclus. ix. 9 μετὰ ὑπάνδρου γυναικὸς μὴ κάθου τὸ σύνολον,
Syr. (cf. Geig. p. 289) עם אנחת גברא לא תסנא ממללא. See also *The
Quotations from Ecclus. in Rabb. Literature* by Mr Schechter in the
Jewish Quarterly Review, vol. III. (1891).

6. בְּאִשְׁתּוֹ. This בבא, which is a תוספת, takes the preceding האשה
in the sense *the* (man's own) *wife*. Mr Schechter in Ab. R. N. מבוא פ"ב
(p. x) refers to the ספר יחוסי תנאים ואמוראים contained in the Bodleian
Heb. MS. No. 2199 (Opp. 391), and in פ"ד (p. xix) quotes from it on the
reading באשתו the remark כך מצאתי במשנה נדה אמרו ק"ו באשת חבירו
דוקנית וכן משמע בתנא דבי אליהו ... לפי ששמעתי דלא גרסינן באשתו נדה
אלא באשתו. BCD Rashi No. 170 (p. 118) mention and reject the reading
 י"ם דגרסי בסיפא כל המרבה שיחה עם האשה כשהיא. Ashk. באשתו נדה.

נָדָה גורם וכו'. On the form קַל וָחוֹמֶר. קל וחומר (pl.) קולין
see Geig. p. 288 (וחומרין). מִכָּאן *.ƽ מיכן. כָּל הַמַּרְבֶּה (ƽ).

כל זמן שהאדם מ מרבה, the מ written after האדם *to fill up the line*
being taken from the following word, like the letters מל six lines lower
down. יוֹרֵשׁ גֵּיהִנֹּם (ƽ), or יורד לגיהנם (cf. v. 28). No. 114 יירש.

יורש ל' C. Ecclus. x. 11 κληρονομήσει ἑρπετὰ καὶ θηρία καὶ σκώληκας.

7. נִתַּאי הָאַרְבֵּלִי, the usual reading. ƽ Nos. 92, 170 (cf. Baer
Streane *Chag.* p. 95) מַתַּאי, for which Strack adds the authority of a
Frankf. Siddur of 1306 A D., while himself reading נִתַּי as abbrev. of *Ne-
thanja*. ƽ in Chag. II. 2 נתי איש תקוע, Chall. IV. 11 מתי הארבלי. Ashk.
ברוב הספרים גרסינן מַאתּאיה במ"ם ואלו"ף (sic) ותי"ו ואל"ף ויו"ד וה"י.

---

* See Zunz *Gesam. Schriften* III. 31 (Berl. 1876) on Das Adverbium כאן.

8. ‏הַרְחֵק‎. No. 170 (p. 118) ‏רְחַק‎. Ashk. found ‏רחק‎ in some copies.

‏וְאַל תִּתְחַבֵּר לְרָשָׁע‎, omitted by No. 105. No. 95 ‏ואל תהי חבר לרשע‎.

9. ‏טַבָּאִי‎ (S). Strack ‏טָבִי‎. B ‏טְבָּאִי‎. Cf. ‏טָבִי‎ in Berak. II. 7 (Jost), fem. Tabitha (Acts ix. 40). Geig. "abgekürzt aus ‏טוביה‎."
‏שָׁטֵחַ‎ (S), al. ‏שְׁטַח‎, B ‏שַׁטֵּח‎ with dagesh in teth. Cahn ‏שֶׁטַח‎.
‏כְּעוֹרְכֵי‎ [from Heb. ‏ערך‎] or ‏כאורכי‎ in the same sense, D ‏ויש גורסין כאורכי וההיא היא‎. A ‏כערכי‎. B (=Greek arch as in patriarch) ‏וי"מ כעורכי כמו כארכי‎, comparing ‏חושי הארכי‎ and (of Ephron) ‏אותו היום מינוהו ארכי‎. See in Git. I. 5 ‏כל הַשְּׁטָרוֹת העולים בְּעַרְכָּאוֹת של נכרים...כשרים‎, where A (94 b₁) has ‏ערכאות‎ for ‏ארכיות‎.
‏וּכְשֶׁיְּהִיוּ‎. ‏הַדַּיָּנִין‎. Auth. P. B. ‏הַדַּיָּנִים‎.
‏כְּשֶׁקִבְּלוּ‎, —‏יָן‎, ‏כזכאים‎ D CA (B Ashk.). ‏כְּצַדִּיקִים‎. ‏וכשהיו‎ A or ‏שקיבלו‎ without caph, al. ‏לכשקבלו‎ No. 101 ‏ואף כשקבלו‎.

10. ‏שְׁמָא‎ (S). B ‏שְׁמָא‎, but in § 11 ‏שְׁמָא‎ with shva, segol. Baer Strack Auth. P. B. ‏שְׁמָא‎. C in text ‏זרי‎ for ‏זהיר‎.

11. ‏שְׁמַעְיָה‎ (Ezr. x. 21, 31). S quotes the grammarian ‏השמשוני‎ for the pointing of the 'ayin ‏בשב"א נח לבדו ולא בחטף פת"ח‎. ‏וְאַבְטַלְיוֹן‎, "Pollion römisch, und gräcisirt, vor λ oft ein τ, wie πόλεμος, πτ-, πόλις, πτ-" (Geig.). ‏אָהַב‎ (S). A C B ‏אהוב‎. ‏דַּרְבְּנוֹת‎, S following ‏כל הסדורים‎, but with the suggestion that the resh should have chireq to correspond to Targ. Mal. iii. 1 ‏רִבּוֹנָא‎, Gen. xxiii. 6 ‏קביל מננא רְבוֹנָנָא‎. Cf. ver. 15 ‏רִבּוֹנִי קביל מני‎. A repeats ‏ואל תתיאש מן הפורענות‎ by error from § 8.

12. ‏בְּדִבְרֵיכֶם‎. No. 109 ‏מדבריכם‎. ‏מַיִם רָעִים‎ (C B S). ‏אַחֲרֵיכֶם‎. A B ‏המים הרעים‎. Berak. III. 5 ‏בְּמַיִם הרעים‎ (Jost). C Nos. 92, 95, 103 ‏אַחֲרֵיהֶם‎. No. 113 omits ‏ו׳‎ ‏הבאים אחריכם‎. ‏מִתְחַלֵּל‎ (not ‏מחולל‎ as Ezek. xxxvi. 23), cf. Is. lii. 5 ‏ותמיד כל היום שמי מנואץ‎ (S).

13. ‏הלל ושמאי‎ B ‏הלל ושמאי ולשון המקרא הלל בדברי הימים‎, where it would be more correct to read ‏בדברי] ושמאי [בשופטים‎ ‏הלל‎ ‏הימים‎. Or the MSS. (cf. No. 108) may have a defective reading of the state-

10

ment that הלל was of the sons of Ne'ariah, whose name is found בדברי
הימים. He is so described in the chain of esoteric Qabbalah by R. Abr. of
Granada (c. 1300 A.D.) in ברית מנוחה (*Introd.*). But the former explanation
is preferable.   Jud. xii. 13, 15 הִלֵּל ('Ελλήγ), cf. הֵילֵל in Is. xiv. 12.
שַׁמַּי is found in 1 Chron. ii. 28—45, iv. 17. Some think it a contraction of
שמעיה or שְׁמַעְי.

14. נגד שְׁמָא אבד שְׁמָא (Ashk.). ℭ שמיה (comm. שמה) *bis.* 𝔅𝔇𝔖
(ℭ*𝔖 Cahn).   וּדְלָא מוֹסִיף יָסִיף   שמא...שמיה (cf. Midr. Shem.)
דִילָא... יָסוּף 𝔅. Baer Auth. P. B. וּדְלָא... יָסֵף. Strack יָסוּף... דִילָא.
וְדְמוֹסִיף יוֹסִיף 𝔇 (cf. No. 4) ודלא מוסיף יסיף, and in comm. (see Ta'an.
31 a) ...ודלא מוסיף שאינו סובר בתלמודו ללמד דבר מתוך דבר ואף אינו
[No. 95 וַיֹּאסֶף] מוסיף מן הלילות על הימים יסיף יאסף. This note agrees
with Rashbam's *perush* on Baba B. 121 b.   וּדִישְׁתַּמֵּשׁ 𝔅𝔖
ודאש(ת)מש 𝔇. ודי אשתמש 𝔄 (ולא ודאשתמש באל"ף).   Cf. Ab. IV. 9.
בְּתָנָא או בְּתָנָא al. ,(ref. to Targ. Sheni Esth. ii. 17) בתאנא. 𝔖 says בְּתַנָא,
that it is a rare word, the use of which is accounted for by הרמ"ב (that is
ר' משה בוטריל) on Sepher Jeçirah, f. 34 a [Mant. 1562 A.D.].

15. אֵמָתִי. Targ. for מתי. So 𝔖, with ref. to כתי in the *Aruch*,
where it is maintained that ממתי should be read for מאימתי in Berak. I. 1.
But see Kohut's *Aruch Compl.* vol. v. 287. Notice the remark of 𝔖
והלא התרגום ברוח הקדש נאמר.

16. בְּסֵבֶר. 𝔖 בכל הסדורים כ"ה, but with preference for סָבַר as in
Targ. Gen. xxxi. 2 ית סבר אפי דלבן.   פָּנִים יָפוֹת fem. as Ezek. xxi. 21
(𝔖) אנה פניך מועדות.

17. אוֹמְרוֹת (𝔅𝔖). See other pointings in Cahn. Ashk. ס"א
עומדות.

18. גְּדַלְתִּי (𝔖), usually גִּדַּלְתִּי. See Cahn.   אֶלָּא שְׁתִיקָה
עקר 𝔇. וְלֹא הַמִּדְרָשׁ הוּא הָעִקָּר   משתיקה 𝔅ℭ𝔇𝔖 (𝔄 Ashk.).
No. 113 לא מדרש הוא עקר אלא מעשה. 𝔖 condemns ולא המדרש עקר.
These readings exemplify the tendency to abbreviate familiar expressions
by omission of the article (p. 132).

* The manuscript ℭ is quoted for the consonants only (p. 83).

19. קַיָּם (p. 84), not עומד as in the saying of Shim'on הצדיק in Ab.

I. 2. שנ' אמת כו'. The Scripture proof Zech. viii. 16 is a תוספת.
T. J. Ta'an. 68 *a* (end) quotes the saying of R. Sh. b. G. (with עומד as
in the saying in Ab. I. 2 cited just before) and adds ושלשתן דבר אחד הן
נעשה הדין נעשה אמת נעשה שלום· אמר רבי מנא ושלשתן בפסוק אחד אמת
ומשפט שלום שפטו בשעריכם· Of the three things on which the
world stands (עומד) according to Simon Justus it had been said in like
manner in T. J. Ta'an. ושלשתן בפסוק אחד (p. 134). The inference in both
cases alike is that the פסוק was no part of the saying. The speaker in each
baba being a שמעון, it was the more natural for scribes to fall into the error
of writing עומד על ג' דברים העולם in the later saying. ℭ in text (p. 84)
and No. 101 repeat עומד על התורה from I. 2.

CHAPTER II.

1. רַבִּי. ⅏ רִבִּי with *chireq* under the *resh*. 𝔅 רְ, cf. II. 19 רְבִי טרפון,
and see No. 105 (p. 86) and Baer on Ab. II. 1. "Rabbi" is called רבי רבה
in Chullin 51 a. On רבנות see chap. I. 11, and note that רבוני is found
once in the Mishnah according to ⅏ (64 a₁₉), for the usual רבונו של עולם
(Ta'an. III.). Rapoport in בכורי העתים vol. x. pp. 104 § 9, 109 § 14
(Wien, 1829) discusses the signature of the poet El'azar בירבי יעקב
קליר (קיליר or), explains בירבי as abbrev. of בן רבי [cf. No. מקרית ספר
103, p. 81], and remarks that Ashkenazic scribes have been wont from
of old to write יו"ד יתירה for *segol* or *chireq* and וא"ו יתירה for *cholem*
or *qameç*. לְעוֹשֵׂה וְתִפְאָרֶת (⅏ אחר השי"ן בלא יו"ד הנכון כ"ה),

or לְעוֹשֶׂה ו'. ⅏ לעושה תפארת. R. Israel (cf. Magen Ab.) כל שהיא תפארת
והר' ישראל ז"ל 𝔅 לְעוֹשֵׂהוּ [לעושיהו No. 90, p. 51] תפארת לו מן האדם
פי'...ועלה בדעתי לומ' כי הגירסא היא כל שהיא תפארת לעושהו...ופי' לעושיהו
הוא האל ית' העושה את האדם כמו אם מעושיהו יטהר גבר...ויהיה עתה הפי'
הפך כוונת המפרשים ז"ל ר"ל שלא יברור האדם הדרך שיהא מפואר בה עם
הבריות בלבד רק שיברור הדרך שיהא מפואר בה לפני האל ית'...וראיתי נוסחא
ישנה נראה שהיא ירושלמית וכתי' בה תפארת בלא וא"ו [⅏] וכן מצאתי
ואני יש לי שתא 𝔅 adds בגירסת ר' יצחק בן גיאת ז"ל וזה העירני לפרש כן
סדרי משנה ב' מדוייקים ומנוקדים שנכתבו בירושלם עיר הקדש וכתי' בהם
תפארת לעושה ותפארת כמו שכתו' בכל ספרי ספרד וצרפת. With this com-

pare the extract from No. 90 given on p. 50.   **כְּבַחֲמוּרָה** (𝕾).

𝖆 taking **מַתָּן שְׂכָרָן שֶׁל מִצְוֹת**, .כמצוה חמורה 𝕭 .כחמורה 𝖆

מתן קמוצה as not סמוך, and adding that if it were the תי״ו should still be

as in Prov. xviii. 16 לו ירחיב אדם מַתָּן. 𝕭 (sic) מַתָּן, Baer מַתָּן. Some

copies add [No. 23 עבירה] **שֶׁל עֲבֵירוֹת** [Ashk. ועונשין] .וְעוֹנְשָׁן

ס״א **בָּאַרְבָּעָה** Ashk. .והסתכל 𝖆𝕮 (𝕾). **הִשְׁתַּכֵּל בִּשְׁלֹשָׁה דְבָרִים**

דברים.   **דַּע מַה-לְמַעְלָה** 𝕮 דע למעלה without מה.

עֵין רוֹאָה   𝖆 ראה for רואה (II. 12, 13), and so וראה in Middoth II.

(185 b₂₂).   𝕭𝖘 **בְּסֵפֶר** (al. 'בְּ), and above **דְּפֵסֶר**.

בַּטֵלָה Ashk. .לגור 𝖆 (𝕾), 𝕭 לסוף. **סוֹפָהּ בְּטֵלָה וְגוֹרֶרֶת עָוֹן** 2.

וכל תורת... **לְגָרֵר** (sic) 𝕮 text omits עון וכתב שכך מצא ברוב הספרים

עוֹן.   (𝕾), **וְכָל הָעוֹסְקִים עִם הַצִּבּוּר יִהְיוּ עוֹסְקִים**

al. עמלים for עוסקים in one or both places. 𝕭 יהיו...והעמלים העוסקין

עוסקין ועמלים.   **מַעְלָה אֲנִי**, the usual reading. 𝖆 מעלין, Ashk.

The ואתם מעלים עליכם שכר כאלו וכו' וכתב שכן מצאתי בכל הספרים

pl. might refer to the פמליא של מעלה, cf. St Luke vi. 38 δώσουσιν εἰς τὸν

κόλπον ὑμῶν.   **שְׂכַר הַרְבֵּה** (𝕾). 𝖆𝕭𝕮 Ashk. No. 107 omit הרבה.

נְרָאִין 𝖆 ונראין.   לו לאדם. (𝖆), usually **לָאָדָם** 3.

.הניתן 𝕭, בְּשַׁעַת הַנָּאָתָן...דְּחָקוֹ Baer (𝕾), **בִּשְׁעַת הַנָּאָתָן...דּוֹחֲקוֹ**

עֲשֵׂה רְצוֹנוֹ כִרְצוֹנְךָ כְּדֵי שֶׁיַּעֲשֶׂה רְצוֹנְךָ כִּרְצוֹנוֹ 4.   Nos.

103, 139 י״ג...שיעשה רצונו כרצונך. No. 106 עשה רצונו כרצונך. Some

copies have this *baba* after IV. 19 only, and some in both places. See Nos.

10, 103, 138—140. M. Shelom. ובמדר״ש בשם ר״י ן' נחמיאש כתב שבמשנה

ירושלמי הגי' **ברצונך** בבי״ת והכוונה...ברצון ובשמחת לב כדי שגם הוא

יעשה רצונך **ברצונו** שלפעמים יעשה הקב״ה רצונו של אדם באף וחימה

להענישו באחרונה כענין להשמידו עדי עד אבל כשהוא ברצון אחריתו ישנא

מאד.   **שֶׁיְבַטֵּל רְצוֹן אֲחֵרִים** No. 138 שיבטל רצונו (p. 111),

which was wanted to complete the parallel, אלא שאין דרך כבוד של מעלה

רְצוֹנוֹ מִפְּנֵי רְצוֹנְךָ (𝕭).   M. Shelom. Baer notice that לומר כדי שיבטל

some add the *baba* ראובן בן איצטרובלי אומר אין אדם נחשד בדבר

אלא א"כ עשהו כו׳ (Mo‘ed Q. 18 b), see Aboth R. N. pp. 63, 78.

5. הִלֵּל. Ashk. ר׳ הלל אומר כן הוא רבי הלל ברוב הספרים. On the

other side see No. 108 (p. 90). אַל תִּפְרוֹשׁ. 𝔄ℭ add עצמך un-

necessarily. Nos. דָּבָר שֶׁאֶפְשָׁר לִשְׁמוֹעַ שֶׁסּוֹפוֹ לְהִשָּׁמַע,

90, 133, 170. In 𝔄 add להישמע after שסופו. Rashi אל תאמר על דבר של

תורה שאתה יכול לשמוע עכשיו שתשמע לבסוף אלא לאלתר הט אזנך לשמוע.

...דבר שאיפשר לשמוע וסופו [שסופו?] להישמע...ואל (see p. 54) 𝔓

תאמר שאי איפשר לשמוע אם אינך טרוד ועסוק במלאכה ואיפשר לך לשמוע

דבר תורה עכשיו אפי׳ אם סופו לישמע בפעם אחרת אל תאמר הרי סופו

שאי אפשר No. 23 (cf. Ashk.). לְהישמע ואותו הפעם תלך ותשמיענו (*sic*)

לְהִשָּׁמַע, דבר שאי איפשר לשמוע וסופו להישמע 𝔅 quotes Maim. as reading

in the sense שבתחלתו יראה מכוער וסופו נעים ומקובל, and "Rashbam" as

reading שאיפשר לשמוע. מבנין הקל 𝔖, לְכְשֶׁאֶפְנֶה... תִּפְנֶה but

לְכְשֶׁאֶפְנֶה...תִּפְנֶה. usually *niph.*

6. בּוּר 𝔖, Baer בּוֹר (𝔅𝔖), הוא תאר למי שאין בו תורה ולא דרך ארץ

והוא לשון תרגום כמו...(משלי ל׳) מטול דבורא דבני נשא אנא ובסוטה פרק

היה נוטל. דף כ"ב ע"א אמרו שנה ולא קרא הרי זה בור Here we have

an example of the old way of quoting a *pereq* by its opening words, together

with the modern way of quoting by *folio* and ‘*ammud*. יְרֵא חֵטְא,

𝔖 comparing יְרֵא 𝔅. אשרי כל ירא יי׳ (תלי׳ קכ"ח). וְלֹא הַבַּיְשָׁן

לָמֵד, 𝔖, הבי"ת בקמ"ץ חטף...כמו...בָּשָׁנָה אפרים יקח (הושע י׳), adding

that some copies have הבוישן with *vau* after the *beth* [𝔆𝔅 No. 95]. 𝔅 Baer

Strack Auth. P. B. הַבַּיְשָׁן with *pathach* under the *beth*. It is the practice

of 𝔖 to use the *raphé* mark (as over the *daleth* of למד), to write *mappiq*

under instead of within *he* (as לְעֹשָׂהֿ), to mark accented syllables, and to

accentuate citations from Scripture in the text of Aboth. הַקַּפְּדָן,

שֶׁאֵין אֲנָשִׁים. מַחְכִּים*. מחכם 𝔅. מעינן קפדה בא (יחזקאל ז׳) 𝔖

שֶׁאֵין אִישׁ... ובמקום שאין אנשים להשתדל ולעמוד בפרץ תשתדל 𝔓

See. להיות איש...ובירושלמי (?) בתר דלית גבר תמן תהי גבר והיא היא

הִשְׁתַּדֵּל. No. 170 (p. 118) in T. B. Berak. 63 a. באתר דלית גבר

* See [cf. p. 128] מס׳ כלה והברייתא in Nathan Coronel's חמשה קונטרסים, fol. 11 a (Vindob.

1864 A.D.), for a reading חכם בסחורה.

ס״א **הִשְׁתַּדֵּר** ברי״ש וכן משמע דגרים רד״ק שבת׳   .M. Shelom   .השתדר
בס״ם השרשים השתדר כמו השתדל וגם הרמב״ן בפ׳ משפטים בפ׳ כי יפתה
כתב דיש נוסחאות דגרס השתדר ברי״ש וכן הגיה הרי״א ז״ל בשם רוב הספרים.

7. **גֻּלְגֹּלֶת אַחַת שֶׁצָּפָה**, 𝔖 (איכה ג׳) מים על ראשי (sic) כענין צפה.

עַל דְּאַטֵּפְתְּ אַטְּפוּךְ, 𝔐 No. 170 צפה without *shin*. גולגולת שצפה 𝔐

𝔖 the *daleth* with *shva* ··· he finds׳ כמו שכתבתי בקדיש the בכל הסדורי׳
אשר הציף (דברי י״א) quotes (י״א) ··· בפת״ח and *pe* בשב״א נח pointing *teth*
which אַטֵּפְתְּ and finds the pointing ··· תרגומו די אטיף האל״ף בפת״ח
he adopts בגליון באחת מכדורי קלף .Auth. P. B   .דְּאַטֵּיפְתְּ אַטְּפוּךְ 𝔐
יש משניות שכת׳ בהן דְּעַמֵּפַת עַטְּפוּךְ והיא היא שאותיות א״ח ה״ע
מתחלפות אשה אל אחותה. ויש שכתוב בהן על דְּאַקְפַת (sic) **אֵקְפוּךְ**,
בערוך הביאו בערך עטף בעי״ן על דְּעַטְּפַת   .M. Shelom .מתרגו׳ וקפא ברזלא
see Kohut on קוֹף and עֲטֵף. Observe that the narrative part of the *baba*
is in Biblical Hebrew, while the saying is in a Targumic dialect.

8. **מַרְבֶּה דְאָגָה**. 𝔐 דוי ודאבון נפש שמפחד [דְּוָוֹן=] דָּווֹן מרבה

Midr. ׳תמיד כו   .M. Shelom. דווֹן כך הוא הגרסא בערוך תרגום יגון **דָּווֹנָא**
Shem. (p. 63) כתב הר׳ אפרים ז״ל כי יש משניות מדוייקות שכתוב בהם מרבה
There would thus be left ׳תורה מרבה חיים קנה שם טוב קנה לעצמו וכו
the *six* clauses תורה··· נשים··· עבדים··· שפחות··· נכסים··· מרבה בשר answering to the comment חוזר לומ׳ שכל הרבוויין אין בהם תועלת זולתי (𝔐).
fore ריבוי התורה בלבד. 𝔄𝔅 (comm.) 𝔐𝔅 Ashk. put the נשים clause next be-
M. Shelom. adds (נ״א צדקה) מ׳ תורה . Ashk. omits after חיים to שלום, and
followed by וכמוהו ברוב הספרים ל״ג זה 𝔐 in text חכמה (for חיים),
No. 90 puts מ׳ עיצה מ׳ תבונה מ׳ ישיבה מ׳ שלום מ׳ חכמה מ׳ צדקה קנה וכו׳
marg. מ׳ חכמה מ׳ ישיבה No. 23 . מ׳ שפחות before מ׳ עבדים , with
ויוסיף דעת יוסיף מכאוב . Eccl. i. 18 מ׳ עצה מ׳ תבונה.

קָנָה לוֹ .Ashk. ונמחק מלת לוֹ ··· קנה דברי תורה קנה חיי העולם הבא.

9. **אִם לָמַדְתָּ תּוֹרָה הַרְבֵּה**, .מְהֻלָּל No. 95 מְהֻלָּל.

𝔖 כ״ה הנוכח במשניות ובכבר מדרש שמואל אבל הר״י אברבנאל ולב אבות
(sic) וָמָלִי דאבות וחסדי אבות ופרקי משה ומדרש שמואל בשם הר״ם אלאשקור
עשית 𝔄 .גורסין אם **עָשִׂיתָ** תורה הרבה ונתנו׳ טעם לנירסתם והוא טעם לשבח
תורה ,cf. Nos. 23, 107 (טובה), 170. 𝔐𝔅 Nos. 95, 101. עשית **תּוֹרָתְךָ** 𝔅 comm.
[in text only as far as תור is legible] אם עשית תורתך הרבה אם למדת כל

יָמִיךְ בתורה ועשית כל המצות‎ . Some such comment or the same words in
Ab. II. 19 may have suggested the reading למדת תורה הרבה‎ in II. 9.

נוצרתה ᴁᴄ‎   נוֹצַרְתְּ‎ . תחזק‎ (Ꞩ), al. תַּחֲזִיק‎

10. אֱלִיעֶזֶר...אֶלְעָזָר‎ . ᴁ frequently has the Jerus. forms ליעזר, לעזר‎

without *aleph*, the latter once with points לַעְזֶר‎ (p. 66, line כ״א‎), Gk.
Λάζαρος. On *pathach* for *qameç* see chap. III. 11.   הוֹרְקָנוֹס‎ .

Ꞩ הוֹרְכָּנוֹס‎ with note that הָרְקָנוּס‎ is יותר נכון‎ . ᴃ *prima manu*,
with *caph* altered to כ‎.   חֲנִינָא‎ for חנינא‎ or יה‎—.   ᴄ omits

וָאִילוּ הן‎ . ᴃ (text) אילו‎ without *vau*. ᴃᎦ al. וְאִלּוּ‎ with *dagesh*,
cf. bibl. אֵלֶּה‎ . ᴃ in comm. ואילו הן ר׳...ור׳ אלעזר בן ערך‎ with *vau* before the last name only, quoting bibl. ראובן שמעון לוי ויהודה‎ .

שְׁבָחָן‎ (Ꞩ). ᴃ שְׁבָחָן‎ . R. Jochanan calls the five severally by name without title, ᴄ שאין דרך הרב לקרות לתלמידיו ר׳‎ ᴅ, בלא שום סמיכה‎ . Strack
Dur. notice readings which make him call the first or the last רבי‎ .
כל הסדורים‎ (ᴁᴃᴄ), bibl. שִׁיד‎ . Nos. 23, 158 סוד‎ , in favour of which against
Ꞩ quotes (Dur.) ר׳ שמעון בר׳ צמח‎ .   ᴁᴃᴄᴅᴤ מעין‎ without *caph*.

11. מ׳ אחת‎ or מֹאזְנַיִם‎ (cf. Strack) to balance שניה‎ .   ᴃᴄᎦ אַף‎

עָמָהֶם‎   ᴃ ו‎—. ᴁ om. אף‎ .

12. צְאוּ וְרְאוּ‎ . Abarbanel gives a reading בואו ראו‎ in this *baba*,
but צאו‎ (of ד׳ רעה‎) in the next. Geig. "bibl. לך‎ geh! z. B. Is. xx. 2, Hos.
iii. 1, Koh. ix. 7...vgl. πορευθέντες μάθετε Matt. ix. 13, syr. זלו ילפו‎ ."

דֶּרֶךְ טוֹבָה‎ . ᴄ No. 106 ד׳ ישרה‎ , cf. II. 1. ᴃ in text טובה‎ altered to
יָשָׁרָה‎ , comm. לבקש איזו היא הדרך הטובה‎ .   שֶׁיִּדְבַּק‎ (Ꞩ). Emd. *niph.*

רואה אני את דברי‎ , cf. Sheqal. IV. 7 רוֹאֶה אֲנִי...מִדִּבְרֵיכֶם‎ .   שֶׁיִּדְבַּק‎ .
ר׳ אליעזר מדברי ר׳ יהושע‎ (ᴁ IV. 9, f. 54 a₁₈). ᴄ once רואה אני‎ without
מדבריכם‎ , cf. Rosh ha-Sh. II. 8 רואה אני את דבריך‎ (ᴁ II. 10, f. 61 b₁₀), Baba
B. IX. 1 רואה אני את דברי אדמון‎ (ᴁ xxix. 1, f. 122 a₂).

13. ברוך הוא‎ without אֶחָד הַלֹּוֶה מִן הָאָדָם כְּלֹוֶה מִן הַמָּקוֹם‎

הק׳ הוא קורא מָקוֹם ומפורש בסיפרי‎ (?) לפי‎ ᴃ without art. לוה‎ or לווה‎ (Ꞩ), al.
שהוא מקומו של עולם ואין העולם מקומו שנ׳ ומתחת זרועות עולם, והקדוש‎
ברוך הוא תכף שאנו מזכירין שמו אנו צריכין לברכו שנ׳ זכר צדיק לברכה ואו׳‎
(p. 99) for בן סירא‎ ᴃ, ספר יצירה‎ No. 108 . כי שם י׳ אקרא הבו גודל לאלהינו‎
ס׳פרי‎ . ᴃ adds that יהוה‎ by a kind of Gematria amounts to the same as

מקום.   וְצַדִּיק חוֹנֵן וְנוֹתֵן.   M. Shelom.   ז״ל אבן ה״ר יהוסף ז״ל כצ״ל

כתב ברוב הספרים ל״ג רק ולא ישלם וגו׳.

14.   הֵם אָמְרוּ שְׁלֹשָׁה דְבָרִים (ℨ).   Read   שלשה שלשה
(Strack *genauer*) with 𝔇 Nos. 90 (p. 54), 95 (marg.), 114, 133, 170, M. Shelom.   Dur.   כל אחד מהם אמר שלשה דברים ולזה נכפל במשנה שלשה ב׳
פעמים.   ℬ has a second שלשה but unpointed* and with a line drawn
through it, and reads ממון חברך, marg. נ״א כבוד תלמידך.   The three sayings of ר׳ אליעזר are (1) יהי כבוד (2), אל תהי נוח (3), שוב יום אחד.   Ashk.
on (3) ס״א וכי יודע אדם באיזה יום ימות כו׳, see Ab. R. N. p. 62, Shab.
153 a, Midr. R. on Eccl. ix. 8 בכל עת. (ℨ).   Baer   בְּנֶחָלָתָן שֶׁלֹּא

בְּנַחֲלָתָם, 𝔄ℬ𝔇 מג׳ (𝔇 ם—.). 𝔄ℬℭ שמא.   שׁוּעָל   R. Isr. gives a
reading נחש but prefers שועל (p. 54).   The saying והוי מתחמם וגו׳
is a תוספת from Aboth R. N., for which 𝔇 makes room by reckoning
R. Eli‘ezer's (1) and (2) as one.   M. Shelom.   כתב הר״מ די לונזאנא ז״ל מכאן
עד סוף המשנה נראה מפ״ט [עי׳ ס״פ ט״ו] דאדר״נ שאינו משנה ובהכי אתי
שפיר דלא פשו מ״ג.

15.   עַיִן רָעָה   (𝔄𝔇 No. 90) as in Ab. II. 13, v. 28 is to be preferred. ℭℨ
Ab. R. N. (p. 62) עין הרע, by assimilation to the following יצר הרע.   Notice
in No. 106 the Gematria הרשע=יצר הרע, ὁ πονηρός, and the expression
שנאת חנם שם השם (p. 88).   ℭ חנם for הבריות.   Joma 9 b שם השם.

16.   מָמוֹן.   Syr. ממונא.   Sanh. III. 1 דיני מָמוֹנוֹת בשלשה.   Geig. *blos*
Erweiterung von הממון *...spätbibl.*   חָבִיב עָלֶיךָ כְּשֶׁלָּךְ (ℨ), cf.
IV. 17.   ℭ om. חביב.   Berak. 61 b שממונו חביב עליו מגופו, Sifré 73 a.
וְהַתְקֵן (ℨ), or התקן (𝔄 ין—) without *vau.* Cf. Ab. IV. 23.   ℨ notes that
the *aphel* is used in Targ. as for ושמש אתה הֲכִינוֹתָ מָאוֹר ושמש (Ps. lxxiv. 16), but
התקן is preferred here in the Mishnah as a biblical form, although itself
not found in the Bible, כי המשנה היא שנויה בלשון המקרא כמו שכתב
כת׳ במשניות 𝔇.   שאינה ירושה לך.   הרד״ק בהקדמת המכלול
ונקוד מלמעלה לומ׳ שאין גורסין אותו.

17.   הֱוֵה זָהִיר בִּקְרִיאַת שְׁמַע וּבִתְפִלָּה (ℨ), 𝔇 in text ותפילה.
ותפילה אין אנו גורסין במשנה 𝔇 (comm.) תפלה. without זהיר בק״ש   Read
𝔄ℬℭ𝔇 (ℨ).   אֶלָּא רַחֲמִים וְתַחֲנוּנִים.   ותפלה ותפילין ל״ג No. 170
omit רחמים ו׳, which was perhaps suggested by רחום in the following proof-

* ℬ III. 4 and from III. 9 to the end (exc. v. 27, 28) is mostly unpointed.

text. Berak. IV. 4 ‎העושה תפלתו קבע אין תפלתו תחנונים‎. 𝕮 comm.

‎בעצמך‎ for ‎בפני עצמך‎. Cf. Nos. 2, 54, 90, 92, 103.

‎כ"ה הנוסח‎ 𝔖 18. ‎שָׁקֶד‎ 𝕭𝕮𝔇𝔖 ‎שקוד‎. ‎וְדַע מַה־שֶׁתָּשִׁיב‎ 𝔖

𝔖 continues ‎בספר נחלת אבות ולב אבות ומלי דאבות גם במדרש שמואל‎
‎ודע‎ ‎גם בספר חסדי אבות הביא שתי הנוסחאות והוכיח שהנכון הוא לגרום‎
[Sanh. 38 b] ‎ונם בסנהדרין‎ ‎הובאה משנה זו בלא מלת *ודע ובעל עין יעקב‎
‎ודע ודע‎ ‎הגיה בה מלת‎. But in Sanh. l.c. the insertion of ‎ודע‎ may be accounted
for by the perush ‎כדי כתדע להסיב‎. 𝕭 ‎ודע‎, 𝔄𝕮𝔇 Nos. 95, 133 omit it.
No. 73 (cf. 𝔇 comm.) ‎כדי שתשיב‎. Nos. 23, 39 ‎מה שתשיב‎ ‎ללמוד‎ without
‎תורה‎. M. Shelom. ‎תורה ודע מה שתשיב כצ"ל‎ (sic) ‎ית דלא גרסי' מלות‎
‎ולפי מה שראיתי בספר מסורת התלמוד שם בסנהדרין (דל"ח) דלא גרסינן‎
‎מלת תורה אין צורך לנרום מלת דע ומ"מ איני יודע מי הגיד לו זו הגרסא‎
‎וברמב"ן פ' ויקרא גבי חלבו האליה כתבה בלשון זה הוי שקוד ללמוד תורה‎

‎כדי שתשיב לאפיקורוס‎. ‎לְאַפִּיקוֹרוֹם‎ (𝔖), Baer ‎לְאַפִּי'‎ with segol, al.

𝔇 raphé. 𝕭 ‎'ה את‎ (𝔇 ‎את‎) for ‎ל‎. On ‎אפיקורום‎ see Sanh. 38 b, 99 b, cf.
Moreh Neb. III. 17. Thus far, omitting ‎ודע‎, we have but one saying.

‎וְדַע לִפְנֵי מִי אַתָּה עָמֵל‎ ‎הרי השניה‎ 𝔇, i.e. the 2nd of R. El'azar's
three sayings. 𝕮 adds ‎ומי הוא בעל בריתך‎, cf. Nos. 95, 110, 113.

‎וּמִי הוּא בַּעַל מְלַאכְתֶּךָ‎ his 3rd saying according to 𝔄 Ashk., to which
‎ואין‎ 𝔇 add 𝕭𝔖 ‎ונאמן בעל מלאכתך הג' הרי ג' 𝕮. שישלם לך שכר פעולתך‎
‎ובמשניות שלנו אין כתוב אלא וּמִי‎, Dur. ‎כת' במשניות נאמן הוא‎, cf. § 19.
‎הוּא בַּעַל בְּרִיתֶךָ‎, the three sayings ‎ואין שם ונאמן הוא בעל מלאכתך‎
according to his perush being (1) ‎הוי שקוד‎ (2) ‎ודע לפני מי‎ (3) ‎ומי הוא‎
‎בעל בריתך‎. See also No. 106 (p. 89).

19. ‎קָצַר‎ ‎כ"ה...ולא ר' שמעון‎ 𝔖. In der Bibel nur

Stat. constr. (Strack). ‎בֶּן חוֹרִין‎ or ‎ים‎— (𝔄). Cf. Ab. VI. 2. 𝕮 ‎ולא‎

‎בן חורין אתה‎ Eccl. x. 17. ‎בן חורים‎ ‎לִבָּטֵל‎ (𝔄), which may be read
as qal (No. 23 ‎לִבְטַל‎) or niph. 𝕭𝕮𝔇 ‎לִיטבל‎ 𝔖. ‎לְהִבָּטֵל‎. 𝕮 adds ‎הימנה‎,
𝔇𝔖 ‎ממנה‎.

---

* See authorities for the omission of ‎ודע‎ or of ‎תורה ודע מה‎ in Rabbinovicz ‎דקדוקי סופרים‎
(IX. 107, Mogunt. 1878). The Well of Jacob (No. 291, p. 437 in Benjacob's Oçar) was first
printed in the year ‎הראב"י לפ' נ‎, that is 5271 (=1511 A.D.), in Rashi type. Benjacob's
No. 311, p. 526 is the ‎הקונים‎ of R. Shimsh. ha-Naqdan referred to by 𝔖 on Ab. I. 11 (p. 137),
a MS. of which is in the British Museum.

CHAPTER III.

1. בֶּן מַהֲלַלְאֵל (𝔖), Geig. *Mahallel.* בנ׳ דברים כו׳ as in Ab. II. 1. Ab. R. N. *B.* XXXII. יסתכל אדם בד׳ דברים, cf. *A.* XIX. Dur. 𝔄 את for אתה here and in Baba Q. IX. (110 b_8), Qinnim III. (191 b_{24}). Numb. xi. 15 ואם ככה אַתְּ־עֹשֶׂה לִּי. מֵאַיִן בָּאתָ וּלְאָן אַתָּה הוֹלֵךְ (𝔖). 𝔄ℭ𝔇 Dur. באתה. 𝔄𝔅 No. 23 Ashk. Strack ולאין, ℭ𝔇 Dur. Emd. ולאן. 1 Sam. x. 14 אָן הֲלַכְתֶּם, Jud. xix. 17 אָנָה תלך וּמֵאַיִן תבוא. Ashk. מאין באתה מליחה סרוחה. מְלִיחָה. 𝔄 דע מאין. 𝔇 Nos. 92, 108, 158 מְלִיחה, 112, 114 מלחה. 𝔄 Shebi. II. (13 b_6) הַלָּחָה, Makhsh. VI. 7 (Jost) וְהַלֵּחָה סרוחה. מְטִפָּה, 𝔖 with 𝔅ℭ𝔇 (comm.), cf. Mekhilta on נורא תהלות (Fr. f. 42 a) נותן לאדם בן מטפה של מים. 𝔄 לרמה ותולעה, No. 23 marg. ר׳ ות׳ למקום. 𝔅𝔇𝔖 Dur. למקום עפר ר׳ ות׳, ℭ ורימה with *vau* conj. את החשבון for דין וח׳, No. 103 here and in IV. 32, cf. Dur. No. 113 לתת את הח׳. Ashk. לפני מלכי המלכים (*sic*) ברוך הוא וכתב כן מג׳לתי.

2. רַבִּי חֲנַנְיָה סְגַן הַכֹּהֲנִים. 𝔇 Baer חנינא, 𝔄𝔅ℭ𝔖 (text) Ashk. *Fragm. of T. B.* ed. Lowe (pp. 41, 42, 45) חנניה. Ashk. גם ר׳ חנניה בן דוסא...חכינאי...תרדיון (Ab. III. 3, 7, 13). סגן pl. only in Bible (Ezra ix. 2, Dan. ii. 48, iii. 2). סגן כהניא Targ. 2 Kings xxiii. 4, Jer. xx. 1. Emd. סֶגֶן with שש נקודות, cf. Baer. שֶׁאִלְמָלֵא מוֹרָאָהּ (𝔖), cf. Emd. Baer. Tos. Megil. 21 a ד״ה אלמלא quotes from R. Tam דהיכא שיש אל״ף בסוף אלמלא רוצה לומר א׳ילו לא והיכא דכתיב אלמלי ביו״ד רוצה לומר א׳ילו ה׳יה. 𝔄 שֶׁאִילוּלֵי, cf. bibl. לולי, לולא. Dur. ובמשניות שלנו גרסינן שאלולי מוראה שהיה קשה ענינו, but why קשה? No. 103 מורא מלכות. בְּלָעֲנוּ, 𝔄𝔅ℭ (חיים בלענו גרסי׳) Dur. Geig. (*richtiger als* בלעו *wegen* חיים). 𝔖 בְּלָעוּ objecting that the speaker would not have included himself, Emd. בְּלָעוּ שני קמצין. ℭ text בלעו, 𝔇 ובמשניות מדוייקות כת׳ חיים בלעו. No. 23 בלעונו. Psalm cxxiv. 2, 3 לוּלֵי יי׳ שהיה לנו...אזי חיים בְּלָעוּנוּ.

3. אֲבָל שְׁנַיִם שֶׁיּוֹשְׁבִין וְיֵשׁ בֵּינֵיהֶם דִּבְרֵי תוֹרָה שְׁכִינָה שְׁרוּיָה בֵּינֵיהֶם, 𝔖 with 𝔅ℭ𝔇 (exc. כאלו שכינה). ℭ שיושבין ועוסקין

שהיו...בדברי ת'...ביניהם 𝔄.   בתורה שכינה עמהם found elsewhere. No. 114 in III. 3, 9 שכינה עמהן.

4. **אחד שיושב ושונה** (𝔄). 𝔖 אֵין לִי אֶלָּא שְׁנַיִם מִנַּיִן שֶׁאֲפִלּוּ אֶחָד וֹמניין (𝔅𝔊𝔇) with text of, שֶׁיּוֹשֵׁב וְעוֹסֵק בַּתּוֹרָה שֶׁהַקָּבָּ״ה קוֹבֵעַ לוֹ שָׂכָר במשנת ר' אפרים ובשאר (אפילו). 𝔇 comm. (cf. p. 91 B) does not find this כת' רש״י ז״ל ולא מצינו במשנה כתי' (p. 100 A) 𝔅.   משניות מדוייקות ...R. Isaac Isr. finds it only in the   ייתב בדר וידום אבל רגילים העם לאומרו margin (מבחוץ) of his two Jerus. ש״ס משנה MSS. (p. 139), ...וופרש'י ז״ל וידום משמע כמו כאשר דמיתי כלו' שיהיה מחשב בדברי תורה. כי נטל עליו כי נטל שכרו באותו עסק וי״א נטל כמו סכך וסכות על הארון מתרגמי' ותטלל ע״ב (sic). Cf. "Rashi" in ed. Mantua above-mentioned (p. 118); but in some editions his *perush* has here only the six words איש אל רעהו הרי

בסוף משנת ר' חלפתא מצאתי כתוב כאן שנים, or these followed by (בפי' רש״י) וז״ל לא מצינו...ומתרגמינן ותטיל, see Midr. Shem. p. 93, and Leb Aboth (Salonika, 1565 A.D.). On the latter *baba* (III. 9), with reference to R. 'Obad. of Bertinoro, M. Shelom. has עוד בפירושו ז״ל **כי נטל עליו** לשון סכך אמר המלקט זו הגירסא של ראיית פסוק כי נטל לא נמצאת אצלי בשום מקום אלא במתני' דלעיל גבי חנניא בן תרדיון.   M. Shelom. on **השכינה ביניהם** ע' בתיו׳ט חילופי גרסאות בזה III. 3, 4.   Ashk. after ביניהם ס״א אחד שיושב **ודורש** [= No. 170] שנ'... deletes the rest (§ 4), but adds and reads like 𝔄 exc. כולה. Dur. quotes Rashi on כי נטל עליו in both places, ending here with ואין במשניות שלנו אין לי אלא שנים וכו'.

5, 6. **שאכלו** or שהיו אוכלין. הרי. 𝔅𝔊𝔇𝔖 omit הרי.   No. 170 אלי for אליו 𝔄.   ב.without ה״ד של מקום 𝔊𝔖.   כאוכלי זבחי מתים הרי אלו

7. **ומפנה** , 𝔄𝔅𝔖 (ref. to Leb Ab. and Midr. Shem.) No. 23 Ashk. (וה״ק הניעור...או המהלך...ומפנה לבו...באחת משניהם ה״ז מתחייב) 𝔊𝔇. לְבַטָּלָה (𝔖) or להבטלה, see Dur. Geig.   והמפנה Geig.

8. **נותנין עליו** 𝔇 No. 113 גוזרין עליו.   Gen. xxvii. 40 וּפָרַקְתָּ עֻלּוֹ מעל צוארך.

9. **ר' חלפתא** (𝔖), No. 95 חֲלַפְתָּא.   Baer adds בן דוסא and notes that §§ 13, 14, 16, 17 precede this *baba* in some copies, cf. Nos. 10, 113. Perhaps because some omit it Dur. writes זאת המשנה נכתבה בסדורי תמרתא No. 17, הבבלי 𝔅 (𝔖), אִישׁ כְּפַר חֲנַנְיָה.   Maim. תפלות.

(cf. Dur.) עשרה שהיו יושבין בדין, R. 'Obad. 'שיוש.   The number *five* may be connected with בקרב אלהים ישפוט and the number *three* with בפי' ר"ע (אם) or *vice versa* (בc־S).   M. Shelom. ואגודתו על ארץ יסדה [R. 'Obadiah], ז"ל וי"ס שכתוב בהן וכו' אמר המלקט ע' תוס' פ"ק דסוכה ד' י"ג see the rest quoted above in § 4.   ם quotes Rabbi's דיני ממנות בחמשה against the customary בשלשה, but the *baba* as a whole seems to refer properly to תורה and not דין.   The words בקרב אלהים ישפוט are part of the verse quoted for the number *ten* and should perhaps be struck out— and with them the number *five*, which is not mentioned in Berak. 6 a or Mekh. Jethro בחדש XI. on בכל המקום.   No. 101 omits it and reads:

...בעדת אל בקרב אלהים ישפוט מנין שאפי' שלשה שנ'
ואגודתו על ארץ יסדה...

and ℭ has a transitional reading, agreeing with this up to ישפוט", continuing חמשה שנ' ואגודתו...שלשה שנ' בקרב אלהים ישפוט, and thus *repeating* the 2nd hemistich of Psalm lxxxii. 1. See also Nos. 9, 10, 12, 22, 23, 39, 68, 73, 81—3, 90, 92, 95, 99, 103, 109, 113, 116, 133, 137, 150, 170. Ab. R. N. p. 36 makes ג' שיושבין אגודה an.   On מַנִּין without *vau* conj. see Nos. 108 (p. 91), 158 and Midr. Shem.   ם comm. מניין...מניין אפי' חמשה.   See אפי' בג'...מנין שאפי' שנים שנ' אז נדברו ואין כת' יותר במשנה שנים...שנ' אז נדברו in III. 4 also, and the notes there on כי נטל עליו. ℭ comments upon § 9 next after § 6.

10. א לעזר, בcם אלעזר, S אליעזר.   Some omit בן יהודה. *מכילתי (sic) (S), cf. Baer Geig. Strack.   ם cites בפרשת איש בַּרְתּוֹתָא [Ex. xiv. 30] ויישע as reading איש כפר תותא, but under xiv. 15 the Venice edit. of 1545 A.D. (f. 12. 1) and the editions of Weiss and Friedmann have איש ברתותא.   In the parallel in Jalq. I. רל"ג as Friedmann remarks (Mekh. 29 b, note 17) the reading is אלעזר בן עזריה אלעזר בן יהודה; but Jalq. II. תקס'ה on Hab. iii. 14 reads איש כפר ביתר; אלעזר בן יהודה.   א 64 b has בית תר in two lines for ביתר (Jost Ta'an. IV. 6 בֵּתָּר).   See also Ta'an. 24 a with Rabbinovicz ס'ד III. 142 (ז); and see Bacher's *Agada der Tannaiten*, I. 442, note 2.   S Baer שָׁאָתֶּה the *shin* with *qameç* as Jud. vi. 17 שָׁאַתָּה מדבר עמי.   Dur. וגם זאת המשנה אינה בסדורי תפלות.

* See מכילתי likewise in No. 108, f. 61 b, presumably for ין—, as R. Jonah on ר"נ בנו של הנשיא ר'י"ה (Ab. II. 2) quoting the Mekhilta כמכילתין. כענין שאמרו במכילתין. I have not seen a *parashath* וירוש in any edition.

11. רִבִּי יַעֲקֹב אוֹמֵר הַמְהַלֵּךְ בַּדֶּרֶךְ‎ (ℭ). al. שמעון or עֲקִיבָא,

קוֹדֵר הֲלַכְתִּי‎ Job xxx. 28. ל״ג יְחִידִי‎ ℭℬ. Rashi see 'Beth Habchira'.

מִשְׁנָתוֹ* 𝔄 with *pathach* for *qameç*, which was illustrated by the annexed

footnote in the first edition of ℬ𝔄. דברי אבות העולם‎. ממשנתו‎

מַה־נָּאֶה אִילָן זֶה‎ (ℭ). 𝔄 repeats this, No. 101 omits it and repeats

the ניר‎ (al. נירא‎) clause. Dur. ונם זו המשנה אינה כתובה בסדורי תפלי'‎

מַעֲלֶה‎ Dan. iv. 7 וַאֲלוּ אִילָן‎. ולשון המשנה מה נָאוֶה אילן זה‎

עָלָיו הַכָּתוּב‎, 𝔄 not Baer Targ. Job xxx. 4 כ״ה בכל הנוכחאות‎ הכתוב‎

הֲרִי זֶה מִתְחַיֵּיב‎...ℬ דיבר לא ושלום וחם‎. דהא לא כת' ביה קרא ℭ ממש‎

הכת'‎. בדבר כזה לפיכך הוא או' כאילו מתחייב בנפשו ולא נתחייב ממש‎

Ashk. מעלין עליו כאילו מתחייב וכו' וכן הגיה ג״כ במתני' דבסמוך‎.

12. ℭ משום אומר ינאי בר' אומֵר‎... אוֹמֵר...אוֹמֵר‎ 𝔄 No. 109

כָּל הַשּׁוֹכֵחַ‎ ר' מאיר אומ'‎ with marks of erasure over the first אומר‎.

תַּלְמִיד ℭℬ. מתלמודו‎. No. 95 אחר‎. ℬ om. (ℭ). דָּבָר אֶחָד מִמִּשְׁנָתוֹ‎

וְגוֹ'‎ ℭ abbrev. ושכח תלמודו מעלה עליו כאילו מ' בנ' ℭ as 𝔄. חכם שׁ'‎

הא אינו מתחייב עד‎ Ashk. (𝔄ℭ). כל ימי חייך‎ and אשר ראו עיניך‎ for

* כ״א ממשנתו‎ : וא״ת למה נורת הפתח תחת הנון בכ״י שלפנינו וי״ל‎
שבם״י דומה נורת הקמן לפתח סתתחתיה חירק אבל לפעמים הפתח בלבד‎
עומד במקום הקמן לגמרי‎. והרי דבר נפלא שראיתי בספר גור אריה (וזה‎
פרוש לפרוש רש״י על התורה להגאון מהר״ל מפראנ) על הפסוק בראשית י״ח‎
ג' ו ז ל : לגדול שבהם אמר וקראם כלם אדוני' פי' הא דכתי' אדוני דמשמע‎
לשון רבים מדלא כתי' אדוני בחירק ואם״כ אמר אל נא תעבור דמשמע לשון‎
יחיד אלא האמירה היא לאחד וקראם כולם אדוני' לכן קאמר אדוני בלשון רבים‎.
וא״ת אי לשון רבים הוי למכתב אדני בפתח דמשמע לשון רבים וי״ל בקמן‎
משמע לשון יחיד וגם לשון רבים וכן מורה הנקודה שהוא קמן והוא מורכב מן‎
פתח שהוא לשון רבים ומן חירק שהוא לשון יחיד ולפיכך הם שהוא קדום‎
נקוד בקמן לפי שהקב״ה יחיד ודרך כבוד אומרים לו לשון רבים ומפני שכאן‎
הוא מדבר לגדול וקראם כולם אדונים לכן קאמר אדני בקמן סהו' ליחיד‎
ומדבר אותו בלשון רבים וזה שכיון רש״י לפרש על וַיֹּאמֶר ה': לגדול שבהם‎
אמר וקראם כולם אדונים כדי לתרן לשון אדני בקמן‎.

שיסירנו‎ ℭ‎, שיישב ויסירם מלבו‎ 𝔄𝔅𝔇𝔖‎, שיישב לו...ומחק מלת‎ בנפשו‎.
ומצאתי נוסחאות משניות קדומות עד שישכיל וידיחנה מלבו‎ Dur.

13. No. 107 וכל שאין יראת חטאו קודמת לחכמתו אין חכמתו מתקיימת‎,
so Midr. Shem. with איֽת דגרסי‎. ℭ חנינא for חנני‎.

14. 𝔇 omitting הוא היה‎, וכל שמעשיו מרובין מחכמתו חכמתו מתקיימת‎ 𝔇
וכל שאין‎ No. 107. וכל שחכמתו‎ the clause (here and in §§ 15, 20) אומר‎
מעשיו מרובין מחכמתו אין חכמתו מתקיימת‎, against which Midr. Shem.
writes שאין צורך להחליף הגרסא‎. ℭ text omits the *baba*.

15. (𝔖). No. 95 הַבְּרִיוֹת‎. Mishnah שְׂרוּחַ הַבְּרִיּוֹת נוֹחָה הֵימֶנּוּ‎
Shebi. (end) (Jost), 𝔄 17 a המנו‎ and המינו‎. רוּחַ חכמים נוֹחָה הֵימֶנּוּ‎.

16. No. 95 אַרְכִּינָס‎, cf. Strack. 𝔖 הָרְכִּינָס‎ the *he* with short *qameç*.

(𝔖). שֵׁינָה שֶׁל שַׁחֲרִית וְיַיִן שֶׁל צָהֳרַיִם...וִישִׁיבַת בָּתֵּי כְנֵסִיּוֹת‎
ר׳ דוסא בן ארכינס אומר שְׁנָת שחרית וְיַיִן צהרים...וישבת כנסיות‎ Ashk.
No. 109 om. ׳צ וְיַיִן של‎. 𝔄𝔅𝔄𝔖 הילדים‎, 𝔇𝔅 ילדים‎. 𝔇𝔅 Nos. 95, 101 om. בתי‎.
Baba M. 24 a בבתי כנסיות של נכרים‎.

17. 𝔖 (after (המועדות והמפר בריתו וְהַמַּלְבִּין פְּנֵי חֲבֵרוֹ בָּרַבִּים‎
של אברהם אבינו והמגלה פנים בתורה שֶׁלֹּא כַהֲלָכָה‎ אף על פי שיש בידו
תּוֹרָה‎ ומעשים טובים. So editions of Sanh. 99 a*, but with והמלבין‎ next
before בידו‎. אע׳ם שיש בידו‎. 𝔅 expounds it before מגלה פנים‎. 𝔇 reads
הגיה הַמְּאָדִים‎...וכתב עוד שברוב (p. 91 D). cf. No. 108. Ashk. וְהַמְּאָדִים‎
𝔄 Ashk. Nos. 23, 39, 114, הספרים ל׳ג והמאדים פני חבירו ברבים כלל‎.
170 om. שֶׁלֹּא כַהֲלָכָה‎. 𝔇 שלא כהלכה אין אנו גורסין במשנה‎.
𝔅 quotes Rashbam as reading מֵעֲשִׂים טוֹבִים‎ without תורה [𝔇 ל׳ג תורה‎],
and adds וכן מצאתי בשית׳ סדרי משנה שלי ומפו׳ בירושלמי דפאה‎. T. J.
Peah I. 1 (16 *b*₂₆) הפורק עול והמיפר ברית והמגלה פנים בתורה אע׳פ שיש‎
תורה תְשׁוּבָה‎ ומ׳׳ט cf. Ab. R. N. (p. 82). No. 10 בידו מעשים טובים‎, cf.
Baer. No. 109 om. טובים‎. ℭ ...תורה ומ׳׳ט‎ שלא כהלכה והמלבין‎.

18. 𝔖 הֱוֵה קַל לְרֹאשׁ וְנוֹחַ לְתִשְׁחֹרֶת‎, without note or comment. 𝔄 הוי קל ראש ונוח תשחורת‎, omitting *lamed* perhaps by error before ראש‎. 𝔅 והוי רך כקנה‎ but rightly before תשחורת‎. הקל את ראשך‎
שהולך לכאן ולכאן וזריז כאדם קל להקביל פני ראש העיר ושופטיה‎, see Nos.

---

* Rabbinovicz ד׳׳ס IX. 297 (ı) shews that והמלבין...‎ is an interpolation in Sanh. *l.c.*

119, 133, 151. Ab. R. N. *B.* XXXI. (p. 68) ‏דברים מאהבין את האדם לבריות‎ ‏ג'‎

‏יד פשוטה ושולחן ערוך וקלות ראש‎ . See in Kohut's *Aruch* under

‏קל‎ (VII. 90 *a*) ‏...בפ' עקביה הוי קל לראש. ראש דמאי‎, and in three Cam-

bridge University MSS. of the *Aruch* (1) Addit. 376 ‏ראש‎. ‏הוי קל לראש‎.

‏דמאי‎ (198 a), (2) Addit. 472 ‏דמאי‎ ‏בר'‎ . ‏הוי קל ראש‎. (3) Addit. 473. 2

‏קל לראש‎ 𝕮 (2 b). ‏הוי קל . ראש דמאי‎.

19. ‏מרגילין לערוה‎, 𝕭𝔇𝔖. 𝕮 ‏לדבר עבירה‎. 𝕬 ins. ‏את האדם‎.

20. ‏מָסוֹרֶת סְיָג לַתּוֹרָה‎ (𝕾). Ashk. ‏ס"א מסרות‎, cf. 𝕬𝕮 comm.

‏מסורות‎ כנון אילו שכותבין בגליון הספרים היא מסורת 𝕭 No. 95. (p. 84)

‏מַעֲשְׂרוֹת סְיָג לָעוֹשֶׁר‎, 𝔖 with 𝕭𝕮𝔇. Ashk. ‏בכל הספרים‎ . ‏הגדולה‎.

‏וי"א מעשרות סייג‎ (VI. 14), cf. 𝕬 No. 23. Kohut *A. C.* on ‏סג‎ ‏זה‎ ‏מצאתי‎ ‏לא‎,

‏לתורה‎, cf. ‏תשובות הגאונים‎, p. 18 *b* (Lyck, 1864 A.D.), and Tos. Yomtob.

𝕭𝕮𝔇𝔖 omit ‏הוא היה אומר‎ (𝕬) and begin with ‏מסורת‎ (𝕭𝕮 ‏ומ'‎) (𝔖

or ‏מעשר ת‎ (𝕭).

21. Between ‏שׁ'‎ and ‏שנברא בצלם‎ (𝕬), 𝕮𝕭 No. 101 insert the

four words ‏שנברא בצלם‎, to which 𝕭𝔖 add ‏חיבה יתירה נודעת לו‎

‏כן הוא הנוסח הנכון בשני הפעמים‎ (‏שֶׁנִּבְרָא בְּצֶלֶם‎ on) 𝔖. (‏בצ' אלהים‎ .al)

‏הראשוני' בלא זכירת אלדים עד שמביא הפסוק כי בצלם אלדים והטעם מבואר‎

‏חיבה יתירה‎ 𝕭 (ix. 6). ‏עשה‎ for (Gen. i. 27) ‏ברא‎ text 𝕮 . ‏במדרש שמואל‎

‏נודעת לו כלום' חיבה יתירה חיבבו שנברא בצלם אלהים עצמו שנ' כי בצלם‎

‏אלהים בצלם אלהים עצמו עשאו המקום. ואית דלא גרסי הא [ר"ל אלהים]‎

‏דכיון דאין לצור דמיון ולא תמונה מי שאומר כזה חיישי' שמא מין הוא. ואף‎

‏כי בצלם אית מתרג' ארן בצלמא יי' עבד ולא בצלמא דיי' ובעברי היקף‎ (*sic*)

‏גדול בצלדין של בצלם הטעם להבין פתרונו כמו שפירשו בהכל חייבין‎

‏בוייעלו עולות וכן נקוד כי בצלם בצֶּ֔לם‎ . I have not seen ‏בצלם‎ with *zaqef*

gadol in the Bible. 𝕭 refers above to ‏לפיסוק טעמים‎ in Chag. 6 b where the

punctuation of Exod. xxiv. 5 by accents is discussed, cf. Megil. 3 a ‏ויבינו‎

‏שכר פיסוק טעמים‎, Nedar. 37 a ‏במקרא אלו פסקי טעמים‎. Abarbanel on this

baba gives ‏בצלמא יי' ברא...עבד‎ as Targ. ‏אונקלום‎ (Gen. i. 27, ix. 6). Modern

texts of Onqelos do not give these renderings, but see Targ. Jon. Gen. i. 27

‏בצלמא יי' ברא יתיה‎. Berliner's Targ. Onk. has ‏אל' בְּצֶלֶם‎ in both verses.

22. ‏חביבין ישראל שנקראו בנים למקום‎, 𝕬𝕭𝕮𝔇𝔖. al. ‏בנים‎

‏בנים‎ ‏שנ'‎ ‏להם‎ ‏נודעת‎ ‏יתירה‎ ‏חיבה‎, 𝕮𝕭 omit- ‏למקום‎. without

ting ‏שנקראו בנים למקום‎ (𝕬𝕭𝔖) before ‏שנ'‎.

23. ‏חֲבִיבִין יִשְׂרָאֵל שֶׁנִּתַּן לָהֶם *כְּלִי חֶמְדָּה‎ 𝔄 Ashk. ‏כלי‎

‏חיבה יתירה נודעת להם‎ .‏כלי חמדה שבו 𝔅𝔄,‏שבו נברא העולם‎

‏כלי חמדה 𝔅,‏שניתן להם כלי שבו נברא העולם‎ 𝔄 (ℭ). ‏שנ' כי לקח טוב‎

‏𝔅 ...‏כלי חמדה שבו‎ .𝔇 omits ‏חיבה יתירה נודעת להם‎ .   Dur. on

§§ 21—3 .‏בצלם אלהים‎ ...‏בצלם‎ .‏ומצאתי בתפלות צרפתות נוסחא יפה‎...

‏בנים‎... ‏בנים למקום. כלי חמדה. כלי חמדה שבו נברא‎

‏העולם.‏ ולפי נוסחא זה החיבה היתירה תוספת היא על החיבה הראשונה‎...

‏אדם‎ ‏עולה מ"ה ומ"ם‎ He gives the Gematria ‏ולא גרסינן במשניות‎ ‏ה"א, and remarks ‏ה"א בשלימותו עולה פ"ו כמנין אלהים‎

‏שנאמר בנים‎... Ashk. ‏שלנו אלא בקצת נוסחאות שנא' כי לקח טוב‎...

.‏שנאמר כי לקח טוב‎... ‏בס"א ל"ג הני תרי שנאמר‎

24. ‏הַכֹּל צָפוּי‎ .Ashk ‏צפון‎ ‏אית דאמרי הכל צפון‎, cf. p. 122.

‏וְהָרְשׁוּת‎, 𝔅 Emd. (‏ה"א קמוצה ורי"ש שוא"ת),‏ but in I. 11, II. 3 ‏רְשׁוּת‎ as

(𝔅). ‏וּבְטוֹב הָעוֹלָם נִדּוֹן‎ ‏רשה‎ s. r. ‏רד"ק,‏ see in ‏מגזרת ראש‎ if

Emd. ‏וּבְטוֹב‎ ‏טי"ת חלומה דגושה),‏ (בי"ת פתוחה רפויה. ‏נָדוֹן‎ (‏נו"ן קמוצה).

,‏נ"א אבל לא על פי רוב המעשה‎ (𝔄), 𝔅 marg. ‏והכל לפי המעשה‎ ‏לפי רוב 𝔅𝔅𝔄.

ℭ ‏לא הכל לפי רוב‎ 𝔇 ‏אע"פי שיש‎ ‏אבל לא על פי רוב המעשה‎...

‏בעולם חוטאי' ויש עושין צדקה וזכות, העולם נידון בטובתו של הק' שאינו‎

‏הולך אחר רוב מעשיהן המקולקלין‎... ‏שהעולם ניזון בטובתו של הק' כך קיבלתי‎

‏אבל לא לפי רוב המעשה כדפרי'.‏ ואני מצאתי במשניות הכל לפי רוב המעשה‎

Midr. Shem. finds in a *perush* ascribed to R. Ephraim with a doubt

whether it is not Rashbam's ‏ובמשניות הרב ר' אפרים‎ ‏גרסינן ובטוב‎...

‏העולם נדון והכל לפי רוב המעשה כלומר אע"פ שיש בעולם חוטאים ויש בהם‎

‏עושי צדקה וזכיות‎... ‏העולם נידון וניזון בטובתו של הקב"ה‎... ‏שרוב מעשיו‎

‏על אדם הם מקולקלים‎. This must be from a recension of ‏פי' רי"ש‎ contain-

ing a reference to ‏משנת ר' אפרים‎ *and other Mishnaioth*, as 𝔇 on Ab.

III. 4 (p. 147), for which 𝔅 50 a₂₁ has ‏במשנאות‎. 𝔅 quotes 'Rashbam' on § 24

(p. 92 E), and adds ‏והרמב"ם והרמ"ה ז"ל גורסין לפי רוב המעשה אבל לא‎

‏על פי המעשה‎. See also Nos. 23, 90, 95, 107, 112—14.   𝔇 on § 24

---

* 𝔇 ‏ויקר מכלי חמדה‎ ‏תורה שהיא כלי חמדה שנ'‎, the ‏פסוק‎ (Prov. xx. 15) having been

disguised by adaptation to the phrase to be illustrated. See also Nahum ii. 10 ‏וכבוד מכל‎

‏כלי חמדה‎. No. 158 [‏ר"ל שפתי דעת‎] ‏וכלי יקר‎ ‏וגומ'‎ ‏דכת' יש זהב ורב פנינים‎. At (a manu-

script of ‏פי' רי"ש‎ in my possession, which was quoted in edit. 1) has an intermediate reading

‏שפת חמרה‎, and No. 108 reads ‏יש זהב ורב פנינים וכלי יקרה שפת חמדה‎ with *resh*.

ועד כאן מדברי ר' עקיב' וההוא נמי דהכל נתון בערבון. ואני מצאתי בתוספתא
ועד כאן מדברי ר' ישמעאל הן ונ"ר שיבוש הסופר דא"כ מקמי מילתיה דר'
הוספה ב, See in Mr Schechter's Aboth R. N., עקיבא הוה ליה למיתנינהו

א'ר ישמעאל הכל נתון בערבון (p. 162), **לנוסחא א**. At Nos. 108, 158
before **ובטוב**. between the hemistichs of § 24, that is to say
to R. Ishmael, הוי קל 18 ascribe **ABCDS** The texts of
19 שחוק וקלות ראש to R. 'Aqiba, 26 אם אין תורה to R. El'azar b. Azariah,
and read הכל צפוי in 21, 25 but not in 24. **B** comm. on 24
עקיבה. **C** on 25 להו 'ר' עקיבא קאמ' להו. נם אלה דברי ר' עקיבא.

25. **הַכֹּל נָתוּן בְּעֵרָבוֹן**. **C** אינמי בערבין (p. 85), cf. No. 113.

וּמְצוּדָה פְרוּסָה, ע' ערוך ערך סעד וא'ת דגרסי בערבים. M. Shelom.
S הצד"י פעם בחול'ם פעם בשור'ק quoting Eccl. ix. 12, Ezek. xiii. 21.
(S). ***וְהַפִּנְקָס פָּתוּח** ומצודה No. 95 **BCD**, with art., והמצודה **A**
והפנקס פת' 109 om., החנות פתוחה No. 103 om. פתוחה **ABCDS**.

(S). **וְכָל הָרוֹצֶה לִלְוֹת יָבֹא וְיִלְוֶה**, (כ"ה הנוסח הנכון) **S**, Emd. (וילוה קל).
ס"א וכל הרוצה ליטול בא. **C** omits the clause. Ashk. בא ולוה **BD**.
(S). **וְהַגַּבָּאִין מַחֲזִירִין תָּמִיד**. נ"א ליטול בא ונוטל. **B** marg. ונוטל.
לר' **D** (text) **ABC**, מִדַּעְתּוֹ **S**, תדיר **BD** Emd. Dur. מחזרין **A**. לדעתו See
[מדעתו § 2 Jost] **A** Parah XII. 3 in Makhsh. VI. 5, ושלא לדעתו].

(S). **עַל־מָה־שֶׁיִּסְמְכוּ וְהַדִּין דִּין אֱמֶת וְהַכֹּל מְתֻקָּן לִסְעוּדָה**
C (comm.) **D** No. 10 Dur. על מי. **BD** Dur. Emd. שיסמוכו. Emd. אם
מותקן **A**. והדן דן אמת' או והדין דיין' או והדין דין אמת.

26. **אם אין חכמה אין יראה** and *vice versa*, **ABD** (text) **S**.
Ashk. בס"א אם אין יראה אין חכמה וכו'. and **D** comm. has this order.

אם אין דעת אין בינה and *vice versa*, **ABDS** Ashk. as against the
reverse order אם אין בינה אין דעת וכו' mentioned in M. Shelom.
D Dur. mention a reading **יש תורה יש קמח** (No. 10 וויש ק') for אם
אם אין דרך ארץ אין תורה אם אין תורה **C**. אין תורה אין קמח
אין חכמה אם אין חכמה אין יראה אם אין יראה אין בינה אם אין בינה אין
דעת אם אין דעת אין קמח אם אין קמח אין תורה.

27. **שֶׁעֲנָפָיו מְרֻבִּים וְשָׁרָשָׁיו מְעָטִין וְהָרוּחַ בָּאָה** (Eccl. v. 1
(מְעַטִּים), **S** וכתב רבי יצחק אבן גיאות (*sic*) ז"ל כי דגש מי"ת מעטים לתפארת

---

* See pl. פינקסיות in Kelim XXIV. 6 (**A** 203 a).

11

𝔖 condemns the form מוֹעֲטִין found ברוב הנוסחאות as belonging to a פ״י verb, but it is used for מְמוֹעֲטִין. 𝔄 מְעוּטִים, 𝔇 (text) ‎‑ין. 𝔅 הרוח without *vau* conj. 𝔄 (cf. Strack) באתה, 𝔇 בָאת. 𝔖 (Jer. xvii. 6) שֶׁנֶּאֱמַר

וְהָיָה כְּעַרְעָר בָּעֲרָבָה וְלֹא יִרְאֶה כִּי יָבוֹא טוֹב וְשָׁכַן חֲרֵרִים בַּמִּדְבָּר אֶרֶץ מְלֵחָה וְלֹא

תֵשֵׁב.   **אֲפִילוּ כָּל הָרוּחוֹת בָּאוֹת עָלָיו אֵינָן מְזִיזוֹת** (𝔄).

וְכָל שֶׁמַּעֲשָׂיו... וַאֲפִלּוּ כָּל הָרוּחוֹת שֶׁבָּעוֹלָם בָּאוֹת וְנוֹשְׁבוֹת בּוֹ אֵין מְזִיזִין 𝔖 אֲבָל כֹּל... שֶׁאֲפִלּוּ... אֵין מְזִיזוֹת... וְאִית דְּגָרֵס׳ **נוֹשְׁפוֹת** 𝔇 ..אוֹתוֹ מִמְּקוֹמוֹ שֶׁנֶּאֱמַר וְהָיָה כְּעֵץ שָׁתוּל (Jer. xvii. 8) 𝔖. כְּמוֹ נָשַׁפְתָּ בְרוּחֲךָ (Ex. xv. 10)

עַל מַיִם וְעַל יוּבַל יְשַׁלַּח שָׁרָשָׁיו וְלֹא יִרְאֶה [כתיב יִרְאֶן] כִּי יָבֹא חֹם וְהָיָה עָלֵהוּ רַעֲנָן ס״א לְאִילָן **שֶׁנְּפַֿיִן** וכתב. Ashk. וּבִשְׁנַת בַּצֹּרֶת לֹא יִדְאָג וְלֹא יָמִישׁ מֵעֲשׂוֹת פֶּרִי

כָּךְ הִיא (No. 170) Dur. (cf. עוֹד... הִנֵּי תְּרֵי שֶׁנֶּאֱמַר יֵשׁ סְפָרִים דְל״ג לְהוּ הגירסא בסדורי תפלות אבל במשניות אין שם פסוקים הנזכרים במשנה. ובמקום ענפיו יש **נוֹפָן** ובמשניות אחרות ראיתי הגירסא כמו שהיא בסדורי תפלות.

28. **ר׳ אֶלְעָזָר חִסְמָא** M. Shelom., ‎בלי יו״ד (i.e. not חיסמא). 𝔖 בֶּן. חִסְמָא, 𝔄𝔅𝔇𝔇 om. בֶּן. Geig. חַסְמָא *ohne* בן, cf. No. 23. No. 95 חַסְמָא. ר׳ לְעָזָר 𝔄. את דגרסי הסמא בה״א. Ashk., הסמה 𝔄 Terum. III. 5 (18 b) ר׳(א)לְעָזר הסמה with *cheth*, Baba M. xvii. 6 (115 a), Nega. vii. 2 (217 b) הסמא with *he*, cf. והפסה with *he* for *cheth* in Par. i. 7 (222 a).

הֵן הֵן גּוּפֵי הֲלָכוֹת 𝔖 with 𝔅𝔇𝔇 (עיקר הלכות למשה מסיני. 𝔄 No. 109 הֲלָכוֹת תְּקוּפוֹת 𝔄 Chag. גּוּפֵי תוֹרָה, which requires the pointing (cf. 73, 151). התר נדרים פורחין באויר ואין להם על מה שיסמכו **הלכות שבת** (67 a) I. 11 וחגיגות ומעילות כהררין תלויין בסערה מקרא ממועט והלכות מרובות הדינין ועבורות הטהרות והטומאות והעריות יש להן על מה שיסמכו **והן הן גופי תורה.** הן הן הן הנה אותם שני דברים 𝔇 **תְּקוּפוֹת וְגִמַטְרִיָּאוֹת**   **פַּרְפְּרָיוֹת** 𝔖 כתב התשבי וז״ל גימטריא היא מלה יונית ממש לשון חשבון. 𝔄 וגימטרייה או מנין ברפי על הגימ״ל. 𝔄 Nos. 23, 95, 170 כ״ה בערוך... 𝔖 ‎‑יות, No. 95 𝔄 26‎₁₀ פרפראות, 𝔄𝔅𝔇𝔇 (pl.). ‎‑יאות 𝔅𝔇𝔇 פרפרותיו Shab. xxiii. 2 וכ״ה במכלול. (𝔄 39 a).

CHAPTER IV.

1. **אֵיזֶהוּ חָכָם הַלּוֹמֵד מִכָּל אָדָם** (𝔖). 𝔄 אי זה הוא, 𝔅 אי זהו, בכל הנוסחאות 𝔖 prefers לוֹמֵד here, but finds למד (see II. 6) so, 𝔇𝔇 איזהו. איזה הכם הלמד לכל אדם כך M. Shelom. ‎‑יד 𝔅, (comm.) 𝔇, (text) 𝔄𝔇

הָשְׂכַּלְתִּי the caph with pathach and הגיה ונקד הר'ר יהוסף ז'ל

ethnach, (ℭ). והוא אחד מן פתח'ין דספרא (ℭ). ℭ𝔅𝔄 (cf. Midr. Shem.) add the remainder of Ps. cxix. 99 כִּי עֵדְוֹתֶיךָ שִׂיחָה לִי, which 𝔅 (but with the note ואין סיום המקרא כתוב במשנה) expounds thus במקום כלום' ששאר בני אדם מטיילין ומשיחין בדברי שחוק אני משיח ומטייל בדברי תורתך כל היום. Notice the bibl. use of שיחה in a good sense.

2—4. ℭ om. מגבור. 𝔄 once אישרך for —יך. 𝔅ℭ𝔇 No. 114 לְעוֹלָם המ'ם נקראת בשב'א נע ואיננה דגושה ℭ, הַמְבַבֵּד, בעולם 𝔄 הבא. הַמְהַלֵּךְ, and so in iii. 7 כמשפט מ'ם הבינוני מבנין הדגש שאחר ה'א חידיעה, המחלל 17, המקבל with מ rapheh, but in i. 3 המשמשין with בּ dageshed after the ה and note to that effect.

5. לְמִצְוָה קַלָּה וּבוֹרֵחַ. al. ins. כחמורה or כבה' from ii. 1. Tos. כבחמורה Emd. ל'ג בס'א...ואי גרסינן לה צ'ל כלחמורה Yom Tob הוי בורח, comm. ברת text ℭ. כחמורה נ'ל לגרום.

6. בֵּן (from בוז) with qameç as Prov. xiii. 13, not pathach as Zech. iv. 10 כי נחי העי'ן, which as רד'ק writes is unusual כי מי בז ליום קטנות. ℭ quotes ואל תהי מפליג (ℭ). On משפטם להנקד בקמ'ץ ופעלי הכפל בפת'ח Ab. ii. 5 thus אל תאמר דבר שאיפשר לשמוע שסופו להישמע, and so 𝔅 ending לשמוע כו'.

7. רְבִּי לְוִיטַס אִישׁ יַבְנֶה (ℭ), 𝔅 om. איש יבנה. M. Shelom. בלא ליטס (sic) but ר' בלא וי'ו הניהו הר'ר יהוסף ז'ל שכן מצא ברוב הספרים וי'ו must mean לויטס not וּם—, cf. Baer on Ab. i. 3 אנטיגנוס...ברוב סדורינו הוא בוי'ו אחרי נון...אך הרבינם נמצא בלי וי'ו (יבמות ט'ז) וכן לויטס Kohut A. C. v. 23 b, לויטס 25 b, Gk. Λευΐτης. His saying is מאד מאד הֱוִי שִׁפַל רוח שתקות אנוש רמה ℭ𝔄 ins. (𝔅𝔇), בפני כל האדם, cf. § 14, D. E. Zuta ii. Rashi רמה ותולעה, cf. Ab. R. N. B. (p. 74).

רְבִּי יוֹחָנָן בֶּן בְּרוֹקָה אוֹמֵר כָּל הַמְחַלֵּל (ℭ), al. ברוקא. 𝔄 by טעות סופר gives the saying כל המחלל in the name of R. Levitas, omitting מאד מאד וכו' and the name of R. Jochanan. אֶחָד שׁוֹגֵג ואחד חילול 𝔅, על חלול (cf. R. Jon.) (ℭ), וְאֶחָד מֵזִיד בְּחִלּוּל הַשֵׁם No. 101 אחד בחלול ℭ. ואחד בשוגג ואחד במזיד as No. 170 (p. 120), but without בח' השם, cf. Dur. 61 a.

8. ‏וב בנו‎ **𝕮𝕭**, ‏ר' ישמעאל בנו‎ (‏ומלי דאבות ונחלת‎ ‏אבל בספר לב אבות‎).

‏ר' יוסי או‎ No. 10, ‏ר' שמעון או'‎ 𝕯. ‏בנו‎ .om (‏אבות כתוב רבי ישמעאל בנו‎)

‏אין מספיקין‎ ‏ללמד‎ ‏ע"מ‎) (after is quoted by 𝕭 as a reading peculiar to

Rashi (p. 101 E), cf. Dur. R. Obad. (‏אין‎... ‏וי"מ‎... ‏בשביל שיקרא רבי וגורסין‎

‏מספיקין‎), *perush* Rashi. See Nos. 54, 55, 81, 113, 170. 𝕯𝕭 ins. ‏לשמור‎

(𝕮 No. 101 with *vau* conj.) before ‏ולעשות‎, cf. Dur. 61 b.

9. ‏רִבִּי צָדוֹק‎ (𝕭) or *mit Kodex de Rossi* 138 ‏צָדוּק‎, Σαδδούκ (Strack).

𝕭𝕮 (‏בהן‎), 𝕾 with 𝕬, ‏אַל תַּעֲשֵׂם עֲטָרָה לְהִתְגַּדֶּל בָּהֶם‎

‏אַל‎...‏תַּעֲשֶׂהָ עֲטָרָה לְהִתְגַּדֶּל־בָּה‎ Baer (‏אַל‎.) 𝕯 (text om. ‏תלמידי חכמי' אל‎)

with the words ‏ואל תעש עצמך כעורכי הדינים ואל‎ ‏תפרוש מן הצבור‎

‏במשניות גם בכי"י ובסדור‎ (II. 5, I. 9) in brackets before ‏תעשה‎, and note

‏רפ"ז‎ [A.D. 1527] ‏ובמחזור רומא הגרסה‎...‏אל תעשה עטרה וכו' ואשר סגרתי‎

‏בספר‎. ‏איננו שם וראה מדרש שמואל‎ Leb Aboth finds this interpolation

‏ויש ספרים שכתוב‎ [cf. Nos. 101, 103] and adds, ‏אל תעשם עטרה‎ with ‏אחד‎

‏אל תעש עטרה להתגדל בה‎ 𝕮 comm. ‏אל תעשׂ עטרה להתגדל בה‎.

No. ‏קורדום‎ (𝕬𝕮𝕯 Ashk.), exc. 𝕮𝕯 or ‏מהם‎ (𝕬𝕮𝕯 Ashk.), exc. 𝕮𝕯 ‏ולא קרדום לאכו(ו)ל מהן‎

(‏וי"ס שבת'‎). Leb Ab. ‏ממנה ר"ל מן העטרה‎, ‏לחתוך בהם‎ 𝕭𝕭. ‏לאכול מהם‎ 92

Dur. ‏לחפור בהם‎. Emd. (ref. to Shab. XVII. 2 and Beçah IV. 3) ‏ושם תראה שאין‎

Baba, ‏נכון לגרוס כאן לחפור בהם שאין הקרדום עשוי לחפירה כי אם המרה‎

M. 82 b. ‏במרא ופסל וקרדום‎. Cf. also *Aruch Compl.* ‏עֲרַךְ מַרְדָּם‎ (VII. 190).

Nedar. 62 a (Wien, 1863) ‏ר"א בר ר' צדוק אומר עשה דברים לשם פעלם‎

‏ודבר בהם לשמם‎ [‏לשם שמים‎ Dur. 62 a] ‏אל תעשם עטרה להתגדל בהם ואל‎

‏תעשם קורדו' להיות עודר‎ [Dur. ‏עובד‎] ‏בו וק"ו ומה בלשצר שלא נשתמש אלא‎

‏בכלי קודש שנעשו‎ (‏כלי‎) ‏חול נעקר מן העולם המשתמש בכתרה של תורה על‎

‏אחת כמה וכמה‎. See Tos. Sotah 4 b on ‏נעקר‎, Rashi and ha-Rosh on Nedar.

l.c., Sifré II. § 48 (Fr. f. 84 b), Buber's Midr. Tehillim Ps. xxxi. (p. 240),

'Derech Erez Sutta,' c. II., p. 11, ed. Tawrogi (Königsb. 1885 A.D.), who reads

‏וכקרדום לבקוע בו‎ [Midr. T. ‏לעטר‎] and ‏כעטרה להתעטר בהם‎ ‏בהם‎, with variants

‏ולא‎ ‏לכרות, לחתוך, לאכל‎. Ha-Rosh *l.c.* has ‏להתעטר‎ as *perush*, and reads

‏וְכַךְ הָיָה הִלֵּל אוֹמֵר‎ ‏ואל‎ for ‏תעשם‎. ‏ועניינם אחד‎, ‏וכן‎ or ‏ככה‎ [bibl.] (𝕭).

or ‏הא כל הנאות‎ as in I 14. 𝕾 ‏ישתמש‎, 𝕬 ‏אשתמש‎ ‏דורש‎ No. 170

‏חא‎ 𝕾 (I. 330). ‏עֲרַךְ אֵת‎ 𝕬𝕮𝕯 Ashk. Dur., and see *Aruch Compl.* ‏הנאות‎,

‏במשניות כתוב שכל‎ ‏הנהנה‎ ‏ורש"‎ with note ‏לָמַדְתָּ שֶׁכָּל הָאוֹכֵל הַנֶּאוֹת‎

‏כתב ה"ג כל הנאות אבל בספר מדרש שמואל ולב אבות ומלי דאבות ונחלת‎

‏אבות‎ [f. 53. I, Ven. 1566] ‏בכולם כתוב שכל האוכל הנאות כמו שהוא בפנים‎

בכי"י and so וכן הוא *בצרור המור פ' כי תשא פסוק על בשר אדם לא ייסך והאוכל ובמחזור שאלוניק (Baer). **הָאֹכֵל** הנאות *prima manu* altered to [cf. לאכול מהם] with the second *vau* above the line. למדת as in Emd. Baer may be from some *perush*, cf. f. 106. 3. No. 101 ולא בה..אל תעש. נוטל **נֹטֵל** חַיִּין (א), . קורדום לאכול מהם...הא כל הנאות

10. וְכָל הַמְחַלֵּל... גּוּפוֹ מְחֻלָּל (). Baer quotes Bemidb. R. תני רבי יוסי אומר כל המכבד את התורה גופו מכובד על הבריות 3 .VIII וכל **המבזה** את התורה גופו **מבוזה** על הבריות שנאמר כי מכבדי אכבד המבזה...מבוזה לבריות (p. 68) xxxII. *B* .N .R .Ab) Ab. iv. 4). **וּבֹזַי** יקלו

11. רַבִּי יִשְׁמָעֵאל . ר' שמעון C. No.170 add בנו (א), ר' **יִשְׁמָעֵאל** ב"ר יוסי, M. Shelom. בַּר רַבִּי יוֹסֵי. Rashi (in Midr. Shem. ed. 1876 A.D.) וְנִזָּל Ashk. Emd.) ה"ג ר' שמעון בנו של ר' יוסי אומר. נ"א רבי ישמעאל as Lev. v. 21 או בגזל, and so גזל in Ab. II. 8 with *qameç, çere*, not *segol, segol* as by error ברוב הספרים (). וְהַגַּם לִבּוֹ ...וְגַם רוּחַ (), but Emd.

והגם לשון תלמוד ומנחי עי"ן הוא...וראוי להיות **קָמוּץ** לקיום הנח אלא דאזיל בנסות עיינין . שנהגו לקרותו בפת"ח עשאוהו כדמות סמוך ואינו נכון †בעל צדה לדרך רום עָינַים, with ref. to Sotah 5 a and Targ. for Prov. xxi. 4 to shew that a תלמיד חכם should have in him חלק שמיני שבשמינית of *gassuth*, גס being by Gematria 63. הרי זה before שוטה.

12. קִבְּלוּ דַעְתִּי שֶׁהֵן רַשָּׁאִין וְלֹא אַתָּה (), not as קיבלו. אין במשניות הוא. אלא אתה. Dur. שאין רשאין הם, with marg. No. 103 in דן יחידי Notice on .היה אומר והכל הוא משנה אחת עם הקודמת דתנינן אל תהי דן יחידי שאין דן יחידי אל אחד. א"ר יהוד' T. J. Sanh. 18 a בן פזי אף ה"בה אין דן יחידי שנאמר וכל צבא השמים עומדי' עליו מימינו ומשמאלו.

13. ר' **יוֹחנן** (א), BDS Dur. יונתן, C נתן, cf. Nos. 10, 92. זאת המשנה. Dur. מענין ובטלו הטוחנות (קהלת י"ב) , לְבַטֵּלָה מֵעֹנִי דלנוה מסדורי תפלות. It is quoted in Buber's Tanchuma, מבוא ס"ב, be-

---

* The *Bundle of Myrrh* is a work on the Pentateuch by ה"ר אברהם סבע הספרדי, see Benjacob's *Oçar ha-S.* p. 513, No. 212, and Steinschneider's Bodleian *Cat. Lib. Hebraeorum* col. 706. The writer remarks (f. 87. 1, Ven. 1567 A.D.) that השם is משה transposed, so that זכרו תורת משה עבדי הוא כמו זכרו תורת השם

† See in צדה לדרך, f. 214 b, ed. Sabionetta (c. 1567 A.D.). The author, R. Menachem ibn Zerach ben Aharon, died in the second half of cent. 14. See Steinschneider's Bodleian *Catalogue*, col. 1741.

מתוך הדחק...הריוח, and with ר׳ יונתן בר יוסי אומר העושה מצוה אחת ginning
for מעוני...עושר and an application to almsgiving.

14. מְמַעֵט בְּעֵסֶק‎ ℨ (cf. Eccl. xii. 3) ℭ Nos. 90, (cf. 92), 101, 170,
Bert. om. *beth**. 𝔄 מעט עסק, Strack מְעַט. 𝔅 ו(מ)מעט עסק וע(ו)סק
with (מ), (ו) shewing faintly after erasure and a *vau* above סק, and in comm.
𝔅 הוי מַעֵט בעסק. והוי מעט עסק לומ׳ שהמעט בעסק הוא טוב ונעים כנ״ל
with and ,ממעט .for abbrev as מעט pointing ,בסחורה שתעשה עסקיך מועטין
Dur. הוי שפל מאד מאד [iv. 7] וכבר נאמר למעלה. ממוע׳ for מועטין.

אִם בָּטַלְתָּ מִן   ותהיה 𝔄. רוּחַ והוא הוסיף בפני כל אדם.

הַתּוֹרָה, ℨ not *piel* as בכל הסדורים but *qal* as Eccl. xii. 3, ובטלו הטוחנות,
and so Dur. 𝔅𝔅 comm. בטלת (ℭ תה—.). 𝔄 ביטלת with *yod*.

יֶשׁ לָךְ

בְּטֵלִים הַרְבֵּה כְּנֶגְדָּךְ (.ℨ). 𝔄 om. כנגדך. Dur. ואם המשנה זאת וסוף
עמלת [עֹסֶקְת 𝔅 comm.] בתורה לא כתבוה בסדורי תפלות, cf. No. 10.

יֶשׁ שָׂכָר הַרְבֵּה לִתֶּן לָךְ omitting לו (𝔄𝔅ℭ). Baer... ℨ ends ובס״א
יש לי בטלים ואם עמלת בתורה יש לי...כאלו. Ashk. שכר הרבה נתן לך
נאמרו מפי הקב״ה...וכך יש בסנהדרין פ׳ עשירי א״ר שמעון [𝔄 128 b₂₀] אם
אתה עושה דין בעיר הנדחת מעלה אני עליך כאלו אתה מעלה עולה כליל
לפני, where Jost has אמר הקב״ה after שמעון. See Sanh. 111 b and Rabbin.
ד״ס ix. 361 (h).

15. קָנָה לוֹ פְּרַקְלִיט...קַטֵּיגוֹר (.ℨ). קונה 𝔅𝔅. No. 107 פרקלט
without *yod*. M. Shelom. ומצאתי שכתב הר״מ די לונזאנו ז״ל הג׳ פרקליט
קטיגור 𝔅. ומלת (*sic*) יונית היא. Targ. Job xxxiii. 23 מלאכא פרקליטא 𝔅,
רכיל וכן דילטור רכיל בגימטריא ושניהם לשון יוון, where the Gematria is of
the species הכולל (p. 132), unless we should read דילטורא (=260). 𝔅 con-
ואני נהוג לפרש קטיגור קטי תגרא כלומ׳ בעל קטטה ותגר או קני tinues
or תְּשׁוּבָה...כִּתְרִים לִפְנֵי הַפּוּרְעָנוּת. תגרא וסניגור סני תגרא

התשובה היינו (.ושניה׳ נכוני׳) ℨ‎, בפני. 𝔅 quotes Rashbam as objecting that
תריס הוא 𝔅 and reading ת״ט and תורה (p. 92). תָּרִים, θυρεός. מעשים טובים
המגן של פני אדם במלחמה...לשון תרים חנויות Baer (quoting Targ. Gen.
ת״י מימרי תריס לך...תריסי גבריא...ונטל (7 .xv. 1, 2 Sam. i. 21, 1 Sam. xvii
תריסא...ונקוד הרי״ש בְּצֵרִי בסדור רפ״ו וכן נקוד בכל מקום בתרגום וכן

הרגל הקריאה והוא במשקל כאב זאב זעיר‏ .Levy *Chald. Wörterbuch*, II. 560
בעלי תריסין Berach. 27 b ‏...תְּרֵיסָא (תְּרֵים) תְּרֵים‏, (1868 A.D.), *die heftig dis-*
putirenden Gelehrten. Dur. ‏מנן בלשון ערבי תורס‏. See *Aruch Compl.*
‏ערך תרס‏ (VIII. 282).

16. ‏כָּל כְּנֵסָה שֶׁהִיא לְשֵׁם שָׁמַיִם‏, 𝔖 cf. ‏דְּבֵלָה‏ (note on I. 1) not
כנסיה (𝕮) as ‏בכל הנוסחאות‏ . 𝕬 ‏כנסה‏, 𝔅 ‏כנסיה‏, 𝔇 ‏כנסייא‏. Strack reads
כנסיות .pl from *Rückbildung* a is [Baer] ‏כְּנֵסָה‏ remarking that ‏פְּנֵסָה‏
כנסת...מאן דגרס ‏בשש‏ and on I. 1, ‏כנסיה‏, Emd. here ‏תלמודית‏ (III. 16).
‏לשם מצוה‏ Ashk. ‏נקודות לא משתבש...ומאן דגרס בהמשה לא משתבש‏
as ‏לשום שמים‏, cf. 𝕬. Dur. 66 b ‏נוסח המשנה לשם מצוה‏ . 𝔅𝕮 ‏ברוב הספרים‏,
𝔇 ‏לשם‏.

17. ‏רִבִּי אֶלְעָזָר בֶּן שַׁמּוּעַ...חָבִיב עָלֶיךָ כְּשֶׁלָּךְ‏ (𝔖). 𝕮 ‏אליעור‏
as II. 14. 𝕬𝕮𝔇 Ashk. om. ‏בן שמוע‏. 𝕬𝔅𝕮𝔇 Ashk. Nos. 90, 112, 114, 170
(cf. ‏חביב עליד ככבוד חבירד‏ M. Shelom. quotes (*sic*) ‏הר״מ אלמשנוני‏
Midr. Shem. p. 161) as reading ‏כשל חברך‏ with 'Rashi,' and ‏הרב מקוצי‏
(auth. of ‏סמ״ג‏), Ashk. and ha-Meiri for ‏ככבוד חברך‏. Baer ‏כְּשֶׁלָּךְ‏ as
‏בחר לנו אנשים‏ 9 Dur. ‏כשלך‏ with note ‏וכן כתבה‏ Rashi on Exod. xvii.
רבינו שלמה ז״ל בפירוש התורה בפרשת בשלח וכן אמר רבי אליעזר בפרק
שני אבל בכאן רבינו שלמה ז״ל כתב חביב עליך ככבוד חבירך וכן כתבה
רבינו יונה ז״ל וכן במשניות שלנו ופירשוה קרוב לכבוד הביריך‏ . See Berliner's Rashi f. 62 b, Mekhilta ed. Fr. f. 53 b, Tanchuma ‏בשלח‏ § 26 (Lubl.
1879 A.D.), Ab. R. N. *A.* XXVII. (p. 84), *B.* XXXIV. (p. 76), *Aruch Compl.*
(IV. 180). ‏כבד‏ . Emd. ‏ככבוד‏ 𝕮, (𝔖) ‏כְּמוֹרָא רַבָּךְ‏ ‏כשלך...רבך · כ״ף‏
‏קמ״ץ‏.

18. ‏בַּלְמוּד שֶׁשָּׁגְגַת הַלִּמוּד‏, 𝔖 ‏בלמוד · כ״ה בקצת נוסחאות וכן הוא‏
במדרש שמואל וגם הביא נוסח שכתוב בו ‏תלמיד‏ ופירש שניהם...ובקצת
נוסחאות כתוב בכאן ‏תלמוד‏...מלת תלמוד סובלת שני פירושים האחד הוא
סתם למוד והשני הוא למוד הגמרא כדאיתא בפרק אלו מציאות דף ל״ג ע״א
שנו‏ § 6 ‏ויקרא‏ Tanchuma. ‏וז״ל בתלמוד אין לך מדה גדולה מזו וכו׳
במקרא לא נמצא שם מעניין למוד‏ Note that ‏רבותינו שגגת תלמוד עולה זדון
רק תארים‏ (𝔖).

19. ‏וְכֶתֶר שֵׁם טוֹב עוֹלֶה עַל גַּבֵּיהֶן‏, 𝔖 (Ps. cxxix. 3) ‏על גבי חרשו‏
‏חורשים‏). 𝕮 ‏כתר‏ without *vau* conj. before ‏כהונה‏. 𝔇 Ashk. Nos. 5, 12,
23, 95, 101 omit ‏עולה‏, which 𝕬𝔅𝕮𝔖 Dur. retain. Emd. on the word in

§ 18 and here ℭ. עולה קמו"ץ· עולה סגו"ל .עַל גביהן על ידיהן בא שם טוב
so 𝔇 (cf. No. 108) but with the further note כך קיבלתי ולי נר' על ·לאדם
רבי אומר עשה רצונו... 𝔅 .גביהן למעלה מכולן...כת' טוב שם משמן טוב
(II. 4), with marg. אין זה מקום זה המשנה and comm. משנה זו נשנית למעלה
בפרק שני בשם ר"ג זקנו של זה ישנאה כאן...ובשיתא סדרי משנה שלי אינה
ℭ comm. של רצונו עשה .שנויה כאן בכלל ושמא הסופרים טעו וכתבוה כאן
See Nos. 116, 138—140. Midr. Mishlé on Prov. ix. 10, f. .מקום כרצונך...
32 a ed. Buber, ...אומר עשה רצונו **אֱלִיעֶזֶר** 'ר תמן תנינן.

20. **נְהֹרָאי** 'ר, 𝔄 as twice at the end of Nazir (94 a). 𝔅ℭ𝔇𝔖𝔄
with *vau*, Baer Strack רי— without *aleph*. See 'Erub. 13 b, Shab. 147 b*
הִיא תָבוֹא .ולמה נקרא שמו ר' נהוראי שמנהיר עיני חכמים בהלכה
אַחֲרִי or שהיא (𝔄ℭ), 𝔅𝔇𝔖—יך. al. אֹו שֹ or אֹו שֹ, cf. Ab. R. N. *B.*
XXXIII. (p. 73). From ס"ד VII. 353 on Shabb. 147 b it appears that the
München MS. has ואל תאמר שהיא תבא אחריך in the margin only and not
in the text, and that it omits the whole *baba* § 20 in Aboth IV. Cf. in
Midr. Mish. on Prov. ii. 4 (Bub. p. 49) תמן תנינן ר' נהוראי אומר הוי גולה
.למקום תורה ואל תאמר שהיא תבוא אחריך, ואל בינתך אל תשען

21. **יַנַּאי** 'ר (𝔄𝔅𝔖 Dur.), Baer Strack יַנַּי ℭ𝔇 הוא היה אומר
without name. **מִשַּׁלְוַת הָרְשָׁעִים וְאַף לֹא מִיִּסוּרֵי הַצַּדִּיקִים**
(𝔖). מִשֵּׁלְוַת רשעים No. 92 without points. 𝔄 לֹא משלַת, 𝔅 לא משלות.
𝔖לְווֹת רשעים ואף לא ייסורי 𝔇 (לא om.). משלות...אף לא מייסורין של ℭ,
אני קיבלתי...ולי נר'...שהרי אין בידינו **מִשַּׁלְווֹת** , and in comm. הצדיקים,
ויש גורסין...מִשַּׁלְוַת. and in comm. ...שלות הר' אף לא יסורי הצ'. Dur. רשעים.
מיסורי...וכן היא במשניות שלנו.

22. **רַבִּי מַתְיָא בֶּן חָרָשׁ...מַקְדִּים שָׁלוֹם לְכָל אָדָם** (𝔖).
Baer מַתִּתְיָה as 1 Chron. xxv. 21, abbrev. מתיא 𝔄, 𝔅—יא, ℭ𝔇 מתיה 𝔄
מַתְיָא 1 Chron. ix. 15 חָרָשׁ Emd. מן הלוים מי שנקרא נמצא בד"ה (אט)
חרש בשש נקודות· וכבר נהגו לומר חרש קמוץ· שמא מהעדר ידיעה עשאוהו
בשלום· דבק Emd. שלום לכל 𝔅 Dur. שלום לכל 𝔄ℭ𝔇, כמו חרש עצים
𝔄ℭ האדם with art. **וְאַל תְּהִי רֹאשׁ לְשׁוּעָלִי'** (𝔖), 𝔄 ולא ראש
והר"ר מנחם לבית מאיר ז"ל כתב...לשועלים שנא' Midr. Shem. p. 169
בית הבחירה Cf. [משלי י"ג] הולך אֶת חכמים יחכם ורועה את (sic) כסילים ירוע
27 b, Tos. Yomtob, R. Jonah.

---

* On Nehorai see also Blumenthal's *Rabbi Meir*, cap. 1 (Frankf. a. M. 1888 A.D.).

23. **בפרוזדוד...לפרוזדוד**, a (exc. ל for ב) B. a פרוזדוד again
with *daleth, daleth* twice in Nid. II. 5 (237 a). B גרסי בשני דלתין בפרוזדוד
[marg.] כדמתרגם יונתן [בן עוזיאל] ואולם לכסא עשה פרסידא, corrected by
erasure of *vau* before פרסידא, which is for אֶלָם המשפט D פרוזדוד בדלת.
תרגום אולם המשפט פרוזדורא Dur., ואולם לכסא מתרגם ופרוזדודא.
Ashk. פרוזדוד בדלי״ת וכתב כן מצאתי, cf. Nos. 5, 10, 23, 81, 107, 112,
114, 116, 157. S דור— *bis*, but in comm. לפרוזדוד (בלשון אשכנז וירהויז)
i.e. *Vorhaus*), the minute last letter being apparently a *daleth*. Nos. 90,
92 פרוסדוד with *samech, daleth, daleth*. C No. 109 פרוסדור, cf. Kimchi
cited below on 1 Kings vii. 7. Tosefta Berak. VII. (Zuck. p. 17$_{10}$)
העולם הזה בפני העולם הבא אלא כפרוזדור [נ״א כפרוצדר] מפני [נ״א בפני]
טרקלין. R. Sa‘adyah in מאמר ט (73 b),
Const. 1562 A.D.) reads לִפְנֵי העוה״ב, and so Ab. R. N. *B.* XXXIII. (p. 73).
aC לפני, BDS בפני S. BS (a ין—), CD וה' with *vau*.

ויש כפרים כתוב בהם Dur. שתעלה No. 112 (S), **כְּדֵי שֶׁתִּכָּנֵס לְטַרְקְלִין**

טַרְקְלִין נָאִין, pointing to a complete transliteration of τρικλίνιον mistaken for two words. Redaq on 1 Kings vii. 7 פורסדרא לבית דינא עביד
ופירוש פורסדא בית שער כמו שאמרו התקן עצמך בפרוזדו' כדי שתכנס
שִׁבְעָה [=] שנה טובה see the לְמַרְקְלִין נָאִין ויש נוסחאו' פרוסדור בסמ״ך
לפ״ק (Zech. iii. 9)] Bible (Ven. 1617 A.D.), and cf. R. Jonah on this *baba*.

24. **יָפֶה שָׁעָה אֶחָת**, S שעה חד is for **רֶגַע אֶחָד** in Targ. Exod.
xxxiii. 5. Dan. iv. 16 בשעה חדא. a 231 a$_{11}$ שעה אחת. **מִכָּל חַיֵּי**
הָעוֹלָם הַבָא (aBCDS), Dur. *so R. Sa‘adyah in* [ibid.] האמונות 'ס, *Rashi*,
Maim. and R. Jonah, לחיי העולם הבא וגורסי הגירסא משנין ויש. No. 92
CD without *vau*, יפה aC (BS), **וִיפֶה...בָעוֹלָם הַבָא** כחיי 114, לחיי
לעולם.

25. **בֶן אֶלְעָזָר**. a הביריך for חביריך. C om. אֶת. S (cf.
II. 3) בְּשַׁעַת, the ש with *pathach* להרחיב על העי״ן, instead of *shva* as Exod.
ii. 3 שְׂפַת היאר. Emd. the *shin* קמוצה. **בְּשָׁעָה שֶׁמֵּתוּ מֻטָל לְפָנָיו**,
S with aBCD. Emd. מוטל קמוץ S, מוטל. השלכה ענין ופירושו. D comm.
כך דרש ר' (2), **וְאַל תְנַחֲמהוּ** כו'...דהיאך יתנחם תנחם ומתו מוטל לפניו (1)
תנחומ' בפרש' שלח לך ובספר ערוך מצאתי שכן מפורש בהגד' ילמדינו הכתחלת
סנדל יחידי בפרשת שלח לך...**וְאַל תְנַחֲמנּו בְשָׁעַת אֶבְלוֹ** מניין אתה למד
מהקב״ה כשגלו ישר' לבבל...בקשו מלאכים לנחמו א' להם הק' אל תאיצו
לנחמני מאי אל תאיצו אין אילו תנחומים אלא ניאוצים הם לפני Kohut

(I. 85. 1) gives this דרש with the reading בשעה שמתו מוטל לפניו, refers to
Yalq. Bemidb. עד אנה on שתמ״ד [f. 224 a, Fr.'a. M. 1687 A.D.], and remarks ובתנחומ׳ שלנו חסר Dur. ...וי״ש גורסין ואל תנחמנו **בשעת אבלו**
בספרי ספרדיים וכן היה גורס רבינו יונה ז״ל בשעה שמתו מוטל לפניו וכן
היא הגירסא במשניות שלנו וכן כתב רבינו משה ז״ל בפרק חמישי מהלכות
דעות...איך יקבל תנחומין באותה שעה· ונראה שהסופרים **שינו הגירסא**
מפני שמצינו שאחר קבורת המת היו נעשין שורות ומנחמין האבל כמו
שנזכר באבל רבתי...אבל אין לשנות הגירסא שלא אמר בימי אבלו ולא
בשעת אבלותו אלא בשעת אבלו כלומר בשעה שהוא מתאנח באבלו No. 10
_נו (ע׳ אל), תנחמהו (ע׳ נָחַם), **a**ᏰᏜ *Aruch* (ע׳ אל **&** *Aruch* בשעת אבלו
וְאַל תִּשְׁתַּדֵּל. *Aruch* (ע׳ שדר) אל תשתדר, where see Kohut's note
(VIII. 35). Dan. vi. 15 הֲוָה מִשְׁתַּדַּר להצלותה.

26. **וּבְכָשְׁלוֹ אַל יָגֵל לִבֶּךָ** (Prov. xxiv. 17), aᏰ ובהכשלו, ᏟᎠᏰ.
ובכ׳. **a** No. 101 end at לבך. ᏰᏟᎠᏰ add פן יראה יי׳ ורע בעיניו
(ver. 18), **&** attaching the vowels of יְהֹוָה and an accent
to two *yods* thus יְֽיָ and adding a third *yod* above the former two and a
fourth inverted below them so as to make a tetragrammaton.
חרון אפו לא נאמר אלא אפו כלמד שמוחלין לו על כל עונותיו No. 107 Ᏼ, of
which Ꭰ has מלמד...עונות written but partly erased. Dur. ולא היתה נראית
גירסא זו גרסת הראשונים ז״ל אלא פירשוה והוצרכו לומר שלא חידש שמואל
פסוק הוא R. 'Obad. Bert. הקטן דבר אחר אלא רגילותו לומר פסוק זה תדיר
הר״ר יהוכף ז״ל מחק ממלת פן M. Shelom. במשלי אלא...היה רגיל כו׳
יראה וכו׳ וכ׳ על מה שפי׳ ר״ע ז״ל פסוק הוא במשלי וכו׳ פי׳ זה מגונמנם כי
לא אמר **היה אומר** ונ״ל דקאי על מה דקאמר לעיל ואל תשתדל לראותו
בשעת קלקלתו ועל זה קאמר שמואל הקטן אומר על לשון זה בנפול אויבך
זאת המשנה דלגוה מכאן בסדורי תפלות וכתבוה **בפרק** Dur. אל תשמח ע״ב
חמישי. No. 10 has Shem. ha-Qatan's saying in Pereq v. only, where
No. 101 *repeats* it ending כל עונותיו. See also Maim. R. Jon.

27. **הַלּוֹמֵד יֶלֶד...וְהַלּוֹמֵד זָקֵן** (**&**), לָמֵד Ꭰ with *pathach*, çerê.
אבִיהָ, Dur. Ᏼ לָמד תורה, Ꮯ לומד. No. 109 לזקן...לילד, cf. Midr. Shem. **a**
bibl. אֲבִיָה. No. 170 אֲבִיָה. ᏰᏟᎠᏰ אביה, Ꭰ ו״יה.—. Dur. זאת המשנה
דלגוה מסדורי תפלות משום שם רשעים ירקב ונראה כי קודם שיצא לתרבות
רעה היתה שגורה בפי התלמידים ואחר כך משנה זו לא זזה ממקומ׳ כמו
לדְיוֹ כְּתוּבָה. שאמרו... קבל האמת ממי שאמרו See also M. Shelom.
עַל נְיָּר, **&** taking *yod, yod* as implying *dagesh*, as also in שׁיִּרי (Ab. I. 2),
although בכל הסדורים נקודה הנו״ן בשב״א והיו״ד בפת״ח. Baer Strack

Auth. P. B. נִיר with *shva, qameç*. Emd. נִיר with one *yod* and note

נייר· תלמודית, without remark on the pointing. 𝕸 נִיר with *chireq* under

the first *yod* [Arab. نِير, *fila conjuncta*], הוא אותו כלף שעושין הקלפים

ובתשובות הגאונים מצאתי הוא אותו שעושין מצמר גפן שנקרא קוטון

ב' שכורכין בו שירים [*נ"א שיראין*] הבאים מארץ ישמעאל ועודנו חדש הדיו

נדבקת בו ועומדת ימים רבים כתיבתו וקורין אותו קַאנד†.

28. 𝕸𝕭𝕯 (𝔖). הַלּוֹמֵר תּוֹרָה מִן הַקְּטַנִּים ... וְהַלּוֹמֵר מִן הַזְּקֵנִים

תורה 𝕭 𝕸, לָמֵר 𝕮𝕯. לוֹמֵד 𝕮 𝕯 ...תורה מן הז' 𝕮 (*sic*)...הלומד מן הזקנים

om. בבלי No. 101 והלומד מן הגדולים No. 109 מק'...מן הז' 𝕯, מהק'...מהז' 𝕭

for הבבלי.

29. ,רַבִּי אוֹמֵר אַל תִּשְׁתַּכֵּל בְּקַנְקַן 𝔖 השתכל with *sin* as in II. 1,

III. 1. Ashk. Emd. מאיר 'ר. Emd. בְּקַנְקַן. Strack with art. בַּקַּנְקַן, No. 95

קַנְקַן. 𝔄 Baba M. XIII. 11 (113 a) בקנקינים, Ohol. VI. 2 (208 b)

בְּמָה (𝔖), Emd. שיש סגי"ל :במה קמוץ, that is אֶלָּא בְּמַה-שֶׁיֵּשׁ בּוֹ

שֶׁיֵּשׁ-בּוֹ. 𝕮 כל...יין ישן and om. וישן by error. 𝕭𝕮𝕯𝔖 Dur. om. *shin* of

זאת המשנ' ג"כ דלגוה מסדר תפלות לפי שהיא Dur. on 28, 29 שאפילו

דומה לראשונה אלא שהראשונה היא בלמדי' ולא נמצאת בזאת המסכתא

מַחֲלוֹקֶת אלא בזאת המשנה. Cf. No. 10.

30, 31. ,ר' אֶלְעָזָר הַקַּפָּר 𝔄 לִיעֶזֶר, Ashk. אלעזר...בלתי יו"ד. Jer.

הַיְלוֹדִים. Gen. I. 20 לְהַחֲיוֹת (*hiph.*), 𝔖 ref. to Midr. Shem. ר"ל

in use. No. 23 Ashk. להחיות (*qal*). לַהֲחָיוֹת, but without proof that *niph.* from היה was להחיות את נפשם Baer

𝕮 ולהיוודע, 𝕭 ...ולהיודע. ולה' ולה' 𝕭𝔖 with *vau* conj. twice, the former לֵידַע לְהוֹדִיעַ וּלְהִוָּדַע.

erased in the text of 𝕭. 𝔄 by error להודיע ולהודיע. שֶׁהוּא אַל הוּא

(𝕭𝕯𝔖), 𝔄𝕮 Ashk. om. אל הוא. 𝔄𝕮𝕯...עד הדיין. 𝕭 העד 𝔖 in reverse

order הדיין...העד, cf. Midr. Shem. וְהוּא עָתִיד לָדוֹן בָּרוּךְ הוּא

(𝔖), al. לדין. שֶׁאֵין לְפָנָיו. 2 Chron. XIX. 7 אין עם יי' אלהינו עַוְלָה

---

* The manuscript A† (p. 152 n.) has מן צמר נפן שכורכין בו שיראין, omitting ...קוטון (Arab. and Fr. *coton*), and reading correctly שֵׁירָאִין, *silks*, see שֵׁירָא in Buxtorf *Lex. Chal. Tal. et Rab.* col. 2383 (1640 A.D.), and שֵׁר in Kohut *A. C.* VIII. 156.

† Professor Bevan remarks that קאנד must be for כאנד, i.e. the modern Persian كَاغَذ

paper; and that the word must have been employed by the Arabs in the Middle Ages, for

the Lisān al-'Arab (c. 1300 A.D.) says that الكَاغَذ is well known, and is a Persian word

Arabicized. The same work gives the form كَاغَد also, as a dialectical variety of كَاغَذ.

לֹא עוֹלה .וּמַשָּׂא פָנִים וּמַקַּח־שֹׁחַד, ﬡ ולא...ולא with *vau* conj. twice and om.
ﬡ remarks that מֶקַח וּמֶמְכַּר רוב המון בני ישראל say מ' וּמ' wrongly for מ' with
chireq (Chron. *l.c.*, Lev. xxv. 25, 33). ﬨ נקוד מֶקַח ויש נקוד ובמשנה יש.

מַקַּח ואני אום' שהאום' כן משתבש דלשון תורה לחוד ולשון חכמים לחוד.
Emd. justifies מַקַּח (constr. חַ־) by pl. מַקְּחוֹת (Nehem. x. 32). Dur. 74 b
No. 101, אין כאן ודע משניות ﬨ .שֶׁהַכֹּל שֶׁלּוֹ. ומ"ם מקח היא בחיר"ק,
בא בחשבון, ﬡﬨ (בּ), וְדַע שֶׁהַכֹּל בָּא לְפִי הַחֶשְׁבּוֹן. ודע כי הכל
No. 108 בא ל'. בא .om שהכל לפי חשבון ﬡ .בא לידי ﬠ (cf. R. Jon.) with
ודע in margin. ﬢ comm. והכל בא לפי .om ודע.

32. ﬢﬡ שב', No. 107 ששאול, ﬡ (בּ), שֶׁיֵּשׁ בִּשְׁאוֹל בֵּית מָנוֹס לָךְ
No. 109 שיש ב', ﬡ comm. שֶׁהֵשׁ ﬨ שהש' ב'. לומר שהש' ﬡﬢﬨ No. 92 om. לָךְ,
ﬢﬡ (text) ﬨ ואל יבטיחך comm. מנוס לך ﬢ .שיש לך בשאול ﬢﬡﬨ with *vau*.
רוב הספרים כמאירי ורי"א שיש בשאול והר"ר יהוסף ז"ל הגיה M. Shelom.
שבשאול וכ' כן הגירסא ברוב הספרים וכן נ"ל עיקר...ומחק מלת אל נם מחק
מלת ברוך הוא דבריש מתני' [31 §] ומלות (*sic*) הקדוש דבסוף מתני' [32 §]
No. 101 ליתן דין .om וחשבון. הוא הקב"ה. ﬨ ends Ab. R. N. *B.* xxxiv.
(בּ), וְעַל כָּרְחָךְ אַתָּה חַי...מֵת .שיש לך בשאול בית מנוס (p. 76)
al. חָךְ. Tosafoth Yeshanim to Kethub. 30 a in reverse order ונרסי' ע"כ אתה
מֵת וע"כ אתה חַי והוי כמו המתים להחיות והחיים לידון, see marg. of Tos.
l.c. on הכל בידי שמים.

CHAPTER V.

1. מַאֲמָרוֹת. sing. בְּמַאֲמָר אֶחָד, constr. מַאֲמַר (Esth. i. 15, ii. 20,
ix. 32). וּמַה תַּלְמוּד לוֹמַר (omitted by No. 101), cf. Ab. III. 12.
מה תלמוד הני ויאמר ויאמר מה אנו למידין מהן comm. ﬡ .לומר .om ﬡﬨ
כלום' היה יכול comm. ﬡ, הֲיָה יָכוֹל ﬡ .יש תלמוד Baba Q. 104 b (*sub fin.*)
אֶלָּא לְהִפָּרֵע (בּ), ﬨ ליפרע. חַ־א for חַ־, Gen. ii. 4 בהבראם. להבראות
אלא ליתן שכר...וליפרע No. 101 in reverse order.

2, 3. שבכל (בּ), No. 170 שֶׁכָּל הַדּוֹרוֹת הָיוּ מַכְעִיסִין לְפָנָיו.
ﬡ No. 101 (cf. M. Shelom) מכ' ובאין, ﬡ om. היו in § 2. ﬡ את המבול, ﬢﬡ
וק' עליו, ﬢﬡ מי, Ashk. om. *vau*. ﬢﬡ וְקִבֵּל שְׂכַר כֻּלָּם, את מי.
No. 101 ככנגד כולן ש'. Jerem. xv. 15 אפך לְאָרֶךְ אפים ﬨ om. in § 3.

4. ‏נְסִיּגֹת‏ from ‏נָפֵּין‏, as Esth. vi. 1 ‏אֶת סֵפֶר הַזִּכְרֹנוֹת‏ sing. ‏זִכָּרֹן‏.
‏𝔖𝔅‏ without ‏הִיא‏. ‏כְּמָה חִיבְּתוֹ‏

5, 6. ‏עֵשֶׂר...עֲשָׂרָה‏, § 6 ‏וְעֶשֶׂר...עֲשָׂרָה‏ § 5 text in ℭ. ℭ comm. agrees
with 𝔄 (exc. ‏הק׳‏ for ‏הקב״ה‏). Note that ‏עֲשָׂרָה‏ should go with a masc. noun,
‏עֶשֶׂר‏ with fem. 𝔅 ‏בָּבָא זוֹ כָּךְ הִיא כְּתוּבָה בְּרֹב סִיפְרֵי מִשְׁנָה עֲשָׂרָה נִיסִּים‏
‏כוּ׳ וְאֵין כַּת׳ בָּם י׳ מַכּוֹת כוּ׳ וְאוֹמ׳ הָיִיתִי שֶׁזֶּה הַכַּת׳ בְּמַחֲזוֹרִים שֶׁלָּנוּ עֶשֶׂר‏
‏מַכּוֹת הֵבִיא פִּי׳ הוּא...אֲבָל מָצָאתִי אַחֲרֵי כֵן מוּגָה בְּמִשְׁנָה דְּווֹקְנִית שֶׁהוּגָהּ‏
‏עֶשֶׂר מַכּוֹת...חָסְרָה בְּהַרְבֵּה נוּסְחָאוֹ׳ אֲבָל 𝔖. מִמִּשְׁנַת ר׳ אֶפְרַיִם עֶשֶׂר מַכּוֹת כוּ׳‏
‏נִמְצֵאת בְּסֵפֶר לֵב אָבוֹת וְמָלֵי דְּאָבוֹת וּבְסִדּוּרֵי קְלַף וְנָכוֹן הוּא וְכֵן נִרְאָה‏
‏מִגִּירְסַת רש״י‏. Cf. Ab. R. N. *A.* p. 95, *B.* p. 99, Dur. 78 b.

7. ‏עֲשָׂרָה נְסִיוֹנוֹת‏ 𝔖. ‏טָעוּת וְנָפַל נִקְבָּה לְשׁוֹן עֶשֶׂר כָּתוּב הַסֵּפְרִי׳ וּבְכָל‏
‏הַקב״ה‏, ‏הַמָּקוֹם‏ 𝔅ℭ𝔇 𝔖. ‏זֶה בַּסּוֹפְרִי׳ מִפְּנֵי הַפָּסוּק...זֶה עֶשֶׂר פְּעָמֵי׳‏.

8. ‏עֲשָׂרָה נִסִּים נַעֲשׂוּ לַאֲבוֹתֵינוּ בְּבֵית הַמִּקְדָּשׁ‏ (𝔖). ℭ ‏נַעֲשׂוּ‏
‏בְּמִקְדָּשׁ‏, 𝔄 ‏בְּבֵית ה׳‏ ‏לֹא‏. om. ℭ ‏לֹא הֵפִילָה כוּ׳ כְּבָר פֵּרַשְׁתִּיו הֵיטֵב בְּמַסֶּכֶ׳‏
‏יוֹמָא בַּפֶּרֶ׳ רִאשׁוֹן‏ The ten miracles, which are numbered as they stand in
𝔄𝔅ℭ𝔇, are enumerated as below in Joma 21 a, b. For the various readings see ד״ס vol. IV. :

‏דְּתָנָן עֲשָׂרָה נִסִּים נַעֲשׂוּ בְּבֵית הַמִּקְדָּשׁ · ¹וְלֹא הֵפִילָה אִשָּׁה מֵרִיחַ בְּשַׂר הַקֹּדֶשׁ ·‏
‏²וְלֹא הִסְרִיחַ (נ״א הִתְלִיעַ) בְּשַׂר הַקֹּדֶשׁ מֵעוֹלָם · ⁴וְלֹא נִרְאָה זְבוּב בְּבֵית הַמִּטְבָּחַיִם ·‏
‏³וְלֹא אֵירַע קֶרִי לְכֹהֵן גָּדוֹל בְּיוֹם הַכִּיפּוּרִים · ⁵וְלֹא נִמְצָא פָּסוּל בָּעוֹמֶר וּבִשְׁתֵּי‏
‏הַלֶּחֶם וּבְלֶחֶם הַפָּנִים ⁸עוֹמְדִים צְפוּפִים וּמִשְׁתַּחֲוִים רְוָוחִים · ⁹וְלֹא הִזִּיק נָחָשׁ‏
‏וְעַקְרָב בִּירוּשָׁלַיִם מֵעוֹלָם · ¹⁰וְלֹא אָמַר אָדָם לַחֲבֵירוֹ צַר לִי הַמָּקוֹם שֶׁאָלִין‏
‏בִּירוּשָׁלַיִם. פָּתַח בְּמִקְדָּשׁ וְסִ״יס בִּירוּשָׁלַיִם אֵיכָא תַּרְתֵּי אַסְרְנִיְיתָא בְּמִקְדָּשׁ‏
‏דְּתַנְיָא׳ ⁶מֵעוֹלָם לֹא כָּבוּ גְּשָׁמִים אֵשׁ שֶׁל עֲצֵי הַמַּעֲרָכָה · ⁷וְעָשַׁן הַמַּעֲרָכָה אֲפִילוּ‏
‏כָּל הָרוּחוֹת שֶׁבָּעוֹלָם בָּאוֹת וּמַנְשְׁבוֹת בּוֹ אֵין מְזִיזוֹת אוֹתוֹ מִמְּקוֹמוֹ וְתוּ לֵיכָּא.‏
‏וְהִתְנִי רַב שְׁמַעְיָה בְּקַלְנְבוֹ שִׁבְרֵי כְּלֵי חֶרֶס נִבְלְעוּ בִּמְקוֹמָן...אִיכָּא נָמֵי אַחֲרִיתִי‏
‏דְּאָ״ר יְהוֹשֻׁעַ בֶּן לֵוִי נֵס גָּדוֹל הָיָה נַעֲשֶׂה בְּלֶחֶם הַפָּנִים סִלּוּקוֹ כְּסִדּוּרוֹ שֶׁנֶּאֱמַר‏
‏לָשׂוּם לֶחֶם חֹם בְּיוֹם הִלָּקְחוֹ.‏

Ha-Meiri counts them up in the order 12436758910, M. Shelom. quotes
Ashk. for the variation 346, and 𝔖 Dur. Emd. have the order of ha-Meiri.
𝔖 brackets 6—7, quotes Rashi for their exclusion as *baraitha* on the
authority of Joma *l.c.*, and makes up the number ten by resolving the fifth
miracle into three. This solution is given by 𝔅 (cf. No. 108), but with
an alternative, namely that in Joma ‏פָּתַח בְּמִקְדָּשׁ וְסִ״יס בִּירוּשָׁלַם‏ is an
objection to including 9, 10 which were not wrought in the ‏מִקְדָּשׁ‏; that 6, 7
are there proposed in place of the two rejected; 5 is then counted as one

only, and the number עשרה is finally made up of 12435867 with *ninthly*
the בלועין or disappearances of refuse, and *tenthly* the miracle of the bread
which was still hot ביום הלקחו. 𝔐 in (2) וְלֹא הִתְלִיעַ, No. 108
אֶרֶע, 𝔖. (3) 𝔄𝔅ℭ𝔐 אירע with *yod*, סימן...הִתְלִיעַ. 𝔄 קדש without art.
with *chateph pathach* comparing (*sic*) וארע מימרא דיי Targ. for ויקר יי
(Numb. xxiii. 16), and noticing a form אורע with *aleph, vau* in Targ. Ruth
ii. 3; אבל בחיר'ק האל'ף לא נמצא בשום מקום. Strack אֶרַע (*yod* after
aleph as *In allen Zeugen*), Baer אֲרַע (without *yod*), Emd. אִירַע with note
ארע מהארמית. Emd. 'ג לְבַ, Strack קְרִי with *shva*. (4) 𝔖 קְרִי לַכֹּהֵן גדול,
בבית הַמַּטְבָּחַיִם as pl. from מַטבח (Isai. xiv. 21)*, Emd. 'מִטְבַּ, Baer Strack
מַטְבָּ. 𝔄 בית without השמוש ב'ת. (5) 𝔖 פָּסוּל, 𝔄ℭ𝔐 פס', 𝔅ℭ פיסול.
Emd. פסול מהכבדים ע'מ בכור צבור, but the use of the verb in *qal* only
favours פָּסוּל with 𝔇 *rapheh*. (6) 𝔄 את המערכה 𝔅 את עצי, ℭ אש שעל
נצחה, 𝔐 No. 107 אש של עצי 𝔖 את אש 𝔖 (𝔄), 𝔅ℭ𝔇𝔖 ניצחה (7) גבי
מד'ג מהכבד לא משתבש...ומד'ג מהקל נמי ל'מ כי לשון חכמים. Emd.
בירושלים לחוד. ℭ עמוד 𝔐 את, om. לעמוד 𝔐. (9) ℭ לא without *vau*. 𝔖
(96 כש'), שְׁאֲלִין 𝔄 𝔖. ℭ𝔅𝔖 Nos. 73, 90, 92, 103, 107, 114 שאלין (10) מֵעוֹלָם.
cf. Bert. Tos. Yomtob Dur. 81 a Kohut *A. C.* v. 45 on לן (1). 𝔅 𝔖 כשעולין ל
Ashk. וצ'ע. ועוד כ' שאלין בירושלים הספרים גרסינן כשעולין וצ'ע.

9.

𝔇𝔖 עם חשיכה (𝔄𝔅 No. 92), ℭ adds נבראו בין השמשות.
ערב שבת עם 𝔖 marg. ש' ערב. 𝔄 33 a (Shab. II. 6), בְּעֶרֶב שַׁבַּת בֵּין
ופי מחק מלות בע'ש ומלות ואלו הן וכ' כך מצאתי. Ashk. חשיכה
הבאר (𝔄𝔇𝔖), 𝔅ℭ פי without *vau*. Nos. 103, 133, Mekhilta Ex. xvi. 32 (Fr.
51 a) omit the words. Numb. xxii. 28 אֶת פִּי הָאָתוֹן, Targ. Jon. (ed. Wien,
1859 A.D.) עשרתי פתגמין אתבריאו בתר שכלול עלמא במיעלי שבתא ביני
שימשתא מנא וּבִירָא וחוטרא דמשה ושמירא וקשתא וענני יקרא ופום ארעא
ת'ר עשרה דברים Pesach. 54 a, b. וכתב לוחי קיימא ומזקי ופום ממלל אתנא
נבראו בע'ש בין השמשות אלו הן בְּאַר ומן וקשת הכתב והמכתב והלוחות
קברו של משה ומערה שעמד בה משה ואליהו פתיחת פי האתון ופתיחת פי
הארץ לבלוע את הרשעים וי'א אף מקלו של אהרן שקדיה ופרחיה וי'א אף
המזיקין וי'א אף בגדו של אדם הראשון (cf. ד'ס VI. 156), and above on 54 a
והא תניא י' דברים...אלו הן בְּאַר והמן...ר' יהודה אומר אף as *baraitha*
‡ הצבת הוא היה אומר צבתא בצבתא מתעביד וצבתא קמייתא מאן עבד.

---

* 𝔖 points the *mem* with *chireq*, but quotes Isai. xiv. 21 as if for *mem, pathach*.

† Emd. writes מד''ג or מ''ר for מאן דגרס, *he who reads*, cf. IV. 16, V. 16.

‡ Notice the application of the saying צבתא בצבתא... at the end of Tosefta 'Erubin
(Zuck. p. 154), and see on נופי הלכות p. 154 of these notes.

With these authorities and Sifré II. § 355 (Fr. 147 a) read הבאר *omitting*
פי** which (so far as I know) is not adequately explained in any *perush*.
שהיו יצר' או' עליו עלי פ‏ .פרש"י ז"ל שפתח פיו ואמ' שירה עלי באר ענו לה ‏בּ
באר. The Zohar (בלק, Brody 201 b), quoted by David Loria on Pirqe
R. El. xix., reckons *three mouths*, including פי הבאר, and says תלת פומין
וְהִמָּכְתָּב ‏(ק), with מַכְתָּב in *perush* אלין אתבריאו ע"ש בין השמשות.
as ‏נ"א, cf. Kohut *A. C.* iv. 357 on כתב, Teshub. ha-Geon. Lyck 36 a (1864 A.D.).
מ‏ (cf. Rashi) וְהַמַּכְתָּב עט שבו נחרתו הלוחות שקורין גְּרֵייפְּא ואני קיבלתי, and
משה הַמַּכְתָּב‏ ‏עט...הלוחות ויש גורסין וְהַמַּכְתָּב, cf. ‏ב. R. Ephr. in Midr. Shem.
‏(קמ), ‏בשׂ add ‏רבנו וּקְבוּרָתוֹ‏ ‏ק שנ' ולא ידע איש את קבורתו (דברי ל"ד)
וְיֵשׁ אוֹמְרִים‏ ‏, cf. ‏ב Dur. כנוסח הסדורים שכתוב בהם קברו and not
אַף הַצָּבַת בַּצְּבַת הָעֲשׂוּיָה‏ ‏(ק), ‏קמד צבת without art., ‏ב ‏צ"ה (om.
‏(ויש אומ). ‏קב העשויה‏ ‏or ‏-ויה, ‏מד הע' with art. See also No. 170.
Dur. זאת המשנה דלגוה מסדורי תפלות, cf. Nos. 10, 73, and see on the *baba*
Tos. Yomtob and Geiger's *Lehrbuch zur Sprache der Mischnah*, pp. 58—60
(Breslau, 1845 A.D.).

בִּפְנֵי מִי‏ ‏10. שִׁבְעָה דְבָרִים בַּגּוֹלֶם‏ ‏(ק), ‏מ נאמרו בגולם.
וּבְמִנְיָן‏ ‏, ‏בחכמה ‏בב No. 92 add שֶׁגָּדוֹל הֵימֶנּוּ‏ ‏(מ), ‏א ממנו...לפני.
‏(מ —)‏-יין, ‏ב וי"ג בחכמה ובמנין, cf. ‏א 'Ed. I. 5 (136 a). ‏מ (cf. ‏מ comm.)
explains these words, but with note במשניות אין כת'. Ashk. מלות מחק
שׁוֹאֵל כַּהֲלָכָה וּמֵשִׁיב כָּעִנְיָן‏ ‏, הללו ושוב כ' ס"א בחכמה גרסינן
שואל כ' (קמד Nos. 23, 92 and Ashk. ‏ס"א בשם). ‏בשׂ in reverse order
עַל מַה שֶׁלֹּא שָׁמַע‏ ‏א בעין. Dur. ‏בְּעִנְיָן with *beth*, ‏מ, ‏וּמ ‏כהלכה without *vau*, ‏ב ‏ועל שלא. See D. E. Zuta on the דברים ‏ז. Ab. R. N. *B.*
עֲשָׂרָה‏ ‏דברים בגולם ועשרה בחכם (p. 110).

פּוּרְעָנִיּוֹת‏ ‏11. ‏ק the *'ayin* with *chateph pathach*, מפני רבוי התנועות
‏פָּרְעָנִיּוֹת‏. Emd. *'ayin* ‏ח"פ and *nun* פּוּ"ם מלא‏. Baer פְּרָעָנִיּוֹת No. 108.
‏בשׂ after בָּאִין‏ ‏ins. לעולם. ‏ק גּוּפֵי עֲבֵרוֹת‏ ‏with ‏קמדב, ‏מ comm. ‏-ה.
שֶׁל‏ ‏(2) ‏al. באה רעב שֶׁל בְּצוּרַת בָּא No. 108. In case (1) גופין של עבירה
מְהוּמָה וְשֶׁל בְּצוּרַת‏ ‏‏בשׂ. ‏מ comm. ‏ות—with note שמעתי מהו לשון ‏אב
וְשֶׁל בְּצוּרַת‏ ‏, ‏א ושל בצורת ha-Meiri om. ‏(בצ'...מהומ'), No. 108. בַּצּוֹרוֹת.

---

* For באר without י see also p. 190 of the famous R. Judah b. Barzilai of Barcelona's
perush on יצירה ‏ס' in *Mekize Nirdamim* (Berl. 1885 A.D.). He flourished about the beginning
of cent. xii.

𝔇 and א״ס in M. Shelom.   מצורה.   (3) שֶׁל כָּלָיה (Emd.), 𝔖 כַּלָּה bibl.

שבעה   𝕮 text defectively   בָּלָה. bibl. cf. but ,(Isai. x. 22) כְּלָיוֹן חרוץ

מיני פורענות באין על שבעה גופי עבירו׳ מקצתן רעבים ומקצתן שביעים גמרו

.שלא לעשר רעב של כלייה באה

12.   וְעַל פֵּירוֹת שְׁבִיעִית (𝔖), 𝔄   שבעיות.

13.   וְעַל עֲוּוֹת הַדִּין וְעַל הַמּוֹרִים בַּתּוֹרָה (𝔖), al.   עיווות   𝔅 ועל

.המורים פנים בתורה ,cf. iii. 17.   עַל עֲבוֹדָה זרה (𝔄𝔅𝔖), 𝔇 עו״די ע״ז.

Nos. 95, 101   Ashk. (cf. 𝔄)   הַשְׁמֵט.   שמיטת (𝔖), 𝔅𝔇   שְׁמִטַּת הָאָרֶץ

השמטת.   𝕮 (omitting ע״ז), ועל   גלות בא לעולם על שפיכות דמים ועל

.שמיטת הארץ ועל גילוי עריות

14.   מְרוּבָּה (𝔄𝔅), 𝕮𝔇𝔖   מתרבה   𝕮 דברים   בא.רבעה.   **החג שבכל**

שָׁנה ושנה (𝔅𝔖 No. 95), 𝔄𝕮 om. ושנה.   𝔇 once החג, then   החג שבכל

ישנה ושנה, and in comm. החג של סוכות שבכל שנה.   For the second

עָנִי (𝔄𝔅𝔇𝔖), 𝕮 has שני.   It is not unusual to find ע or עו interchanged

with ש, cf. 𝔄 9 a (Demai vii. 1) ומעשר עָנִי for שני, 13 a (Shebi. i. 6) אילנות

עַל שלשה for של, 97 a (Git. vi. 9) זו הלכה שלח, a good reading, preserved

also in תום׳ רי״ד [Ben Jac. Oçar p. 623, No. 27], in place of which Surh.

Jost have זו הלכה העלה.

15.   זו מדה בינונית...זו מדת סדום (𝔅𝕮𝔇𝔖), 𝔄 om. זו...זו.

of שלך ושלי שלי and שלי ושלך שלך of the חסיד   𝔄 Ashk. No. 23

the רשע, exc. that 𝔄 omits a שלך by ט״ם.   Dur. (on שלך...שלך ושלך שלי

...כך היא הגירסא בספרים כולם אבל במשניו׳ ישנות writes (שלי ושלי שלי

שבאו מארץ ישראל שהם מנוקדות יש גירסא יותר מדוקדקת והיא שלי ושלך

.שלך חסיד שלך שלי ושלי שלי רשע

16.   נוֹחַ לכעוֹם...יֵצֵא שכרו (𝔄𝔅𝕮𝔇𝔖), Ashk. Dur. ha-Meiri No.

101   לָרְצוֹת 𝔖, M. Shelom. לרצות (niph.), or qal.   Emd. ומ״ד   יצא הפסדו.

בתפלות ספרדיות pointed as qal Dur. finds   בפת״ח מהכבד משתבש,

supports this by Psalm lxxvii. 8 ולא יוסיף לרצות עוד, and adds on the

current reading לְרַצוֹת (quoting Job xx. 10 בניו ירצו דלים), that the piel

may mean לרצות את עצמו, cf. iv. 25 אל תרצה.

17.   מְמַהֵר לשמוֹעַ...יֵצֵא שכרו 𝔄𝔅𝔖 Dur. (ומבמשניות גרסין ממהר)

Emd. (ממהר צ״ל).   𝕮𝔇 No. 92 מהר.   Dur. suggests that the scribes fell

into error in putting יצא שכרו before יצא הפסדו in § 16 שרצו להשוות בין

cf. No. 95) בְּלָמֵידִים‎ has 𝕭 ,(𝕬𝕭𝕮𝕾) For .בתלמידים‎ שתי המשניות

M. Shelom.).‎ חכם‎ (𝕬𝕭𝕾), 𝕮𝕯 זה חלק טוב‎. No. 107 om. זה.

18. שִׁיתָנוּ 𝕭 .שִׁיתָנוּ 𝕬𝕯𝕭‎, (𝕮𝕾) יתנו אחרים והוא לא יתן‎ ,רוצה שיתנו‎

ואין אנו גורסין במשנה רוצה אלא אלא בראשון גרסי' רוצה שיתן ולא יתנו כו' 𝕭.

thrice for לא‎, 𝕮 רשע...ולא יתן ולא...חסיד אל שיתן‎ .𝕬 אל

19. הראוי היה בה"מ בלי‎ .בית‎ 𝕬 ,(𝕾𝕭) בהולכי לבית‎ (𝕭𝕮𝕯𝕾)‎. Emd.

עוֹשֶׂה וְאֵינוֹ הוֹלֵךְ שָׂכַר עֲשִׂיָה בְּיָדוֹ‎ .למ"ד או בהולכים לבה"מ

כ"ה בכל הנוסחאות המדוייקות ולא מַעֲשֶׂה כנוסחאות קצת הסדורים 𝕾‎, cf.

Dur. 88 a. 𝕮𝕯𝕾 שכר מעשה 𝕭‎, עשייה‎. 𝕬 omits the clause.

20. סְפוֹג וּמִשְׁפָּךְ מִשְׁמֶרֶת וְנָפָה‎ ....Emd. משמרת מחודשת במשקלה

שמוציאה 𝕭 .שהוא מ' 𝕬𝕮‎, הם', 𝕭‎ ,שמכנים 𝕭𝕬 .ולא נמצא לו משקל בשמות

bis. 𝕬𝕮 שהוא מ'‎ in both cases, and 𝕾 in the former, 𝕭 in the latter

case. 𝕬 124 a (Sanh. ii. 8) מַסְתַּפֵּג‎ ולא כשהוא‎, 165 b (Chul. v. 3, 4)

and 227 a (Tahar. i. 1) סוֹפֵג את הארבעים‎. 20 b (Terum. viii. 6) מִשְׁמֶרֶת

הַמְנָפָּה‎ חרסים מתוך השוקת‎ 224 a (Par. vii. 8) של יין.

21, 22. 𝕾 תְּלוּיָה בְּדָבָר‎ four times with נ"א‎ (= ר' עובדי' נירסת)

adding בָּטֵל‎ as an epithet of דבר‎, and note* בעל סדר היום‎ וכן הגיה החסיד

עולמית 𝕮 without vau. 𝕾 בְּטֵלָה אַהֲבָה‎ .במשניות שלו כפי' הרמב"ם

לעולם‎. M. Shelom. quotes the reading of ר' ע"‎ above-mentioned and con-

tinues כך שמעתי מפי החכם החסיד‎...בבי"ת גרסי' אמנון בתמר‎ זו אהבת

ההר' מסעוד אזולי נ"ע מצאתי מוגה ג"כ כך במשנתו של הה"ר יהוסף‎

עיקר‎ וכן נ"ל ודוד יהונתן‎ זו אהבת‎ ברוב ספרים דגרסי'‎ וכתב ז"ל אשכנזי‎. See on M. Azulai in part i. of שם הגדולים‎, letter Mem No. 70. He

flourished about 1612 a.d. No. 108 (f. 67 a) בתנא דבי ר' אליהו

תלויה בדבר זו אהבת בלק ובלעם שאינה תלויה בדבר זו אהבת אברהם יצחק‎

יעקב להקב"ה‎, see c. 28 in ed. מינקאווי"ץ‎ (Minkowce), 1798 a.d., which reads

בלעם ובלק...ויעקב‎ (f. 79 b), and so ed. pr. Ven. 1598 a.d. (f. 44 b).

23, 24. מחלוקת שמאי והלל‎ (or מ'‎ זו), 𝕬𝕮 Nos. 4, 10, 13 (ש'‎ בית

'Erub. ברוב הספרים שמאי בְרישָׁא‎. M. Shelom. (ובית ה'‎), 39, 101,.114, 157.

13b שמקדימין דברי ב"ש לדבריהן [של ב"ה]‎. הלל ושמאי 𝕭𝕮 שום 𝕭𝕮𝕾

for שם‎ (𝕬𝕭𝕾). 𝕾 זו מַחֲלוֹקֵת קֹרַח וְעֲדָתוֹ‎ with 𝕭𝕯 (exc. ע'‎ וכל),

𝕬𝕮 תו של קרח‎—. 𝕯 comm. om. זו exc. בזו מחלקתו של קורח‎ In

No. 10 מחלוקת‎ comes before אהבה‎, cf. Dur. 89 a.

---

* The author of the *Seder ha-Yom* was R. Moses ben Judah Machir, who wrote about the beginning of cent. xvi. See 'Kore ha-Dorot' ed. Cassel f. 42 a, 48 a (Berl. 1846 a.d.).

25. 𝕮 before אין מספיקין has חטא הרבים תלוי בו ואין.

26. וזכות masc., 𝕬 —יה. זכות 𝕭𝕮𝕯𝕾, 𝕮𝕯𝕾, תלוי 𝕭𝕮𝕾 (𝕬𝕭). 𝕬 omits the *baba* יָרָבְעָם חָטָא וְהֶחֱטִיא אֶת הָרַבִּים חֵטָא הָרַבִּים תָּלוּי בּוֹ שֶׁנֶּ׳ עַל חַטֹּאות יָרָבְעָם אֲשֶׁר חָטָא וַאֲשֶׁר הֶחֱטִיא אֶת יִשְׂרָאֵל (1 Kings xv. 30, cf. xiv. 16). 𝕮𝕯 ישראל for the first הרבים, and י׳ בן נבט *bis*. 𝕭 וחטא with *vau*, 𝕯 וחטאת הרבים תלייה בו No. 114, וי— for תלייה.

27, 28. Ashk. agrees throughout with 𝕬 (p. 78) except in some minutiae of spelling and in reading שלשה, שיש בידו for יש וש׳ with *vau*, גבוה masc., and מה for ומה. 𝕯 reads כל מי תלמידיו, רוח pl. throughout, before שחת after הרשע with the 2nd בלעם, אבינו with 3rd and 4th אברהם, נפש אנשי דמים ומרמה לא יחצו ימיהם ואני אבטח בך the remainder of the verse אוכלין בעולם הזה ונוחלין לעולם הבא שנ׳ להנחיל...אמלא and at end.

𝕮 begins defectively כל מי שיש בידו שלשה דברים הללו מתלמידיו של בלעם הרשע אברהם אבינו עין טובה and continues very much as 𝕯, but has the order רוח, נפש, and has מה without *vau*, as 𝕾 finds בכל הנוסחאות המדוייקות. 𝕬𝕮𝕯 Ashk. Nos. 4, 101, 133 conclude with the introverted parallelism {abb′a′}, in which the disciples of Abraham are mentioned in the extreme, and those of Bil'am in the intermediate clauses. The collocation of bb′ (with mention of בלעם של תלמידיו followed by קללתם) is in accord with the principle of Baba B. 14 b סמכינן חורבנא לחורבנא ונחמתא לנחמתא, and the introversion gives an auspicious ending ואוצרותיהם אמלא, cf. 𝕬 48 b (Pes. x. 3) מתחיל בגנות ומסיים בשבח, 206 a (end of Kelim) אין 66 a (Megil. III. 8) אשריך כלים שנכנסת בטומאה ויצאת בטהרה זה שהוא עומד לקרות בתורה צריך שיהא, T. J. Meg. 74 b מפסיקין בקללות. פותח בדבר טוב וחותם בדבר טוב The order {aa′bb′} as in 𝕭𝕾 makes it necessary to go on to the end of Psalm lv. 24, so as not to stop at באר שחת, as is indeed done also in 𝕮𝕯, although with their order of clauses this is unnecessary. 𝕭 (written briefly) reads thus (1) כל מי שיש בידו שלשה דברים *הללו מתלמידיו של אברהם אבינו וכל מי שיש [שאן .marg] בידו מה בין תלמידיו של ב״ה לת׳ של (2). של׳ דב׳ הללו מתלמידיו של בל הרשע תלמידיו של א״א עין ט׳ ונפש ש׳ ורוח נ׳ תלמידיו של ב״ה עין רעה (3). א״א (ו)תלמידיו של א״א אוכלין העולם הזה ונוחלין (4). ונפש קצרה ורוח גבוהה העולם הבא שנ׳ להנחיל...אמלא· אבל תלמידיו של ב״ה יורשין גיהנם ויורדין לבאר שחת שנ׳ ואתה...ואני אבטח בך, but the clauses (2), (3) are marked for transposition, and (4) is altered at the beginning by marginal addi-

---

* Baer הַלָּלוּ as pl. of הַלָּה (Kohut *A. C.* III. 206), quoting passages of the Gemara and one from Mishn. M. Sheni, where 𝕬 (III. 3, f. 23 a) reads הללו מחוללים...והלה עושה צורכו במעותיו. In 𝕭 (4) *shva* remains at the beginning under the place of *vau* conj. erased.

tions and erasure thus ח״ל של ת׳ ב״ה של א״א לת׳ של א״א תלמידיו בין מה
אוכלין. Note in (2) the order בלעם...אברהם, and in (3) קצרה [found also
in ℭ comm.] for רחבה, with the remark of Dur. שכתוב הרבה ספרים ויש
דברים No. 95 בהם נפש קצרה ושמא תיקון סופרים הוא לכנותו לגנאי
דברים הללו...דברים אֲחֵרִים ⅀. טובים הללו...רעים הַלָּלוּ, with note
that הללו is for bibl. האלה. But הללו [Auth. P. B. הַלָּלוּ] disconnected
from the things עין טובה וכו׳ is out of place, אחרים is not indispensable,
and both should be omitted as by ⅍ Ashk. ⅀ rejects the reading אוכלין
העולם הזה ונוחלין העולם הבא (נ״א יורשין) and prefers to read, according
to רש״י פי׳ [and with ℭ⅍], אוכ׳ בָּעוֹלָם הזה ונוח׳ לָעוֹלָם הבא. But all these
are doubtless developments from an older one-clause reading as in ⅍ Ashk.

29. יְהוּדָה בֶּן תֵּימָא. ⅍ Pes. 112a Chag. 14a ר׳ יהודה. No. 10 בן
טבאי. Aboth ends at אביך שבשמים according to the statement of ⅍
on this *baba* (p. 23),

חסלת מסכת אבות.

⅍ goes on to say (p. 23) that Shemuel ha-Q.'s בנפל אויבך (iv. 26) was commonly repeated here to introduce הוא היה אומר בן חמש שנים, but sometimes written here only. ⅍ and others simply write Shem. ha-Q. for הוא.
R. Israel remarks (p. 52) that בן חמש is not מן אל מסכתא, and sometimes
we find it only in Pereq vi., as in Nos. 83, 160 (2). In Nos. 10, 80, 81, 92
it stands last in Pereq v.; but since it ends with death it was natural to
move it to some place within the chapter, *um einen so düsteren Schluss zu
vermeiden* (Strack). It is commented upon twice over in ℭ and No. 19 (1).
See also Nos. 13, 42, 54, 77, 95, 109, 161. M. Shelom. (on הוא היה
בשימושא רבה מייתא לה בשם שמואל הקטן וכן בן העתיקה (,אומר בן חמש
הב״י [בית יוסף] א״ח כס״י [סוף סימן] Tur. Or. Chay.] ל״ח בשם שמושא רבא
דתנן שמואל הקטן וכו׳ בתוי״ט שהאריך להוכיח שאינה מסדר מסכתא
זו עש״ב וגם כה״רר יהוסף ז״ל מחקה לכל מתני׳ וכתב בכל הספרים לא
מצאתי משנה זו.

30. לְגֵיהִנָּם. Emd. (⅀), al. עַז פָּנִים לַגֵּיהִנַּם וּבוֹשׁ פָּנִים לְגַן עֵדֶן
וּבוֹשֶׁת, a reading which may have come from Mass. Kallah or some *perush*
as No. 108 שיש בו בושת פנים. Although No. 170 with 'Rashi' writes of
this *baba* עד כאן כת׳ במשנה (p. 121), ⅍ may be right in excluding it;
for the repetition of גיהנם and גן עדן after § 28 (acc. to ⅍ Ashk.) does not
commend itself, and עז פנים may be a qualifying appendix by some early
editor to the praise of עזות in § 29. Dur. זאת המשנה דלגוה מסדורי

תפלות.   שֶׁתִּבָּנֶה עִירְךָ ... יְהִי רָצוֹן in this place (𝔄𝔖, not 𝔅ℭ𝔇)

looks like a survival from a time when the chapter ended here. 𝔇 at the end of Pereq R. Meir שיבנה בית המקדש. 𝔄 190 b (Tam. VI. 7) on mention of *beth elohenu,* שיבנה רצון יהי. Strack שֶׁתִּבָּנֶה עירך (*niph.*), Emd. שתבנה קל. Psalm li. 20 תִּבָּנֶה חומות ירושלם את ציון ברצונך היטיבה.

𝔇 brings in עז פנים only as a *baraitha,* and concludes its appendix to the text of Pereq v. (but with the criticism ר׳ יהודה נראה לגרום הכותב ולי (הנשיא דכך היא שנוייה במסכת כלה*) as below :

עז פנים   תניא ר׳ נתן אום׳ עז פנים לגהינם ובוש פנים לגן עדן.
ר׳ אליעזר אום׳ ממזר ר׳ יהושע אום׳ בן הנדה ר׳ עקיבא או׳ ממזר ובן הנדה
אף לא עמדו אבותיו על הר סיני ועל כולם אליהו כותב והק׳ חותם אוי לו
לפוסל את זרעו ולפוגם את משפחתו ולנושא אשה שאינה הוגנת לו שכל
הנושא אשה שאינה הוגנת לו אליהו כופתו והק׳ רוצעו וכל הפוסל פסול וא׳
שמואל במומו פוסל [Qiddush. 70 a].   סוף אדם למות וסוף בהמה לשחיטה
הכל למיתה הן עומדין :

ר׳ אבא אום׳ אשרי מי שגדל בתורה ועמלו בתורה ועושה נחת רוח ליוצרו
וגדל בשם טוב ונפטר בשם טוב מן העולם ועליו א׳ שלמה בחכמתו טוב
שם משמן טוב ויום המות מיום הולדו [Berak. 17 a].   למוד תורה הרבה
כדי שיתנו לך שכר הרבה ודע שמתן שכרן של צדיקים לעתיד לבא :

ר׳ חנניא בן עקשיא כו׳.

31, 32.   והפן or בן.-- וַהֲפוֹךְ , 𝔖 or ---יך, והפך 𝔄𝔅ℭ𝔇   בן בג בג...והפך בה.
וכולך בה   בה for א--.   דכולה 𝔄𝔇   ומלך (𝔄 No. 92), No. 133
99, 108 , Nos. 5, 12, 95,   דכולא בה סמא.   Notice Nos. 12 וכולה בה, 23 ובה, 103 דכלה נ״א,
בלי, (כו׳ בה ובה 150 , Possibly   כלה without *vau* gave rise to והפך בה.
as *perush* תהוי בה to כולך בה and that by ס״ב in expanded forms of the saying, and
תהגה 𝔅 תחזי to ס״ט by that and.   Dur. quotes סיב ובלה בה ובה תקזי׳
as a reading derived from ומינה לא תזוע סאין לך טובה הימנה [מדה .om]
Ab. R. N., and omits the words in Rabbinic type, cf. No. 133.   לא תזוע תזוו 𝔇
with תזוו as *perush*.   Dur. on 31—32 זהו סוף הפ׳ החמישי ובסדורי תפלות
ששי ראש פ׳ עשאוהו.   Nos. 101, 161 have these sayings in the margin
of chap. v. as well as in chap. VI. On the identification of their authors
by Gematria see (beside Aboth commentaries) R. Judah b. Barzilai on
Sepher Jeçirah, p. 7 (Berl. 1885 A.D.). The *Tanna de-Bé Eliyahu Zuta*
c. 17 reads *Jochanan* b. Bagbag.

Pereq v. in 𝔅 ends thus, (mg. בה דכלא) בה והפך בה אומר בג בג בן
(לד) שאין תזוו לא ומנה .tחזי ו״ג .תהוי ו״ג (mg. תהגה ובה בה ובלי וסיב

---

* The editions of Mas. Kallah have ר׳ יהודה without הנשיא.

מדה טובה הימנה" בן הא הא אומר לפום צערא אגרא׳, next before this come

the three *baboth* (1) ...בשמים בן תימא יהודה (2). הוא היה אומר עז פנים

with *baraitha* to וכל הפוסל פסול של עולם followed by ואינו מדבר בשבחו.

בן (1) reads לגן עדן after ₡ . הוא היה אומר בן חמ׳ש...מן העולם (3)

בג בג אומר הפוך בה והפיך בה דכולא בה ובה תהוי ומינה לא תזוז שאין...

ר׳ יהודה הנשיא או׳ (4). הוא היה אומ׳ בן חמש (3). בן הא הא (2). היומנה

עז פנים with *baraitha*, and ר׳ אבא...לעתיד לבוא and, ר׳ , and סליק פירקא. ₰ in-

serts בן and בן בג בג and ends with הוא היה אומר בן חמש after § 30, and

הוא היה then, פרק חמשי (f. 68 b—72 b) writes אגרא No. 108 after הא הא.

תניא ר׳ נתן אומר בברייתא היא ונהגו לומרו בסוף, and אומר בן חמש

בן (1) has ₯ at the end of Pereq vi. בעשרה מאמרות...סליק פרקא.

בג בג אומר הפוך בה והפיך בה דכולה בה ובלה בה ובה תהוי ומינה לא

יהי רצון מלפניך יי׳ (3). בן הא הא (2). תזוע שאין לך מידה טובה הימנה

אלהינו ואלהי אבותינו שיבנה בית המקדש במהרה בימינו · ר׳ חנניא בן

עקשיא... Nos. 84, 154, 165 have an exceptional form of Pereq vi.,

and Nos. 10 (cf. 134), 83, 97 have Seven Peraqim.

INDEX.

The pages hereinafter referred to are those of the second edition of *Sayings of the Jewish Fathers,* published in 1897.

AN INDEX TO
SAYINGS OF THE JEWISH FATHERS.

1. SUBJECTS.

2. PASSAGES OF THE NEW TESTAMENT.